United States of America
US and Canadian Navigable Waters

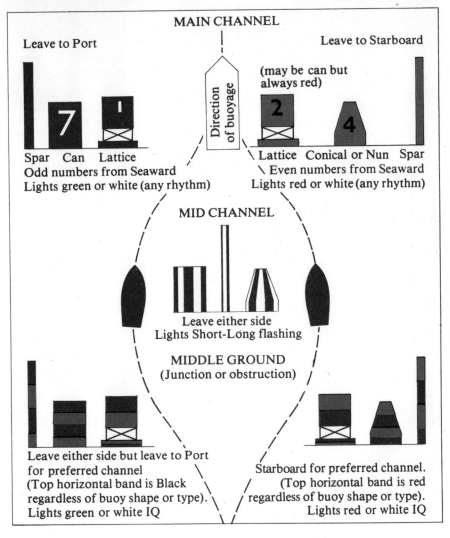

MAIN CHANNEL

Leave to Port

Leave to Starboard

Direction of buoyage

(may be can but always red)

7

1

2

4

Spar Can Lattice
Odd numbers from Seaward
Lights green or white (any rhythm)

Lattice Conical or Nun Spar
Even numbers from Seaward
Lights red or white (any rhythm)

MID CHANNEL

Leave either side
Lights Short-Long flashing

MIDDLE GROUND
(Junction or obstruction)

Leave either side but leave to Port
for preferred channel
(Top horizontal band is Black
regardless of buoy shape or type).
Lights green or white IQ

Starboard for preferred channel.
(Top horizontal band is red
regardless of buoy shape or type).
Lights red or white IQ

Special Buoys
(All US waters)

These have no special shapes and no numbers (they may be lettered).
Lights are white, fixed, flashing or occulting.

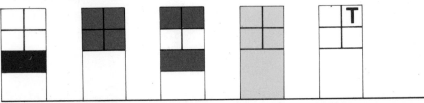

Fish net   Dredging   Special purpose   Quarantine   Anchorage

THE SAILING DICTIONARY

Joachim Schult

Translated and extensively revised
by BARBARA WEBB

ADLARD COLES LIMITED
GRANADA PUBLISHING
London Toronto Sydney New York

Published by Granada Publishing in
Adlard Coles Limited, 1981

Original German Title
SEGLER-LEXICON
Published by Klasing & Co GmbH
4800 Bielefeld 1, German Federal Republic

Granada Publishing Limited
Frogmore, St Albans, Herts AL2 2NF
and
36 Golden Square, London W1R 4AH
866 United Nations Plaza, New York, NY 10017 USA
117 York Street, Sydney, NSW 2000, Australia
100 Skyway Avenue, Rexdale, Ontario, Canada M9W 3A6
61 Beach Road, Auckland, New Zealand.

Copyright © Adlard Coles Limited
ISBN 0 229 11619 1
Phototypesetting by Parkway Group, London and Abingdon
Printed in Great Britain by
Mackays of Chatham Ltd

Author's introduction

Over the past few decades the branches of knowledge relating to the sport of sailing have proliferated. The need for a comprehensive specialized dictionary compiled for those who build, buy, equip and sail boats has become more and more pressing in view of the growing number of different types of boats and the increasing variety of gear and equipment available. With numerous boat shows and sailing schools, as well as thousands of sailing clubs, sailing is not simply a sport but an important industry and a part of the economy that deserves to be taken seriously. The highly specialized terms cannot be learnt overnight, but become familiar with use.

Originally only sailing boats and ships could be used for transport over long distances, and the language of the sea is the oldest of the really idiomatic tongues. A very great number of words and phrases that have been used for centuries to enable mariners and navigators to handle vessels safely and to exchange information about their experiences are still in use, and they have been joined by an ever-increasing number of new terms and expressions as building materials change and the range of sailing expands.

Sailing language today covers so vast a field because, within its unique and rich traditional framework, it has embraced so much from other technical subjects. Not only has the number of relevant subjects increased as technology has advanced, but also the need to delve into them further. The modern sailor in charge of his yacht requires a solid foundation of seamanship, nautical affairs, weather and the rule of the road, plus some knowledge of mathematics, physics, geography, astronomy, hydrography and other technical matters if he is to conduct his vessel as safely as possible. As well as the manual skills of the boatbuilder, sailmaker, rigger and mechanic he must know about his engine, and be able to check the worth of his costly electric and electronic equipment. When racing and competing for prizes and cups, often at great expense, he needs to know the meaning of the terms used in connection with tactics, tuning, racing rules and ratings.

The development of sailing into a sport within reach of the man in the street resulted from the introduction of glassfibre reinforced plastics about 20 years ago, an event as revolutionary in its way as the discovery of electricity or radio, or the invention of the motor car and aeroplane. Suddenly skills and experience developed through the centuries became unimportant, and many technical terms became virtually superfluous, but in their place came a host of new words, mostly unknown to the great majority of sailors, relating to the new materials and building methods. The exchange of experiences and understanding between sailors becomes absolutely impossible without a comprehensive specialized dictionary, as exists for many other sports and technical subjects.

At this period of radical change, I have selected over 4000 technical terms, and have tried to preserve the established and well-proven words and phrases by defining them accurately while, at the same time, including authentic definitions for new terms. Sometimes a word with several meanings or a vague definition has to be given a new, correct and etymologically clear definition. By following the references in the text, the reader will recognize the interdependence of the words and phrases, and become accustomed to how they are used in context.

In spite of the large number of terms defined it may be that some have been forgotten or omitted, and I would be glad to receive suggestions as to what should be added.

Joachim Schult

Note on the English edition

It is, of course, impossible to translate a dictionary; for example the word 'back' has five nautical meanings listed in the German edition and four in the English, and only one of those meanings is common to both tongues, although three of the other German meanings have an English equivalent which has been included in this adaptation.

The practical comments and the information in Herr Schult's text have been retained wherever possible, provided that they are relevant for English-speaking sailors. Sometimes they appear in the definitions of different terms, often they have had to be amended, shortened or extended. I have also retained his method of using terms that are defined elsewhere in the dictionary, and many of these are italicized to make further reference simple. Not every word that is defined is in italics, for example the definition of a basic word such as clew refers the reader to other basic words by italicizing *foot, leech* and *outhaul,* but it is assumed that a reader looking up angle of attack will know the meaning of mainsail and spinnaker, and further reference is therefore to *boundary layer, camber* etc. By following the italicization, somebody starting from, say, the definition of coastal navigation should be able to find all the terms relevant to *plotting instruments, charts,* and *compass.*

The English language is said to have the richest vocabulary of all, and my aim has therefore not merely been to find an English equivalent for every German term, but to try to include all those English terms for which there is no German equivalent. The original text has been broken down into subjects, such as sails, rigging, rules of the road etc, and many extra terms and phrases have been added in every case. This enabled several experts in their fields to check some particularly specialized subjects, and I am grateful to Tony Marchaj for his advice on aerodynamics and hydrodynamics, John Leather on construction, Conrad Dixon on navigation, John French on electronics, Alan Watts on weather and seas, and Jeremy Howard-Williams on sails, before the whole was reassembled into alphabetical order. An interesting point is that the terms which have been most hotly debated prior to publication are traditional words, the meaning of which has often become less precise, or even altered, over the years. Herr Schult mentions in his introduction that sailors now have to delve deeply into technology, and his delving has certainly extended his translator's research into aspects that are normally glossed over or taken for granted.

SI units and conversion factors are included, first because they are being used increasingly in scientific work, secondly because today's teenagers, educated on Joules and Newtons, are unfamiliar with the fps system used by their parents. A list of abbreviations is also included.

Particular attention has been paid to the differences between US and UK usage and, to avoid repetition, the definition is given under the UK term; the US equivalent is listed in alphabetical order and the reader referred to the relevant entry. UK spelling is used throughout, except in those definitions that relate purely to a US term, but differences in spelling are indicated for each alphabetical entry. The reader's attention is drawn to three points peculiar to this dictionary:

1. GRP/FRP: UK glassfibre, US fiberglass reinforced plastics.
2. IRPCS: abbr for International Regulations for Preventing Collisions at Sea.
3. Tidal stream or current: an all-embracing term to cover the US terms tidal and non-tidal currents as well as the UK terms currents and tidal streams.

Barbara Webb
June 1981

iv

Abbreviations

abbr.	abbreviation
ABS	American Bureau of Shipping acrylonitrile-butadiene-styrene
Ac	altocumulus
AH	amp-hour
Al	aluminium
Al or Alt	alternating light
AMVER	Automated Mutual Assistance Vessel Rescue
AP3700	Sight reduction tables
AR	aspect ratio
As	altostratus
B	beam; rated beam (IOR)
BCF	bromochlorodifluoromethane
BFO	beat frequency oscillator
BMAX	maximum beam (IOR)
Bn	beacon
Bol	bollard
C	Celsius
Cb	cumulonimbus
CB	centre of buoyancy
CBF	centreboard factor (IOR)
Cc	cirrocumulus
CCA	Cruising Club of America
Cd	candela
CE	centre of effort
CG	centre of gravity Coastguard station
CGF	centre of gravity factor (IOR)
Ci	cirrus
CLR	centre of lateral resistance
COGAID	Coast Guard Assistance Instruction Data
Co-lat	complement of latitude
Coll	Colloquial
Colregs	US CG contraction for International Regulations for Preventing Collisions at Sea
cov	covers
CPA	closest point of approach
CQR	patented anchor

CRT	cathode ray tube
Cs	cirrostratus
Cu	cumulus copper
CUT	Co-ordinated Universal Time
CZD	calculated zenith distance
D	rated depth (IOR), drag
DF	direction finder/finding
Dia	diaphone
Dir.Lt	direction light
d.lat	difference of latitude
d.long	difference of longitude
Dn	dolphin
dr	dries
DR	dead reckoning
DW	track for deep draft vessels
DWL	designed waterline
E	east mainsail hoist length (IOR)
ED	existence doubtful
EHF	extremely high frequency
E.Int	equal intervals
EP	estimated position
EPF	engine and propeller factor (IOR)
EPIRB	Emergency Position-Indicating Radio Beacon
expl	explosive
F	fixed light Fahrenheit
FD	Flying Dutchman
F_H	heeling force
F Fl	fixed and flashing light
Fl	flashing light
f.p.s.	foot, pound, second system
F_R	driving force
FRP	fiberglass reinforced plastics
FS	flagstaff
F_S	side force, lift
g	acceleration due to gravity
GHA	Greenwich hour angle

GM	metacentric height	long	longitude
GMT	Greenwich mean time	LOP	line of position
GP	geographical position	LP	longest perpendicular (IOR)
Gp Fl	group flashing light	LRBC	Lloyds Register Building Certificate
Gp Occ	group occulting light	LRP	low rigging penalty (IOR)
GRP	glassfibre reinforced plastics	Lt Ho	lighthouse
HA	hour angle	Lt V	light vessel
HAT	highest astronomical tide	LW	low water
Hc	altitude at chosen position (Sight reduction tables)	LWL	load waterline
		MA	mechanical advantage
HF	high frequency	MAF	movable appendage factor (IOR)
Hg	mercury	MEKP	methyl-ethyl-ketone-peroxide
HO 249	Sight reduction tables	MF	medium frequency
hp	horse power	MHHW	mean higher high water
HW	high water	MHW	mean high water
Hz	Hertz	MHWS	mean high water springs
I	foretriangle height (IOR)	MHz	megahertz
IALA	International Association of Lighthouse Authorities	MLLW	mean lower low water
		MLW	mean low water
IHO	International Hydrographic Organization	MLWS	mean low water springs
IMO	International Maritime Organization	Mo	morse
Int Qk Fl	interrupted quick flashing light	MORC	Midget Ocean Racing Club
IOR	International Offshore Rule	MR	measured rating (IOR)
IQ	interrupted quick light	MSL	mean sea level
IRPCS	International Regulations for Preventing Collisions at Sea	N	north Newton
Iso	isophase (light)	NACA	National Advisory Committee for Aeronautics
IYRU	International Yacht Racing Union		
J	Joule foretriangle base (IOR)	n.mile	nautical mile
		NOS	National Ocean Survey
JOG	Junior Offshore Group	Oc, Occ	occulting light
K	Kelvin	ODAS	Ocean Data Acquisition System
k	kilo-	OOD	officer of the day
kH	kilohertz	ORC	Offshore Racing Council
kn	knot	OSTAR	Observer Single-handed Trans-Atlantic Race
kW	kilowatt		
L	lift	P	mainsail hoist length (IOR)
LAT	lowest astronomical tide	PA	position approximate
lat	latitude	Pb	lead
LB	lifeboat station	PD	position doubtful
LBP	length between perpendiculars	PFD	personal flotation device
LF	low frequency	PPI	plan position indicator
L Fl	long flashing light	PVC	polyvinylchloride
LHA	local hour angle	Q, Qk Fl	quick light, quick flashing light
LMT	local mean time	q	dynamic pressure
LOA	length overall	q.v.	please see

R	resistance		**T.M.**	Thames measurement
R, Rk	rock		**TMF**	time multiplication factor
Ra	radar		**TZD**	true zenith distance
RC	non-directional or omnidirectional radio beacon		**UHF**	ultra high frequency
			uncov	uncovers
RD	directional radio beacon		**UQ**	ultra quick light
RDF	radio direction finder/finding		**USYRU**	United States Yacht Racing Union
RG	RDF station		**UT**	universal time
RNLI	Royal National Lifeboat Institution		**v, V**	velocity
RORC	Royal Ocean Racing Club		V_A	apparent wind
RSA	rated sail area (IOR)		**Var**	variation
RT, R/T	radio telephone		**VHF**	very high frequency
R_T	resultant hydrodynamic force		$V/\sqrt{L}$	speed to length ratio
RYA	Royal Yachting Association		**VLF**	very low frequency
S	south		**Vmg**	speed made good to windward
SAR	search and rescue		**VQ**	very quick light
Sc	stratocumulus		V_S	boat speed
SHA	sidereal hour angle		V_T	true wind
SHF	super high frequency		**W**	west
SHP	shaft horse power		**whis**	whistle
SI	Système Internationale d'unités		**Wk**	wreck
SINS	ship's inertial navigation system		**WMO**	World Meteorological Organization
SLP	safe leeward position		**Z**	azimuth (Sight reduction tables)
SMF	spar material factor (IOR)		**ZD**	zenith distance
SOLAS	safety of life at sea (convention)		**Zn**	zinc
SORC	Southern Ocean Racing Conference			
SOS	· · · — — — · · · save our souls		Symbols	
SSB	single sideband		⊕	rock awash at chart datum
St	stratus		μ	micro- (prefix)
TCF	time correction factor		♈	Aries
Ti	titanium		⊕	built under survey (Lloyds)
			Δ	displacement (weight)
			∇	displacement (volume)

A = Alfa: white and blue *swallow-tailed code flag*. As a single letter signal means 'I have a diver down; keep well clear at slow speed.' *Morse code:* •—(dot dash).

Aback 1. A sail is aback when the wind strikes it on what would normally be its *lee* side. 2. *Square sails* are *braced* aback, with their *yards* trimmed so that the wind strikes the forward side of the sails, to help the vessel to *go about* or *lose way* (similar to *backing* a sailing boat's jib). 3. Taken aback: the sails are backed inadvertently, probably owing to a wind shift.

Abaft Further *aft* than, as in abaft the mast; towards or nearer the *stern* than.

Abaft the beam Indicates direction from the boat, i.e. the sector on both sides from *abeam* to *astern*, as in wind from abaft the beam, side lights shine over a sector from right *ahead* to two points abaft the beam etc. US: the sector from abeam to broad on the *quarter*, i.e. through 45°.

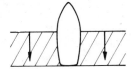

Abandon All crew members leave a vessel that it is considered impossible to save.

Abandonment A *race* declared void by the *race committee* after the *starting signal* has been made, perhaps because the boats are not making the minimum speed prescribed owing to light breezes, or because the crews could be endangered in strong winds. The signal is *code flag* N. The race can be re-sailed at the race committee's discretion.

Abate The *true wind* abates or moderates when it blows less strongly than before. When a sailing boat *bears away* onto a *run* the wind appears to abate, but this is deceptive; it is not the true wind but the *apparent wind* that blows less strongly when running.

Abeam Indicates direction from the boat, at right angles to the *fore-and-aft line*.

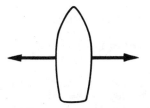

Aboard Inside or on board a vessel. Close aboard is close alongside.

A-bracket The metal struts which support the *propeller shaft* after it has emerged from the hull are usually angled either side with a cross brace, in the form of an inverted letter A.

Abreast Said of boats on parallel *courses* and *abeam* of each other; line abreast, several boats are equally spaced and abreast of each other.

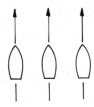

ABS 1. Abbreviation for acrylonitrile butadiene styrene, a thermoplastic material used for the *series production* of small boats. ABS sheeting is formed to the shape of the *mould* by a vacuum process. 2. Abbreviation for American Bureau of Shipping, a *classification society* similar to Lloyds Register of Shipping.

Accelerator A chemical substance (cobalt or amine based) added to *resin* when making a *GRP/ FRP moulding* to enable the *polymerization* reaction to occur more quickly at room temperature of 15–20° instead of 50°C. *Pot life* is shortened. The accelerator must be suitable for use with the *catalyst*, and they must never be mixed together before being added to the resin because they may explode. Accelerator is either supplied separately, or already mixed with the resin.

Accelerometer or **Acceleration indicator** An additional facility provided with some electronic *logs*; small rates of change in boat speed are shown on an expanded scale so that the crew can see clearly whether the boat sails faster or slower in response to a change of course, sail *trimming*, shifting crew weight etc.

Accidental gybe (US or **uncontrolled jibe**) On a dead *run,* the boom swings over and the boat *gybes* herself before the crew is ready. Occurs when the helmsman does not notice that the wind has shifted to blow on the *lee* side of the sail, which is suddenly slammed right over to the opposite side. The boom can injure a crew member, knock a man overboard, and damage or be damaged by the lee *shroud.* Rigging a *foreguy* or *preventer* helps to avoid an accidental gybe.

Accommodation (US **accommodations**) Spaces on board where the crew live, eat and sleep.

Accommodation ladder Ladder, hung over the side or stern, almost always removable but may be part of the *stern pulpit.* A swimming ladder must extend far enough into the water to enable a swimmer to get back on board.

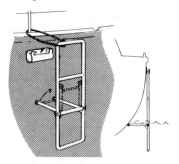

Accommodation plan Additional to the *lines plan;* gives the lay-out of the below deck areas, viewed from above, with the size and position of berths, galley, stowage spaces etc.

A Class catamaran The smallest of the *catamaran* classes. The boats are sailed single-handed, and the maximum measurements permitted are LOA 18ft (5.49 m), overall beam 7.54 ft (2.30 m), sail area 150 sq ft (13.94 sq m). A spinnaker may

be set only if its area is included in the total sail area.

Act of God A natural occurrence which could not have been foreseen; nor could damage have been averted by human efforts. The term is used in relation to *distress,* damage, or misfortune at sea.

Admiral's Cup A challenge prize named after Sir Miles Wyatt, who was Admiral of the *RORC* when the first competition was held in 1957. National teams of three offshore racing yachts compete. Originally the races were open to yachts of over 30 ft or 9.14 m waterline length, but in 1979 they were restricted to yachts with an *IOR rating* of not less than 30 ft and not more than 40 ft. The biennial races are run in conjunction with Cowes Week, and consist of three inshore races counting single points, the Channel Race, which is about 225 n.miles long and counts double points, and the *Fastnet Race* 605 n.miles long, treble points. Competitors score points individually, and their total scores for the four races are added to find the winning team.

Admiralty anchor Traditional *anchor* with a fixed or folding *stock* set at right angles to the arms; also called fisherman anchor.

Adrift 1. Not attached to the sea-bed or the shore; at the mercy of wind and current. 2. Said of an object broken free of fastenings or (coll.) missing.

Advanced line of position (US) See *transferred position line.*

Advection fog or **sea fog** When relatively warm moist air flows over a colder surface the lower layers are cooled, and fog forms over both land and sea. Sea fog occurs frequently near the coast in spring and early summer when warmer air from over the land flows over the cooler sea. It also forms at sea when air passes from a region of

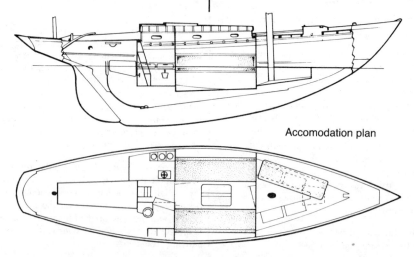

Accomodation plan

warmer sea to one where the sea is colder; the Grand Banks fogs are typical, and occur when warm Gulf Stream air flows over the cold waters of the Labrador Current. Sea fog often persists, but is replaced by cloud if winds are above 14 knots.

Aerial or **antenna** Different types of aerial are needed for various purposes on board. The *loop, Bellini-Tosi* or *ferrite rod* aerial of a *direction finder* and the *scanner* of a *radar* set are *directional aerials*. The first three receive signals, but the last both transmits and receives. Rod, whip or di-pole aerials are required for radio communication. Often part of the *rigging* is used, and this must be electrically insulated from spars and superstructure by special strain *insulators* that will withstand the stresses of the rigging; an emergency aerial should then also be carried in case the boat is dismasted.

Aerodynamics Branch of physics concerned with the motion of air and other gases.

Aerofoil (UK) or **airfoil** (US) The cross-section of a body, such as an aircraft wing, shaped to cause a change in the velocity of the fluid (air) flowing over it. A sail is curved in order to guide the flow of air, and so converts wind energy into forward motion. A hydrofoil, such as the keel, centreboard or rudder, is shaped similarly but the fluid is water. In both cases the effect is the same whether a body is moving into a still fluid or the fluid is approaching a stationary body. For example, when a curved sail is trimmed to a certain *angle of attack,* air is diverted from its normal path, streamlines are more widely spaced to windward of the sail, air flow is decelerated and pressure rises; to leeward the streamlines are constricted, air flow is accelerated and pressure drops (Bernoulli's principle). The resultant force is composed of *lift,* acting at right angles to the wind direction, and *drag,* acting with the wind. A high lift to drag ratio is desirable. The main factors involved are *aspect ratio,* the *camber* or fullness of the sail, and the angle of attack, i.e. sail cut, sail tuning and sail trimming.

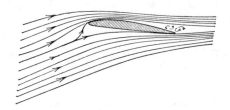

Afloat 1. *Floating,* supported by water, as opposed to *beached, aground, ashore* etc. 2. At sea, as opposed to on shore.

A-frame See *bipod mast.*

Aft Near, towards or at the *stern;* opp of *forward* and *fore.*

After Nearer the *stern,* often as a prefix as in afterbody, afterdeck; opp of *fore, forward.*

Afterbody The part of the hull form abaft the *midships section;* c.f. *forebody.*

Aftercabin When a boat has more than one cabin, the one further aft, often abaft a *centre cockpit* and beneath the afterdeck.

Afterdeck The *deck* abaft amidships, usually abaft the *cockpit.*

Afterpeak Space aft, immediately forward of the *stern.*

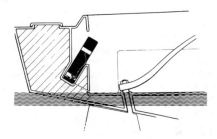

Age allowance *IOR* Mark IIIA may be applied to reduce the *rating* of older boats slightly, and so enable them to race more fairly against newer designs. May be 0.2% of the *time multiplication factor* deducted for each year prior to a certain date, (e.g. in 1979 prior to 1977) or 2% of the TMF deducted for a boat of a certain age, e.g. 5–9 years old.

Aground 1. Partly or completely resting on the *bottom.* 2. The *IRPCS* require vessels aground to display signal *shapes* by day, exhibit certain lights by night and make *sound signals* in *restricted visibility.* These vary according to the size of the vessel, and full details are printed in the IRPCS but, if a vessel is seen exhibiting two all-round red lights or three *balls* forward in a vertical line or if, in restricted visibility, a *bell* is heard being rung rapidly, preceded and followed by three distinct strokes on the bell, the vessel exhibiting or making the signals is aground. The regulations concerning lights and shapes will not apply to vessels under 12 m in length after the 1981 IMO decision comes into force.

Ahead Indicates the direction of an object beyond the *stem* of a boat, whether moving or stationary; e.g. a landmark may be sighted right ahead. Also forward movement of the boat, as in the engine order 'full ahead'. Opp *astern*; c.f. *clear ahead.*

Ahoy Shout made to attract attention when *hailing* a vessel, often in conjunction with her name, as 'Cormorant' ahoy.

A-hull To ride out a gale with no sail set and the *helm* lashed to *leeward*. The boat usually lies roughly *broadside* on to the seas.

Aid to navigation Any object on land or sea, sited or anchored to warn a sailor of a danger, or to enable him to fix his position; may be a *buoy, beacon, lighthouse, radio beacon, leading line, daymark* etc. The position of an aid is marked on a *chart* together with such details as shape, colour, *lights, topmarks,* and *fog signals,* so that it can be identified by the navigator.

Airfoil (US) See *aerofoil.*

Air mass A mass of air with reasonably uniform *humidity* and temperature at all layers, covering some thousands of square miles. Air masses may be described as polar or tropical, and continental or maritime according to the source region: they are cold or warm according to whether the temperature of the air near the surface is below or above that of the land or sea beneath. Air masses are modified when they leave the source region, mainly by being warmed or cooled by the surface beneath them.

Alee To *leeward;* esp in the US helmsman's warning when he has put the helm down to *go about,* 'helm's alee'.

All-round light (UK) or **all-around (32-point) light** (US) A *light* that is *exhibited by a vessel* and is visible all around the horizon. The *IRPCS* require vessels of certain categories to display one or more all-round lights, either alone or in conjunction with other lights, to inform other vessels of their condition or occupation. The minimum range of visibility varies with the size of the vessel, and is specified in the IRPCS.

All standing See *bring up,* and *gybe.*

Aloft Above deck, up the *mast* or *rigging,* as in to go aloft.

Alongside Berthed in line with or beside another vessel, a jetty, pier etc, as in come, go, moor and lie alongside.

Altering course Under *racing rule 35,* a *right-of way* yacht may not alter course to prevent another from keeping clear or to obstruct her, except as

specified in the rule. She may well be disqualified if she does not *hail* before making an unforeseen alteration of course.

Alternating light A light, exhibited as an *aid to navigation,* which shows more than one colour on the same *bearing* during each *period.* The *character* of an alternating light may be continuous, *flashing, group flashing* or *occulting.* Chart abbr Al, formerly Alt.

Altitude The angular distance of a *heavenly body* above the *horizon. Sextant* or observed *altitude* is that measured with a *sextant* or *octant* by an observer, and is the angular distance above the *visible horixon. Apparent altitude* is the angular distance above the *sensible horizon,* after sextant altitude has been corrected for *index error* and dip. *True altitude* is the actual altitude of a body above the *rational horizon,* i.e. apparent altitude further corrected for *refraction, semi-diameter* and *parallax.* Calculated altitude (*intercept method*) is the true altitude a body would have at an *assumed position.* Tabulated altitude, the true altitude a body would have at a *chosen position,* is found in the *Sight Reduction Tables* (Hc).

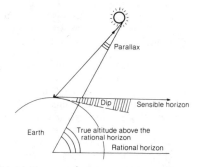

Altitude Correction Tables Tables printed in the *Nautical Almanac* giving the corrections to be applied when *sights* are taken of heavenly bodies: (a) the upper and lower *limb* of the sun – *apparent altitudes* from 0–90°, including corrections for *refraction, semi-diameter* and normal *parallax;* lower limb values are added: (b) stars and planets – refraction only; subtract: (c) *dip* – for *heights of eye* to 155 ft (48 m); subtract: (d) tables for the upper and lower limb of the moon, and a separate table for horizontal parallax.

Altocumulus (Ac) White or grey medium level patch, sheet or layer cloud, like cotton wool balls and streaks.

Altostratus (As) Greyish or bluish fibrous veil of sheet or layer clouds at medium level; a watery sun can be seen through them, and they often accompany a *warm front* or *occlusion.*

Aluminium (US **aluminum**), Al. Marine alloy of aluminium, often used for racing keelboats because strength is allied to light weight. Widely used for spars. Can be welded and does not rust, but care is required to avoid *galvanic corrosion,* and copper- or mercury-based paints must be avoided. At present more costly than *GRP/FRP* for keelboats and larger craft. *Specific gravity* 2.7. See also *anodize.*

Amateur Under the IYRU *racing rules,* a *yachtsman* who engages in yacht racing as a pastime, as distinguished from a means of obtaining a livelihood (paid *hand*). One or more amateurs must be on board during a race.

America's Cup The first challenge prize for sailing yachts, put up in 1851 by the Royal Yacht Squadron, originally as the Hundred Guinea Cup. America's Cup racing has influenced design since then. In 1851 the schooner 'America', fig A (LOA 101 ft 9 in, 31 m; beam 22 ft 6 in, 6.8 m; draft 11 ft 6 in, 3.5 m; displacement 170 tons, 172.7 tonnes; sail area 5263 sq ft, 489 sq m) beat the élite of British yachts in a race round the Isle of Wight, taking the cup across the Atlantic where it has stayed ever since. The largest defender was 'Reliance' in 1903, fig B (LOA 142 ft 8 in, 43.5 m; sail area 16,160 sq ft, 1501 sq m). *J-class* yachts, originally gaff-rigged (fig C), but later bermudan-(US marconi-) rigged, competed in the 1930s (LOA about 120 ft, 36.5 m; sail area about 7500 sq ft, 700 sq m) fig D. Since 1958 races have been sailed between *12-Metres,* fig E (LOA about 66 ft, 20 m, sail area about 1800 sq ft, 167 sq m). The boats race without *handicap* over a triangular course about 24 n.miles long off Newport, RI, on the east coast of the USA, the match winner being the yacht that first wins four races.

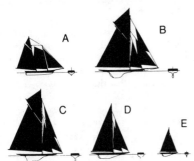

Amidships or **midships** The centre part of the boat, both *athwartships* and *fore-and-aft,* thus both between the *port* and *starboard* sides and between the *forward* and *after* parts of the boat.

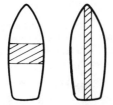

Amp-hour Of batteries, the number of amps that can be taken at a steady rate of discharge, often quoted for 10 or 20 continuous hours, e.g. a 250 AH battery supplies 25 amps for 10 hours, or 12½ amps for 20 hours.

Amplitude 1. The *true bearing* of a *heavenly body* when it is *rising* (or *setting*), measured in degrees from the east (or west) points on the observer's horizon towards north or south. 2. Of the *tide,* half the *range,* i.e. the difference between mean tide level and either *high water* or *low water.* 3. Of a *wave,* half the height, i.e. half the vertical distance between crest and trough. See also *modulation.*

AMVER *Automated Mutual-Assistance Vessel Rescue* q.v.

Anabatic wind Local wind that flows upwards, as opposed to a katabatic wind that flows downwards. Generally occurs in mountainous areas.

Analogue display Measurements obtained by an instrument are indicated by a pointer moving along a scale, which is often a graduated dial. It is easy to read, particularly for circular presentations such as DF compass. Where absolute values are required, measurements can be given *digitally* very accurately, say to six decimal places.

Anchor Verb (see *anchoring*) and noun. Heavy metal device dropped to the bottom on the end of a cable or rode to hold a vessel in a certain position. The most popular modern types of anchor are the *CQR* (*plough* or plow anchor), *Danforth* and *Bruce.* Older anchors include the *fisherman* (or Admiralty or folding *stock*) and *mushroom anchors.* A *folding anchor* is often used by dinghies. The *holding power* of older types relies more on weight than on shape, but modern designs combine greater holding power with lighter weight, and a modern anchor is often 20% lighter than an equivalent fisherman. The weight of anchor required depends both on the size of boat and on the type of sailing planned, i.e. whether

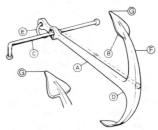

cruising or racing in estuaries or offshore, for temporary *kedging* etc. *Classification societies* list the weights recommended for various sizes of vessel. The main parts are A, shank; B, flukes which dig into the ground; C, stock which stabilizes the anchor; D, crown which connects the main parts; E, ring to which the cable is bent; F, arms; G, bill. The type of sea-bed also determines how well an anchor will hold (see *holding ground* and *anchoring*).

Anchorage A suitable place for a vessel to anchor. Should be protected, shallow with good *holding ground*, little *tidal stream or current*, and preferably near a *weather shore. Swinging room* is required, and objects should be visible on shore on which to take a *bearing* to check that the anchor is *holding*. An anchorage is indicated on *charts* by an anchor symbol or the abbr Anch.

Anchor bed and **chocks** Strong, shaped deck fitting, or a moulding on a *GRP/FRP* deck, to which the anchor is secured. Alternatively wooden or plastic chocks, fastened to the deck, are shaped to carry the fluke, crown, shaft etc. Some boats have an anchor well forward, closed by a lid when the anchor is stowed.

Anchor buoy *Buoy* or *float* on the end of the *tripping line,* which is secured to the crown of the anchor. Indicates the anchor's position, and enables it to be raised by the tripping line if the cable parts or, if the anchor cannot be broken out and raised normally, to be pulled forward clear of the obstruction.

Anchor cable or rode Chain, wire rope or rope connection between a vessel and her anchor. Chain cable does not *chafe* and, because it weighs more, hangs down in a curve (see *catenary*), which helps the anchor to hold. Whereas in normal weather *scope* should be roughly six times the depth of water when using rope cable, only four times the depth of water is adequate for chain cable, and the boat then needs less *swinging room*. Dinghies use light rope cable but, in keelboats, larger diameter rope cable is easier to handle, although unnecessarily strong, and part of the advantage of the lower weight of rope is therefore lost; the *chain locker* also has to be larger than when chain cable

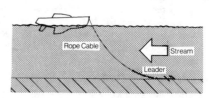

is used. A length of chain (leader) should generally be inserted between rope cable and the anchor; its weight ensures that the pull is parallel to the sea-bed, and this helps the anchor to bite. When rope cable is attached directly to the anchor it can chafe on a foul bottom with protruding objects such as rocks. The leader also acts as a shock absorber and, like an anchor weight and catenary, reduces *snubbing. Classification societies* list the sizes of chain and rope cable recommended for various sizes of craft.

Anchored vessel The *IRPCS* require a vessel at anchor to display a signal *shape* by day, exhibit certain lights by night and make *sound signals* in *restricted visibility*. These vary according to the size of the vessel, and full details are printed in IRPCS but, if a vessel is seen displaying one black *ball* by day or a *bell* is heard being rung rapidly for five seconds at intervals of not more than one minute (not preceded and followed by three strokes on the bell), the vessel exhibiting or making the signals is at anchor. Boats under 20 m in length exhibit a white all-round *anchor light* forward. Although a boat under 12 m in length is not obliged to ring a bell, she must be able to make some other efficient form of sound signal in restricted visibility.

Anchoring In the broadest sense anchoring involves selecting a suitable anchorage, preparing the anchor cable and letting go the anchor, belaying the cable, checking with a *transit* (US range) or by taking *bearings* that the anchor is not *dragging*, and hoisting a black *ball* or an anchor light to show that the vessel is at anchor. A boat that lies midway between two anchors is said to be *moored*.

Anchor light or **riding light** An *all-round* white light, visible for at least two miles, exhibited forward where it can best be seen, to show that a boat of less than 50 m in length is at anchor. On a sailing boat is usually shackled to the forestay, and hoisted to a suitable height by the jib halyard. Full details of lights to be exhibited by vessels of various sizes are printed in the *IRPCS*.

Anchor watch Watch kept when a vessel is at anchor to check whether the anchor is *dragging*, to *veer* more cable if necessary, and to call out the watch in an emergency.

Anchor weight (US or **sentinel**) Weight or heavy object attached to a ring which slides over the

anchor cable. The weight is lowered on a line to increase the *catenary* of the cable, especially in fresh winds; this increases *holding power* and reduces *snubbing*.

Anchor winch See *windlass*.

Anemometer Instrument that measures wind speed; in sailing boats its sensor is normally mounted at the masthead. Semi-circular cups on the ends of horizontal arms catch the wind and revolve around a vertical shaft. The speed of rotation indicates wind speed which is displayed on a dial, usually in or near the cockpit.

Aneroid barometer See *barometer*.

Angle of attack or **angle of incidence** The angle between the direction of flow of a fluid and the direction of the *chord* of an *aerofoil* or *hydrofoil*. For example the angle between the direction of the *apparent wind* and the chord of the sail (see *force* fig.) or the angle between the direction in which the boat moves through the water and the chord of the centreboard or rudder. For a sail the

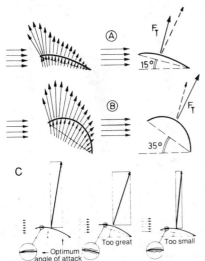

optimum angle varies considerably with *camber*, that of a flat-cut mainsail (A) being roughly 15–20°, whereas a full sail such as a spinnaker set on a reach (B) is trimmed to a much greater angle of 25–35°. In practice, *telltales* (C) sewn to the sail show at a glance whether the sail is trimmed to the correct angle of attack or not, because they give a visual indication as to whether air flow in the *boundary layer* is *laminar* or *turbulent*.

Angle of cut The smaller of the two angles made when two *position lines* are laid off on a chart and cross each other. An angle of 90° gives the least error.

Angle of vanishing stability The point on a *stability curve* where *righting moment* is zero at a certain angle of heel. The optimum conditions on which the stability curve is based deteriorate rapidly, and the boat will capsize earlier, if the crew (live ballast) accidentally slip to leeward, if gear on board shifts when the boat heels, or if she ships water.

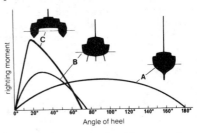

Annual change *Variation* changes continuously because the position of the *magnetic north pole* alters. Printed inside most *compass roses* on charts is information as to whether variation at that place is westerly or easterly, the value for variation at the time the chart was printed, and the amount of change in one complete year.

Anode The positive electrode of a galvanic cell from which current flows into the negative cathode via the electrolyte (sea-water): the electrode which corrodes, and the less noble metal in the *galvanic series*. Anodic protection: see *cathodic protection*.

Anodizing *Aluminium* is given a *corrosion*-resistant coating. The aluminium is made the anode in a cell and, when a current passes through the electrolyte (often chromic or oxalic acid), a layer of oxide forms on the aluminium. May also be coloured. Masts and booms are often anodized.

Answering pendant A red-white-red-white-red *code pendant*, hoisted at the *dip* when a hoist of

Answering pendant

signal flags is seen, and hoisted fully when the signal has been understood. Is also hoisted by a signalling station to indicate that the *International Code of Signals* (1969) is being used. Racing, means 'All races not started are *postponed*'.

Answer the helm A boat is said to answer the helm when she alters course in response to the helmsman's deflection of the *rudder*. A boat cannot respond unless she is making *headway* or *sternway*, and is then said to have steerage way. Sometimes a boat refuses to answer the helm, for example if a strong wind is blowing on her superstructure, in a high following sea, when *broaching*, or if she loses steerage way when close-hauled and suddenly *headed* by the wind.

Antenna See *aerial*.

Anticyclone High pressure area enclosed by widely spaced *isobars*. In the central part, where pressure is highest, wind speeds are low, skies are clear or slightly cloudy, and precipitation is rare. Winds blow outwards from the centre, clockwise in the northern hemisphere, but circulation is counterclockwise in the southern.

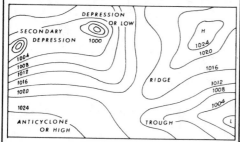

Antifouling paint Poisonous paint applied to the underwater surfaces of a boat to prevent or restrict *fouling* by *marine* life, such as algae and barnacles. Paints with a high copper content can be applied to wooden and *GRP/FRP* hulls, but not to steel or light alloy hulls on account of the danger of *galvanic corrosion*. Paints containing mercury or tin may be used on metal hulls, but only over suitable primers. Soft antifouling has to be applied immediately before launching, because it loses toxicity when it dries in the air. Hard paints which remain toxic for long periods out of the water are applied to dinghies and boats that are trailed.

Antron Trade name for American *polyamide* fibres made by duPont and used for making rope.

Apeak Of an *anchor cable*, up and down or nearly vertical, just before the anchor is broken out.

Apogee The point in the moon's orbit where she is furthest from the earth; the apogean *tide* which occurs at this time has small *range*. C.f. *perigee*.

Apparent altitude The *altitude* of a *heavenly body* above the *sensible horizon*, i.e. sextant altitude corrected for *index error* and *dip*. To obtain the *true altitude*, further corrections have to be applied, in the case of sun and moon for *refraction, semi-diameter* and *parallax*.

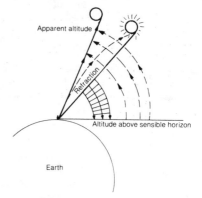

Apparent noon The time of the upper *meridian passage* of the *true sun* when it is on the *observer's meridian;* the time that it reaches its greatest *altitude*.

Apparent solar time Time relative to the *true sun* that is visible in the heavens; the *local hour angle* of the sun ± 12 hours. C. f. *mean solar time*, based on a fictitious mean sun. Clocks and watches measure the passage of mean time, which differs from apparent time by the *equation of time*, as tabulated in the *Nautical Almanac*.

Apparent wind or **relative wind** The wind felt by the crew, the direction of which is indicated by the burgee, when a boat is moving *over the ground*, as opposed to the *true wind*, which blows over water nearby and is felt on a boat lying motionless at anchor. It is the apparent wind that blows on the sails which, helped by the hull, convert its energy into forward motion.

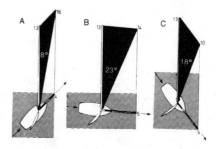

Apparent wind velocity (speed and direction) can be found with a *vector diagram*, and is the resultant of true wind and the wind that arises as a result of the boat's motion over the ground (boat speed); the latter blows in the opposite direction to that in which she moves, but not necessarily opposite to that in which she is heading (see *tide*

wind). Given a true wind of constant velocity, the apparent wind velocity varies with the *point of sailing*. In the figures, true wind direction and speed (13 knots) are shown by the white arrows, and boat speeds of 4, 5 and 5 knots by black and white arrows.

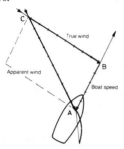

When two forces act at a single point (A), and are represented both in magnitude and direction by the adjacent sides of a parallelogram (CB and BA), the diagonal of the parallelogram drawn from that point (CA) represents the magnitude and direction of the resultant of the two forces. Thus the black arrows in the fig. p. 8 show the velocity of the apparent wind and, as can be seen, in each case its direction is nearer the bow than that of the true wind; the difference in direction is greatest when the wind is abeam and decreases progressively as the boat luffs up or bears away. When the boat runs dead before the wind, the directions of the true and apparent winds coincide. Apparent wind speed is much the same as true wind speed when the wind is abeam, but becomes progressively greater than true wind speed when the boat luffs up, and progressively slower when she bears away.

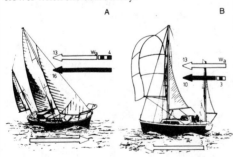

In figures A and B the true wind is blowing at 13 knots, but the apparent wind propelling boat B, running downwind at 3 knots, is only 10 knots; whereas boat A, close-hauled, is making 4 knots towards it and the apparent wind is therefore blowing at 17 knots.

Apron Member, fastened inside the *stem*, to which the *planking* is secured. See *construction* fig.

Arc The curved part of the frame of a *sextant* or *octant*. Has a toothed rack in which the *index*

bar's worm wheel engages, and is either engraved in degrees or in degrees, minutes and seconds.

Arc bottom A hull with a *chine* and a curved bottom, which is an arc of the circumference of a circle, e.g. Star class boats.

Archboard Solid chock of wood at the aft end of a *counter* stern.

Archimedes principle Owing to upthrust (buoyancy), a body that is totally or partially immersed in a fluid appears to lose as much weight as the weight of the fluid it displaces. The weight of a floating boat is equal to the weight of the water she displaces (i.e. that of the volume of the water displaced by her *underwater body* up to the *waterline* at which she is floating). Hence the volume of the immersed hull, multiplied by the *density* of the water in which she floats, equals the weight of the displaced water. Because the density of water varies with *salinity*, the same boat will be more or less deeply immersed in different areas, and her *displacement* varies in consequence.

Arc to time A conversion table in the *Nautical Almanac, Reed's* etc, enabling degrees of *longitude* to be converted into time, and vice versa: 15° longitude = 1 hour; 15′ longitude = 1 minute; 15″ longitude = 1 second; 4 minutes = 1° longitude; 4 seconds = 1′ longitude.

Argos Method of locating vessels at sea. The vessel's transmitted coded signal is received by an orbiting satellite, which in turn transmits the vessel's position to a telemetering station on earth. Used in Trans-Atlantic and other long-distance races to enable the organisers to pinpoint the competitors' positions.

Aries, First point of The point where the *ecliptic* crosses the *celestial equator* on about March 21st (the vernal equinox). *Greenwich Hour Angle* and time of *meridian passage* are given in the *Nautical Almanac* as if Aries were a star, because it is used as the datum point for the 57 listed stars. The GHA of a heavenly body is found by adding the body's *Sidereal Hour Angle* to GHA Aries. The symbol for Aries is ♈.

Arm The part of an *anchor* between the crown and the fluke.

Arm the lead The hollow base of the *lead* is filled with grease or soap, formerly with tallow, so that a sample of the bottom is brought up when taking a *sounding*. This can help the navigator to determine his position, because the quality of the bottom is marked on charts. Also gives an indication as to how well the *anchor* will hold (see *holding ground*).

Ash A tough, flexible wood of which many items of equipment may be made, such as cleats, boathooks, oars, ensign staffs and gratings. *Specific gravity* 0.74.

Ashore On the land, or aground.

Aspect ratio In general usage the aspect ratio of a sail is taken to be the length of the *luff* to that of the *foot,* as in fig (b), i.e. the luff to foot ratio. In aeronautical terminology a sail's aspect ratio is the ratio of the length of the luff to mean width, i.e. length of luff squared divided by sail area in the case of a triangular sail, as in fig (a). A tall

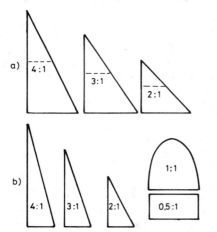

narrow sail has a high aspect ratio, whereas a lower broader sail has a low aspect ratio. The former performs better when the boat is close-hauled, but low aspect ratio sails, such as gaff and square sails, are more efficient when broad reaching and running. The aspect ratio of a rudder is depth:*chord,* and that of a keel is depth:fore-and-aft length. Abbr AR.

Assumed position The position at which a vessel is assumed to be, when using the *intercept* (Marcq St. Hilaire) *method* of celestial navigation. May be her *dead reckoning* position or her *estimated position.*

Astern Direction beyond the *stern,* behind the boat, opposite to *ahead.* Also movement through the water in that direction, as in the engine order, 'slow astern'.

Astrolabe Astrolabes were complicated instruments with which astronomical calculations were

made from very early times, the oldest known dating from 150 BC. The much simpler navigational astrolabe measured the *altitude* of the sun and stars, and the figure shows an instrument dated 1468. Replaced by the backstaff and, eventually, by the *sextant.*

Astro-navigation Navigation by means of observations of stars, more widely used as synonymous with *celestial navigation,* i.e. observations of heavenly bodies.

Astronomical triangle See *PZX triangle.*

Astronomical twilight The period when it gradually becomes less dark before sunrise, and when darkness increases after sunset; starts in the morning and finishes in the evening when the sun's centre is 18° below the *rational horizon.*

Athwart, athwartships, thwartships At right angles to the *centreline* of the boat; side to side; inside the boat, whereas *abeam* is a direction outside the boat.

Atmosphere 1. The air which envelops the earth. The lower layer of the atmosphere is the troposphere above which is the stratosphere; these are separated by the tropopause. Above the stratopause, which is about 30 miles above the earth, are the D-, E- and F-layers of the ionosphere. 2. Former metric system unit of pressure, replaced by the *bar:* 1 atmosphere = 1.01325 bar = 101325 N/sq m.

Atmospheric pressure or **barometric pressure** Pressure related to the weight of air above a place, i.e. to the top of the atmosphere. Varies with height, temperature and *latitude,* and was formerly measured in inches or millimetres of mercury, but the unit now used is the *millibar,* one thousandth of a bar. The International Standard Atmosphere, 1013.2 mb (760 mmHg, 29.92 inHg) is based on atmospheric pressure at sea level at 15 °C. Mercurial *barometers* are calibrated to read correctly at mean sea level at 0 °C and standard gravity 9.80665 m/sec^2, i.e. virtually at latitude 45°.

Atrip Said of the *anchor* when it has just been broken out but is still touching the bottom.

Aurora Borealis and **Aurora Australis** Luminous phenomena which occur at heights of over 60 miles. Aurora Borealis, also called the Northern Lights, is seen most frequently in high latitudes within the Arctic circle, and Aurora Australis similarly within the Antarctic Circle. Electrically charged particles from the sun are diverted towards the *magnetic poles* by the earth's *magnetic field,* and collide with gases in the atmosphere. Earth's magnetic field is disturbed, and the *magnetic compass* is often affected.

Automated Mutual-Assistance Vessel Rescue System (AMVER) US Coast Guard-operated system whereby the movements and positions of vessels at sea are reported to the AMVER Center in New York. A vessel known to be in the vicinity of another that is in distress can then be effectively integrated into the Search and Rescue efforts by the AMVER Center.

Automatic Direction Finder *Radio direction finding* instrument. The components are an *aerial* (for example *cross-loop*), receiver and *bearing* indicator. Automatically takes bearings of marine *radio beacons, omnidirectional* radio beacons or other transmitters. The bearing is either read on the dial, which is set to the *magnetic course*, or is shown as a trace on a cathode ray tube. Originally a medium and long wave aid, but can now be obtained in a form that allows reception of almost all *frequencies,* including VHF bands.

Automatic pilot or **autopilot** Electronic equipment that enables a boat automatically to follow a *compass course* or, when controlled by a wind *vane,* a course relative to wind direction. Many types are available and vary greatly in sophistication, efficiency and price. A special *compass* with a sensor compares the boat's *heading* with the *rudder* position. When a course error occurs, a hydraulic unit or electric motor moves the rudder in the direction which will reduce the error; as this action is often fully proportional, the rudder is in the midships position when the error is reduced to zero. The names of the controls differ according to the manufacturer. The rudder control adjusts the amount of rudder applied to alter course; the amount required varies with the sea state and the boat's characteristics. The weather or *yaw* control adjusts the width of the deadband; this is an arc within which the boat is allowed to swing either side of the compass course, and respond naturally to the seas before the drive motor is actuated. The trim, *weather helm,* bias or standing helm control keeps the rudder at a slight angle to the centreline, either to allow for weather helm when under sail, or to offset the *wheel effect* of the propeller when under power. Only larger vessels require a counter rudder control. See also *tiller steering system.*

Auxiliary Frequently used term for a sailing boat that has auxiliary power, i.e. with an *inboard* or *outboard* petrol or diesel engine. Also abbr for auxiliary engine.

Auxiliary engine *Inboard* or *outboard* petrol or *diesel* engine, fitted to a boat designed primarily for sailing to enable her to make way at a reasonable speed in calms, and to operate without sails

when leaving a berth, coming alongside etc. Two newer forms of transmission are *sail-drive* and *outdrive.* About 4 hp (3 kW) per 100 sq ft (10 sq m) of sail area is normally adequate.

Avast Order to stop an activity such as *heaving, hauling* etc. May be reduced to 'vast'.

Awash Level with the surface of the water which just washes over an object, such as a boat, rock or other feature. The chart symbol for a rock awash at *chart datum* is a vertical cross with a dot in each quadrant

Aweigh Said of the *anchor* when it has been broken out, and is no longer holding the vessel.

Awning A protective canvas cover that generally extends the full width of the boat to protect an area, such as the *cockpit, coachroof* and *deck,* from hot sun, and to keep out rain. Important when sailing in tropical and sub-tropical waters.

Often fitted to larger dinghies and small cruisers to provide or extend *accommodation.* May be in several parts, laced together and hung over the boom. Some have pockets for *battens* or rods, which extend the canvas and are rigged above the boom supported by wires leading from the ends of the batten pockets or from a central point to the mast.

Azimuth 1. Angle PZX in the *PZX triangle.* The angle at the *zenith* between the observer's meridian (the *meridian* that passes through the observer's zenith) and the *great circle* that passes through both the *heavenly body* and the observer's zenith. The azimuth angle is measured in degrees from 0–180° east or west from the observer's meridian, and is named from the elevated pole, i.e. from the north pole in the northern hemisphere and from the south pole in the southern. 2. The true *bearing* of a heavenly body, measured from north or south in degrees.

Azimuth mirror Similar to an azimuth ring, but the mirror or prism stands centrally over the card, not on the rim.

Azimuth ring or **circle** Ring which fits on top of a *compass;* carries a prism with which horizontal *bearings* can be taken, and may also have a mirror and shades for taking bearings of *heavenly bodies.*

B

B = **Bravo:** *swallow-tailed* red *code flag.* As a single letter signal means 'I am taking in, or discharging, or carrying dangerous goods'. *Morse code:* — • • • (dash dot dot dot). When racing is flown to indicate that the yacht intends to make a *protest.*

Baby stay   Or *inner forestay*, q.v.

Baby staysail or **inner staysail**   A small *headsail* set by offshore racing boats on the baby stay or inner forestay.

Back   1. To back a sail: a *jib* or *headsail* is backed when it is held or sheeted to *windward* so that the wind strikes it on the side that is normally to *leeward*. Pushes the bow round, and helps a boat that is slow *in stays* to *go about*, or to avoid getting *in irons* when tacking in a heavy sea. The jib is also backed when a boat is hove to (see *heave to*), and to put her on the desired tack when getting under way from a *mooring* or after *weighing anchor*. 2. To back an *anchor:* to lay out a second,

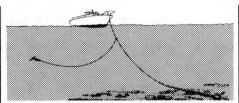

reserve anchor or *kedge,* the two cables being connected to each other, when high seas or strong winds make an anchorage unsafe, and especially if there is a *lee shore* close by, or if the *holding ground* is poor. In the US the term also relates to rigging a sentinel (UK *anchor weight*) on the rode. 3. To back oars: when *rowing* (pulling), to reverse the action, so causing the boat to slow, stop or make *sternway*. She will turn on the spot if one oar

is backed and the other operated normally. 4. Of wind: it backs when it shifts to blow from a direction that is further anti- or counterclockwise. To back and backing refers to a change in direction of the *true wind,* and should not be confused with *heading* and *freeing winds* which are related to the boat's course. The opposite of to back is to *veer.*

Backing blocks, chocks or **plates**   Where a fitting is under heavy load, such as an eyebolt through-bolted to the deck, a wooden block, a metal backing plate or extra layers of GRP/FRP provide greater strength and distribute the load more widely.

Back splice   The end of a rope or line is finished by unlaying the *strands* for a few inches, making a *crown knot* and tucking the strands back down the rope.

Back or **quarter spring** *Mooring line* (q.v.) which is made fast to a point aft in the boat, and which runs forward to a *bollard* on shore or to another boat moored alongside.

Backstay A *stay* that supports a *mast* from *aft.* In *bermudan-rigged* (US marconi-rigged) boats leads from the masthead to a *chain plate* at the *stern,* or to a *bumpkin.* Some boats have twin standing backstays, others have *running backstays* or runners, which extend from the *hounds* to a point on the deck alongside the cockpit. (See *rigging* fig.) Part of the backstay may be used as a radio aerial (see *insulator*). In *square-rigged* ships the backstay leads from near the head of a mast to a point at the sides *abaft* the *shrouds.*

Backstay adjuster A fitting that adjusts the tension of the backstay and so *tunes* the *rig.* In smaller boats may be a *turnbuckle* (UK or rigging screw) or a *tackle;* in larger boats a hydraulic cylinder or *wheel tensioner* can alter the length of the rigging wire by up to 8 in (200 mm).

Backstay lever See *runner lever.*

Backstaysail An unusual sail set by a *bermudan-* (US marconi-) *rigged sloop* when *reaching* or *running* in light breezes. The *head* extends about half way up the backstay, and it is tacked down to the deck near the mast. In effect a *mizzen staysail* for a boat without a mizzenmast.

Backwater 1. A quiet part of a river, out of the main current. 2. To reverse the motion of a *rowing boat* by pushing on the *oars* instead of pulling.

Backwind Air flow is deflected by a sail, or by the sails of another boat, onto the *lee* side of another sail. The *mainsail* is backwinded by a *headsail* if the headsail sheet is led too close to the *centreline,* the wind being exhausted from the *leech* of the headsail onto the lee side of the *luff* of

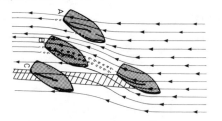

the mainsail. When a *close-hauled* boat is in the *safe leeward position,* close ahead and to leeward of another boat, the wind exhausted by her sails is deflected onto the lee side of the following boat's headsail; the backwinded boat either has to bear away to fill her sails, or tack to clear her wind.

Baffle plate Vertical plate fitted *fore-and-aft* or *athwartships* inside tanks of all sizes. The fluid can pass through holes in the plates, but sudden and dangerous surging in response to the boat's motion is prevented.

Baggwrinkle (or **baggy rinkle** or **bag a wrinkle** etc) Old rope yarns teased out and plaited together, padding etc, which is wound round stays, shrouds and other parts of the rigging to protect sails, sheets and spars from *chafe.*

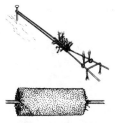

Bail or **bale** 1. To remove *bilge water* that has been shipped, or that has accumulated in the *bilges* or *cockpit* as a result of a leak, rain etc, using a bailer, bucket or scoop. 2. Fitting, often on end of boom, to which a sheet or other line may be led.

Bailer (or **baler**) or **scoop** A container with which water is bailed out of a boat. Formerly wooden or metal, now usually made of plastics and either flat and broad, or round with a handle.

Balance The ability of a boat to stay on a steady course without having to apply *helm.* Balance is largely a question of design and hull shape. Aerodynamic forces act on the sails through the *centre of effort,* and hydrodynamic forces act on the *lateral plane* through the *centre of lateral resistance.* These are not the geometric centres of the areas, and they shift with the trim of the sails, the point of sailing and the attitude of the hull. To be well balanced a boat must be correctly trimmed

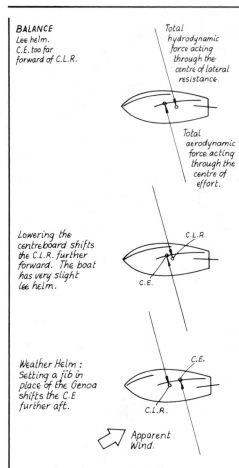

BALANCE
Lee helm.
C.E. too far
forward of C.L.R.

Total hydrodynamic force acting through the centre of lateral resistance.

Total aerodynamic force acting through the centre of effort.

Lowering the centreboard shifts the C.L.R. further forward. The boat has very slight lee helm.

C.L.R.

C.E.

Weather Helm : Setting a jib in place of the Genoa shifts the C.E further aft.

C.E.

C.L.R.

Apparent Wind.

(crew weight can be shifted), and the sails sheeted to the correct angle for the point of sailing. An unbalanced boat has *weather helm* or *lee helm*, because the lines of action of the forces acting through the CE and CLR are too widely separated. The rudder then has to be kept over permanently to hold her on course. Balance can often be improved by altering mast *rake;* raking it further forward moves the CE further forward to reduce weather helm, and vice versa. Temporary corrections can be made under way; lee helm can be countered by reducing headsail area or increasing mainsail area to shift the CE further aft, or by moving crew weight forward or lowering a centreboard to shift the CLR further forward. Weather helm can be reduced by increasing sail area in the foretriangle, by reducing mainsail area (perhaps by *reefing*) or by flattening the mainsail to reduce its effect, thus shifting the CE further forward, or else by moving crew weight further aft and adjusting the centreboard to bring the CLR further aft.

Balanced rudder A *rudder* which, like the *spade rudder* in the figure, pivots about a *stock* which is not at the *leading edge* of the blade but some distance further aft. Because part of the blade area

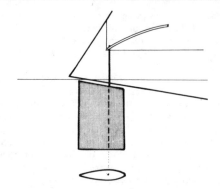

lies ahead of the stock, *torque* is reduced and less power is needed to turn the rudder.

Balance lug See *lugsail.*

Baldheader 1. A *square-rigged* vessel with *stump topgallant* masts, and therefore no sails above the *topgallants.* 2. A *schooner* without *topmasts.* 3. Now a boat with no *headsails* set.

Bale See *bail.*

Ball 1. A signal *shape* displayed as prescribed by the *IRPCS* by a vessel at *anchor* (one), *not under command* (two) or *aground* (three). Also used to signal other information, with or without other signal shapes. A ball is black, with a diameter of not less than 0.6 m, but a vessel under 20 m in length may hoist smaller balls. For convenience in smaller boats they are often cloth with a wire frame, or two flat folding discs which appear to be round when fixed at right angles to each other; some are inflatable. 2. Soft iron balls or spheres are sometimes mounted each side of the compass to reduce *deviation.*

Ballast Additional weight placed low in the hull to improve *stability* and to enable a boat to carry more sail, especially when *on the wind.* May be an external ballast keel bolted on outside the hull, or inside ballast secured inboard under the cabin *sole.* Sometimes can be moved to alter the *trim* of the boat (but see *rating certificate*). When racing in dinghies the weight of wet clothing is limited because it acts as ballast. The crew are regarded as live ballast. Also used as a verb.

Ballast keel A mass of ballast, generally lead or iron, streamlined and bolted to the *keel* to increase *stability* and to prevent a *keelboat* from *capsizing.* Lead is preferable to iron, both because of its

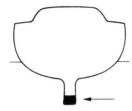

greater *density* and because it does not affect a *magnetic compass*. Gold is forbidden for *America's Cup* yachts. See *construction* fig.

Ballast ratio The ratio of *ballast* weight to the total *displacement* of the vessel, expressed as a percentage.

Balloon jib General term, rarely used now, for a large, full, overlapping *headsail* set when *reaching* in light breezes.

Ball terminal A *swaged* stay or shroud *terminal* with a solid ball on the end; this is inserted into a hole either in the mast or in a *tang*.

Balsa wood The lightest of woods, the *specific gravity* of which varies from 0.0962 to 0.248. End-grain balsa is often used as the spacing material between two *GRP/FRP laminates* (*sandwich construction*) and has superior mechanical properties to foam plastics.

Bandwidth Sidebands are created either side of a radio *carrier wave* when it is *modulated*. Bandwidth is the total amount of space required to transmit the radio signal, i.e. upper sideband plus lower sideband. *Single sideband* transmission bandwidth is half that of double sideband. The term is also used to define the passband of receiving apparatus.

Bank 1. An extensive area where the water is shallower than the surrounding area, but generally sufficiently deep for vessels to cross; often good fishing grouund such as Dogger Bank, Grand Banks. 2. The sides or shores of a river, canal, lake etc. The left bank of a river is on the left when looking downstream.

Bar 1. A *shoal* close by a river mouth or harbour entrance, consisting of particles of sand, mud and debris transported downstream by water and deposited where the current slows. Generally builds up parallel to the coastline and across the entrance to a river. In bad weather, a heavy *ground swell* and *breakers* on a bar can capsize a dinghy, while keelboats must beware of touching the bottom in

wave troughs. Many bars change shape during winter storms, and the entrance channel then has to be rebuoyed or the *leading line* altered annually. 2. *SI* unit of pressure: 1 bar = 1000 millibars = 10^5 Newtons per square metre = 0.986923 atmospheres = 750.1 mmHg = 29.53 inHg.

Barbed ring nail (US **serrated nail**) Monel or silicon bronze nail for fastening wooden parts. Easily hammered in, but the ribbed swellings along its length have sharp barbs that grip the wood fibres, and make it difficult to withdraw the nail when making repairs. Sold under many trade names, such as Anchorfast, Gripfast, Stronghold.

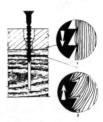

Barber hauler A control line, mainly used in racing dinghies; is attached to a ring or block on the *jib sheet*, and adjusts the angle of *lead* in either the horizontal or vertical plane. Named after Manning and Merritt Barber of California.

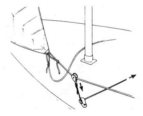

Bareboat charter Only the vessel is chartered, i.e. with no crew.

Bareheaded Said of a boat that has no *headsail* set while changing sails.

Bare poles No sails are set, and the boat is driven only by the force of the wind on the spars and rigging. When *riding out a storm* in heavy weather, running under bare poles is an alternative to *heaving to,* but frequently warps, lines or a *sea anchor* have to be *streamed* to slow the boat and prevent her from being *pooped* by following seas, or burying her bows right under.

Barge 1. A flat-bottomed, shoal-draft, high-sided, beamy boat that carries cargo inland or very near the coast. 2. Before the start of a race, illegally to force a passage between a boat to *leeward* and the starting mark.

Barnacle A marine crustacean (cirripedes) whose calcareous plates form a cone-shaped shell. Attaches itself to the bottom of a boat that is not protected by *antifouling paint*.

Barograph Instrument which continuously records *atmospheric pressure*. A lever and pen, connected by a system of levers to an aneroid *barometer*, make a trace on a chart wrapped round a clockwork drum which rotates once in seven days. The variation in pressure can be seen visually, but barographs are little used on small sailing boats because they would be put out of action by the rapid motion.

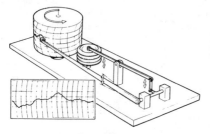

Barometer Instrument which measures *atmospheric pressure*, currently in *millibars*, formerly in inches or millimetres. A sailing boat does not carry a mercury barometer (based on Torricelli's principle) but an aneroid barometer, which is a partly evacuated, sealed metal box. This has a thin corrugated face (or two faces kept apart by a spring), which reacts to changes in atmospheric pressure. The reaction is transmitted by a system of sensitive levers to a pointer, which indicates pressure on a graduated dial. Coll glass.

Barometric pressure See *atmospheric pressure*.

Barque or **bark** Three-masted *sailing ship*, the two forward masts (*foremast* and *mainmast*) are *square-rigged*, the *mizzenmast* is *fore-and-aft rigged*. Only the aftermost mast of a four- or five-mast barque is fore-and-aft rigged.

Barquentine, barkentine or **barkantine** Three--masted *sailing ship, square-rigged* only on the *foremast*; the *main-* and *mizzenmasts* carry *fore-and-aft* sails. All except the foremast of barquen-

tines with more than three masts are fore-and-aft rigged.

Barrel buoy A barrel-shaped *aid to navigation*; floats lengthwise and marks special areas.

Basin An area of water that is almost entirely land-locked or enclosed by structures. May be tidal or completely enclosed.

Basket A signal which, under the *IRPCS*, may be displayed by a *vessel engaged in fishing* if she is under 20 m in length, instead of two cones apexes together.

Batten A thin flexible strip, originally wooden but now usually plastics; is fed into a batten pocket at the *leech* to support the *roach*, generally of a *mainsail* or mizzen but sometimes of a *headsail*. Length is frequently limited by class rules, and the position may be specified. Sometimes battens have a small line attached so that they can be withdrawn more easily when *reefing*. See also *fully-battened*. Battens are also used to extend *awnings*.

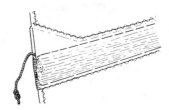

Batten down In heavy weather, when seas are running high, to close all openings and to secure firmly all *hatches, sliding hatches, scuttles, skylights* etc to prevent seas from breaking through and flooding the boat. Sometimes a tarpaulin is securely fastened to the hatch *coaming*, and held with battens and wedges.

Batten pocket A pocket sewn roughly at right angles to the *leech* of a sail. It is either shaped to hold the batten safe after it has been slipped in, or is closed by ties to prevent the batten from working out.

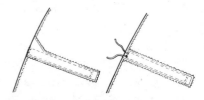

Batten-seam planking A method of constructing wooden hulls. The *seams* of the *planks* are backed inside by battens to which the planks are fastened.

Battery drain The more electrical fittings and electronic appliances there are on board, the greater the drain on a boat's batteries. A *generator* is often required for recharging batteries.

Bay Broad concavity in the coastline; the indentation landward is generally less than the width.

B Class catamaran A *catamaran* racing class; the boats are sailed by a crew of two, and the maximum measurements permitted are overall length 20 ft (6.10 m), beam 10 ft (3.05 m), sail area 235 sq ft (21.84 sq m). A spinnaker may be set only if its area is included in the total sail area. The *Tornado* is a B Class catamaran.

Beach 1. To run a vessel ashore or on to a beach deliberately. 2. Area of shore covered with an accumulation of debris (such as sand, pebbles, shingle and shells), which is shifted by wave action. A greater expanse is uncovered at low water than at high water.

Beacon A mark erected on land or on the bottom in shallow waters to guide or warn shipping. The position is marked on *charts*. UK may be lit or unlit, is of a particular shape or carries *topmarks* so that it can be identified from a distance. US a daybeacon is unlit. Chart abbr Bn. See also *radio beacons*.

Beam 1. One of the main dimensions of a boat; her breadth. Overall beam is measured from the outside of the *skin, planking* or *plating* at the widest point. Waterline beam is measured similarly at the *designed waterline* but, in practice, varies with *displacement*. (See *construction* fig.) Moulded beam is breadth measured between the inside surfaces of the skin. For rated beam and BMAX see *International Offshore Rule*. 2. Transverse member that supports the *deck*. 3. The direction of an object from the boat is said to be on the beam when it is at right angles to the *centreline*. UK: forward of the beam is between right *ahead* and *abeam*, abaft the beam is between right *astern* and abeam; US: forward of the beam is between *broad on* the bow and on the beam, while abaft the beam is between on the beam and broad on the quarter (i.e. between 45° and 90°, and between 90° and

135° from dead ahead respectively). 4. Path along which light from a lighthouse or pulses from e.g. a radar aerial are concentrated.

Beam ends A boat is said to be on her beam ends when she is heeled over so far that the deck beams are vertical, or nearly so.

Beam reach A *point of sailing;* reaching with the wind roughly at right angles to the boat's *fore-and-aft line*.

Beam sea Seas that travel at right angles to a boat's course; the wave troughs and crests are parallel to her *fore-and-aft line*.

Beam wind A wind that blows at right angles to the boat's *fore-and-aft line*.

Beamy Describes a boat that has greater than average beam for her length.

Bear Verb relating to the direction of an object from an observer, e.g. a lighthouse may bear 220°. See *bearing*.

Bear away (more rarely, **bear up**) To put the *helm* up, to *windward,* so that the boat alters course to *leeward,* away from the wind. The sails are trimmed to the new course by *easing* the *sheets.* Opp to *luff up.*

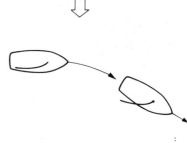

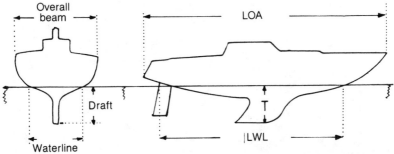

Bear down To approach another vessel or some object, especially from windward.

Bearers Supports on which an engine, floorboards etc rest.

Bearing The direction of an object from an observer. A bearing is given as an angle between the direction of the object and a line of reference. A *true bearing* is referred to the direction of *true north*, a *magnetic bearing* to *magnetic north* and a *compass bearing* to *compass north*. A *relative bearing* is referred to the ship's *head*, i.e. to her fore-and-aft line. Bearings are obtained e.g. with the *hand-bearing compass, radio direction finder*,

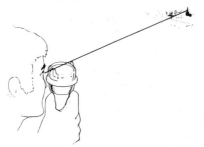

transits and *radar* to fix the vessel's position. When taking bearings of two objects, the angle of cut at which the bearings meet when they are laid off on the *chart* should be as near 90° as possible to minimize error, and should not be less than about 30°. Whenever possible, bearings should be taken of three objects, and should differ by about 60°. A nearer object is preferable to a more distant object, because an error of 2° in the bearing of an object 15 miles away results in an error in the boat's position of over half a mile, whereas the error is only 2 cables, 0.2 of a mile, if the object is 6 miles away. The bearings of *leading lines, light sectors* etc are given from seaward on charts and in publi-

cations such as the *List of Lights;* they are always given as true bearings. Bearings of *radio beacons* are great circle bearings (see *half convergency*). See also *cross* and *four point bearings, bearing angle on the bow* and *doubling the angle on the bow.*

Bearing angles on the bow (UK) or **Two bearings and a run between** (US) When a boat is sailing along a coast, *distance* off can be found by taking *relative bearings* of an object, whether marked on the *chart* or not, provided that the *tidal stream or current* is not setting across her *course.* The angles required are in pairs (either to starboard or to port), e.g. 30° and 54° as in fig 1. The navigator calculates the distance made good *over the ground* between point A, when the object bears 30° and point B, when it bears 54°, taking into account *leeway* and the beneficial or adverse effect of any tidal stream. If the boat stays on the same course, her distance from the object when it is abeam at C will be the same as the distance made good over the ground between point A and point B. A further check can be made as in fig 2 by calculating the distance sailed over the ground from B to D, when the object bears 78°. At D distance off will be double the distance sailed from B to D. Other pairs of angles that can be used as in fig 1 are: 22° and 34°, 25° and 41°, 26½° and 45°, 32° and 59°, 35° and 67°, 37° and 72°.

Bearing-out spar See *jockey pole.*

Bearing sight A ring carrying two sights, a tube, or sighting vanes through which an object is

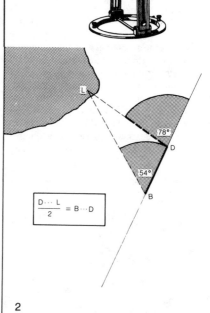

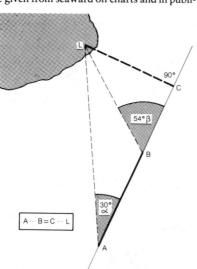

1

2

BEAUFORT SCALE

Wind speed

Knots	Force	Metres per sec	Feet per sec	Miles per hour	km per hour
1	0 Calm	0.0–0.2	1	1	1
1–3	1 Light air	0.3–1.5	1–5	1–3	1–5
4–6	2 Light breeze	1.6–3.3	5.1–10.9	4–7	6–11
7–10	3 Gentle breeze	3.4–5.4	11–17.9	8–12	12–19
11–16	4 Moderate breeze	5.5–7.9	18–26	13–17	20–28
17–21	5 Fresh breeze	8.0–10.7	26.1–35.2	18–24	29–38
22–27	6 Strong breeze	10.8–13.8	35.3–45.4	25–30	39–49
28–33	7 Near gale	13.9–17.1	45.5–56.2	31–38	50–61
34–40	8 Gale	17.2–20.7	56.3–68	39–46	62–74
41–47	9 Strong gale	20.8–24.4	68.1–80.2	47–54	75–87
48–55	10 Storm	24.5–28.4	80.3–93.4	55–63	88–102
56–63	11 Violent storm	28.5–32.6	93.5–107	64–72	103–117
64+	12 Hurricane	32.7+	108+	73+	118+

viewed; is fitted over the *steering compass* to enable *bearings* to be taken.

Beat Noun and verb: to sail towards an objective to *windward*, following a zig-zag course *close-hauled* on alternate *tacks*. The boat *goes about,* changing from *port tack* to starboard tack and back again. If the direct line between the place where the beat starts and the objective is not exactly in line with the wind direction (e.g. in a narrow channel) one tack will be longer than the other, and the *long tack* (q.v.) should be sailed first in case the wind shifts.

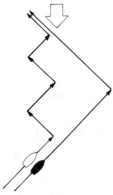

Beat Frequency Oscillator, BFO. An oscillator arranged to mix with the incoming signal, so producing an audible beat. A *direction finder* receiver BFO is switched on when taking *bearings* of *radio*

beacons to enable the signal to be heard clearly against a noisy background.

Beaufort notation Letter code indicating weather conditions, now largely replaced by the World Meteorological Organization code (see *weather code*); e.g. b = blue sky, 0–2/8 clouded: bc = partly clouded, 3/8–5/8: c = cloudy, 6/8–8/8: d = drizzle: f = fog: g = gale: kq = line squall: m = mist: o = overcast: q = squally: r = rain: s = snow: t = thunder: z = haze.

Beaufort scale of wind force A scale devised by Admiral Sir Francis Beaufort in 1808, grading winds by the effect of their forces on the amount of sail that a full-rigged frigate could carry. The scale was adopted internationally in 1874, and extended to forces 0–12 in 1939, Beaufort's criteria being replaced by descriptions of the effects on land and at sea. Now the scale goes to force 17, and includes wind speed in *knots*, metres per second and, sometimes, kilometres or miles per hour, as well as describing the sea and giving probable wave heights. Weather forecasts often predict winds in terms of *forces* and, because *wind pressure* increases as the square of wind speed, it is important to remember that an increase of only one force, from 4 to 5, or 5 to 6, means a 100% increase in wind pressure. The scale from force 0–12 is given above and opposite. When increased to force 17 the details are:
Force 12 32.7–36.9 m/sec, 64–71 knots,
73–82 mph

BEAUFORT SCALE

| Wind pressure | | | | | | | Wave heights | | |
Knots	lb/ft²	kg/m² (mb)	Sea criterion	Probable ft.	m.	Maximum ft.	m.
1			Sea like a mirror.				
1–3	0.02	0.1 (0.01)	Ripples with the appearance of scales are formed, but without foam crests.	0.3	0.1	0.3	0.1
4–6	0.08	0.4 (0.04)	Small wavelets, short but more pronounced. Crests glassy but do not break.	0.6	0.2	1	0.3
7–10	0.27	1.3 (0.13)	Large wavelets. Crests begin to break. Foam glassy, perhaps scattered white horses.	2	0.6	3	1
11–16	0.67	3.2 (0.32)	Small waves, becoming longer, fairly frequent white horses.	3	1	5	1.5
17–21	1.3	6.3 (0.62)	Moderate waves, longer, many white foam crests. Chance of some spray.	6	2	8	2.5
22–27	2.3	11.2 (1.1)	Large waves begin to form; white foam crests more extensive everywhere, probably some spray.	10	3	13	4
28–33	3.5	17.3 (1.7)	Sea heaps up, white foam from breaking waves begins to be blown in streaks along the direction of the wind.	13	4	18	5.5
34–40	5.4	26.5 (2.6)	Moderately high waves, longer, edges of crests begin to break into spindrift. Well marked streaks of foam.	18	5.5	25	7.5
41–47	7.7	37.7 (3.7)	High waves, dense streams of foam. Crests begin to topple, tumble and roll over. Spray may affect visibility.	23	7	33	10
48–55	10.4	51.0 (5.0)	Very high waves, long overhanging crests. Whole surface of the sea white. Tumbling of the sea heavy and shock-like. Visibility affected.	29	9	41	12.5
56–63	14.0	68.3 (6.7)	Exceptionally high waves. Sea completely covered with foam. Edges of crests everywhere blown into froth. Sea completely white with driving spray.	38	11.5	52	16
64+	16.0+	78.5+ (7.7+)	Air filled with foam and spray. Sea completely white with driving spray. Visibility very seriously affected.	45+	14+		

NB: 1. Knots are given in accordance with traditional divisions. If based on m/sec, Force 4 is 11–15 knots, Force 5 16–21 knots.
2. Ft/sec, m.p.h. and km/hr are based here on figures for m/sec.
3. Pressure based on figures given for mb.
4. Wave heights based on metres, as estimated for the open sea.

Force 13 37.0–41.4 m/sec, 72–80 knots, 83–92 mph
Force 14 41.5–46.1 m/sec, 81–89 knots, 93–103 mph
Force 15 46.2–50.9 m/sec, 90–99 knots, 104–114 mph
Force 16 51.0–56.0 m/sec, 100–108 knots, 115–124 mph
Force 17 56.1–61.2 m/sec, 109–118 knots, 125–136 mph

Becalmed To be unable to move because of lack of wind, such as when under a steep coast, in the lee of trees, large steamers etc where it is dead calm.

Becket 1. A becket *block* has a metal loop or eye to which a line can be attached, such as the *standing part* of a tackle or a line that prevents the block from tumbling. 2. Rope handle. 3. Loop made in the end of rope or wire rope.

Bed 1. As in engine bed, anchor bed etc, the framework, support, housing etc on which it rests. 2. The bottom of the sea, river, lake etc, i.e. of any body of water.

Bedding compound A flexible, putty-like substance with which a watertight seal is made; for example is applied to a fitting before it is bolted or screwed to the deck.

Bee-block A chock fitted to one side of the boom, usually with one or two holes through which the *reef pendant* is rove.

Before Forward of, nearer the *bow;* before the *beam,* a direction from the boat in the sector between *abeam* and right *ahead* (but US see beam 3.).

Before the wind To *run* with the wind aft, with *sheets* eased right out. The *true* and *apparent winds* blow in the same direction.

Belay 1. To make a line fast by taking turns round a *belaying pin, cleat* etc. For example as in (1) take a *round turn* round the cleat, follow this with several figure of eight turns (2). Figs 3 and 4 show a *half hitch* taken to jam the line, but this is forbidden by some skippers who prefer to use a further round turn. 2. Order to cease, e.g. belay *hoisting.*

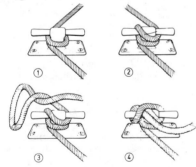

Belaying pin Vertical pin to which *halyards* and other parts of the *running rigging* are belayed, often fitted in a *fiferail, spider band* etc.

Bell 1. In *restricted visibility* a vessel over 12 m in length that is at *anchor* or *aground* is required by the *IRPCS* to ring a bell as prescribed in the regulations. Smaller vessels are not obliged to ring a bell, but must be able to make some other efficient form of sound signal. An ordinary hand bell is easier to stow and cheaper than a traditional ship's bell. 2. The ship's bell is struck to mark the

passage of time, each stroke marking half an hour, e.g. 8 bells when the *watch* changes after four hours. 3. (or cup) A bell-shaped fitting on the mast into which the *spinnaker pole* is thrust; often slides on a track fastened to the forward side of the mast.

Bell buoy Anchored *aid to navigation* which has several swinging clappers that sound the bell as the buoy moves in response to waves. May also be operated electrically.

Bellini-Tosi A fixed *directional* cross-loop *aerial,* often used in conjunction with a *goniometer* (q.v.), with two loops set at right andles to each other. The advantage is that the aerial can be mounted permanently, say at the masthead to avoid induced error from rigging. The *bearing* of the *radio beacon* is found by turning the search coil of the goniometer, which is normally installed in the cabin or wheelhouse.

Belly The *camber,* draft or *fullness* of a sail. A sail is said to belly out when it is full of wind.

Below Beneath the deck. To go below is to go into the cabin.

Bend 1. Verb: to connect two ropes with a knot; to attach a rope to a *spar,* ring etc, as when making the *anchor cable* fast to the anchor ring. 2. Noun: the knot made, as in *fisherman's bend* etc. 3. To prepare a sail for *hoisting; a mainsail* is either *laced* to the spars, or the *bolt rope* is fed into the *grooves* in *mast* and *boom,* or the *slides* are fed onto *tracks; the foot* is extended by the *outhaul.* A *headsail* may be *set flying,* fed into a grooved *headfoil* or *luff spar,* or *hanked* to the *stay. Halyards* are *shackled* to the *heads* of the sails, and *sheets* to the *headsail* and staysail *clews.*

Bendy mast See *flexible mast.*

Beneaped or **neaped** Said of a vessel that has *run aground* at *high water* and does not refloat at the following high water because the *tides* are *taking off* (*range* decreases); also of a vessel that cannot leave a dock or port for the same reason.

Bermudan cat A bermudan-rigged (US marconi-rigged) boat with no *headsail* and the *mast stepped* well forward. See also *una rig.*

Bermudan cat

Bermudan cutter A boat with a *jib-headed mainsail* and two *headsails,* i.e. *jib* and *staysail.*

Bermudan cutter

Bermudan ketch A two-masted bermudan-rigged (US marconi-rigged) boat; the *mainmast* is taller than the *mizzenmast* aft, and relatively taller than that of a *yawl*. See also *ketch*, for definition of ketch and yawl.

Bermudan (UK), **marconi** (US) or **jib-headed mainsail** Unlike a *gaff sail, lugsail* or *spritsail*, is a triangular sail, hoisted up the mast by a single *halyard* shackled to the *head*, which is reinforced by a *headboard*. The *roach* is usually extended at the leech by *battens* which are pushed into batten pockets sewn to the sail at varying heights above the *clew*. (See also *fully-battened*.)

Bermudan rig Alternatively termed bermudian or Bermuda rig in the UK, and jib-headed or marconi rig in the US. Instead of a quadrilateral *gaff sail, lugsail, spritsail* etc, a bermudan-rigged boat has a tall mast with a triangular mainsail that sets without a gaff, sprit or *yard*. This rig was introduced to Europe in about 1920, but had long been used for sporting and fishing boats in Bermuda where light winds predominate; the tall, lightweight mast enabled sails to be set higher where wind speed is greater (see *wind gradient*). The majority of modern sailing boats are bermudan-rigged.

Bermudan schooner Two-masted bermudan--rigged (US marconi-rigged) boat; the *mainmast* aft is as tall or taller than the *foremast*.

Bermudan sloop A boat with a single mast, *jib-headed mainsail*, and, normally, only one sail set in the *foretriangle*. The boat in the figure is *masthead-rigged*; others are *fractional-rigged*.

Bermudan yawl Two-masted bermudan-rigged (US marconi-rigged) boat; the shorter *mizzenmast* aft is relatively shorter than that of a *ketch*. See also *yawl*, and for definition of yawl and ketch, see *ketch*.

Bermuda Race An *offshore race* from Newport RI to Bermuda, 635 n.miles in length. One of the first of the offshore races, and the oldest still being run regularly (by the *Cruising Club of America*). The first Bermuda Race, starting from New York, took place in 1906 with three yachts competing. Since 1926 has been run in alternate even years.

Berth 1. A place where a vessel can lie for a period. Must be suitable for her *length* and *draft*, and could be *alongside*, bow or stern on to a *pier* or *pontoon*, between *piles*, at a *mooring buoy* or on a *trot*. Often allotted by the harbour master, but in less congested waters the skipper may be able to select his own berth. The boat must be properly secured so that she is safely moored, whatever the direction and strength of the wind and *tidal stream or current*. 2. To berth is to put a vessel in a berth. 3. A sleeping place on board, generally built in, where the crew can sleep securely regardless of the motion of the boat, e.g. *quarter berth, pilot berth, root berth*. A settee berth serves as a seat by day, and a *leeboard* or *bunkboard* is required to prevent the sleeper from rolling out when the boat heels. A hinged *pipe cot* is often fitted forward. Hammocks are not normally found in sailing boats. Many cruisers have a *dinette* which converts into a double berth at night. 4. To obtain a position or appointment as a member of the crew is to find a berth. 5. To give a vessel, obstruction, or danger a wide berth is to keep well clear.

Beset A vessel that is hemmed in or endangered by wind, *tidal stream or current* or, especially, ice.

Beveling The angle where one part of the boat meets another is often considerable; for example, the *frames* have to beveled to match the varying curvature of the *planking* or *plating*. Metal frames are measured to the *moulded* line from the forward edge in the forepart, and from the after edge in the afterpart of the boat, so that the angle of the frame matches the hull planking or plating. The bevel is measured from the after edge of wooden frames in the forepart, and from the forward edge in the afterpart, because the outstanding edges can be worked until they fit.

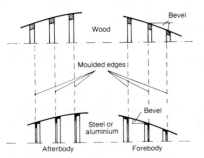

Biased starting line A *starting line* that is not set at right angles to the direction of the *true wind*. In

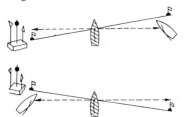

the absence of other factors, the end of the line that is closer to the weather mark is the end to be favoured.

Bias stretch *Sail cloth* stretches more when a load is applied at 45° to the *warp* and *weft*. Good cloth stretches less and *recovers* better than cloth of lower quality. Sails are cut in such a way that the unsupported load (e.g. on the leech) is taken by the warp or weft, and not diagonally.

Bi-colour lantern The *IRPCS* permit a vessel under 20 m in length to carry a single lantern that exhibits both the required *side lights*, red to port and green to starboard, each shining over an arc of

112.5°. This is mounted forward on the centreline, usually on the *pulpit*.

Bifurcation buoy (US) *Aid to navigation* that marks the junction of channels; UK *junction buoy*, q.v.

Big boy Alternative for *blooper* (q.v.), but is also used (especially in the US) to mean a *staysail set flying* on the *centreline*, often under a *spinnaker*.

Bight 1. A loop in a rope or line. 2. Curve hanging down between the two ends of a rope or line. 3. A large open indentation into the coastline, which is penetrated less deeply than by a bay.

Bilge The rounded part of the boat where the *bottom* curves up towards the sides. If the curve is abrupt the boat is said to have a hard or firm bilge, as opposed to a slack or soft bilge when the curve is gentler. C.f. *hard chine* figure in contrast. As an

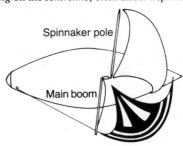

adjective, relates either to the *bilges* (q.v.) as in bilge paint, or to the bilge, as in bilge block, which supports a vessel's bilge when she is on shore, in dry dock etc.

Bilgeboard One of the two boards that are raised and lowered in the same way as a *centreboard*, but

which are located near the bilge either side of the hull instead of on the *centreline*. They are lowered to reduce *leeway*. There is more space in the centre of a bilgeboard dinghy, because there is no centreboard case, but water can enter when the boat heels unless the bilgeboard *trunks* extend to the deck. Bilgeboard *scows* draw very little water and are extremely fast; they are generally very beamy, with flat bottoms and two rudders.

Bilgeboarder A sailing boat with bilgeboards. An *IOR* bilgeboarder proved so successful in offshore races that a heavy *rating* penalty was introduced to discourage such designs.

Bilge keel 1. One of two *keels* fitted either side of a motor vessel's hull to resist *rolling;* may also reduce *leeway*. 2. Similar *ballasted* bilge keels may be fitted to a sailing boat in place of a single central keel, or in addition to a shallow central keel, to provide *lateral resistance;* the ballast may be integral or bolted on externally. 3. Long bilge strakes fitted along the bilge either side to protect the planking, e.g. when running aground or when a dinghy is dragged along a stony beach.

Bilge keeler A sailing boat with twin bilge *keels* to provide *lateral resistance* and *stability,* in place of a single central keel. Easy to trail, stays upright when *aground*, and *draws* less water because the bilge keels are shallower than a normal keel, but *windward performance* is poor because more lee-

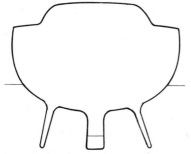

way is made than by a normal keelboat. An additional central keel is sometimes provided when twin keels alone would provide insufficient stability, and these boats are even easier to trail and take the ground still better.

Bilge paint Synthetic resin paint applied to the *bilges* to conserve the inside of the hull and to provide protection against any oil, grease and fuel that is mixed with the bilge water.

Bilge pump Pump with which water is removed from the *bilges*. *Capacity* must be adequate for the size of boat. The *piston pump* is the simplest design, and is manually operated, as is the more efficient *diaphragm pump*. *Submersible electric pumps* are also available, and may be operated by the inboard or outboard engine. Another type reacts mechanically to the movement of the surface of the water which actuates a lever; this keeps the boat dry when left unattended at her berth for a long period. With all pumps the suction tube must lead from the lowest point of the bilges, or from the pump well, and a *strum box* or strainer is required round the open end to prevent debris from blocking the pump. Manually operated pumps are often fitted in the cockpit and must be sited where they can be manned for a long period if necessary.

Bilges The lowest part inside the hull, above the *keel* and beneath the cabin *sole,* where bilge water collects. Gas detectors or bilge sniffers can be fitted to detect the presence of heavy fumes which sink and can cause explosions, while bilge or exhaust blowers expel the fumes before the engine is started.

Bilge stringer Longitudinal member fitted at the *turn of the bilge* to support the *frames*. See *construction* fig.

Bilge water The water that collects in the *bilges;* is generally dirty and accumulates as a result of spray, rain, condensation, leaks, spillage etc. Runs to *leeward* when the boat heels, especially when close-hauled, and affects *transverse stability* adversely. The level of the water in the bilges should be checked regularly, and the boat pumped dry whenever necessary. Bilge water level alarms are available.

Bill 1. (or pea) The pointed extremity of an anchor *fluke*. 2. A narrow promontary.

Binnacle Strong housing which protects the *compass* from being struck or damaged by seas etc. Usually incorporates lighting, and often has *corrector magnets,* or *soft iron spheres* and *Flinders Bar,* so that *deviation* can be reduced. In larger sailing boats is often mounted on the *steering pedestal,* so that the helmsman at the wheel can read the card through the aperture or transparent part of the hood. Generally brass, wood or *GRP/FRP* to avoid affecting the compass needle; may be designed for overhead mounting with a *reflector*.

Bino-compass Proprietary name for a small *compass* designed to clip on to the rim of the object glass of *binoculars,* so that a *bearing* can be taken of an object viewed through the glasses.

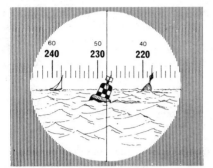

Enables reliable bearings to be taken of objects that would otherwise be too distant.

Binoculars Magnifying instrument with two connected telescopes, one for each eye; a monocular has only one telescope. Considerable magnification is required for marine purposes, such as identifying *aids to navigation,* and the exit pupil diameter must be adequate for work at night and in twilight. The instrument must both be light enough to handle on an unsteady platform and have a field of view large enough to enable distant objects to be found easily, or moving objects followed. Typical sailing boats binoculars are 7×50, i.e. sevenfold magnification and 50 mm object glass diameter. Greater magnification is unsatisfactory owing to the boat's motion, and lower magnification is inadequate. Increasing the diameter of the object glass or objective lens (the lens which is further from the eye, and through which light rays enter) increases weight excessively, and the 7.1 mm exit pupil diameter of 7×50 glasses (object glass in mm divided by magnification) is suitable for work in a dim light when the human eye's pupil is dilated. The field of

view of 7×50 binoculars is generally about $7.4°$ and covers an area about 388 ft in diameter at 1000 yards, or 124 m at 1000 m. Weight varies and is about 40–46 oz (1.1–1.3 kg). Other terms used by some manufacturers are relative brightness $(50/7)^2 = 51$, and twilight performance, $\sqrt{50 \times 7} = 18.7$, both in the case of 7×50 binoculars.

Bioluminescence The sea becomes luminous at night because microscopic marine organisms emit light when water is disturbed. Is particularly apparent in bow and stern waves. Formerly called phosphorescence because the phenomenon was thought to be caused by phosphorous in the water.

Bipod mast or **A-frame** A mast with two legs splayed athwartships. Generally one is stepped on each of the hulls of a *catamaran,* and the sail sets between them.

Bite The *anchor* fluke bites into the ground.

Bitter end The inboard end of a rope, line or cable, which may or may not be made fast to the bitts.

Bitts Strong vertical fitting on deck to which *mooring lines* or the *anchor cable* are secured. Two bitts are often fitted to larger boats, and may extend to the *keel* so that a heavy load is well distributed over the *hull,* for example when the whole weight is taken by the bitts while the boat is being towed off the ground. The bitter end of the cable, rope or line may be made fast to the bitts.

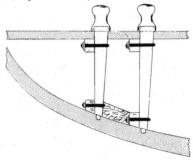

Black band A band (normally black but of some other colour if the *spar* itself is black) painted on the *mast, boom* etc. The inner edge of the band indicates the limit to which the *head* of the sail may be hoisted, the *tack* pulled down or the *clew* hauled out. These limits may not be exceeded when a boat is racing.

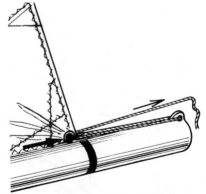

Blade 1. One of a *propeller's* spiral fins, shaped like a screw thread. 2. The flat part of the *oar* that is dipped into the water. 3. The underwater part of the *rudder,* which is turned to alter course.

Blanket To take the wind from another boat's sails. In the figure, boat A is being blanketed by boat B which is to *windward;* A is being slowed

and will probably be overtaken. Obstructions such as trees, woods, hills and buildings also interfere with a boat's wind, and she may be blanketed or caught in eddies when to *leeward* of them. The strength and direction of the wind are affected both to windward and to leeward of the obstruction.

Blast A *sound signal* given on a whistle or siren when manoeuvring. A short blast lasts about 1 second, a prolonged blast 4–6 seconds.

Blind arc or **sector** 1. Area where a *radar* or *sonar* display is obscured. Echoes are either absent or reduced in amplitude because there is some obstruction to radiation. 2. The area masked by the genoa or other obstruction, where the helmsman cannot see.

Blistering Air bubbles trapped in a *GRP/FRP laminate* as a result of inefficient wetting out, *osmosis* etc. The air expands when heated by the sun and the bubbles burst, allowing water to enter the *moulding*. The voids have to be cleaned out and filled with a polyester *filler*.

Block Has a roller or sheave which turns on a pin between the two wooden, metal or plastics

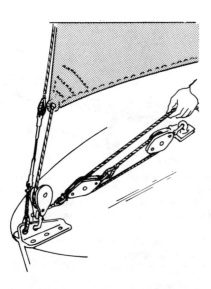

cheeks. Lines are rove through blocks either to change the direction of pull, say of a *halyard* passing over a single block with one sheave, or to reduce effort. *Double, fiddle* and *sister* blocks have two sheaves, treble blocks have three. When the *mainsheet* is rigged as a *tackle* made up of several blocks with a rope *fall*, the sail can be *hardened* with less effort; see *tackle* for reeving to advantage or disadvantage. See also *ratchet, foot, snatch* and *cheek blocks*, and *becket*.

Block coefficient The ratio of the immersed volume of the *displacement* to the volume of a circumscribing block with sides equal to the vessel's immersed *length, beam* and *draft*:

$$C_B = \frac{\text{displacement}}{\text{LWL} \times \text{waterline beam} \times \text{draft}}$$

Indicates the fineness or fullness of a hull; the smaller the block coefficient the finer is the *underwater body*. Values for yachts vary between 0.35 and 0.55, those for passenger liners from 0.50–0.65, fast container ships 0.55–0.75 and large oil tankers 0.75–0.88.

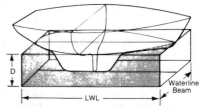

Blocking diode A one-way device that controls the flow of electric current. It is incorporated in a circuit so that, e.g. mutual discharge between two separate batteries is prevented, but power from both can be used as required.

Blooper Alternatively called big boy. A very full sail, set on the opposite side to the *spinnaker* to

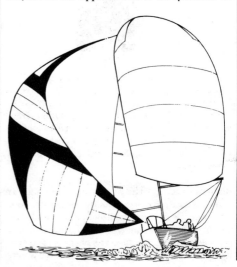

balance the pull of the spinnaker on a *broad reach*, particularly when racing offshore. The *IYRU* rules do not allow two spinnakers to be set at the same time, but the blooper ranks as a *headsail* and is *set flying* to leeward. It is tacked down to the stem, and often is not fully hoisted, the head sagging some distance to leeward of the mast to let the sail catch wind round the leech of the mainsail, which reduces forward visibility. Has to be *handed* before gybing.

Blow As a noun relating to wind, usually strong, as in a hard blow. As a verb, to blow up is to freshen; wind speed increases.

Blue Peter *Code flag* P, blue with a white rectangle inside; flown in harbour means 'All persons should report on board as the vessel is about to proceed to sea'. May be used at sea by a fishing vessel, meaning 'My nets have come fast upon an obstruction'. Before the start of a race it is broken out as the *preparatory signal*, five minutes after the warning signal, and means that the race will start exactly five minutes later.

Blue Ribband Is held by the vessel with the record time for crossing the North Atlantic between Ambrose Lighthouse off New York and the Scilly Isles. In 1838 the 'Great Western', 1340 tons GRT, averaged 8 knots whereas the present holder, the 'United States' (51,500 tons GRT), averaged 36 knots in 1952. The fastest crossing for a sailing vessel stood at 12 days and just over 4 hours by the 'Atlantic' in 1905 (an average of 10.4 knots for the 3014 n.miles travelled, which included a *day's run* of 342 n.miles), until July 1980, when Eric Tabarly of France sailed the 55 ft *hydrofoil trimaran* 'Paul Ricard' across in 10 days, 5 hours and 14 minutes.

Blue-water The deep sea, well offshore, as opposed to coastal waters; often used in the US as an adjective, e.g. blue-water racing. The Blue-Water Medal is awarded annually by the *Cruising Club of America* to an individual to mark the year's most meritorious example of seamanship.

Board 1. To go on to or into a boat. 2. When *beating* to *windward* the stretch sailed on one *tack* before *going about*. If the objective is not directly to windward one board or tack is long, the other short. 3. The side of the boat, as in starboard, inboard, outboard, overboard, freeboard.

Boardboat Small centreboard dinghy with one sail, low *topsides* and a shallow *well* rather than a *cockpit*. The hull is not unlike that of a surfboard.

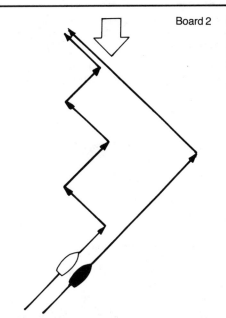

Board 2

Boarding ladder Ladder hung over the side or stern to enable the crew to board. May be wooden, a *Jacob's ladder* with wooden rungs suspended on ropes, or a lightweight alloy folding or collapsible ladder. The permanent safety ladder in the figure normally forms part of the *stern pulpit*, but can be lowered when required. A person who has fallen overboard can operate it by pulling the cord marked A. A *folding step* is an alternative aid to boarding a boat with high *topsides*.

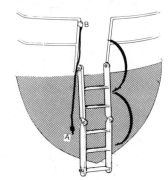

Boardsailor (UK) The person who sails a *sailboard*.

Boat Essentially a small open craft, but the term is often applied to larger vessels. The US Federal Boat Safety Act defines a boat as a vessel manufactured, chartered or used primarily for non-commercial purposes, or a vessel that carries six or less passengers for hire.

Boathook A pole, generally of wood or light alloy, with a hook at one end. The crew uses it to *fend off*, pull on an object, pick up a *mooring* *buoy* etc. In small dinghies the boathook may also serve as a *whisker pole*. Some are telescopic and others are shaped at one end for paddling.

Boat roller A long roller, often inflatable, roughly 8–12 in (20–30 cm) in diameter, generally made of tough PVC, on which a boat can be rolled over a beach or ramp without damaging her bottom.

Boatswain or **bo'sun** In larger vessels is the man responsible for the efficient working of *ground tackle*, *rigging*, sails etc.

Boatswain's or **bo'sun's chair** A seat, which may have a safety strap and pockets for tools, on which one of the crew is hoisted *aloft* to work on the sail, mast or mast fittings.

Boatswain's or **bo'sun's locker** Stowage space for spare gear, such as blocks, hanks etc.

Boatyard A yard where boats are built and, generally, repaired. Often has a *slipway*, *marine railway*, *travel-lift* or *crane* for *launching* and *slipping* boats.

Bobstay A *stay* from the *stem* to the outer end of the *bowsprit;* counters the upward pull of the *forestay*. Is generally heavy wire rope, chain or a metal rod to avoid stretch.

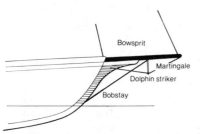

Body plan Part of the *lines plan* which shows the shape of the transverse or athwartships section of the hull (called *sections*). The right-hand half shows the half-sections of the *forebody* at each *station,* and the left-hand half those of the *afterbody*.

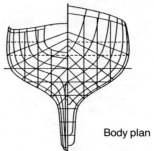

Body plan

Bollard Strong fitting, firmly bolted to the deck, to which *mooring lines* etc are *made fast*. There are many designs and types, such as *mooring*, open, raked and *staghorn bollards*. Similar but much larger bollards on quays and piers are used when mooring alongside. Chart abbr Bol.

Bolt 1. Standard measure of a length of *canvas*, roughly 39 yards (35.5 m). 2. A *fastening;* see also *keelbolt*.

Bolt rope Rope sewn to one or more edges of a sail, either to reinforce the sides or so that the sail can be fed into a *grooved spar*.

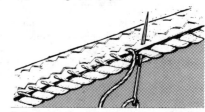

Bonded stores Duty-free stores for use on board a vessel that is sailing beyond specific confines. The stores must be kept under seal until the vessel has passed these limits.

Bone in her teeth The foam seen at the *stem* of a fast-moving vessel.

Bonnet Strip of canvas, laced to the foot of a *square sail*, *headsail*, *staysail* or *lugsail* to increase the area when the wind is light; is unlaced and removed when the wind freshens. Bonnets are banned under the *IOR*.

Boom 1. *Spar* that extends the *foot* of the sail bent to it, e.g. mainboom, mizzen boom, spinnaker boom. Often attached to a *mast* at one end by a *gooseneck* or universal joint. Most booms are made of light alloy or wood, and generally either have a *track* to take the *slides* sewn to the sail or a *groove* into which the *bolt rope* is fed. 2. A spar, rigged outboard from larger vessels at *anchor* or on a *mooring,* to which boats can be secured. 3. Floating barrier that protects waters by closing an entrance, sometimes to exclude enemy vessels. See also *jib-boom* and *boom-jib.*

Boom claw See *reefing claw.*

Boom crutch, sometimes **crotch** See *crutch.*

Boom jib or **boom staysail** A *jib* that must be smaller in area than the *foretriangle* because the *foot* is attached to a *spar* (US club, UK boom) which swings from side to side forward of the mast. The single sheet leads to a block which slides athwartships on a *horse,* and does not need to be

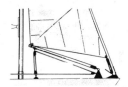

manned when the boat is *tacked* and *gybed;* the sail (often called a self-trimming jib) is therefore generally set in short-handed cruising boats. Sometimes the forward end of the *club* is attached to a pedestal aft of the stay; the shorter radius adds fullness to the sail as the sheet is eased.

Boomkin See *bumpkin.*

Boom out On a run, to thrust the *jib* or *genoa* out to windward with a *spinnaker pole, whisker pole, jib-stick* or *boathook* so that it fills with wind instead of being *blanketed* by the *mainsail.* A small sail can be held out by hand.

Boom strap Boom fitting to which the upper mainsheet *block* is shackled. A double block may be used, or two boom straps, each with a single block to spread the load. The sail cannot be *roller reefed* because the strap is fastened to the boom, and sail area is either reduced by *points* or *jiffy reefing.* Mainly fitted to dinghies which do not reef sails.

Boom vang A number of different fittings and systems are used to pull the boom down, keeping it horizontal on all *points of sailing* and, especially, preventing it from lifting on a *broad reach* or *run* when the pull of the *mainsheet* is predominantly horizontal. If the boom is allowed to lift, the sail *twists* instead of maintaining much the same *angle*

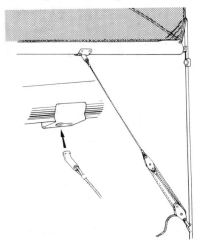

of attack from head to tack. UK and US terminology differs in that kicking strap or kicker is generally used in the UK when the boom is pulled down towards the *centreline* near the mast or to the mast itself, whereas boom vang is used mainly for a temporary *tackle* which holds the boom down to the side, say to the *toe-rail* or to the *headsail sheet track.* In the US boom vang is used

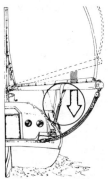

for both types. In a small dinghy a simple line may suffice, or a tackle rigged between the mast foot and a key on the boom, about one-third of its length from the mast. A *kicker lever* or *wheel*-type *turnbuckle* (UK or rigging screw) provides more power for larger boats, and hydraulic kicker rams are fitted to some competitive keelboats.

Boot top or **topping.** A narrow strip of contrasting colour applied between the *bottom paint* and the topside *enamel,* unless *antifouling* is taken above the *waterline.* Dark colours are often preferred because they disguise the discoloration resulting from oil and scum on the surface of the water. As well as improving the appearance, the boot top indicates the boat's waterline and therefore enables the crew to check her *trim*.

Bore Tidal pheonomenon which occurs where tidal *range* is large, usually in shallow converging estuaries at *spring tides*. A steep wave develops and advances up-river just after *low water*.

Boss The centre of the *propeller* into which the blades are fixed, and through which the end of the propeller shaft passes. Often streamlined to improve water flow.

Bo'sun See *boatswain*.

Bottlescrew Alternative UK term for a *turnbuckle* or rigging screw, but increasingly rarely heard now.

Bottom 1. The lower immersed part of the *hull*. 2. The bed of the sea, river, lake or other body of water. The quality of the bottom (its composition) is printed on charts, and a sample can be obtained by *arming the lead*.

Bottom boards Removable light boards fitted in the bottom of small boats to keep weight off the *planking*, and to distribute the load over the *frames*.

Bottom paint Special paint applied to the wetted surface of hull, keel and rudder to discourage *marine fouling* and *corrosion*, and to keep *friction* to the minimum. *Antifouling paint* is applied to boats that are not hauled out after a sail, and *varnish* or *enamel* to those that can be cleaned before each race. See also *hard racing antifouling*, *graphite paint*.

Bound 1. The destination of a vessel, as in homeward, eastward, outward bound. 2. Held in harbour, as weatherbound, fogbound.

Boundary layer The region between a surface, such as a sail or hull, and the undisturbed fluid (air or water) streaming past. The particles move more slowly in this layer than in the main stream owing to *friction*, and flow may be *laminar* or *turbulent*; see *telltales*. The rougher the surface and the greater the turbulence the thicker is the boundary layer. Wind speeds are similarly affected in the layer near the surface of the earth; the wind is slowed by surface friction, and speed increases at greater heights above earth (see *wind gradient*).

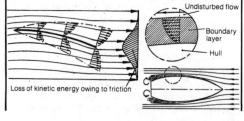

Loss of kinetic energy owing to friction

Bouse or bowse To haul, usually downwards, on a rope or *tackle*.

Bow The forward part of a vessel; not the foremost member, which is the *stem*, but the whole area just abaft the stem. The bows are the sides between the stem and *amidships*. The shape of the bow varies with the type of vessel and seaworthiness. *Overhangs* may be long or short, non-existent in the case of a straight-stemmed craft. See also

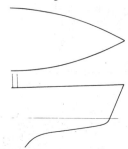

spoon, clipper bow. Directions from the boat are given as, UK, on the bow, 45° from the *head*; fine on the bow, between right *ahead* and 45°; broad on the bow, between 45° from the head and *abeam*: US, broad on the bow, 45° from dead ahead; on the bow, from dead ahead to 45°; forward of the beam, from 45° to abeam.

Bow and beam bearing See *four point bearing*.

Bower anchor Main *anchor*, carried forward, heavier than a *kedge*.

Bow fast See *bow line*.

Bow fender (UK also **bow pudding**) Rubber, plastics or rope *fender*, either permanently fitted to the bow or hung over it when required, to absorb shocks forward and to prevent damage caused by the *anchor cable* or *mooring lines*. Should be attached centrally as well as to both bows.

Bow line 1. UK or bow rope, US or bow fast: a *mooring line* (q.v.) attached to the bow and running to a *bollard* or ring ashore, or to a *pile* or *mooring* when lying alongside another boat. 2.

Term formerly used in respect of the part of the *buttock lines* forward of the *midship section* in the *profile plan,* as in bow and buttock lines. 3. Line or rope which keeps the weather *leech* of a *square sail* taut when the ship is *on the wind,* or which is used to hold the staysail of a barge aback when winding or tacking.

Bowline 1. A knot tied in the end of a line to make a loop that will neither slip nor jam, and that can be undone after it has been subjected to tension. Probably the most important knot of all because it can be used for so many purposes, such as when mooring alongside, or to attach a lifeline round the crew's chest in place of a *safety harness.*

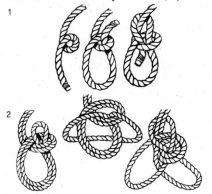

2. A bowline on the bight, made with doubled line as in the figure, provides two non-slip loops which can be separated to form a substitute *boatswain's chair* when hoisting a man aloft, or when recovering a man who has fallen overboard; one leg is placed in each bight. 3. A running bowline forms a noose; a bowline is made around the *standing part.*

Bow plate Metal fitting at the *stem* to which the headsail is tacked down; incorporates the *forestay* deck fitting.

Bow rail (US) See *pulpit.*

Bowse See *bouse.*

Bow shackle See *harp shackle.*

Bowsprit Strong fixed *spar,* generally extending almost horizontally forward from the *stem* to which it is fastened, often with a *gammon iron.* Relatively rarely seen in modern sailing boats, and then mainly with a *clipper bow* or *cutter* rig, the *jib* being set on the foremost *stay* leading from the masthead to the outer end of the bowsprit. Unless very short, a bowsprit is supported by *shrouds*

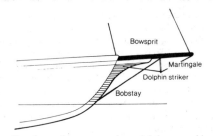

leading from the outer end to each bow, and by a *bobstay* to the stem; in sailing ships it may be extended by a jib-boom, braced by a *dolphin striker* and *martingale* stay and guys, and sometimes further extended by a flying jib-boom. A running bowsprit can be run in and out through a *cranse-iron,* while spike or horn bowsprits serve both as bowsprit and jib-boom.

Bow wave Part of the wave system generated by a boat moving through water; at the bow divergent waves spread out diagonally and a transverse wave is also formed between them, both systems moving forward with the boat. A *displacement*

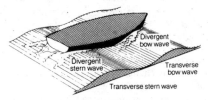

boat cannot escape from her wave system and, at *hull speed* (V/√L = 1.34), the length of the transverse wave generated matches her *waterline length.* A *planing boat* can escape owing to *dynamic lift;* the bow wave then shifts aft to about mast level, and the forebody lies ahead of and above the wave.

Box compass A *compass* that is housed permanently in a box.

Box the compass To recite the thirty-two *points of the compass* clockwise from north, or to recite the thirty-two points and the quarter points. The term boxing the compass is sometimes applied to the wind when it is particularly fluky and unsettled, switching irregularly between various points of the compass.

Brace 1. *Square rig:* rope (US line), attached to the yardarm, with which the *yard* is swung round to a different angle. Is rove through brace pendants and named after the sail it serves, e.g. main topgallant brace. To brace up is to haul on the *lee*

brace and ease the *weather* brace to bring the yard nearer to the *fore-and-aft line* and the ship closer to the wind, i.e. comparable to *hardening* in the mainsheet. To brace in is to ease the lee brace and haul on the weather brace to set the sail squarer, like *easing* the mainsheet. To brace aback, similar to *backing* the jib, is to allow the wind to strike the sail from ahead. 2. (Aus) the *spinnaker guy,* q.v. 3. A *rudder* fitting; a strap with a *gudgeon* or *pintle* at the forward end.

Brackish Mixture of fresh and salt water, as is found in estuaries, marshes etc. *Salinity* varies between 0.05–17.50 parts per thousand. The boundary of brackish water in estuaries is marked by the deposit of sediment suspended in river water, and by a change of plant and animal life where salinity becomes too high for freshwater species and too low for marine species.

Braided or **plaited rope** Between eight and sixteen *strands* are plaited into rope by machine. Given the same material and size of rope, *breaking strength* is below that of *laid rope,* but the rope is softer and has less tendancy to *kink* or *snarl* up. Is

preferred for sheets, which are heavily stressed by continously changing loads, and which are often made fast in jam cleats. Some braided ropes have a central *core* made of low-stretch fibres, the sheath being more fleecy and less slippery. Formerly made of cotton, but now of *synthetic fibres.* See also *double-braided.*

Brail Rope or line which gathers a *fore-and-aft* sail to the *mast.* Also to gather up a sail in this way.

Brave West Winds The *prevailing* westerly winds that blow in temperate latitudes in both hemispheres.

Breaker 1. Portable water container, a cask or tub. 2. The *crest* of a wave breaks or collapses either on account of strong winds, or when it meets a contrary *tidal stream or current,* or over a shoal where the *shelving* sea-bed flattens the circular *orbit* in which water particles move, the effect at the surface being that seas become steeper and more unstable and the crests break. The energy released is enormous, and pressure can amount to well over 1 bar (roughly one ton per square foot).

Breaking load or **breaking strength** The load at which a fitting, rope, wire rope etc will part or break. The breaking load in tons for manila, hemp or sisal rope can be found roughly by squaring the circumference in inches and dividing by three; coir has about one-fifth the strength of manila; nylon rope is roughly three times and polyester twice as strong. These approximate figures are for new rope, and decrease as the rope wears. The safe working load is one-sixth of the breaking load.

Break out 1. To break out the *anchor* is to pull it out of the ground, either by heaving on the *cable* manually, or with the help of a *windlass, capstan* or *winch.* 2. To *harden* the *sheet* of a *headsail* or *spinnaker* that has been hoisted *in stops* (or any other device or line rigged for a similar purpose), so as to break the stops and allow the sail to fill. 3. In the case of a flag, a *slippery hitch* is made round the rolled up flag with the part of the *halyard* that does not hoist it; the flag can then be broken out with a pull after it has been hoisted. 4. To open cargo, nowadays often a bottle of spirits or beer.

Breakwater 1. A low, curved or vee-shaped rail or *coaming,* fitted on the *foredeck* at the forward end of the *cockpit* of an open boat so that water is deflected to either side and runs overboard instead of into the boat. 2. Stone, steel or concrete structure built to protect a harbour from the force of seas, breakers etc.

Breasthook Wooden chock or crook fitted at the top of the *stem;* holds the two *shelves* or *gunwales* at the sides of the boat together. See *construction* fig.

Breast rope (US **breast line**) *Mooring line* (q.v.) that runs at right angles to the centreline; usually one runs from the bow and one from the stern to the shore or to another boat alongside.

Breeches buoy A life-ring running on a *whip;* has canvas breeches in which a man is hauled ashore when rocket apparatus is used to save life.

Breeze A good sailing wind; in the *Beaufort scale* is described as light, force 2, 4–6 *knots;* gentle, force 3, 7–10 *knots;* moderate, force 4, 11–16 knots; fresh, force 5, 17–21 knots. See also *land* and *sea breeze.*

Bridge Many low bridges can be opened to allow vessels with masts to pass through, and bridge fees often have to be paid. The *vertical clearance* of a fixed bridge is printed on charts (i.e. the height above *MHWS* - UK, or *MHW* - US of the highest point of the bridge span). See also *flying bridge.*

Bridgedeck Transverse structure between the *cabin* and the *cockpit;* provides transverse strength. The mainsheet track or compass is often fitted here.

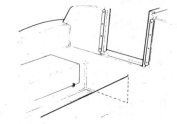

Bridle In sailing boats, a *span* of wire which is made fast at each end, with a line attached to the mid-point; for example the bridle rigged for the *spinnaker pole* spreads the load of the *downhaul* to the two ends rather than concentrating it at a single point. Also a wire attached either side of an obstruction, such as the mainsheet bridle (or *horse*) on which the lower *mainsheet* block travels from side to side above the *tiller*.

Brig Two-masted *sailing ship, square-rigged* on both masts.

Brigantine Two-masted *sailing ship, square-rigged* on the *foremast* but *fore-and-aft rigged* on the *mainmast*.

Brightwork The *varnished* parts of a boat.

Bring up 1. To moor or anchor. 2 To be brought up all standing is to come to a sudden stop, e.g. when the wind shifts suddenly and the sails are caught *aback*, or when a boat *runs aground* with her sails set.

Bristol fashion Smart, as in the phrase 'shipshape and Bristol fashion'.

Broach, or broach to Owing to heavy *following seas*, or to an error made by the helmsman when *running* or *gybing*, the boat slews round and *luffs up* uncontrollably, *heeling* dangerously as she does so. In high seas she may be *broadside* on in the trough of the wave and, unless she is *dismasted*, can be *capsized* or rolled over by the next breaking crest. Many modern *light displacement* boats with short keels broach when *close reaching* under spinnaker, because the *centre of effort* is well aft and is offset to *leeward* as the boat heels while the *centre of lateral resistance* tends to shift forward because the bow is depressed. The rudder is often

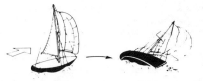

half out of the water, and is unable to counter the force couple resulting from the wide separation of the CE and CLR.

Broad on Direction from the boat, as in broad on the *bow*, UK roughly 45° from right *ahead* and *abeam;* broad on the *quarter*, between 45° from *astern* and abeam: US, directly off the bow or quarter, 45° from ahead and astern.

Broad pendant A *flag* with a *swallow-tail*, similar to *code flags* A and B. Is flown by a commodore in the Royal Navy, and by the *flag officers* of UK yacht clubs; the vice-commodore's has one ball (round patch) in the *hoist* and the rear-commodore's two.

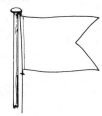

Broad reach Verb and noun: the *point of sailing* between a *beam reach* and a *run*. The wind blows over the *quarter*, further aft than abeam but not from dead astern; the sheets are eased well out.

Broadside Parallel to the side of a boat, e.g. broadside on to the waves.

Broken water Breaking turbulent water, especially in an area that is otherwise smooth.

Bruce anchor Modern *anchor* with excellent *holding power*, made in one piece with three *flukes* shaped like a scoop.

Bubble sextant Can be used for taking *sights* of *heavenly bodies* when the *horizon* is invisible; a bubble indicates the horizontal. Much used in aircraft but not suitable for sailing boats.

Bucket 1. Has a line attached to the handle so that water can be gathered, and may be weighted on one side to make it dip under the water. Collapsible canvas buckets are easier to stow. 2. US slang for a boat (often derogatory).

Bulb bow A *bow* with an underwater projection at the stem, just below the *cutwater*, designed to reduce *wave-making resistance*.

Bulb keel A *keel* that is bulb-shaped when viewed from forward or aft; has a streamlined cylindrical lump of lead or iron *ballast* along the bottom, e.g. as in the Tempest and Star classes.

Bulkhead A partition below decks; stiffens the structure and separates one compartment from another. Is often fitted beneath a deck-stepped mast to provide support. In smaller boats bulkheads are fitted athwartships; more rarely one may also be fitted longitudinally. A *collision bulkhead* may be built in forward, and watertight bulkheads are sometimes provided to divide a vessel into watertight compartments. The engine compartment bulkhead is often insulated to reduce noise. In large vessels there may be a watertight door, but smaller boats usually have a simple door or an opening through which the crew can pass.

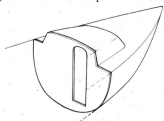

Bulldog grip, or **wire rope grip** or **clamp** Like a short U-bolt with threaded ends over which is passed a strong bridge, tightened down by nuts to clamp two wires together. Generally used to make a temporary eye or to join the two broken ends of a parted wire rope as an alternative to *splicing*, or in pairs to insert a length of wire rope. They should be fitted with the U gripping the end and the bridge the *standing part*, so that only the end is crimped.

Bull rope A rope led from a *mooring buoy* to the *bowsprit*, to prevent the bow from bumping into the buoy at *slack water*, or when the boat is *wind rode*.

Bullseye A round, hard-wood, metal or plastics eye through which a line is rove. Serves to guide the line or alter the *lead*, and may be fitted on a *track*.

Bullseye

Bulwarks A solid extension of the *topsides* above deck, higher than a *toe-rail*, sometimes knee-high but more often hip-high. Serves to prevent the crew from falling overboard, and keeps out the sea, as opposed to a *lifeline* (guardrail) which consists simply of stanchions supporting wire rope lines around the sides. *Freeing ports* are essential to allow spray and water on deck to flow overboard. Usually only fitted to motor fishing vessels and larger craft.

Bumpkin, boomkin or **bumkin** 1. *Spar* which projects aft from the *stern,* and to which the *backstay* or the foot blocks for the *mizzen* sheet may be attached. 2. Formerly, short spar projecting outboard from the quarters for the main brace block, or from the stem for the foresail clew line.

Bunk A built-in sleeping place. Also verb, to share quarters with; to bunk down is to get into a bunk.

Bunkboard or **leeboard** Hinged or removable wooden plank, or sailcloth stretched along the open side of a *berth* when at sea, and stowed under the cushion in harbour. Is rigged to prevent a sleeping crew from falling out to leeward when the boat heels.

Bunt The middle portion of a *sail*.

Bunting 1. Material of which *flags* are made. 2. Collectively, flags.

Buntlines Lines or ropes which haul up the central lower part of a *square sail* to *furl* it.

Buoy Floating object made of plastics, rubber, sheet steel, wood or cork; indicates the position of an object on the bottom, such as the *anchor* or the *ground tackle* of a *mooring buoy*. Many *aids to navigation* are buoys laid for a specific purpose such as to mark a channel, wreck, isolated danger, landfall or prohibited area. They can be identified by their shape (*conical, can, nun, spherical, spar,* *pillar*), colour (mainly red, black, green, white or yellow, sometimes striped or banded in two colours), and by the *characteristic* of the *light* exhibited. Some are unlit, others are numbered and/or named, many carry *radar reflectors* and sound *fog signals*. See *buoyage system*. Also used as a verb: to buoy is to lay a buoy to mark an object or position. See front endpapers for illustration.

Buoyage General term embracing the *aids to navigation* laid in accordance with a buoyage system.

Buoyage system Many different buoyage systems are in operation throughout the world, but considerable progress has been made by IALA, the International Association of Lighthouse Authorities, towards establishing two alternative systems to be adopted world-wide. *IALA A* (red to port entering port) is a combined *lateral/cardinal system* laid in European waters and elsewhere. In North American waters the basic system is lateral, red to starboard entering port, but there are minor differences on the Intracoastal Waterway and in the Western Rivers; there is also a Uniform State Waterway marking system (see *United States buoyage system*). See front endpapers for illustration.

Buoyancy or **flotation** The upward thrust exerted by a liquid, such as water, on an immersed or partly immersed body such as a hull, caused by displacement of the liquid. A boat only remains buoyant if the part of the hull below the *waterline* is watertight and, to ensure that she will float even when full of water, say because of a leak, buoyancy (US flotation) bags and tanks, *watertight bulkheads* etc may be fitted; suitable inaccessible areas may also be filled with foam. A *displacement*

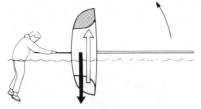

boat floats, whether she is at rest or moving through the water, on account of the hydrostatic force of buoyancy but, given large enough sail area and adequate *stability*, a lightweight dinghy can *plane* at high speed in stronger winds as a result of *lift*, a hydrodynamic force.

Buoyancy aid (UK) or **life vest** A life-preserver, worn by the crew to help him to float if he falls in, or if the boat *capsizes*. Is less bulky than a *life-jacket*, but does not provide as much buoyancy, and does not necessarily keep him face upwards in the water when unconscious.

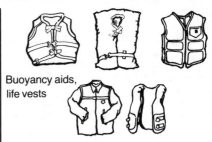

Buoyancy aids, life vests

Buoyancy (US **flotation**) **bag** Tubular or cushion-shaped inflatable bag, which is fastened beneath the *side deck, foredeck* or *afterdeck* of a dinghy to keep her afloat, even when full of water. Also makes it easier to *right* a *capsized* dinghy.

Buoyancy (US **flotation**) **material** Apart from bags, tanks and compartments, blocks of foamed plastics may be fitted beneath decking and *thwarts*, and areas such as a compartment, mast or inaccessible part of the boat may be filled with foam to help a boat to float when full of water. See also *masthead float*.

Buoyancy (US **flotation**) **tank** or **compartment** Watertight compartment in the hull, often beneath the *side decking* or *foredeck* of a sailing dinghy. Keeps her afloat when full of water, after *capsizing* or when she has *turned turtle*.

Buoy rope A light line which either connects a buoy to the object it is marking, such as an *anchor*, or to the chain attached to that object.

Burdened A term used especially in the US for the *give-way vessel* which does not have right of way, and has to keep clear of another vessel with right of way.

Burgee A triangular *flag*, occasionally *swallow-tailed*, worn at the *masthead;* the *hoist* is about two-thirds the length of the *fly*. Shows the insignia of the sailing club or yacht club of which the owner is a member. *Flag officers* fly a swallow-tailed *broad pendant*. The burgee pivots on the burgee stick which, in the case of boats with tall masts, is a thin metal or wooden stick, hoisted by an endless burgee *halyard*. The burgee must fly clear above the *truck* if it is to indicate wind direction effectively. See *rigging* figure.

Burr (UK usually **roove**) Copper washer that fits over the pointed end of a copper boat nail, which is then hammered (*clenched*) over it to rivet a wooden hull etc.

Bury A boat is said to bury her bows when they dip beneath a wave instead of lifting to it.

Bustle Offshore racing yachts with *fin and skeg* configuration often have a bustle which connects the *ballast keel* to the *skeg*, on which the *rudder* is hung. This relatively shallow streamlined projection from the keel is designed to reduce *wave-making resistance*, and to counter the tendency to *squat* when the bow lifts to waves by providing *buoyancy* aft. The bustle forms an important part of the underwater lateral area of fast *IOR* yachts.

Butt Joint where the ends of wooden *planks*, plywood sheets or steel or light alloy *plates* meet. A butt is backed with a butt block or strap, which bridges the joint and is normally twenty times as wide as the plank is thick. A *scarph* is an alternative joint for wooden parts.

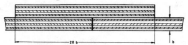

Butterfly or **bulkhead ventilator** Circular *ventilator* with slits that are opened and closed by turning a knob. Normally is fitted on vertical doors, *bulkheads, lockers* etc, but is not spray proof.

Buttock Longitudinally rounded part of the underbody aft between the *stern* and the after part of the *bilge,* lying between one quarter and three quarters of the half breadth either side.

Buttock lines Vertical fore-and-aft sections through the hull, perpendicular to the *waterline* and parallel to the *centreline.* They appear as straight lines in the *body* and *half-breadth plans,* and as curves in the *profile plan.* They are generally labelled with letters, working outwards at uniform intervals from the centreline, and give an indication of the fineness of the ends.

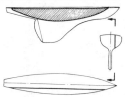

Buys Ballot's Law The Dutch meteorologist, Buys Ballot, defined his Law in 1857; if you stand facing the *true wind*, lowest pressure lies to your right in the northern hemisphere and to your left in the southern. Because the wind at the surface does not blow parallel to the *isobars* but is deflected and blows at an angle towards the centre of a *depression,* the centre is at an angle approximately 20° behind your outstretched right arm in

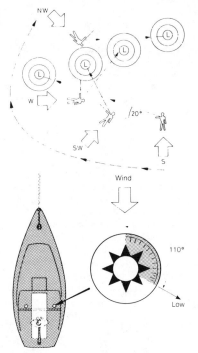

the northern hemisphere; this knowledge enables a suitable course to be selected. When a boat is making way, true wind direction only coincides with that of the *apparent wind* when the boat is running, so the direction of the true wind either has to be calculated or found by bearing away onto a run. When at anchor or on a mooring, the passage of a depression can be observed by checking the direction of the centre periodically.

By the head (and **by the stern**) A boat is said to be down by the head (or stern) when she is *trimmed* so that she does not float on an *even keel,* parallel to or on her *designed waterline;* her bow (or stern) is more deeply immersed than the designer intended, while her stern (or bow) is less deeply immersed.

By the lee The boat is on a *run* but the wind, instead of blowing from dead *astern*, blows from the same side as that on which the mainsail is setting. Often leads to an *accidental gybe* when the wind gets behind the sail and blows on its *lee* side.

By the wind *Close-hauled*, q.v.

C = Charlie: blue-white-red-white-blue *code flag.* As a single letter signal means 'Yes, affirmative' or 'The significance of the previous group should be read in the affirmative'. *Morse code:* —•—• (dash dot dash dot).

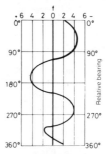

Cabin   The sheltered area in which the crew live and sleep. In very small boats with a single cabin, there may be only sitting headroom, or a *coachroof* to provide standing headroom, and the crew also cook in the cabin. In larger boats there may be more than one, e.g. forward and after cabins, or a separate *galley,* while still larger boats may have cabins for individual passengers and crew.

Cabin cruiser   A *motor boat* with a cabin and sleeping *berths.*

Cable   1. Chain or rope that is made fast to the anchor. See *anchor cable.* 2. Nautical measure of length: one tenth of a *nautical mile,* approximately 608 ft, 200 yards and 100 *fathoms.*

Cable-laid   When *making rope,* three right-hand (*hawser-laid*) ropes are laid up left-handed, i.e. nine *strands* in all.

Cable ship   Vessel equipped to lay and raise cables, easily recognized by the large roller at the bow. Depending on size can carry up to 3000 n.miles of cable aboard. When engaged in cable-laying is classed as a *vessel restricted in her ability to manoeuvre* (q.v.), and exhibits the appropriate lights and *shapes.*

Cadet   1. An *international* dinghy class for young people aged 8–17, designed by Jack Holt and bult of *marine plywood* or *GRP/FRP.* LOA 10 ft 6¾ in (3.22 m), beam 4 ft 2 in (1.27 m), weight rigged 120 lbs (54 kg), sail area 56 sq ft (5.16 sq m),

spinnaker 49 sq ft (4.25 sq m). 2. Mnemonic frequently used when correcting courses and bearings as described under *compass course:* Compass → ADd → East → True.

Calendering   Part of the *finishing process* of sail-cloth. Involves twin heated rollers which can apply over 100 tons pressure to the cloth to straighten and smooth it.

Calibration   The determination of instrumental errors so that measured values can be corrected and an accurate measurement obtained. *Logs* are calibrated over a *measured distance,* and *echo sounder* readings can be checked against the *lead-line. Direction finders* must be calibrated owing to instrumental and, in particular, *quadrantal errors,* which are often caused by continous metal loops on board such as rigging, lifelines, window frames, or by other aerials. Such errors vary according to

the ship's *heading* relative to the *bearing* of the transmitter, and are established by swinging the boat (see *swinging ship*) when within sight of a transmitting *radio beacon.* The *true bearing* of the beacon is compared with radio bearings taken every 10°, and a calibration table or curve is drawn up. Portable DF sets also have to be calibrated and, afterwards, must always be operated in the same place on board.

Call sign   The letters and/or numbers transmitted by radio stations, and those alloted to *registered* (US *documented*) ships and boats with R/T equipment for identification purposes.

Calm   Force 0 in the *Beaufort scale;* wind speed under one *knot,* sea smooth and unruffled, like a mirror. A calm is generally found in the centre of an *anticyclone,* or inland at night. There are extensive areas of persistent calms in the *doldrums.*

Camber   1. A cloth sail has a cambered profile, as opposed to the symmetrical profile of a keel or rudder. The amount of *lift* developed varies considerably with camber, a flatter sail being preferable for *close-hauled* work in fresher breezes to avoid excessive *heeling*. In lighter breezes, and when the wind is free, greater *fullness* is required to increase drive. The degree of curvature and the position of maximum camber can be altered by

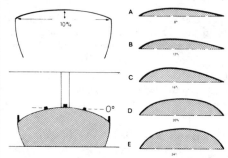

adjusting such controls as the *cunningham, downhaul* and *outhaul*, by altering *mast bend*, or with a *flattening reef*. Camber is quoted as a proportion or percentage of the *chord*, and varies from about $1/12$ or 8.3% for a flat-cut sail (A) to $1/6$ or 16.6% for a very full mainsail (C) and $1/4$ or 25% for a spinnaker (E). The most effective *angle of attack* varies with sail camber. 2. The convexity of the *deck* athwartships; adds to the integral strength of the hull, and helps the deck to shed water, as well as making it easier to stand on the *weather* side when the boat heels.

Cam cleat Two toothed cams, mounted on springs which force them together, hold a rope fast so that it does not have to be *belayed* to a *cleat*. Is often used for a *sheet*, which is gripped by the cams but can be freed instantly with a sharp upward tug.

Camjammer See *stopper*.

Canal Artificial waterway, dredged or cut for the passage of vessels.

Canal effect When two boats lie close together on separate moorings they are drawn towards each other, owing to the drop in pressure that occurs when water flow accelerates as it passes between the hulls. The same venturi effect occurs when a boat lies alongside a pier in a tidal stream, when two vessels meet in a canal, and when a small boat goes too close to a larger vessel.

Can buoy Anchored *aid to navigation*, the part above water appearing to be virtually cylindrical with a flat top. *IALA A: port hand mark* left to port when entering a harbour etc, red. *US buoyage:* port hand mark when entering, black. *Western*

rivers, port side when sailing upstream. (See front endpapers.)

Cancellation Under the *racing rules*, a race which the race committee decides will not be sailed thereafter (whether before or during a race). The signal is *code flag* N over the first *substitute* (US repeater).

Candela (cd) The basic *SI* unit for luminous intensity, e.g. of lights exhibited by vessels, lighthouses, distress signals etc.

Canoe Small simple boat, propelled by paddles; originally made of wooden laths and animal skins, later of canvas and now, frequently, of plastics. The *International 10 sq m* sailing *canoe* was developed from theses craft.

Canoe body A *round bilge*, shallow, beamy *hull* to which a separate *keel* is bolted. Typical of *fin and skeg* configuration hulls.

Canoe stern The shape resembles a canoe when viewed from above; the *stern* curves to a point, and the *overhang* is moderate. The *rudder* is hung on the *keel* beneath the stern, and does not extend above the *waterline*.

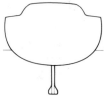

Canton One of the four quarters of a flag. The *jacks* of the US and UK *ensigns* are in the upper inner canton.

Canvas 1. Alternative word for *sails*. 2. The material of which a sail is made, whether of natural or synthetic fibres.

Cap Strong fitting with two holes; usually one is square and fits over the head of a *lower mast;* the upper mast is drawn through the other round hole and is held fast by a *fid*. The *jib-boom* is drawn through the *bowsprit* cap.

Capacity 1. The load that a boat can carry safely, i.e. crew, stores etc. In the US many small boats have to exhibit a capacity plate stating the limits that may be carried in terms of people and weight of stores etc. 2. Of a *bilge pump*, relates to the quantity of water that can be pumped overboard in a given period; the larger the boat the greater the capacity required.

Cape Land that projects into the open sea, such as Cape Horn and the Cape of Good Hope.

Capful of wind A light, short-lived puff of wind; just enough to fill the sails.

Capping A wooden strip round the top of a member such as the gunwale.

Cap shrouds *Shrouds* that lead from the top of a mast, e.g. from the cap of a *lower mast*, down to the *chain plates* at the sides. In *bermudan-* (US marconi-)*rigged* boats usually lead from the *masthead* over *spreaders* and down to the sides.

Capsize 1. The boat overturns. A *keelboat* or motorboat is said to have capsized when she turns keel uppermost, but a capsized dinghy may be either floating with her mast and sail lying on the water, or she may have turned turtle lying with mast pointing downwards. A keelboat with a *watertight* or *self-draining cockpit* normally *rights* herself owing to the weight of her *ballast keel*, sometimes after the load has been eased when she is *dismasted*. A dinghy on the other hand has to be

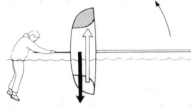

righted by the efforts of her crew, and the method varies according to the boat, the weather and the number of crew. Her *centreboard case* must be high enough to be clear above the water even when she is *awash*, and she must have adequate *buoyancy* (US flotation) *tanks* and *bags*, so positioned that her *centre of gravity* lies near the *keel* and her *centre of buoyancy* near the *deck*, even when full of water. The *centreboard* can be used as an effective lever to right her. 2. A *coil* of rope is capsized when it is turned over.

Capsizing moment When a boat heels in response to the wind and the *centre of gravity* lies to leeward of the *centre of buoyancy*, *righting moment* is negative and acts in the same direction as *heeling moment*; the boat capsizes.

Capstan Manually, electrically or hydraulically operated machine for hauling heavy ropes or lines. The drum or barrel rotates round a vertical spindle, whereas a *windlass*, used for similar purposes, has a horizontal shaft. Capstans are normally only fitted to larger yachts near the bows for *anchoring*,

kedging or *warping*. That in A was turned by men who pushed on the capstan bars, inserted into sockets in the drumhead; the ship's fiddler sometimes sat on top, playing as he went round, and the sailors sang sea shanties as they slowly raised the anchor.

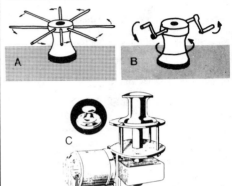

Car See *traveller*.

Carbine hook Link with a spring closure, fitted between ropes or a rope and part of the rigging. When used with *safety harness* should have a spring-loaded sleeve to prevent accidental opening.

Carbon fibre Extremely strong reinforcing material consisting of threads or filaments extruded through a spinneret, stretched, dried and heated. The carbonized type has low modulus and high stretch, the graphitized type high modulus and low stretch. *Specific gravity* is 1.5–2.0, i.e. lower than that of glass, but the material is extremely expensive.

Cardan shaft A *propeller shaft* with a *universal joint* next to the engine; allows it to flex.

Cardinal point One of the four chief *points of the compass:* north, east, south or west.

Cardinal system A *danger* is marked by a *light buoy* laid in one of the four *quadrants*, NW–NE, NE–SE, SE–SW, SW–NW; the buoy indicates where navigable water can be found relative to a cardinal point of the compass (whereas channels are marked by *lateral system* buoys, regardless of the direction in which the channel runs). For example, a north cardinal mark, laid to the north of a danger or a feature in a channel such as a bend or junction, indicates that water is deepest to north of the mark, or that north is the safe side on which to pass. *IALA A* cardinal marks are black and yellow horizontally striped *pillar* or *spar* buoys, and carry two large black cone *topmarks* (See front endpapers):
North: topmarks point up; black over yellow; light *very quick* (VQ) or *quick* (Q).

East: topmarks form a diamond shape, base to base; black, yellow, black; light VQ(3)5 s (i.e. very quick light flashing three times every 5 seconds) or Q(3)5 s.

South: topmarks points down; yellow over black; light VQ(6) plus a *long flash* every 10 seconds or Q(6)+L.Fl 15 s.

West: topmarks points together; yellow, black, yellow; light VQ(9)10 s or Q(9) 15 s.

Note that the character of the lights corresponds to the hours on a clock face: 3 for east, 6 for south and 9 for west, and that the cones 'point' to the black band(s) on the mark.

Careen To *beach* a vessel and haul her over on to one side so that the other side of the *bottom* can be examined, cleaned, painted or repaired.

Carling or **carline** or **carlin** (US or **header**) Fore-and-aft member which provides support for the inner ends of *half beams* at hatches, skylights etc. See *construction* fig.

Carrick bend Connects two heavy *warps* or *hawswers* that are too inflexible for other knots to be used. The warps take up the shape of a figure of eight when the ends are *stopped*, as at B.

Carrier wave The *frequency* at which a radio signal is transmitted. With a few exceptions (such as the unmodulated carrier waves used for some *morse* and *radio beacon* signals) the information to be sent is superimposed by *modulating* either the *amplitude, phase* or frequency of the carrier wave. For *single sideband* transmission, the carrier and one sideband are suppressed.

Carry away A *spar* breaks, or rope or wire *parts* as a result of a strong wind or heavy seas.

Carry sail A boat is said to carry sails when they are *hoisted*.

Carry way Owing to momentum, a boat continues to move through the water after stopping engines, *easing* sails right out, *luffing head to wind* or stopping *rowing*. A large ship may carry her way for anything up to four miles, and this has to be taken into account when sailing in shipping lanes. See also *forereach, shoot up.*

Car-top dinghy Small dinghy, light enough to be carried on a roof rack.

Carvel-built Wooden *planks* are laid flush, edge to edge, and fastened to *frames* to form a water-

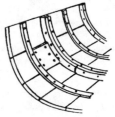

tight *hull* with *caulked seams* and a smooth outside surface. More complicated and expensive to build than a *clinker* hull, but generally preferred for keelboats.

Cast 1. A single *sounding*, taken with the *lead* and line. 2. To cast the lead is take a sounding. 3. When *weighing anchor*, to turn the boat before she starts to make way, usually by *backing* the jib so that she pays off on the desired tack.

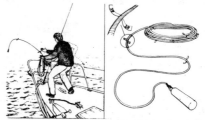

Cast off To let go a rope or line, such as the dinghy *painter*, the line attached to a *mooring buoy*, or a *tow-rope*. Some prefer the term let go.

Cat Widely used abbreviation for *catamaran*. See also *cat-boat*.

Catalyst A substance that alters the rate of a chemical reaction but itself remains unchanged. When making a *GRP/FRP moulding* is the organic peroxide *hardener* which initiates *polymerization* reaction of the *resin* (the cure). Has to be stored in a cool dark place because it decomposes in light and warmth. Must be suitable for use with the *accelerator*, and must not be mixed with it before being added to the resin because accelerator mixed with catalyst can explode.

Catamaran Sailing boat with twin *hulls*, connected by cross beams, developed from light but seaworthy Polynesian craft. Has greater *initial stability* than a centreboard dinghy or keelboat and, although unable to sail as close to the wind, is faster than a *monohull* in spite of overall beam

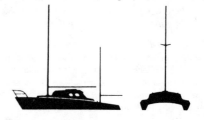

being greater because, thanks to the very narrow hulls, *frictional* and *wave-making resistance* are low. There are four restricted international racing classes A, B, C and D, and *hydrofoils* are permitted. The *Tornado*, a B class catamaran, was first selected as the Olympic catamaran class in 1976. Some large cats have been built and have proved their seaworthiness in Trans-Atlantic races and by sailing round the world, but catamarans have always been outnumbered by monohulls.

Cat-boat A boat with one *mast stepped* near the *bow*, and no *headsail*. Popular rig for single-handed dinghies such as the *Optimist*. The sail may be *gaff-* or *jib-headed*, a *spritsail* etc. The term is extended to cat-schooners and cat-ketches, i.e. *schooners* and *ketches* with the forward mast stepped near the bow and no headsail. See also *una rig*.

Catenary The curve made by a chain, wire or rope that is hanging between two points, e.g. by an *anchor cable* between the anchor and the bow, or by a *tow-rope* or line between tug and tow. Greater catenary reduces *snubbing*, and in the case of anchor cable also helps the anchor to hold because a more horizontal pull helps the fluke to dig in deeply. See also *anchor weight*.

Cathedral hull form A central *hull* has *sponsons* either side so that surface friction is reduced when air is channelled between hull and sponsons. The central hull may be shallower than the sponsons which may be faired into the hull, as in the *dory*. Alternatively hull and sponsons may be veed, with hull draft exceeding that of the sponsons; the *section*, viewed upside down, then has a similar appearance to a cathedral with central nave and two side aisles, viewed in silhouette from the west. See also *tunnel hull*.

Cathode The negative electrode of a galvanic cell into which current flows from the positive anode via the electrolyte (sea water): the electrode which does not corrode, and the more noble metal in the *galvanic series*.

Cathodic or **anodic protection** Protection against *galvanic corrosion* is required whenever different metals are positioned close to each other, because sea-water acts as an electrolyte and a galvanic cell is formed. If a bronze propeller has to be fitted to a steel hull, a *sacrificial anode* made of zinc or magnesium is attached to the hull nearby; this corrodes more readily than the hull, because the anode is baser or less noble in the *galvanic series* and protects the hull from corrosion.

Cat's paw 1. A hitch with which to attach a load to a hook. Two loops are formed, and each is twisted several times about itself before being hung on the hook. 2. A light and short-lived puff of breeze which slightly ripples the smooth surface of calm water. May be the first indication of a new breeze.

Caulk or **calk** To make the *seams* between wooden planks watertight. *Oakum* is forced into the seams with a caulking wheel or caulking mallet and iron, and is then payed, traditionally with pitch, now with caulking compound. Caulking cotton is used for smaller seams but, with the advent of *GRP/FRP* hulls without seams, caulking is an obsolescent skill.

Cavil or **kevel** Piece of wood fitted horizontally across two vertical timbers or *bulkwark* stanchions. Ropes may be belayed round the ends or to *belaying pins* if fitted.

Cavitation As a *propeller* rotates a partial vacuum is formed. Water rushes in to fill the vacuum, tiny bubbles form and, when they collapse, they pound the propeller causing pitting or erosion of the *blades* and reducing propeller *efficiency*.

CCA *Cruising Club of America*, q.v.

C Class catamaran International *catamaran* racing class. The boats are sailed by a crew of two, and the maximum measurements permitted are overall length 25 ft (7.62 m), beam 14 ft (4.27 m), sail area 300 sq ft (27.87 sq m). A spinnaker may be set only if its area is included in the total sail area. C Class catamarans compete for the *International Catamaran Challenge Trophy* (the Little America's Cup).

Cedar Light wood, mainly used for planking racing dinghies. Has few knots, is easy to work and resists rot. *Specific gravity* about 0.49.

Ceiling The inside vertical lining of the sides of the hull, fitted at the face of *frames* to allow air to circulate, so discouraging condensation and damp. Wooden laths are often used. A continous ceiling also protects berths and interior fittings from *bilge water*, which swills up the sides when the boat heels.

Celestial Pertaining to the sky or heavens.

Celestial equator Also called the equinoctial or equinoxial; the *great circle* in the celestial sphere where the celestial sphere is cut by the plane of the earth's *equator*. (See *PZX triangle* fig.)

Celestial horizon See *rational horizon.*

Celestial meridan *Semi-great circle* that joins the celestial poles; corresponds to a terrestrial *meridian.*

Celestial navigation A vessel's position when out of sight of land is determined by observing *heavenly bodies;* their positions in the celestial sphere are given in the *Nautical Almanac.* Their *altitude* is measured with a *sextant* or *octant*, time with a *deck watch* or *chronometer* and, usually, the navigator requires tables or a scientific or navigational electronic calculator in order to find a *position line.*

Celestial poles The points on the celestial sphere where the earth's axis, if produced, would cut the sphere; the elevated pole is the pole nearer to the observer (i.e. north in the northern hemisphere).

Celestial sphere An immense imaginary sphere with its centre at the earth's centre. Sun, moon, stars and planets are assumed to be on its surface, regardless of their actual distance from the earth. Although it is in fact the earth that rotates eastwards, *heavenly bodies* are treated as if they were points moving westward. Celestial poles, meridians and equator correspond to their terrestrial counterparts.

Celestial triangle See *PZX triangle.*

Celsius or **centigrade scale** Scale of temperature 0° is the melting point of ice, 100° the boiling point of water. Absolute zero is −273.15°. To convert to *Fahrenheit*, multiply by 1.8 (⁹/₅) and add 32; to convert from Fahrenheit, subtract 32 and multiply by 0.555 (⁵/₉).

Centigrade See *Celsius.*

Centreboard (US **centerboard**) A board that is lowered through a slot in the *keel* to reduce *leeway* by providing *lateral resistance.* Unlike a *daggerboard*, usually pivots about a bolt in the centreboard trunk, and is often raised and lowered by a line, wire, chain or *tackle;* sometimes one is provided to raise the centreboard and another to lower it. Some larger sailing boats, especially those designed for shoal waters, have a centreboard which extends below a shallow *ballast keel.* Most dinghy centreboards are streamlined, and are made of marine plywood or plastics, but metal centreplates are also used. The *centre of lateral resistance* shifts when the centreboard pivots as it is raised and lowered; this affects *balance* and, consequently, *weather* and *lee helm.*

Centreboard (US **centerboard**) **boat** or **centreboarder** (US **centerboarder**) A boat with a centreboard. May be a relatively beamy, capsizable sailing dinghy with *righting moment* provided by crew weight rather than by a *ballast keel*, or a large sailing boat with a shallow *keel* plus a centreboard. The latter performs well on all *points of sailing*, and can cruise in shallower waters when the board is raised, but suffers from the disadvantages that the board may bend or become jammed in its case. An *IOR rating* penalty and *inclining test* have been introduced in recent years to discourage centreboard offshore racing yachts, which rely on hull form and *inside ballast* for *stability*, because of doubts as to the ability of such yachts to *right* themselves after a *knockdown.* Centreboard dinghies designed for cruising are more robustly built, heavier, have higher *topsides* than a *planing* dinghy, and may have an *awning* under which the crew can shelter or sleep.

Centreboard case (US **centerboard trunk**) A long narrow casing, running fore-and-aft, fastened to the *keel* either side of the centreboard slot; usually extends above the *waterline.* Houses the raised centreboard and supports the upper portion of the centreboard when it is lowered. *Daggerboard* and *bilgeboard* cases perform a similar function.

Centreboard (US **centerboard**) **hoist** Line or fitting which raises and lowers the centreboard. Sometimes a *downhaul* is required in addition to pull a wooden centreboard down to the desired position.

Centre (US **center**) **cockpit** A common arrangement in *motor-sailers;* the *cockpit*, generally *watertight*, is positioned nearer amidships than normal. Divides the accommodation into forward and after cabins, and enables the crew to sit and work further from the ends where they are less affected by the boat's *motion*. The weight of the crew, engine etc is concentrated nearer her *centre of gravity*.

Centreline (US **centerline**) The fore-and-aft line running between *bow* and *stern*, i.e. along the vertical plane midway between the sides. Transverse measurements are taken from the centreline.

Centre (US **center**) **mainsheet** A *mainsheet* led between an upper *block* attached about half way along the *boom*, and a lower block, which usually slides on an athwartships *track* near the centre of the *cockpit*, whereas a stern mainsheet is led between the end of the boom and the *transom* or *afterdeck*.

Centre (US **center**) **of buoyancy** The *centre of gravity* of the water displaced by a floating boat, a point which is identical to the imaginary centre through which the force of *buoyancy* may be assumed to act. The center of gravity is usually above the centre of buoyancy of a dinghy, but

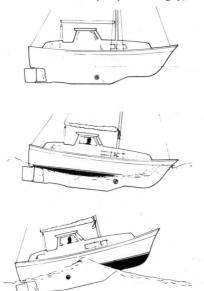

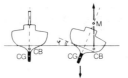

Metacentric height = GM

below the CB of a keelboat (see centre of gravity fig, p. 44). When the boat floats upright the CB and CG are vertically above or below one another, but when the boat heels the CB wanders sideways, and may shift well to one side if the transverse *sections* are suitably shaped. The position of the CB at small angles of heel determines the *metacentre*, and the *initial stability* of a boat can be gauged from the *metacentric height*. The centre of flotation is often also termed the CB, and shifts further forward and aft when the boat pitches in waves and when she is trimmed by the head or the stern.

Centre (US **center**) **of effort** 1. The static geometric centre either of a single sail, or of the area of several sails. 2. The point at which all the forces acting on and developed by the sail(s) can be assumed to be concentrated. The position of the geometric centre (1) can be found in the same way as described for the *centre of lateral resistance*. Alternatively the geometric CE of a triangular sail is at the point of intersection of lines joining the mid-point of each side to the opposite corner. To find the geometric CE of headsail and mainsail combined, first calculate the ratio of the area of the larger sail to that of the smaller sail, then draw a line to connect the CEs of the two sails, and divide the line inversely in the same ratio; the shorter distance is between the combined CE and the CE of the larger sail.

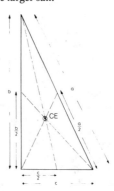

In practice the true CE, the *centre of pressure* at the point at which the forces act (2) (see *force* fig), is not identical with the geometric centre, and its position varies constantly with sail *camber*, *angle of attack* and wind speed. Given the same *aspect ratio*, the true CE of a flat sail will be nearer the luff than that of a full sail; it wanders towards the geometric centre as the angle of attack increases.

The positions of the geometric and true CEs shift both horizontally and vertically when a sail is reefed.

The geometric CE of a well *balanced* boat lies a short distance forward of the geometric CLR, the distance (lead) being usually 5–10% of waterline length.

Centre (US center) of flotation   The centre of the *waterplane* area.

Centre (US center) of gravity   The point through which all the constituent parts of the weight of a boat can be assumed to act. The position of the CG does not alter when the boat heels, but in a dinghy will shift to windward when the crew sits out. In keelboats it is normally lower than the *centre of buoyancy,* but in dinghies it is higher.

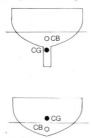

Centre (US center) of gravity factor   One of the elements of the *IOR* rating formula. An *inclining test* is conducted to determine *righting moment* at very small angles of heel. A minimum value of tenderness ratio is stipulated to discourage excessively unstable designs.

Center of lateral plane (US)   See *centre of lateral resistance.*

Centre (US center) of lateral resistance   The CLR is often taken to be the geometric centre of the area of the *lateral plane,* a static point that can be found by cutting out the shape of the underwater profile in stiff board, and balancing it on the point of a needle so that it does not tilt in any direction. It is easier to hang the board from a number of different points one after another, the CLR being at the point of intersection of several plumb lines. When a boat is designed, the relative positions of the *centre of effort* and the CLR are important and govern her *balance* (q.v.), because the aerodynamic *forces* act through the CE and the hydrodynamic forces through the CLR (see force fig). The *under-*

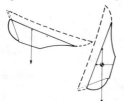

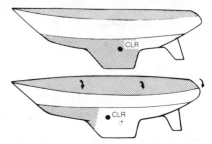

water body is not a flat plate but a streamlined *hydrofoil* past which water flows. The true CLR, the centre of pressure through which side force and *resistance* act, does not coincide with the geometric centre, and shifts as the boat heels or trim alters; it wanders further forward when the boat heels and when she is close-hauled, but further aft when she is reaching. The CLR shifts when the crew of a dinghy move their weight forward, aft or athwartships, and when the centreboard or lifting rudder is raised or lowered.

Centre (US center) of pressure   The total forces acting on an *aerofoil* such as a wing or a sail, or on a *hydrofoil* such as a hull or rudder, can be assumed to be concentrated at a single point, the centre of pressure. That through which the aerodynamic forces act on a sail is the true *centre of effort,* and that through which the hydrodynamic forces act on the underwater area, including centreboard and rudder, is the true *centre of lateral resistance.* Neither coincides with the static geometric centres of the areas, and the positions vary with trim, angle of heel, sail camber, the point of sailing etc.

Centreplate   (US   centerplate)   A   metal *centreboard,* q.v.

Centrifugal force   When a body rotates in a circle about a centre point, centrifugal force is the force that acts outwards, away from the centre. Centripetal force is the force that acts in the opposite direction, towards the centre; the forces are in equilibrium.

Centripetal force   See *centrifugal force.*

Certificate of Registry   The official document giving the measurments and construction details of a vessel, issued when she is *registered* (US *documented*) with the appropriate national authority.

C-flex   *GRP/FRP* reinforcement consisting of unidirectional glass rods, alternating with *roving,* and held together with open weave cloth. May be laid like planking with the rods running fore-and-aft, or used with *chopped strand mat* or woven roving to provide extra strength in a certain direction.

Chafe Verb and noun: damage or wear resulting from friction. When two objects are in contact for a long period, the rubbing action causes wear, e.g. where *mooring lines* pass through *fairleads,* where sails are in contact with parts of the *standing rigging* etc. Particularly vulnerable places are (1) Where the mainsail presses against the spreaders when running, (2) where a slack topping lift or lee runner rubs against the batten pockets and mainsail leech generally, (3) where the genoa leech rubs against the spreader end when close-hauled, (4) where the genoa foot bears on the lifeline or pulpit when reaching, (5) where the spinnaker foot rubs against the forestay or pulpit if it is trimmed in too tight, (6) where sheets and guys rub on lifelines and shrouds, (7) where mooring lines rub on bulwarks, shrouds etc. Chafing gear such as *baggywrinkle* and *shroud rollers* are fitted to protect parts from chafe.

Chain 1. Length of interlocking iron or steel links, which may be plain or reinforced with studs (stud-link chain). Chain cable connects a vessel to her *anchor;* the *classification societies* specify the diameter suitable for various sizes of vessel. If a *windlass* is fitted, the chain must be calibrated, and the links must match the pattern of the *gipsy* (US wildcat). 2. A group of linked transmitting radio stations consisting of a master and several slaves (see *master station*). 3. Chain of soundings (US), see *line of soundings.*

Chain locker Compartment, usually near the bows, in which the *anchor cable* is stowed.

Chain pipe (UK or **navel pipe**) A pipe which passes through the deck, and through which the

anchor cable is led to the chain locker. May have a watertight cover, or a hinged cover with a slot which holds one of the links of the chain.

Chain plate A fitting which is bolted to the structure, and to which *shrouds* or *backstays* are attached; distributes the load more widely over the hull (see *rigging* fig). Often a broad flat strip of metal bolted to the sides, with an eye at the top to which the *turnbuckle* (UK or rigging screw) is shackled. Normally is laminated into a *GRP/FRP moulding,* and may be taken down to the *keel* for added strength.

Championships Races, usually run as a *series,* to find the champion of a racing class, whether area, national, North American, European or World Champion.

Chandlery The items of nautical gear required to fit out a vessel, such as ropes, blocks, shackles, cleats etc. 2. The shop which sells such items, and which is run by a *ship chandler.*

Channel 1. Natural or dredged navigable waterway through shoals, rivers, islands, harbours etc. Important channels are generally marked by *buoys* and *beacons,* and are usually lit; smaller channels and those not used by commercial shipping are often unlit and marked by *perches* rammed into the mud. Channels used by shipping should be avoided by sailing boats whenever possible. 2. An arm of the sea, or a wide strait, e.g. English Channel. 3. Radio communication: a specific band of *frequencies,* such as Channel 16, the Distress, Safety and Calling frequency 156.8 MHz.

Character or **characteristic of a light** A light exhibited as an *aid to navigation* has a character that enables it to be identified, generally by the sequence and duration of the light and dark intervals, sometimes by variation in *intensity* or change of colour. A *fixed light* is continuous and steady, an *alternating light* shows more than one colour on the same *bearing.* The sequence of light and darkness that is exhibited by a *rhythmic light* is repeated regularly, the duration of each sequence being the *period. Occulting:* light is of longer duration than darkness. *Isophase:* the duration of light and darkness is the same (US equal intervals). *Flashing, quick flashing, very quick flashing* and *ultra-quick flashing:* light and darkness alternate continuously at a certain rate, the duration of darkness being longer than that of light. Frequently

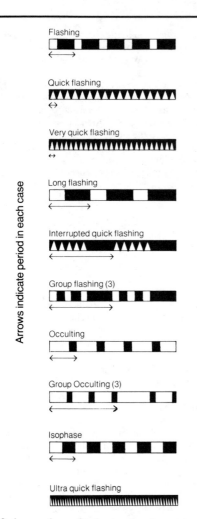

Flashing

Quick flashing

Very quick flashing

Long flashing

Interrupted quick flashing

Group flashing (3)

Occulting

Group Occulting (3)

Isophase

Ultra quick flashing

Arrows indicate period in each case

flashes and occultations occur in *groups*. The character of lights is printed on *charts*, in publications such as *Reeds Nautical Almanac*, and details are given in the *List of Lights* (UK except of light buoys under 8 m).

Charley Noble The *galley* smoke funnel.

Chart Printed map representing part of the earth, giving many details about the area covered by water, and those details concerning land that are of interest to the navigator. The scale of charts varies (see *natural scale*): small scale *gnomonic* charts, covering part of or an entire ocean, are required when planning and making long voyages; medium scale charts provide considerably more information about a much smaller area, usually by the coast; large scale charts are very detailed and are required for entering harbours, and for waters where navigation is particularly difficult. Details given in the *title* include *scale,* units (metres, feet, fathoms), *projection* and *chart datum*.

Most charts used on board sailing boats are *mercator* projection, the *meridians* being drawn parallel to each other and at right angles to the *parallels of latitude; bearings* and *courses* are laid off as straight lines. The *compass roses* are true roses, based on *true north,* sometimes with a half arrow indicating the direction of *magnetic north,* more often with a full rose based on magnetic north inside the true rose. Because mercator projection distorts the shape of features by enlarging them progressively towards the poles, *distances* are measured against the *latitude* scale printed along both sides, at the latitude of the distance being measured; one minute of latitude equals one *nautical mile.*

The information provided on, say, a medium scale chart includes: coastline and natural features, prominent buildings, landmarks; details of principal offshore *aids to navigation* such as *buoys, lights, fog signals, lighthouses; dangers* such as *rocks, eddies, wrecks;* details of *traffic separation* schemes, *submarine cables, vertical clearance, prohibited areas; soundings, depth contours* and the composition of the *sea-bed;* information about *tidal streams and currents,* and cautions. *Symbols and abbreviations* are used to enable all this information to be printed, and booklets (US chart No 1, UK chart No 5011) are published to enable the navigator to interpret the chart. Older charts are printed in two colours, but most countries now show land as yellow or buff, *drying* areas which cover and uncover as green, shallower water as blue and deep water as white. Purple draws attention to lights, warnings and limits.

The navigator lays off courses on charts and plots the vessel's *position* with the help of visual and radio bearings, *sights* etc. Many charts are printed for special purposes, e.g. *harbour plans, routeing* (US pilot) and *latticed charts.* In the UK the Hydrographic Office of the Admiralty produces charts covering most areas of the world in varying scale, and Canadian waters are charted by the Canadian Hydrographic Service. In the US the National Ocean Survey, NOS, charts cover coastal waters, the Great Lakes, rivers and harbors; the Defense Mapping Agency charts cover the high seas; the US Army Corps of Engineers are responsible for charts of the Mississippi river and tributaries. *Small craft charts* are printed by the NOS for use in small vessels in US waters and, like the UK charts produced by private firms such as Stanford or Imrays, they fold up small like a road map. When buying a chart, check that it has been corrected recently in accordance with *Notices to Mariners.* The date and number of the correction is usually entered at the bottom.

Chart datum Reference level on charts. *Soundings* are given below chart datum; the heights of *drying features* which cover and uncover are given above chart datum and are underlined. The datum level selected varies according to

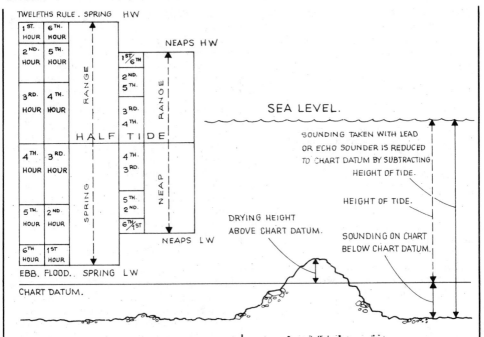

country and area, and is stated in the *title;* in most tidal waters the level selected is so low that only exceptional tides fall below it, e.g. UK metric charts, LAT, *lowest astronomical tide;* fathoms charts, MLWS, *mean low water springs.* US Atlantic charts are based on MLW, *mean low water,* and Pacific charts on MLLW, *mean lower low water;* consequently depths are often shallower than the soundings printed on the chart, especially at low water *spring tides.* Charts covering non-tidal waters may be based on MSL, *mean sea level* (UK), but many other levels are used, and each chart must be checked. In tidal waters the same reference level is used for tidal predictions, heights in official *tide tables* being given as heights above chart datum. Heights of features permanently above sea level are not referred to chart datum but, in UK charts, to MHWS, *mean high water springs* or MSL and, in US charts, to MHW, *mean high water.*

Charter To hire a boat that is fitted out and ready to sail. Normally sailing boats are chartered for cruising either bareboat (without a crew) or with paid hand(s). The charter party, which needs to be checked carefully, is an agreement that includes clauses covering liability, insurance, damage, cruising range and replacement of lost gear.

Chart magnifier A magnifying glass used to read the small print on charts. Many incorporate a light so that the navigator can read the chart at night without turning on the cabin lights; some fold up so that they may be pocketed.

Chart magnifier

Chart table Flat surface on which the navigator works, generally fitted near the *companion.* Should be large enough to spread out a chart, and often has *fiddles* to prevent instruments slipping off. Lighting must be adequate but shaded so as not to interfere with the helmsman's night vision, and may be in the form of a *chart magnifier.* Chart tables sometimes incorporate a drawer or other stowage space where charts can be kept flat when not in use. A rack is often provided nearby for instruments, and shelving for reference books.

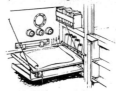

Cheat the tide When there is a *foul tidal stream or current,* to sail where it is least strong, usually close by the shore where there may even be favourable *eddies.*

Check 1. To ease out gradually and carefully, keeping the rope or line under tension. 2. A boat's *way* is checked when it is reduced by controlled tension on a line ashore, or by motor.

Check wire   A light wire sewn into the luff of some sails to prevent too much stretch, e.g. in a gaff mainsail where the *gaff jaws* should not be hoisted above a *mast band* which protects the mast against chafe.

Cheek block   A *block* that is flat on one side so that it can be fastened to the structure or to a *spar*.

Cheeks   1. Wooden blocks at the side of a *spar* or a part, such as the rudder cheeks either side of the *rudder stock*. 2. The sides of a *block*. 3. Brackets fitted at the side of a mast below the top to support the *trestle-trees*.

Cheesecutter   Peaked cap.

Cheese down   *Coil* a rope or line in a tight spiral to make it look neat.

Chine   The line where the *bottom* of the hull meets the side at an angle, as in *hard chine* and *double chine* boats.

Chinese gybe (US **jibe**)   The *boom* swings over on to the new side when the boat gybes, but the upper portion of the sail, or the *gaff* of a gaff-rigged boat, remains on the original side. Generally occurs when the boat gybes *accidentally*. The lower part of the sail and the boom have to be gybed back on to the original side before making a controlled gybe.

Chinese lug or **junk rig**   Rig used by many sea-worthy junks up to the present day, and successfully used by smaller cruisers since 1960. Well-known Chinese lug-rigged boats include 'Jester', which has been raced single-handed across the Atlantic on numerous occasions, and the two-masted 'Galway Blazer', which has sailed round the world. Like a normal *lugsail,* the sail extends forward of the mast, which therefore has little effect on airflow. The *full length battens* maintain

the shape of the sail, while sheets, each attached to the ends of two battens, lead down to the main-sheet block aft and control the *camber* of that part of the sail. *Reefing* is simple; as much sail as is necessary is folded between the battens which lie on top of each other. Although the rig appears complicated it is easy and light to handle.

Chip log   A traditional method of measuring boat speed with a wooden quadrant, the log chip, weighted along the arc so that it floated upright, and attached to a log line, which it pulled off a drum. The log line was knotted every 47 ft 3 in (14.4 m), and time was measured with a 28-second sand glass. The number of knots pulled out in 28 seconds indicated the boat's speed. The same principle can be used if a modern *log* or speed-ometer fails. A makeshift log chip is attached to a

piece of nylon line about 100 ft (30 m) long, and a knot is tied about 15 ft (4.5 m) from the chip. Let the line run out to this knot and, with a stopwatch, measure the time that it takes a further 84 ft 5 in (25.7 m) of line to run out. This length is 50/3600 of a *nautical mile*, so speed in *knots* = 50 divided by the number of seconds taken. E.g. line runs out in 10 seconds, 50 divided by 10 = 5 knots. See also *Dutchman's log*.

Chock   1. Backing pieces or filling fitted where there is a great load, e.g. beneath a *windlass* and where the *mast* passes through the deck. 2. (US) as *fairlead,* a wooden, metal or plastics fitting with curved arms through which a *mooring line* or *cable* is led, usually fitted at the bows and stern or quarters. 3. Block of wood or plastics, often shaped, attached to the deck so that an object can rest on it and be secured to it.

Chock-a-block or **two-blocks**   Said of two *blocks* of a *tackle* that have been pulled together until they touch.

Choke the luff   To jam a line or *tackle* by pulling the *hauling part* of the *fall* between the *sheave* and the line rove through the *block,* in such a way as to prevent the line from running out. The choke is the opening between the sheave and the shell of the block.

Chop and **choppy**   Noun and adjective: disturbed water; the seas are short and steep, but not high.

Chopped strand mat or **glass mat**   Mat formed of irregular chopped filaments of glass, about 1–2 in (25–50 mm) long, used for *hand laid-up GRP/ FRP mouldings*. Available in several grades (1,

1½ or 2 oz/sq ft, 300, 450 or 600 g/sq m are the most common). *Tensile strength* is much the same in all directions.

Chord The chord of a sail is the straight line between *luff* and *leech;* that of the rudder is the straight line between the *leading* and *trailing edges.*

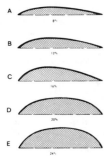

Chord line Term used by some sailmakers for the line applied to a sail at right angles (approximately) to the mast. Gives an indication as to how the sail curves at that height above deck, and the position of maximum *camber.*

Chosen position When using *Sight Reduction Tables* for celestial navigation, a position chosen to give a whole number of degrees of *latitude* and *longitude.* The tabulated *altitude* for the chosen position is found in the tables and compared with the *true altitude* at the observer's position.

Chronometer Very accurate timepiece, often hung in *gimbals* in a special case. Keeps *Greenwich Mean Time* and is not adjusted; any gain or loss is allowed for when determining the vessel's position (see *rate*). Today GMT is given regularly by radio *time signals,* and quartz wristwatches are very accurate. The figure shows the oldest known chronometer.

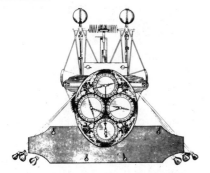

Chronometer error Gain or loss in minutes or seconds by comparison with GMT. Accumulated error is based on the daily *rate* of gain or loss since the previous time check.

Chute Slang for *spinnaker* (esp US). See also *spinnaker chute.*

Circular radio beacon (US) See *omnidirectional radio beacon.*

Circumnavigation To sail completely round something large, such as an island, but especially to sail round the world and either return to the departure port, or cross the outward-bound track. When circumnavigating east to west, the boat covers a longer distance in the *trade wind* zone in lighter winds than when sailing west to east, when the distance is shorter but conditions much harder in the *Westerlies* of the southern hemisphere. In both cases the boat sails downwind, and is helped by the *ocean currents* that result largely from *global wind circulation.*

Cirrocumulus (Cc) High white clouds composed of small elements; dappled, rippled, mackerel sky.

Cirrostratus (Cs) High transparent whitish cloud covering all or part of the sky; often produces a halo phenomenon round sun or moon. Warns of deterioration in the weather when accompanied by a falling *barometer,* and is then often followed by a *warm front* with rain.

Cirrus (Ci) Very high detached white clouds that form in patches, streaks or narrow bands. Tufted cirrus or mare's tails, accompanied by a falling *barometer,* gives warning of an approaching *depression* and its *warm front.*

Civil twilight The periods when it gradually becomes less dark before sunrise and darker after sunset; starts in the morning and finishes in the evening when the sun's centre is 6° below the *rational horizon.* There is sufficient light to measure the *altitude* of a *heavenly body* above the horizon, and bright stars are visible.

Clam cleat Trade name for a nylon *cleat* with strong sides, ridged to hold a line that is under a constant load. The line is pulled back and down to engage in the vee-shaped groove, and can be released instantly with an upward jerk. Vertical, horizontal and lateral cleats are obtainable, as well as *bollards* with a central clam. They can be fitted for many purposes, such as for cleating *sheets, halyards, outhaul* etc.

Clamp. 1. UK: a horizontal member fitted inside the *shelf* in way of *mast, shrouds* or *davits* to provide extra support. 2. US (or beam clamp): a longitudinal member which runs parallel to the upper edge of the hull from bow to stern inside the *frames,* and to which *deck beams* are secured (UK shelf).

Clap on canvas To set more sail.

Class 1. Boats normally race in *keelboat, dinghy, sailboard* or *multihull classes. Manufacturer's class* boats are as nearly identical as possible; the building rules for *one-design class* boats are strictly controlled, but there is more freedom of choice over fittings; in *development classes* there are certain measurement limitations such as overall length, sail area, weight; boats that race in the *level rating* or *ton classes* must be below a certain *rating*, and the same applies to *metre boats*. Sailing boats of different types and sizes can race against each other in *handicap classes. International classes* are recognized by the *IYRU*, and *national classes* by the national authority of a country. *Olympic classes* are those used for the Olympic Games. Before a boat can compete in a race for her class, she has to be measured and a rating or *measurement certificate* issued. Class emblems are displayed on the mainsail. 2. See *classification society*.

Class emblem Indicates the class to which a boat belongs, and is exhibited either side of her *mainsail*. May be a letter(s), number(s) or symbol.

 Puffin   Tornado

Classification society The class or classification of a vessel depends on her *construction*, materials, *scantlings* etc as laid down by a classifiction society and confirmed by a *surveyor*. There are a number of such societies, such as the American Bureau of Shipping, Germanischen Lloyd, Bureau Veritas and *Lloyd's Register of Shipping*. The latter assigns ✠100A1 to sailing boats built to the highest standard, 100A when built in accordance with Lloyd's rules, ⊤ if built under survey; the suffix 1 indicates that she carries anchors, cables and warps adequate for her size. A boat classified 100A has to be surveyed periodically to retain her classification. A Lloyd's Register Building Certificate (LRBC) can be obtained as an alternative for a newly-built boat up to 66 ft (20 m) in length, say for a *GRP/FRP* production boat, provided that she has been built in accordance with Lloyd's rules and under the supervision of Lloyd's surveyors. First the Hull Moulding Release Note is issued to the moulder/builder when a Lloyd's surveyor deems the work satisfactory; the Hull Construction Certificate and Machinery Installation Certificates are issued after the work has been approved, and all these are sent by the owner to Lloyd's to obtain the LRBC.

Claw off To *beat* to windward off a *lee shore* with some difficulty. To work clear of a dangerous coast, when there is a strong *onshore wind* and high seas, calls for a boat that performs well to windward when *close-reefed*.

Claw ring See *reefing claw*.

Clear 1. To free or disentangle a line so that it will run freely through *blocks, fairleads* etc. 2. (adj) Opp of *foul*, i.e. a line that is not entangled, or a clear *berth* where a vessel has room to swing without touching another boat or grounding. 3. Weather: a clear sky is cloudless; clear weather, good visibility, no fog; to clear up indicates an improvement, clouds diminish, visibility improves. 4. To avoid a danger or obstruction, such as another boat, by keeping sufficiently far away, e.g. to keep clear, or to clear a shoal on port tack. 5. All clear aft: report from the crew that *mooring lines* have been *cast off* and are clear of the *propeller*. See also definitions under clear and clearing below.

Clear ahead/astern A term used in the *racing rules*. A yacht is clear astern of another when her *hull* and equipment are abaft an imaginary line projected *abeam* from the aftermost point of the other's hull and equipment; the other yacht is clear ahead. If neither is clear astern the yachts *overlap*. A yacht clear astern must keep clear of a yacht clear ahead.

Clearance 1. Space between two objects or points that are close to each other, such as the tip of the *propeller blade* and the hull or rudder. 2. Certificate showing that the departing or arriving vessel has been cleared or *entered* at the custom house, and that immigration and health authority requirements have been satisfied. Sailing boats arriving at a foreign port fly the *Q flag* to request *pratique* and clearance, which is normally granted by a customs officer who boards the boat, and to whom imported goods are declared and duty paid, where appropriate. He often also deals with immigration and health requirements. See also *clear customs* and *vertical clearance*.

Clear customs When sailing from one country to another, to satisfy *customs* requirements before leaving port by presenting the *ship's papers* and obtaining permission to leave; UK, yachts are required to inform customs before departure, and failure to do so (or failure to fly the *Q flag* and report arrival from abroad) may result in a fine. The term is often used in the UK to mean reporting the arrival of a sailing boat from a foreign country and obtaining *clearance* (q.v.), i.e. entering.

Clearing bearing (US **danger bearing**), **clearing line** or **danger line** A *bearing* or line that leads a vessel clear of a *danger*. By inspecting the *chart* the navigator can often find two identifiable features or landmarks that will keep a vessel clear of a danger if they are either kept in line or just *open*.

In the figure the vessel will clear the shoal if the two clearing marks are kept in line, but clears it by a wider margin if the nearer mark is kept open to right of the church. Should the nearer mark be unidentifiable, the clearing bearing of 029° magnetic can be used, and the navigator then checks with the *hand-bearing compass* to ensure that the bearing becomes no less than 029°.

Clear wind A wind that is not reduced or deflected by the sails of other boats, or by obstructions on the water or on land. When racing it is important to have a clear wind, especially when starting in a big fleet. A boat may clear her wind by bearing away and sailing fast to break through an opponent's *wind shadow*, by tacking to avoid her *dirty wind*, by luffing to avoid being *blanketed*, etc.

Cleat 1. A wooden, plastics or metal fitting with two horns around which a rope is *belayed*. Is designed to take a pull horizontal to the line of the horns, and the line must therefore be led flat to the cleat avoiding an upward or outward pull. Where

possible, a cleat should be so arranged that its centre line is at 15° to the direct pull of the rope. 2. Other types are designed for speedier crewing, the rope being jammed instead of belayed; see *cam, clam, jam* and *tubular cleats*. 3. To cleat is to belay, i.e. to make a rope fast to a cleat.

Clench or **clinch** A method of fastening two wooden parts, especially the two overlapping *planks* of a *clinker-* or clench-*built* boat. The boat nail or rivet is driven through the planks, and the pointed end turned over a roove or *burr*.

Clevis pin A locking pin, headed at one end, with an eye at the other through which a split ring is passed to prevent accidental withdrawal.

Clew 1. The after, lower corner of a *fore-and-aft sail* where *foot* and *leech* meet. (See *sail* fig.) Reinforcing patches, into which the clew eye is worked, take the load applied at the clew by the *outhaul* of a *mainsail* or *mizzen*, or by the *sheet* of a *headsail* or *staysail*. 2. The outer lower corners of *square sails* and *spinnakers*, where the leeches meet the foot. Formerly spelt clue.

Clew garnet In *square-rigged* ships the rope (US line) or *tackle* which hauls the clew of the *course* up to the *yard* when the sail is *furled*. Clew lines serve the same purpose for smaller and higher square sails.

Clew outhaul The line which tensions the *foot* of the *mainsail*. A simple line is adequate for dinghies but, aboard larger boats, a *tackle* or mechanical device such as the worm gear in the figure is required to pull the sail out towards the boom end and to adjust sail *camber*. Pulling the clew towards the after end of the boom flattens the sail for a *beat*; greater fullness for downwind sailing is obtained by easing the tension, so that the foot slips back slightly towards the mast.

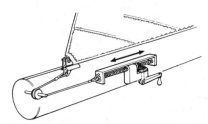

Cliff Land that rises almost vertically from the water. When cliffs are high, an *offshore wind* usually gusts and slants down at an angle, making a sailing boat heel more than normal.

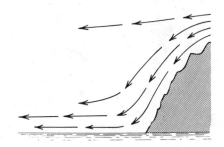

Climate The meteorological conditions that prevail throughout the year in a particular area or place, as governed by its latitude, height above sea level, ocean currents, vegetation etc. Broadly divided into polar, sub-polar, temperate, subtropical and tropical zones.

Climbing rung Light alloy step attached to the mast with pop rivets; useful not only when *rigging* is damaged or requires attention, but to increase the *range* of *visibility* and to determine distance off an object by varying *height of eye*.

Clinker-built or **lapstrake,** sometimes **clench-** or **clencher-built** Method used to build wooden boats from earliest times. The lower edge of each *plank* overlaps the upper edge of the plank below it like a roof tile. Lighter timbers replace the heavy *frames* of a *carvel-built* boat. The overlapping *clench*-nailed seams provide considerable strength. *GRP/FRP* hulls can also be moulded to appear like clinker, the ridged construction increasing strength. Reverse clinker is rare.

Clinometer (sometimes **inclinometer**) An instrument with a pendulum and graduated arc, or a curved spirit level, usually fitted to a transverse *bulkhead* in the cabin so that the angle of *heel* can be measured (i.e. the angle between the vertical, when the vessel lies upright, and her attitude when heeled). The mounting plate of some spherical porthole-type *compasses* incorporates a clinometer scale.

Clipper Fast nineteenth-century sailing ship, designed primarily for speed. Clippers sailed during the Gold Rush between the west and east coasts of North America via Cape Horn, carried tea from China to London, and were engaged in the Australian wool trade. They made 14–20 knots and, in tea races, took about 100 days to sail from China to England. The clipper bow is characteristic of the vessels, which had fine ends with concave *waterlines* forward and aft, a *length-to-beam* ratio

of about 5, and considerable *deadrise*. The 'Cutty Sark', launched in 1869 and the only surviving British tea clipper, lies at Greenwich: hull length 224 ft (68.3 m), beam 36 ft (11 m), sail area 32,800 sq ft (3047 sq m), draft 20 ft (6.1 m), displacement 2100 tons (2134 tonnes). The 'Wavertree', though somewhat later and not strictly a clipper, engaged in a similar trade and is preserved at South Street Seaport Museum in New York.

Clipper bow The *stem* is concave and curves aft of the straight line between stemhead and *waterline*. In modern keelboats is often combined with a *bowsprit* which is sometimes very short.

Close To draw near to another vessel or the land. Close aboard or close alongside: very near to.

Close fetch See also *close reach*.

Close-hauled A *point of sailing,* defined in the *IYRU racing rules* as when a boat is 'sailing by the wind as close as she can lie with advantage in working to *windward*'. The boat sails on *port* or *starboard tack, pointing* as close to wind as is efficient with her sails *hardened* right in; i.e. without *pinching*. When she sails close-hauled on alternate tacks she is *beating*. A boat is able to sail towards the wind because the *lift* force produced by air flow over the curved sail draws her forward,

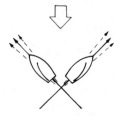

while the *lateral area* underwater discourages her from making *leeway*. The helmsman has to find the best compromise between pointing high and sailing fast (see *speed made good to windward*). In stronger winds the boat *heels* to a considerable angle, and in dinghies this has to be countered by *sitting* (US hiking) *out*, or by using a *trapeze*, while the *mainsail* can be made flatter by adjusting the *cunningham, mainsheet traveller* and other control lines, or by *bending the mast*.

Close reach The *point of sailing* between *close-hauled* and *beam reaching*. Sails are not sheeted in quite as far as when hard on the wind, and a *reaching genoa* or *star-cut* spinnaker may be set.

Close-reefed Said of a boat when all possible *reefs* have been taken in and *canvas* reduced to a minimum.

Closest point of approach (CPA) When operating *radar,* the closest that two vessels will approach each other if neither alters course or speed.

Close-winded Describes a boat that sails efficiently when *pointing* very close to the wind.

Cloth One of a number of strips or panels of *canvas,* seamed together to make a sail. See also *sailcloth*, entries below and *sail* fig.

Cloth construction The make-up of cloth. A particular material may be made up of a large number of fine low *denier* or *decitex yarns,* or a smaller number of thicker yarns. Because *mainsail* cloth is subjected to greater loading on the *weft* than the *warp*, its construction often incorporates extra strong weft yarns; whereas a *genoa* is more likely to be made of cloth with equal thickness warp and weft. However, different requirements need different constructions, sometimes in the same sail.

Clothing Sailors need clothing appropriate for all weathers, whatever the size of the boat; non-slip sailing shoes or boots, protection from sun, *foul weather gear* including waterproof hood or sou'wester, windproof jacket and warm pullovers. *Wet suits* are often worn by dinghy sailors in colder waters. Thermal underwear may possibly be worn for night sailing. Special gloves for sailing have roughened, hard-wearing palms. See also *life-jacket* (US *personal flotation device*) and *safety harness*.

Cloth weight Different weights of *sailcloth* are required for *working, light-weather* and *storm sails,* and weights also vary with the size of the sail itself. British cloth weight is given in ounces per square yard or grammes per square metre, but American cloth is only 28½ ins wide and designation of the same gauge of cloth therefore differs in UK and US by about 20%. America produces more cloth than any other country, and weights are therefore usually quoted in US ounces in English-speaking countries. Sail cloth weights range from about $^5/_8$ oz US, $^3/_4$ oz UK, 27 g/sq m for a light-weather spinnaker, through 3–5½ oz US, 4–7 oz UK, 128–235 g/sq m for a jib about 270 sq ft (25 sq m) in area, to 7 oz US, 9 oz UK, 300 g/sq m for a 160 sq ft (15 sq m) storm trysail. The figure compares A, the metric g/sq m with B, UK ounces and C, US ounces. 1 UK oz/sq yd = $^{19}/_{24}$ (roughly $^4/_5$ or 0.8) US oz/36 in × 28.5 in = 34 g/sq m: 1 US oz/36 in × 28.5 in = $^5/_4$ (1.25) UK oz/sq yd = 42.8 g/sq m: 1 g/sq m = 0.03 UK oz/sq yd = 0.023 US oz/36 in × 28.5 in.

Cloud Visible collection of minute water droplets or ice in the air, caused by the condensation of water vapour. *Stratus* – grey layers, sheets: *cumulus* – lumpy with flat bases and cauliflower-like rounded tops: *cirrus* – fibrous or feather: nimbus – rain-bearing.

Cloud amount The proportion of cloudy sky to the total area of the sky, generally given in eighths, sometimes in tenths. Cloud amount is shown on weather maps by varying the *station circle* symbol from a clear sky, empty white circle, to completely overcast, a solid black circle. A St. Andrew's cross in the circle indicates that the sky is obscured and the amount of cloud cannot be estimated.

Clove hitch A useful hitch for attaching a line to a vertical or horizontal spar or rope, or to a handrail, mooring bollard, ring etc.

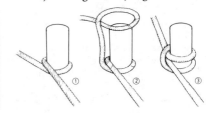

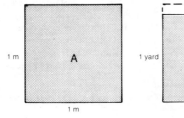
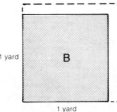
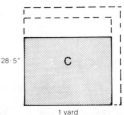

Club 1. UK more often boom. A short *spar* at the foot of a self-trimming *staysail* or *boom jib*. The sail moves to leeward automatically like the mainsail when the boat is tacked or gybed, and the *sheet* can be left permanently cleated. The boom must be shorter than the distance between the *stay* and the *mast*. Popular for cruising boats sailed short-handed. 2. See *Yacht Club*.

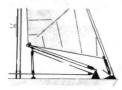

Clump A heavy block of concrete or iron to which a *mooring buoy* is attached, used in place of an expensive *anchor*. When calculating *holding power*, the *density* of the material has to be compared with that of a metal anchor.

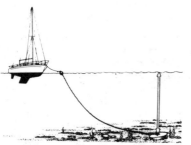

Clutter Unwanted echoes from waves (sea clutter or sea return), rain, snow etc which appear on a *radar screen*. Echoes from nearby waves appear near the centre of the *Plan Position Indicator* and, in heavy weather, can hide a small vessel or buoy. A small boat should therefore hoist a *radar reflector* high in the rigging so that she can be detected by other larger vessels against the background of clutter, especially when near shipping lanes. Sea clutter can be reduced with the sensitivity time control (also called swept gain or sea clutter control); this reduces gain most at the centre of the display, but progressively less as range increases. The differentiator (or fast time constant, or rain clutter control) reduces rain clutter and has an equal effect at all parts of the PPI.

Coachroof (US **trunk**) The part of the *cabin* that is raised above *deck* to provide height in the cabin.

Is usually forward of the cockpit and has side decks to port and starboard. See *construction* fig.

Coaming Vertical structure surrounding a *hatch, cockpit, skylight* etc which prevents water entering. May be of wood or part of a *GRP/FRP moulding* which, in the case of the cockpit coaming, may be broadened to form the base for the *sheet winches* or *cleats*. See *construction* fig.

Coast 1. Where land meets the sea; the limit of land. The narrow strip of the coastline, details of which are printed on charts. Is often taken to include a much broader strip inland. 2. To sail along a coast.

Coastal current A *current* which follows the trend of the coast, just seaward of the zone of breaking *surf*.

Coastal navigation Navigation largely within sight of land and exclusive of *celestial navigation*. The navigator requires *charts, plotting instruments, pilots, tide tables* and *tidal stream atlases, List of Lights* and, if a *direction finder* is carried, a *List of Radio Aids* (UK). The boat should at least carry a *steering compass* so that the correct *course* can be followed, a *hand-bearing compass* for taking *bearings*, a *lead* or *echo sounder* for measuring depth of water, a reliable clock or watch, and a *log* for measuring distance sailed through the water. The boat's *position* is fixed by obtaining *position lines*. See *bearing, dead reckoning, horizontal* and *vertical sextant angles, line of soundings, running fix, three-point problem, transit* and position line.

Coast chart (US) Medium scale *chart*, 1:50,000 to 1:150,000, normally 1:80,000; used when sailing along a coast, entering channels, bays and harbors, or when seeking an anchorage (UK equivalent medium scale).

Coastguard (US **Coast Guard**) In the UK the organization responsible for Search and Rescue operations in UK waters; maintains radio watch on *distress frequencies* and has direct liaison with the *Royal National Lifeboat Institution,* Coast Radio stations, the armed services, the fisheries department and *Lloyds*. Is also charged with co-ordinating measures to deal with oil spillage, as well as watching and reporting on passing shipping from coastguard stations around the coast, organizing cliff rescues etc. The US Coast Guard is a military organization and, as such, is part of the armed forces of the United States. It has similar duties to the British Coastguard, but operates its own *lifeboats* and aircraft; it is also responsible for law enforcement and the maintenance of *buoys, lighthouses* and *aids to navigation* (in the UK these are maintained by *Trinity House*).

Coastland Strip of land just inland of the coastline; may include sand dunes, marshes, saltings etc.

Coastline The limit of land where it meets the sea, i.e. the limit of the area affected directly by the sea and waves.

Coast pilot See *pilot, 2.*

Coast radio station The UK Post Office and the US Federal Communications Commission each maintains a chain of radio stations round the coast. *Radio telephony:* listening watch is maintained on VHF Channel 16 (156.80 MHz) and on 2182 kHz, the *Distress, Safety and Calling frequencies.* In the UK watch is also maintained from 0900–1700 hrs local time daily, except on Sundays, on 2381 kHz, and working frequencies on VHF and/or MF are assigned to each station. In the US several long range communications stations which monitor 500 kHz are maintained by the Coast Guard.

Cocked hat (UK) or **triangle of position** (US) The triangle formed when three *position lines* fail to meet at a single point. The smaller the triangle the less the uncertainty, because the boat's *position* should be somewhere in the cocked hat. The position is either taken to be at the centre of a small triangle or, when it is larger and there is some danger to be avoided, at the apex that would place her nearest to the danger.

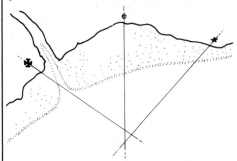

Cockpit In decked boats a space, lower than deck level, where the crew can sit or stand. Raised *coamings* discourage water from entering, but *watertight* or *self-draining cockpits* (q.v.) are preferable at sea. Some boats have more than one cockpit, so that the area for the helmsman is separate from the area where the crew work. In sailing dinghies and dayboats the cockpit is the entire undecked portion.

Code flag One of the *International Code of Signals flags,* used for communication at sea. See back endpapers.

Codline Natural fibre three-stranded *cordage,* now largely replaced by small diameter synthetic fibre line.

Coefficient As applied to sailing boats, a number of coefficients are used as non-dimensional shape factors, usually determined empirically. Coefficient reflects the relationship between the *force,* such as *drag,* D, sail area S_A and the *dynamic pressure* of wind, $q = mv^2/2$, i.e. $D = C \times S_A \times q$. The drag coefficient C in the above expression does not remain constant, but depends on the sail shape (geometry), together with the angle of the sail to wind direction (*angle of attack* or incidence). See also *block, lateral plane, midship section, prismatic* and *waterplane coefficients.*

Coffee grinder Powerful *sheet winch* fitted to large sophisticated racing yachts such as those competing for the *America's Cup* or *Admiral's Cup.* A separate pedestal with two handles, often fitted beneath the deck to reduce *windage,* is operated at a distance from the winch drum(s) to which it is linked by shafting and a gearbox, which enables one of several drums or gears to be selected.

Cogaid Short for (US) Coast Guard Assistance Instruction Data. Gives information on *distress,* towing, helicopter lift, R/T etc.

Coil 1. To arrange a rope or line neatly in rings so that it will run out without getting *snarled* or so that it can be *stowed* tidily. *Right-hand lay* rope is coiled clockwise, *left-hand* counterclockwise. The crew should never stand in or on a coiled line because he can be thrown overboard if the line runs out. 2. A quantity of rope when coiled, or a single ring of a coil. 3. Rope may be bought by the coil.

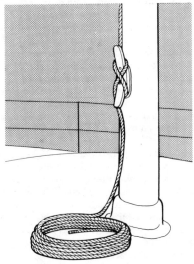

Coir Strong coarse filaments obtained from coconut husks and made into cheap, flexible but rather weak rope. Being light in weight and springy was often used for *tow-ropes*. Floats and is easy to pick up. Now used for making mats, *chafing* gear etc, but otherwise has been replaced by *polypropylene* rope.

Col A saddle-shaped area between two *anti-cyclones* and two *depressions,* which form a high-low-high-low pattern around the col.

Co-latitude The complement of the observer's *latitude,* i.e. 90° minus latitude. Side PZ in the *PZX triangle* (q.v.); the arc between the elevated *celestial pole* and the observer's *zenith.*

Cold front The line where a mass of cold air following a *depression* meets warmer air ahead. The cold air thrusts beneath the warm air and lifts, it, heavy clouds form and there is rain, which is often heavy, and sometimes thunder with strong gusts from different directions. Weather and visibility improve when the cold front has passed, and pressure rises.

Cold moulding Wooden construction with a high strength to weight ratio. Thin veneers are glued together over a framework or *mould,* and the adhesive *cures* without being heated.

Collision Although a vessel is often said to have been in collision with a pier or other fixed structure, a collision is more narrowly defined in marine insurance as contact between two vessels at sea, or between a moving vessel and a light vessel or a *wreck* that could be saved. Contact with fixed structures, wreckage, flotsam etc is not considered collision. The *International Regulations for Preventing Collisions at Sea* specify in great detail how vessels must behave in order to avoid collision, as well as laying down what *lights* and *shapes* must be *exhibited* and what *sound signals* must be made. The *IRPCS* stipulate that vessels shall always proceed at a safe speed, that action to avoid collision must be made in ample time, and that alterations of course and speed should be large enough to be readily apparent to another vessel. After a collision, international maritime law requires a vessel to give whatever assistance is needed by the other vessel, in so far as she is able to do so without endangering the lives of those on board. See *risk of collision.*

Collision bulkhead A strong, watertight, transverse *bulkhead,* sometimes built into seagoing craft to ensure that they will stay afloat when holed near the stem, say as a result of a collision, or of hitting *flotsam* or driftwood. A watertight door or hatch provides access, so that the space forward of the bulkhead can be used for *stowage,* often as a *chain locker.*

Collision course When two vessels are sailing in such directions that they would collide if they maintained their courses and speeds, they are on collision courses; if the bearing of the other vessel remains constant, a risk of collision exists, and the give-way vessel must take action to avoid it.

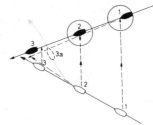

Collision mat A greased cloth or canvas mat which is drawn over the area where a boat has been *stove in,* to prevent water from entering. The boat can then be pumped out and the leak repaired from inside. A modern alternative operates like a strong umbrella, and is pushed through a hole from inboard, extended, and pulled back to clamp tight against the hull to make the boat watertight.

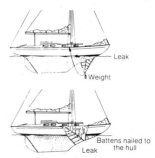

Colours (UK) or **colors** (US) The national *ensign.* Morning colours: the ensign and other *flags* are hoisted by all vessels at 0800 in the summer and 0900 in the winter. Evening colours (US making colors), lowering the ensign at sunset or at 2100, whichever is the earlier. If the crew will not be on board at sunset, flags are lowered before they disembark.

Colregs demarcation line Colregs is the US *Coast Guard* contraction for the *International Regulations for Preventing Collisions at Sea.* A demarcation line, entered in purple on a chart, marks the boundary between waters where US *rules of the road* are in force and waters where Colregs apply.

Combination buoy (US) *Aid to navigation* that exhibits a light and makes a sound signal.

Combined lantern (UK) or **combination light** (US) Either a *bi-colour* lantern exhibiting red and green *side lights,* or a *tri-colour* lantern exhibiting a white *stern light* in addition.

Come about To *tack* or go about, i.e. to change from *port tack* to *starboard tack* or vice versa without *gybing.*

Come home Said of the *anchor* when it is dragged towards the boat.

Come to anchor Drop *anchor.*

Come up with A boat reduces the distance between herself and another vessel ahead, which she overtakes.

Committee boat The vessel from which the *race officers* start a race, and from which *course* and *starting signals* are made. Should preferably be positioned at the end of the *starting line* where the competing boats concentrate to start with a *clear wind* on *starboard tack,* so that the race officers have a good view of competitors' actions. Under the *racing rules* may be a limit mark of the starting line or rank as an *obstruction.*

Commodore. The highest ranking *flag officer* of a *yacht club* or *sailing club;* some clubs also have an Admiral, which is an honorary position.

Companion or **companionway** The main *hatch* and the adjacent area where the *cabin* is entered. The steps into the cabin are generally steeper and have narrower treads than those on land.

Compass The most indispensable of all navigational instruments. A compass needle always points to the *north,* with *gyro compasses* giving the direction of *true north,* and *magnetic compasses* that of *magnetic north* (see *magnetic compass*). Using this information the navigator may find the *bearing* of an object, and set a *course* to steer. Magnetic compasses are generally used in sailing boats, and are *gimballed* so that the card remains horizontal regardless of the boat's motion. Some modern compasses are spherical, often with internal gimbals and *compensating magnets;* others are flat, semi-domed or domed, and the figures on the compass card are magnified when the glass above is curved. The domed compass

gives the impression that the compass is spherical, but it is actually half-spherical with a flat bottom that limits the angle to which the card can tilt; like the flat-bottomed compass it is usually hung in gimbals. The porthole-type, mounted on the bulkhead abaft the cabin, may have a completely transparent bowl so that it can be read in the cabin as well as in the cockpit. Many modern compasses have 45° *lubber lines* in addition to the normal lubber line against which the boat's course is read. The compass may be housed in a *binnacle,* flush-mounted horizontally or vertically, suspended in a bracket or bulkhead mounted. See also entries below under compass, and *bino-, hand-bearing, grid, electronic, projector, reflector, repeater, tactical* and *telltale compasses.*

Compass adjuster Expert who checks *compass error, compensates* the instrument with *corrector magnets* to reduce *deviation,* and draws up the *deviation table.*

Compass adjustment buoy or **beacon.** Laid or erected to facilitate the determination of *deviation* when *swinging ship.*

Compass bearing The direction of an object from an observer relative to *compass north,* as found with a *magnetic compass* that is disturbed by an external force. Has to be corrected for *deviation* to obtain the *magnetic bearing,* and again for *variation* to obtain the *true bearing,* as described under *compass course.*

Compass bowl Container in which the compass card is suspended. Generally made of brass, which does not affect the compass needle, and filled with oil or a mixture of alcohol and distilled water to damp down the movement of the card.

Compass card Card to which the compass needles or bar magnets are attached. Is almost always balanced on a jewelled pivot upon which it rotates (a modern innovation has a floating card and magnet). Formerly the card was *graduated* in

points, but now almost all are graduated from 0–360°. Some cards have degrees marked around the circumference and 8, 16 or 32 points marked nearer the centre in addition. Cards to be viewed from above are flat or dished, but many modern compasses are edge-graduated so that they can be viewed from the side as well. See also *tactical compass.*

Compass course The angle between *compass north* and the vessel's *fore-and-aft line;* the *course* steered or to be steered by the helmsman, who checks the course he is following against the *steering compass.* Differs from the *magnetic course* by the value of *deviation* for that particular course, and from the *true course* by compass error,

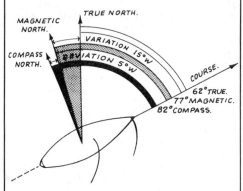

which is deviation plus the value of *variation* for that particular locality. When correcting (US uncorrecting) a true course to a magnetic and compass course, westerly deviation and variation are added, easterly subtracted; when correcting a compass course to a true course, westerly deviation and variation are subtracted and easterly added.

Compass error (total) The error of a *magnetic compass* resulting from the effects of both *variation* and *deviation,* i.e. the difference between *true north* and *compass north.*

Compass monocular and **binoculars** Magnifying instruments which incorporate a compass so that *bearings* can be taken of distant objects, or by short-sighted sailors.

Compass needle Magnetized steel rod(s) or bar magnet(s) attached beneath the compass card. Because the card can pivot freely, the needle of a *steering compass* (subject to *deviation* as well as *variation*) indicates the direction of *compass north,* which differs from *true north* by the amount of total *compass error.* The needle of a compass that is affected solely by the earth's magnetic field (such as a *hand-bearing compass* held absolutely clear of all disturbing influences on board) aligns itself with the *magnetic meridian,* which differs from the true meridian by the amount of variation alone.

Compass north The direction indicated by the north-pointing needle of a *magnetic compass* when disturbed by an external force. Differs from *true north* by the amount of total *compass error;* this is an addition of *variation,* which is constant for any one particular place, and *deviation,* which differs for each compass installation. A *hand-bearing compass,* held in such a position that it is not subject to deviation, aligns itself with the *magnetic meridian,* and the bearing obtained has to be corrected only for variation to obtain the *true bearing.*

Compass pivot A vertical pin in the compass bowl, with a sharp point on which the centre of the compass card rests.

Compass rose A circle printed on a *chart,* representing the true compass, and graduated clockwise from 0–360°. There is generally a second concentric rose inside, which is rotated east or west of *true north* by the amount of *variation* at the date of publication so that it points to *magnetic north.* This is also graduated in degrees, and may have a third rose inside graduated in *points.* The details of variation and *annual change* are usually printed inside the rose. Sometimes there is only a true rose; half an arrow then indicates the direction of magnetic north, and details of variation are printed nearby.

Compass safe distance To avoid deflecting the *magnetic compass,* electronic instruments such as *radar, echo sounder* and *direction finder* must not be installed too close to it. The distance should be stated in the installation instructions. The compas must also be sited far enough from fixed iron objects, such as the engine or ballast keel, and beyond the field set up by electrical circuits, to avoid excessive *deviation.*

Compass stabilized See *plan position indicator.*

Compensate To reduce the *deviation* of a *magnetic compass* as much as possible by adjusting or fitting *corrector magnets,* or *Flinders Bar* and *soft iron spheres,* to counteract or neutralize the effect of fixed ferrous fittings, electrical circuits and equipment on board. Many modern compasses have internal compensators which can be adjusted to counteract deviation.

Complements Numerals 1–9 in the *International Code of Signals* which add to the meaning of a particular *hoist* of letters.

Composite construction Method of building *hulls* using more than one material. Originally metal *frames* with wooden *planking,* later *GRP/ FRP* over a *moulded plywood* hull.

Composite track The track followed by a vessel when she is unable to follow a *great circle* course all the way to her destination, e.g. on account of

Compass rose

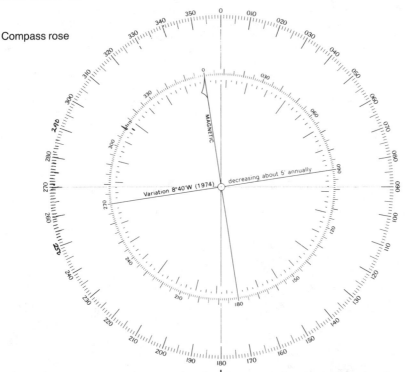

ice. She may start on a great circle course, skirt the ice on a *rhumb line* course, and finish on a great circle course.

Condensation If air temperature drops and the air becomes fully saturated (*dew-point*), any further drop in temperature causes condensation, and tiny droplets form. The air cannot hold the water and various forms of *precipitation* result. Condensation occurs in cabins on the ceiling, on bulkheads and the deckhead when a boat lies at a mooring without adequate ventilation, and is caused by the difference between air temperature inside and air or water temperature outside, particularly at night when the temperature of deck and hull drop below the dew-point of the moist air inside the cabin.

Cone 1. A signal *shape*, displayed as prescribed in the *IRPCS* either point up, point down or in combination with other shapes. A *sailing vessel* using her auxiliary engine as well as sails must exhibit a cone point downwards forward in the rigging. Two cones, points together, are hoisted by certain *vessels engaged in fishing*. Two cones, bases together, form a *diamond* shape. A cone is black, and base diameter is not less than 0.6 m,

but a vessel under 20 m in length may hoist a smaller cone. Those for sailing vessels are generally collapsible, made of plastics or alloy, or of cloth with a wire frame; some are inflatable. 2. Storm cones are hoisted at UK coastal stations when gales are expected (see *storm warnings*). 3. *Top-mark*, e.g. as fitted on cardinal system buoys.

Cone terminal See *swageless terminal*.

Confused Said of seas that run in more than one direction, and are disorderly; generally the result of a shift in wind direction, but also occur in a *race*, near harbour walls and where *tidal streams or currents* meet.

Conical buoy (UK) Anchored *aid to navigation*; the part above water appeas to be cone shaped, point up, the sides are straight or nearly so. *IALA A, starboard hand mark*, green, occasionally black; left to starboard when entering a harbour, river etc. See also *nun* (US) buoy, and front endpapers.

Conjunction When two *heavenly bodies* are in the same direction from the earth they are said to be in conjunction. C.f. *opposition*.

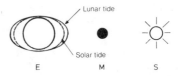

Consol and **Consolan** Similar radio navigation systems, the former operating in Europe, the latter in North America. A boat's position can be found by using only a simple radio receiver and special Consol *charts,* which are normal charts overprinted with labelled Consol *position lines.* A Consol *radio beacon* transmits the station identification signal, followed by a long continuous tone and then a series of dots and dashes. The number of dots (or dashes) is counted until they are lost in the continuous equisignal which follows, after which the number of dashes (or dots) is counted to

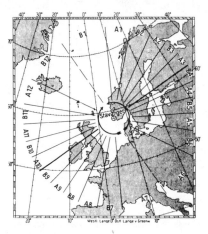

the end of the signal. The total number of dots and dashes counted is subtracted from 60 and the remainder divided by two: e.g. 40 dashes – equisignal – 14 dots: 60 minus 54 (the total counted) = 6, divided by 2 = 3. The figure is added to each count and the signal is therefore 43 dashes and 17 dots, which places the ship on a particular position line. A second position line obtained from another Consol transmitter gives a *fix.* Range is normally 1,000 miles during the day and 1500 by night, but accuracy at longer ranges is not as good as that of other long range navigation systems.

Constant bearing A *bearing* that does not alter although the vessel is moving. When two boats are on *collision courses* the bearing of one from the other remains constant, and the vessel whose duty it is to keep clear must take avoiding action.

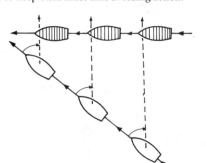

Construction Boatbuilding methods have changed because timber, originally the only material available, has almost entirely been superseded by *GRP/FRP, steel, aluminium, marine plywood* and *ferro-cement.* In traditional wooden construction the *keel* is laid first on keel blocks and the *stem* and *sternpost* are *scarphed* to it. *Moulds* are set up and braced to provide a framework, and *ribbands* are bent around them. *Frames* or *timbers* are sawn or bent to the shape of the *hull,* and are fastened to the keel between the

Sheer plan	8 sternpost	17 shelf
	9 horn timber	18 rib
1 stem	10 stern knee	19 bilge stringer
2 breasthook	11 deadwood	20 length overall LOA
3 apron	12 rudder trunk	21 load waterline LWL
4 wood keel	13 rudder	22 bilges
5 keelson	14 tiller	23 hull
6 ballast keel	15 deck	24 net registered
7 keel bolts	16 beam	tonnage

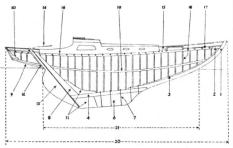

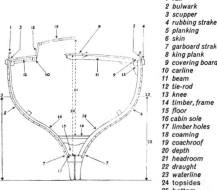

Half-sections
1 rail
2 bulwark
3 scupper
4 rubbing strake
5 planking
6 skin
7 garboard strake
8 king plank
9 covering board
10 carline
11 beam
12 tie-rod
13 knee
14 timber, frame
15 floor
16 cabin sole
17 limber holes
18 coaming
19 coachroof
20 depth
21 headroom
22 draught
23 waterline
24 topsides
25 bottom
26 freeboard

moulds. The hull *planking* is fastened to the frames and timbers. The lowest strake near the keel, the *garboard,* is *rabbeted* into the keel, and the *hood ends* of the planks are rabbeted into the stem and sternpost. Many of the terms are retained in other forms of construction. See also *batten-seam planking, cold moulding,* moulded plywood, *stitch-and-glue, strip planking, sandwich construction,* and *cloth construction.*

Contender A very fast single-handed racing dinghy with a *trapeze,* designed by Miller and

Whitworth. An *international class*. LOA 16 ft (4.88 m), beam 4 ft 8 in (1.42 m), weight rigged 228 lbs (104 kg), sail area 120 sq ft (11.1 sq m).

Continental air mass *Air mass* that forms over land, as opposed to a maritime air mass. Continental-tropical if formed in the sub-tropical belt, continental-polar if formed in the polar regions.

Continental shelf The area surrounding the continents where water is shallower than in mid-ocean, usually taken as extending to a depth of 600 ft (200 m). Depths increase considerably beyond the continental shelf.

Contour Line on a *chart* joining points that are the same height above a reference plane (often *MHWS* on UK charts or *MHW* on US charts) or the same depth below *chart dataum* (*MLWS* or *LAT* on UK charts, *MLW* or *MLLW* on US charts).

Control 1. (or control line) A line that controls the shape and set of the sails, such as a *cunningham, outhaul, boom vang*. 2. A lever or other device that controls the operation of machinery, such as a gear lever or throttle. 3. A number of electronic aids, engines etc are operated at a distance by remote control.

Control-luff See *stretch-luff*.

Convection Heat in a fluid is transferred from one place to another by movement of the fluid itself, e.g. air heated by warm ground becomes less dense and rises (see *land* and *sea breezes*).

Convergence Zone of earth's atmosphere, such as the *Intertropical Convergence Zone* near the equator, where the upward motion of air is accompanied by inward horizontal motion near the surface of the earth. In the case of oceans, an area where currents meet and, usually, surface water sinks. C.f. *divergence*. See *global winds* fig.

Convergency of the meridians Any two *meridians* cut the *equator* at right angles, and gradually converge as *latitude* increases until they meet at the *poles*. A *great circle* intersects two meridians at different angles, and the approximate difference between the angles is found from the formula:

convergency = *difference of longitude* × sin mean latitude.

The meridians on *mercator* charts appear as parallel lines that do not converge and *great circle* (radio) bearings have to be corrected to mercatorial bearings before they can be laid off (see *half convergency*).

Co-ordinated universal time The speed of

rotation of the earth varies minutely and *Greenwich Mean Time*, which is based on the assumed regularity of the *mean sun*, loses or gains micro-seconds with this speed irregularity. Co-ordinated universal time is based on the atomic second, which is the SI unit of time and is defined as the duration of 9,192,631,770 periods of the radiation corresponding to the transition state of the caesium atom 133. The atomic second is almost identical to the GMT second (1/86,400 of the mean solar day), and the adjustment of the latter in leap seconds can sometimes be detected when the pips which indicate the exact time are increased from six to seven.

Co-ordinates The position of a point within a certain grid or frame of reference is determined by co-ordinates. For example, those that pinpoint the position of a place on the surface of the earth are its *latitude* and *longitude*, i.e. its distance north or south of the *equator* and its distance east or west of the *Greenwich meridian*. The spherical co-ordinates that fix the position of a *heavenly body* in the *celestial sphere* are its *hour angle* and *declination*. In *coastal navigation* a *fix* is obtained with co-ordinates such as two *bearings* (*cross bearings*), a bearing and an angle (*vertical* and *horizontal sextant angles* plus a radio or visual bearing) or two angles (*three-point problem*).

Co-range line On a chart connects places where the *range of tide* is the same.

Cordage Collective term for fibrous rope, whether made of natural or synthetic fibres. The former are mainly *manila, sisal, hemp, coir* and *cotton*, the latter mainly *nylon, polyester* and *polypropylene*. See *rope-making*. Cordage is either measured by circumference or diameter, and the approximate equivalents are:

Diameter	Diameter	Circumference
2 mm	$5/64$ in	$1/4$ in
3 mm	$1/8$ in	$3/8$ in
4 mm	$5/32$ in	$1/2$ in
5 mm	$3/16$ in	$5/8$ in
6 mm	$1/4$ in	$3/4$ in
7 mm	$9/32$ in	$7/8$ in
8 mm	$5/16$ in	1 in
10 mm	$13/32$ in	$1 1/4$ in
12 mm	$15/32$ in	$1 1/2$ in
14 mm	$9/16$ in	$1 3/4$ in
16 mm	$5/8$ in	2 in
18 mm	$11/16$ in	$2 1/4$ in
20 mm	$13/16$ in	$2 1/2$ in
22 mm	$7/8$ in	$2 3/4$ in
24 mm	$15/16$ in	3 in
28 mm	$1 1/8$ in	$3 1/2$ in
32 mm	$1 1/4$ in	4 in

Core 1. In *sandwich* (q.v.) or cored construction, the material that separates the two *GRP/FRP laminates*. Often foamed plastics, or end-grain balsa. 2. The jute or wire centre around which wires are twisted to form a *strand* of *wire rope* (c.f. *heart*). 3. The inner strands of synthetic fibre ropes around which a sheath is *braided*, e.g. a *Kevlar* core with a braided polyester sheath.

Cored construction (US) See *sandwich construction*.

Coriolis force Force named after the French physicist, Gustave-Gaspard Coriolis. Because the earth rotates, a moving object is accelerated at right angles to the direction in which it is moving. In the northern hemisphere acceleration is to the right, in the southern to the left. The effect is greatest at the poles and becomes progressively less towards the equator where it is nil. Coriolis force affects the *global circulation of winds,* such as the *trade winds*, which consequently blow from the north-east north of the equator, but from the south-east to the south of it. Also affects *ocean currents*.

Corposant See *St. Elmo's fire*.

Corrected time When *handicap racing,* a boat takes a certain time to complete the *course;* this is the *elapsed time.* The *time allowance* is then applied to find the corrected time. The winner is the boat with the shortest corrected time.

Correction A number of values have to be corrected for known erorrs. A *compass bearing* or *course* is corrected to *true* by allowing for *deviation* and *variation* (see also *uncorrecting,* US); a *sextant altitude* is corrected by allowing for *sextant errors, height of eye, refraction, parallax* and *semi-diameter;* a *DF* bearing is corrected for *half-convergency* and DF errors in accordance with the *calibration* table, and so on. Corrections to *charts* are made subsequent to their publication to keep them up to date, and are entered by the chart agency or the navigator as instructed in *Notices to Mariners.* When buying a chart it should be checked to ensure that corrections are up to date.

Corrector (US **compensator**) **magnet** Magnet placed in a *binnacle* by a *compass adjuster* to eliminate or reduce the *deviation* of a magnetic compass. Many spherical compasses have internal magnets that can be adjusted, often with a screwdriver.

Corrosion Destruction or eating away of metal through chemical or electro-chemical reaction with water, air or chemicals. See *galvanic corrosion, rust.*

Crevice corrosion, from which stainless steel

suffers in particular, occurs in threaded joints and in a crevice between two surfaces, even when they are of two similar metals or if only one surface is metal.

Brass, a mixture of copper and zinc, can become dezincified, leaving a porous mass of copper which has virtually no strength, and only special marine brasses (bronzes) should be used in hull construction.

Stray-current corrosion can occur when a boat is connected to a shore supply of electricity if there is a fault in the insulation.

Corten steel A high-strength, low-alloy steel made by the US Steel Corporation.

Co-tidal line Connects places where a tidal undulation occurs at the same time. *Charts* with co-tidal lines are of value when *reducing soundings* taken offshore to *chart datum* because they enable the navigator to calculate the *height of tide.*

Cotter pin (US) or **split pin** (UK) Soft metal pin, folded back on itself to form an eye at one end. Is pushed through an aperture, and the two parts are opened out and bent back to prevent the pin from withdrawing accidentally.

Cotton Natural fibres spun into yarns from which ropes and sails are made. Now largely replaced by synthetic fibre materials.

Cotton counts The number of hanks of cotton, each 840 yards long, which will weigh one pound; this gives a gauge of coarseness. To convert into *denier*, divide 5315 by the cotton counts, and vice versa.

Counter Above the *waterline* the *stern* extends beyond the *rudder stock* and terminates in a small transom (archboard), providing a broad afterdeck abaft the cockpit. A long counter increases waterline length when the boat heels, and provides *reserve buoyancy,* but long *overhangs* at bow and stern can cause *sagging.* Modern counters (2) are therefore usually short and are frequently *raked* forward instead of aft.

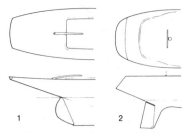

Countercurrent A *current* that sets in the opposite direction to the flow of the main current, such as the Equatorial Countercurrent which flows eastward between the westward flowing North and South Equatorial Currents, and the Agulhas Current which runs contrary to the Southern Ocean Current.

Counter rudder A boat may swing further than intended when the helm is put over to alter course; counter rudder is then applied to check the *yaw*, and this is particularly necessary immediately after *gybing* in strong winds and high seas to prevent *broaching*. The helmsman is said to 'meet her' with counter or opposite rudder.

Counter stern An overhanging stern with a *counter*.

Couple Two forces acting on a body are equal and opposite, their lines of action are parallel to each other, but are separated by a certain distance. The moment of the couple is the perpendicular distance between the two lines of action multiplied by one or other force, e.g. righting couple, the forces being gravity and buoyancy.

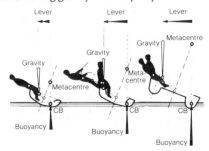

Course 1. The direction in which a vessel is being, or is to be steered. *True, magnetic* and *compass courses* are the angles between the vessel's fore-and-aft line and the directions of true, magnetic and compass north respectively. Courses are normally given in degrees, rarely in *points of the compass* these days. The course to be *made good over the ground* is laid off on the *chart*, and the course to steer is found by calculator, by arithmetic or by drawing a *vector diagram* (q.v.) to allow for the effects of the *tidal stream or current; leeway* also has to be allowed for when close-hauled or reaching. The true course on the chart is converted

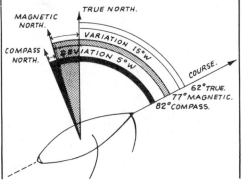

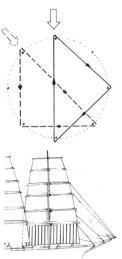

to a compass course by adding westerly, or subtracting easterly *variation* and *deviation*. To find the *track* made good over the ground, the navigator converts the compass course to a true course by adding easterly or subtracting westerly deviation and variation, and allows for the effects of the tidal stream or current and leeway as above. 2. Sailing boats compete in races by sailing round a course one or more times; normally they cross the *starting line* and then *round* or pass a number of *marks,* leaving them to port or starboard as instructed, and complete the course by crossing the *finishing line.* Marks of inshore and inland courses may be specially laid *buoys,* but for *off-shore races* aids to navigation such as *light vessels* or *light buoys* are generally selected. 3. One of the *square sails* bent to the lowest *yard* on each mast of a square-rigged sailing ship; forecourse (or foresail) on the *foremast,* main course (or mainsail) on the *mainmast,* crossjack on the *mizzenmast.* The yards are trimmed by *braces,* and the *clews* of the courses by sheets leading aft and *tacks* leading forward.

Courtesy flag The national *flag* (not the *ensign,* though this is often used, particularly the red ensign in the UK) of the country being visited by a foreign yacht; is flown from the *starboard spreader* or *rigging.*

Cover 1. When racing, to stay between an opponent and the next mark. This often involves tacking every time the other boat tacks, to ensure that she does not benefit from a wind shift. 2. The boat cover and *cockpit* cover protect the boat or cockpit, whether at a mooring or on land, and prevent rain water from filling the *bilges*. 3. The sail cover is laced over a sail when the boat is moored to keep it dry and to prevent deterioration of the fibres caused by ultra-violet rays, pollution etc. See also *covers*.

Cover factor The closer the *warp* and *weft* of *sailcloth*, the higher the cover factor, the lower the *porosity* and the greater the driving force produced.

Covering board or **plank sheer** The outermost *deck plank*, laid over the *frame* heads where deck and *hull* meet. Covering (US): see *sheathing*. See *construction* fig.

Covers Said when a feature such as a rock, wreck or sandbank is covered with water at some state of the tide, but is uncovered at low tide, i.e. (UK) a *drying feature*. Chart abbr cov.

Cowl A cover that is fitted above a *ventilator*; can be rotated to face whichever direction suits the wind and the *point of sailing*. The opening either collects and directs air into a cabin or compartment, or exhausts air from them. Now generally made of flexible plastics or synthetic rubber so that it will give, for example when in contact with a headsail sheet or the crew's foot.

CQR anchor Patented *anchor* with good *holding power* (see *plough anchor*). The letters are variously said to stand for Coastal Quick Release, Carlos Quincey Rudd or, simply, 'secure'.

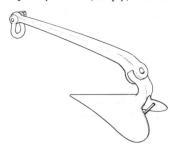

Crab 1. (esp US) To make *leeway*. 2. To catch a crab; when rowing the oar is *feathered* excessively under water, and the blade jerks clear when the oarsman pulls on it, often causing him to fall backwards. 3. A small *winch*.

Cradle Frame which supports a vessel on land, or when she is being *launched* or *slipped*.

Craft Any type of ship or boat, most often applied to a smaller vessel. Singular and collective noun.

Crane 1. machine that lifts, e.g. cargo into and out of the hold of a ship. Keelboat *masts* are generally *stepped* with the help of a *derrick, sheer legs* or a crane, and sailing boats may be lifted out of the water by a crane or *Travel-Lift* instead of being hauled out on a *slipway* or *marine railway*. 2. Short projecting bracket at the *masthead* or at the end of a *spar; stays* may be attached to it, and it may carry a *block* or the *spinnaker halyard sheave* clear of the spar.

Crank Said of a boat that *heels* too easily; the term *tender* is used more frequently.

Crans, crance or **cranze iron** Iron band to which *stays* are attached, fitted at the forward end of the *bowsprit*. May have a second hole through which the *jib-boom* passes.

Crazing Fine cracks that appear on the *gelcoat* surface, generally as a result of applying too thick a gelcoat, using unsuitable *resin*, or the wrong mixture, such as too much *catalyst*. Varnish may also craze.

Crest The highest point of a *wave* (opp *trough*), or of a hill, mountain etc.

Crew The ship's company who sail, cook and navigate the boat. The number of the crew is often limited by *class* rules to a maximum and/or minimum, i.e. single-handed classes, two-man dinghies, ton classes. In dinghies the word may relate to all on board, or to all except the *helmsman*. As a verb: to crew is to work as a member of the crew.

Cringle A rope loop, usually with a metal *thimble*, worked into the *bolt rope* at the *tack, clew* or *head* of a sail. For *points* and *jiffy reefing*, cringles are provided along the *luff* and *leech* of the sail, at either end of each line of *reef points*.

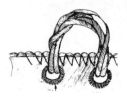

Cripple To damage wire rope by leading it over a sharp edge, or bending it at too acute an angle so that it is permanently kinked.

Cross bearing The vessel's position is (or should be) at the intersection of two *bearings* taken of two objects marked on the *chart*, the bearings being obtained by *hand-bearing compass* or radio *direction finder*. The nearer the *angle of cut* is to a right angle the more reliable will the *fix* be. Whenever possible a check should be made, either by taking a bearing of a third object, a *horizontal sextant angle* of the two objects, or a *vertical sextant angle* of one of the objects if its height is known.

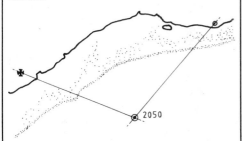

Crosshead bollard A strong deck fitting to which a line may be *belayed* in many ways without making a *hitch* or bend.

Crossing 1. Two vessels are said to be crossing when one passes ahead of the other. When two *power-driven* vessels are crossing, and there is a *risk of collision*, the one that keeps clear is the vessel which sees the other on her own *starboard* side, provided the other vessel is not *overtaking*. Where possible the give-way vessel should avoid crossing ahead of the other when there is any risk of collision. In the figures the ship will cross ahead of the sailing boat. Had the bearing of the ship remained unchanged, she would still have

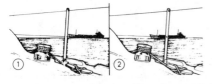

been seen just astern of the stanchion after a period had elapsed (assuming that neither boat had altered course) as in fig 1, and the boats would have been on *collison courses*. A sailing boat using her engine would then have had to give way. 2. When crossing *traffic separation zones* or traffic lanes, a vessel should always cross at right angles without allowing for *leeway* or tidal *set*, so that her profile and/or navigation lights are presented at 90°.

Crossing the line A ducking ceremony in which old hands dressed up as Neptune and his retinue initiate those people who are crossing the equator for the first time.

Crossjack 1. Lowest *yard* on the *mizzenmast* of a *square-rigged* sailing ship. 2. Lowest *square sail* on the mizzenmast. Pronounced cro'jack.

Cross-linked winch Two *winches* are linked together with shafting and a gearbox, so that a sheet or warp can be hauled taut, using the power available from two winches at the same time.

Cross-loop aerial See *Bellini-Tosi.*

Cross seas Confused seas that form when two wave systems run in different directions and meet at an angle, such as where wind-raised seas meet an ocean swell.

Cross-staff See *Jacob's staff.*

Crosstrees 1. See *spreaders.* 2. In a *square-rigged sailing ship*, which has a *topmast* above a *lower mast*, thwartship pieces of timber fitted above the *trestle-trees* to support the *top.* Smaller crosstrees at the topmast head provide support for the *topgallant mast.*

Crowd on sail To set more than the usual amount of sail.

Crowfoot Small lines radiate from a central eye, e.g. as used to spread an *awning* when the eye is attached to a *topping lift.*

Crown 1. Where the shank and arm of the *anchor* meet. 2. The top of the bow of a *shackle*. 3. The head of a *block*. 4. Alternative term for deck *camber*, q.v.

Crown knot A knot made in the end of a line to prevent it from unlaying. Usually combined with a *wall knot*, or finished as a *back splice.*

Crow's nest A small *look-out* position high on the mast.

Cruise Verb and noun: to cruise is to make a leisurely voyage (the cruise), taking at least several days and visiting a number of places, which may be close together or at some distance from each other.

Cruiser or **cruising boat**   A sailing boat with a cabin, fitted out for *cruising*, often for long periods. More attention is paid to comfort than when a boat is designed primarily for racing. The design, *rig*, gear and equipment carried vary according to the waters where she will sail, the degree of comfort required and the owner's taste. Many *multihulls* are designed expressly for cruising.

Cruiser-racer   A boat designed and fitted out for both cruising and racing. Generally faster than a cruiser of comparable size, and more comfortable than an out-and-out racing boat.

Cruising Club of America, CCA   Leading American club concerned with both cruising and racing (e.g. organizes racing on the East Coast of the USA including the *Bermuda Race*); founded in 1922 and based in New York. The CCA *rating* rule

Rating = 0.95 (length ± beam ± displacement ± sail area ± freeboard ± iron keel allowance) × ballast ratio × propeller factor

for *offshore racing* yachts was used in the western hemisphere until 1970, concurrently with the *RORC* rule on the eastern side of the Atlantic and elsewhere. Elements of both the CCA and RORC rules have been retained in the *International Offshore Rule*.

Cruising speed   *Economical speed* at which to run an engine, i.e. low fuel consumption, good power output and minimum wear of engine parts.

Crutch   1. Correct but rarely heard term for a *rowlock* (US oarlock), which is shipped in the *gunwale* to provide the fulcrum for an *oar* when rowing. 2. Or boom crutch: a single vertical support with a curved top in which the *boom* rests when the sail is lowered; is removed when sailing. A folding scissors crutch is made of two pieces,

bolted together close beneath the boom. These open out into an X shape, the legs being held firm by chocks on deck. *Gallows* perform the same function, but are not removable.

Cuddy   A small shelter forward in a small sailing or motor boat, especially in a *dayboat*.

Cumulonimbus   (Cb)   Massive cloud which towers miles upwards from a horizontal base some half mile above the sea, often with a horizontal anvil-shaped top. May be accompanied by *thunder* and rain or hail, and often generates its own squally winds.

Cumulus (Cu)   Fair-weather cumulus, the cotton wool clouds with flat bases and tops that only swell slightly upwards, are often seen on summer days when there is a *sea breeze*. Gusty winds accompany larger cumulus with brilliant white swelling tops and darker, level bases. Cumulus congestus towers upwards for a mile or more, and may develop into *cumulonimbus*.

Cunningham, or **cunninham eye**, or **cunningham hole**   A simple but effective method of altering sail *camber* by means of a line, rove through a *cringle* in the *luff* of the sail above the *tack*. When the cringle is pulled down towards the boom or tack fitting, the mainsail or headsail becomes flatter, and the position of maximum camber shifts further forward towards the *leading edge* of the sail, which is then a more efficient shape for *close-hauled* sailing, especially if the wind *freshens*. US also ooker. Named after Briggs Cunningham of New York.

Cure   Noun and verb: the hardening of synthetic *resin* or of a *GRP/FRP moulding*. An unsaturated resin cures from a fluid to a solid state, the process being speeded up by the addition of a *catalyst*.

Current   Horizontal movement of water. UK: relates to the horizontal movement that results from natural causes such as wind, *density*, gravity (rivers) etc, but not from the *tide*-raising forces of the sun and moon; in the US this is termed a non-tidal current. The US term *tidal current* relates to horizontal movement resulting from the tide-raising forces, and is not used in the UK. See also *ocean current*.

Current diagram (US)   See *vector diagram*, 2.

Current rose *Vector diagram* that shows the direction and *rate* of a *tidal stream or current* during a 12-hour (*semi-diurnal tide*) or 24-hour (*diurnal tide*) period.

Curtain When paint or varnish is applied too thickly to a vertical or nearly vertical surface it sags, forming curtains in the shape of runs down the surface.

Curve of areas A line representing *waterline length* is divided, usually into ten equally spaced parts. Lines (ordinates) are drawn at right angles to this base line, the length of each representing the underwater area of the *section* at that ordinate. The volume of the *displacement* is calculated from the area between the curve and the base line, and the coefficient of the combined areas is the *prismatic coefficient*.

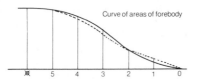

Curve of areas of forebody

Custom-built As opposed to *stock production*, a one-off boat built to the owner's requirements.

Customs Officials who deal with the payment of legally imposed customs duties, and to whom imported goods have to be declared. They are informed of a vessel's intended departure from a country and, on arrival in a foreign country or when returning from abroad, the vessel flies the *quarantine flag Q* to request *clearance* by customs, health and immigration officials. A UK sailing boat that fails to fly a Q flag and report her arrival, or to advise customs of her departure, may be fined.

Cut Verb and noun: the way in which the individual *cloths* of a sail are seamed together to provide the sail area required, and the desired degree of *fullness* throughout the sail. The relative strengths of *warp* and *weft* and *bias stretch* have to be taken into consideration when the cloths are assembled. The *luff* and *foot* are *rounded* (A) so that the required *camber* is obtained (B) when the sail is set on a straight mast and boom.

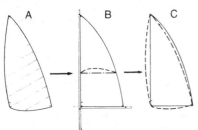

Cutless bearing A neoprene bearing in which the *propeller shaft* turns. Usually straight-sided (octagonal or more) to allow water to flow through, to lubricate and cool the bearing.

Cut splice Two lines are *spliced* together, the end of each being spliced some distance along the other to form an oval *eye* between the splices.

Cutter 1. A single-masted boat with *mainsail* and more than one *headsail*. Cutter rig is popular for cruising boats because sail area is divided roughly equally between the mainsail and the headsails, which consist of *jib* and *staysail*, sometimes with a *jib topsail* as well. Several sizes of headsail can be set, and are relatively easy to change to suit the weather, being smaller than the one headsail set in a *sloop*. Older cutters have a

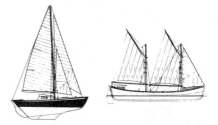

gaff mainsail, with or without a *topsail*, and a *bowsprit*. 2. A boat designed for sailing as well as for *rowing* (pulling) by a crew, usually of twelve; mainly used by navies and youth organizations. 3. The vessel in which pilots wait for incoming vessels requiring their services and to which they transfer after piloting an outward bound vessel is often termed a pilot cutter.

Cutwater The forward edge of the *stem* near the *waterline* where it cuts the water.

Cyclone Name given to a *tropical revolving storm* in the southern Indian Ocean; occurs most frequently between December and April. Most cyclonic storms in the Bay of Bengal occur between May and December, and in the Arabian Sea between April–June and September–December. The US term extra-tropical cyclone relates to a *depression*, i.e. a low pressure area.

Cyclonic wind Wind circulation about a low pressure area. In the northern hemisphere circulation is counterclockwise, in the southern hemisphere clockwise. The surface winds blow at an angle of about 20° to the *isobars* over the sea, but at a greater angle to them over land.

Cylinder A signal *shape* which, under the *IRPCS*, may be displayed by a *vessel constrained by her draft*, and therefore unable to manoeuvre freely. The cylinder is black with a minimum diameter of 0.6 m and a height of twice its diameter.

D

$D = $ **Delta:** yellow-blue-yellow *code flag*. As a single letter signal means 'Keep clear of me – I am manoeuvring with difficulty'. *Morse code:* — • • (dash dot dot).

Dacron Trade name of *polyester* fibres made by duPont in the USA; used for making rope and sail cloth.

Daggerboard A board that is raised and lowered vertically in the daggerboard trunk or case. Serves the same purpose as a *centreboard* (provides *lateral resistance*), which differs only in that it pivots about a bolt. Capping prevents a daggerboard from being pushed too far down and, usually, friction provided by shock cord pressing against the *trailing edge* is adequate to hold it in the desired position when fully or partly raised. Preferred for small dinghies and children's boats because it requires less space than a centreboard. The main disadvantage is that it usually jams or is damaged when running aground because it cannot pivot up into the boat.

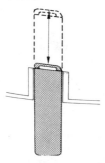

Dan buoy 1. A temporary *mark* laid, for example, to mark the end of a *starting line,* an *obstruction,* danger etc. A flag flies from a spar which passes through a float, the spar being weighted at the bottom to keep it upright. 2. Similar apparatus that can be launched to mark the position of a man who has fallen overboard. Often specified as safety equipment that must be carried when *racing offshore,* e.g. *IOR,* and then has a 12 in orange flag flown from an 8 ft spar, which is attached to a *lifebuoy* that provides 30 lbs *buoyancy.* Has a *drogue* and a water-activated battery connected to a light at the top of the spar.

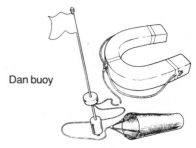

Dan buoy

Danforth anchor A patented lightweight *anchor* with great *holding power;* has often been imitated. The flat flukes have pointed bills which lie close together, and the stock which passes through the crown is attached to them. Depending on the type of *sea-bed* can hold up to one hundred times its weight. Also known as the Meon anchor.

Danger (US usually **hazard**) All hazards to surface navigation such as *rocks, wrecks, reefs* and *shoals* are drawn on *charts* and, in busy waters, are also marked by *aids to navigation* such as buoys, lighthouses and beacons to give warning to shipping. Other dangers entered on charts include *overfalls, tide-rips, eddies, breakers* and *kelp.*

Danger angle *Vertical* and *horizontal sextant angles* can be used to ensure that a vessel keeps a safe distance from a danger. The angle subtended by an object, the height of which is known, is the same at all points on the circumference of a circle, the centre of which is the object and the radius of which is the distance from the object. Tables are printed, e.g. in *Reed's,* giving distances, heights and angles, and the navigator finds the angle subtended by, say, a lighthouse of known height when the boat is at a safe distance from the danger. The formula is:

$$\text{distance} = \frac{\text{height}}{\tan \text{angle measured}}$$

(See vertical sextant angle). In the figure p. 69 the danger lies between the lighthouse and the vessel, and the navigator checks with the *sextant* that the

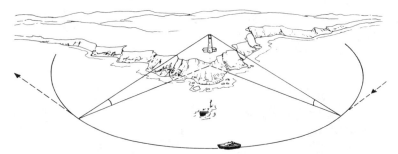

angle becomes no greater than that found in the table; if the vessel were between the lighthouse and the danger he would check to see that the angle became no smaller.

Similarly the angles subtended by two landmarks are the same at all points on the circumference of circles. If the danger lies roughly midway between the objects, the horizontal danger angle can be found on the chart by measuring the angle made by lines to the objects from a position that is at a safe distance outside or inside the danger. When the boat has to stay outside the danger, the navigator checks that the angle becomes no greater; if the safe course is inside the danger the angle must become no smaller.

Danger bearing and **line** See *clearing bearing.*

Dangerous quadrant and **semicircle** In the northern hemisphere, the quadrant lying forward and to the right of the *path* of a *tropical revolving storm* (q.v.), and the semi-circle to the right of its path. In the southern hemisphere they lie to the left of its path. The areas are on the same side as the typical direction of *recurvature,* and should be avoided if possible. When in the dangerous quadrant, a sailing boat overtaken by a tropical revolving storm *heaves to* on whichever tack takes her away from the centre.

Date line The International Date Line is based on the 180th *meridian,* but is modified to keep all those islands in one group on the same side of the line. The date changes when a vessel crosses; it is put back a day when crossing in an easterly direction, and forward a day when crossing westward; the time remains unchanged.

Datum See *chart datum* and *tidal datum.*

Davit Small crane fitted on board to hoist and lower the *dinghy* and other heavy gear. Generally mounted in pairs at the *transom* of larger yachts. A *tackle* or *winch* is usually required to raise the load.

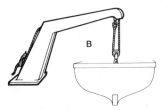

Day 1. As opposed to night, the period when the sun is above the *visible horizon* between sunrise and sunset. 2. Broadly, the period during which earth turns once about its axis. The actual duration of a day is based on successive transits across a *meridian* by a *heavenly body.* The duration of the *apparent solar* day varies considerably, because the speed at which the *true sun* moves along its elliptical path (the ecliptic) is not constant. The duration of the *mean solar* day is 24 hours (the civil day), and is based on the movement of the fictitious *mean sun* at a constant speed of $15°$ *longitude* per hour. The daily difference between apparent and mean solar days is given in the *Nautical Almanac* under *Equation of Time.* The *sidereal* day, based on two successive transits of a star across the same meridian, is 23 hrs 46 min 4 sec, but the *lunar* day is about 24 hrs 50 mins.

Daybeacon See *daymark,* 1.

Dayboat, daysailer A *keelboat* or *centreboarder,* often with no *cabin,* designed for day-time sailing. Always has a large *cockpit,* and may have limited accommodation or a *cuddy,* but is not normally fitted out for extended cruising or racing, although some classes do race.

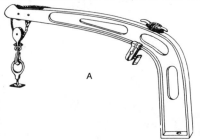

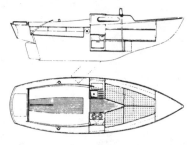

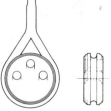

Daymark 1. UK: a large unlit *beacon* (US day-beacon). 2. US: Large geometric shape fitted on top of a *buoy, pile* or *dolphin,* generally to mark the side of a channel. Square green daymarks are left to port when entering from seaward or sailing clockwise round North America, and red triangular daymarks are left to starboard. Pointers are being phased out. Mid-channel marks have octagonal black and white vertically striped daymarks. 3. US *shape* (q.v.) shown by a vessel to indicate her occupation or class.

Day's run The distance made good *over the ground* in *nautical miles* in 24 hours, traditionally from noon to noon but now, with radio aids, often reckoned from 0000–2400 hrs. The time between, e.g. two noon *sights* is exactly 24 hours only when a boat is sailing due north or south, because the time at which a noon sight is taken varies with *longitude.* In small cruising boats 100 n.miles is considered a fair day's run, and Sir Francis Chichester averaged 131 n.miles for 226 days when circumnavigating the world in 'Gipsy Moth V' in 1967. The record day's run for a large sailing yacht is 342 n.miles, held by 'Atlantic', winner of the 1905 Trans-Atlantic race.

D Class catamaran The largest of the International *catamaran* classes. The boats are sailed by a crew of three, and length and beam are unrestricted, but sail area is limited to 500 sq ft (46.45 sq m). A spinnaker may be set in addition, the maximum area permitted being 800 sq ft (74.32 sq m).

Dead Exactly: as in dead *astern* or *ahead,* exactly in line with the *centreline;* dead *run,* running with the wind aft, e.g. when the objective is exactly downwind.

Dead calm No breeze at all and an absolutely smooth sea, *Beaufort force* 0. The wind is sometimes said to be blowing 'straight up and down'.

Deadeye Circular wooden *block,* generally with three holes to take a *lanyard,* grooved around the circumference so that it can be *spliced* into a *shroud* like a large *thimble;* the lanyard is passed through it to set up the standing rigging. Superseded by *turnbuckles* (UK or rigging screws).

Deadlight Metal cover clamped over a *portlight* or *scuttle* in bad weather to prevent water entering if the glass is broken by a heavy sea. US: also piece of heavy glass set in a door, deck etc to admit light; does not open.

Dead reckoning A term applied more loosely by many small boat sailors and aviators than by the navy. The dead reckoning position of a vessel is very approximate, and is calculated from the *course* steered and the *distance* sailed *through the water* only, without allowing for the effects of *tidal stream or current* and *leeway.* The more accurate *estimated position* is then plotted on by allowing for these effects. Frequently small boat sailors do not differentiate and speak of an estimated position as a dead reckoning position. The dead reckoning or estimated positions can only be found at any moment if every alteration in course has been noted in the *log-book,* together with the time and *log* reading showing the distance sailed through the water. Courses and distances can then be plotted on from the last *fix* or *observed position.* A DR position can also be found with the help of *traverse tables* by calculating *d.lat* and *departure* from the course(s) and distance(s) run. The term is thought to be derived from deduced or ded. reckoning. UK: a DR position is conventionally marked on the plotting chart by a cross and its time of origin; US by a half circle.

Deadrise or **rise of floor** The vertical distance between a line horizontal to the *keel* and the *chine* or the *turn of the bilge* above it. The deadrise angle is that made by a line horizontal to the top of the keel and a line from the top of the keel to the chine or the turn of the bilge. A flat-bottomed boat has no rise of floor, but a deep vee hull has a large deadrise angle.

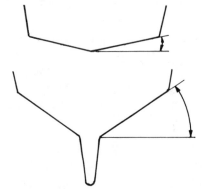

Deadwood Wooden members that form part of the centreline structure, usually between *sternpost* and fuller sections amidships, but sometimes also forward. In *GRP/FRP* construction this space may be foam-filled to provide *buoyancy,* because it is too narrow for tanks or stowage. See *construction* fig.

Decca An extremely accurate low frequency navigation system which, because the special receivers have to be hired from the Decca Navigator Co Ltd, is mainly confined to larger vessels that are in constant use. Continuous *phase*-locked radio signals are transmitted by a *master* and three slaves (red, green and purple), and are compared in the Deccometer (the receiver), which gives the zone letter and number of the lane in which the vessel is situated. This is referred to a Decca *chart,* which has a lattice overprinted in the three colours, with labelled *hyperbolic position lines*. Two or three position lines *fix* the vessel's position. Of the 43 chains that operate world-wide, 23 are in Northern Europe, 4 in North America and 5 in South Africa.

Decitex Often written d'tex. The standard unit for gauging coarseness of *yarns* or filaments used in *cloth construction*. One tenth of a *tex* (q.v.); to convert to *denier* multiply by 0.9.

Deck Covers the *hull,* i.e. the virtually horizontal surface on which the crew walk. In larger ships there are several decks, the weather deck being the one exposed to the elements. See also *foredeck, side deck, afterdeck, whaleback, flush* and *raised decks. See construction* fig.

Deck beam A thwartship member that rests on the *shelf* (US clamp) and supports the deck.

Decked As opposed to a half- or quarter-decked boat, one that is closed entirely by a deck.

Deck filler plate A watertight screw-down cover fitted on deck above the tubing that leads to fuel and water tanks.

Deck fitting Any fitting that is attached to the deck.

Deckhead The underside of a deck. In the same position as the ceiling of a room on shore (but the *ceiling* of a boat or ship is a lining for the sides of the *hull*).

Deckhouse An enclosed structure that stands on a deck, usually to provide accommodation.

Decklight 1. Small prism or piece of heavy glass, strong enough to be trodden on, fitted in the deck to provide light below. 2. A deck, *mast* or *spreader* light may be fitted on the mast or spreaders to

illuminate the decks for working at night. Not one of the *navigation lights.*

Deck plan Detail drawing showing the lay-out of the deck, viewed from above, i.e. shows the position of the *cockpit, winches, fairleads, mast* etc.

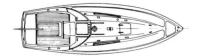

Deck plate or **eye plate** 1. Plate, attached to the deck, to which a fitting such as a block is shackled. (See *rigging* fig.) 2. US: disk covering the opening of a fuel or water tank.

Deck watch A very accurate watch used when taking *sights.*

Declaration Form signed at the end of a race declaring that *class* and *racing rules,* and the *sailing instructions,* have been complied with.

Declination Angular distance in degrees, minutes and tenths of minutes of a *heavenly body* north or south of the *celestial equator,* i.e. of the two co-ordinates that pinpoint the position of the body on the *celestial sphere* the one that corresponds to terrestrial *latitude* (see *PZX triangle* fig). Is tabulated in the *Nautical Almanac* hourly for sun, moon and planets, and for one day in three for stars.

Deep 1. An area where the water is particularly deep. 2. See *lead line.*

Deep draft route In *traffic separation schemes* etc the route recommended or advisable for vessels that *draw* a lot of water, because they cannot navigate safely elsewhere; should be given a wide berth whenever possible by sailing boats that draw little water. Fines would be heavy if a collision in a deep draft route were caused by the negligence of a sailing boat's crew; she should always cross speedily, at right angles to the route, ignoring tidal *set* or *leeway*. On charts the abbreviation for 'track for deep draft vessels' is DW; deep draft (US) is DD.

Deep vee A boat with a considerable *deadrise* angle of over about 5°.

Defaced Said of an *ensign* with the symbol of a club, authority or organization in the *fly*.

Degree One degree equals 60 minutes or 3600 seconds. The circumference of the earth at the *equator* is divided into 360 equal parts, each subtending an angle of one degree at the earth's centre. *Longitude* is given in degrees, minutes and seconds from the *prime meridian*, longitude 0°, east and west to 180°. Similarly *meridians* connecting the north and south *poles* are divided into 180 parts, each subtending one degree at the earth's centre, and *latitude* is given in degrees, minutes and seconds from the equator, latitude 0°, north and south to the poles, 90°N and S. The earth takes 24 hours to turn through 360°, and 15° of longitude can be expressed as 1 hour, or 4 minutes of time as 1° of longitude.

Delaminate The breaking asunder of parts that have been *laminated* together.

Delta anchor Type of *anchor* developed from the *Danforth*; has much the same *holding power*. The divided shaft is fixed to a single broad fluke.

Denier Under the traditional system, inherited from the real silk industry, the coarseness of a *yarn* or *filament* of natural or synthetic fibre is known in *cloth construction* by its denier, which is based on the weight in grammes of 9000 m of the yarn or filament. The higher the number the coarser the yarn. The denier is 90 if a spool or cop of yarn 9000 m long weighs 90 grammes, and the yarn may be made up of 3 filaments each of 30 denier, 6 of 15, etc. The system is being replaced by the *decitex*. To convert denier to decitex divide by 0.9.

Density The mass per unit volume of a substance, given e.g. in lbs/cu ft (f.p.s.) or kg/cu m (*SI*). The maximum density of pure water, at 4 °C, is 62.428 lb/cu ft, 1000 kg/cu m; that of sea water varies, being affected by temperature (less dense as temperature rises) and *salinity* (more dense as salinity increases), but is generally taken as 64 lb/cu ft, 1025 kg/cu m. The mass density of air at 15 °C and normal atmospheric pressure is 0.0766 lb/cu ft, 1.227 kg/cu m. In SI units the *specific gravity* (relative density) of any substance is numerically equal to its density, i.e. pure water

1.0, salt water approximately 1.025.
1 lb/cu ft = 16.0185 kg/cu m = 0.0160185 g/cu cm:
1 lb/cu in = 27.6799 g/cu cm:
1 kg/cu m = 0.062428 lb/cu ft:
1 g/cu m = 62.428 lb/cu ft = 0.0361273 lb/cu in:

Departure 1. The last *fix* obtained by a vessel when outward bound. 2. The *distance* in *nautical miles* that a vessel has sailed to eastward or westward, whatever her *course* may be.

Depression, low or (US) **extra-tropical cyclone** Area of relatively low pressure, enclosed by closely-spaced *isobars* (steep *pressure gradient*). Winds circulate round a depression in a counter-clockwise direction in the northern hemisphere, but clockwise in the southern, the surface winds blowing inwards at an angle towards the centre where pressure is lowest. The lower the central pressure and the steeper the pressure gradient the stronger the winds will be. The position and

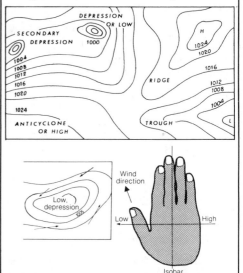

passage of a depression can be established by *Buys Ballot's Law*, independently of a weather report, or by holding your hand outstretched horizontally with the thumb pointing exactly downwind (*true wind*). In the northern hemisphere use your right hand and the low will be at right angles to your hand and to the left; high pressure will be to the right. In the southern hemisphere use your left hand; the low will be on your right, high pressure to your left. Similarly if you lay your hand on a weather map with the fingers parallel to the isobars your thumb indicates the direction of the true wind.

Depth 1. The distance between the level of the water and the sea-bed or bottom at any place or time. In tidal waters depth varies according to the

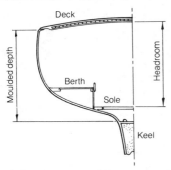

state of the *tide;* in non-tidal waters depth varies seasonally and with meteoroligical conditions. See *soundings.* 2. Moulded depth is the vertical distance from the horizontal plane passing through the top of the *keel* to the underside of the *deck* amidships at the sheer line or *gunwale.* 3. See *IOR.*

Depth alarm An electronic accessory for an *echo sounder* or, sometimes, a facility built into the set. Gives an acoustic warning when depth of water measured decreases below or increases above a set level. Various forms exist.

Depth contour Contour joining points that are the same depth below *chart datum.*

Depth sounder See *echo sounder.*

Derelict Gear, cargo or vessel which has not been sunk but *abandoned* by the crew who at that time had no intention of returning to recover it.

Derrick *Spar* or boom for hoisting and lowering heavy weights.

Designed draft The *draft* of a vessel calculated by the designer or naval architect and shown in the *lines plan.* In practice a boat often draws more than her designed draft.

Designed waterline. The *waterline* drawn on the *lines plan* as calculated for the fitted-out vessel. In practice the waterline at which she floats varies with the load carried and with the *density* of the water in which she is floating.

Designer The creator of a sailing boat; a specialist who may or may not be a *naval architect.* The design can only be used with his permission, usually on payment of a fee. The designer provides the *lines plan, table of offsets, sail plan* and all details required for construction and completion. Many boats are designed to a specific *rating* at the request of an individual.

Deterioration A general worsening of the weather, usually with stronger winds, precipitation and, possibly, reduced visibility.

Development or **restricted class** A racing *class* in which certain measurements are limited, such as maximum *sail area,* overall *length* or minimum weight, but others are left free for the individual designer to develop as he pleases. There is often a great variety in hull shapes, sail plans etc, but the boats race against each other without *handicap.* Some development classes are the *International 14* and Moth, Merlin-Rocket, National 12, *catamaran* and *metre classes.*

Deviation The needle of a *magnetic compass* settles along the line of force of earth's *magnetic field,* i.e. along a *magnetic meridian,* except when it is deflected by iron or steel nearby, by electrical circuits, or by electronic equipment, in which cases it points to *compass north.* Deviation is the angle between the direction to which the compass needle points and the magnetic meridian. Easterly deviation is subtracted when converting a *magnetic bearing* or *course* to *compass,* but added when converting a *compass bearing* or *course* to magnetic. Conversely westerly deviation, when the compass needle points west of the magnetic meridian, is subtracted when converting from compass to magnetic and added when converting

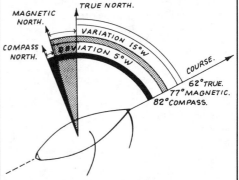

from magnetic to compass. Whereas *variation* differs from place to place but, at any spedific position, the value is the same whatever the boat's course and for every compass, deviation differs for every compass and with the course being steered, but the value of deviation on any specific course is the same in whatever part of the world the boat is sailing. The amount of deviation on a number of *headings* is determined by *swinging ship* and drawing up a *deviation table* or *curve* for the *steering compass;* excessive deviation can be reduced by adjusting or compensating with *corrector magnets.* Loose iron or steel tools, portable radio etc must not be left lying near the compass, because they also cause deviation which, resulting from objects that are not fixed, differs from that established by swinging ship, and is temporary. See also *heeling error.*

Deviation table and **curve** These show the value of *deviation* in degrees east or west of the *magnetic*

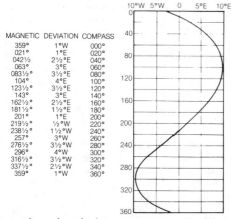

MAGNETIC	DEVIATION	COMPASS
359°	1°W	000°
021°	1°E	020°
042½	2½°E	040°
063°	3°E	060°
083½°	3½°E	080°
104°	4°E	100°
123½°	3½°E	120°
143°	3°E	140°
162½°	2½°E	160°
181½°	1½°E	180°
201°	1°E	200°
219½°	½°W	220°
238½°	1½°W	240°
257°	3°W	260°
276½°	3½°W	280°
296°	4°W	300°
316½°	3½°W	320°
337½°	2½°W	340°
359°	1°W	360°

meridian when the boat is on various *headings*. The values found by *swinging ship* (q.v.) are for *steering compass* deviation caused by the proximity of fixed ferrous objects and electronic equipment etc, and are applied when correcting a *compass course* to a *magnetic course* and vice versa. The difference between the *magnetic bearing* and the *compass bearing* is usually found at 20 or 22½° intervals, and the table is laid out so that it can be entered with the compass course or the magnetic course. The figures can also be set out in the form of a graph or deviation curve, which gives the value of deviation for every heading, and this in turn enables a more detailed deviation table to be compiled.

Devil's claw or **chain hook**   Two-pronged metal claw that is dropped over the side of a cable *link*. Is often secured to a deck fitting with a rope or wire rope, e.g. to hold the anchor cable temporarily.

Dew   *Condensation* of water vapour on solid objects when temperature falls beyond the saturation point of air, i.e. below *dew-point*.

Dew-point   The temperature at which the *relative humidity* of a mass of air reaches 100% due to cooling; e.g. if one cubic metre of air contains 15 grammes of vapour and the temperature drops, dew-point is about 15 °C. In the cabin, when air heated in daytime comes into contact with surfaces cooled at night, *condensation* occurs on the deckhead, ceiling etc when air is cooled below dewpoint. Outside, fog or precipitation forms when moist air is cooled.

DF   *direction finder,* q.v.

Diagonal   An additional diagonal plane shown in the *lines plan*, mainly to help to *fair* up the lines,

especially at the *turn of the bilge*. Appears in the *body plan* as a straight line and cuts the *frames* as nearly at a right angle as possible. The curve(s) showing the intersection of the diagonal(s) with the hull is (are) drawn on the *half-breadth plan* on the opposite side of the centreline to that showing the half *waterlines*.

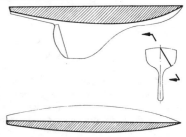

Diagonal or **mitre** (US **miter**) **cut**   The sail is assembled from *cloths* that run at right angles to both *leech* and *foot;* they meet at the *mitre seam* which bisects the angle at the *clew* and meets the *luff* roughly at right angles. The *headsail sheet lead* is approximately along the extension of the mitre.

Diagonal planking   Wooden construction that provides a smooth outer surface to the *hull*. In double-diagonal construction the planking is usually laid at 45° to the *keel*, and a second layer is generally laid at right angles to the first but sometimes fore-and-aft or as illustrated. There is often a layer of calico or neoprene between the skins. Triple diagonal planking has a third layer; this may be laid fore-and-aft or parallel to the first layer. The hull is strong and *frames* can be light.

Diamond   A signal *shape*, displayed as prescribed in the *IRPCS* by vessels *towing* and being towed when the length of the tow exceeds 200 m. A diamond, formed of two black cones base to base, is hoisted in conjunction with black *balls* by a *vessel restricted in her ability to manoeuvre,* and by one engaged in dredging or underwater operations. The topmark of an IALA east cardinal mark is two black cones bases together, forming a diamond.

Diamond of error *Hyperbolic position lines* obtained from radio signals generally meet at an acute angle, and errors allowed for either side when laying them off on the chart result in a diamond-shaped area within which the vessel's position should be. The further the vessel is from the transmitting stations the larger the diamond of error will be.

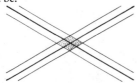

Diamonds *Shrouds* that support the top of the *mast;* instead of terminating at the deck as in A and C they pass over the upper *spreaders* and are attached by *turnbuckles* (UK or rigging screws) to the lower spreader fitting on the mast as in B.

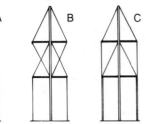

Diaphone A *fog signal* sounded as an *aid to navigation;* low-pitched and powerful, often with a grunt at the end. Made by compressed air. Chart abbr Dia (UK) and DIA (US).

Diaphragm pump A highly-recommended non-choke *bilge pump* which does not have to be fitted vertically like a *piston pump,* but can be operated horizontally or at an angle. A lever (1) actuates an oval or round metal plate (2) which is connected to the sides of the pump housing by a synthetic rubber membrane or diaphragm (3). When the diaphragm is raised (lower fig) bilge water enters through the suction inlet (4); when it is lowered the inlet valve is closed and the outlet (5) opens, permitting water to flow overboard. Capacity varies with size from 35–136 litres per minute (7½–30 British gallons, 9–36 US gallons per minute). Boats over 30 ft (9 m) LOA require pumps with a capacity of about 90 litres (20 British or 24 US gallons) per minute. A single-acting pump sucks in water when the handle is moved in one direction and discharges it when the handle is moved back, but double-action pumps suck and discharge on every stroke; the capacity and the effort required when pumping are greater with double-action pumps.

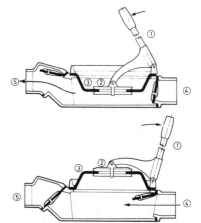

Diesel engine Two-stroke or four-stroke internal combustion engine invented by Rudolf Diesel (1858–1913). Pure air is sucked into the cylinders and the diesel oil, which is injected when the air has been compressed to the maximum, ignites automatically. Uses fuel more efficiently than petrol (US gasoline) engine. Diesel fuel is safer, having a much higher *flash-point* (over 55°).

Difference of latitude (d.lat) and **difference of longitude (d.long)** Given any two positions on the earth, d.lat is the angular distance between them, measured along a *meridian* cut by the two *parallels of latitude* that pass through the positions. D.long is the angle made at the pole by the two meridians that pass through the positions, and is measured along the *equator*. If two positions are 48°40′N 25°30′W and 46°25′N 15°18′W, d.lat will be 2°15′, d.long 10°12′.

Digital read-out Measurements obtained by an instrument are shown as figures, instead of by a pointer moving along a scale. The absolute values are easier to read, and can be very accurate, but often a more fluent visual impression can be obtained from *analogue display.*

Dinette Sitting area in the cabin, often with two settees either side of a table fitted athwartships. Is usually converted into a double *berth* at night, generally by lowering the table to seat level and laying the back cushions on it.

Dinghy 1. A small open boat for rowing, fishing etc. Many can be propelled by an *outboard* as well as by *oars*. May be used as a *tender* to a larger boat 2. Often used in respect of a *sailing dinghy* (q.v.)

Dip 1. Of the *horizon:* an observer's eye is at a certain height above the surface of the earth, and dip is the angle between the horizontal plane through his eye and the apparent direction of the *visible horizon*. The value that has to be subtracted when taking a *sight* or a *vertical sextant angle* is given in the dip correction table in the *Nautical*

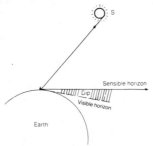

Almanac. 2. A *compass needle* suspended absolutely freely lies along the line of total force of earth's *magnetic field;* it pivots in response to the horizontal component and tilts in response to the vertical component of the line of total force. The angle of dip, which is the angle between the horizontal and the line of total magnetic force, varies from $0°$ at the magnetic equator, where the needle is horizontal, to $90°$ at the magnetic poles; the needle is vertical, north-seeking end down at the north magnetic pole, but south-seeking end down at the south magnetic pole. A compass needle which is correctly balanced for the magnetic equator therefore tilts at other parts of the world, and some compass manufacturers counterbalance the needle differently according to the area in which the compass will mainly be used, while others position the card and needle slightly off centre, with the centre of gravity below the pivot point. 3. At the dip: a *flag* that is not fully hoisted, see *answering pendant*. See also *dip the ensign*.

Dipping light A light that appears and disappears on the horizon (see *horizon range*).

Dipping lug See *lugsail*.

Dip-pole gybe (US **jibe**) When *gybing*, the *spinnaker pole* is not detached from the mast; the outboard end is disengaged from the original guy or tack, dipped beneath the forestay, and clipped

on to the new guy or tack when the boat has gybed.

Dipstick Measures how much oil is in the engine sump, or the quantity of liquid in a fuel or water tank.

Dip the ensign To lower the *ensign* briefly as a salute. It is not rehoisted until the vessel being saluted has dipped and rehoisted hers in acknowledgment.

Direction A line between an observer and some specific point on the horizon. The direction of wind is given as the *point of the compass* from which it blows, but the *set* of a *tidal stream or current* as the direction towards which it sets.

Directional aerial or **antenna** An *aerial,* such as the *loop* or *ferrite rod aerial* of a direction finder; enables the *bearing* of a transmitter to be found because the signal is weakest when the loop is turned broadside on to the path of the radio waves, or when the ferrite rod is end on to the transmitter. Directional aerials also transmit radio waves over a limited arc, e.g. the rotating *scanner* of a *radar* set or the leading bearing provided by a directional radio beacon.

Directional radio beacon (US or **radio range**) A beacon designed to help vessels to enter or leave port etc in *restricted visibility*. The vessel only receives a continuous signal when in the *fairway;* usually if she is to port of the leading bearing when entering, only dots will be received, but error to starboard allows reception only of dashes. Chart abbr RD.

Directional stability The ability of a boat to stay on a steady course without having to apply *helm*. Is largely governed by the shape of the *underwater body*. A boat trimmed *by the stern*, with great lateral underwater area, a long *keel*, full *entry* and deep *forefoot* has greater directional stability than one trimmed by the head with a short keel or *centreboard* and flat *bottom. Balance* (q.v.) is the term more often used for sailing boats.

Direction finder or **radio direction finder** (DF or RDF) A radio receiver with a *directional aerial* with which the *bearing* of a *radio beacon* is found (see *radio direction finding*). DF sets vary in complexity from a simple hand-held instrument, complete with integral *ferrite rod* and *compass,* to a sophisticated and costly *automatic direction finder*. Most small boat DFs have a ferrite rod or a *loop* aerial. When this is turned through a full circle, the volume of the signal rises and falls, passing through two broad maxima $180°$ from each other and, half way between them, through two narrow minima or *null* points, which are easier to distinguish aurally with the help of earphones. To find the bearing, the aerial is turned until the null is obtained; a ferrite rod is then end on to the radio beacon, but a loop is at right angles to the direction of the station. A *sense* aerial is often fitted to avoid any possiblity of a 180° error resulting from there being two nulls. Some DF sets consist of a *Bellini-Tosi* or fixed cross-loop aerial and a *goniometer,* the nulls then being found by turning a search coil control. A null meter may be incorporated with a DF set, and enables the minima or maxima to be found visually, as well as facilitating sense determination. With automatic DF no manual rotation is required, and the bearing is displayed either on a rotating scale or by a digital read-out or, occasionally, by a trace on a cathode ray tube. Latterly an easily-operated portable digital direction finder has been produced. Installation and instrumental errors must be established by *calibration* (q.v.), however small and simple the set may be and, once a calibration table or curve has been drawn up, a portable DF should always be operated in the position where it was calibrated.

Direction light An *aid to navigation* which marks a channel, harbour entrance, passage etc by showing a light over a narrow *sector;* chart abbr Dir Lt. May have warning sectors either side and, often, the warning sector to starboard being green and that to port red when entering harbour. The navigator is then aware immediately that the vessel is standing into danger to that particular side.

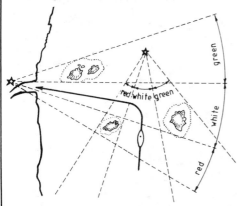

Dirty wind Wind that is distrurbed and deflected by the sail of a boat, such as the wind exhausted by the sails of a boat in the *safe leeward position,* q.v. Extends 2–3 times mast height to windward, and 7–8 times to leeward and astern.

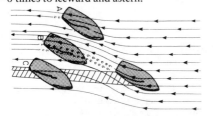

Discrimination The ability of a *radar* set to show, as separate echoes, two *targets* that are close in terms of range or bearing, such as a tug and tow. See *resolution.*

Disembark To leave a vessel and go ashore.

Dismast To break the mast, perhaps in a storm or collision, or when part of the *standing rigging* fails.

Displacement The weight of the water displaced by a floating vessel is equal to the weight of the vessel (Archimedes principle), and is given in pounds, tons, kilogrammes or tonnes. The symbol Δ is usually used to denote displacement as a weight, which varies with the number of crew and the weight of fittings, stores, drinking water and fuel carried aboard. Displacement as a volume, usually indicated by the symbol ∇, varies with the *density* of the water in which the vessel floats, as can be seen by comparing a boat's *waterline* in a lake with that when she is at sea.

Displacement hull or **boat** A hull or boat that displaces its own weight in water; is supported only by *buoyancy,* even when moving at full speed, whereas a *planing* hull or boat can exceed *hull* (or displacement) *speed,* $V/\sqrt{L} = 1.34$. Cruising boats, offshore racers, motor sailers and heavy dinghies are included in this category, but not light racing dinghies which plane.

Displacement to length ratio This ratio gives an indication of the potential speed of a hull and, for example, indicates the difference between a *planing* hull and a *displacement hull.* Given displacement in tons and *waterline length* in feet, the formula

$$\frac{\text{Displacement}}{(0.01\text{LWL})^3}$$

gives values of about 55 to 100 for planing dinghies with crew, over 150 for light displacement keelboats, and 300–500 for heavy displacement yachts. Changing to the metric system, with length in metres and displacement in tonnes,

$$\frac{\text{Displacement}}{(0.1\text{LWL})^3}$$

gives figures of about 2.0–3.6 for planing dinghies, over 5.3 for light displacement keelboats and 11–18 for heavy displacement cruisers.

Display The visual presentation of information received from instruments, such as echoes received from *echo sounders, radar* or *sonar,* speed from *anemometers* or *logs,* etc. See *digital* and *analogue.*

Disqualification A boat is disqualified from a race if she infringes any of the *racing rules,* unless she retires or an alternative *penalty* (q.v.) is performed. When *series racing* she scores a greater number of points than the last boat to finish, and often a greater number than a boat that has retired.

Distance At sea distance is measured in *nautical miles, cables* and feet, or nautical miles and metres, whether it is the distance between, say, two ports, a vessel and a feature on land, two vessels, or two *fixes.* Distance run may be *through the water,* as measured with a *log,* or *over the ground,* with allowance has been made for the effects of *tidal stream or current* and *leeway.* On *charts,* distances are measured against the *latitude* scale bordering

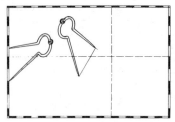

the sides, one *minute* of latitude equalling one nautical mile. The measurement must be taken at the same latitude as the position on the chart because, on *mercator* charts, the scale increases towards the pole. On some inland charts, such as the Great Lakes charts, distances are measured in statute *miles.* Distance off is the distance between the vessel and some object such as a light vessel, the coast etc.

Distance of the visible horizon Varies with the *height of eye* of the observer. To a man sitting in a dinghy with a height of eye of 3 ft (1 m) above sea level, the *horizon* is 2n.miles distant, but at 7 ft (2 m) in the cockpit of a cruiser it is 3n.miles distant and, if he stands on deck and is 10 ft (3 m) above the water, the horizon will be 3.6 n.miles distant. The navigator can estimate the distance from a light on the horizon, or some other object that comes in sight over the horizon, with the formula:

Distance in n.m. $= \sqrt{(ht\ of\ eye)\ (ft)} \times 1.15$

or

$\qquad = \sqrt{(ht\ of\ eye)\ (m)} \times 2.075$

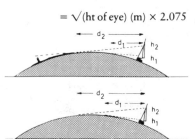

Distinguishing number The number exhibited by a boat on her *mainsail* and *spinnaker,* and on the *headsails* of *IOR* boats. In some *classes* is issued by the national authority, in others by class associations. A *class emblem* and *national letter* are often displayed in addition.

Distress A vessel is in distress when in danger and unable to save herself without outside assis-

tance, e.g. when she *springs a leak* and is sinking, or catches fire, or is severely damaged in a *collision.* May be owing to an *Act of God,* or caused by failure of gear or crew. She may make a distress call by radio telephone using the prefix *Mayday* for R/T or *SOS* in morse code, or by *EPIRB,* or may use visual *distress signals,* q.v. Under the Geneva Convention a vessel is expected to assist any person found at sea in danger of being lost, to proceed with all possible speed to the rescue of persons in distress and, after a collision, to render assistance to the other vessel and her crew or passengers in so far as she can do so without endangering the lives of those on board.

Distress frequency By international agreement, the following radio frequencies are allotted for *distress, urgency* and *safety* messages:

(a) Radio telephony: VHF Channel 16 (156.80 MHz) is monitored by most *coast radio stations,* the UK *Coastguard* and US Coast Guard, lifeboats, most military search and rescue (SAR) aircraft and many large merchant vessels. Small craft safety traffic is often passed on the working *frequencies* 156.3 MHz (Channel 6) in the USA and 156.375 MHz (Channel 67) in the UK. VHF range is restricted to line of sight (25–50 miles). MF 2182 kHz is monitored by all the services which guard VHF Channel 16, and by large fishing vessels. An automatic alarm may be fitted to give notice of a distress call when the operator is absent, and is actuated by the two-tone alarm signal. MF range is much greater than VHF.

(b) Radio telegraphy: 500 kHz, which is monitored by most organizations concerned with SAR.

(c) Aircraft frequencies: 121.5 MHz (civil aviation emergency channel) and 243.0MHz (military aircraft, some SAR organizations and some lifeboats).

To ensure priority for distress calls, *radio silence* is mandatory throughout the world when a distress call is heard and during the silence periods (three minutes past every hour and half hour on R/T, and three minutes past every quarter and three quarter hour on W/T). All the frequencies listed under (a) and (b) are also used as the initial calling frequencies to establish contact with a shore station, before switching to a working channel for routine radio traffic.

Distress procedure (radio communication) RADIO TELEPHONY The internationally recognized R/T *distress frequencies* are Channel 16 (156.8 MHz) VHF, and 2182 kHz MF, and the silence periods reserved for R/T distress calls are the three minutes past every hour and half hour. In an emergency, however, any frequency may be used at any time if it appears probable that assistance may thereby be gained more quickly.

(a) If an alarm signal generator is fitted, the R/T two-tone warbling signal is sent continuously for a period of betsween 30 seconds and 1 minute.

(b) The R/T distress call should not be addressed to any particular station, and consists of:
 1. MAYDAY MAYDAY MAYDAY
 2. THIS IS (name of vessel) (name of vessel) (name of vessel)

(c) The R/T distress message follows the distress call and consists of:
 1. MAYDAY
 2. Name of vessel
 3. Position (latitude and longitude, or true bearing and distance in n. miles from a known or charted geographical position, e.g. '324° 2 miles from the Skerries, off Holyhead'.)
 4. Nature of distress
 5. Aid required (including number of persons requiring aid)
 6. If time allows, the position is repeated
 7. OVER

(d) If immediate reply is not forthcoming, the equipment is checked and the distress call is the repeated.

The *urgency* (q.v.) signal PAN PAN is used when the calling station has a very urgent message to transmit concerning safety, but circumstances do not justify the use of the MAYDAY distress signal.

RADIO TELEGRAPHY The internationally recognized W/T distress frequency is 500 kHz, and the silence periods reserved for W/T distress calls are the three minutes past every quarter and three quarter hour. In an emergency, however, any frequency may be used at any time if it appears probable that assistance may thereby be gained more quickly.

(a) If the apparatus is manual, the W/T distress call should not be addressed to any particular station.
 1. Transmit the distress call (SOS three times, the word DE, the *call-sign* of the vessel in distress three times).
 2. If possible, allow two minutes for radio officers to reach their apparatus.
 3. Transmit the distress message consisting of SOS, the call-sign of the vessel in distress and, as for R/T (c) 3–5, the position, nature of distress and aid required.
 4. Transmit two dashes, each of 10–15 seconds duration, to assist in direction finding.

(b) If an automatic keying device is fitted:
 1. Set the control to ALARM, so that 12 four-second dashes are sent in precisely one minute.
 2. If possible allow two minutes for operators to reach their sets.
 3. Set the automatic keying device control to

DISTRESS, so that the distress call (above, 1), followed by two dashes (above, 4) is automatically transmitted every twelve minutes until the battery runs down or the transmitter is switched off.

Distress signal The *International Regulations for Preventing Collisions at Sea* list internationally recognized visual and audible signals to be made or exhibited together or separately to indicate distress or need of assistance. Use of these signals, or of any others which might be confused with them, is prohibited except for the purposes of indicating distress.

(a) a gun or other explosive signal fired at intervals of about a minute;
(b) a continuous sounding with any fog-signalling apparatus;
(c) rockets or shells throwing red stars fired one at a time at short intervals;
(d) a signal made by radiotelegraphy or by any other signalling method consisting of the group $\cdots - - - \cdots$ (SOS) in the Morse Code;
(e) a signal sent by radiotelephony consisting of the spoken word '*Mayday*';
(f) the International Code signal of distress indicated by N over C;
(g) a signal consisting of a square flag having above or below it a ball or anything resembling a ball;
(h) flames on the vessel (as from a burning tar barrel, oil barrel, etc);
(i) a rocket parachute *flare* or a hand flare showing a red light;
(j) a *smoke* signal giving off orange-coloured smoke;
(k) slowly and repeatedly raising and lowering arms outstretched to each side;
(l) the radiotelegraph alarm signal;
(m) the radio telephone alarm signal;
(n) signals transmitted by emergency position-indicating radio beacons. (See *EPIRB*.)

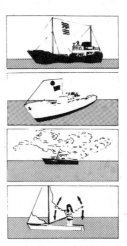

The IRPCS note two further signals, (a) a piece of orange-coloured canvas with either a black square and circle or other appropriate symbol (for identification from the air): (b) a *dye marker*.

Distress transceiver See *EPIRB*.

Ditchcrawling (UK) See *gunkholing*.

Ditty bag Small canvas bag in which a seaman keeps his personal belongings.

Diurnal inequality Successive *semi-diurnal tides* have differing *high* and *low water* heights, and the interval between successive high waters differs because the *declination* of the moon changes as she orbits the earth. When the moon is on the *equator*, i.e. when declination is 0°, the heights of successive high waters are the same, but when the moon's path is at an angle to earth's equator, she passes from the northern to the southern hemisphere and back as she orbits the earth. There is then a higher and a lower high water, and a higher and lower low water during the course of each day, as is usually the case with semi-diurnal tides.

Diurnal tide A tidal cycle with only one *high* and *low water* every *lunar day*, such as occurs in the Gulf of Mexico, whereas a *semi-diurnal* tide has two cycles daily.

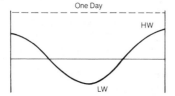

Divergence Zone of earth's atmosphere, such as the sub-tropical divergence zones at about 30° N and S, where the downward motion of air is accompanied by outward horizontal motion near the surface of earth. In the case of oceans, an area where currents flow away from a particular point, usually where water wells up from beneath the surface. C.f. *convergence*, and see *global winds* fig.

Dividers Navigation instrument for measuring *distances* on *charts*. Two hands must be used for

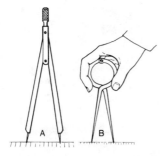

the type in fig A, but B can be opened or closed by squeezing the top or the legs with one hand.

Diving Under the *IRPCS* a vessel engaged in diving operations and *restricted in her ability* to manoeuvre exhibits the *lights* and *shapes* prescribed for a vessel so restricted, plus other lights and shapes according to whether she is at *anchor* or *under way,* and to indicate whether an obstruction exists on either side of her. If she is too small to exhibit the shapes prescribed, e.g. an inflatable dinghy, a rigid replica of International *Code flag A,* not less than 1 metre in height, must be exhibited and means 'I have a diver down, keep well clear at slow speed'.

Dock 1. An area of water artificially enclosed so that the depth of water inside can be controlled. A *wet dock* is a non-tidal basin. Vessels can be repaired inside a *dry dock* or *floating dock*. Also to dock, when a vessel is admitted to a dock. Docks: a general term relating to all the port installations. 2. Often used more widely, especially in the US, for a place where vessels can moor, i.e. pier, wharf etc; hence dock fees, docking lines etc.

Documentation A yacht enrolment and license is issued in the US to a vessel of over 20 tons net that is used purely for pleasure, and a yacht license to a vessel between 5 and 20 tons, provided that the owner is a US citizen. The owner has to produce a title paper, such as the builder's certificate or bills of sale to prove ownership, the vessel is measured, and the official number allocated is carved on the main beam together with her net tonnage. The yacht's name and home port must be marked on the hull, usually at the stern, and she may fly the yacht ensign. UK see *registration*.

Dodger or **weather cloth** Canvas screen fitted to give the crew in the *cockpit* protection from wind and spray. Generally laced to the *lifeline* (guardrail) with enough space left beneath to allow water to run off the decks. The boat's name is often printed on the outside so that she can be identified if in *distress*.

Dog To secure from movement, either equipment or a rope/chain, with a metal bar or clamp, or length of rope.

Doghouse A raised area at the after end of the *cabin* top to provide standing room. Also applied to a raised shelter over the forward part of the *cockpit*.

Dog watch To break the *watch* cycle, the first and last dog watches are two hours long instead of the normal four: 1600–1800 and 1800–2000 hrs.

Doldrums Extensive low pressure area near the *equator*, lying between the NE and SE *trades;* (see *global winds* fig); characterized by calms and light variable winds, interspersed with torrential rain, thunderstorms and, sometimes, squalls. Follow the sun to lie rather further north during the northern summer, and move further south during the northern winter.

Dolphin A mooring post or group of *piles* to which a vessel's *mooring lines* may be secured; chart abbr Dn (UK) and Dol (US). US: a *daymark* may be fitted on a dolphin to mark a channel.

Dolphin striker Short *spar* fitted perpendicular to the *bowsprit* cap to extend the *martingale* stay; supports the *jib-boom* in the same way as *jumper* struts on the mast extend the topmast jumper stays.

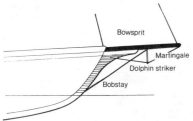

Doppler effect First described by the Austrian physicist Christian Doppler in 1849; when the source of a sound is moving in relation to a stationary observer the apparent *frequency* changes (e.g. a police siren sounds higher when it is approaching an observer than when it is moving away). The difference in frequency is proportional to the speed of the sound source in relation to the stationary observer. The Doppler effect is made use of in *satellite navigation* and by a *Doppler log*. Doppler radar measures frequency shift to determine speed and range.

Doppler log Instrument that measures boat speed by using the Doppler effect. Two *transducers*

may be required for sailing boats, one either side of the hull to allow for *heeling*. They can be installed in-hull with the faces bonded to the outer skin. The transducer transmits an ultrasonic signal directed forward, and part of the signal is reflected back to the transducer by small air bubbles or particles in suspension in the water. During this period the boat moves forward through the water, and the *frequency* of the reflected signal is therefore higher than that of the transmitted signal. Frequency increases proportionally to boat speed and, by measuring the frequency shift, speed and distance sailed *through the water* can be displayed. When the signal from a Doppler log is reflected back from the sea-bed the change in frequency indicates speed and distance *over the ground*, but the considerable power requirement and the size of the equipment precludes the use of bottom-locking in small craft.

Dorade ventilator A vent pipe is built into a box which has holes through which spray and water drain onto the deck. Only air can enter the cabin because the vent pipe is separated from the *cowl* by baffles. Named after the US ocean racer 'Dorade'.

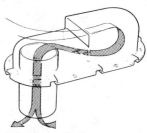

Dory 1. Small, light, flat-bottomed *rowing boat* with a triangular sail used by fishing vessels; often has removable *thwarts* so that one can be stowed inside another. Roughly 13 ft 9 in–21 ft (4.2–6.5 m) long and 3 ft 3 in–5 ft (1.0–1.5 m) beam. A small dory crossed the Atlantic as early as 1867. The Finn, Ulari Givikoski, left New York in 1953 in a larger schooner-rigged dory 'Turquois', 36 ft (11 m) LOA, 8 ft 3 in (2.5 m) beam, and made his way home via Newfoundland, Ireland, Den Helder and Wilhelmshaven. 2. Small open *tender,* usually *GRP/FRP*, of *cathedral hull* form, almost rectangular in plan view.

Double To succeed in *rounding* a feature, such as a cape or head.

Double block *Block* with two *sheaves* of the same diameter fitted side by side. A block with two sheaves one above the other is a fiddle or sister block.

Double bottom   An inner *bottom* built above the outside *skin*. In many *GRP/FRP* dinghies the watertight space between the bottoms is filled with foamed plastics to increase *buoyancy*. This adds to safety as well as strength.

Double braided   *Braided* or plaited rope, particularly suitable for sheets, with a braided *core* around which is a braided sheath. Must be carefully made so that core and sheath bear proportional loads.

Double chine   A fairly unusual form of construction with two *chines* either side of the *keel*. The *section* is more like a *round bilge* hull than *hard chine*.

Double diagonal   See *diagonal planking*.

Double-ender   A boat with a pointed *stern* and *bow*, and therefore roughly the same shape at either end. A double-ender only sails forward whereas a *proa* (q.v.) has a bow at either end and is designed to sail in either direction.

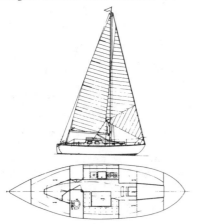

Double head rig   Modern term for a rig with two

headsails set forward of the mast, often used of a sloop when temporarily setting a staysail inside a genoa or other jib. Whereas the two headsails set by a *cutter* are the *jib* and *staysail*, those of modern rigs are normally a *tallboy, inner staysail*, etc with a genoa, or a *spinnaker staysail* or *big boy* with a *spinnaker*.

Double-luffed   Said of a sail, the *luff* of which passes round a *stay* or *spar* and is attached to itself, e.g. with a zipper, or stitched.

Double planking   Two layers of wooden *planking* laid *fore-and-aft*.

Double sheet bend   Similar to a *sheet bend*, but with an extra turn taken for security.

Double tide   A *tide* which either has two *high waters* or two *low waters* in each tidal cycle, for example as occurs off Cowes, Isle of Wight.

Double up   To put out extra *mooring lines*, e.g. when a storm is expected.

Doubling   1. The area where the upper end of a *lower mast* overlaps the lower end of the mast above it. 2. Area where material is doubled to increase the strength of part of a sail, spar or the hull.

Doubling the angle on the bow   A method of finding distance off by taking *relative bearings* of an object, which need not be marked on the chart.

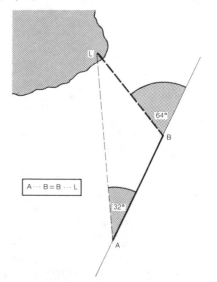

As in the figure, the second angle is double the first, 32° and 64°. The navigator calculates the distance made good *over the ground* between A and B, taking into account the time, boatspeed, the adverse or beneficial set and rate of the *tidal stream or current* (this method cannot be used when the tidal stream sets across the boat's course) and *leeway*. The triangle LAB is an isosceles triangle, and the distance made good therefore equals the distance between the vessel and the object at the time the second bearing is taken.

Douglas Scale International *Sea* and *Swell* scale which grades seas and swell in much the same way as the *Beaufort Scale* grades winds; 0 = calm, 8 = precipitous, 9 = confused; 00 = no swell, 88 = long and heavy, 99 = confused swell. See also *sea state scale*.

Douse or **dowse** 1. To lower a sail quickly. 2. To extinguish a light quickly.

Dowel Circular piece of wood glued into a plank etc to cover the countersunk head of a bolt or screw.

Downhaul A rope or line with which an object such as a spar or sail is pulled down. A downhaul pulls down the *gooseneck* to tauten the *luff* of the *mainsail*. (See *rigging* fig.) The *spinnaker pole* downhaul prevents the pole from lifting. May also be a line attached to the head of a jib or spinnaker led down the luff to the *stemhead fitting* and back to the cockpit so that the sail can be hauled down quickly to the deck.

Down helm The order to put the *tiller* to *leeward* so that the boat will *luff up*. The helm is said to be a-lee.

Downstream The direction towards which a stream flows; in the case of a river, towards the sea.

Downwind Direction to *leeward*. To sail downwind is to *run*.

Downwind performance When a boat sails on a dead *run* the *apparent wind* which propels her is least strong in relation to the strength of the *true wind,* and it sometimes pays to *tack downwind* with the sails trimmed to the correct *angle of attack*. The boat *broad reaches* fast on alternate tacks and often reaches her objective more quickly than when taking the direct and shorter route. If she sails 10–30° either side of the direct course, she will sail about 20–30% further. The fastest course to her destination depends largely on the sails she is able to set.

Dowse See *douse*.

Draft (UK often **draught**) 1. The vertical distance from the lowest point of the *keel* to the *waterline:* the depth of water at which a vessel floats. See below for fig. The draft of a *centreboard boat* may be quoted as hull draft with centreboard raised, or with centreboard when it is down. *Designed draft* is calculated from the *lines plan* (q.v.), and may be less than actual draft when fitted out and carrying stores and crew. Draft varies with water *density* (*salinity* has to be taken into account when the boat is measured for a *rating*) and with *displacement*. 2. The flow, *camber* or fullness of a sail.

Drag 1. The *anchor* drags when it fails to hold and slides over the *sea-bed,* perhaps because *holding ground* is poor, or because insufficient cable has been *veered* and the pull on the anchor is not horizontal. *Bearings* are taken after anchoring to check whether the anchor is dragging; although two bearings are preferable, one taken on an object lying roughly abeam soon shows if the anchor is holding. An alternative check is to watch whether two objects on shore that are in line remain so; if they open the anchor is dragging. 2. The *force* that acts in the same direction as that of the flow of air over an *aerofoil* such as a sail, or of water over a

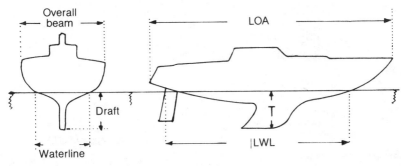

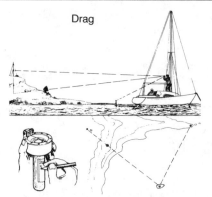
Drag

hydrofoil such as the hull. Synonymous with *resistance*, which term is now used mainly in the UK in connection with hydrodynamics. Total aerodynamic drag is composed of *frictional, induced* and *form drag*; hydrodynamic resistance has additional *wave-making, eddy-making* and *heeling* components. See *force* figure, D and R. 3. To search for an object on the sea-bed with a *grapnel*. 4. US: the amount by which the *draft* of a vessel aft exceeds her draft forward. 5. US: alternative term for *drogue*.

Drag angle The aerodynamic drag angle is the angle between the direction of total or resultant aerodynamic *force* and the direction of *lift*, which acts perpendicular to the *apparent wind* direction. The hydrodynamic drag angle is the angle between the direction of the side force (lift) and the resultant or total hydrodynamic force. The sum of the two angles equals beta, the angle between the boat's course and the direction of the apparent wind. See *force* figure, ϵ_A, ϵ_H and β.

Dragon *International* racing keelboat *class*, designed in 1928 by Johan Anker, formerly wooden but now also *GRP/FRP*. Three crew and a spinnaker. An *Olympic class* from 1948 to 1972. LOA 29 ft 2 in (8.89 m), beam 6 ft 5 in (1.96 m), displacement 3743 lbs (1698 kg), sail area 286 sq ft (26.6 sq m).

Draw 1. A vessel is said to draw a certain amount of water, say 6 ft 6 in or 2 m. That is the depth of water she requires to *float*, and it matches her *draft*. 2. A sail draws when it is hoisted, full of wind and propelling a boat.

Drawstring (US) See *leech line*.

Dredged channel A channel that is deepened to a specified minimum depth, which is marked on *charts*. Sediment is removed from the bottom by dredging.

Dredger (US **dredge**) A vessel designed for dredging a channel. Sediment is removed from the sea-bed or river bed by means of a suction pipe or an endless chain of buckets, and the material is then dumped at a spoil ground, at sea, or is used for land reclamation.

Dress a mast To attach all *shrouds, stays* and fittings, and *reeve* the *halyards* prior to *stepping* the mast.

Dress ship or **dress overall** On special occasions vessels at anchor or in harbour, including sailing boats, hoist the set of *International Code flags* and *pendants* on a line running from the stem to the top of the mast(s) and down to the stern. They should be evenly spaced and as symmetrical as possible, with two square flags between pendants and the swallow-tailed A and B flags at each end. No *ensigns* should be incorporated in the dressing line. The *burgee* is flown at the *masthead* for local festivities, the ensign at the masthead on national occasions.

Dries Chart abbr dr. (UK) and Uncov (US). See *drying feature*.

Drift 1. To be carried by a *tidal stream or current*, and/or to be driven by the wind when the sails or engine are not propelling the boat through the water. 2. (UK) The distance that a vessel is carried by a tidal stream or current in a given time when no other factors need to be considered, i.e. the drift of a vessel would be 3 miles in 2 hours when the tidal stream is making 1½ *knots*. 3. (US) The velocity of a *tidal* or non-tidal *current*, given in knots, except in rivers when it may be given in mph (UK rate). 4. Drift angle: see *turning circle*.

Drift or **wind drift current** A horizontal movement of the water in the oceans, caused by wind blowing from one direction for a long period.

Drifter 1. A fishing vessel that lies to her nets. 2. A very lightweight *headsail* set when *close-hauled* or *reaching* in light breezes of force 1 and under. *Cloth weight* about ¾−1½ oz US, 1−2 oz UK, 30−70 g/sq m. 3. Coll. a race run in very light breezes (sometimes drifting match).

Drinking water (US **potable water**) An adequate supply of drinking water has to be carried on board, the usual allowance being half a gallon or 2¼ litres per man per day. When racing this could be viewed as unwanted excess *ballast,* and many long-distance race regulations specify the minimum quantity to be carried, and how it must be stowed. Water tanks may be of rubber, plastics or metal, and require an air-vent or breather that must be higher than the filling aperture. Each should have a drain cock and *inspection cover* large enough to enable the inside to be cleaned. Large tanks should have *baffles*. Built-in tanks are usually fitted near the keel where they do not affect *trim* and *stability* adversely. If the tank is filled on deck the filler cap must be watertight. *Fresh water* obtained from taps on shore in some countries is not necessarily suitable for drinking before it has been boiled or purified. See also *fresh water*.

Driver 1. *Fore-and-aft sail* set on the aftermost mast of a *full-rigged ship* or *barque*. Alternative term for *spanker*. 2. The fifth and aftermost mast of a five-masted sailing ship.

Driving force The component of total aerodynamic force that acts in the direction of the boat's course through the water. The value of this useful force, which varies with the square of wind speed and with the area of the sail, depends largely on the crew's ability to trim the sails and tune the rig correctly while keeping the boat on the desired heading. See *force* fig F_R.

Drizzle Very small closely-spaced droplets of rain with a diameter of under 0.5 mm. Reduces *visibility* and often occurs after the passage of a *warm front*. Is associated with warm *air masses*.

Drogue (US or **drag**) or **sea anchor** An open-ended cone or pyramid shape, generally made of stout canvas, *streamed* in *heavy weather* to slow a boat, or to keep her bow or stern on to wind and seas, so that she can take breaking crests more easily. Has a *tripping line* attached to the narrow end so that it can be recovered. Lighter and more practical drogues have been developed, but the advisability of using a drogue at all continues to be disputed.

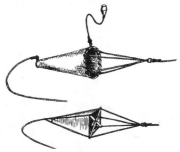

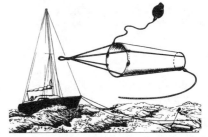

Drop astern 1. To fall astern of another boat, whether intentionally or not. 2. To move an object lying outboard, such as the dinghy, further aft.

Drop keel See *retractable keel*.

Drum sextant See *micrometer sextant*.

Dry 1. Describes a boat that does not leak and ships little water. 2. A boat is pumped dry when the *bilges* are emptied.

Dry card compass A *magnetic compass* which is virtually useless on small boats, because there is no liquid in the bowl to damp the card when it reacts to the boat's *motion*.

Dry dock An artificial enclosure which is built into the bank, and into which a vessel can be moved; the gate is closed to exclude the sea, and the water inside is pumped out so that she can be repaired. When the work is completed the dry dock is *flooded,* so that the vessel can leave once the water level inside matches that outside.

Drying feature (UK) Feature, such as a *rock,* bank or the *foreshore,* that is covered at *high water* but uncovered at *low water*. Large areas are coloured green on modern charts. Drying heights are given in metres or feet above *chart datum* (q.v.), and are underlined to differentiate them from *soundings,* which are below chart datum. Alternatively they may be entered as 'dries x metres'. Features continuously above sea level do not dry, and heights are measured above a datum level such as *MHWS* (UK) or *MHW* (US).

Drying harbour (US **harbor**) A harbour, generally small, that dries out at *low water*.

Dry out In *tidal waters* a boat that *grounds* may dry out if the *ebbing* tide recedes so far that she is left *high and dry*. Instead of hauling a boat out of the water she can be beached or dried out alongside a quay wall deliberately, so that the bottom can be scrubbed or painted. A keelboat which dries out regularly on her mooring at each tide can be fitted with *legs* to keep her upright.

Dry rot Timber decay, usually occurring in moist warm conditions owing to poor *ventilation*.

D-shackle A *shackle* with straight sides.

Dugout Primitive type of boat hollowed in one piece from a tree trunk, usually partly by burning. The sides may be braced by *deck beams,* and *freeboard* increased with additional wooden *planking.* The famous dugout 'Tilikum' was sailed round the world by John Voss in 1901–5.

Dumb compass See *pelorus.*

Dune A low hill, beyond the limit of wave action, composed of sand blown by the wind.

Duplex operation Simultaneous two-way radio communication, as when using an ordinary telephone; and ordinary conversation can be held without the need to switch between receive and transmit. Its use at sea is invariably via the public correspondence service. C.f. *simplex.*

Duration of rise and **fall** The time interval between *high water* and the preceding or following *low water.*

Dutchman's log A very simple method of finding approximate boat speed. All that is needed is a stopwatch and a measured distance marked along or below the *lifeline* (guardrail). A boat making one *knot* sails 6076 ft (1852 m) in one hour, or 1.69 ft (0.514 m) per second. This distance is multiplied by 10, measured and marked on the boat, i.e. 17 ft or 5.14 m. A floating object such as a piece of wood or board is thrown over the bow at least 3 ft away from the *topsides* and, when the boat is making one knot, it will take 10 seconds for the piece of wood to move from abeam of the forward end of the measured distance to the after end. At 2 knots it takes 5 seconds, at 5 knots it takes 2 seconds. If some other marked distance is used, length in feet divided by time in seconds multiplied by 0.6 gives the approximate speed in knots (or length in metres divided by seconds and multiplied by 2). The *rate* of a *tidal stream or current* can be found in this way when at *anchor.*

Duty Tax or charge payable to customs on imported goods etc. Duty free: goods exempt from customs duty.

Dye marker A chemical which spreads a bright orange dye over the surface of the water downstream, say of a *liferaft* or of a person who has fallen overboard. Enables searching aircraft in particular to locate a vessel or individual in *distress.*

Dynamic lift Hydrodynamic force generated when a vessel moves fast over the water, whereas *buoyancy* is a hydrostatic force. *Displacement boats* are always supported by buoyancy alone, whether motionless or moving at full speed, but *light displacement planing boats* with relatively large sail area benefit from dynamic lift when the *speed to length ratio* exceeds about 1.6. They are then *semi-planing,* and are supported by both lift and buoyancy. Pure *planing,* when the hull is supported only by dynamic lift, occurs at a speed to length ratio of about 3.4.

Dynamic pressure or **velocity pressure** The pressure experienced when a stream of fluid is brought to rest; pressure exerted by virtue of fluid motion (kinetic energy). Dynamic pressure (q) therefore $= \frac{1}{2}mv^2$. Given mass density of air of 0.0765 lb/cu ft, and wind velocity v,

$$\frac{1}{2} \frac{\text{density}}{\text{acceleration due to gravity}} =$$

$$\frac{1}{2} \frac{0.0765}{32.2} = 0.00119$$

q (lbs/sq ft) $\quad = 0.00119 \times v^2$ (v in ft/sec)
$\quad\quad\quad\quad\quad = 0.0034 \times v^2$ (v in knots)

Given mass density of air 1.23 kg/cu m.
q (Newtons/sq m) $= 0.615 \times v^2$ (v in metres/sec)
$\quad\quad\quad\quad\quad\quad = 0.163 \times v^2$ (v in knots)

The mass density of fresh water is about 62.4 lb/cu ft (1000 kg/cu m) or 1 tonne/cu m; that of salt water is about 64 lb/cu ft (1025 kg/cu m), and the dynamic pressure of salt water is therefore:
q (lbs/sq.ft) $\quad = 0.995 \times v^2$ (v in ft/sec)
$\quad\quad\quad\quad\quad = 2.84 \times v^2$ (v in knots)
q (Newtons/sq m) $= 513 \times v^2$ (v in metres/sec)
$\quad\quad\quad\quad\quad\quad = 136 \times v^2$ (v in knots)

E = Echo: blue-red *code flag*. As a single letter signal means 'I am altering my course to *starboard*'. *Morse code:* • (dot).

Earing Small line *spliced* into the *cringle* of a sail, e.g. at the corners at the head of a square sail. Often applied to the ropes attached to the *luff* and *leech* cringles for *reefing* purposes.

Ear, on her A boat is said to sail on her ear when she *heels* excessively.

Ease 1. To let out a rope or line gradually, especially a sheet so that a sail sets less close to the *fore-and-aft line*. Sheets are eased when the boat *bears away* or when the wind *frees*. 2. Of the *helm*, to reduce the rudder angle slightly so as to make a less abrupt alteration of course. 3. To ease her is to let the boat *luff* slightly when *close-hauled* in a strong wind.

East A *cardinal point* which lies 90° clockwise from north on the *compass rose* and *card*. The direction towards which earth rotates.

Easterly To the east, of variation, course, tidal stream or current etc, but from the east in the case of wind.

Eastern Adjective that differentiates between two similar areas, features etc by locating them with reference to the *cardinal point*, e.g. eastern seaboard, or eastern *quadrant*, (which is bounded by NE and SE).

Easting The distance that a vessel makes good towards the east.

Eastward Direction towards the east, e.g. an easterly current sets eastward.

Ebb The period during a tidal cycle when the sea level is falling; the period between *high water* and *low water* is the ebb tide. See *tide* fig. This term is often also applied loosely to the horizontal motion of the *tidal stream* (US *tidal current*), both as verb and noun, i.e. to flow and the flow away from the land in estuaries, harbours etc, or in the direction associated with a falling tide.

Ebb stream (UK) or **ebb current** (US) The horizontal flow of water associated with a falling (ebb) *tide;* in estuaries etc is outgoing. After a period of *slack water* the *flood stream* (US flood current) starts, and in the case of a *rectilinear* (US reversing) stream often flows in approximately the opposite direction. See also *ebb*.

Echo sounder or **depth sounder** Electronic depth-finding instrument. The velocity at which sound travels through water varies with water temperature and *salinity* but, for echo-sounding purposes, is taken in the US and UK to be either 4800 ft per second, or metrically as 1500 m/sec (i.e. at 20 °C and 20 $\%_{oo}$ salinity). The distance that a sound wave travels through water to an object and back can be found by measuring the time that elapses between transmission and the reception of the reflected sound. The echo sounder's *transducer* converts an electric pulse into a sound wave which travels to the sea-bed (or to some other object such as an underwater obstruction, shoal of fish etc), and is echoed back to the transducer. Most small boat echo sounders are directly calibrated to show the elapsed time in terms of feet, fathoms and/or metres, i.e. half the two-way distance travelled by the sound wave; thus 1/10th of a second would read as 40 fathoms or 75 m and 1/100th of a second as 24 ft or 7.5 m. Normally there are two depth range scales, e.g. 0–60 ft and 0–60 fathoms, or 0–20 m and 0–120 m. Many displays have an arm which rotates at a constant speed appropriate to the depth scale. A neon bulb or LED (light emitting diode) on the end of the arm flashes at zero when the pulse is transmitted, and again when the echo(es) returns. Other echo sounders have a meter which is switched on when the pulse is transmitted, and off when the echo returns; the longer the meter circuit is working the further the pointer moves along the scale, integration providing a steady reading. Other presentation methods include digital and cathode ray display, or paper recording.

Whereas digital and meter types only record

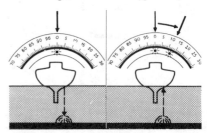

depth, to the experienced eye the flashing display gives some indication of the type of sea-bed, e.g. the echo is weaker and broader when returned from a soft muddy bottom, but strong and clear with a sharply defined edge if the bottom is hard sand or gravel; it also shows secondary responses, say from a shoal of fish, as weaker echoes. The graphic or recording echo sounder provides even more detailed information, and this can be referred to as required, for example when comparing chart *soundings* with recorded depths.

Because sound travels more slowly in fresh water and at colder temperatures, the depth indicated in these conditions is greater than actual depth, but in very warm water when salinity is high the error is on the safe side. A single transducer is often installed to one side of the centreline, roughly amidships, or on the centreline forward of the keel. Two may be required for sailing boats, one each side at the turn of the bilge to allow for heeling; a gravity switch or a manual change-over switch selects which of the two will operate. Through-hull installation enables greater depths to be measured than in-hull installation, because considerable sound is lost by dissipation in the hull. The advantages of in-hull mounting are that no hole has to be made in the hull, and the transducer can be withdrawn for inspection more easily, or its position changed if found to be unsatisfactory. See also *depth alarm*.

Eclipse Of a *light* exhibited as an *aid to navigation*, the dark interval between the appearances of light.

Ecliptic *Great circle* inclined at an angle of 23°27′ to the *celestial equator;* the apparent path of the sun in the *celestial sphere*.

Economical speed The speed at which a boat travels the greatest distance through the water on a given quantity of fuel; may be found by motoring over a *measured distance* at a certain number of engine revolutions per minute and noting both speed and fuel consumption. This is repeated at different engine speeds so that a table or *polar diagram* can be drawn up, based on distance in *nautical miles* per gallon or litre, and giving the *endurance* on a full tank. The economical speed is generally 20–40% below maximum rpm. *Displacement boats* have greater endurance at lower rpm, whereas a *planing boat's* economical speed is at higher rpm.

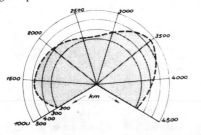

Eddy Water or wind moving in a circular direction, or in a direction different or opposite to that of the main stream or wind direction. Water eddies are often found in bays, harbour entrances and between *groynes,* and are sometimes marked on charts. Provided that the water is deep enough, their reverse direction can be extremely useful when sailing against a *tidal stream* that is generally adverse.

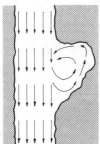

Eddy-making resistance The part of the total *resistance* of a hull or sail that is attributed to the formation of eddies, owing to appendages such as the propeller strut or reef points. Sometimes taken to include differences in pressure resulting from the hull shape (i.e. *form drag*).

Edge-fastening See *strip planking*.

Efficiency The ratio of the useful energy output to the energy input; for example, of a *propeller* is the ratio of the thrust developed to the power delivered to the propeller.

Elapsed time When *handicap racing,* the time taken by a boat to complete the course, i.e. the time between the *starting signal* and the moment that she crosses the *finishing line*. Each boat's *time allowance* is then applied to her elapsed time to find the *corrected time*. The boat with the shortest corrected time is the winner.

Elasticity The ability of a material to resist stresses and to recover its original shape and size after a load has been removed. The modulus of elasticity is the ratio of stress to strain in a material, stress being the load transmitted, and strain the resulting deformation. As in the case of materials such as wire, rod, fibres etc, Young's modulus relates to the change in length when under tension or compression. See also *stretch*.

Electrolysis Word frequently used loosely (esp in US) in place of *galvanic corrosion*.

Electro-magnetic log A *log* based on Faraday's principle that, when a conductor of electricity moves in a *magnetic field,* an electrical current is induced in the conductor (i.e. in the water), proportional to the speed of the relative movement. The log has a coil, which produces a magnetic field, and two probes or sensors, which project a very small distance from the hull and pick up the induced voltage. Considerable amplification is required to produce the speed signal. A voltage to frequency converter then converts speed to distance run.

Electronic compass Modern *compass* which senses earth's *magnetic field* electronically.

Elevated pole The *celestial pole* that is above the horizon and nearer the observer, i.e. the north pole when in the northern hemisphere.

Elevation Of *lights* exhibited as *aids to navigation*, the height of the light itself above sea level, UK usually above *MHWS*, US above *MHW*. The elevation of all lights (UK excluding those on *buoys* under 8 m) is given in the *List of Lights*. Admiralty *charts* give the elevation of lights exhibited by lighthouses, towers etc.

Embark To go on board a boat.

Emergency, degrees of (radio communication) *Distress, urgency* and *safety* messages, in that order, take priority over all other radio traffic. Each message is preceded by a different signal, radio telephony signals being based on French words and radio telegraphy signals consisting of morse code letters.
(a) Distress: MAYDAY in R/T, or SOS in W/T, indicates that a vessel or aircraft is in grave and imminent danger and requests immediate assistance; the implication is that there is immediate danger to life. Anyone in a position to respond to a distress call is legally bound to render assistance, and the situation automatically imposes *radio silence* on those not involved.
(b) Urgency: PAN-PAN in R/T, or XXX in W/T, precedes messages concerning the safety of a vessel, aircraft or person. The message has priority over all communications except distress and, although radio silence is not imposed, all stations must avoid interfering with the message which follows.
(c) Safety: SECURITE (pronounced say-cure-e-tay) in R/T, or TTT in W/T, is normally sent by a shore station to indicate that an important navigational or weather warning is to be transmitted.

Emergency equipment A useful list is given by the *Offshore Racing Council*: separate *navigation lights* and power source, *storm sails, jury steering* equipment, marine radio transmitter and receiver in addition to a radio receiver for weather bulletins, and the equipment listed under *safety equipment* (q.v.). See also *EPIRB*.

Emergency Position Indicating Radio Beacon See *EPIRB*.

Emergency rations Stores and water, either kept permanently in the *liferaft*, or stowed where they are instantly accessible in case of need. Vitamin-enriched concentrated food for 5–10 days (about 2 lbs, 1 kg per head) plus 3–6 pints (1½–3 litres) each of drinking water in cans are required. Part of the latter may be provided by chemicals that convert sea water into fresh water.

Enamel Hard gloss paint applied principally to the *topsides*, but sometimes to the *bottom* of boats that are hauled out after each race or sail.

End fitting A fitting on the end of a *spar*, such as that which protects the end of the *spinnaker pole* and enables it to be attached to the spinnaker guy or tack at one end and to the mast at the other. The end fitting on the main boom may have eyes to which the *topping lift* and *mainsheet block* can be shackled.

Endurance The time during which, or the distance that, a boat can motor with a full fuel tank at a certain rate of engine revolutions. See also *economical speed*.

Energy The capacity for doing work; potential energy by virtue of the body's position, kinetic energy by virtue of the body's motion. The *SI* unit of energy is the *Joule*.

Engine Almost all keelboats have *auxiliary engines*, often fitted inboard, not only to enable them to make way in calms or to supplement sails when the wind is light, but because an engine is essential in many busy waters and when entering or leaving a *berth*, say in a congested marina. *Diesel* engines are safer and more reliable than petrol (US gasoline) engines, but are heavier and noisier. Smaller boats with relatively little accommodation, tenders etc may carry an *outboard engine*. Most boat engines are water-cooled, either directly by sea water or indirectly by fresh water, which circulates in an enclosed circuit and is cooled in a *heat exchanger* by sea water. A few engines are air-cooled, and some boats have keel cooling or skin-tank cooling fitted, the fresh water in the closed circuit being cooled when it passes through pipes or tanks in contact with the sea or the skin. See also *outdrive, sail drive, vee drive, water-jet propulsion, cruising* and *economical speeds, endurance, propeller, reduction* and *reverse gear*.

Engine and propeller factor One of the elements of the *IOR rating* formula. Relates to the weight and position of the engine (Engine Moment Factor) and to the size and type of the *propeller,* its depth of immersion and shafting (Drag Factor).

Engine beds or **bearers** Supports to which the engine is secured once it has been properly aligned with the *propeller shaft;* distribute the load and stresses over a portion of the hull. The engine rests on mountings which may be flexible to absorb and reduce vibration and noise. The installation may be enclosed in a box-like housing or, in larger vessels, there may be a separate engine room. Adequate *ventilation* and *insulation* is required.

Ensign The national *flag,* worn at or near the *stern* of a vessel to show her nationality. In the US there is a special yacht ensign, exclusively for pleasure boats. In the UK sailing yachts wear a red ensign, unless boats owned by members of a certain club are permitted to wear a white or blue ensign or a *defaced* red or blue ensign, in which case a *warrant* is required. The only club whose members may obtain a warrant for their boats to wear a white ensign is the Royal Yacht Squadron.

Ensign staff Staff from which the ensign is flown; is inserted into a socket at the *stern,* and is usually removable.

Entering On arrival at a foreign port or when returning home from abroad, a vessel is entered at the custom house, the *ship's papers* are presented, and no-one on board may leave before permission has been given and *pratique* granted. In the case of sailing boats, the *customs* officer often boards the boat and deals with customs, immigration and health requirements, collects duty payable etc.

Enterprise *International class* two-man racing dinghy, designed by Jack Holt with a *double chine* hull. LOA 13 ft 3 in (4.04 m), beam 5 ft 3 in (1.6 m), weight rigged about 253 lbs (115 kg), sail area 113 sq ft (10.5 sq m).

Entrance or **entry** The forward part of the *hull* below the *waterline.*

Entry form Before taking part in a race a form, generally much as specfied in *racing rule* 18, completed to give the owner's name and address, the boat's *national letter(s)* and *distinguishing number, rig, rating* or *class* and *hull* colour. The entrance fee is usually enclosed, and a *measurement* or *rating certificate* often has to be sent as well.

Ephemerides or **ephemeris** A *nautical almanac.* Annual publication giving the positions of *heavenly bodies* hourly or daily throughout the year, as well as other data useful for *celestial navigation.*

EPIRB In its simplest form, an Emergency Position Indicating Radio Beacon transmits a distinctive signal on one of the *distress frequencies,* so that rescuers may *home* onto it. More sophisticated units sweep a band of frequencies, and others can both transmit and receive. Most have a folding or telescopic aerial, and are submersible, buoyant and self-righting; some also give the two-tone alarm on 2182 kHz. Range from a portable emergency transmitter in a liferaft varies from about 5 miles on Channel 16 (VHF, line of sight), through 25–27 miles on 2182 kHz up to as much as 200 miles with aircraft on distress frequencies (121.5 MHz or 243.0 MHz).

Epoxy Basically a compound of one oxygen and two carbon atoms.

Epoxy adhesive A glue, sold in liquid or powdered form with a separate *hardener;* has exceptionally high holding power, and can be used for glass, metal etc.

Epoxy paint Is usually supplied in two-pack form, and is very suitable for *topsides, decks* and *superstructure* because it provides excellent resistance to chemicals and abrasion. Can also be used with glassfibre cloth to provide an absolutely watertight and strong *sheathing.* Epoxide resin *primers* containing powdered zinc are excellent for protecting steel hulls from rust.

Epoxy resin Preferable to *polyester resin* because mechanical properties are better, and because lower shrinkage enables parts to be built more accurately. The extra strength of the *laminate* is offset by higher cost, slower *curing* and greater *viscosity,* which make work more difficult.

Equal intervals (US) See *isophase.*

Equation of time (See fig on p. 91) The excess of *mean solar time* over *apparent solar time,* i.e. the difference between time related to the visible *true sun* and time related to the fictitious *mean sun.* On December 25, April 15, June 14 and September 1 the figure is zero, when the equation of time changes from positive to negative and vice versa (see fig). The highest positive value of 14 min 16 sec occurs on February 12, and the extreme negative value of 16 min 24 sec on November 3. The value of the Equation of Time is given in the *Nautical Almanac* for every 12 hrs.

Equator The *great circle* half way between the *poles, latitude* 0°. See also *celestial equator.*

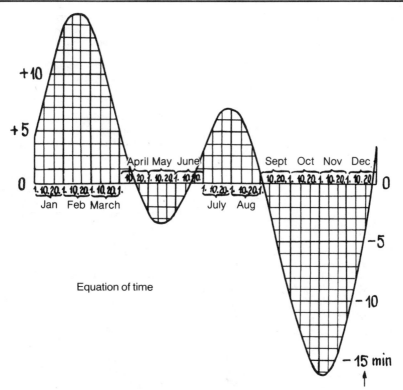

Equation of time

Equatorial trough See *intertropical convergence zone*.

Equilibrium The resultant of all the forces acting on a rigid body is zero, and the resulting moment is also zero. For example a boat at rest and on an even keel on the water is in a state of equilibrium, because the force of buoyancy equals the opposing force of gravity and the resulting force is zero; the resulting moment is also zero because both forces act vertically along the same line. If a boat under sail is to be directionally stable (balance), all forces have to be in equilibrium, such as heeling force and righting force, and the forces that act through the centres of effort and lateral resistance.

Equinox The days on which the sun, following its path along the *ecliptic*, crosses the equinoxial (the *celestial equator*), i.e. March 21/22 and September 22/23. Day and night are of equal length, 12 hrs.

Estimated position The vessel's position worked up from a previous *fix* or *observed position*. First the *dead reckoning* position is calculated from the *course(s)* and *distance(s)* sailed *through the water*; then the effects of *leeway* and *tidal stream or current* are plotted on to find the estimated position, which is more accurate than the DR position. UK: an EP is conventionally marked on the plotting chart by a triangle with a dot inside, with its time of origin; US, by a square with a dot in the centre.

Estuary An area of salt water at the mouth of a *tidal river*. Is connected to the sea, partly enclosed by land, and the *tidal streams* (US *tidal currents*) are affected by the river currents.

Europe *International* single-handed *one-design* class racing dinghy, designed by Alois Roland and made of wood and/or GRP/FRP. LOA 11 ft (3.35 m), beam 4 ft 6½ in (1.38 m), weight rigged 139 lbs (63 kg), sail area 80 sq ft (7.5 m).

Even keel A boat floats on an even keel when she floats parallel to her *designed waterline*, is neither down *by the head* nor by the stern, and is not *heeling*. Sailing dinghies, in particular, should not normally be allowed to heel excessively on any *point of sailing*, because heeling reduces the *projected sail area* (c.f. A and B in the figure) and increases hull *resistance*. When the wind is very light it does pay to heel the boat slightly in order to reduce *wetted area* and to help the sails to fill.

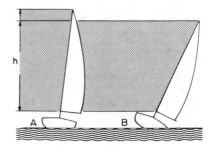

Existence doubtful On *charts* marks the position of an unconfirmed *danger;* chart abbr ED.

Ex-meridian altitude *Latitude* is obtained by taking the *altitude* of a *heavenly body* shortly before or after its *meridian passage,* for example when a noon sight is impossible because the sun is temporarily obscured.

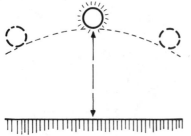

Expanded or (US) **foamed polystyrene** Very light and buoyant foamed material that provides *buoyancy* either by filling a hollow space such as an inaccessible part of the hull, or a mast; may also be made into blocks, but these are easily damaged.

Expanded scale Some electronic instruments are provided either with a single dial, part of the scale of which is magnified or, more frequently, with a separate dial with a greatly magnified scale. This enables the crew to see instantly how the boat reacts to changes in sail trim, course etc, e.g. *accelerometer,* and the close-hauled and running dial of a *wind speed and direction indicator.*

Explosive or **gun** *Fog signal* made as an *aid to navigation,* e.g. by a light vessel. An explosive charge is fired. Chart abbr (UK) expl. and (US) explos.

External ballast As opposed to *inside ballast,* is bolted to the *keel* from outside, i.e. a *ballast keel.*

Extra-tropical cyclone (US) See *depression.*

Extrusion Long metal or plastics tube or shape with a constant cross-section, formed by forcing molten material through a die. Light alloy masts and polyester yarn are extrusions, and the method is also used to form hollow or solid shapes which may be very complicated, and which could either not be made, or not be made economically in any other way.

Eye 1. Loop or eye splice, especially at the upper end of a *stay* or *shroud;* may be passed over a *mast, spar* or *cleat.* 2. A hole in a sail with a metal ring that is either punched in, fitted by hydraulic press or sewn in by hand to protect the cloth from *chafe.* Takes a *shackle,* the seizing that attaches a *slide, hank* etc. 3. Loop in rope or hole in a fitting through which a line may be *rove* (e.g. *bull's eye),* to which a line is shackled or made fast, or into which another fitting slips. 4. Eyes of a boat; right forward, the foremost part.

Eye bolt A metal bolt with an eye at one end. Passes through the structure and is held by a nut over a *backing* plate, or reinforcing piece.

Eyelet A small hole in a sail, awning, sailbag etc, sometimes stitched, but usually has a metal *grommet* through which a *lacing* is passed.

Eye of the storm The relatively calm centre of a *tropical revolving storm* where there are few clouds and where pressure is lowest. Seas are high and confused. Winds are strongest close by the eye, which should be avoided whenever possible. See *navigable* and *dangerous semicircles.*

Eye of the wind Directly upwind; the direction from which the *true wind* blows.

Eye plate Strong fitting, bolted or screwed to the structure, often with a *backing* piece on the underside of the deck, e.g. when fitted as an anchorage for a *shroud.*

Eye splice A permanent eye *spliced* in the end of a rope or wire rope so that it can be shackled to a fitting, sail etc. A *thimble* eye or hard eye is spliced around a thimble; a soft eye has no thimble. Each strand of natural fibre rope is *tucked* at least three times, but a minimum of five tucks is required for more slippery synthetic fibre ropes. *Swaging* and *Talurit* (US Nicopress) splicing is now preferred for wire rope.

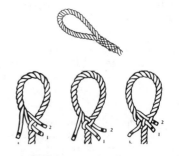

Eye terminal A *terminal* with an eye to which a *turnbuckle* (UK or rigging screw) or *shackle* may be attached.

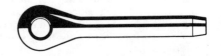

F = Foxtrot: white *code flag* with a red diamond. As a single letter signal means 'I am disabled, communicate with me'. *Morse code:* • • — • (dot dot dash dot).

Fahrenheit scale   Scale of temperature: 32° is the melting point of ice, 212° the boiling point of water. For conversion factors see *Celsius*.

Fair   1. A curve in the *lines plan* is fair when it runs smoothly with no hard spots, humps or hollows. When the curve is transferred to the *mould loft* floor, a batten is used to draw a fair line, and is held to the desired curve either by nails or by suitably shaped weights. The flexibility of the battens varies according to the radius of the curve. Similarly a surface is fair when it curves smoothly (e.g. with no *knuckle*). 2. To fair is to ensure that all the lines are fair before commencing construction, or to ensure that a part or fitting offers the minimum *resistance*, e.g. a *skin fitting* may be faired into the hull. 3. A rope is given a fair *lead*, with no awkward bends, to avoid *chafe*. 4. Advantageous or favourable, of wind, weather and *tidal stream or current*.

Fairlead   1. Fitting through which a working line is *rove* to alter the direction of the *lead*. May be a *bull's eye* fastened to the structure (sometimes combined with a *jam cleat*), a *turning block* fastened to a strong point, or an adjustable *sliding fairlead* mounted on a *track*, etc. 2. (US *chock*): fairleads at the *bows*, *stern* or *quarters* are usually open in the centre with arms either side bent over to keep a *mooring line* in place. The arms may be straight, or angled (continental type) as in the figure.

Fair sailing   The fundamental *racing rule* is that a yacht shall participate only by fair sailing, superior speed and skill and, except in *team races*, by individual effort.

Fair tide   Frequently used term for a fair *tidal stream* (US *tidal current*), i.e. one that helps the boat towards her destination.

Fairway   The main channel in a body of water such as a river or estuary; shallows either side are often marked by *buoys*, sometimes by *perches*; *mid-channel buoys* may mark the centre of the channel. A busy fairway should be avoided by small boats whenever possible.

Fairway buoy   (UK) marks the navigable limits of the fairway, either *port* or *starboard hand*. (US) a *mid-channel buoy* (q.v.).

Fair wind   A wind which blows from a direction that enables a boat to sail towards her destination without having to *tack*.

Fake   One turn in a *coil* of rope. To fake down is to coil a line with the running end on top (sometimes flake).

Fall   1. The rope or line rove through the *blocks* of a *tackle* (q.v.), especially applied to the hauling part. 2. The *barometer* falls when *atmospheric pressure* decreases. When the *pressure gradient* is steep, the barometer falls quickly and gives warning of strong winds associated with a *depression*.

Falling tide   When water level drops during the *ebb*, between *high water* and *low water*, as opposed to a *rising tide*.

Fall off   To *point* less high; the boat falls away to *leeward* of her intended *course*.

Fall wind   A *katabatic wind*, q.v.

False keel   1. Supplementary *keel*, usually streamlined and replaceable, fitted below the main keel to protect it from damage when running aground. 2. The wooden pieces that fill the spaces aft, and sometimes forward, of the *ballast keel* to complete the *underwater profile*.

False tack Tactic employed when racing to break away from an opponent that is *covering* closely. The boat pretends to tack, but only luffs head to wind and pays off on the original tack, hoping that the opponent is misled into going about.

Fashion piece Wooden member at the edge of the *transom* to increase the landing for the *plank* ends.

Fast 1. Secure. 2. US: alternative for *mooring line*. No longer used in this sense in the UK.

Fastenings General term for the screws, bolts, rivets, nails and even *treenails* that hold the various parts of a boat together. Silicon bronze and stainless steel are widely used, also monel, special bronzes, copper (nails), and sometimes galvanized iron and steel.

Fastnet Race A 605-mile race, first sailed in 1925 and now run in alternate and uneven years; starts at Cowes in the Isle of Wight, passes the Scilly Isles, round Fastnet Rock off the south-west tip of Ireland and finishes at Plymouth. Boats competing in the *Admiral's Cup* score treble points for their Fastnet result.

Fathom Obsolescent measurement of length, used especially for depths: 1 fathom = 6 ft = 1.83 metres. The length of outstretched arms, approximately one-hundredth of a *cable* and one-thousandth of a *nautical mile*. The unit for *soundings* on fathom charts.

Fathom chart (UK) *Soundings* are given in fathoms and feet, heights in feet, Gradually being replaced by *metric charts* on which measurements are in metres.

Fathom line *Contour line* on a fathom chart connecting points that are the same depth below *chart datum*. A fathom line encloses an area where the water is less deep.

Faying edge One of the two edges that meet at a joint. To fay is to fit two pieces of wood together so closely that the joint is virtually invisible.

Feather 1. When *rowing*, to turn the blades of the *oars* parallel to the water on the backstroke. 2. On *weather maps*, feathers and *pennants* are drawn on *wind arrows* to indicate the strength of the wind. Under the World Meteorological Organization method, half a feather represents

5 *knots,* and a full feather 10 knots. No feather indicates winds of up to 2 knots, one half feather 3—7 knots, etc. 3½ feathers therefore indicates 35 knots, i.e. a wind speed between 33 and 37 knots. Some countries adopt a system based on one half feather per *Beaufort wind force* and, in this case, 3½ feathers indicates force 7, 28—33 knot winds. It is advisable to check which system is adopted for a particular weather map because, given 3½ feathers on the arrow, wind pressure could be up to 70% higher under the WMO system. In the US, wind speed is usually quoted as the equivalent in mph. 3. In strong winds a sail can be feathered to reduce *heeling* without easing the *mainsheet;* the mast is bent to windward at spreader level so that the topmast curves to leeward, increasing sail *twist* and opening the leech to allow air to flow out freely. Pointing high and feathering is often preferable to *spilling wind* while sailing full and by, because *Vmg* is greater.

Feathering propeller The *blades* can be turned to lie *fore-and-aft* so that *resistance* is reduced when the boat is *under sail*.

Feeder Claw shaped fitting, loosely attached by a short line at the base of a *headfoil* (and sometimes below a mast groove opening). The sail luff is led between the two arms of the feeder, held in the correct position for entry into the luff groove opening.

Female mould A hollow mould in which, e.g. a hand laid-up *GRP/FRP* hull is constructed, giving a smooth outer surface. Normally the female mould is made over a male *plug;* the inside shape of the female mould matches the outside of the finished hull.

Fender (US also fend-off) Any device hung outboard to absorb the shock when coming *alongside* and to protect the hull when moored alongside. Generally a resilient cushion-like device with a tough cover; may be round, oval or sausage-shaped, and inflated or made of rubber,

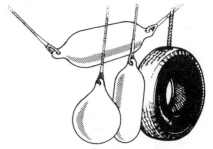

cork covered with sailcloth, foam-filled poly-ethylene weighted to hold it in position etc. Fenders are often fastened permanently to the *topsides* or *rubbing strakes* of smaller *launches* and *tenders* (see *fendering*) or at the *bow* and the corners where the *transom* meets the topsides.

Fenderboard A plank suspended horizontally outboard of two or more fenders to bridge the gap between them.

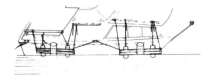

Fendering Protective fender attached all round the *gunwale* of a *tender* or *launch*. Is preferable to individual fenders which can slip to one side. Formerly usually rope, often canvas-covered, now generally made of plastics or synthetic rubber, and may be solid or hollow with a rectangular or D-section, sometimes with an anodized light alloy strip inserted.

Fend off 1. To push a boat clear of another boat or object, either by hand or with the *boathook* etc; similarly to push an object away from the boat. 2. See *fender*.

Ferrite rod A *directional aerial*, mainly used with a portable *direction finder*, and to receive medium and long wave transmissions. The conductor is wound round a horizontal rod core of ferrite, which is a scientifically processed ceramic oxide of iron. Ferrite can be magnetized by a weak magnetic field, and can retain some of its magnetism when the magnetizing field is removed. When the end of the rod points towards the transmitter, the minimum signal is received (*null*), and when the rod is broadside on the signal is strongest (maximum).

Ferro-cement A hull is constructed by making a framework of rods, covering them with mesh or chicken wire, and plastering the whole with a strong cement. The material cannot be attacked by marine borers, but boats under 65 ft (20 m) long are relatively heavy. The first such boat was built by a Frenchman, Lambot, in 1848. Bob Griffiths' 'Awahnee', 53 ft (16.15 m) has twice sailed round the world.

Ferrule A compression sleeve, made of soft metal, through which the end of a wire rope is fed when forming an *eye* by the *Talurit* (UK) or Nicopress (US) processes. When squeezed tight under pressure, the soft metal cold flows between the strands and wires which are tightly gripped. Copper ferrules are used for stainless steel wire rope, and light alloy ferrules for galvanized iron.

Fetch 1. The distance travelled by the wind across open water, either from land to *windward*, or from the area where the wind started to blow. Fetch is a major factor governing the growth of *waves*, i.e. given an *offshore wind* of constant strength, the height of waves close by the weather shore is small, but as fetch increases the waves grow, their height and length increasing proportionately with distance from the shore. 2. To reach an objective, especially a *mark* in the *course*, without tacking when racing; e.g. fetch the mark on port tack. 3. See also *reach*.

Fiberglass (US) See *glassfibre*. US only. FRP is the abbreviation for fiberglass reinforced plastics (UK: GRP).

Fibre (US **fiber**) Natural or synthetic material from which *cordage* and sails are made. The fibres are spun into *yarns*, which are either woven into *cloth* or twisted into the *strands* that are *laid* or *braided* to form rope.

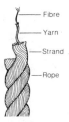

Fibreglass (UK) Trade name for *glassfibre*, q.v.

Fid 1. Wooden or iron bar that is passed through a hole in the *heel* of an upper *mast* to locate it. 2. Tapered wooden tool for *splicing* heavy rope, and for sailmaking. c.f. *marlinespike*, which is metal and smaller.

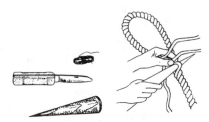

Fiddle Raised wooden framework bordering a cabin table, chart table etc to prevent objects from falling off when the boat heels; may be removable. Often plural.

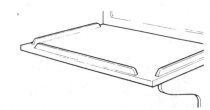

Fiddle block A *block* with two *sheaves,* one above the other on separate pins; is supposed to look rather like a violin because the upper block is larger. Mainly fitted to racing dinghies because *windage* is low.

Fiferail Piece of timber fitted horizontally around a mast, pierced to carry *belaying pins.*

Fifty-fifty A *motor-sailer,* designed to perform equally well under sail or power.

Figure-of-eight knot (UK) or **figure-eight knot** (US) A *stopper knot,* shaped like an 8, made in the end of a line to prevent it from unreeving through a block, fairlead etc.

Filament A single *extrusion* of synthetic fibre, often of great length (as much as a mile or more). Is twisted with others to form *thread* or *yarn,* used in cloth-weaving and rope-making.

Fill 1. To fill the sails is to steer the boat so that the wind acts on the sails, or to trim the sail so that it is distended by the wind. 2. US: Synonymous with weft (q.v.).

Filler 1. A substance, usually in powder form, added to *resin* when making a *GRP/FRP moulding* to reduce the cost or to give the resin certain properties, such as to increase *viscosity* and to reduce the effects of abrasion. The proportion of filler should never exceed 20%. No filler is used for transparent mouldings such as hatches. 2. A composition with which holes or the grain of wood is filled before the first coat of paint or varnish is applied. Small repairs to a GRP/FRP *laminate* can be made with *polyester* filler, and this provides a sealed surface. 3. Chemical (often melamine resin) added to sailcloth in the *finishing process* to increase stability, and reduce *bias stretch* and *porosity.* Modern processes enable the filler to

adhere to the weave well, but a good check is to crumple a small sample in the hand and look for marble crazing, or possibly flaking of the surface. Some fillers can give a stiff feel to the cloth, and this is acceptable to small racing boats but not suitable for cruising yachts.

Fin 1. A small metal or plastics plate projecting beneath the *hull* aft to promote *directional stability* and to provide a degree of *lateral resistance;* normally only fitted to *surfboards, sailboards* and some fast *runabouts.* 2. See *fin keel.*

Fin and skeg configuration The *keel* is short and well separated from the *rudder,* which is hung right aft on a separate *skeg.* Sometimes there is a *bustle* between the fin and the skeg.

Fine As opposed to *full,* is descriptive of a boat with a narrow but graceful hull, with a high *length to beam ratio* and a fine *entry* (narrow, sharp bow).

Fine on (UK) Direction from the boat, as in fine on the *bow,* between dead *ahead* and 45° from ahead: fine on the *quarter,* between 45° from *astern* and dead astern.

Finish The surface of *topsides* and, particularly, the *underwater body* has to be smooth to keep *frictional resistance* to a minimum. Some paints can be burnished to give a mirror-like finish, others are rubbed down with very fine grade *wet-and-dry sandpaper.*

Finishing A boat finishes a race when any part of her *hull,* crew or equipment in normal position crosses the *finishing line* from the direction of the *course* from the last *mark,* after fulfilling her penalty obligations if any. An acoustic signal may be made by the race officers, say with a *foghorn.*

Finishing line The line a boat has to cross in order to finish a race. Under the *racing rules,* may be a line between two *marks,* between a mark and a mast or staff on the *committee boat,* or the extension of a line through two stationary posts, the outer limit of which may be marked by a buoy.

Finishing process Treatment to sailcloth after it has been woven, in order to improve stability, impermeability and surface polish. Includes scouring, drying, heat relaxation to shrink and set the weave, impregnation with chemical *fillers*, surface coating with polymer to improve polish, and finally *calendering*.

Fin keel A short *keel*, usually bolted to the *hull* after it has been completed; see *fin and skeg configuration*.

Finn *International class* single-handed racing dinghy, designed by Rickard Sarby, and an *Olympic class* since 1952. LOA 14 ft 9 in (4.5 m), beam 4 ft 11½ in (1.517 m), weight rigged 319 lbs (145 kg), sail area about 115 sq ft (10.68 m).

Fireball *International class* high-performance two-man *scow*-type racing dinghy with a *trapeze* and a spinnaker, designed by Peter Milne; built of *marine plywood* and/or *GRP/FRP*. LOA 16 ft 2 in (4.928 m), beam 4 ft 5 in (1.359 m), weight rigged 175 lbs (79.4 kg), sail area 123 sq ft (11.45 sq m).

Fire extinguisher Foam, powder or fluid-filled device for fighting fuel, electrical and other fires on board. Must be readily accessible, and of a type approved by the national authority. Many countries specify the number and type that must be carried by various types and sizes of craft. An automatic BCF (bromochlorodifluoromethane) extinguisher can be fitted in the engine compartment, and reacts to the rise in temperature when an engine catches fire, but BCF and BTM extinguishers should not be used in confined spaces where the toxic fumes could poison the crew. The US Coast Guard prohibits the use of chlorobromethane and carbon tetrachloride extinguishers for this reason; carbon dioxide and dry chemical extinguishers are approved. A woven glass blanket smothers flames effectively.

Fire prevention In addition to fire extinguishers, many countries specify that an electrically shielded blower must be fitted to expel fumes from the engine compartment before the engine can be started; regulations vary from country to country. Fire retarding material is often used in certain places on board, and delays the spread of a fire by at least half an hour. *Intumescent* paint can also be applied. Bilge sniffers detect the presence of fumes in the bilges, and bilge blowers expel the fumes. See also *flame arrestor*.

First point of Aries See *Aries*.

Fish A temporary repair to a *spar* that has sprung or been weakened; a piece of timber is lashed to it.

Fisherman 1. A person who fishes. 2. Coll. a fishing vessel. 3. A *fisherman staysail*, q.v.

Fisherman anchor Traditional *anchor* with two *flukes* and a fixed or folding *stock* set at right angles to the arms. Also called Admiralty anchor.

Fisherman's bend Often used to bend a *cable* to an *anchor*. A *round turn* is taken round the ring, and the first *half hitch* passes through it. The end can be *stopped* to the *standing part* after the second half hitch has been made.

Fisherman's knot Two small lines of equal thickness can be joined temporarily by tying a simple *overhand knot* in the end of each around the *standing part* of the other line. Useful when there is insufficient time to *splice* them together.

Fisherman staysail Light weather reaching sail set between the masts of a *ketch* or *schooner* to make use of the space not taken up by other sails. Sometimes known as a gollywobbler.

Fishing vessel Broadly a vessel that is used by fishermen when catching fish. Under the *IRPCS* a *vessel engaged in fishing* is one whose manouevrability is restricted by the apparatus being used; this includes nets, lines or trawls but not trolling lines. Thus, pleasure craft with short lines or other small gear are not accorded the privileges given to commercial fishing vessels by the IRPCS.

Fit out 1. To prepare a boat for sea at the start of a season, or before her *maiden voyage*, by providing and fitting all the gear, equipment etc. 2. To complete a bare hull by fitting all the cabin furniture, deck fittings etc.

Fitting General term applied to gear that is not part of the boat's structure, but is attached to *hull, deck, rigging* etc, such as *cleats, fairleads, stemhead fitting* etc.

505 *International class* high-performance two-man racing dinghy with spinnaker and *trapeze*, designed by John Westell. LOA 16 ft 6½ in

(5.05 m), beam 6 ft 2 in (1.88 m), weight rigged 280 lb (127 kg), sail area 200 sq ft (18.58 sq m).

Fix The position of the vessel as plotted from *position lines* obtained by *hand-bearing compass, direction finder, echo sounder, sextant* angles etc. An observed position, found by measuring the *altitude* of a *heavenly body,* is termed a fix by some people. *Estimated* and *dead reckoning positions* are calculated. A fix is conventionally marked on the plotting chart by a circle with a dot inside, with its time of origin.

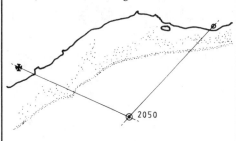

Fixed and flashing light A fixed *light,* exhibited as an *aid to navigation,* that *flashes* more brilliantly at regular intervals; chart abbr F Fl. Fixed and group flashing lights are fixed lights varied by groups of several brilliant flashes.

Fixed light A white or coloured light that shines continuously with no change in *intensity;* chart abbr F. Not exhibited by a floating aid to navigation (apart from some privately laid buoys in the US).

Flag Oblong, square, triangular or swallow-tailed piece of coloured material, often bunting, or pieces of different colours assembled in various patterns. The material is generally stitched at the *hoist* to a strong piece of canvas through which a line passes; the top of the line has an *eye,* or passes round a *toggle* to which the flag *halyard* is bent; the lower end may have an eye, swivel or clip. Flags are measured by the length of the hoist (height) and the *fly* (length). The flags worn include the *ensign* (vessel's nationality), *burgee* (owner's yacht club), *courtesy flag* (of country being visited), *house* (private), *racing* and *protest* flags (when racing); the *International Code flags* consisting of letters and numerals are flown singly or in groups for visual communication. (See back endpapers).

Flag etiquette Flags are flown at certain positions and at certain times in accordance with tradition and usage and, although there is great similarity in etiquette between countries, the small boat sailors of some nations are more punctilious than those of other lands in observing etiquette. The *ensign* is worn aft, the *burgee* at the *masthead,* and a *courtesy flag* or *house flag* at the *starboard*

spreader. In harbour, ensigns are lowered at sunset and hoisted at 0800 in the US and UK from March 25–Sept 20, but at 0900 in the winter. All flags are lowered before leaving the boat for more than a few hours and, apart from the burgee which serves to indicate wind direction, they are also normally lowered at night, and in heavy weather when under way. See also *dip, half-mast, dress ship.*

Flag officer One of the highest ranking officers of a yacht or sailing club; i.e. the commodore, vice-commodore or rear-commodore (more rarely, President or Vice-President) who are all entitled to fly a club *broad pendant.* Some clubs also have an admiral, which is an honorary or courtesy rank above that of commodore. In navies, ranks equivalent to a rear-admiral and above.

Flagstaff A wooden or metal mast on shore from which flags are flown, such as a yacht club *burgee, signal flags, storm warnings* or harbour signals. The *ensign* is flown on board from the *ensign staff.* UK usage, no flagstaff on board; US usage, may also be on board. Chart abbr FS.

Flake and **flake down** Rope is laid out on deck in a figure of eight pattern so that it will run out easily. *Fake* and flake are often used interchangeably for *coiling,* and for a single loop of rope in a coil. To flake down is to lay a sail in folds either side of the boom.

Flame arrestor A metal screen mounted over the carburettor air intake to prevent fire or explosion caused by backfiring. A legal requirement in the US.

Flammable Different countries set different limits below which a substance is deemed to be flammable, e.g. the US National Fire Protection Association defines a flammable liquid as one with a *flash point* below $38\,°C$ or $100\,°F$; in Germany the limit is $21\,°C$ or $70\,°F$. It is not just the substances themselves, such as petrol (US gasoline), butane and propane gas, that are dangerous, but the vapours which form a combustible mixture when combined with oxygen; being heavier than air they sink to the bottom of the engine compartment or bilges and then ignite. The term inflammable is often used in the UK.

Flare 1. Of *topsides,* curvature outwards towards the *gunwale, beam* being greatest at deck level (c.f. *tumblehome*). 2. Pyrotechnice device; red and orange flares indicate *distress,* but a white flare may be ignited to avert a collision by drawing attention to the boat's presence. Flares must be kept in a dry place and, because their life is short, they must be replaced regularly. A hand-held rocket produces a red parachute flare, which is ejected at about 100 ft and burns for 40 seconds at

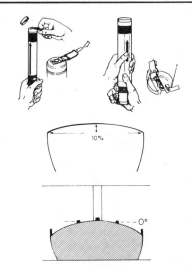

40,000 *candela*. To pinpoint a vessel's position in daylight, orange smoke hand flares produce smoke for 50 seconds, while buoyant flares last for three minutes. Two-star red rockets fire two red stars at heights of over 200 ft at an interval of three seconds, and are small enough to be stowed in a *life-jacket*. Plastic packs can be obtained, containing the flares required by vessels, either when sailing offshore, or in coastal waters. The figure shows how easy they are to ignite.

A UK aircraft engaged in Search and Rescue fires green flares at five to ten minute intervals while searching. A vessel in distress should wait for the green flare to die out, fire two red flares at 20 second intervals (to allow the aircraft to line up a *bearing*), followed by a further red flare when the aircraft is either overhead or appears to be going badly off course.

Flashing light A light, exhibited as an *aid to navigation*, which flashes repeatedly at regular intervals. The duration of light is less than the duration of darkness; chart abbr Fl. See also *quick, very quick, fixed and flashing, ultra quick, group flashing lights*.

Flash point The lowest temperature at which a volatile liquid such as fuel gives off enough vapour for it to be ignited by a spark or flame when it is mixed with air. The lower the flash point the more dangerous is the substance.

Flat 1. A level area of mud, sand etc, generally of considerable extent and connected to the shore; uncovers at *low water*. 2. A flat sail is one with less *belly* or curvature than a *full* sail.

Flat-bottomed Describes a boat with a flat bottom, such as a *barge* or US *scow*. No *deadrise*.

Flatten Take steps to make a sail flatter through use of *halyard, cunningham, flexible mast* etc.

Flatten in Sometimes used as an alternative to *hardening* in a sail, i.e. to pull the sail closer to the centreline by hauling on the sheet.

Flattening reef or **roach reef** Flattens a mainsail by decreasing the area and *fullness* or *flow* of the sail at the *foot*. A special eye 6–8 in (15–20 cm) above the *clew*, and often the *cunningham hole* above the *tack* too, are pulled down to the boom.

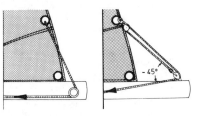

Flaw 1. A sudden gust of stronger wind. 2. A weak point in material, usually caused in manufacture but sometimes natural.

Flexible coupling An engine, bedded on flexible mountings to reduce noise and vibration, must have a flexible coupling between the propeller shaft and the drive output to absorb the movement; may be soft discs or a *cardan shaft*.

Flexible or **bendy mast** The flexibility of an unstayed mast, such as that of a *Finn*, depends on its construction, but the stayed mast of a high-performance racing dinghy or keelboat, such as a *Flying Dutchman* or *Star*, can be deliberately bent athwartships or fore-and-aft to vary sail *camber* to suit the point of sailing and wind strength. In light breezes and when the wind is free a full sail is required, with maximum camber. This is obtained with a straight mast (A). For fresher winds and close-hauled sailing the mast is bent (B) to flatten the sail by drawing forward some of the *round* cut into the luff. Sail camber can also be altered without bending the mast by adjusting *controls*, such as the cunningham and outhaul, or with a *flattening reef*. A bendy boom is sometimes used as well.

Flinders Bar A soft iron bar fitted vertically to the *binnacle* to compensate for *compass error* caused by vertical induced magnetism.

Float 1. A boat floats when the force of *buoyancy* acting upwards balances the force of gravity (her *displacement*) acting downwards. 2. Buoyant object used to mark the position of something on the bottom, or connected to a fishing net. 3. Term sometimes applied to the small *outriggers* outboard of the main central hull of a *trimaran*. 4. See *masthead float*.

Floating bridge Powered floating structure which pulls itself across a river or narrow entrance, usually along chains or wires.

Floating dock Trough-shaped watertight structure with high sides between which vessels are repaired. Is partially submerged by flooding *pontoon* tanks so that the vessel can enter. The water is then pumped out, and the dock rises to float above water level, providing a working platform on which the ship is painted, repaired etc.

Flog A sail flogs when it whips wildly from side to side.

Flood 1. The period during a tidal cycle when the sea level is rising, i.e. the period between *low water* and *high water*, is the flood *tide*. The term is often also loosely applied to the horizontal motion of the *tidal stream* (US *tidal current*); as verb and noun, to flow and the flow towards the land in estuaries, harbours etc or in the direction associated with a rising tide. 2. To fill boat, river or container to overflowing. 3. To fill, e.g. a ballast tank to increase *stability* or correct *trim*.

Flood mark Shows the level reached in abnormal circumstances by flood waters on a particular date.

Flood stream (UK) or **flood current** (US) The horizontal flow of water associated with a rising (flood) *tide*. In estuaries etc is ingoing. After a period of *slack water* the *ebb stream* starts and, in the case of a *rectilinear* (US reversing) *stream*, often flows in approximately the opposite direction.

Floor Not a horizontal surface to walk on but a *transverse* structural *member* fitted across the *keel* to connect the *heels* of *frames* and the bottom *planking* or skin to the keel. *Keel bolts* often pass through the floors. See also *construction* fig.

Floor

Flotation See *buoyancy, buoyancy material* and *tanks*.

Flotsam Cargo or wreckage floating on the water after a vessel has sunk.

Flow Alternative term for the *fullness* or *camber* of a sail.

Fluke The flattish plate or shovel-shaped part at the end of the arm of an *anchor;* bites into the ground.

Fluky Light winds which vary frequently and considerably in direction and strength are said to be fluky.

Flush-decked Describes a boat with a deck all on one level, interrupted only by the *cockpit* at a lower level; the *cabin* does not extend above the deck, which is absolutely clear to work on. Generally only found in boats where standing *headroom* is available without need of a *coachroof* (US trunk). The *accommodation* is lit by transparent hatches or *decklights*.

Fly 1. The part of a flag farthest from the *hoist*. 2. The horizontal length of a flag from hoist to fly. 3. A small *pennant* at the masthead, see *masthead fly*.

Flyer When racing, a boat is said to take a flyer when the helmsman chooses an extreme course, e.g. by taking a very long tack well away from the majority of the fleet, possibly when hoping for a wind shift.

Flying See *set flying*.

Flying bridge A higher steering position, built above the wheelhouse of a power cruiser to give the helmsman better visibility. Controls usually duplicated are wheel, speedometer or log, echo sounder and, possibly, radar screen.

Flying Dutchman *International class* high-performance two-man racing dinghy with a *trapeze* and a spinnaker, designed by Uwe van Essen, and an *Olympic class* since 1960. LOA 19 ft 10 in (6.05 m), beam 5 ft 7 in (1.7 m), weight rigged 364 lbs (165.11 kg), sail area 200 sq.ft (18.58 sq m).

Flying jib The foremost *jib*; in *square-rigged* ships is tacked down to the *jib-boom* or flying jib-boom.

Flying proa See *proa*.

Fo'c's'le Abbreviated form of *forecastle*, q.v. (which is always pronounced fohksl).

Fog *Visibility* is reduced to below 0.5 n.miles or 1 km, owing to the condensation of water vapour into minute water droplets. The four lowest numbers on the visibility scale, 90 to 93, relate to fog, 90 being the most dense. The main types of fog encountered at sea are *advection fog* (sea or coastal), and *radiation* or ground *fog* that has formed over land but drifted seaward. Is also formed when two very different *air masses* meet, for example when a *warm front* approaches and the warm air flows over cold air; this type is called precipitation, mixed or frontal fog. See also *steam fog, sea smoke*.

Fog detector light Powerful bluish-white light with which a *lighthouse* keeper detects the presence of fog. Chart abbr Fog Det Lt.

Foghorn A horn with which fog signals are made. The *IRPCS* term is *whistle*, q.v.

Fog signals *Sound signals* prescribed by the *IRPCS* to be made in *restricted visibility* by day or night. They indicate the type of vessel, whether she is *making way, under way, at anchor, aground* etc, and are made with a *whistle, bell* or gong. Fog signals are also sounded by *lightvessels, buoys, lighthouses* etc; the sound made is indicated on *charts* and given in the *List of Lights*.

Folding anchor or **folding grapnel** An *anchor* with four flukes, which spread out like an umbrella and are held in place by a ring (A). They fold flat along the shank when stowed (B). *Holding power* is lower than that of a *fisherman*, and they are generally only used by dinghies or sometimes as *kedge* anchors for *dayboats*.

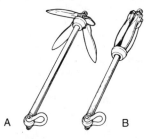

A   B

Folding propeller A type of propeller designed to reduce *drag* when under sail; water streaming past the hull folds the blades together in line with the propeller shaft, except when the engine is turning the shaft; the blades then swing out automatically owing to *centrifugal force* . Only suitable for lower power (5–50 hp) engines that run at 500–1500 rpm.

Folding propeller

Folding step Hinged light alloy or bronze step, about 2½ × 3½ in (60 × 90 mm) in size, which can be bolted to the *transom* of boats with high *freeboard*, or elsewhere as required.

Following sea and **wind** Seas that move in the same direction as the boat is heading; wind blowing from astern. In high following seas and strong winds it may be necessary to *stream* a warp to slow the boat and prevent her from being *pooped*.

Foot 1. The lower edge of a *sail*, whether quadrilateral or triangular. 2. The lower few feet of the *mast*. 3. Verb: to foot well is to sail fast. 4. Measurement; unit of length:
1 ft = 12 in = 30.48 cm = 0.3048 m;
1 m = 3.28084 ft;
1 sq ft = 0.092903 sq m;
1 sq m = 10.7639 sq ft;
1 cu ft = 0.0283168 cu m;
1 cu m = 35.3146 cu ft.
For further conversion factors see *density*.

Foot or **turning block** Fitted to alter the direction of *lead*, often of a *sheet*.

Footrope 1. Part of the *bolt-rope* along the foot of a sail; is often fed into a *groove* in the *boom*. 2. Or horse; stout rope stretched beneath the *yard* of a *square-rigged* ship, or beneath *bowsprit* and *jib-boom*, supported at intervals by stirrups. Sailors stand on it with their chests over the yard or bowsprit when handling sails.

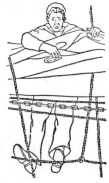

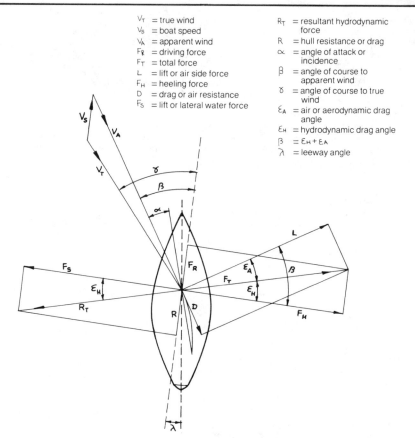

V_T = true wind
V_S = boat speed
V_A = apparent wind
F_R = driving force
F_T = total force
L = lift or air side force
F_H = heeling force
D = drag or air resistance
F_S = lift or lateral water force

R_T = resultant hydrodynamic force
R = hull resistance or drag
$\propto$ = angle of attack or incidence
β = angle of course to apparent wind
δ = angle of course to true wind
ε_A = air or aerodynamic drag angle
ε_H = hydrodynamic drag angle
β = $\varepsilon_H + \varepsilon_A$
λ = leeway angle

Force 1. The *Beaufort scale* grades winds by the effect of their forces on sea and land; the speed of wind at each force is given in the scale (p.19). 2. Some of the dynamic forces that act when a boat under sail moves through the water are shown in the *vector diagram* (above). V_T is the *true wind*. The sail is set at an *angle of attack* α to the *apparent wind* V_A, which is the resultant of true wind and boat speed V_S. The aerodynamic forces are shown acting at the *centre of effort* (CE). Total aerodynamic force F_T is composed of L, *lift* (or air side force), which acts at right angles to the direction of the apparent wind, and D, *drag* (or air resistance), acting in the same direction as V_A. Angle ϵ_A is the aerodynamic drag angle, and angle ϵ_H is the hydrodynamic drag angle; the sum of these drag angles equals β, the angle of the *course* to the apparent wind direction. γ is the angle of the course to the true wind. F_T is resolved into two components; F_R acting in the direction of the boat's course is *driving force*, and F_H acting at right angles to it is *heeling force*. The resultant hydrodynamic force R_T is shown acting at the *centre of lateral resistance* (CLR), and is composed of F_S, lift (or side force water), acting at right angles to the course sailed through the water, and R, hull drag or *resistance*, acting in the direction

opposite to that in which the boat is sailing. Angle λ is the *leeway* angle, i.e. the angle between the boat's *heading* and the actual course she sails through the water. The static forces of *buoyancy* and gravity are not shown. In wind tunnels, total force is found by measuring lift and drag separately. In the figure the aerodynamic and hydrodynamic forces are shown acting at a single point but, normally, the CE and CLR are separated; the CE usually lies forward of the CLR.

Total aerodynamic force varies as the square of wind speed (as well as with the angle of attack, *camber* and *aspect ratio* of the sail). Total force can be nine times greater when the boat is close-hauled than when on a dead run, because apparent wind speed is over 30% greater than true wind speed when the boat is close-hauled, but about 40% slower when sailing downwind. 3. Action that alters the state of rest or the state of motion of a body, measured in Newtons (*SI*), poundals or lb force (f.p.s.) or kilogramme force, kilopond (metric).

1 N = 7.233 poundals = 0.224809 lbf = 0.101972 kgf; 1kgf = 9.8066 N;
1 poundal = 0.138255 N = 0.031081 lbf;
1 lbf = 4.44822 N = 32.174 poundals.

Fore Towards or nearer the *bows*, as opposed to *aft, after*.

Fore-and-aft Parallel to the line between *stem* and *stern*; at right angles to *athwartships*.

Fore-and-aft line The *centreline* (q.v.) between *stem* and *stern*; in line with the *keel*, and midway between the sides.

Fore-and-aft rig 1. Sails are set in the fore-and-aft line, parallel to the *centreline*, as opposed to *square rig* when they are set on *yards athwartships*. The normal rig for sailing dinghies and keelboats alike. *Sloops, cutters, cat-boats, ketches, yawls* and *schooners* are all fore-and-aft rigged. 2. Professional seaman's uniform of jacket and peaked cap.

Fore-and-aft sail A sail set in the fore-and-aft line, as opposed to a *square sail*, which is set *athwartships*. *Lugsails, lateen sails*, all *jib-* or *gaff-headed* sails attached to a *mast* by the *luff* (*mainsail, mizzen* etc), *headsails* (such as *jib, genoa*), *mizzen staysail* and other *staysails, spinnaker, tallboy* and *big boy* (set flying, i.e. not attached to a mast or stay) are all classed as fore-and-aft sails.

Fore-and-aft schooner Schooner rigged fore-and-aft on two or more masts, i.e. with no square sails.

Forebody The part of the hull form forward of the *midship section*; c.f. *afterbody*.

Fore cabin or **forward cabin** In boats with more than one living area, the cabin forward.

Forecastle The part of the accommodation below the *foredeck* and *forward* of the *mast* of a sailing boat, or above the foredeck in a motor vessel with an enclosed forecastle erection. Pronounced fohksl

and often abbreviated to fo'c's'le (placing of apostrophes may vary).

Foredeck In sailing boats, that part of the *deck* that is *forward* of the *mast* and *coachroof* or cabin *trunk*; covers the forward part of the hull.

Foredeck hand The member of the crew who works on the foredeck; changes *headsails, gybes* the *spinnaker pole*, handles the *anchor* etc.

Forefoot The part of the *forebody* immediately abaft the forward end of the *stem*, below water. The shape may influence the boat's *balance* and her behaviour in seas. The forefoot of older heavy displacement sailing boats was relatively narrow and well veed, whereas that of a modern *IOR* offshore racer is fuller and flatter.

Foreguy Rope or line led forward from the end of a *boom, spinnaker pole* etc; allows the spar to swing forward but no further aft. May be rigged to the mainboom when running as a *preventer* to avoid an *accidental gybe* should the wind shift, the boat *yaw* or the helmsman make a mistake. A *tackle* may be needed to adjust trim under load.

Forehatch A *hatch* forward, usually in the *foredeck*.

Foremast The forward *mast* in a vessel that has two or more, except in a *yawl* and *ketch* when the forward and taller mast is the mainmast.

Forepeak Compartment right forward, immediately abaft the *stem*, usually used for stowing ground tackle, mooring lines, fenders or spare gear. In sailing boats the term is often used in place of *forecastle*. In motor boats may be a watertight compartment.

Forereach 1. Make *headway* when *shooting up* into the wind with the sails shaking. The distance that a boat *carries* her *way* depends largely on her type (heavy boats shoot further), and the size of the waves. 2. To gain ground on and overtake

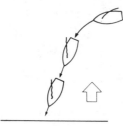

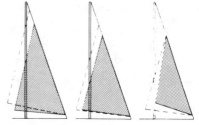

another vessel on the same course. 3. Make headway when *hove to*.

Foresail 1. In *square-rigged* ships, the lowest sail on the *foremast*, i.e. the fore *course*. 2. The sail set on the after side of a *schooner's* foremast; may be *jib-* or *gaff-headed*, or extended by a *wishbone* boom. 3. Often used as an abbreviation of fore-staysail, namely the *headsail* set on the *forestay*.

Foreshore All that part of the shore that is covered at *high water springs* and uncovered at *low water springs*.

Forestay In almost all sailing boats and dinghies, the foremost *stay* to which the *jib* or *genoa* is *hanked*; runs from high on the *mast* to the *stemhead* or *bowsprit*, providing *fore-and-aft* support for the mast. (See *rigging* fig.) In *sailing ships*, leads from the lower *foremast* stayband to the stem or bowsprit. See also *inner forestay*.

Forestay sag The amount by which the forestay falls away from a straight line due to weight and to wind pressure on the headsail; causes aerodynamic inefficiency.

Foretriangle Broadly, the triangle formed by the *forestay*, *mast* and *foredeck*. *Headsails* suitable for all winds can be set in this area, which is larger in a *masthead-rigged sloop* than in a *seven-eighths* or *three-quarter rigged* sloop because the forestay

extends right to the top of the mast. A large fore-triangle is generally preferred because airflow over a *staysail* is not disturbed, as is that of a sail attached to a mast at the *leading edge*, and the sail therefore generates more drive. Often only part of the foretriangle area is rated. See also *International Offshore Rule*.

Fork terminal A *terminal* with an open fork at the end, secured with a *clevis pin*.

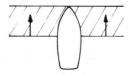

Form drag That part of total aerodynamic *drag* that is due to shape, mainly of the sails but also of spars, mast and standing rigging. Form drag is caused by pressure being lower in the *wake* of a moving object, and is low at a small *angle of attack* but increases as the angle of attack increases. Similarly is a part of total hydrodynamic *resistance*.

Forward Towards the *bows*; nearer the bows; the part of the boat near the bows, as to go forward. Opp *aft* and *after*.

Forward of the beam A direction from the boat, i.e. the sectors to *port* and *starboard*, bounded by right *ahead* and *abeam*.

Foul 1. A foul *anchor* has its *cable* caught on its *flukes*, or the flukes caught on an obstruction on the *bottom*. 2. The opposite of *clear*, e.g. a rope that does not run through a block because it is *snarled*. 3. Breach of the rules when racing. See also below, p. 105.

Foul anchorage An area that is unsuitable for anchoring owing to underwater obstructions such as rocks, seaweed or cables which could result in the anchor becoming foul.

Foul berth A *berth* where a boat cannot *swing* at the *turn of the tide* without *grounding* or striking another boat.

Foul bottom 1. Describes the *bottom* of a boat when weed and barnacles grow on it, because *antifouling* was either not applied or has lost its toxicity. 2. Also used to describe *foul ground*.

Foul coast A coast with *off-lying dangers*, such as rocks, breakers or shoals, i.e. the coast is not clear.

Foul ground *Sea-bed* that is unsuitable as an *anchorage* owing to submarine cables, wrecks, rocks, or other obstructions.

Foul tide Frequently used term for a foul *tidal stream* (US *tidal current*) that *sets* in the opposite direction to a boat's course to her destination.

Foul weather Stormy, with heavy rain or strong wind, hence. . .

Foul weather gear General term (mainly used in the US) for waterproof protective clothing such as *oilskins, sou'westers* etc.

Foul wind An adverse wind that is either blowing from the direction of the boat's destination, or in a direction that forces her towards a danger.

Founder Of a vessel, to fill with water and sink.

Four point bearing (UK) or **bow and beam bearing** (US) When the *tidal stream or current* is running parallel to the coast, *distance* off can be found by taking two *relative bearings* of any object on shore, the first when it bears four points or 45° on the bow, the second when it is abeam and bears 90°. The distance made good *over the ground* (calculated from the time taken and the speed of the boat through the water, adjusted to allow for *leeway* and the helpful or adverse effect of the tidal stream) between A and B in the figure equals the distance between the vessel and the object D at position B. The first bearing can be taken at point

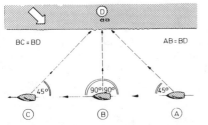

B, when the object is abeam, and the second when it bears 135°; distance BC then equals BD. Because the distance between the vessel and the shore is not known until the object is abeam or later, *bearing angles on the bow*, or *doubling the angle on the bow* are preferable methods if the navigator wishes to clear an off-lying danger.

470 *International class* two-man racing dinghy with a *trapeze* and spinnaker, designed by André Cornu. An *Olympic class* since 1976. LOA 15 ft 5 in (4.70 m), beam 5 ft 6½ in (1.68 m), weight rigged 264 lbs (119 kg), sail area about 130 sq ft (12.08 sq m), spinnaker about 130 sq ft (12.08 sq m).

420 *International class* two-man racing dinghy with a *trapeze* and a spinnaker, designed by Christian Maury. Very widely distributed. LOA 13 ft 9¼ in (4.20 m), beam 5 ft 6½ in (1.69 m), weight rigged 220 lbs (99.79 kg), sail area 110 sq ft (10.22 sq m).

F.p.s. system Measurement system based on the foot, pound and second. Replaced by *SI* units for scientific work, and gradually being phased out in the UK.

Fractional rig As opposed to a *masthead rig,* the *forestay* of which extends to the top of the mast, the forestay of a yacht with fractional rig extends only part of the way up, i.e. as in *three-quarter* and *seven-eighths rigs.*

Frame Rib-like *transverse* structural *member* which stiffens the *hull* and dictates its shape. In wooden construction is sawn to shape from grown or built-up timber, or is *laminated.* When bent it is called a *timber.* When building a *round bilge* hull the frames are fitted after the *moulds* have been set up; *planking* is then fastened to the frames. See *construction* fig.

Frap Bind tightly or secure with a rope or line; especially to tie halyards keeping them off from the mast to stop them from rattling noisily in the wind when in harbour.

Free 1. To clear, e.g. a sheet that has got caught on a fitting. 2. To sail free is to *reach* or *run.* 3. Of wind, see *freeing wind* and *free wind.*

Freeboard The vertical distance between the

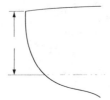

waterline and the top of the *deck* at any point along the hull. The freeboard of a boat with normal *sheer* is least at a point slightly aft of *amidships*, and increases towards *bow* and *stern*. A seaworthy boat must have adequate freeboard, and this varies according to how deeply she is immersed and, consequently, with the weight of crew, stores etc.

Freeing port   Fitted in *bulwarks* to allow water on deck to flow overboard.

Freeing wind   A wind that shifts to blow from a direction nearer the stern of the boat (opp *heading wind*). If the wind shifts when two boats are *beating* on opposite *tacks*, it will free for one which can then either *luff up* or *ease* her sheets, but it will head the other boat which has to *bear away* to keep her sails full. The wind also appears to free temporarily in a gust because, when *true wind* speed increases with no change of boat speed or direction, the *apparent wind* blows from further aft; boats on opposite tacks are then both able to luff up. When on a reach the sails can be eased out when the wind frees.

Free wind   The wind is said to be free when it blows from a direction *abaft the beam*.

Frequency   The number of cycles or oscillations per unit of time in a vibrating system, e.g. radio, sound or sea waves. The *SI* unit of frequency is the Hertz (Hz), one cycle per second. 1 kilohertz, kHz = 1,000 Hz (10^3 Hz): 1 megahertz, MHz = 10^6 Hz: 1 gigahertz, GHz, = 10^9 Hz. The human ear can detect sounds at frequencies roughly between 20 Hz and 20 kHz, lower frequencies being subsonic and higher ultrasonic. Frequency equals speed of wave (electromagnetic radio waves travel at 300,000,000 metres per second) divided by wavelength, and can be found from the formula:

$$\text{Frequency in kHz} = \frac{300,000}{\text{wavelength in metres}}$$

The following frequencies are used by navigational systems and aids, and for radio communication:
Omega 10.2, 11.333 and 13.6 kHz
Sonar 15–250 kHz
Loran C 100 kHz
Decca Main chain 70–130 kHz, Two range 170–180 kHz, High Fix 1700–2000 kHz
Echo sounders about 150 kHz
Consolan 192–194 kHz
Consol 257–363 kHz
Marine *radio beacons* 285–350 kHz
Radio telephony: MF 1605–3800 kHz: HF 3.0–30 MHz: VHF 156–174 MHz
Loran A 1850, 1900, 1950 kHz
Radar 9,200–9,500 MHz
See also *distress frequency* and *propagation.*

Fresh breeze   *Beaufort force* 5, 17–21 *knots.*

Freshen   The *true wind* is said to freshen when its speed increases. When a boat luffs up, say from a broad reach to a close reach, *apparent wind* speed increases, even when the speed of the true wind does not alter.

Freshen the nip   To alter the position of a line under load, so that *chafe* occurs in a different place.

Fresh gale (US)   *Beaufort force* 8, 34–40 *knots.* WMO term: gale.

Fresh water   An opposed to *salt* and *brackish water*, fresh water is found in rivers, canals, lakes etc, and has a salt content of under 0.05 parts per thousand. *Density* is lower, and this is taken into account when a boat is measured in a river for a *rating* or *handicap*. The *specific gravity* of pure water is 1.00, and maximum density is at 4 °C. The term fresh water includes water suitable for drinking, but the fresh water that is supplied for purposes such as boilers is not necessarily drinking water, and in some countries fresh water must be boiled or purified before it is drunk. Can also be distilled from sea water.

Frictional resistance or **skin friction**   The part of the total *resistance* of a hull moving through water, or of a sail over which air flows, that is caused by fluid sliding over the surface of the foil in the *boundary layer;* depends largely on the area and roughness of the surface, and the speed at which

Band			Frequency	Wavelength	
4	VLF	very low frequency	3–30 kHz	10–100 km	myriametric
5	LF	low frequency	30–300 kHz	1,000–10,000 m	kilometric
6	MF	medium frequency	300–3,000 kHz	100–1,000 m	hectometric
7	HF	high frequency	3–30 MHz	10–100 m	decametric
8	VHF	very high frequency	30–300 MHz	1–10 m	metric
9	UHF	ultra high frequency	300–3,000 MHz	10–100 cm	decimetric
10	SHF	super high frequency	3–30 GHz	1–10 cm	centimetric
11	EHF	extremely high frequency	30–300 GHz	1–10 mm	millimetric

the fluid flows. Frictional resistance increases as the square of speed and, at slower speeds, resistance is predominantly due to friction. *Antifouling* is applied to the bottom of a keelboat to prevent marine fouling, which increases roughness and skin friction, while the *wetted surface* of a racing dinghy is rubbed down and made as smooth as possible. The frictional resistance of sails depends on the quality of the sailcloth and is very low when modern materials such as *dacron* and *terylene* and used. See also *Reynolds number*.

Front Sloping boundary between *air masses* of different temperatures; there is a marked change in the weather and, in the northern hemisphere, the wind *veers* as the front passes. A *warm front* slopes gently forward towards the direction in which it is travelling, and warm air replaces cold air. A *cold front*, where cold air replaces warm air,

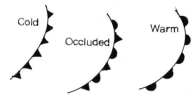

slopes backwards at a steeper angle and travels faster, catching up the warm front and forming an *occluded front*. The *weather code* symbols for occluded, warm and cold fronts are shown in the figure; a quasi-stationary front has triangles and semi-circles on opposite sides.

Frontogenesis A *front* forms or is intensified.

Frontolysis A *front* weakens and disappears.

Froude, William British engineer and naval architect (1810–1879) who successfully used models etc in an experimental tank at Torquay. He stated that hull *resistance* could be divided into independent components, namely *frictional* and residual *resistance*, the former being found to depend on the smoothness and length of the body while the latter followed his Law of Comparison. See also below.

Froude number A dimensionless number: v/√L × g, where v is speed, L length of vessel and g acceleration due to gravity. Indicates the similarity in the pattern of *waves* generated by boats of different sizes but with the same *ratio* of *speed to length*. The same pattern is generated by a model and by the full-size boat when the ratio of the square of speed to *waterline length* is the same. In consequence a model built to a scale of 1:100 is towed in a tank at one-tenth of the speed made by the full-size vessel.

FRP (US) Abbreviation for fiberglass reinforced plastics (see *GRP/FRP*).

Full 1. Of the boat, as opposed to *fine;* descriptive of a relatively *beamy* rounded boat, as in full-lined, full bow, full-bottomed etc. 2. Of speed, maximum as opposed to slow: as in full speed ahead or astern. 3. Of a sail, as opposed to *flat;* with considerable curvature. 4. Of a sail, as opposed to *lifting* or *slatting;* a sail that is drawing and full of wind.

Full and by *Close-hauled* with all sails full and drawing; sailing fast rather than *pinching*.

Full-length battens The battens used in a *fully-battened sail*, q.v.

Full moon When sun and moon are in *opposition* and the moon's surface is fully illuminated by the sun. *Spring tides* usually, but not invariably, occur shortly afterwards.

Fullness or **camber** or **draft** or **belly** The degree to which a sail curves. Fullness is built into the sail by the sailmaker by varying broad seam (the taper of the individual *cloths*), and by cutting *roaches* into the *luff* and *foot*. The fullness or *camber* of a sail can be adjusted to wind strength and the *point of sailing* by adjusting *controls* such as the *cunningham* and *outhaul*, by altering *mast bend* etc, a fuller sail being required when the wind is light and the boat sailing free, whereas a flatter sail is desirable in a fresh breeze when close-hauled to avoid excessive heeling.

Full-rigged ship Carries *square sails* on all her three (or more) *masts*.

Full rudder The maximum angle to which the *rudder* can be turned, but not necessarily the angle at which the rudder produces the greatest turning moment. A dinghy's rudder can often be turned to 90°, but is generally most effective at an angle of about 40° to the *centreline*.

Full sail 1. A boat under full sail has all normal sails set and not *reefed*. 2. A full sail is not *flat*, but has considerable *camber*. 3. A sail is said to be full of wind when it is drawing without *lifting*.

Full sail breeze A moderate to fresh wind, *force 4–5*, in which a vessel can carry full sail and make maximum speed.

Fully-battened sail (UK) or **sail with full-length battens** (US) Normally a *mainsail*, but occasionally a *staysail* supported by many *battens* which run from *luff* to *leech*. They slip into batten pockets and give flexible *sailcloth* a semi-rigid aerofoil shape. Sail *camber* can be altered to suit the strength of the wind and the *point of sailing* by pushing the battens in further to increase *fullness*. Were popular in *gaff-* and *bermudan-rigged* (US marconi-rigged) racing dinghies, but most modern

racing dinghy classes prohibit full-length battens, and they are now seen almost exclusively on *catamarans*. They are considered too unhandy and unreliable for offshore cruisers, apart from those that are *Chinese lug-rigged*.

Funneling Winds blowing along a valley or between mountains may be accelerated markedly when the *isobars* follow the line of the valley. The same effect is felt inland between high buildings.

Furl Roll up or gather and lash a lowered sail with *sail tiers* or *shock cord* to prevent it from blowing about. *Square sails* are furled by gathering them up and lashing them to the *yards*.

Furling gear 1. Fitted so that a *headsail* can be rolled round the *forestay*, a *luff spar* or its own *luff wire* instead of being lowered. Headsail area can only be *reefed* if there is a luff spar and the furling gear incorporates strong bearings top and bottom. The rotating drum to which the *tack* of the sail is attached may be turned by a single line to roll up the sail, but finer adjustment is possible if there are two lines. In some systems the luff spar rotates round a fixed stay; in others the stay itself revolves, and swivels must be incorporated close beneath the mast *tang* and by the drum. Furling gear is also available for *mainsails*. See also *Ljungstrom rig*. 2. System of hooks and shock cord with which a lowered mainsail is furled close to the *boom*, ready for the sail cover to be laced over it, if one is used.

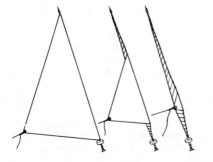

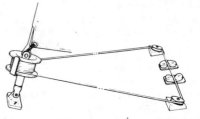

Futtock Part of a wooden hull *frame* that is made in several pieces.

Futtock shrouds Wire rope, chain or iron rods that connect the futtock band on the *lower mast* to futtock plates secured to the side of the *top*; counter the pull of the *topmast rigging*, and support the top. Not related to futtock above, but probably deriving from foothook.

G

G = Golf: yellow-blue-yellow-blue-yellow-blue *code flag*. As a single letter signal means 'I require a *pilot*'. When made by fishing vessels operating in close proximity on the fishing grounds means 'I am hauling my nets.' *Morse code:* — — • (dash dash dot).

Gaff A *spar* which extends the upper part (the *head*) of a quadrilateral gaff sail. The *peak* is the upper outboard end; the inboard end has *jaws*, or else a *saddle* with parrel beads, that fit round the mast. C.f. *gunter-rigged*, a modern development. Normally a gaff is hoisted by the peak *halyard* at the outer end, and by the throat halyard at the mast end, but some are hoisted by a single halyard attached to a *span*.

Gaff cutter A *cutter* with a gaff *mainsail* and more than one *headsail*; often carries a *topsail*.

Gaff-headed As opposed to a triangular *jib-headed* sail, a quadrilateral sail with the *head* attached to a gaff.

Gaff jaws Wooden or metal claw-like horns projecting from the gaff; they partly encircle the mast and are held there, often with *parrel* beads threaded on a jaw rope. A wooden mast may be protected from *chafe* by a *mast band*. See also *saddle*.

Gaff ketch A *ketch* with a gaff *mainsail*; the *mizzen* may be gaff- or *jib-headed*, or a *spritsail*.

Gaff ketch

Gaff-rigged *Fore-and-aft rig* with quadrilateral fore-and-aft gaff sail(s) set on the mast(s).

Gaff-rigged cat A boat with one *mast* stepped near the *bow*; sets a gaff sail and no *headsail*.

Gaff sail Quadrilateral *fore-and-aft sail*, the *head* (upper edge) of which is attached to a gaff while the *foot* is extended by a *boom*. The *luff* (leading edge) is usually *laced* to the mast or held to it with *hoops*; the after edge is the *leech*. The lower corners are the *tack* at the *gooseneck* and the *clew*; the upper corners are the *throat* near the mast and the *peak*. Is usually hoisted by peak and throat *halyards*, but may be hoisted by a single halyard attached to a gaff *span*.

Gaff schooner See *fore-and-aft schooner*.

Gaff sloop A boat with a single *headsail* and a gaff *mainsail*.

Gaff topsail A triangular sail set above the gaff, the *halyard* being led to the *masthead* and the *sheet* to the *peak* of the gaff. The *tack* is attached to a long line, which leads to the deck where it is *belayed*. C.f. *jackyard topsail*.

Gaff yawl A *yawl* with a gaff *mainsail*. The *mizzen* may be *gaff*- or *jib-headed*, or a *spritsail*.

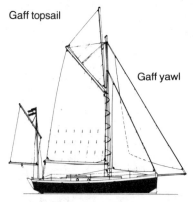

Gaff topsail

Gaff yawl

Gale In the *Beaufort scale*, a near gale is force 7, 28–33 *knots;* a gale is force 8, 34–40 knots; a strong gale is force 9, 41–47 knots. Gale warnings are broadcast in weather forecasts, and storm signals are made on coasts (see *storm warnings*).

Galley Area where food is prepared and cooked.

Gallon Measure of volume (e.g. fuel or water) or capacity (e.g. *bilge pump*). 10 UK gallons is approximately equal to 12 US gallons.
1 UK gal = 4.54609 litres = 1.2009416 US gals.
1 UK gal = 3.7854 litres = 0.83268 UK gals.
1 litre = 0.219969 (0.22) UK gals = 0.26417 US gals.

Gallows Permanent framework, extending almost to the sides of the boat; supports the *boom* when the sail is lowered, when *reefing,* or when a *trysail* is set. A *crutch* is removable.

Galvanic corrosion *Corrosion* that occurs when two metals are immersed in sea-water, which acts as an electrolyte. A galvanic cell is formed and current flows from the *anode* (the less noble metal which corrodes) into the electrolyte, and from the electrolyte to the *cathode,* the more noble metal (see *galvanic series*). To avoid corrosion, the fastenings with which fittings are attached should be made of the same metal, or of one which lies close in the galvanic series; paints containing copper, mercury or bronze must not be applied to light alloy hulls, and *sacrificial anodes* may be required. The latter are made of zinc or magnesium and will corrode in preference to more noble metals, so providing cathodic protection.

Galvanic series The metals are listed from the most noble (*cathode*) to the least noble, i.e. most base, (*anode*), which corrodes: gold, platinum, graphite, silver, titanium, monel alloy, nickel, copper, brass (70/30), silicon bronze, cupro-nickel, gunmetal, brass (60/40), stainless steel (passive), manganese bronze, tin, lead, chromium plate on nickel on steel, stainless steel (active), cast iron, steel, aluminium, zinc, cadmium, galvanized iron, magnesium. See *galvanic corrosion.*

Galvanize To coat iron with a layer of zinc to protect it from *corrosion.* Although a zinc coat can be sprayed on, hot-dip galvanizing is more effective, the object being completely immersed in molten zinc.

Gammon iron Iron band which clamps the *bowsprit* to the *stem.*

Gangway 1. A long narrow plank that connects a boat to the shore. May have treads and a handrail or *manrope* to help maintain balance when boarding or disembarking. 2. Opening in the side of a vessel, or in the *lifelines* (q.v.) through which people embark or disembark.

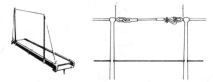

Garboard strakes The *strakes* of planks immediately either side of the *keel.* See *construction* fig.

Gas detector or **bilge sniffer** Instrument that detects the concentration of explosive fumes in an enclosed space. Gives a visual, and often an audible warning.

Gashers (UK) See *whiskers (2).*

Gasket 1. Short piece of line or shock cord, or strip of canvas, which gathers a lowered sail to the *boom, pulpit* etc. See *sail tier.* 2. Watertight packing in a gland or joint. 3. US: seal around a watertight door or where wires etc pass through a watertight bulkhead.

Gate See *mast gate.*

Gate start An alternative method of *starting* a large fleet. The line is not between anchored marks or stationary posts, but extends from the *committee boat* to a motor boat following close behind the pathfinder. He is one of the competitors and sails away from the committee boat *close-hauled* on *port tack.* The remainder of the fleet cross behind the motorboat on *starboard tack* wherever and whenever they wish.

Gate valve A stopcock or *seacock* which closes a pipe by turning a shutter through 90°; usually operated by a lever, which should lie along the pipe when the gate is open and across it when it is shut.

Gather way To start to move through the water.

Gear 1. Part of mechanical equipment (such as *winches*) and the engine; see *reduction* and *reverse gear.* 2. General term applied to the fittings, equipment, rigging etc required for operating a boat, also often used for the crew's clothing and private possessions.

Gear ratio 1. Of a *winch:* the ratio of the number of handle revolutions to the number of drum revolutions. C.f. *mechanical advantage (2)* and *power ratio.* 2. Of an engine: see *reduction gear.*

Gelcoat When making a *GRP/FRP moulding,* the gelcoat is the first coat of *resin* applied to the *mould,* and becomes the outer, unreinforced layer after the *laminate* has been removed from the mould. Pigment is usually added first to provide a coloured moulding. The gelcoat is very thin, about 1/50th of an inch (0.5 mm), and has to be touch dry before proceeding with the *laying-up.* The quality of the moulding is indicated by that of the gelcoat, which protects the underlying laminate from chemical action, abrasion etc. Faults which appear in the gelcoat later, such as *hairline cracks* or *pinholes,* are an indication of poor quality and have to be repaired.

Gel time or **setting time** The time it takes for a *resin* to set to a gel after *catalyst* and *accelerator* have been added.

General chart (US) *Chart* with a *natural scale* between 1:150,000 and 1:600,000.

Generator Machine which converts mechanical energy into electrical energy. Power consumption on board (current drain or battery drain) varies according to how many electronic instruments are used, and the amount of electric lighting and accessories fitted. Normally batteries are charged by an alternator or dynamo driven by the engine, or by a separate auxiliary generator, but this involves carrying too much fuel when making longer voyages in small boats. Several ingenious water- or wind-powered generators have been designed to provide power, e.g. for an *autopilot* when crossing oceans, or to keep batteries charged while the boat lies unattended. *Solar cells* may also be used in areas where sunshine can be relied upon.

Genoa A large *overlapping headsail* set in light to fresh winds on all courses from *close-hauled* to a *broad reach,* sometimes *boomed out* on a *run.*

Named after Genoa in Italy where it was introduced by the Swede, Sven Salen in 1928. *Cloth weight* varies from 3–5 oz US, 4–6 oz UK, 135–200 g/sq m for a light-weather genoa, up to 8 oz US, 10 oz UK, 340 g/sq m for a heavy genoa.

Genoa sheet The *sheet* which trims the genoa. May sometimes be led to a block near the outer end of the boom. See also *headsail sheet lead.*

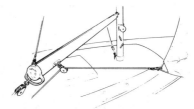

Gentle breeze *Beaufort force* 3, 7–10 *knot* winds.

Geographical north pole The earth rotates about an axis, and the end of the axis that is 90° north of the *equator* is the geographical north pole; *true north.*

Geographical position (GP) The point on the earth where a line from a *heavenly body* to the earth's centre cuts the earth's surface. The heavenly body would be at the *zenith* of an observer situated at its geographical position. US: sometimes called ground position.

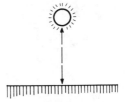

Geographical range The maximum distance at which a light can be seen at night, or at which an *aid to navigation* or some feature can be seen by day, limited only by the observer's *height of eye,* the *elevation* or *height* of the light or object, *refraction,* and the curvature of the earth. The formula is:

Geographical range in *nautical miles* = 1.15 × ($\sqrt{H}$ + $\sqrt{h}$) where H = elevation, and h = height of eye in feet.

Geographical range in *nautical miles* = 2.075 × ($\sqrt{H}$ + $\sqrt{h}$), given H and h in metres.

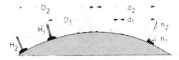

Geostrophic wind The wind that blows at about 2000 ft (600 m) above the earth when the accelerations produced by *pressure gradient* force and *Coriolis force* balance, i.e. the accelerations which result from variations in *atmospheric pressure* between two places and from earth's rotation. The geostrophic wind blows parallel to straight parallel *isobars*, and above the surface layer affected by friction, normally at a speed that is about 150% of that of the wind close above the sea. In the northern hemisphere low pressure is to the left and high pressure to the right.

Ghost To make *headway* slowly when there appears to be no wind.

Ghoster A light, full *headsail*, set in light breezes of force 2 and under; *cloth weight* 1½–2½ oz US, 2–3 oz UK, 60–100 g/sq m.

Gilguy (US) A gadget, such as a lanyard or piece of shock cord which prevents the *halyard* from *slatting* against the mast.

Gimbals Method of suspending an object such as the *compass*, a cooker or paraffin lamp so that it remains horizontal regardless of the boat's *motion*. Consists of two concentric rings which are pivoted at right angles to each other, generally one being pivoted *fore-and-aft* and the other *athwartships*. A cooker may be semi-gimballed, and is then suspended so that it stays level when the boat *heels* or *pitches* but not both.

Gipsy or **gypsy** 1. UK: wheel fitted on one side of a *windlass* and recessed to take the *links* of chain when the *anchor* is being raised (US *wildcat*). The calibrated chain links must match the pattern of the gipsy. 2. US: drum which is fitted to one side of a windlass, and around which turns are taken with with rope anchor cable when the anchor is being raised (UK *warping drum*).

Girder A longitudinal member fitted to increase fore-and-aft strength. In *GRP/FRP* construction, wooden or metal girders may be *laminated* to the shell.

Girth The circumference of the hull from sheer

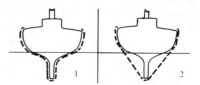

line to sheer line. When a chain or tape is used for measuring (2) the shortest distance or chain girth is found, rather than girth at the skin (1).

Girth station When measuring a boat for an *IOR rating*, the positions forward and aft at which the *girths* are equal to 0.5B (forward girth station, FGS), 0.75B (forward inner, FIGS), 0.75B (after, AGS) and 0.875B (after inner girth station, AIGS); B is rated beam. In some cases these basic stations are relocated. Other rating rules incorporate girth measurements.

Give a lee To position a boat to *windward* of something, such as a person in the water, so as to provide some protection from the wind, and to break the force of the seas.

Give-way vessel In the *IRPCS*, the vessel whose duty it is to keep clear of another; she has to take early and substantial action by altering course in good time, and in such a way that the other vessel can see that she is taking appropriate action to avoid a *collision*.

Glass Often used colloquially for *barometer*, especially with regard to *tendency*, e.g. rising glass.

Glasses Colloquial for *binoculars*.

Glass fibre (US **fiber**) A thin, flexible, spun thread or filament of glass with high *elasticity*, great *tensile strength* and low *stretch*. The reinforcing material used for *GRP/FRP mouldings*. E-glass, which is usual for marine purposes, has an alkali content of under 1% and absorbs virtually no water, but cheaper A-glass has an alkali content of about 15% and is not used for boatbuilding. About 200 filaments are bundled into a strand which is woven into cloth, tape etc. Other forms of glass fibre reinforcing materials include *chopped strand mat*, *surfacing tissue*, scrim, *roving*, *C-flex*.

Glassfibre reinforced plastics, GRP (UK) The US term is fiberglass reinforced plastics, FRP, but fibreglass is a British trade name and the term cannot therefore be used in the UK for the products of other manufacturers. As opposed to unreinforced plastics, from which items such as buckets and containers are made, *GRP/FRP* is a *laminate* composed of *glass fibres* and *resin*. The higher the proportion of glass fibres in a laminate, the stronger it will be and the higher the quality, but the cost is also greater. With *chopped strand mat* reinforcement the proportion of glass is about 28%, with glass cloth or scrim 55%, and with woven *roving* 45%. Solid glassfibre sinks, and *buoyancy* (US flotation) *tanks* or *bags* are required to keep a *capsized* boat afloat, but with *sandwich construction* a foam core between two laminates of solid GRP/FRP provides buoyancy. See also *epoxy* and *polyester resin*.

Global wind circulation The earth is not heated uniformly by the sun's rays, and air would circulate northwards and southwards in cells if earth did not rotate. Warm air rising at the *equator* would flow towards both *poles* at high altitude, sink at the high pressure belts at about 30° N and S, and flow back to the equator near the surface. Similarly cold surface air at the poles would flow towards the equator to about 60° N and S where, having been warmed, it would rise to flow back to the poles at high altitudes. Between them would be a cell in which air would circulate in the opposite direction, rising at the *convergence* zones at 60° N and S, and falling at the *divergence* zones at 30° N and S. However, because earth rotates, *Coriolis force* causes an acceleration at right angles to the direction of motion; winds do not blow north and south to and from the equator, but in a more easterly direction when blowing towards the poles, and in a more westerly direction when blowing towards the equator (see fig).

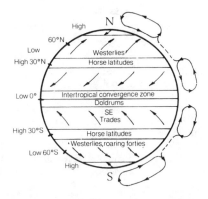

In the *trade wind* belts the NE and SE trades blow at the surface towards the equator from the sub-tropical divergence zones at about 30° N and S. At the *Intertropical Convergence Zone* (the *doldrums*) air rises and flows back at high altitudes to the sub-tropical divergence zones, as the SW and NW anti-trades respectively. Similarly polar winds flow near the surface from the poles to the sub-polar convergence zone, where they rise and flow back to the high pressure zone at the poles. Between these two cells the prevailing surface winds are westerly; many *depressions* form when warm tropical air meets cold polar air, and they chase each other eastward through these temperate latitudes, often in quick succession. This rather

idealized broad outline is greatly modified by geographical features, especially by land masses.

Gnomonic projection The *chart* is taken to be a flat plane touching the spherical earth at a point (the tangent point). Straight lines from the earth's centre, passing through points on the surface, are extended until they reach the chart. Distortion increases with distance from the tangent point, *great circles* appear as straight lines, *meridians* converge towards the poles and *parallels of latitude* are curved. Gnomonic projection is used for small *scale* charts (UK 1:13,500,000–1:32,000,000) because, on longer voyages, the shorter great circle course is preferable to a *rhumb line* course. It is also used for very large scale charts and *harbour plans* which cover only a small area of the earth.

Go about To change from one *tack* to another by *luffing* and turning the *bows* through the wind. See also *tack (2)*.

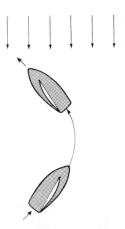

Gong 1. When visibility is restricted, the *IRPCS* require a vessel over 100 m in length to sound a gong in the after part immediately after ringing a *bell* forward, when *anchored* or *aground*. 2. A *fog signal* sounded by an *aid to navigation* such as a buoy; may be sounded mechanically, by hand, or by the action of waves.

Goniometer or **radiogoniometer** A *direction-finding* instrument used in conjunction with a fixed cross-loop (*Bellini-Tosi*) aerial. Two fixed field coils in the goniometer are mounted with their axes at right angles to each other, and a search coil between them is rotated; the *bearing* of a *radio beacon* is found from the direction of the signal *null*.

Gooseneck Fitting which attaches the *boom* to the *mast*, allowing it to move in all directions, i.e. to lift, drop and move sideways. The simplest is a hook on the boom which fits into an eyebolt on the mast. Dinghies often have a round pin with a

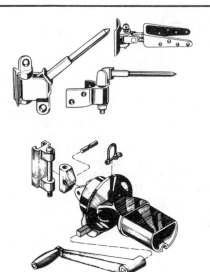

squared section forward, which engages a square hole in a plate on the end of the boom. A sliding gooseneck moves up and down a *track* fastened to the mast. The gooseneck often incorporates *roller reefing* gear.

Goosewing To *boom out* the *headsail* to windward on a run with a *whisker pole* or *spinnaker pole* connected to the mast, or to hold the windward sheet outboard, so that the sail fills on the opposite side to the *mainsail* instead of being *blanketed* by it.

Grab rail, line and **handle** Rails and handles may be fitted at suitable heights above and below decks to grab at when the boat *heels, rolls* or *pitches*. A grab line may be fitted around the *topsides* of a dinghy to be grasped after *capsizing*, as well as round *life-rafts* and *lifeboats*.

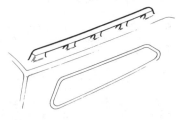

Gradient wind Flow of wind above the surface friction layer along a curved path; cyclonic when *centrifugal force* acts in the opposite direction to *pressure gradient* force, but anticyclonic when it acts in the same direction. The gradient wind is stronger than the *geostrophic wind* when curvature is anticyclonic, but less strong when it is cyclonic, and the greater the path curvature the greater the difference between gradient wind speed and geostrophic wind speed.

Graduation or **notation** A *compass card* may be graduated in degrees or *points* of the compass. Circular: the degrees run clockwise from north 001–360°. Quadrantal (rare): the four quadrants are each graduated in degrees from 0° (north and south) to 90° (east and west), south-east being S45°E. Points: the card is marked in 32 points, each of 11°15'; quarter points between them, each of 2°48'45" are sometimes employed.

Granny knot An incorrectly tied *reef knot*, which must not be used on board; when made with larger rope it slips, but it jams when tied with smaller lines.

Graphite paint A copper-based paint containing graphite, generally applied to planing dinghies and high performance dayboats such as Stars and Dragons. The top coat has to be *rubbed down* with fine grade sandpaper if the boat is to *plane* at maximum speed.

Grapnel A small light *anchor*, usually with four *flukes*, used for recovering objects from the *sea-bed* such as an anchor cable. May be used as a light anchor for dinghies, but the folding type is easier to stow.

Grating Lattice-type floorboards fitted, e.g. over the cockpit *sole* to keep feet clear of water and to keep the sole clean. Metal gratings may be fitted to protect a *skylight* or to provide a platform above an engine.

Great circle Any circle on the surface of the earth, the plane of which passes through the centre of the earth, cutting it into two equal halves. The *equator* is the only *parallel of latitude* that is a great circle, but all *meridians* are semi-great circles, and the number of other great circles is infinite. A portion of a great circle is the shortest distance between two points on the earth's surface (A). On *gnomonic* projection charts it appears as a straight line, but on *mercator* charts (B) as a curve. Radio *bearings* are great circle bearings.

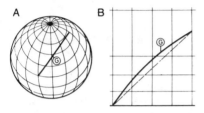

Great circle sailing The *course* selected follows a great circle, rather than the longer *rhumb line* course. A great circle course is, in fact, a succession of rhumb line courses, unless a boat is sailing due north or south, or along the *equator*.

Great Lakes rules of the road Rules of the Road valid for US vessels in the Great Lakes and connecting tributaries, and in the St. Lawrence as far east as Montreal; also valid for all other vessels in the Great Lakes waters under US jurisdiction. There are minor differences from the US *Inland Rules* and the *IRPCS;* for example at night a *sailing vessel* not only exhibits red and green *side lights*, but also shines a torch towards an approaching *power-driven* vessel.

Green seas Solid water taken aboard, not foam or spray; also to ship green water, to take it green.

Green stage The period during which a *GRP/ FRP moulding* matures and gradually becomes hard.

Greenwich Hour Angle, GHA The angle at the *pole* between the *Greenwich meridian* and the *meridian* through a *heavenly body*, measured westwards. The GHA of a heavenly body = GHA *Aries* + the *sidereal hour angle* of the body. *Local Hour Angle* = GHA plus easterly *longitude* or minus westerly longitude.

Greenwich mean time (GMT) or Universal Time *Local mean time* at the *prime meridian;* the Greenwich Hour Angle of the *mean sun* at any particular moment. GMT plus easterly *longitude* or minus westerly longitude equals local mean time; when west of the Greenwich meridian LMT is behind GMT, but when east of Greenwich LMT is ahead of GMT. GMT is the time kept in *zone* zero. The *chronometer* or *deck watch* is set to

GMT, and *time signals* are GMT, because observations and calculations in *celestial navigation* are based on the Greenwich Hour Angle.

Greenwich meridian The *prime meridian, longitude* 0°, which passes through the Greenwich observatory. Longitude is measured from 0–180° east and west of the Greenwich meridian.

Gribble A small marine borer that eats wood.

Grid steering compass A transparent rotatable grid cover, marked in degrees around the circumference, is fitted above a normal *magnetic compass*, and has two parallel lines and a central pointer. The *course* is set by turning the grid cover to the desired *heading*, and the helmsman steers by keeping a clearly marked line on the *compass card* parallel to the line on the grid cover. In some compasses the parallel lines on the cover form a T, which is aligned with three lines on the compass card.

Gripe 1. Member joining the *stem* to the *keel*. 2. A boat that gripes carries too much *weather helm* and continuously tries to *luff up* towards the wind.

Grommet 1. A ring made by unlaying a length of rope and using one strand. The strand is formed into a circle and then taken spirally round again twice, being laid in the space where the other two strands lay originally, and the two ends are tucked against the lay to complete the grommet. Used in canvas work, in a boat with *slings*, to hold oars in *thole pins* etc. 2. Brass eye fitted into a hole in canvas to take a line, lacing etc.

Groove Instead of *slides* and a *track*, many *masts*, *spars* and some *forestays* have a groove into which is fed the *bolt rope* that is sewn along the *luff* and *foot* of a *mainsail*, the luff of a *headsail*, and in the case of a *gaff sail*, sometimes along the *head* as well.

Groove

Grooved luff (head) stay See *headfoil*.

Ground To *run aground* or touch the *bottom*, whether accidentally or, as when rowing ashore, deliberately. After grounding accidentally, a sailing dinghy can often be refloated by raising the *centreboard* and shoving off with a paddle, but a keelboat may have to be *heeled* well over, or lightened by removing gear if she cannot be hauled off by laying out a *kedge*, or with outside assistance. See also *middle, spoil, holding ground* and *over the ground*.

Ground swell Where depths decrease, such as over *shoals, banks* and *bars, a swell* becomes shorter and steeper, and the water is full of sand whipped up from the sea-bed.

Ground tackle A general term for the *anchors, cables* and all the gear required when *anchoring*. Also the components of a *mooring*, such as anchor or *clump*, chain cables, *buoy rope, swivel* etc.

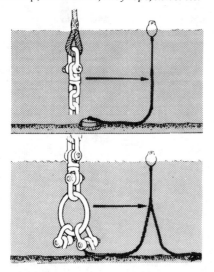

Ground wave A radio wave which travels along or near the surface of the earth, as opposed to a *sky wave* which is reflected back to earth by the ionosphere. The range of ground waves decreases as their *frequency* increases, and medium frequency is therefore used for long distance radio communi-

cation, while very high frequency is restricted to line of sight coastal and ship-to-ship communication.

Group flashing light A *light* exhibited as an *aid to navigation*. Groups of a specific number of *flashes* are separated by *eclipses* of longer duration; chart abbr Fl ( ). Composite group flashing: the number of flashes in a group differs and alternates in a single *period*, e.g. Gp Fl (3 + 4), in each period there is a group of three flashes, an eclipse, a group of four flashes and a second eclipse.

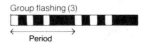

Group flashing (3)

Period

Group occulting light A *light*, exhibited as an *aid to navigation*, which *eclipses* at least twice at regular intervals during one *period*, the total duration of light being longer than the duration of darkness; chart abbr Oc ( ). Composite group occulting: the number of occultations in a group differs and alternates in a single period, e.g. Gp Occ (2 + 3), in each period there is a group of two occultations, followed by light, and a group of three occultations, followed by light.

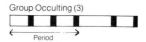

Group Occulting (3)

Period

Grow The direction in which the *anchor cable* leads from the vessel.

Groyne (UK) or **groin** (US) A low structure, often made of wood or stone, built like a dam at right angles to the shore to control the direction of water flow. May be erected to encourage or discourage silting, or to prevent erosion. *Eddies* often occur between groynes.

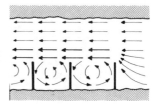

GRP/FRP Abbreviation used in this dictionary, GRP being the UK abbr for *glassfibre reinforced plastics* and FRP the US abbr for fiberglass reinforced plastics.

Guardrail or **lifeline** Safety lines fitted round a boat to prevent the crew from falling overboard. See *lifeline* and c.f. *bulwark*.

Gudgeon A *rudder* fitting. The eye or socket into which the *pintle* (q.v.) is slipped.

Gunkholing (US) Cruising in uncrowded shallow waters, gunkholes being waters too shallow for commercial shipping, such as coves, bays, small rivers etc.

Gunter rig A *spar* (gaff, sometimes called yard) is hoisted to form a considerable, almost vertical extension of the mast above the *masthead*. Although the sail has four sides, the angle at the *throat* between the *head* and the *luff* is extremely obtuse, and the rig differs very little in appearance and aerodynamic efficiency from triangular *bermudan* (US marconi) *rig*. Preferable for boats that are trailed because the mast is so much shorter. Is thought to have been invented by Edmund Gunter.

Gunter schooner Two-masted boat, the *main-mast* aft being the same height or taller than the *foremast*; both are gunter-rigged.

Gunwale Broadly, the upper edge of the side of a boat (US also rail). A wale is a strong *strake* fastened to the side of a wooden hull, the gunwale being the *longitudinal member* at the *sheer*. The term is often applied to a wale fastened outside the *skin*, sometimes to a *stringer* fitted inside the top strake above the *timberheads*.

Gust Sudden increase in wind speed, of short duration; in the northern hemisphere the wind often *veers*. Gusts occur particularly frequently in *thunderstorms* and when *warm* and *cold fronts* pass, also along cliffy coasts when they strike downwards at an angle and cause boats to heel more than usual. When gusty winds are forecast, the wind is likely to shift and increase considerably in strength from time to time.

Guy A line attached to the end of a *spar* to hold it in position, such as the spinnaker guy (or brace, Aus), which is attached to the spinnaker tack, leads through the spinnaker pole end fitting to a block or sheave right aft and forward to a winch or direct to the crew. A *foreguy* leads forward from the boom, an afterguy leads aft.

Gybe (UK) or **jibe** (US) To change from one *tack* to the other by turning the *stern* through the wind, as opposed to tacking or going about when the *bows* pass through the wind. The helmsman *bears away* until the wind strikes the opposite side of the *mainsail*, which usually has been *hardened in*, the *boom* and sail swing over to the opposite side, and the helmsman immediately has to counteract the boat's tendency to *luff up* sharply; at the same time the *sheet* is *eased* rapidly. The *spinnaker* can be kept full and drawing while the boat is gybed, the pole being moved from one side to the other and the sheet and guy adjusted.

In light breezes or when racing in dinghies the *mainsheet* may not be hardened in, and the boat is then gybed all standing; the boom swings from square out on one side to square out on the other, assisted by the helmsman or crew who grabs all the parts of the mainsheet and pulls the sail over at the right moment. The faster a dinghy is sailing the safer it is to gybe because, on a run, the *apparent wind* strength decreases as boat speed increases. See also *dip-pole gybe*.

As defined in the *racing rules*, a yacht begins to gybe when, with the wind aft, the *foot* of her mainsail crosses her *centreline*, and she completes the gybe when the mainsail has filled on the other tack. While gybing during a race, she must keep clear of other yachts that are on a tack.

Although gybing used to be a slow and often risky affair, when boats had long booms, *gaffs* and *running backstays* which had to be manned on either side, modern yachts and dinghies can be gybed quickly and easily. Whereas with some modern *catamarans* gybing is preferable to tacking, just as used to be the case with *square-rigged* ships, there are occasions (e.g. to avoid the possibility of *broaching* in high seas) when it is better to alter course from one *broad reach* to the other by *close-hauling,* tacking and then bearing away to a broad reach instead of gybing. Gaff-rigged boats and those with running backstays may find this preferable, in spite of the extra time it takes, because there is more time to set up the lee runner, which becomes the windward runner on the new tack; the mast is supported permanently and there is no danger of a *Chinese gybe.*

A boat is sometimes said to be on port or starboard gybe when she is running or on a very broad reach with her boom to starboard or port respectively. The term is not used in the *IRPCS* or the racing rules. See also *accidental gybe* and *wear.*

Gybe-o (US **jibe-o**) Helmsman's warning that he is putting the helm up to gybe; the crew must man the sheets and be prepared for the boom to swing over rapidly to the other side.

Gypsy See *gipsy.*

Gyro compass This *compass* indicates the direction of *true north,* because it operates without relying on *magnetism.* The axis of a gyroscope which is spinning rapidly points in a certain direction and, by making use of the effects of gravity and the rotation of the earth, the gyro compass is made to seek true north. Current models are based on the two-gyro principle and rotate at about 20,000 rpm but, although more accurate than a *magnetic compass,* are not suitable for small sailing boats because they require a relatively stable platform.

H = Hotel: white and red *code flag*. As a single letter signal means 'I have a *pilot* on board'. *Morse code:* •••• (dot dot dot dot).

Hail 1. To shout loudly to another boat. When racing, a *right-of-way* yacht must hail before making an unexpected alteration of course, except when she has *luffing rights;* she may hail to claim that she has established an *overlap*, or for *room* to tack at an *obstruction*. She may also hail '*mast abeam*' to prevent or stop another boat from luffing her. 2. A form of precipitation that often occurs during *thunderstorms;* pieces or balls of ice 5–50 mm in diameter are formed when water droplets in the air are swept up to a great height in *cumulonimbus* clouds and cooled.

Hairline cracks Tiny, barely noticeable cracks crazing the *gelcoat* of a *GRP/FRP moulding;* they are a sign of poor quality and require attention to avoid trouble when water, oil or chemical substances permeate the unprotected *laminate* beneath, when the gelcoat may start to break off. Possible causes are too thin a gelcoat, too early an application of the first layer of laminate, or too weak a moulding.

Half beam A *deck beam* which does not extend the full breadth of the boat but stops at a *carling*, e.g. at the *cockpit*, in way of the *coachroof* (US trunk), *hatches* etc. See *construction* fig.

Half breadth plan Part of the *lines plan;* shows the shape of half the symmetrical hull, viewed from above, as a series of horizontal cross sections, the *waterlines*. The *diagonals* are often drawn on the other side of the *centreline*.

Half convergency A *bearing* on a *radio beacon* is a *great circle* bearing and, if the beacon is further than 50 miles distant, is converted into a mercatorial bearing before being plotted on a *mercator* chart. The difference is greatest when vessel and beacon are due east and west of each other. The approximate formula is:
Half convergency = ½ *difference of longitude* × sin mean *latitude*. The correction is always applied towards the *equator* (i.e. in the northern hemisphere the correction is added to a great circle bearing between 000° and 180° but subtracted from one between 180° and 360°; the reverse applies in the southern hemisphere).

Half-decked Part of the *hull* is decked; usually there is a *foredeck, side decking* and, possibly, a small *afterdeck*.

Half ebb (or **half flood**) Terms sometimes used to describe a *tide* that is half way between *high* and *low water*, (or half way between low and high water).

Half hitch The simplest knot; a turn is taken round the *standing part*. Rarely used alone, but is part of many bends such as a *round turn and two half hitches, fisherman's bend* etc.

Half mast A *flag* or *ensign* flown part of the way down an *ensign staff* or *flagstaff*, usually as a sign of mourning, whether national or on the death of the owner or a yacht club officer. The ensign should be first hoisted right up before being lowered to the dipped position, and the reverse procedure adopted when lowering at sunset.

Half model   Model of half the hull of a boat, reduced in scale generally by 1:20 or 1:40, and mounted on a board. Formerly served as a model to which the full scale boat was built.

Half tide   Water level is half way between *high* and *low water* levels. Thus a half-tide rock is awash at half tide, and a half-tide harbour can only be entered or left during the last half of the *flood* and the first half of the *ebb. See tide* fig.

Half Ton Class   A *level rating* class, the maximum *rating* being 22.0 ft. A typical boat's measurements are LOA 32.83 ft (10 m), LWL 24 ft (7.30 m), beam 9.7 ft (2.95 m), draft 5.75 ft (1.75 m), displacement 9000 lbs (4.1 tonnes), ballast keel 3,740 lbs (1.7 tonnes), mainsail area 172 sq ft (16 sq m), genoa 344 sq ft (32 sq m), foretriangle 225 sq ft (21 sq m). The Half Ton Cup, the Coupe Internationale Atlantique, was presented by the Société des Régates Rochelaises. Five races are sailed; three Olympic courses, single points, about 22 n. miles long, plus two offshore races lasting about 27 hours and 54 hours, counting 1.5 and double points respectively (about 125 and 250 n. miles long). National teams of three boats compete for the Coupe du Marquis de Lareinty Tholozan, presented by the Cercle de la Voile de Paris. The number of crew is five.

Halyard or **halliard**   Line or rope, wire rope or *tackle* with which a *sail, spar, flag* etc is hoisted up a *mast* or *staff*. Each is named after the sail or object it serves, e.g. spinnaker, main and burgee halyards. Is either *belayed* to a *cleat* or fed onto a *halyard winch*, and may also be tensioned by *swigging* or *sweating up*. Originally for hauling a *yard* aloft.

Halyard lock   A device at the top of the mast; keeps the *luff* absolutely taut after the load has been taken off the *halyard*, which consequently can be lighter, so saving weight up high. In the figure a ball (1) in the halyard close above the *headboard* engages in a catch (2). Sail *camber* is thus not affected by a stretching halyard. There are other types.

Halyard or **reel winch**   *Winch* for *hoisting* sails with a wire rope *halyard*, which is wound round

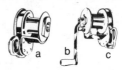

and stored on the drum like a fishing line. Generally has a brake to stop the halyard running back. Drum capacity varies with wire diameter, for example the same drum can take 118 ft (36 m) of 1/8 in (3 mm) wire, or 56 ft (17 m) of 3/16 in (5 mm) wire. The case (a) guides the wire onto the drum, and prevents it from springing off; the winch handle (b) is removable; (c) is the friction brake. A secondary track is often provided to increase the *power ratio* for the last few turns and to reduce crimping. Some have two *gear ratios*, say a high gear of 1:1 for rapid initial hoisting and a low gear of 4 or 5:1 for tensioning. The advantages are that the deck is kept clear by the mast and that wire, being smaller in diameter, takes up less room than rope, but these are offset by the facts that the halyard may jam on the reel, and that operation is rather slower than with an ordinary winch and a rope-tailed wire halyard.

Hambro line   Thin line made of three *strands* of tarred *hemp yarn*.

Hampered vessel   Earlier versions of the *IRPCS* stated that smaller power-driven vessels should not hamper the safe passage of vessels which could navigate safely only inside a narrow channel, but the verb hamper does not appear in the current IRPCS. The term hampered vessel is, however, often used to describe a vessel which is unable to manoeuvre freely owing to her occupation or condition, and is therefore unable to give way; she could be *not under command* or a *vessel engaged in fishing, restricted in her ability to manoeuvre* or *constrained by her draft*, e.g. a minesweeper, trawler, *dredger* or cable-layer at work, or a deep-draft vessel in a *narrow channel*, tug with *tow* etc.

Hand   1. To lower a sail. 2. To haul in the *log*. 3. Of features and objects, indicates direction to one or other side in relation to the vessel, e.g. a *port hand buoy* is left to port when entering a channel, but is left on the *starboard* hand when outward bound. 4. A member of the crew, as in foredeck hand, one who works on the foredeck. Hence single-handed, a vessel with one crew, and short-handed, a vessel with less crew than she normally requires. A paid hand is a crew member who is not an amateur and, when a difficult job has to be done, all hands are called on deck.

Hand-bearing   compass   Portable   *magnetic compass* with which visual *bearings* can be taken. Almost all have some form of illumination so that they can be used at night (battery or beta). The traditional type has a normal *compass card* and

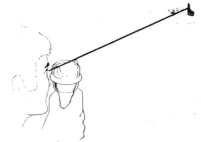

relatively large bowl; the bearing is taken by aligning a mark on the compass glass with the object, and with a notch in the prism mounted on the rim of the compass. There are several much more compact modern designs, some of which are considerably easier to use; latterly a digital type has appeared. See also *bino-compass, compass monocular.*

Handed *Winches* or engines are said to be handed when they are mounted in pairs and rotate in opposite directions.

Handicap In order to enable boats of different types and sizes to race against each other, they are either measured and given a *rating* (e.g. *IOR*), or past performance is compared (e.g. *Portsmouth Yardstick*). Each competitor has a *time allowance*, which is applied either to the time the boat takes to complete the *course* (time on time) or to the length of the course (time on distance), the former system being preferred in the UK and the latter in the USA. Hence handicap racing, class etc.

Hand laid-up A method of building *GRP/FRP mouldings*, which is expensive on account of the manual labour involved. *Chopped strand mat* and woven *roving* are laid by hand (as opposed to being sprayed by a gun) over or in a *mould*, impregnated with *resin*, and rolled or brushed to press the reinforcing material down and to force out air bubbles. The one smooth surface obtained is the outer *gelcoat*, which is the first layer to be applied to the mould. The *laminate* is made up of several layers of glassfibre reinforcing materials and resin, and better control of thickness is possible than with *spray moulding*.

Hand over hand To haul on a rope or line continuously by using alternate hands without pausing, each hand taking the load in turn.

Hand pump See *piston pump*.

Handrail, handhold A wooden or metal rail which can be grasped to steady a person working on or below deck. Often fitted on the *coachroof* (US trunk). Below deck, part of a *bulkhead* or cabin fitment may have a hole cut in it to provide a handhold to grasp. US: the *lifeline* (guardrail) is sometimes termed handrail.

Handsomely To lower away on a *tackle*, or to *hoist*, or to ease out a line gradually and carefully; formerly slowly, now generally at a steady rate, without delaying or hurrying.

Handy Describes a boat that *answers the helm* well and is easy to manoeuvre. The shorter and deeper the *keel* or *centreboard* and the nearer the *rudder* to the *stern*, the quicker a boat will turn; for example a sailing dinghy is handy.

Handy billy A *tackle* with one single and one double *block*, with a hook or *tail* on each, kept ready to apply extra power where needed.

Hanging knee Wooden or metal *knee* attached vertically to connect a *deck beam* to the *hull*.

Hanging locker A locker in which to hang clothes.

Hank (UK) 1. or **snap** (US) A fitting made of stainless steel, bronze, nylon etc by which the *luff* of a *staysail* is held to a *stay*. May be a simple hook shape, or a spring-loaded *piston hank*. Because hanks increase *windage* and disturb airflow, many racing boats use a *headfoil*; others *set* a headsail *flying*, but the *leading edge* has to be taut. To hank on is to attach a sail to a stay with hanks. 2. *Small stuff* is often sold by the hank.

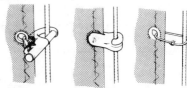

Harbor chart (US) See *harbour plan*.

Harbour (UK) or **harbor** (US) A natural or artificial area of water where vessels can safely *anchor*, tie up to *mooring buoys*, go *alongside* etc.

Harbour (UK) or **harbor** (US) **dues** Payment for the use of a harbour. The amount varies according to the length and type of boat, how long she is in harbour, and whether she is moored alongside, anchored or secured to a mooring buoy.

Harbour (UK) or **harbor** (US) **master** The man in charge of a harbour. He is contacted on arrival so that he can allocate a *berth* to the boat, and harbour dues are usually paid to him.

Harbour plan (UK) or **harbor chart** (US) A large scale plan or *chart* which provides very detailed information about a small area. *Natural scale* 1:50,000 or greater, but may be as large as 1:5,000.

Hard 1. (not US) A firm part of the foreshore where the crew can land; often artificial with a gravel or concrete surface over which boats can be hauled, or dinghies and small boats launched on trailers and trolleys. 2. Of the *helm*, see hard down.

Hard a-lee Helmsman's warning that he is putting the helm down and *going about*. Mainly US, the UK equivalent being *lee-o*.

Hard and fast Said of a vessel that has *run aground* and is unable to get off immediately.

Hard chine or (US) **vee bottom** As opposed to *round bilge*, the *bottom* meets the *topsides* at an angle. This form of construction is popular for wooden boats because it is easier to build. Virtually restricted to plywood boats since the introduction of *GRP/FRP*. See also *double chine*.

Hard down, hard up and **hard over** Of the *helm*, when the *tiller* is put as far as possible to *leeward* (down), to *windward* (up) or to one or other side (over).

Harden or **harden in** To haul in the *sheets* and bring the sail closer to the *centreline*; the opposite of *easing*. The sheets should be hardened in when the boat *luffs up* or when the wind *heads*.

Hardener Chemical added to *polyester resin, epoxy adhesives* etc to initiate *polymerization* (see *catalyst*).

Hard on the wind *Close-hauled* with the *sheets hardened* right in, *pointing* as close to the wind as possible without *pinching*.

Hard racing antifouling A very poisonous paint which maintains toxicity in air for eight weeks without being immersed, and is therefore suitable for wooden or *GRP/FRP* boats which are not left in the water but are trailed or kept on shore.

Contains heavy metals and is unsuitable for metal hulls because *galvanic corrosion* is initiated. When applied to a racing boat, can be *rubbed down* wet with fine grade wet-and-dry sandpaper to reduce *skin friction*.

Harp or **bow shackle** A *shackle* with curved sides, whereas a *D-shackle* is straight-sided.

Hatch An opening in the *deck* which provides access to the *accommodation*. May be round, oval or rectangular, and has a raised *coaming* round the edges to prevent water entering the boat when the hatch is open and a hatch cover(s) which fit(s) over the coaming. The forehatch usually has a

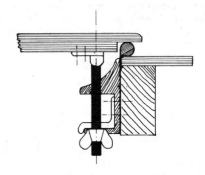

hinged cover which may be translucent, and hatch clips similar to that in the figure so that it can be screwed down tight over a sealing strip and made watertight. The main *companion* hatch is usually a sliding hatch.

Hatchboard See *washboard*.

Haul 1. To pull on an *anchor cable*, or on a line or rope such as an inhaul, outhaul, downhaul or uphaul. 2. Of wind: US to *veer*, q.v. UK: haul ahead, the wind *heads;* haul aft, the wind *frees*. 3. A boat is said to haul her wind when she *luffs up*. 4. US: see *haul out*.

Hauling part The part of the *fall* of a *tackle* to which power is applied.

Haul out (US often just **haul**) To take a boat out of the water, usually on a *cradle* or, if a sailing dinghy, on a *trolley*, whether after a sail, to *lay* her *up*, or to inspect or repair the *bottom*.

Haven A place where a vessel can take refuge from the weather, and which can be entered at *low water*.

Hawse 1. When a vessel is lying to two *anchors*, the area between the *bows* and the anchors; foul hawse when the *anchor cables* cross each other, open hawse when they are clear. 2. Coll: sometimes used as an abbr for *hawse hole*.

Hawse hole A hole in the *bulwark* through which the *anchor cable* passes. In large vessels, the cable runs through a heavy hawsepipe in which a *stockless anchor* may be stowed when not in use.

Hawser Heavy rope or wire used on larger vessels for *towing, berthing* etc.

Hawser-laid When making rope, three *strands,* consisting of *yarns* twisted *left-handed,* are *laid right-handed.* Ropes used on board are normally hawser-laid, and are stronger than four-stranded *shroud-laid* rope of the same size.

Hazard A *danger* to navigation. Hazard is preferred in the US, danger in the UK.

Haze *Visibility* is reduced to 0.5–1 n.mile (1–2 km) by invisible dry particles in suspension in the air. *Relative humidity* is under 95% (c.f. *mist*).

Head 1. The *bow* or forward part of a vessel, ship's head; hence *heading* (q.v.) and to head, i.e. to sail in a certain direction. 2. The upper end of vertical parts of a boat, such as the *rudder* head, *masthead, stemhead, timberhead.* 3. The upper corner of a triangular *jib-headed* sail to which the *halyard* is *bent* or *shackled (see sail* fig.). 4. The upper edge of a quadrilateral sail such as a *gaff sail,* i.e. the edge between the *throat* near the mast and the *peak* at the outer end of the gaff. 5. The upper edge of a *square sail.* 6. US: the toilet or WC. The UK term is heads. 7. A fairly high and steep part of the land that projects into the sea. 8. The seaward end of a pier or similar structure. 9. Of wind, opposite of to free; to shift in direction, blowing from a direction nearer the bow (see *heading wind* and *head wind and sea*).

Headboard Wooden, metal or plastics reinforcement at the head of a triangular sail, especially the *mainsail.* May be of varying shape to distribute the load applied by the halyard. Unless otherwise prescribed in class rules, size is limited fore-and-aft to 3% of the *boom* length because it affects the shape of the *roach.*

Header 1. See *heading wind.* 2. US: See *carling.*

Headfoil Streamlined fairing with groove into which the headsail luff slides. May be formed by two mating light alloy *extrusions* which fit over the existing wire *forestay,* or may be a single rod.

Sometimes has one groove, but usually has two which may be side by side or one forward and one aft of the foil. A *feeder* at the base of the groove facilitates entry of the sail. An efficient headfoil reduces *forestay sag,* provides a clean *leading edge* and enables sail drill to be speeded up, particularly when replacing one headsail with another. Its smooth surface also means that a collapsed spinnaker is more likely to slide off than wrap round it. Other terms are used by various manufacturers, such as luff foil, luff groove extrusion, grooved luff stay, and foil. Luff groove devices, the term used in the *IOR,* carry a small penalty.

Heading The direction in which a boat's head is pointing, her *course.*

Heading wind, or **header** or **knock** The wind shifts to blow from a direction nearer the *bow* (opp *freeing wind*). When on a *reach,* the sails have to be *hardened in* when the wind heads. If the wind shifts when two boats are *beating* on opposite *tacks,* one will be headed and have to *bear away* to fill her sails, but the wind frees for the other, which can *luff up* or *ease* sheets. The wind also appears to head temporarily when the speed of the *true wind* drops, because the *apparent wind* then blows from nearer the bow; boats close-hauled on opposite tacks would then both be headed.

Head-on The *IRPCS* require that *power-driven* vessels meeting on *reciprocal* or nearly reciprocal courses must both alter course to *starboard* to avoid collision.

Headroom The distance between the cabin *sole* and the *deckhead* is standing headroom, and may be based on a tall man of 6 ft 2 in (1.88 m), or an average man of 5 ft 8½ in (1.74 m); often limited to a small area near the *companion.* A tall man requires about 3 ft 2 in (0.96 m) sitting headroom beneath *side decks,* and an average man 2 ft 11½ in (0.90 m).

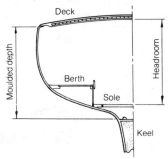

Head rope (US **head fast** or **line**) *Mooring line* which runs forward from the *bows* to a *bollard* on shore, to a *pile* or to some other object.

Heads UK: the toilet or WC. The term is used in the singular in the US.

Headsail Any sail set forward of the *mast*, or of the *foremast* if there is more than one mast. Most *sloop-rigged* sailing dinghies set a single headsail, the *jib*, whereas a *cutter* sets a *staysail* abaft a jib, sometimes with a *jib topsail* above it. Headsails of varying shapes and sizes are set in the *foretriangle* to suit the wind strength and *point of sailing*, the normal *working sail* being a jib or flat-cut *genoa*. A large *reaching genoa, star-cut spinnaker, big boy, spinnaker* etc may be set in lighter breezes and on downwind courses. A smaller and often heavier *spitfire* or *storm jib* is set in strong winds.

Headsail sheet lead The *sheet* attached to the headsail is normally led to a point on the deck which is approximately on the extension of the line that bisects the angle at the *clew*. One end runs through a *fairlead* or *block* to *port*, and the other to *starboard* of the *mast*, then back to the crew or to the *sheet winch* in the *cockpit*. The *leeward* sheet is the one hauled taut, except when the headsail is *boomed out* or *backed* deliberately. The sheet has to be led correctly if the sails are to develop full power; for example, if it is led too close to the *centreline*, air exhausted from the headsail *leech* may *backwind* the *mainsail* at the *luff*. A simple dinghy with one headsail usually has a fixed fairlead on the side deck, but more sophisticated racing dinghies and keelboats generally have a *sliding fairlead* mounted on a *track* so that it can be moved further forward or aft according to which sail is set, and to adjust sail *camber* to the *point of sailing* and the strength of the wind. Thwartship tracks are also fitted, the fairleads being positioned further inboard in light breezes and further outboard in fresher winds; a *barber hauler* serves the same purpose. Some

sliding fairleads for small boats incorporate a *jam cleat*, others just have a block or eye. The jib sheet of smaller boats is held by the crew, but that of larger boats is led aft to the cockpit, often to a sheet winch, and *cleated*.

Head sea Seas that approach from the direction in which the boat is heading.

Head spring or **fore spring** *Mooring line* made fast to a point near the *bows;* runs aft to a *bollard* on shore or to a boat *alongside*.

Headstay Alternative term for *forestay;* runs from high on the mast to the *stemhead fitting*.

Head to wind The *stem* points exactly into the wind, whether the boat is at *anchor* or *under way*.

Head up 1. To sail closer to the wind, to *luff up*. 2. A head-up display is one where instrument readings are projected electronically onto the windshield of a powered vessel.

Headway Movement forward through the water, *stem* first, as opposed to *sternway* when movement is stern first.

Head wind A wind that blows from the direction towards which the boat wishes to sail; opp *fair wind*. A boat under sail has to *beat* to reach her objective.

Heart 1. The jute or hemp rope in the centre of *wire rope*, around which the *strands* are laid (c.f. *core*). Fills the space between the strands, which bed themselves into it. When the wire is dressed with oil, the lubricant is squeezed out and protects the inner surfaces of the strands. 2. The inner strand of *shroud-laid* rope.

Heat exchanger When an engine is cooled indirectly, fresh water circulates in a fully-enclosed circuit, and is itself cooled in the heat exchanger by sea-water.

Heave 1. To pull strongly on a rope or line, often with the help of a *winch* or *windlass*. 2. To throw, as in heaving line, heave the lead. 3. The vertical motion of a vessel as she is lifted by seas or swell. 4. To become visible, as heave in sight when a vessel appears over the horizon.

Heavenly body Sun, moon, planet or star. The positions of stars are given for every third day in the *Nautical Almanac,* but the positions of the other bodies are given hourly. See *declination, Greenwich Hour Angle, Sidereal Hour Angle, Aries*.

Heave short To heave in on the *anchor cable* until the boat is nearly over the anchor.

Heave the lead   Take a *sounding* by casting the *lead* and line into the water some distance ahead of a moving boat.

Heave to or **lie to**   Dinghies or keelboats heave to simply by *tacking* in the normal way, but the *jib* is left sheeted on the original side so that it is *backed;* the *helm* usually has to be *lashed* to *leeward* to keep the boat balanced. When hove to the boat makes little or no *headway* but considerable *leeway,* and lies relatively quietly. A boat may heave to in light weather, say when waiting or when identifying landmarks. In heavy weather she rides the waves more easily when hove to under

storm jib and *trysail,* and lies with the wind and sea about two points (20–25°) *forward of the beam.* The *slick* that she leaves to windward when she makes leeway causes most seas to break some way before reaching her, and many sailors prefer to heave to when *riding out* a storm.

Heaving line   A light, flexible line thrown to bridge the gap between a boat and, say, a man on shore when coming *alongside.* A heavier rope, such as a *mooring line* or *tow-rope,* is attached to one end; a *monkey's fist* may be made in the other, or a weight attached to it to help it fly through the air. Several *bights* are held in the throwing hand, and the remainder is held neatly *coiled* in the other hand so that the line can run out freely to its full extent when thrown. See also *messenger.*

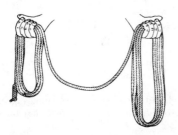

Heavy air (US) Strong wind.

Heavy displacement   A relatively heavy *hull* that displaces a greater amount of water than the *light displacement* hulls favoured today. Often has a long keel.

Heavy weather   Rough; high seas and strong winds.

Heel   1. To lean over to one side; a temporary condition when the boat turns about her longitudinal axis in response to a heeling force, usually the wind. Repeated inclination to either side is *rolling;* if the state of inclination is continuous the boat is said to *list.* A boat may be heeled deliberately by the crew, for example to help the sails to fill and reduce *wetted area* in light breezes, or to try to *refloat* a boat that has *run aground* by shifting weight and/or using wind pressure. A boat that heels easily is said to be *tender,* one that heels less easily is *stiff.* Waves also cause a boat to heel and roll. 2. The inboard or lower end of a *spar.* 3. The lowest point of the *keel, rudder, frame* etc. See also *mast heel.*

Heeling error   *Magnetic compass error* that occurs when a boat heels because of the change in the relative positions of the compass and, say, the engine or iron ballast keel. If heeling error is appreciable and cannot be reduced satisfactorily with *corrector magnets,* it may even be necessary to draw up two *deviation tables,* one for port and one for starboard tack.

Heeling force   The component of total aero-

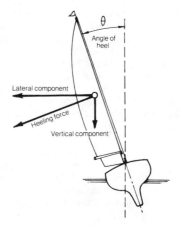

dynamic force that acts at right angles to the boat's course through the water. Has both a lateral component acting horizontally, and a vertical component acting downwards. Heeling, which causes hull *resistance* and *weather helm* to increase, is countered in dinghies by *sitting* (US hiking) *out* or using a *trapeze*. See *force* fig.

Heeling moment The product of heeling force F, acting through the *centre of effort,* and the distance a, between the CE and the *centre of lateral resistance.* When the boat is in a state of equilibrium, heeling moment is equal to *righting moment.* Heeling moment can be decreased by reducing the area of sail set so as to lower the CE, or by pulling the centreboard part way up to raise the CLR. A heeling moment is applied during an *inclining test* by suspending weights outboard.

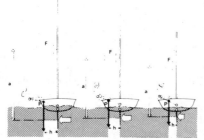

Height The vertical distance between a point and a reference datum level. Heights of natural features above sea level are given on UK *charts* above *MHWS* in tidal waters and above *MSL* elsewhere, in feet on fathom charts and in metres on metric charts; on many US charts heights are given above *MHW.* Heights of *drying features* which cover and uncover are given above *chart datum,* and are usually underlined, i.e. above *LAT* or *MLWS* on UK charts, and above *MLW* on US Atlantic charts or above *MLLW* on US Pacific charts. Heights of *lighthouses* etc are given under height of structure in the *Lists of Lights,* but the height of the light itself is given under *elevation.*

Height of eye Owing to the curvature of the earth, the distance that an observer can see is limited by the height of his eye above the surface of the water. The formula for finding the distance from the observer to the horizon can be found under *distance of the visible horizon* (see also *geographical range).* Approximate distance off can be found by varying the height of eye. Height of eye also affects *sights* and *vertical sextant angles;* see *dip.*

Height of tide The distance between sea level and *tidal* (chart) *datum* at any instant. Tables and curves are provided in *Tide Tables* so that heights can be calculated for any time between *high* and *low water.* See also *twelfths rule* and *chart datum* fig.

Height of wave Vertical distance from crest to trough.

Helm The *tiller* or *wheel,* and all the *steering gear.*

Helm or **rudder angle** The angle the *rudder blade* makes with the *centreline.* Is exactly equal to the angle the *tiller* makes with the centreline, but is not necessarily the same as the *angle of attack* (i.e. when the boat is altering course – see *rudder). Resistance* increases when the helm is at an angle.

Helm angle indicator A pointer which moves over a graduated arc, indicating the angle between the *rudder* and the *centreline.*

Helmsman The member of the crew who steers the boat with the *tiller* or *wheel.*

Hemp Fibres up to 10 ft (3 m) long obtained from the hemp plant. Formerly widely used to make rope which was particularly suitable for sheets, *tensile strength* being high and *stretch* low, but has been superseded by synthetic fibres except for small sizes of cordage.

Herculon Trade name for American *polypropylene* fibres used for making rope.

Hertz *SI* unit of *frequency,* named after the German physicist Heinrich Hertz (1857–1894). One hertz Hz = one cycle per second: 1 kilohertz, kHz = 1000 Hz (formerly 1 kilocycle, kc): 1 megahertz MHz = 1,000,000 or 10^6 Hz: 1 gigahertz GHz = 10^9 Hz.

High 1. An area of high pressure, an *anticylone.* 2. A boat is said to *point* high when she sails close to the wind, and higher when closer.

High and dry Said of a vessel that is *aground* and surrounded by drying *sea-bed* after the tide has *ebbed.*

Highest Astronomical Tide (HAT) The highest level predicted, based on any combination of astronomical conditions.

Highfield lever Tensioning lever, used especially for *running backstays*. See *runner lever*.

High focal plane buoy (UK) Anchored *aid to navigation* with a tall central structure so that the light can be seen from a greater distance. Often laid as a *landfall buoy*.

High seas 1. All parts of the seas and oceans that lie beyond the Territorial limits, i.e. beyond the jurisdiction of states, and not included in the *Territorial Waters* or internal waters of states, 2. Seas are said to run high when they are big.

High water, HW The time in a tidal cycle when *height of tide* is greatest; the highest level reached by that *tide*. HW *springs* and *neaps* are the maximum and minimum HW heights respectively that occur during half a *lunar month*. When there is *diurnal inequality* there is a higher HW and a lower HW daily. See *tide* fig.

Hike out US equivalent of to *sit out* (UK) or swing (Aus). Hence hiking board (see *sliding seat*), hiking stick (see *tiller extension*), hiking strap (see *toe strap*). Other aids enable the crew to keep their weight outboard for long periods so as to keep a sailing dinghy on an *even keel*, for example a handle fitted to the side deck. See also *trapeze*.

Hitch A knot with which a line is attached to an object, such as a *clove hitch* or *timber hitch*.

Hog *Fore-and-aft member* fitted over the *keel* to provide landing for the *garboard strakes*.

Hogging The *hull* is higher *amidships* than at the *bow* and stern. Often a sign of age, although a boat may be designed and built with hogged (*reverse*) *sheer*. A hull is only supported along its whole length when the surface of the water is smooth. If wave lengths exceed her overall length, she bends upwards amidships, slightly but

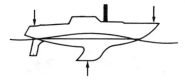

measurably, and her *overhangs* droop. The opposite is *sagging*.

Hoist 1. The length of a triangular sail from *head* to *tack*, measured along the *luff*. 2. The depth of a *square sail*, measured at the centre from head to *foot*. 3. To raise an object vertically with a *halyard*, line or *tackle*, e.g. a sail, spar or *flag*. 4. Of a flag, the vertical side nearest the *staff*, and the dimension of that side. 5. A collection of objects being hoisted. 6. A group of *signal flags* hoisted together to send a message. 7. A line with which an object is raised, often in the form of a *whip* or tackle, such as the centreboard hoist.

Hold 1. The part of a vessel where cargo is stowed. 2. The *anchor* holds when it is not *dragging* but has bitten into the *sea-bed*.

Holding ground The composition of the *sea-bed* determines whether an *anchor* will hold well or not, and the quality of the bottom is printed on *charts*. Sand (A) and clay (B) are good, but rocks (C) and weed (D) are poor holding ground. Mud and shingle (E and F) generally lie above a firm bed, and a heavy well-designed anchor is required.

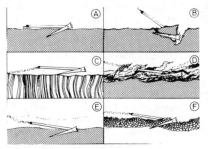

Holding power The holding power of an *anchor* depends on its weight and design. If the design is good, a lighter anchor will hold as great a weight as a considerably heavier anchor of less effective design.

Holding tank In which sewage is held on board, instead of being pumped into the water.

Hold water To stop a boat propelled by *oars* by holding the *blades* vertical in the water.

Holiday An area unintentionally overlooked when painting, varnishing or *paying* a seam.

Hollow leech A *leech* which curves inwards towards the *luff*, as on a *jib*. Whereas a *mainsail* leech curves outwards beyond the direct line between *head* and *clew*.

Hollow mast As opposed to a solid *spar*, has a hollow section and, when wooden, is assembled from several pieces. Now hollow masts are mainly light alloy *extrusions*.

Home 1. As in *sheet* home, *hoist* home; to haul on a rope or line until the sail fills or is fully hoisted, or until the end of the sheet or halyard is fully home to the *block* or *sheave*. 2. To steer directly towards a *radio beacon* using a *direction finder*. The *bearing* of the beacon becomes the boat's *course*, and caution is essential when homing on a coastal beacon or on a light vessel in restricted visibility. A vessel can home from great distances, e.g. if the *magnetic compass* fails or is unreliable in an area of abnormal magnetic variation; provided no *drift* occurs the vessel will follow a *great circle* course, which is the shortest route to her destination. The effects of drift are usually serious and, although the spacial error diminishes as the range reduces, the best procedure is to note the radio bearing and compass reading simultaneously; the compass course is then followed. If drift occurs it will show as a divergence between DF and compass which increases with time.

Hood end The end of a *plank* where it fits into the *rabbet* on the *stem* and *sternpost*.

Hook 1. Coll for *anchor*. US: a *kedge* is often termed a lunch-hook. 2. *Snap, pelican, carbine* and *sister hooks* are required for a variety of purposes on board.

Hook reefing or **shock-cord reefing** Similar to *points reefing*, but with light *shock-cord* led through *eyelets* along the sail between the *luff* and *leech cringles*. After the reef cringles have been pulled down to the boom by the *pendants*, the shock-cord is slipped over hooks either side of the boom to confine the *bunt* of the sail. This avoids the time-consuming tying of individual *reef points*. Light line can also be used.

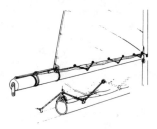

Hoop Wooden ring which encircles the *mast*, holding the *luff*, usually of a *gaff sail*, to the spar.

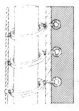

Horizon The *visible horizon* is the circle around an observer where sea and sky appear to meet. Its distance from an observer depends on his *height of eye*. The *sensible horizon* differs by the value for *dip* from the visible horizon. Observations of *heavenly bodies* are based on the *rational* or celestial *horizon*, which passes through the centre of the earth, and which is parallel to the sensible horizon.

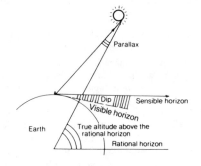

Horizon glass The fixed glass mounted on the *sextant* frame. One half is clear glass through which the horizon is viewed, the other half is silvered. The image of the *heavenly body* or object is reflected by the *index glass* to the horizon glass, which in turn reflects the image to the observer's eye.

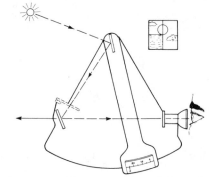

Horizon range The moment when a light appears above or disappears below the horizon can be used to find the distance of the vessel from the light at that moment, provided its *elevation* and the observer's *height of eye* are known. When the observer is in the cockpit, at h1, the distance from the observer to the horizon, d1, is added to the distance from the light to the horizon D1 (formula under *geographical range*). If the observer is higher (in the figure by the spreaders), the horizon range d2 + D2 is greater because of his increased height of eye.

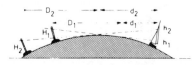

Horizontal cut *Genoas* and bermudan *mainsails* are often cut horizontally, the *cloths* being seamed together so that the *weft* runs at right angles to the stress line between the *head* and the clew. The *camber* required can easily be obtained with broad seam, i.e. by tapering the cloths. A horizontally cut *spinnaker* has the cloths at right angles to the leeches and usually a vertical seam down the middle of the sail.

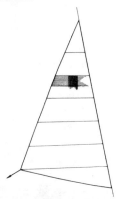

Horizontal sextant angle A horizontal angle between two landmarks, measured with the *sextant*, provides a *position line* which is an arc of a circle. The centre of the circle, on the circumference of which lie the observer and both landmarks, is found by subtracting the sextant angle measured, alpha, from 90°. From both landmarks draw lines at an angle of 90° minus alpha to the line joining the two landmarks. The centre of the circle is where these two radii intersect. When alpha exceeds 90°, the lines are drawn at an angle of alpha minus 90°, and the centre lies landward of the line connecting the two landmarks. (See three-point problem fig.)

Horn 1. The arm of a *cleat*, usually one of two. 2. One of the two projections from the *gaff* that form the *jaw*. 3. A *fog signal* sounded as an *aid to navigation*, the tone of which differs and may also vary in pitch. A diaphragm is vibrated electrically or by compressed air.

Horn timber *Fore-and-aft member* sloping up from the *keel* to form the backbone of the *counter*. See *construction* fig.

Horse 1. A bar, wire etc on which the lower *block* of the *mainsheet tackle* or that of a self-trimming *boom jib* travels athwartships, sliding over to *leeward* when the boat changes *tack*. A *track* is usually preferred for the mainsheet nowadays. 2. A shoal. 3. See *footrope*.

Horse latitudes High pressure area where winds are light and variable, lying approximately between 30 and 35° N and S between the *trade wind* belts and the belts of *westerlies* in the temperate zones. So called because sailing ships in earlier centuries made such slow progress that horses being transported to the American colonies died from lack of food and water, and had to be thrown overboard. Also called the variables, and subtropical high pressure belt. See *global winds* fig.

Horse power Unit of power: in the f.p.s system one hp raises 1 lb 500 ft per second; in the metric system 1 hp raises 75 kg one metre per second. The power output of auxiliary engines is measured in horsepower or kilowatts (*SI*). Indicated horse power is the power developed in the cylinders; brake power, measured at the output shaft, is lower owing to mechanical losses; shaft horse power (SHP) is the power delivered to the propeller shaft.
1 hp (f.p.s) = 0.7457 kW = 1.0139 hp (metric);
1 hp (metric) = 0.735 kW = 0.9863 hp (f.p.s.);
1 kW = 1.36 hp (metric) = 1.34 hp (f.p.s.).

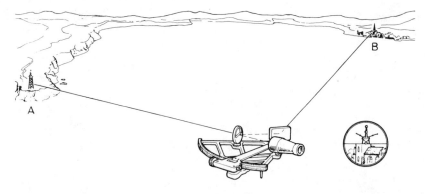

Horseshoe lifebuoy A *lifebuoy,* shaped like a horseshoe, which a person in the water does not have to lift over his head; is therefore preferable to a circular ring.

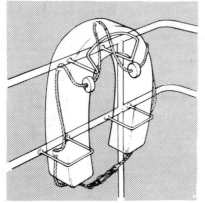

Hose clip or (UK) **jubilee clip** A clip that encircles hose and is drawn tight by turning the screw,

which engages in the notches in the clip. Makes a leakproof connection between hosing and *skin fittings,* engine etc.

Hounds 1. Place on the mast where *shrouds* and *stays* are attached. 2. Wooden shoulders below the *masthead,* originally to support *trestle-trees* and to form rests for *eyes* of *rigging.*

Hour angle The angle at the *pole,* measured westwards in units of arc or time, between the *observer's meridian* and the *meridian* passing through the *heavenly body* observed. Angle ZPX in the *PZX triangle.* The hour angle is found by adding easterly *longitude* to, or subtracting westerly longitude from the *Greenwich Hour Angle.* (In North America the term meridian angle may be used in place of hour angle, but is measured east or west from 0–180°). See also *Sidereal Hour Angle.* See *PXZ triangle* fig.

House To stow or secure in the proper or safe place.

House flag The private *flag* of the owner(s) or of a shipping company. Is worn at the starboard spreader, except when the vessel is abroad in which case the *courtesy ensign* is worn at the starboard spreader (starboard being the senior side of the vessel) and the house flag at the port spreader.

Hovercraft Amphibious air cushion or ground effect machine. Travels over land or sea, larger craft serving as ferries, e.g. across the English Channel. First successfully developed by Sir Christopher Cockrell.

Hove to Past tense of *heave to,* q.v.

Hulk An old hull unfit for sea, often used for storage.

Hull The actual body of a vessel, excluding *superstructure, masts, rigging, rudder.*

Hull down Said of a distant vessel when only masts, sails and/or superstructure are visible above the horizon.

Hull speed The maximum speed that a *displacement boat* can make as governed by her

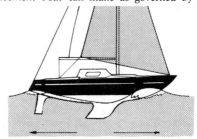

waterline length, i.e. $V/\sqrt{L} = 1.34$ where L is waterline length in feet and V is speed in *knots;* $V/\sqrt{L} = 2.42$ (L metres, V knots), $V/\sqrt{L} = 4.5$ (L metres, V km/h) or $V/\sqrt{L} = 1.25$ (L metres, V m/sec). At hull speed, the length of the wave made by the boat moving through the water matches the boat's waterline length. See also *speed to length ratio.*

Humidity The dampness of the *atmosphere.* Absolute humidity is the amount of water vapour in grammes per cubic metre of air; *relative humidity* (q.v.) is the amount of moisture present in one cubic metre of air, expressed as a percentage of the amount of moisture that would be present if the air were saturated.

Hurricane 1. *Tropical revolving storm* in the North Atlantic and Caribbean; occurs most frequently between July and October. Figure A shows

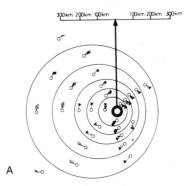

A

the extent of a hurricane, and the direction and strength of the winds. B shows the waves that are formed, and how a dangerous cross sea develops. 2. In the *Beaufort scale*, hurricane is force 12, wind speed over 64 *knots*, 118 km/h or 32 m/sec.

Hurricane

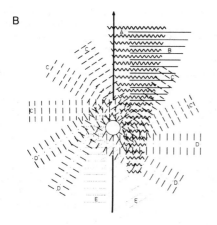

B

Hydraulic systems Apart from hydraulically-operated *steering, windlass, capstan* and transmission, hydraulic systems are fitted to many offshore racing boats, particularly to adjust the tension of the *backstay* and inner forestay, and to control the *kicker* strut which raises or lowers the boom as required. Hydraulic *outhauls, spreader* adjusters, *mast partners* etc are also fitted occasionally. Pressure is transmitted through a hand pump by means of a non-compressible liquid in flexible piping, enabling remote controls to be sited at a convenient position.

Hydrodynamics The branch of physics concerned with the motion of liquids, whereas hydrostatics relates to liquids at rest.

Hydrofoil 1. A body with a cross-section shaped to cause a change in the velocity of the liquid (water) flowing over it (c.f. *aerofoil*). 2. A flat, angular or curved foil, designed to produce sufficient hydrodynamic lift to raise the hull of a vessel above the water. The term is also applied to the boat that has hydrofoils attached to her hull so that, when she is moving fast enough under power

or sail, hydrodynamic lift raises the *wetted surface* of her hull clear of the water; she is then supported only by the foils. Hull *friction* and *wave-making resistance* are eliminated, and far less wind power is required to overcome the resistance offered by the foils. Even very light sailing boats with large sail area rarely achieve the speed required, and the problem of *transverse stability* has not often been resolved. The hydrofoil 'Mayfly' has held the class A sailing speed record of 23 knots since 1977.

Hydrography The science of surveying the waters of the earth, such as oceans, seas and rivers, together with the land bordering the waters. The measurements taken, published in the form of *charts, pilots* etc, enable the navigator to guide his vessel safely from one place to another.

Hydrostatic drive A transmission system in which the normal shafting that connects the engine to the *propeller* is replaced by flexible hydraulic lines through which oil is pumped by the engine, forcing it to a turbine mounted near the propeller. The turbine rotates the *propeller shaft*. A control valve enables the engine to idle in neutral, or reverses the propeller's direction of rotation. Although the installation is lighter in weight than with shaft transmission, and the engine can be mounted wherever desired, say in the forepeak, beneath the cabin sole, or in the afterpeak above the propeller, hydrostatic drive is less efficient than normal transmission or *sail drive*.

Hydrostatic pressure Pressure exerted on a motionless body in all directions. Water pressure varies with depth and *density,* the density of the water being multiplied by the head. In sea water, the average density of which is 64 lbs/cu ft (1.025 tonnes/cu m), pressure at a depth of 33 ft (10 m) is 14.7 lb/sq in (1 bar).

Hygrometer Instrument for measuring *humidity,* normally a wet-and-dry bulb thermometer; now called a *psychrometer,* q.v.

Hyperbolic navigation Radio navigation systems such as *Omega, Loran* and *Decca* are based on hyperbolic *position lines,* a hyperbola being a curve composed of those points that all have the same difference of distance between two fixed points, called the loci. Generally a chain consists of one *master* station, linked with three *slave* stations, all transmitting accurately timed signals. A hyperbolic position line is obtained, because the receiver on board measures either the difference in time of reception or the difference in *phase* between the master station signal and that of one of the slave stations, i.e. the loci. A second position line, usually from the same master and a second slave, *fixes* the vessel's position. Special *latticed charts* are required, and are overprinted with hyperbolic position lines.

I

I = India: yellow *code flag* with a black circle. As a single letter signal means 'I am altering my course to *port*'. *Morse code:* • • (dot dot). In races indicates that the one-minute period relating to the *round-the-ends* starting rule has commenced. When flown on a yacht which is racing, means 'I acknowledge having infringed a rule of Part IV Rights of Way'.

IALA Maritime Buoyage System A The International Association of Lighthouse Authorities' international *buoyage sytem* (red to *port*), adopted in European and other waters, is gradually replacing many national and international buoyage systems, except in areas such as North America where, traditionally, the *lateral system* has long been based on red to *starboard* when entering port. Elsewhere red *can* buoys have been left to port. IALA A combines a lateral system, with red can buoys to port and green (sometimes black) *conical* buoys to starboard marking a channel, with black and yellow *cardinal pillar buoys* laid in the *quadrant* on the safe water side of a *danger*. There are also red and black pillar buoys marking *isolated dangers*, and red and white *spherical safe water marks*, laid e.g. in the centre of a fairway. Special marks are yellow, of any shape, and may carry yellow St. Andrew's cross *topmarks* and exhibit yellow lights. In every case *spar* buoys are an alternative to the shapes stated above. See front endpapers. IALA System B (red to starboard but otherwise similar) may be introduced to US waters later.

Iceboat A light hull with a sail or sails trimmed like those of a sailing boat; moves over the ice on three steel or bronze runners. Because resistance is very low, it is much faster than a sailing dinghy and can achieve speeds of 100 mph, the world record being 146 mph. There are several single-handed and two-man classes. See also *Scooter*.

IMO International Maritime Organisation (IMCO, Intergovernmental was Maritime Consultative Organisation), an international advisory and consultative body based in London. Since 1959 has been concerned with establishing the

highest standards for safety at sea. See also *SOLAS*. Amendments to the 1972 *IRPCS*, expected to come into force about June 1983, are as follows: (a) a vessel under 12 m in length will not be required when *aground* to exhibit two *all-round* lights at night or three *balls* by day; (b) a *sailing vessel* under 30 m in length will be permitted to use a *tricolour lantern*; (c) a *power-driven* vessel under 12 m in length may exhibit *side lights* and, in lieu of separate *masthead* and *stern lights*, an all-round white light.

Impeller Screw-like device which is rotated by the action of fluid flowing past (e.g. component of some *logs* and *generators*) whereas a *propeller* is rotated mechanically to propel an object through a fluid.

Impeller log A *log* with a small impeller fitted outboard, often with a deflector to keep it free of weed; has a small magnet which creates a pulse every time the impeller rotates. The pulse rate increases with speed, and distance sailed *through the water* is recorded electronically and displayed on a dial, together with boat speed. The impeller is often retractable for cleaning and inspection. See also *Sumlog*.

Inboard Within a vessel or nearer *amidships*, whether on *deck* and inside the *lifeline* (guardrail) or *below* decks.

Inboard engine An *auxiliary engine* fitted inside the boat.

Inboard-outboard Alternative term for *outdrive*, q.v. Auxiliary power is supplied by an inboard engine coupled to an *outboard* drive unit.

Inch Unit for measuring length: 1 in = 2.54 cm; 1 cm = 0.393701 in: 1 sq in = 6.4516 sq cm; 1 sq cm = 0.155 sq in; 1 cu in = 16.3871 cu cm; 1 cu cm = 0.0610236 cu in. For other conversion factors see *pressure*.

Inclining test A test to establish the *stability* of a boat. Such a test is carried out to find the *Centre of Gravity Factor* when a boat is measured for an *IOR rating*, because a boat can only achieve the speed expected from her length and sail area if her stability is adequate. An object of known weight is hung at a measured distance outboard at the BMAX station, normally at the end of the spin-

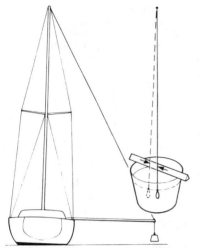

naker pole, and the angle of heel, both to port and starboard, is found by measuring the deflection of a pendulum on a manometer gauge. A normal *clinometer* is not sufficiently precise, but the angle of heel can be measured more accurately by suspending a plumb bob on a cord of certain length, attached to a point on the centreline, such as the cabin deckhead. The plumb bob may be submerged in a bucket of water to steady it, and a longer cord gives a more accurate measurement. See also *ultimate stability.*

Index bar or **arm** The moving arm of a *sextant* or *octant*. The quick release clamp disengages the worm wheel from the toothed rack on the *arc*, and enables the index bar to be moved quickly until the object comes into view in the *horizon glass.* The *micrometer* screw (or the tangent screw of a *vernier*) is then turned to measure the angle exactly.

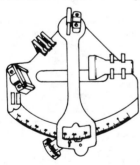

Index error Adjustable *sextant error;* the *index glass* is not parallel to the *horizon glass* when the index mark is at zero. The value of the error is the difference between the zero mark on the *arc* and an actual zero measurement. When the horizon is viewed directly and forms a straight line, i.e. when the index glass is parallel to the horizon glass, the sextant reading should be zero; when off the arc (beyond the zero graduation), the sextant is reading too low, the value of index error is positive

and has to be added to every reading; when on the arc (within the graduated scale), the instrument is reading too high, and negative index error has to be subtracted. The sextant must be checked regularly for index error by lining up the horizon.

Index glass or **mirror** The mirror which is attached to the index bar of a *sextant* or *octant* and moves with it. Reflects the image of the object viewed to the fixed *horizon glass.*

Induced drag or **resistance** That part of total drag that arises from the difference between the pressure on the windward side of a sail and that to leeward. Air tries to reduce the pressure difference by flowing over and round the head and foot. With a high *aspect ratio* sail, induced drag is a relatively small part of total drag, but increases in importance when aspect ratio is low, such as with a gaff sail. Induced resistance also occurs at a centreboard, keel etc.

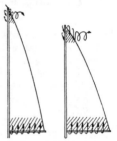

Inertial navigation A modern navigation system for large vessels; gives an accurate *dead reckoning* position by use of gyros, accelerometer and a computer. Known in the UK as SINS – Ship's Inertial Navigation System.

Inflatable dinghy Often abbreviated to inflatable. A dinghy made of neoprene rubber or other sheathed synthetic cloth; filled with air and can be deflated to be stowed on board. Has several separate air chambers, and may have wooden floorboards, *thwarts* and a bracket for an *outboard,* as well as *oars* or *paddles.*

Inglefield clip Interlocking C-shaped metal or plastics clips, mainly used to connect two *flags* or a flag to a *halyard;* occasionally used for light sail halyards.

Inhaul A line which hauls something *inboard,* such as the *jib tack* from the *bowsprit* end, as opposed to an outhaul which pulls outboard.

In irons (or **In stays** US) Said of a boat that is *going about* but loses momentum and stops *head*

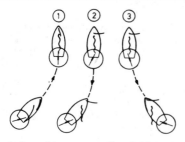

to *wind,* unable to *pay off* and fill her sails on either *tack.* Usually occurs when the boat *pitches* in a heavy sea, or is slow *in stays.* She can be helped to go about by *backing* the jib. In the figure the boat has come head to wind and is in irons; when she starts to make *sternway* the *tiller* has to be put over in the opposite direction to that when she makes *headway.* If the rudder is turned to port (tiller to starboard as in 2), the boat falls back on her original tack; if it is turned to starboard (tiller to port as in 3) the bow swings to port onto the intended tack.

Initial stability The *transverse stability* of a boat at a small angle of *heel,* i.e. her ability to counter the commencement of a *heeling force* by heeling only slightly. A beamy dinghy with form stability has high initial stability, whereas a keelboat with a ballast keel and low centre of gravity is less stable initially. See *stability curve.*

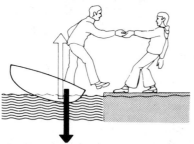

Inland rules of the road (US)   Rules valid in all US inland waters within the *Colregs Demarcation Lines* – basically in harbours, rivers and inland waterways apart from those where *Western Rivers* or *Great Lakes* rules are in force. There are many minor differences from the *IRPCS,* especially with regard to lights. The important difference relates to right of way between two vessels under sail, approaching each other so as to involve *risk of collision.* When new US rules are issued, they are expected to accord with the IRPCS, but at present (1980):

(a) a vessel running free keeps out of the way of one that is close-hauled;

(b) a vessel close-hauled on port tack keeps out of the way of one that is close-hauled on starboard;

(c) when both are running free with the wind on different sides, the vessel with the wind on the port side keeps out of the way of the other;

(d) when both are running free with the wind on the same side, the vessel to windward keeps out of the way of the vessel to leeward;

(e) the vessel with the wind aft keeps out of the way of the other vessel.

Inland waters   Navigable waters wholly or almost entirely enclosed by land. The term internal waters is also used; navigable waters within a state.

In line   When two marks or the two lights of a *leading line* (US range) are in line, the vessel is sailing exactly on the leading line. A reliable *position line* free of *compass error* is obtained when two landmarks or buildings marked on the chart are identified and come into line (US range, UK *transit*); the vessel must be somewhere on the seaward extension of the line connecting them.

Inner forestay or **babystay**   An additional shorter *forestay* seen on many offshore racing boats and cruisers; runs from a point on the *mast* below the forestay to a *deck plate* roughly midway between the *stem* and the mast, which it supports from forward. Can be tensioned to control the degree of *mast bend.* The inner foresail or baby staysail may be set on it, or the *storm jib* in heavy weather.

Inner jib   When two or more *jibs* are set forward of a *staysail,* the jib nearer the mast.

Inner staysail or **baby staysail**   Small light-weather sail set beneath a *genoa* when *close-hauled* or *reaching; cloth weight* varies from $2\frac{1}{2}-5\frac{1}{2}$ oz US, 3–7 oz UK, 100–230 g/sq m.

Inshore   Nearer to or towards the shore. As an adjective, near the coast.

Inshore waters   UK *weather forecast* term; waters within 12 miles of the coast.

Inside ballast   *Ballast,* whether fixed or movable, that is carried inside the *hull,* as opposed to an external ballast keel bolted onto the outside of the hull. Includes ballast that is secured within the shell of a *GRP/FRP* hull.

Inside yacht   Under the *racing rules,* the inside yacht nearest a *mark* or *obstruction* has to be given *room* by the outside yacht(s), provided she has established an *overlap* before she is within two of her overall lengths of the mark.

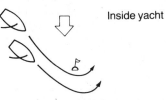

Inside yacht

In sight An object such as a landmark comes into sight either when it appears over the horizon at the limit of *geographical range,* or when it can be identified at the limit of meteorological *visibility.*

Insignia See *class emblem.*

Inspection cover Watertight cover for an aperture in a tank, buoyancy compartment etc, which it seals; is removed to ventilate, inspect, clean or paint the interior.

In stays 1. UK: when a vessel *goes about,* her position when *head to wind.* 2. US: synonymous with *in irons,* q.v.

In stops Rotten cotton or stopping twine is tied round a sail to keep it gathered while it is being *hoisted.* The stops break when the *sheet* is *hardened,* and the sail then fills at the desired moment. Ordinary elastic bands can be used in place of stopping twine when hoisting a *headsail* or *spinnaker,* as in figure a. Another alternative is

A

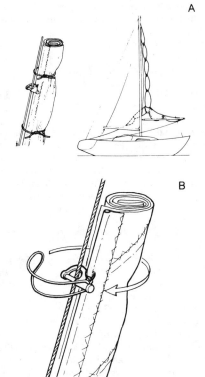

B

C

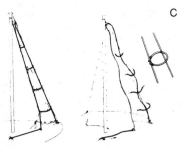

light shock cord, at least twice the length of the luff, and this can be used repeatedly (see figure c). The short lines spaced along it are hooked round the sail, which is broken out by uncleating the shock-cord to ease the tension. The hooks come free and the shock-cord can be retrieved when the sail has filled.

Insulation Material attached as a lining to part of the structure to reduce noise or condensation and/or to discourage the passage of heat, e.g. as fitted to the engine compartment.

Insulator When part of the backstay or a shroud is used as a receiving or transmitting *aerial,* insulators are inserted to separate the aerial from the rest of the boat; they have eyes or terminals at either end so that they can be attached to the rigging. *Breaking strength* normally exceeds that of the rigging wire, and varies from about 9000

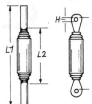

to 22,000 lbs (4080–9980 kg). Simple porcelain insulators are effective, but the topping lift can get caught in the grooves. Others are made of stainless steel, and are embedded in a nylon injection moulding. Insulators often have to be inserted to break the loop formed by the lifeline and pulpits, which frequently causes radio interference.

Insurance Marine insurance policies insure against losses occurring at sea as a result of fire, explosion, sinking, collision, stranding, weather etc, and generally also cover theft, damage to other vessels, pontoons etc, injury to a member of the crew, and so on. Often only two-thirds cover is provided for masts, spars and sails when racing, and deductions are usually made for wear and tear on such items as outboards, sails and rigging, whether damage or loss is incurred racing or cruising. Many policies limit the cruising waters, and extra premiums may be required when sailing beyond certain limits. Insurance may be compulsory, for example when competing in certain races, and a high level of third party cover is always advisable. The degree of cover provided should be checked carefully when comparing premiums, especially in the case of a boat that is trailed overland.

Intensity The intensity of a light, measured in *candelas,* governs its *luminous range.* The intensity of sound signals is measured in decibels. *Navigation lights* exhibited by vessels must be visible at the prescribed distance, and the minimum luminous intensity is laid down in the *IRPCS.*

Intercept The difference between the true *zenith distance* and the calculated zenith distance of a *heavenly body,* measured in n. miles from the *assumed* or *dead reckoning* position along the *line of bearing* of the body's *geographical position (azimuth).* It is measured away from the body if CZD is less than TZD, but towards the body if CZD is greater. Similarly the difference between the *true altitude* and the tabulated or calculated altitude of a body when using *Sight Reduction Tables,* measured from the *chosen position* along the azimuth, towards the body if true altitude is greater than tabulated altitude, and away from the body if tabulated altitude is greater.

Intercept method or **Marcq St. Hilaire method** A *position line* is obtained by comparing the known *zenith distance* (90° minus *true altitude* = true zenith distance) between a position on the earth's surface and the *geographical position* of a *heavenly body,* with the calculated zenith distance, between an *assumed position* and the same geographical position, the difference between the two being the *intercept* (see above and *PZX triangle*).

International 10 sq m canoe A single-handed high performance sailing *canoe* with centreboard and sliding seat; one of the oldest and fastest single-handed sailing *monohull* classes, having originally been developed 100 years ago from a canoe, with sails added; beam is exceptionally small. LOA 17 ft (5.20 m), beam 3 ft 3 in (1.10 m), weight rigged 130 lbs minimum (63 kg), sail area 10 sq m.

International Catamaran Challenge Trophy Trophy competed for by *C-class catamarans.* So far has been won by Australia, Denmark, USA and UK. Coll referred to as the Little America's Cup.

International class A *class* of racing boats granted international status by the *IYRU* and raced in at least five countries. Category 1 are IYRU-controlled, category 2 by an international class organization. Amendments to class rules have to be approved by the IYRU. Some international classes are: *Dragon, Soling, Flying Dutchman, Finn, 470, Contender, Tornado* and the *metre classes.*

International Code of Signals. Internationally agreed signals, listed in the Code book, which enable vessels to communicate at sea either by *signal flags, morse code* (visually with lights or acoustically) or a letter code (*radio telephone*). The set of signal flags consists of 26 rectangular or *swallow-tailed* letter *flags,* 10 numeral *pendants, 3 substitutes* (US repeaters), and the code flag and *answering pendant.* The most important single letter signals are given here as the first entry under each letter of the alphabet. Signals consisting of more than one letter or numeral, such as a *hoist* consisting of several flags hoisted together, provide more detailed information.

International Fourteen *Development class* racing dinghy for two crew, with a *trapeze* and spinnaker; high-performance. LOA 14 ft (4.267 m), beam 5 ft 6 in (1.676 m), dry hull weight 225 lbs (102.1 kg), sail area 190 sq ft (17.65 sq m), spinnaker about 220 sq ft (20 sq m).

International nautical mile 1852 metres, 6076.115 feet (see *nautical mile*).

International offshore rule, IOR Current international measurement rule for offshore racing yachts, adopted in 1970 and based on elements of the American *CCA* and British *RORC* rules. This comprehensive rating rule is so complicated that a computer is required for the calculations but, briefly, and omitting all adjustments for different types and designs:
    Rating (feet) = MR × EPF × CGF × MAF × SMF × LRP × CBF
where MR is the measured rating (see below) EPF the *Engine and Propeller Factor* (q.v.), CGF the Centre of Gravity Factor (see *Inclining test*), MAF the Movable Appendage Factor which relates to underwater surfaces such as trim tabs that are able to induce assymetry in the underwater shape, SMF the Spar Material Factor (1.000 in the case of wooden, aluminium or steel alloy and *GRP/FRP* spars), and LRP the Low Rigging Penalty, which applies when the upper end of any rigging, apart from the spinnaker pole uphaul, is attached to the

mast below a point 25% of the genoa halyard height above its low point of measurement; CBF, centreboard factor, applies only to centreboard yachts.

MR =

$$\left[\frac{0.13L \times SC}{\sqrt{B \times D}} + 0.25L + 0.2 \times SC + DC + FC\right] \times DLF$$

L, rated length, is length between *girth stations* forward and aft, less the forward and after overhang components (which evaluate the contribution made by the overhangs to the sailing length of the boat) so that L = LBG − FOC − AOCC; B, rated beam, is measured at the section where beam is greatest (BMAX being maximum beam at this station), often at a point one-sixth of the length of BMAX below the sheer line. D is rated depth, based on immersed depth at specific stations forward, aft and amidships. DC is draft correction and FC freeboard correction; they are based on the difference between actual draft and freeboard and a proportion of rated length. DLF, the displacement length factor, based on rated length, rated beam and midship depth immersed, has a maximum value of 1.1.

SC is sail area value, based on RSAT, Rated Sail Area Total, which combines the RSA for each sail. RSAT = RSAF + RSAM + SATC (Sail Area Total Correction) in the case of a single-masted yacht, namely the RSA of foretriangle and mainsail, but YSAC, the combined RSA of mizzen and mizzen staysail is included in the case of yawls and ketches.

RSAF =

$$0.5IC \times JC \left[1 + 1.1 \left(\frac{LP - JC}{LP}\right)\right] + 0.125JC(IC - 2JC)$$

RSAM = 0.35(EC × PC) + 0.2 EC(PC − 2E) (jib-headed)

C in each case is 'corrected': I is the foretriangle height (intersection of forestay and mast to the level of the sheer line abreast the mast): J is the foretriangle base (from the leading edge of the mast to the foremost stay): LP is the longest perpendicular, usually 1.5JC (but, if longer than 1.5JC, either clew to luff of largest genoa, plus forestay perpendicular if a luff groove device or wrap-around jib is used, or clew of headsail set on inner forestay to foremost stay): E is the length of the mainsail foot from the after side of the mast to the black band on the boom: P is the mainsail hoist length between black bands on the mast at head and tack.

The *rating certificate* issued gives all the measured and calculated values, as well as the rating which, although given in feet, is not a linear measure. Often the *time multiplication factor* is given as well. See also *RORC classes.*

International Regulations for Preventing Collisions at Sea Abbreviated in this dictionary to IRPCS, and by the US Coast Guard to Colregs. The inter-

nationally agreed rule of the road, designed to ensure the safety of vessels at sea. Applies to all vessels upon the high seas and in all waters connected therewith navigable by seagoing vessels. Although special rules relating to inland waterways, rivers, lakes etc are not prohibited, they must conform as closely as possible to the international regulations. Part A covers application, responsiblity and definitions; Part B the steering and sailing rules; Part C *lights* and *shapes;* Part D *sound* and light *signals;* Part E exemptions. Annexes give details of lights, shapes, sound signal appliances and *distress signals.* See also *rules of the road, Inland* (US), *Great Lakes* (US), and *Western Rivers (US).*

International (sometimes **IYRU**) **rule** Not to be confused with the IYRU *racing rules.* This relates to design, and was originally introduced in 1906, but subsequently amended. Racing yachts built to rate in accordance with the rule include 6-, 8-, 10-, 12-, and 23-metre yachts. The formula is

$$R = \frac{L + 2d + \sqrt{S} - F}{2.37}$$

d being the difference between chain *girth* and skin girth, F freeboard and S sail area (all metric). L is not length overall but length as defined in the rule. Although the boats of one class all have the same rating, they are far from identical and individual measurements such as length, sail area etc vary considerably. 12-metres have competed for the *America's Cup* since 1958. 5.5-metres were built to a different formula (see *metre classes).* 23-metres were very similar to the *J class.*

International waters All waters apart from *territorial* or internal *waters.*

International Yacht Racing Union, IYRU Founded in 1906, is the authority for yacht racing and has sub-committees responsible for *racing rules* (q.v.), building regulations for *international classes* etc. Runs world and other championships for many classes, including *Olympic classes.* National sailing authorities such as the United States Yacht Racing Union (USYRU) and the British Royal Yachting Association (RYA) are affiliated to the IYRU.

Interrupted quick (flashing) light A *light,* exhibited as an *aid to navigation,* that *flashes* rapidly but is interrupted regularly by a long *eclipse;* chart abbr IQ, formerly Int. Qk. Fl. Exhibited by US junction buoys. The IALA A quick flashing rate is 50−60 times a minute, the US rate not less than 60 times a minute.

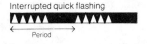
Interrupted quick flashing

Intertropical Convergence zone or **Equatorial trough** The area between the NE and SE *trade wind* belts where pressure is low, air rises, winds are light and variable with many calms, interspersed with torrential rain, squalls and thunderstorms. See *global winds* fig.

Intracoastal Waterway An almost entirely sheltered route, nearly 2500 miles in length, which follows rivers, waterways, bays and one canal from Trenton in New Jersey, south to Florida and on to Brownsville, Texas. The *buoyage* is laid in accordance with the basic US *lateral system,* i.e. red to starboard and black to port when sailing from NJ to Florida and Texas, the main difference being that buoys have yellow bands, while daymarks have yellow lines beneath the numbers, and reflecting red borders on triangular daymarks (starboard hand), or green reflecting borders on square daymarks (port hand).

Intumescent resin A fire-retardant *resin* applied to a *GRP/FRP laminate*. Swells up and forms a protective crust which insulates the surface to some extent.

Inversion Normally the temperature of air decreases with height, but when there is a temperature inversion the reverse is the case, and temperature increases with height. *Fog* often forms beneath an inversion.

Inverter Rotating machine or solid state power device which converts direct current (DC) into alternating current (AC).

Inwale Inside *fore-and-aft* strengthening *member* fitted at the upper edge of a small boat.

Ionosphere Ionized layers in the upper part of the *atmosphere*, 50–100 miles (80–160 km) above the earth. Electro-magnetic radio waves with a frequency of over 2 MHz and lower than about 50 MHz are reflected, making short wave radio communication possible across continents and oceans.

IOR *International Offshore Rule*, q.v.

IRPCS Abbreviation used in this dictionary to mean the *International Regulations for Preventing Collisions at Sea*, q.v.

Isobar A line on a *weather map* connecting places where *atmospheric pressure* is the same. Isobars are closely spaced around *depressions*, but widely spaced around *anticyclones*, and the more closely they are spaced the greater the difference in pressure and the stronger the winds. They show the positions of *ridges, cols* and *troughs*, and

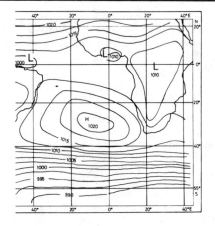

enable a general picture of the weather to be built up. The figure shows an isobaric chart of the South Atlantic.

Isobath Contour line connecting places of equal depth.

Isochrone Line connecting places where times are the same.

Isoclinal line Line connecting all places where magnetic *dip* is the same.

Isodynamic line Line connecting all the places where the value of horizontal magnetic force is the same.

Isogonal or **Isogonic line** Line of equal magnetic *variation*. The agonic line connects those places where variation is nil.

Isohaline Line joining places where the *salinity* of sea-water is the same.

Isolated danger A danger surrounded by deep water. An isolated danger mark is laid over it. The *IALA A pillar* or *spar buoy* has black and red horizontal bands, carries two large black spherical *topmarks* and, if a light is exhibited, the character is *group flashing* (2), white. See front endpaper.

Isophase (US **Equal Interval**) *Light* exhibited as an *aid to navigation*, the duration of the light being equal to the duration of darkness; chart abbr Iso or E Int.

Isotach Line joining places where wind speeds are the same.

Isotherm Line connecting places where temperature is the same, or where mean temperature over a long period is the same. Isotherms relate to temperatures of both air and water; the figure shows the South Atlantic surface water temperatures.

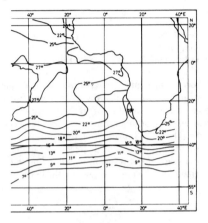

IYRU *International Yacht Racing Union, q.v.*

J

J = **Juliett:** blue-white-blue *code flag*. As a single letter signal means 'I am on fire and have dangerous cargo on board; keep well clear of me'. *Morse code: •— — —* (dot dash dash dash).

Jack A small *flag* worn at the jackstaff forward by naval vessel, e.g. when at anchor; usually the union flag or national flag. The *pilot* jack is a small national flag surrounded by a white border.

Jackass rig Any unusual combination of *rig,* such as a jackass barque, which is a *sailing ship square-rigged* on the two forward masts but *fore-and-aft rigged* on the other two.

Jackstaff Staff at the bow from which the jack is flown by warships.

Jackstay 1. Iron rod or wire rope which is fitted on top of a *yard,* and to which the *head* of a *square sail* is bent. 2. Holds the head or *luff* of a sail such as a *topsail* close to a *spar* or *mast.* 3. Taut rope or wire rope secured between two points for some purpose, such as rigging an awning, or to provide the connection between ship and shore when rescuing the crew with a *breeches buoy.* 4. The loose wire fitted to the lower part of the luff of a *boom jib,* carrying the *hanks,* so that the sail may slide down the *stay* unhindered by the restraint of the fixed *clew.*

Jackyard *Spar* to which the *luff* or *foot* of a jackyard topsail is bent.

Jackyard topsail Triangular topsail, not unlike a *gaff topsail,* but the luff and foot are laced to yards which extend the sail beyond the *topmast* and the *gaff.*

Jacob's ladder or **jack ladder** Has wooden rungs (rounds) supported by rope either side, and is

lowered to enable, e.g. a *pilot* to board or leave a vessel, or to recover a person from the water. Possibly named after the ladder in Jacob's dream.

Jacob's staff and **cross-staff** Similar simple instruments with which the *altitude* of a *heavenly body* was measured prior to the invention of the *sextant.* One or more transoms (cross-pieces) were moved back and forth along the staff, which was graduated in degrees or degrees and minutes; the lower edge of the transom was lined up with the horizon and the upper edge with the body.

Jam cleat or **jamming cleat** One *horn* is stubby and the other extends at an angle from the base, so that the sheet or halyard can be cleated quickly with a single turn, the rope being jammed in the tapering slot after it has been passed round the short horn. The term may also be applied to a *cam cleat,* a stainless steel cleat with a veed notch, and see *tubular jam cleat.*

Jammer See *stopper.*

Jaw 1. See *gaff jaw.* 2. The distance along a rope between one *strand* and the next time the same strand appears. Long-jaw rope is loosely *laid* (soft-laid) and flexible, short-jaw is hard-laid and tight.

J Class The largest of the classes built to the *Universal Rule*

$$R = \frac{0.18L \times \sqrt{S}}{\sqrt[3]{D}} = 76 \text{ ft}$$

L being length, S sail area and D displacement. These were the fastest racing yachts to be built, and competed for the *America's Cup* in the 1930s. 'Ranger' for example, was 135 ft 2 in (41.2 m) LOA, 21 ft (6.4 m) beam, 15 ft (4.57 m) draft; she displaced 166.5 tons (169 tonnes) and carried 7950 sq ft (738 sq m) of sail.

Jeers Heavy *tackle* for hoisting and lowering the lower *yards* of a *square-rigged* vessel.

Jetsam Gear or cargo deliberately thrown overboard to lighten a sinking ship.

Jet stream A high altitude wind that blows strongly in a narrow belt near the *tropopause.*

Jetty UK: a structure which projects roughly at right angles from the shore, and alongside which ships and boats can moor. US: similar structure but built to protect harbor entrances or, like a groin (UK *groyne*), to direct *tidal currents.*

Jib Triangular *headsail* set on a *stay* forward of the *mast:* in *cutters* the forward of the two headsails, often tacked down to the *bowsprit.* The only *working sail* set forward of the mast and *mainsail* of *sloops*, but a larger *genoa* is often substituted. When jibs vary in size they are called No. 1, No. 2 etc, No. 1 being largest.

Jib-boom The spar that is the extension of the *bowsprit*, on which it is housed; the flying jib-boom is a further extension. Lateral support is given by *shrouds*, and the pull of the *headstay* is countered by the *martingale* stay, which passes over the *dolphin striker.*

Jibe US spelling of *gybe*, q.v.

Jib-headed As opposed to *gaff-headed*, a triangular sail, as set on *marconi-rigged* (UK *bermudan-rigged*) boats.

Jib sheet The *sheet* which trims the jib, and which is attached to the jib *clew.* See *headsail sheet lead.*

Jib-stick or **whisker pole** Small light pole with a spike at the outboard end that is poked into the *clew cringle*, so that the jib can be held out to windward when running. The inboard end is connected to a fitting on the mast, or has a jaw which fits round it.

Jib topsail Is set above the ordinary jib, either *hanked* to the *forestay* or *set flying.*

Jiffy reefing Similar to *points reefing* but quicker. The *luff cringle* is pulled down and slipped over a hook on one side of the *gooseneck*, and the *leech* cringle is pulled down with a permanently rove *pendant* that is either led to a small *winch* mounted on the side of the boom or shackled to a *tackle.* The *bunt* is often left free, but may be gathered with *reef points* for longer periods.

Jigger 1. US coll for *mizzenmast* or *mizzen.* 2. Light tackle with one double and one single block.

Jiggermast 1. The fourth mast from forward in *sailing ships* or *schooners* with more than three masts, stepped abaft the *mizzenmast.* 2. A small mast stepped right aft in some barges etc.

Jimmy Green Sail set below the *bowsprit* of some *square-rigged* vessels.

Jockey pole or **reaching strut** A small *spar*, with a *sheave* in a slot at the outboard end; is attached to a fitting on the mast at the inboard end and is rigged on the same side as the *spinnaker pole.* It extends beyond the *shrouds* and thrusts *spinnaker guy* clear of the shrouds and *lifelines* to prevent *chafe*, especially when reaching with the pole well forward and a *shy* spinnaker set.

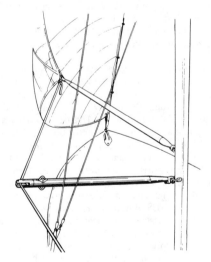

Joker (US) The main valve in a marine toilet.

Joule *SI* unit of energy and work. 1J = 1 newton metre = 0.737561 ft lb = 1 watt second = 2.77778×10^{-7} kW hr.

Jubilee clip See *hose clip.*

Jumper stay A single *stay*, or one of two, that runs forward from the *masthead* over a short jumper strut and back to the mast, to stiffen the upper portion of a *fractional-rigged* mast. See

rigging fig. Generally the jumper stay returns to the mast at *spreader* level, but in racing dinghies the strut may be about midway between the top of the forestay and the masthead, the jumper stay being fastened to the mast at these points. Jumpers may be fitted to fractional-rigged sloops to support the upper part of the mast against the pull of the mainsail and backstay. A single strut is fitted fore-and-aft; when there are two they are fitted at an angle of about 30–45° to the centreline.

Jump the gun To cross the *starting line* before the starting signal has been made. The boat is then *recalled*.

Junction buoy (US) Marks the junction of channels. Horizontal black and red bands; if the preferred channel is on the *port hand* a *nun* buoy, with the top band red, but if the preferred channel is on the *starboard* hand a *can* buoy with a black top band. Lights, when exhibited, are *interrupted quick flashing. See front endpapers.*

Junior Offshore Group (JOG) UK organization founded in 1950. Ran the *RORC* class IV and V *offshore races,* which were introduced in 1951 after 'Sopranino' (LOA 19 ft 8 in, 6 m) had taken part hors concours in the 1950 Santander Race. Has had a great influence on the building of small offshore racing yachts, and on safety regulations, for many years under the chairmanship of Capt John Illingworth. Waterline length was restricted to 15–20 ft, and regulations specified such matters as mast height, *cockpit* size, minimum *freeboard, buoyancy* (US flotation), *ventilation, seacocks, berth* sizes, *lifeline* measurements and the minimum equipment and gear to be carried. Currently runs about a dozen races up to about 150 miles in length, mostly for RORC classes V-VIII.

Junk Chinese sailing vessel with one or more masts. See *Chinese lug.*

Jury 1. A temporary but effective device which replaces lost or damaged gear. A jury *mast* may be made with the *boom* and *spinnaker pole;* a jury *rudder* at its simplest could be a bucket towed on a line and pulled to one side or the other to alter course. An improvised *tiller* can be fitted to the *rudder stock* if part of the steering gear fails. A *headsail* can be set as a jury mainsail, the foot

being attached to the mast and the head to the boom. 2. A jury may be appointed by the *race committee* or organizing authority to hear and decide *protests.* An international jury supervises the conduct of a special *regatta* or *series.*

K = Kilo: yellow and blue *code flag*. As a single letter signal means 'I wish to communicate with you'. *Morse code:* — • — (dash dot dash).

Kamal A navigational instrument, pre-dating the *Jacob's staff*, used by Arab seamen to establish *latitude*. A length of cord, knotted at intervals appropriate to the meridian *altitude* of a *heavenly body* relative to various ports and features along the route, was attached centrally to a rectangular wooden board, the upper and lower edges of which were lined up with the heavenly body and the horizon beneath it. The length of the taut cord between the observer's eye and the board indicated the altitude of the body, from which latitude could be ascertained. The same principle can be used to make a simple rangefinder. A hole is bored through

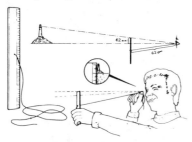

the centre of a 30 cm ruler, graduated in millimetres. A line passed through the hole has a knot tied in it exactly 62 cm from the ruler, and the ruler is held 62 cm away from the eye. The height of the landmark is measured in millimetres from the top of the ruler, and the approximate distance off in n. miles is found from the formula

$$\frac{\text{known height of object in metres}}{\text{measured height of object in mm} \times 3}$$

Thus, if the top of a lighthouse is known to be 18 m above sea level, and the height measured is 12 mm, distance off = 18/36 = 0.5 n. miles.

Katabatic wind Downward-flowing wind that blows because high land loses heat by radiation faster than low-lying land. Where there are snow-covered mountains winds can reach gale force, and may be dangerous.

Kedge An *anchor* that is smaller and lighter than the main anchor; is used to move a boat from one place to another or to anchor temporarily in fine weather, but particularly when the wind drops during a race. 2. Also used as a verb, to kedge. After a boat has *run aground*, a kedge is often run out into deeper water in the dinghy so that the boat can be kedged off, i.e. by hauling on the rope attached to the kedge.

Keel The backbone of a boat; the main *longitudinal member* to which the *stem* is *scarphed* at the forward end and the *sternpost* at the after end. See construction fig. Transverse members such as *frames*, *timbers* and *floors* are spaced along its length. A *centreboard* may pass through a slot in the keel, or a *ballast keel* may be bolted beneath it. The word keel is often applied to all the lateral area that extends beneath the hull to provide *transverse stability* and to resist *leeway*, exclusive of the *hull* itself and *skeg*, *rudder* etc. Consequently, although both *centreboard boats* and *keelboats* have backbone keels, only keelboats have deep ballast keels, and these may be long or short (the former extending a greater distance along the fore-and-aft line than the currently popular short keel).

Keelband Metal strip screwed along a dinghy's keel to protect it from damage when being hauled over a beach. Sometimes termed keel shoe.

Keel block Blocks on which the keel rests in dock, or when the vessel is laid up on land. Blocks may also be placed beneath the bilges.

Keelboat A boat with a *ballast keel*, which may be an integral part of the *hull* structure or bolted on to the outside of a *canoe body*. Most have a single central keel; *bilge keelers* have twin bilge keels; a few boats have all three. Keelboats are used for racing or cruising, and generally have a *cabin*. Some have *drop keels* and others, designed for sailing in *shoal waters*, have a *centreboard* to supplement a shallow ballast keel.

Keel bolt Long, strong bolt that holds the *ballast keel* to the *keel*. Often highly stressed when the boat runs aground. It should be possible to draw

keel bolts from beneath the hull, so that they can be checked for *corrosion* and replaced as necessary. See *construction* fig.

Keelson A longitudinal member fitted parallel to and directly above the *keel* or above the *floors. See construction* fig.

Kelp Large masses of seaweed.

Kelvin *SI* basic unit of thermodynamic temperature, named after Lord Kelvin, the Scottish scientist William Thomson. The scale starts at absolute zero 0 K, which is $-273.15\,°C$ and, as the interval of one degree *Celsius* (centigrade) is the same as the temperature difference of 1 K, the freezing point of water, $0\,°C$ is 273.15 K, while boiling point, $100\,°C$, is 373.15 K.

Ketch Two-masted boat with *fore-and-aft sails,* the *mainmast* forward being taller, sometimes only slightly taller, than the after *mizzenmast.* Several definitions attempt to differentiate between a ketch and a *yawl:* ketch's mizzenmast stepped forward of the *rudder stock,* or forward of the aftermost point of her *designed waterline:* ketch's mizzenmast more than half the height of her mainmast:

ketch's *mizzen* over half the area of her *mainsail.* Essentially the mizzen of a yawl is proportionately smaller than that of a ketch, when compared to the mainsail. The *IOR* does not differentiate between a yawl and a ketch, but classes two-masted boats as yawls if the taller mainmast is forward, or as *schooners* if it is aft.

Kevel See *cavil.*

Kevlar DuPont trade name for a yellowish, long chain polymer, synthetic fibre, with a *tensile strength* greater than stainless steel; called Fiber-B when produced by another manufacturer. When used in sailcloth and rope, is subject to ultraviolet degradation but, when mixed with carbon fibres and protected from the effects of the sun's rays in a moulding such as a hull, adds greater strength for low weight.

Kicker 1. Coll for *kicking strap.* 2. US coll for *auxiliary engine.*

Kicker lever A lightweight and more effective alternative to a tackle-type *kicking strap (boom vang);* the *mechanical advantage* varies between 7:1 and 10:1, depending on its length and design. Cheaper than a *wheel tensioner turnbuckle* (UK or rigging screw).

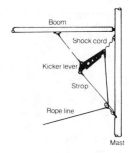

Kicking strap (UK) Line or *tackle* used to pull the *boom* down to keep it horizontal on all *points of sailing,* and in particular to prevent it from lifting on a *reach* or *run.* The usual US term is *boom vang,* q.v.

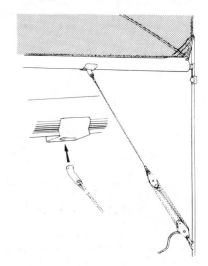

Killick Term sometimes applied to an *anchor;* originally a stone secured to wooden crooks.

Kilo- Prefix used with *SI* units, abbr k. Multiply the unit by 1000 (10^3).

Kilogram(me) Basic *SI* unit of mass. 1 kg = 1000 grammes: 1000 kg = 1 tonne, and 1 kg therefore equals one thousandth of the weight of one cubic metre of pure water at maximum *density.* The international standard kilogramme is a mass of platinum-iridium, kept at Sèvres. For conversion factors see *pressure, pound, density.*

Kilometre (US **kilometer**)   Unit of length, 1000 metres.
1 km = 0.621371 statute miles = 0.539957 n. miles;
1 statute mile = 1.60934 km; 1 n. mile = 1.852 km.

Kilowatt, kW   The basic *SI* unit of power, the watt multiplied by 1000. Under the metric and f.p.s. systems the power output of *auxiliary engines* is measured in *horsepower* (q.v. for conversion factors).

Kinetic energy   The energy possessed by a body by virtue of motion; k.e. = ½ mv^2 where m is mass and v velocity. Is equal to *dynamic pressure.*

King plank   The middle plank of a *laid deck;* runs along the *centreline.* The other planks are often curved and laid parallel to the *covering board;* they are butted to or nibbed into the king plank. See *construction* fig.

Kink   A sharp twist in rope or wire rope that does not clear itself, and prevents the rope from running through blocks, fairleads etc. In wire rope causes the individual wires to break. Rope must be properly *coiled* to avoid kinking.

Kit (US or **knockdown**)   The component parts of a boat supplied for home construction, sometimes partly assembled. The saving in cost over a professionally built boat depends on how comprehensive the kit is, and on how much is left for the purchaser to do. May be *GRP/FRP mouldings,* or wooden parts ready for assembly.

Kite   1. Light-weather sail, such as a *skysail* or *moonraker,* set high on the mast of a *square-rigged ship;* also the highest *fore-and-aft sails.* 2. Coll: a *spinnaker* or other modern light-weather sail.

Knee   Connects two parts that meet roughly at a right angle, e.g. the stern knee joins the *sternpost* or the *transom* to the *keel,* hanging knees join *deck beams* to *frames* or *planking,* lodging knees are fitted horizontally. May be solid or *laminated* wood, steel angle, wrought iron or reinforcements embedded in *GRP/FRP.*

Knife   A clasp knife is essential for a sailor, and should have a hinged *marline spike* as well as a blade; some have a *shackle spanner* instead.

Knock   See *heading wind.*

Knockdown   1. See *kit.* 2. The boat is knocked flat by a sudden *gust* or *squall,* lying on her *beam* ends with the sails in the water. The terms B1 and B2 knockdowns stem from the inquiry following the 1979 Fastnet Race disaster, B1 being a knockdown to horizontal and B2 a knockdown substantially beyond horizontal, including total inversion and a full 360° roll.

Knot   1. Knots, *bends* and *hitches* are all used to tie a line to a spar, to another line or to some other object. Most knots are formed in the end of the rope by twisting it about itself, e.g. *stopper, figure of eight* and *overhand knots,* but a *reef knot* joins two rope ends. The dividing line between knots, bends and hitches is not precise. 2. The unit of speed at sea; one knot is one *nautical mile* per hour   and =   1.852 km/h =   0.5144 m/sec = 1.15 mph (for further conversion factors see *speed).* The term derives from the knots made in the line of the *chip log;* these were counted, as the line ran out over the taffrail, to measure the speed of the vessel through the water. European weather forecasts frequently give wind speeds in metres per second or knots, and these are easily converted: multiply m/sec by two to obtain knots; divide knots by two to obtain m/sec, e.g. 20 m/sec = 40 knots.

Knuckle   A sudden change of curvature in the *hull.*

L

$L = $ **Lima:** black and yellow chequered *code flag*. As a single letter signal means 'You should stop your vessel instantly'. *Morse code:* •—•• (dot dash dot dot). When racing and displayed at sea means 'Come within hail' or 'follow me'. When displayed on shore means 'A notice to competitors has been posted on the notice board'.

Labour Pitch and roll heavily in a seaway, with irregular motion and stresses.

Lacing Long, thin line with which a sail is attached to the *mast, boom, gaff* etc in place of either a *track* and *slides* or a *grooved* spar and *bolt-rope.* Also used for the sail cover, and to rig screens, *dodgers, awning* or cockpit cover.

Lacing eye and **hook** Screwed to the structure to provide anchorages to which an awning, cockpit cover, dodgers etc can be secured with a lacing.

Ladder See *accommodation, boarding, Jacob's* and *side ladders.*

Lagan Gear or cargo thrown overboard from a sinking vessel, but buoyed so that its position is marked to assist subsequent recovery.

Lagoon An area of sheltered *salt* or *brackish water,* largely or entirely enclosed by a small strip of land, such as sandbanks or dunes, or by a barrier reef.

Laid deck Wooden *deck* of narrow *planks, caulked* and *payed* with marine glue or with a seam compound. Often *teak,* left unvarnished to provide a non-slip surface that can be scrubbed with sea-water, sometimes with sand and canvas (formerly with a 'bible' or holystone).

Laid rope As opposed to *braided* rope, the *strands* are twisted round each other to form rope (see *rope-making*).

Laminar flow Fluid flow is smooth, with stream-lines parallel to the foil (c.f. *turbulence*), whether

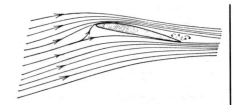

the fluid is air flowing over a sail or water along the hull, centreboard etc. When *telltales* sewn to the sail align themselves with laminar airflow in the *boundary layer,* they lie flat and indicate that the sail is trimmed to the correct *angle of attack.*

Laminate 1. To laminate is to form an object of several layers of material, such as *marine plywood* glued together. A tiller, frame or member can be laminated over curved *moulds,* and will be very strong. Appearance is improved when woods of different colours are used alternately. 2. A laminate

is an object composed of several layers of material, such as layers of *chopped strand mat, roving* or cloth, impregnated with *resin* to which a *catalyst* has been added. Each layer is under $1/25$ in (1 mm) thick and a $1/6$ in (4 mm) laminate consists of 4–7 layers.

Lanby buoy Large Automatic Navigational BuoY: unmanned *aid to navigation* which exhibits a light from a considerable height and gives *fog signals;* often remote-controlled. Frequently laid as a *landfall buoy* and is so large (40 ft or 12 m diameter) that sailors in distress can take refuge on it. Maintenance has proved difficult owing to severe motion in seas, and unmanned automatic light floats, shaped and ballasted more like a lightship, appear to be preferable.

Land To go ashore, or to put someone ashore.

Land breeze A night wind which blows close by the coast in temperate, sub-tropical and tropical latitudes. Land loses heat more quickly than the sea, and cools the air above which sinks and flows

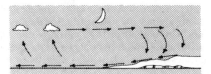

seaward beneath the warmer air offshore. The warm air is forced upwards and flows back towards the land at greater height. The land breeze is not as strong as the *sea breeze* which replaces it by day.

Landfall Land first sighted after a long sea voyage. A vessel makes a good landfall when the land sighted is as expected.

Landfall buoy Generally a *Lanby* or *high focal plane buoy* that exhibits a light at a considerable height so that it can be identified from a greater distance than normal. Is laid to mark the start of a buoyed channel, sometimes well offshore and out of sight of land.

Landlubber A derogatory name for a person who is not a seaman, or who is incompetent on board.

Landmark A conspicuous fixed feature on or near the coast, such as a chimney, tower, church spire or windmill. Many landmarks are marked on charts and help the navigator to fix his position.

Lands (US laps) Where the *strakes* of a *clinker-built* (US lapstrake) hull overlap.

Lantern Housing for one of the *lights exhibited by vessels* at night in the positions prescribed by the *rules of the road;* so constructed that the lights are visible only over the required *sectors.*

Lanyard 1. Short length of line with which an object, such as a knife, is secured. 2. When rove through a *chain plate* eye and a *deadeye* or *thimble,*

replaces a *turnbuckle* (UK or rigging screw); each part has to be hauled tight so that all bear the same load. Now confined to smaller dinghies or emergencies such as turnbuckle failure. 3. May be used to tension the wires in *lifelines* (guardrails).

Lapse rate The rate at which temperature decreases as height increases. The lapse rate is negative when there is an *inversion* and temperature increases with height.

Lapstrake (occasionally **lapstreak**) Alternative term for *clinker,* q.v. Laps (US) are where the strakes or planks of a clinker-built hull overlap.

Larboard Obsolete word for *port,* the left hand side of a vessel when facing forward. Derived from the loading or lade board, to port in most old vessels.

Laser *International class* racing dinghy, strict *manufacturer's* one-design; single-hander designed by Ian Bruce. LOA 13 ft 10½ in (4.23 m), beam 4 ft 6 in (1.37 m), weight rigged 145 lbs (65.77 kg), sail area 76 sq ft (7.06 sq m). The Junior Laser has a smaller sail, 62 sq ft (5.76 sq m) in area.

Lash To secure firmly with cordage, e.g. to lash the boathook or anchor to the deck so that they will not shift in a seaway. Also lash down.

Lashing The line that secures one object to another to keep it in place.

LAT *Lowest Astronomical Tide,* q.v.

Lateen sail Triangular sail set on a long curved yard which runs up obliquely from the bows at an angle of about 45°. The yard is suspended about a third of the way along its length from a very short mast, and its forward end is attached to the bow.

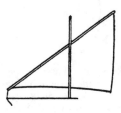

Reefing is difficult, which is typical of light-weather rigs. The felucca and xebec are lateen-rigged, but have more than one mast. The rig may be of Arabian origin, and was used in early times in the Red Sea, Persian Gulf and the Eastern Mediterranean. *Square rig* was developed from it.

Lateral plane or **lateral underwater body** All those parts of the boat beneath the *waterline* that resist sideways movement (*leeway*) *heeling* and *rolling*, i.e. the *bottom, rudder, keel* and/or *centreboard;* the shape can be seen in the *profile plan.* The lateral plane coefficient is the ratio of the actual lateral plane to the area of the circumscribing rectangle with sides equal to the boat's *waterline length* and *draft.*

Lateral resistance Owing to its shape, the *underwater body* offers much greater resistance to sideways motion (i.e. the lateral plane resists *leeway*) than to forward motion through the water. The *centreboard* of a dinghy is therefore lowered to increase the lateral area and lateral resistance when she is *on the wind* and lateral forces are greatest, but it is raised fully on a *run,* when all the wind's energy is converted into forward motion and the boat makes no leeway.

Lateral system A *buoyage system* suitable for marking channels, passages etc with *buoys, beacons* or *perches* to *port* and *starboard;* the *dangers* are marked relative to the vessel's course. *Port hand marks* are left to port when approaching a port or estuary from seaward, when sailing clockwise round a land mass, when sailing upstream in rivers and, in the Great Lakes, when sailing towards the end where water enters. See *IALA A* and *US buoyage. See endpapers for illustration.*

Latitude The position of any place on the surface of the earth is defined by two spherical co-ordinates, latitude and *longitude,* both of which are expressed as angular distances. The *meridian* that passes through place A cuts the *equator* at point B, and the latitude of A is the angle AOB at the centre of the earth. Parallels of latitude are measured in degrees, minutes and seconds north

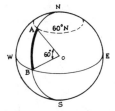

and south of the equator (Lat 0°) to the *poles* (90° N and S) and, with the exception of the equator which is a *great circle,* are *small circles* passing through all places on the earth that have the same latitude. Every degree of latitude represents virtually the same distance on the earth, 60 *nautical miles* (q.v.). On the latitude scale bordering the sides of *mercator charts,* one minute represents one nautical mile, and *distances* can therefore be measured on the latitude scale.

Latitude by meridian altitude The vessel's latitude can be found when a *heavenly body* is on the *observer's meridian,* at which time it has a

greater *altitude* than at any other moment during its daily journey round the earth. The *true bearing* is north or south, 0° or 180°, and the *position line,* which runs E–W at right angles to the bearing, indicates the vessel's latitude. A *sight,* taken at the time of meridian passage, usually a noon sight of the sun, requires little calculation. *Sextant altitude* is corrected to find *true altitude,* and true altitude is subtracted from 90° to give the true *zenith distance:* TZD ± *declination* gives the observer's latitude. If the observer is between the *elevated pole* and the heavenly body, latitude is equal to ZD minus declination when latitude and declination have opposite names (one is north, the other south), but latitude is equal to ZD + declination when they have the same names. If the body is nearer the pole than the observer and they have the same name, declination is greater than the vessel's latitude, which equals declination minus ZD.

Latitude by Polaris Latitude is found by measuring the *altitude* of *Polaris* with a *sextant.* Polaris is so close to the celestial *north pole* that its altitude is almost the same as the vessel's latitude. *Sextant altitude* is corrected first for instrumental error and *dip,* and then in accordance with the Polaris tables in the *Nautical Almanac,* which are entered with LHA *Aries.* The correction is under 1.5°, and calculations are quick and easy. See p. 149 for fig.

Latticed charts Normal charts overprinted with *hyperbolic position lines* for use with *Loran, Decca* and *Omega* navigation systems.

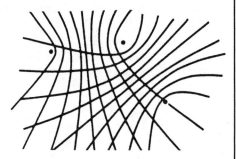

Launch 1. A small power boat, usually open and used for transporting the crew between a larger boat and the shore. 2. To put a vessel into the water, whether for the first time or after she has been *laid up* or *hauled out.* She may be supported in a launching *cradle* as she slides down the launching ramp or slip. Dinghies are usually launched with a *trolley.*

Launching tube (US) See *spinnaker chute.*

Lavsan Trade name for Russian *polyester* fibres, used for making rope and sail cloth.

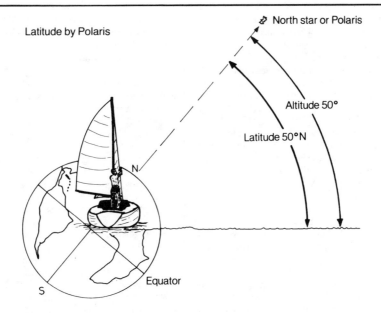

Latitude by Polaris

North star or Polaris

Altitude 50°

Latitude 50°N

Equator

Lay 1. *Strands* twisted together to form rope, e.g. right-hand lay, soft-lay (see *rope-making*). 2. To lay a *course* is to be able to keep to that course, whether a compass course or one to a visible destination such as a headland. 3. To lay a *mark* is to sail directly to it without having to *tack*, the lay line being the most *leeward* course which a boat can sail and still *fetch* the mark.

Lay off To draw a line on the *chart* representing a *bearing* or a *course*.

Lay up 1. To take a boat out of commission for a certain period; she may be laid up either in the water or, as is common with keelboats, on land. 2. To twist *strands* together to form *rope*.

Lay-up 1. A *GRP/FRP laminate* or *moulding*. 2. To make such a laminate or moulding.

Lazarette Small stowage compartment at the *stern*.

Lazy block *Block* which is fitted to a *deck plate*, *track* etc, and which tumbles when there is no tension on the line rove through it.

Lazy guy *Guy* on which there is no strain.

Lazy jack Lines on both sides of the *mainsail*, led from the *topping lift* and under the *boom* so that the sail is gathered automatically to the boom when it is lowered. Often used with gaff sails.

Lazy jack

Lead (Pronounced led) 1. The depth of water can be measured with a shaped piece of lead weighing 5–10 lb (2.5–5 kg), attached to a line marked in *fathoms*, feet or metres. The faster the boat is moving the further ahead must the lead be thrown so that it is touching the *sea-bed* when it is abreast of the leadsman; the line must be vertical

to measure depth exactly. Still used on board sailing boats to measure water that is too deep for a *sounding pole*, and is used, even when an *echo sounder* is carried, to bring up a *sample of the bottom*, and to check echo sounder readings. See also *lead line*. 2. (Pb). Very dense metal of which *ballast keels*, *inside ballast* etc are often made; *specific gravity* 11.3. (Pronounced leed) 3. The direction in which a rope goes. Hence lead or leading *block*, *fairlead* etc, which guide or alter the direction of pull (the lead) of a line. See also *headsail sheet lead*. 4. The distance that the *centre of effort* is forward of the *centre of lateral resistance;* usually expressed as a percentage or fraction of *waterline length*.

Leading edge The forward edge of an *aerofoil* or *hydrofoil*, e.g. the luff of a sail, the forward edge of a streamlined centreboard or rudder. It is rounded, whereas the *trailing edge* tapers.

Leading line (US **range**) Leading lights or marks (US range lights or marks), positioned to indicate the direction of a channel, entrance or passage. When the helmsman keeps the marks or the lights *in line*, the vessel is led clear of *dangers* while she is

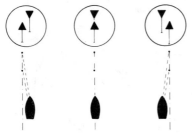

within the limits marked on the *chart* (e.g. between two bends in a river). If she deviates from the correct course, the marks or lights open and the upper light or higher mark, which is further inland, shows to which side of the leading line she has strayed. The *bearing* of a leading line is given from

seaward on charts, in the *List of Lights* etc, and is a *true bearing*. If there is only one leading mark, the helmsman has to keep the bearing steady to follow the leading line.

Lead line The line attached to the *lead;* is used when *sounding*, and is marked at intervals or metres of fathoms as follows:

fathoms	quantity	metres
– (deep)	1	one strip of leather (and 11, 21 etc)
two strips of leather	2	two strips of leather (and 12, 22 etc)
three strips of leather	3	blue bunting (and 13, 23 etc)
– (deep)	4	green and white bunting (and 14, 24 etc)
white linen (and 15)	5	white bunting (and 15, 25 etc)
– (deep)	6	green bunting (and 16, 26 etc)
bunting (and 17) red	7	red bunting (and 17, 27 etc)
– (deep)	8	blue and white bunting (and 18, 28 etc)
– (deep)	9	red and white bunting (and 19, 29 etc)
square of leather with hole	10	square of leather with hole (and 20, 30 etc)
– (deep)	11	one strip of leather
– (deep)	12	two strips of leather
blue serge	13	blue bunting
– (deep)	14	green and white bunting
white linen	15	white bunting
– (deep)	16	green bunting
red bunting	17	red bunting
– (deep)	18	blue and white bunting
– (deep)	19	red and white bunting
cord with two knots	20	square of leather with hole

When the sounding matches a mark, the leadsman

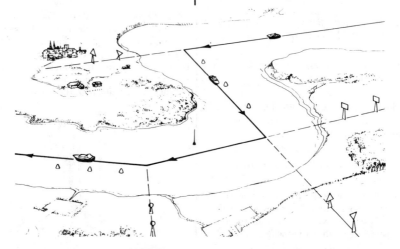

sings out, e.g. 'By the mark, 10', but at the un-marked intermediary fathoms he estimates the sound as 'Deep, 6'. The heavier deep sea lead was used to measure depths of up to about 120 fathoms.

Leadsman The crew who measures the depth of water with a lead and line.

Leak 1. Noun: any unintended opening that permits water to enter; may be in *hull, deck, hatch, portlight* etc. 2. Verb: to let in water involuntarily. A *GRP/FRP* hull normally only leaks at the site of through-hull fittings such as a *stern gland* or water inlet, at the hull-to-deck joint, or when damaged in a *collision.*

Ledge Flat-topped rocky ridge near the shore, close to the surface.

Lee The direction towards which the wind blows, as opposed to *weather* and *windward;* either on board, as lee side, lee helm, or beyond the boat, as lee shore, lee mark. In the lee of an object: sheltered from the wind by, and to leeward of, that object.

Leeboard 1. One of two pivoting boards fitted at the side of a *flat-bottomed* boat to provide *lateral resistance* in place of a *keel* or *centreboard.* Still used by sailing barges and many Dutch boats such as the Tjalk, Botter etc. The leeward leeboard is lowered, but the windward leeboard would be

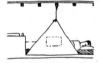

only partly effective when the boat heeled, and it is therefore usually raised alongside the hull to pre-vent damage from twist caused by leeward drift. 2. Alternative term for *bunkboard;* board or strip of canvas fitted along the open side of a berth to prevent the sleeping occupant from falling out when the boat heels.

Lee bow 1. The bow to *leeward.* 2. When racing a boat often goes about close to an opponent's lee bow so that she is in the *safe leeward position,* and can slow her opponent with her *dirty wind.* 3. A boat *close-hauled* in a foul *tidal stream* will sag off

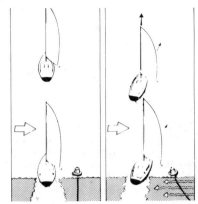

to leeward if it is just on her weather bow, but if *pointing* slightly higher brings the tidal stream onto her lee bow, she will be pushed up to *windward.* The difference between the two tracks made good over the ground is out of all proportion to the small change in course, and this is one of the few times when it pays to *pinch.* 4. A boat on a reach with the tidal stream on her lee bow is set to windward of the direct course to her destination, and she allows for set by pointing to leeward of her direct course. 5. When beating towards a mark to windward, the effect of a tidal stream setting across the wind direction is to make the tack with the tidal stream on the lee bow into the *long tack,* and the other into the short tack. In a steady wind, there would be no advantage to starting on either tack, but it is generally preferable to sail the long tack first because the boat stays closer to the direct line to the mark; the effect of the *tide wind* is to enable her to point closer to the wind when the tidal stream is on the lee bow, but less close when it is on the weather bow.

Leech (sometimes **leach**) 1. The aftermost or *trailing edge* of a quadrilateral or triangular *fore-and-aft sail. (See sail* fig.) 2. The *leeward* side of a *spinnaker* when it is set. 3. The two sides of a *square sail,* and of a spinnaker before it is set.

Leech line (US **drawstring**) 1. A very light line which is led through the leech *tabling* from the *headboard* to the *clew* so that the leech can be tensioned, especially if an old sail has stretched out of shape. Supports a sail that flutters or 'motorboats' too much along the *trailing edge,* and discourages it from sagging to leeward, which affects the shape adversely. 2. Line that runs from the yardarm to the leech of a *square sail;* controls and gathers the sail.

Leech rope Part of the *bolt-rope,* sewn along the leech(es) of a sail.

Lee helm The tendency of a boat to turn her bow to *leeward;* to keep her on course the *tiller* has to be held to leeward. Many boats have lee helm in

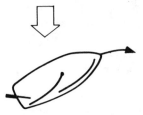

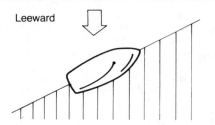
Leeward

light breezes, but slight *weather helm* is desirable, especially in strong winds. To eliminate lee helm, the relative positions of the *centre of effort* and the *centre of lateral resistance* have to be altered, either by shifting the CLR further forward or the CE further aft (see *balance*).

Lee mark See *leeward mark*.

Lee-o The helmsman's warning that he is putting the *helm* down and is *going about*. Hard a-lee is the US equivalent.

Lee rail The leeward *gunwale;* hence lee rail under or awash: said of a boat that is *heeled* well over with the lee gunwale in the water.

Lee runner See *running backstay*.

Lee shore A coast towards which an *onshore wind* blows; the coast to leeward of a boat. A lee shore should be avoided in strong winds which drive a boat towards the land, because she will be *stranded* unless she manages to *claw* her way off. When choosing an *anchorage,* the skipper takes into account any expected or forecast shift of wind direction that could turn the coast nearby into a lee shore.

Lee tide A *tidal stream or current* that runs in the same direction as that towards which the wind is blowing. Waves are longer, and of only moderate height by comparison with waves generated when wind and tidal stream are opposed. When the tide turns to become a lee tide, wave crests are flattened, and breaking seas become less vicious.

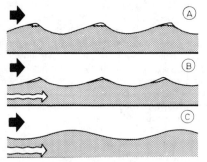

Leeward Downwind, away from the wind, the direction to which the wind blows, e.g. a boat may *bear away* to pass to leeward of an obstruction, or a *bearing* may be taken of a landmark to leeward.

Leeward or **lee mark** When racing the *mark* of the *course* furthest to leeward. The *beat* to the *weather mark* and, often, to the finish starts here.

Leeward yacht In the *IRPCS,* when two *sailing vessels* approach each other and there is a *risk of collision,* the vessel to *windward* has to keep clear. In the IYRU *racing rules,* the leeward yacht is defined as the one of two on the same *tack,* neither being *clear astern,* that is to leeward of the other; again the windward yacht has to keep clear.

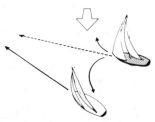

Leeway The sideways drift of a vessel caused only by the wind. Often expressed as the angle between the course steered (*heading*) and the course made good through the water, and most easily measured as the angle between the extension astern of the fore-and-aft line (the reciprocal of her heading) and her *wake* (shows her actual track through the water). The leeway angle is normally between 3° and 7° when *close-hauled,* depending

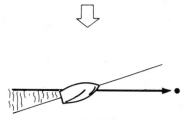

on the underwater profile of the boat (*bilge keelers* usually make more leeway than fin keel boats, *leeboard* barges are also poor performers), and decreases progressively as the boat bears away to a *beam reach* and *broad reach,* becoming nil when she is *running*. Leeway has to be taken into account when calculating the course to steer, and when plotting the course made good, especially when close-hauled. Should not be confused with the *set* (q.v.) of a *tidal stream or current*.

Left bank The bank of a river on the left when facing downstream.

Left-hand lay or **S-twist** Rope made with the *strands* sloping to the left, in the opposite direction to the thread of a corkscrew. Has to be coiled counterclockwise. See also *rope-making*. Also used of twist of filaments when making *thread* for *cloth* weaving. Opposite is Z-twist or right-hand lay.

Left-hand propeller Viewed from aft, the *blades* rotate counterclockwise to move the boat forward (see *wheel effect*).

Left rudder (US) An order to direct the vessel's head to port.

Leg 1. When racing, the distance between *marks*, e.g. windward leg between the lee and windward mark. 2. The distance covered on one *tack* when *beating*.

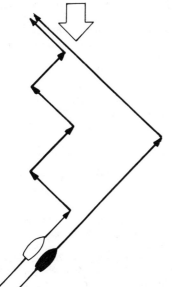

Legs Supports secured to the sides so that a boat will stand upright on the ground when the *tide* falls.

Length 1. The length of a boat, the main dimension, can be measured between various points.

Length overall, LOA, is the extreme length of the *hull* between the foremost part of the *bow* and the aftermost part of the *stern*, normally exclusive of *bowsprit*, *bumpkin*, projecting *pulpit* or *self-steering gear*. Waterline length (the abbreviation LWL stands for load waterline) is the length of the boat between *stem* and stern at water level. The actual waterline length of the floating boat varies from the designed waterline length with the amount of gear and stores carried and with the *density* of the water in which she is floating. Length between perpendiculars (LBP) is length between two verticals at the fore side of the stem and the after side of the rudder post. Sailing length is a vague term relating to her waterline length when *heeled*, and varies with the angle of heel. See also *International Offshore Rule*. 2. The basic *SI* unit of length is the metre. Other linear measurements used at sea include the *nautical mile, cable, fathom*, yard, foot and inch. 3. The length of a wave is the horizontal distance between successive crests or troughs.

Length to beam ratio This ratio indicates the slenderness of a *hull*, length being divided by *beam*. The higher the figure the narrower the hull, e.g. for a boat 36 ft (11 m) LOA and 10 ft (3 m) beam the ratio is 3.6, but given 11 ft (3.35 m) beam the ratio is 3.28.

Length to draft ratio A useful ratio when different designs are compared, length being divided by *draft*. A *shoal draft* boat has a larger length to draft ratio than one with a deep *keel*.

Lenticular rigging Solid *rod rigging* with a streamlined cross-section to reduce *drag*.

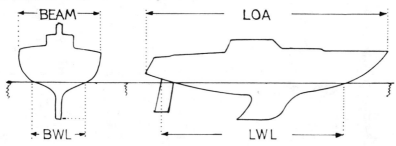

Let fly To let the *sheet* go completely so that the sail is no longer full of wind, as opposed to *easing* the sail out under control.

Let run To allow a line or *anchor cable* to run out quickly under load, as opposed to *checking* or *paying* it out under control.

Level racing Boats race without *handicap*, and generally must be *one-designs* or all below a certain *rating*. The first to finish is the winner. See *Level Rating Class*.

Level Rating Class At present there are six *classes* in which *offshore racing* yachts compete against each other without *handicap*, entries being limited to boats below a certain *rating*. Level rating competition offshore started in 1965 for the *One Ton* Cup, the boats having a maximum *RORC* rating of 22 ft. When the *International Offshore Rule* came into force, the maximum rating became 27.5 ft. The smaller *Mini, Quarter, Half* and *Three-Quarter Ton* classes (16.5 ft, 18.5 ft, 22 ft and 24.5 ft rating respectively) and the larger *Two Ton Class* (32 ft maximum rating) followed later. The term Ton is misleading and does not relate to *displacement;* for example a One-Tonner displaces about 6 tons, and a Half-Tonner about 4 tons; it derives from the One Ton Cup, first competed for in 1907 by the original 6-metres which had to have a keel weighing one ton.

Lever A rigid bar or piece of wood that can be turned about a fulcrum (a fixed point of support) to obtain a mechanical advantage, e.g. as in the figure, to raise a boat's bow. The advantage gained is the ratio of the distance between the fulcrum and the point where power is applied to the distance between the fulcrum and the load. In the figure, leverage is 8:1 and the mechanical advantage would increase if a longer bar were used. Levers are often used for quick adjustment of the tension of *standing* and *running rigging* etc. There are jib halyard levers, mainsail luff tensioning levers, *kicker levers, runner levers* and so on.

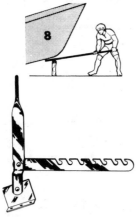

Lie A boat that is not making way is said to lie at *anchor, alongside, a-hull,* quietly etc. To lie off is to stop some distance from the shore or another vessel. To lie over is sometimes used instead of to *heel*. Lie to, see *heave to*.

Lifeboat 1. A seaworthy boat carried aboard a larger vessel to save the lives of passengers, crew etc in an emergency. 2. A shore-based rescue craft, *self-righting* and unsinkable, designed to save the lives of seamen. Inshore lifeboats are *inflatables* with powerful *outboard engines,* and operate near the UK coast. Lifeboats exhibit a flashing blue light on a short mast.

Lifeboat station Place where a lifeboat is housed or moored, ready to assist vessels in distress. Chart abbr (UK) LB and (US) LS S (Lifesaving Station).

Lifebuoy or **life-ring** Circular or, preferably, *horseshoe*-shaped float designed to support a person in the water. Should be stowed within easy reach of the helmsman so that he can throw or drop it instantly. When racing or cruising offshore, should be attached to a *dan buoy* with a flag and a light or self-igniting *smoke float* so that its position is marked.

Lifebuoy light, man overboard light or **waterlight** A fixed or flashing light that marks the position of a man in the water. The recommended type is stowed upside down on board, and starts working immediately it turns right way up to float. A flashing strobe light is used in American waters but is not recommended in Europe.

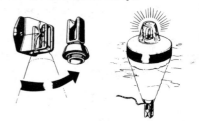

Life jacket (UK), **life preserver** or **Personal Flotation Device, PFD** (US) A buoyant jacket which provides sufficient support to keep an unconscious person afloat for at least 24 hours. Has a collar that keeps him face upwards with nose and mouth clear of the water, and must

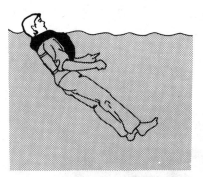

automatically turn him into this position, even if he falls in face downwards. Is normally filled with closed-cell foam, or is inflated by mouth and/or by a CO_2 cylinder, but may be partly foam-filled and topped up by air. *SOLAS* recommends a minimum of 8 kg buoyancy, but Department of Trade regulations specify 35 lbs for adults and 20 lbs for young children (16 kg and 9 kg). US regulations specify minimum flotation limits according to the type of boat and the waters in which the boat will sail (see *personal flotation device*). One life jacket is required for each member of the crew.

Lifeline   1. (or guardrail): lines fitted around the sides of the boat to prevent the crew from falling overboard. They run from the *bow pulpit* to the *stern pulpit* (if fitted), passing through holes in the *stanchions,* which are spaced along the deck, and are secured and tensioned at the aft end by *turnbuckles* (UK or rigging screws) or short *lanyards.* Swage studs are often used, the swage being drawn through the stanchion hole and secured with a screw-on eye. Usually two lifelines are fitted each

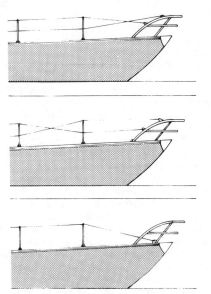

side, at heights which vary according to the size of boat, and which may be specified by national authorities or in race regulations. *IOR* yachts of over 21 ft *rating* must have double lifelines, the upper being not less than 2 ft (60 cm) above deck; the minimum height of the single lifeline specified for yachts below 21 ft rating is 18 in (45 cm), and the maximum gap allowed between wires, or between wire and deck, is 22 in (56 cm). The upper line is often $3/16$ in (5 mm) 7×7 *wire rope* with a PVC covering, the overall diameter of $9/32$ in (7 mm) providing a good grip. Some lifelines are made of *polyester.* A breach or *gangway* may be made in a high lifeline between two more closely spaced stanchions; the short length of lifeline between them is opened and closed with a *pelican hook.* The figures show some alternative methods of keeping the headsail foot clear. 2. The line attached to *safety harness* by which a crew member

fastens himself to the boat; often has two *snap hooks* which can be clipped onto the hand rail, shrouds, stanchions etc, one hook being at the end and one half way long the lifeline. 3. A wire or line attached at either end to a strong point, rigged along or across the deck to provide a handhold for the crew, and to which he can hook his safety harness lifeline when working on deck in heavy weather. 4. A line trailed astern when a person is alone on deck, so that he can grab it if he falls overboard; if it is attached to the helm his weight on the line will make the boat alter course, and

alert those below. 5. Any line used to save life, such as a line attached to a person in the water, or a grab line attached to a lifebuoy or round the side of a dinghy.

Life raft   An inflatable *raft* made of neoprene or special waterproof and airtight sheathed material. It is carried, usually on deck, in a sailcloth bag or plastic valise, and inflates automatically in under one minute. A life raft has two separate airtight chambers, and a double skin bottom, double canopy with supporting tubes, *boarding ladder,*

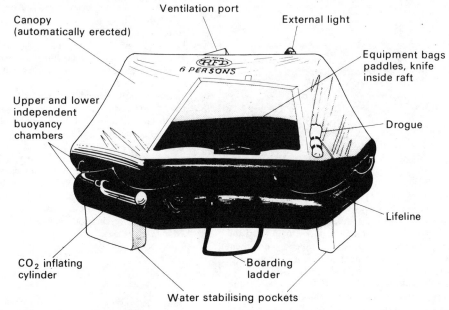

Canopy
(automatically erected)

Ventilation port

External light

RFD
6 PERSONS

Equipment bags
paddles, knife
inside raft

Upper and lower
independent
buoyancy
chambers

Drogue

Lifeline

CO_2 inflating
cylinder

Boarding
ladder

Water stabilising pockets

INFLATED LIFERAFT SHOWING SAFETY FEATURES

lights etc. Carries a *sea anchor, emergency rations,* distress *flares* and, often, an emergency radio transmitter (*EPIRB*). Is required when racing offshore, and carries four to ten people according to its size. Some commonly found features, some of which can be seen in the fig, are as follows:

external water-activated light
canopy
rainwater collector
leak plugs
topping up valve
paddle
CO_2 cylinders
drogue
self-inflating canopy tube
survival pack
painter
blow-off valves
bellows
boarding ladder
grab lines
upper and lower buoyancy chambers
stabilizing pockets
boarding line
sea-water battery

Life vest or (UK) **buoyancy aid** A closed-cell, foam-filled or inflatable jacket worn to provide *buoyancy* when swimming; popular with dinghy crews because it interferes less with mobility than a bulkier *life-jacket*. Does not have a collar to keep an unconscious person's nose and mouth above water, and usually provides less buoyancy than a life-jacket.

Life vests

Lift 1. A line which supports part of the rig, see *spreader, topping* and *spinnaker pole lifts.* 2. The useful force that acts perpendicular to the direction of flow of air or water over a foil. The ratio of lift to *drag* is important, especially when the boat is *close-hauled,* and determines the drag angle, which should be small (see *force* figure, L air, F_S water, and *dynamic lift*). 3. (US also to luff): a sail is said to lift when it is not *hardened* in sufficiently, or if the boat is *pointing* too close to the wind. The wind then strikes the lee side of the sail at the *luff,* close abaft the mast or forestay, and lifts the sail. A sail is at the optimum *angle of attack* when it is full and just not lifting; the helmsman therefore checks that he is pointing as high as he should be by luffing up slightly until the luff starts to lift, and then *bears away* until the trembling stops; similarly, on all other courses, the crew checks that the sail is correctly trimmed by *easing* the sheet until the sail starts to lift, and then hardens it fractionally until the sail is full. 4. (esp US) A favourable wind-shift; the wind frees slightly. Opp of *header.*

Lifting keel A ballasted *keel*, usually with a bulb, which can be raised when sailing by means of a *tackle* or geared crank, to reduce *draft* and *drag*.

Lifting rudder (US also **tip-up rudder**) The *rudder blade* pivots between *cheeks* and can be raised or lowered to the desired depth. Generally fitted to dinghies so that the rudder can be raised part way when running in light breezes, and fully when landing on or leaving a beach. The cheeks are often rounded at the lower edge, and high enough to be clear of the *stern wave*.

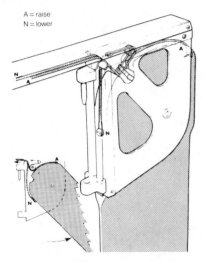

A = raise
N = lower

Light 1. Lights are exhibited by *aids to navigation* such as *lighthouses, buoys* and *beacons*. The *characteristic* of the light enables the aid to be identified, and frequently also informs the observer of its purpose, e.g. that it has been laid to mark an *isolated danger*. Fixed lights are sited on land (apart from a few privately laid US marks). The white, red, green or yellow rhythmical lights exhibited by aids to navigation may be *flashing, occulting, isophase, alternating, morse code, group flashing, group occulting* etc. *Leading lights, direction lights* and *sector lights* can only be exhibited by aids built on land or in shallow water; they indicate direction. Range depends on the *elevation* and *intensity* of the light, and on the meteorological *visibility* at the time; the maximum distance at which it can be seen also depends on the observer's *height of eye*. Attention is drawn to aids that are lit by printing purple splashes on *charts*, which also give the characteristic of the light. A full description of all lights is given in the US Coast Guard's *List of Lights;* the Admiralty *List of Lights* does not include details of beacons or buoys under 8 m. 2. Electro-magnetic radiation, the wavelength being between about 4×10^{-7} to 7.7×10^{-7}. The mean maximum velocity of light is 2.997925×10^8 m/sec, which is 186,281 miles/sec or about 300,000 km/sec. See also *lights exhibited by vessels*.

Light air *Beaufort force* 1, 1–3 *knots*, sea rippled.

Light breeze *Beaufort force* 2, 4–6 *knots*, small wavelets.

Light buoy Anchored *aid to navigation* which exhibits a light with a *character* that enables it to be identified and, often, indicates the purpose for which it was laid, say as a *port hand buoy* marking a channel. Can be used to fix the vessel's position but, unlike a lighthouse built on solid ground, may break adrift or fail to operate. Buoys carry their own source of power.

Light displacement A boat that displaces little water, being relatively light in weight. Most modern offshore boats are light displacement and, given the same expenditure on materials, are more spacious and faster than *heavy displacement* boats. Long *overhangs* are avoided, but the *hulls* are highly stressed. *Marine plywood, GRP/FRP* and light alloy enable hulls to be very strong although light.

Light dues Payment made to contribute towards the maintenance of *light buoys, lighthouses* and other *aids to navigation*.

Lighten ship To reduce a vessel's *displacement* and *draft* by taking off crew or equipment, e.g. when refloating a vessel that has *run aground*.

Lighter A flat-bottomed barge, usually with no means of propulsion, when it may also be called a dumb barge.

Light float *Aid to navigation* like a small *light vessel*, but usually has no crew.

Lighthouse Tower built on solid ground close by the coast, or on a rocky islet; exhibits a light(s), generally makes *fog signals* and often also transmits radio signals. Only structures that do not float can indicate direction, and many lighthouses exhibit lights over limited *sectors*. *Charts* give details of colour, *characteristic*, sectors, *nominal range* and fog signals, US charts give the radio identification signal, usually the *elevation* as well; UK charts give the elevation. The *List of Lights* adds details of position, structure, *phase* and *intensity*. Chart abb Lt. Ho.

Lightning protection To protect a boat from being struck by lightning, the conductor should be sufficiently high above deck for the entire boat to lie within the conical protected zone. An angle of 60° either side of the mast gives about 90% protection, and an angle of 45° gives 99.9% protection; as shown in the figure 30° either side is

effective. The circuit from the top of the mast to the water (ground) should be straight, possibly running from the masthead via the *standing rigging* to the *chain plates* or *keelbolts*. It is often necessary to include a bridging conductor, as in the case of *GRP/FRP* hulls which are non-conducting, so as to avoid damage to the hull if lightning strikes.

Light sector 1. A lighthouse may exhibit one or more lights over one or more sectors; the limits of the sectors are printed on *charts,* and the *bearings* of the sectors are given in *true* notation from seaward in the *List of Lights.* Frequently either the *character* or the colour of the light varies in each sector, so that a vessel knows in which she is situated. 2. The *lights exhibited* by *power-driven*

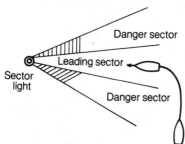

and *sailing vessels under way* show over a prescribed arc of the horizon, the *masthead light* over 225°, each *side light* over 112.5°, the *stern light* over 135° and *all round lights* over 360°. In the US these sectors are given in terms of points (each point being 11¼°), i.e. masthead 20-point, side 10-point, stern 12-point, all-round 32-point light.

Lights exhibited by vessels The *IRPCS* and other *rules of the road* prescribe the lights that a vessel must exhibit from sunset to sunrise, or during the day in *restricted visibility,* so as to prevent collisions. They show whether she is *anchored* or *aground,* her condition or occupation, her position and, when *under way,* her *course* in relation to the observer, by means of exhibiting different colours over specific sectors. Apart from very small boats (e.g. under oars), which are only required to carry

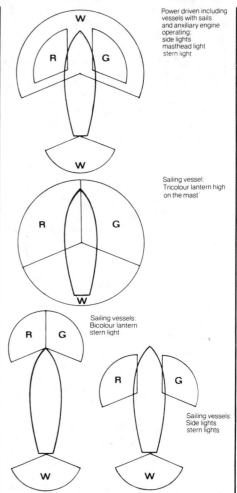

Power driven including vessels with sails and anxiliary engine operating: side lights masthead light stern light

Sailing vessel: Tricolour lantern high on the mast

Sailing vessels: Bicolour lantern stern light

Sailing vessels: Side lights stern lights

a torch or white lantern, all vessels under way at night, including *sailing vessels,* exhibit *side* and *stern lights; power-driven* vessels also exhibit white *masthead light(s).* Minimum range of *visibility* varies with the size of the vessel and, together with details of the vertical and horizontal positioning and spacing, screening, *intensity* and vertical sectors of lights, are specified by the rules of the road. Vessels engaged in dredging, minesweeping and underwater operations exhibit additional lights by night (and *shapes* by day). See also *vessels constrained by draft, engaged in fishing* and *restricted ability to manoeuvre,* also *not under command, pushing, towing,* and *range lights.*

Light tower (US) Platform erected in place of a light vessel, usually manned but may be remote-controlled. Exhibits a light at a considerable elevation.

Light vessel and **lightship** A clearly identified, manned vessel, anchored at an important position as an *aid to navigation.* Exhibits a light at night and in *restricted visibility*, sounds *fog signals*, and may transmit radio signals. *Lanby* buoys, remote-controlled buoys and *light towers* are gradually replacing manned vessels in many waters, but an anchored light vessel provides additional information for *navigators* and *pilots*, because she indicates the *set* of the *tidal stream* or *current* as she swings to her anchor. Chart abbr Lt V.

Light-weather sails Sails made of lightweight *cloth*, set in light breezes and when *running* and *reaching*; generally larger than the equivalent *working sails*. US often just light sails.

Lightweight construction If a boat has to be built to a certain minimum weight, the proportion of *ballast* can be increased by using lightweight materials such as *marine plywood*, light alloy or *GRP/FRP*. Careful design is essential, particularly in the case of *light displacement keelboats*, and strong reinforcing members are required.

Lignum vitae One of the hardest and heaviest of woods, of which sheaves, shaft bearings, fairleads etc were made formerly. Is grown in Central America and is dark and waxy; repels water and weathers well. *Specific gravity* 1.33.

Limb The upper and lower edges of the sun and moon are termed the upper and lower limbs. When taking a sun *sight* with the *sextant*, the *altitude* is normally measured between the horizon and the lower limb; when taking a moon sight only one limb may be visible. In both cases *sextant altitude* has to be corrected for *semi-diameter*, q.v.

Limber holes Holes cut in *floors* or left unfilled to allow *bilge water* to drain to the lowest point of the bilges or to a pump suction. See *construction* fig.

Limiting danger line A line printed on a *chart*; encloses a number of *dangers* or hazards.

Line 1. UK: *cordage* of small size, including *small stuff* such as hambro line, marline or codline. Larger cordage is called rope. 2. US: ropes are called lines as soon as they are used for a specific purpose, regardless of size, e.g. dock line. Thus a warp for towing is called a tow-line in the USA, but more often a tow-rope in the UK. The word line is now used increasingly in the UK for larger ropes, over an inch in circumference, possibly owing to the exchange of publications between the two countries. 3. The *equator*, as in the ceremony of *crossing the line*. 4. See *starting* and *finishing lines*.

Line honours Earned by the boat that crosses the finishing line first when *handicap racing*. When *elapsed times* have been adjusted to *corrected times*, the winner is rarely the boat which finishes first.

Line of bearing The *bearing* of an object is the same from any position on a line of bearing, and the vessel from which the bearing is taken must therefore be somewhere on the line drawn on the *chart* through positions which would all have that bearing. A line of bearing may be obtained visually with a *hand-bearing compass*, by radio with a *direction finder*, or by finding the bearing of an object *relative* to the ship's head.

Line of position, LOP (US) See *position line*.

Line of soundings (US **chain of soundings**) Numerous *soundings* taken at regular intervals. If the depth of water alters quickly, a reliable *position line* can be obtained, but in any case a line of soundings helps to check the vessel's position.

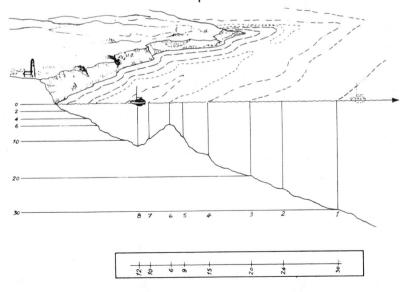

The soundings are noted, *reduced to chart datum* and marked on a strip of paper at intervals corresponding to the speed of the boat *over the ground*. They are then matched to the soundings on the chart by moving the paper parallel to the *track* near the *estimated position*, or near a position line obtained, e.g. by taking a *bearing*.

Lines The shape of the *hull*, as in lines plans, and expressions such as fine or sturdy lines.

Lines plan Set of drawings that shows the external shape of a boat's *hull*. There are always three drawings, and may be more. *Buttock* lines give the shape of vertical sections through the hull, parallel to the fore-and-aft line, and are drawn on the *profile* or sheer *plan*, the view from the side; *sections* are vertical sections at right angles to the centreline, and are drawn on the *body plan*, the view from the end; *waterlines* are horizontal sections at various heights, and are parallel to the waterplane; they are drawn on one side of the centreline on the *half-breadth* plan, the view from above. *Diagonals* are often drawn on the other side of the half-breadth plan, and also appear in the body plan as straight lines. Lines plans are generally drawn to a scale of between 1:10 and 1:100, and are supplemented by the *table of offsets* as well as by *accommodation, sail* and construction *plans* which give details as to layout, materials and *scantlings* etc.

Link Many links interlock to make up chain. Stud-link chain cable is less likely to get snarled up than open-link.

Link shackle The link is opened and closed by screwing or unscrewing the nut.

Liquid compass The bowl of the *magnetic compass* is filled with oil, sometimes with a mixture of alcohol and distilled water. This both steadies the card and reduces wear when the card rotates on the pivot.

List A boat lists when she leans to one side, perhaps because more gear, stores etc have been stowed on that side, perhaps because water has been taken on board, e.g. after springing a leak. A permanent state, as opposed to the temporary state of *heeling*.

List of Lights Official publication that gives details of lights exhibited by all *aids to navigation* (UK except *light buoys* under 8 m), including name, position, *character, phase* and *elevation* of the light, height of structure, *fog signals* etc. The US List includes details of *radio beacons*, whereas the UK List merely mentions the type of radio beacon, i.e. *direction, omnidirectional* etc, there being a separate List of Radio Aids. The US List includes charts showing the location of radio beacons along the coasts and in coastal waters. They are published by the US Coast Guard and by the Hydrographer of the Navy (UK).

List of Radio Aids Annual UK publications which give full details of all radio aids, such as *radio beacons*, radio stations and matters concerning radio communication. Published by the Hydrographer of the Navy.

Litre (US **liter**) One cubic decimetre, one thousand cubic centimetres. For practical purposes, approximately: 1 litre = 1.8 pints; 1 pint = $\frac{1}{8}$ gallon = 0.57 litres. See also *gallon* for conversion factors.

Little America's Cup Correctly the *International Catamaran Challenge Trophy* (q.v.), nicknamed after the America's Cup.

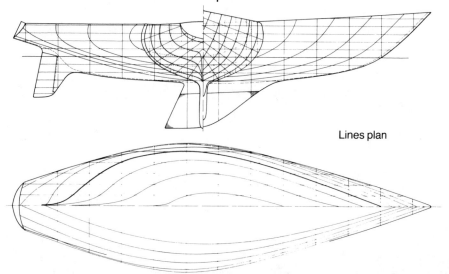

Lines plan

Littoral The zone between the limits of high and low water: the *foreshore*.

Live ballast Movable *ballast* in the shape of the crew, whose weight can be shifted to *trim* dinghies and keelboats, or to keep a boat upright. *Trapezes* and *sitting out* (US *hiking out*) aids increase the effectiveness of live ballast. Many dinghy racing classes limit the weight of *wet clothing* that may be worn by the crew.

Lively Said of a boat that responds quickly to seas; has a short *rolling period*.

Ljungstrom rig (US also **twin-wing**) First tried in 1935 by the Swede, Dr. Fredrik Ljungstrom, on the 22 sq. m skerry cruiser 'Aeolus'. Smooth airflow over the mast and leading edge of the sail is achieved by setting a double sail that encloses the mast, either *loose-footed* or with rigid double *booms* that can be swung out to either side. When

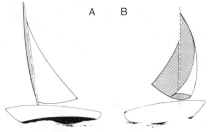

close-hauled and *reaching* both sails set on the same side (A), but when *running* they are separated to set either side, so doubling the sail area. *Reefing* is achieved by rotating the mast to wrap the sail around it. The smooth transition between mast and sail has the same effect as a *wing sail,* and improves airflow on the lee side of the sail, which generates more drive than a mainsail with slides, or one fed into a groove.

Lloyd's Register of Shipping Lloyd's is an association of underwriters, which was formed as a result of meetings in Edward Lloyd's coffee house in London in 1601. Marine underwriters at Lloyd's formed Lloyd's Register of Shipping in 1760. This is the largest and oldest of the *classification societies*, and draws up rules to cover construction methods, materials, *scantlings* etc. Vessels built in accordance with the rules are classed 100A, and are listed in the register; the prefix ⊬ is added if they are built under survey, and the suffix 1 if the vessel carries anchors, cables and warps adequate for her size.

Lloyd's Register of Yachts Publication which first appeared in 1878, listing the yachts built to Lloyd's rules, originally of wooden construction, later of steel and latterly of *GRP/FRP*. The 75th edition, published in 1963, listed the details of over 10,000 yachts for the first time, but publication ceased in

1981. The American edition, giving details of Canadian and US yachts, was first published in 1903, but is now called the North American Yacht Register.

LOA Length overall, see *length*.

Load waterline, LWL In the *lines plan*, is the *waterline* at which a boat is calculated to float when fitted out and ready to sail, i.e. when carrying the load for which she was designed.

Local attraction In certain areas, often owing to concentrations of iron ore on the sea-bed or in an adjacent land mass, *compass* errors occur because the earth's *magnetic field* is irregular. In these areas, which are often marked on charts, the magnetic compass cannot be relied on.

Local Hour Angle, LHA The angle measured westwards at the pole between the *observer's meridian* and the *meridian* through a *heavenly body,* found by adding easterly *longitude* to the *Greenwich Hour Angle* or by subtracting westerly longitude. See *PZX triangle* fig.

Local Mean Time, LMT Time kept in a particular country or part of a country; the local hour angle of the *mean sun* at any particular moment. LMT at a place differs from *Greenwich Mean Time* by the equivalent in time of the *difference of longitude* between the *Greenwich meridian* and the *meridian* of that place. West of Greenwich LMT is behind GMT: e.g. when time in London is 1200 hrs time in New York is 0700 hrs. LMT = GMT + easterly or − westerly longitude.

Lock A chamber with gates either end which are closed when boats or ships inside are raised from a lower level to a higher by filling the chamber with water, or are lowered by draining out some of the water inside. The gate(s) are then opened at one end only to allow vessels to lock in and out when the water level inside the lock is the same as that outside. *Mooring lines* must be carefully secured to keep the boat parallel to the lock wall, in spite of the turbulence caused by the rapid inrush or outflow of the water. A ladder of locks is found inland where there is a great change in level, but in some canals vessels are raised and lowered by mechanical lifts to avoid having to operate a succession of locks. Many small locks, used mainly by pleasure boats, are manually operated by boat owners themselves as they pass through.

Locker An enclosed stowage space anywhere on board, such as a hanging locker for clothes, bo'sun's locker for spare gear, chain locker for anchor cables, sail locker, cockpit lockers under the seats for stowing mooring lines, fenders and other deck gear.

Lodging knee A *knee* fitted in the horizontal plane.

Lofting Drawing the lines of the boat full scale, generally on the *mould-loft* floor, working from the *lines plan* and *table of offsets*.

Log 1. The distance that a boat sails *through the water,* or the speed at which she sails, is measured with a log, which is an essential part of the navigational equipment of any boat that sails out of sight of land or in restricted visibility. The oldest and simplest are the *Dutchman's log* and the *chip log*, both of which measure speed, from which the distance sailed is calculated. The *patent log* has a towed rotator vane and records distance on a mechanical register, often mounted on the taffrail, without using electric current; it often also indicates speed; a later version of this log records distance and speed electronically. *Impeller logs* measure distance sailed and *electro-magnetic logs* measure speed through the water, but both have dials registering speed and distance, and some also indicate acceleration. Venturi-type and pitot tube

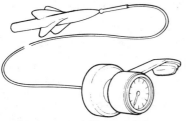

logs measure pressure differential that occurs when water flows past the measuring head, the difference being proportional to speed. A simple hand-held log of this type is held over the side with the open end of the tube pointing ahead; the faster the boat moves the higher does the level of water rise in the tube, which is graduated in *knots*. Electronic strain-gauge type logs have a rod that projects beneath the hull, and the strain on the rod increases proportionally with speed, enabling boat speed to be determined. The *Doppler log* measures either speed through the water or (more rarely, and in commercial shipping) *over the ground.* Many logs have *repeaters* in the cockpit to enable the helmsman to check speed without going below. Logs are *calibrated* by checking the recorded speed or distance against a *measured distance.* 2. The word log is also used as a verb: a boat may be said to have logged 30 miles. 3. Log or log-book: book in which full details of all matters concerning navi-

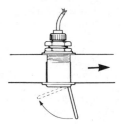

gation are entered or logged such as *courses,* speeds, *distances* run, *bearings, fixes;* in each case the time is also noted. Weather details are also required, i.e. wind direction and *force, sea state, visibility, barometer* readings, temperature, weather forecast etc. Changes of sail, reefing, setting the spinnaker, starting and stopping the auxiliary engine, damage sustained and all other occurrences that affect navigation or safety, or are of interest, are also entered. 4. A written radio log is kept on board a vessel with radio communication equipment. The operator enters details of traffic relating to *distress, urgency* and safety, ship-to-ship and ship-to-shore communication and other details required by the national authority. The log must be made available on request for inspection by an authorized representative of the US Federal Communications Commission, or of the UK Department of Trade or Home Office.

Long-flashing light The duration of the *flash* exhibited as an *aid to navigation* is at least two seconds, followed by a longer period of darkness or less intense light; chart abbr L. Fl.

Longitude The position of any place on the surface of the earth is defined by two spherical co-ordinates, *latitude* and longitude, both of which are expressed as angular distances. The longitude of a particular place P is the angle AOB at the earth's centre, in the plane of the *equator,* made by lines from the centre to the *Greenwich meridian,* OB, and to the *meridian* of the place, OA.

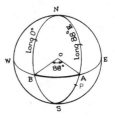

Longitude is measured in degrees, minutes and seconds up to 180° east and west of the *prime meridian* (long 0°) which passes through Greenwich. The distance represented by one degree of longitude varies from roughly 60 *nautical miles* at the equator to nil at the poles.

Longitudinal bulkhead A *bulkhead* fitted longitudinally to separate one part of the accommodation from another.

Longitudinal or **longitudinal member** Any *fore-and-aft member* of the structure fitted to strengthen the boat, such as *stringer, shelf, keelson*. In *GRP/FRP* construction longitudinal stiffening often consists of layers of reinforcing material laminated around a solid or hollow core. See also *sonrib*.

Longitudinal stability A boat is very much more stable in the fore-and-aft plane than in the transverse plane, because length is greater than beam. When sailing downwind the boat does not heel when the wind freshens, and the area of sail *projected* is not reduced; this can lead to damage to sails or rigging, or to dismasting, if the crew underestimate wind strength.

Long splice A permanent connection made between two ropes or lines when the join has to pass through a *block, sheave,* or *eye*. The two ropes are unlaid, crotched or married, and then selected strands are unlaid further with corresponding strands from the other rope laid into the vacant grooves. The resulting pairs are halved in diameter and tied off. Unlike the *short splice* the diameter of the cordage is not increased, but the result is not so strong as a short splice.

Long tack or **long board** When *beating,* the *tack* which is the longer of the two, and which takes the boat closer to her destination. Tacks are of unequal lengths whenever the objective is not directly to *windward,* say when beating up a narrow channel, when a strong *tidal stream or current* is setting across the wind direction, or when the wind shifts after a race has been started. The general rule is to sail the long tack first. In figure 1 both boats sail equally close to the *mark,* but in figure 2 white, on the long port tack, is nearer. Figure 3 shows how much further the white boat has sailed towards the

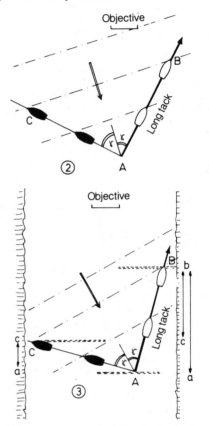

mark (a–b) than black (a–c). If the wind *backs* at this point, C will have *overstood* the mark but, if the shift is about 20°, B will be able to stay on port tack sailing parallel to the shore. If the wind *veers* 20° B will be able to *point* closer to it on starboard tack than C was able to before the wind veered, and will reach it well before C which is unable to lay the mark on port tack.

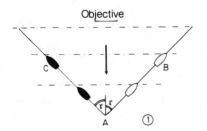

Look-out Visual watch. Also the member of the crew whose duty it is to keep a close watch all round the boat, especially dead ahead, on the lee bow (an area which is often concealed by the headsail), and on the starboard bow, so as to observe the movements of other vessels, look for obstructions, lights, navigation marks etc. A look-out may be posted in the cockpit, at the bows when visibility is restricted, or up the mast to increase *height of eye*. Under the *IRPCS* all vessels must maintain a proper look-out by sight, hearing and all appropriate measures, such as *radar*.

Loom 1. The glow from a light below the *horizon,* seen reflected on clouds; the light is otherwise invisible to direct vision. 2. To appear larger than natural or indistinctly in *fog*. 3. The part of the *oar* inside the fulcrum, including the handle (US sometimes the part between the blade and the handle).

Loop or **frame aerial** or **antenna** A rotating *directional aerial* for *radio direction finding.* Typically such an aerial consists of several turns of insulated wire wound inside the loop core; when the plane of the loop is at right angles to the *radio beacon* the voltages induced are equal and opposite, and this is called a *null* point. As the loop is rotated, the induced voltage unbalance and the signal gradually increase; the strongest signal is received when the plane of the loop is aligned with the radio beacon (maximum). See also *Bellini-Tosi.*

Loose-footed A *mainsail* which is neither connected continuously along the *foot* to a *boom* by *slides* or *lacing,* nor fed into a *groove.* Is either fastened to the boom only at *tack* and *clew* or, as in a *trysail* and *standing lug,* is set without a boom.

Lop 1. Short, choppy seas, not high. 2. US: LOP is abbr for line of position, see *position line.*

Loran LOng RAnge Navigation system. The Loran A *hyperbolic navigation* system, introduced in World War II, has been superseded by Loran C, a similar but more accurate system (normally ± 1500 ft), which combines time difference with *phase* matching. A chain of transmitters, consisting of a *master* and up to four *slaves* which are usually between 350 and 750 n.miles distant, emits synchronized pulses at a *frequency* of 100 kHz, giving a *ground wave* range of 1000 n.miles or more. The receiver on board identifies two transmitters, and measures the difference in the time of arrival of the pulses in microseconds. The time difference is referred to a Loran chart, which is a normal chart overprinted with hyperbolae, each of which connects all the points where the time difference is the same. The vessel will be somewhere on the hyperbolic *position line* which matches the measured time difference, and her position may be fixed by obtaining a second position line, using the same master and a second slave. *Sky wave* zones cover much greater areas than the ground wave zones, but the fixes are considerably less accurate. More sophisticated receivers provide the vessel's latitude and longitude as a read-out, but position can also be calculated using Loran C tables.

Lose way A boat loses way when she slows down and ceases to move through the water.

Loudhailer A device to improve voice communication over longer distances. May be just a funnel-shaped tube, battery-powered or a combination of *foghorn* and megaphone that can also be used for signalling.

Louvre Small slotted *ventilator,* usually fitted in a door; not sprayproof.

Low An area of low *atmospheric pressure;* see *depression.*

Lower To let down a sail, spar, anchor, flag etc (opp *hoist*).

Lowering mast A mast *stepped* on *deck* in a *tabernacle,* and lowered to pass under bridges. A deck-stepped mast can be kept under control while being lowered if a *spar,* the same length as the base of the *foretriangle,* is rigged between the base of the mast and the *forestay,* with a *tackle* between the spar and the *stemhead fitting.* When the tackle is eased, the mast is still supported from forward and, initially, there is little change of angle between the tackle and the spar. Additional lateral support is provided if two spars are used, hinged either side at the *chain plates.*

Lower light The nearer and lower light of a pair of *leading* lights (US range lights). The vessel is not on the leading line when the lights are *open.*

Lower mast The lowest section of a built-up mast; a *pole mast* carrying other masts about it.

Lower shroud *Shroud* which runs athwartships from the *spreaders* (or the lower spreaders if there is more than one pair) to a *chain plate* at the side of the deck. Normally there is either one to port and one to starboard, or two either side, one pair running to a point slightly forward of the mast and the other slightly abaft it. See *rigging* fig.

Lowest Astronomical tide, LAT The lowest level of *tide* which can be predicted to occur under (a) any combination of astronomical conditions that may be foreseen and (b) average meteorological conditions. The reference level (*chart datum*) for UK metric charts and for *heights of tide* (tidal datum) in UK *Tide Tables. Storm surges* may give lower levels of tide than those predicted by LAT criteria.

Low water, LW The time in a tidal cycle when the *height of tide* is least, i.e. the lowest level reached by that *tide*. Low water *springs* and *neaps* are the minimum and maximum low water heights of tide respectively that occur during half a *lunar month. See tide* fig. When there is *diurnal inequality*, there is a higher LW and a lower LW daily.

Lubber line or **lubber's line** The pointer, close to the *compass card*, against which the *course* is read. A compass must be installed so that the line between the *compass pivot* and the lubber line is parallel to the *fore-and-aft line;* the lubber line then corresponds with the ship's *head.* Many modern compasses have additional lubber lines 45° either side of the fore-and-aft lubber line, so that errors caused by *parallax* when the helmsman is sitting on the side deck are eliminated. When *beating,* these also roughly indicate the course that the boat will follow after *going about.*

Luff 1. or luff up: to alter course by putting the *helm* down to *leeward* so that the boat sails closer to the wind or turns into the wind. The *apparent wind* then blows from nearer the *stem,* and the *sheets* have to be *hardened* in. The opposite is to *bear away.* To luff another boat is a defensive racing tactic; see *luffing match.* 2. The *leading edge* of a *fore-and-aft sail;* a *staysail* often has *hanks* (US snaps) sewn to the luff so that it can be

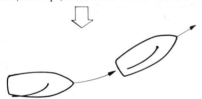

hanked on to the *stay,* and the luff of a *mainsail* either has *slides* seized to it at intervals (they run in or on a *track* on the *mast*), a *bolt-rope* (feeds into the mast *groove*) or is held to the mast with *lacing* or *hoops.* 3. The *windward* side of a *spinnaker* when it is set. 4. US: a sail luffs when the wind *backs* it close abaft the luff, i.e. when the boat is *pointing* just too close to the wind, or when the sail is not trimmed in quite far enough. The UK term is to lift (see *lift* 3).

Luff groove device Light alloy *extrusion,* grooved to take the luff of a *headsail.* See *headfoil* and *sail changing cartridge.* c.f. luff spar. Under the *IOR* the device must be free to rotate and of constant section; twice its diameter is added to LPG (longest perpendicular of jibs) when measuring a headsail.

Luffing match Under the *racing rules,* a *leeward yacht* may luff one or more competitors to *windward* of her to try to prevent them from overtaking to windward, provided that she has luffing rights, which are defined precisely in rules

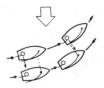

38, 40 and 42; the windward yacht has to respond to avoid a collision, and the leeward yacht may continue to luff until the helmsman of the windward yacht can shout 'mast abeam', or until the yachts involved are more than two boat's lengths apart. The match ends in favour of the windward yacht when she has advanced so far that her helmsman, when sighting abeam and sailing no higher than the leeward yacht, is *abreast* of the leeward yacht's mast (at which moment he may shout 'mast abeam'). The match ends in favour of the leeward yacht when the windward yacht has to go about to avoid a collision, or when the leeward yacht reaches the *safe leeward position* where she slows her opponent by *backwinding* her, so that she has to tack to clear her wind or fall still further back.

Luff-rope The part of the *bolt-rope* that is sewn to the luff of a sail. May be fed into the *groove* in the mast, headfoil, or luff groove device.

Luff spar 1. A flat spar, usually of wood, with a groove into which the luff of the headsail is fed. Typically has a fore and aft dimension of 4–6 in (10–15 cm) as compared with 2–3 in (5–7 cm) of a *headfoil.* Restricted mainly to certain catamarans, and usually included in the sail area measurement. 2. Of *furling gear,* the light alloy *extrusion,* grooved to take the luff of the sail. When the drum is rotated, the sail is wrapped round the spar, luff first.

Luff tackle A *tackle* with one *single* and one *double block,* the *standing part* being attached to the single block. Luff upon luff: the block of one luff tackle is hooked to the fall of another luff tackle.

Luff wire Wire that runs from *head* to *tack* inside the luff *tabling* of a *headsail* to limit stretch.

Lugsail Quadrilateral *fore-and-aft sail*, the *head* of which is attached to a steeply inclined *yard*. The *tack* of the dipping lug is attached to a hook forward and, when *gybing* or *going about*, is unhooked to dip the yard because the sail always

sets to *leeward* of the mast. The standing lug is tacked down permanently to the deck, and the yard is not dipped. The balance lugsail is laced to a boom that projects forward of the mast. Lugsails were often set by fishing boats such as luggers, but now are mainly confined to smaller sailing dinghies. See also *Chinese lug*.

Lull A temporary drop in wind speed.

Luminous range The maximum distance that a light can be seen and identified at a certain time; depends both on the *intensity* of the light and on the meteorological *visibility* at that time (c.f. *nominal range*, based on 10 *n. miles* meteorological visibility). Luminous range is affected by visibility, e.g. given 100,000 cd light intensity, nominal range is approximately 20 n. miles but, when visibility improves to 27 n. miles, the light is visible at double the distance; if visibility deteriorates to 500 m luminous range drops to under 1 n. mile. On modern *charts* the range of lights exhibited by lighthouses is normally given as nominal range.

Lunar day The interval between two successive *transits* of the moon across a particular *meridian*. The lunar day is about 50 minutes longer than the solar day because, during the period that the moon makes one revolution round the earth, the earth itself continues on its path around the sun. This affects the times of the *tides*.

Lunar month, lunation or **synodical month** The time it takes for the moon to orbit the earth from one *new moon* to the next, i.e. to return to the same position relative to the sun: 29 days 12 hrs 44 mins 2.87 secs.

Lunar tide The part of a tidal undulation that is caused by the tide-raising force of the moon. The gravitational effect of the moon is over twice that of the sun because she is so much closer to the earth. The period of the *semi-diurnal* lunar tide is about 12 hrs 25 mins, i.e. half a *lunar day*.

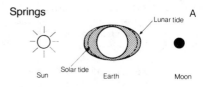

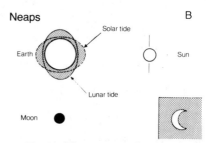

Lux *SI* unit of illumination. The amount of light emitted by one lumen per second (i.e. emitted by a light source of 1 *candela intensity*) on a surface vertical to the light source.

M

M = Mike: blue *code flag* with a white cross. As a single letter signal means 'My vessel is stopped and making no way through the water'. *Morse code:* — — (dash dash). When racing means '*Round* or pass the object displaying this signal instead of the *mark* which it replaces'.

Made good A term applied to *courses, distances* and *speeds*. Sometimes (especially in the US) is restricted to those that have been made good *over the ground*, i.e. when allowance has been made for *leeway* and the *set* and *rate* of the *tidal stream* or *current*, but some authorities also use it in connection with those made good *through the water*. In casual speech may also be applied to the average course steered by the helmsman during a certain period.

Magnet A metal body which attracts particles of iron or steel, and which is surrounded by a *magnetic field. Corrector magnets* are fitted by a *compass adjuster* to eliminate or reduce *deviation*.

Magnetic bearing The angle between the direction of an object and the *magnetic meridian*. A *bearing* taken with a *magnetic compass* that is not disturbed by an external force (not subject to *deviation*). A *true bearing* that has been corrected (US uncorrected) for *variation*, and a *compass bearing* corrected for *deviation* (q.v. for details of correction).

Magnetic compass The lines of force of the earth's *magnetic field* direct the needle of the magnetic compass. The needle is fixed beneath the *compass card* and, because the card is able to pivot freely inside the bowl, the needle aligns itself with the direction of the earth's line of total force, i.e. with the *magnetic meridian*. Its red end is attracted by earth's magnetic north pole and its blue end by the magnetic south pole. The angle between the magnetic meridian and the *true meridian* is called *variation. Deviation* is the angle between the magnetic meridian and the direction to which the compass needle points when deflected by a disturbing influence such as an electrical circuit or a mass of ferrous metal. See also *compass*.

Magnetic course The angle between the *magnetic meridian* and the vessel's *fore-and-aft line*. Like a magnetic bearing (q.v.), is the interim stage when correcting a course from compass to true or vice versa. The direction of a magnetic course only coincides with that of the *compass course* when *deviation* is nil.

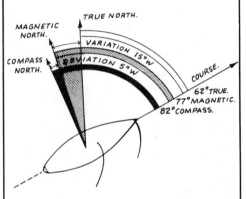

Magnetic disturbance The earth's *magnetic field* is sometimes disturbed by magnetic storms, which cause *compass* errors that cannot be foreseen. See also *local attraction*.

Magnetic field The field of force that surrounds a magnet or a current-carrying conductor, i.e. the area surrounding a magnet in which its magnetic effect can be detected. Electronic equipment and electric circuits on board have to be positioned where their magnetic fields are sufficiently far away from the *magnetic compass* to avoid causing *deviation*.

Magnetic meridian A line of force along which the freely pivoting needle of a *magnetic compass* settles when not disturbed by an external force. Although an undisturbed compass needle is often said loosely to point to the *magnetic north pole*, earth's magnetic field is very irregular, and not all of the magnetic meridians pass through the magnetic north and south poles.

Magnetic north The magnetic rose printed on a chart is based on the *magnetic compass*, and 0° on the magnetic rose is often referred to as magnetic north which, almost always, differs from *true north* by the amount of *variation*. Similarly the magnetic compass, when directed solely by the earth's magnetic force, is often said to indicate the direction of magnetic north. See below.

Magnetic north pole Not a fixed point but an area that is constantly moving its position. It is some way from the *geographic north pole*, and is near Hudson's Bay, roughly 75° N 100° W. A *compass needle* suspended absolutely freely rests vertically, north-seeking end down, at the magnetic north pole (see *dip*).

Magnetic poles The points near either end of a magnet where the lines of force of its magnetic field emerge (red pole) and enter (blue pole). On the earth the positions north and south where a freely suspended magnetic *compass needle* points vertically downward.

Magnetism (terrestrial) The earth can be imagined as having a long magnet in the centre, set at an angle to the axis (between the geographic north and south poles) about which the earth rotates. The north end of this 'magnet' is the *magnetic north pole*, which is a blue pole and, owing to the fundamental law of magnetism that unlike poles attract each other, attracts the red end of the magnetized *compass needle*, while the south red pole of the 'magnet' attracts the blue end of the needle. The needle of a compass is free to pivot, and settles with its axis along a line of force, i.e. it lies in the *magnetic meridian*. The earth's magnetic field is irregular and magnetic meridians do not necessarily pass through the north and south magnetic poles which, in any case, are not fixed points but move constantly. See also *dip*.

Magnetron The transmitting valve used in a *radar* set; produces pulses of high power and very short duration.

Mahogany Wood from which many parts of wooden boats are made, especially planking. Honduras, Brazilian, African, Philippine and other mahoganies vary considerably in weight and quality. *Specific gravity* 0.56–0.85.

Maiden voyage The first voyage made by a boat after construction has been completed.

Main 1. The principal of two or more similar objects, such as the mainmast, main halyard. 2. Coll the *mainsail*. 3. Poetically the high seas, e.g. the Spanish Main.

Mainboom *Spar* which extends the *foot* of the *mainsail* of a *fore-and-aft rigged* vessel with more than one *boom*. When the boat has only one it is simply called the boom.

Mainmast The principal *mast;* in *ketches* and *yawls* the taller forward mast, in other two-masted vessels such as *schooners*, the aftermast; in vessels with three or more masts, the second from forward, aft of the foremast and forward of the *mizzenmast*.

Mainsail The principal sail. 1. A *fore-and-aft sail* set on the after side of the *mainmast;* may be a *bermudan* (US marconi), *gaff* or *spritsail*, and *loose-footed* or bent to the *boom* or *mainboom*. See *rigging* fig. 2. In a *sailing ship*, the lowest *square sail*, the main *course*, bent to the main *yard* that crosses the mainmast.

Mainsheet The *sheet* which controls the *mainsail*. The number of *parts* varies mainly with the area of the sail, and the *mechanical advantage* needed for efficient *trimming*. The lower block may be a *snatch block* to enable the number of parts to be reduced when the wind is light. A centre mainsheet is fitted from a point roughly half way along the

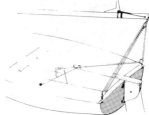

boom to the centre of the *cockpit* or on *deck;* a stern mainsheet is fitted aft from the end of the boom to the *transom* or *afterdeck*. The upper block may be fixed to the boom or to a *boom strap*, or may be adjustable and attached to a *reefing claw* or to a *traveller* sliding on a *track* on the boom. The lower block is usually shackled to a traveller which slides athwartships on a track or, sometimes, on a *horse*.

Mainsheet track A *track* in the *cockpit* or on *deck*, fitted athwartships and sometimes curved so that the pull of the mainsheet is always as near vertical as possible; the mainsail can then set in any position without *twisting*. The mainsheet block

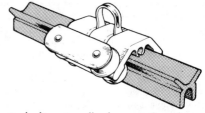

is attached to a *traveller* that runs along the track, and can be fixed at any position. Tracks of different sections are available, and the traveller may slide inside raised rails or have rollers which run on X-section track.

Main ship channel The deepest channel in an area, and the one that can be navigated most easily; generally marked by *light buoys*, sometimes also by *direction* or *sector lights*.

Main staysail A *staysail* set on the mainstay of a *schooner* between the *mainmast* and the *foremast*.

Maintenance All parts of a boat and her equipment need careful maintenance during the sailing season, as well as when *fitting out* and *laying up*. Sails need frequent checking for *chafe* and broken stitching, all parts of the *standing* and *running rigging* must be inspected regularly, *blocks* and sail *slides* must run smoothly, and suspect rigging wire has to be replaced immediately. The paintwork of hull, deck and superstructure needs cleaning and touching up where necessary, particular care being paid to *brightwork* to avoid unsightly black marks where moisture penetrates to the wood. The bottom of a boat kept in the water requires regular attention to remove *marine fouling*, and *antifouling* paint is applied to discourage new growth. All machinery requires greasing, oiling and protecting from *corrosion*. A check should also be made regularly to ensure that no parts are suffering from *galvanic corrosion*.

Make . . . In relation to the progress of a boat: she makes way when she moves through the water; headway when moving ahead; sternway when moving stern first; *leeway* when moving to leeward of her *heading*. She is said to make, say, 5 *knots* when she is moving at a rate of 5 *nautical miles* per hour. Make good – see *made good*.

Make fast To secure a line or rope to a *cleat*, *bitt*, ring, *bollard* etc.

Make heavy weather *Roll* and *pitch* heavily in seas, making slow and uncomfortable progress.

Make port To reach and enter a port.

Make sail To set sails and get under way.

Make water To *leak*, as opposed to *shipping* water over the *gunwale*.

Making When the *ranges* of successive *tides* increase between *neaps* and *springs* they are said to be making, as opposed to taking off or cutting.

Man 1. To provide a boat with a crew. 2. To operate or work, as in to man the windlass etc.

Manila Light brown, hard, smooth natural fibres up to 10 ft (3 m) long, obtained from the abaca plant that grows in the Philippines (hence its name), make very strong, rot-resistant rope; now largely superseded by synthetic fibre rope.

Manoeuvrability (US **maneuvrability**) In the broadest terms, the manoeuvrability of a boat depends on her *balance*, her ability to *answer the helm* quickly, to accelerate as wind speed increases and to *carry way*. All these factors are important when *going about*, *gybing* and manoeuvring in restricted waters under sail, and the crew must also be efficient because sail *trimming* is crucial for good handling qualities.

Manoeuvring (US **maneuvring**) and **warning signals** The *IRPCS* prescribe that the following signals shall be made by *whistle* when vessels manoeuvre in sight of one another (• = short blast, about one second duration; — = long blast, 4–6 seconds):
• I am altering my course to *starboard*
• • I am altering my course to *port*
• • • I am operating astern propulsion
In a fairway or narrow channel:
— — • I intend to overtake on your starboard side
— — • • I intend to overtake on your port side
— • — • Vessel about to be overtaken is in agreement
• • • • I am in doubt regarding your intentions, the so-called Look Out signal
— Warning on approaching a bend, and acknowledgement of such warning
Sound signals may be supplemented by light signals. There are many differences in the *US Inland Waters*, *Great Lakes* and *Western Rivers* rules where signals are frequently exchanged, e.g. vessels when passing (meeting) port to port and at a safe distance both sound one blast, but when passing starboard to starboard both sound two blasts. Four blasts are sounded in case of doubt or danger, except in the Great Lakes where five are sounded.

Manometer Instrument with which the pressure of a fluid is measured.

Man overboard The words shouted when a member of the crew is seen to fall into the water. The vital actions are to throw a *lifebuoy* to him immediately, and to detail one of the crew to watch him continuously, regardless of the boat's actions, so that his position is known. It is best not to sail downwind further than necessary (2) because *beating* is more difficult when shorthanded. After *broad reaching* (3) for a short time,

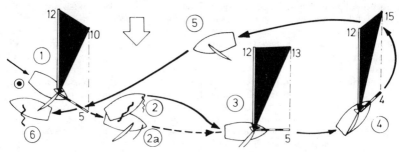

either *gybe* or *go about* (4) on to the opposite tack, returning (5) to *leeward* of the man (6), where sheets are eased right out and the boat brought to a halt. The figure shows how the *apparent wind* (black arrow) varies on the different *points of sailing*, although the *true wind* strength is a constant 12 knots. It is advisable to mark the position of a person in the water because it is not always possible to return immediately, for example if a *spinnaker* has first to be lowered. Many boats carry a *dan buoy*, secured by a line to the lifebuoy that is thrown to him. One alternative is a small pack that is attached to *safety harness;* when this is opened a balloon inflates and flies at about 100 ft (30 m) overhead. A trail can also be left in the water by throwing a series of cushions, empty bottles etc overboard. See also *smoke float, dyemarker*, and *lifebuoy light. Code flag 0* signifies man overboard.

Man overboard light   See *lifebuoy light.*

Man overboard pole   See *dan buoy.*

Manrope   A rope rigged as a handrail for an *accommodation ladder* or gangplank. The manrope knot is a double *wall* and *crown*, and is a *stopper knot* made to prevent the manrope from unreeving through a *stanchion* eye.

Manufacturer's class   Boats built by a single manufacturer, or by several yards under licence, to a single design and as nearly identical as possible, not only in construction but in all details. Fittings and gear are more strictly controlled and *tolerances* smaller than those of *one-design class* boats. The Laser is an example.

Marconi rig   In the UK the term *bermudan*, bermudian or Bermuda rig is preferred. Triangular

fore-and-aft sails are set without a *gaff, sprit* or *yard*. The mast required is very much taller than that of a gaff-rigged boat and, like the tall aerial used for the Marconi transmitter in the early days of wireless, the original spars for this rig required a considerable number of *stays* and *shrouds* for support.

Marcq St. Hilaire method   See *intercept method.*

Mare's tails   See *cirrus.*

Marina   Artificial boat basin with berthing and servicing facilities; usually has banks of finger *pontoons*. Primarily for pleasure craft.

Marine fouling or **growth**   General terms for marine organisms that attach themselves to the *underwater body* and *boot top*, whether vegetable (green and brown algal slimes, seaweeds) or animal (barnacles, mussels, tunicates), especially when a vessel lies in harbour on a *mooring buoy* or at *anchor* for long periods. Boat speed is quickly reduced by 20%, and after a long period from 30–50%. The bottom is painted with *antifouling* to prevent marine growth, and is scrubbed periodically.

Marine glue   Not glue but a flexible compound, such as a rubber-based or oil-and-shellac composition, with which the *seams* of a *laid deck* are *payed*. Must neither become too hard nor too soft when temperature fluctuates, and must remain in contact with the wood.

Marine plywood   Plywood sheets of varying sizes and thicknesses are made to official standards specifically for marine purposes, and no other plywood should be used on board. Quality depends mainly on the adhesive, which should be waterproof and heatproof, and on the core material. Used for *hard chine* hulls (especially those constructed by amateurs), for *bulkheads* and interior joinery and, in very thin sheets, to build *moulded plywood* hulls.

Marine railway (US)   A slip at a boatyard; has tracks leading into the water on which boats are launched or hauled out.

Maritime air mass An *air mass* formed over an ocean, either in the subtropical belt (maritime-tropical air) or in the polar area (maritime-polar air).

Mark 1. An object that marks a position, such as an *aid to navigation*. In races is any object specified in the *sailing instructions* which has to be passed or *rounded* on a required side. Marks are laid or selected to indicate the beginning and end of each *leg* of the *course*. They have to be rounded in the correct order, and left to *port* or *starboard* (often as indicated by red or green flags respectively, flown on the *committee boat*). If a mark is rounded wrongly (a), the boat retraces her course

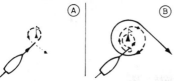

before rounding it in accordance with instructions (b), because the *racing rules* specify that a string representing her *wake* from her start to her finish would have to lie on the required side of each mark. If a boat touches a mark, she either has to retire or exonerate herself by rounding it entirely and then re-rounding or re-passing it without touching it, and leaving it on the required side. 2. See *lead line* for 'by the mark'.

Marline Light two-stranded hemp line, formerly used for *lashing, lacing* etc.

Marline spike A pointed steel tool for *splicing* and other purposes, such as tightening and un-screwing *shackle* pins. Many seamen's knives have a spike. Hence marline spike seamanship: the art of knotting, splicing, seizing etc; and marline spike sailor: one who is skilled in manipulating ropes and lines (terms which are used more frequently in the US than the UK).

Marline spike hitch A marline spike or toggle is placed in the *bight* of a *slip knot* made in a line so that more power can be applied, for example when *whipping* a rope's end, tensioning the outhaul etc.

Marling hitch (sometimes **marline hitch**) A *half*

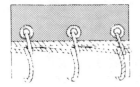

hitch made round a spar or similar object, and repeated at intervals. Can be used to *bend* a sail to a spar that has no track or groove, to secure a sail to the boom when *furling*, etc.

Maroon 1. An explosive signal, usually with a *flare*, made particularly to summon the crew when the *lifeboat* is called out. 2. To leave a member of the crew at some isolated place as a punishment.

Marsh Flat, wet and very soft low-lying land that is often flooded by rain. Salt marshes are flooded by the sea.

Martingale 1. *Stay* which leads from the end of the *jib-boom* to the *dolphin striker* and counters the pull of the *headstay*. In some *sailing ships* there are inner and outer martingale stays, and a martingale backstay between the bow and the dolphin striker, which is sometimes called the martingale boom. 2. Formerly an alternative term for *kicking strap* or *boom vang*.

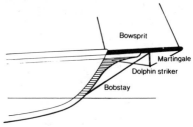

Mast The most important *spar* without which no *sail* can be set. In modern sailing boats may be of wood, steel or plastics, but is generally a light alloy *extrusion*. Wooden masts may be solid or hollow. A *pole mast* is made in one piece, but in *sailing ships* the *lower* (pole) *mast* carries a *topmast*, which in turn carries a *topgallant mast*, etc. A mast may be *stepped* on the *keel*, on *deck*, or in a *tabernacle* in the case of a *lowering mast*. It is normally supported *athwartships* by *shrouds* and *fore-and-aft* by *stays*. May be *flexible*, and bent to alter sail *camber*. Is subject to shock and compression loads when going to windward, but is also highly stressed when the wind is *free* with the *spinnaker* set, especially in fresh winds and a seaway, because the boat's *longitudinal stability* causes the crew to underestimate wind strength. When there is more than one mast each has a different name, e.g. *mainmast, foremast*, and *mizzenmast*.

Mast abeam In the *racing rules*, the words suggested for use by the helmsman of a *windward yacht* to inform a yacht to *leeward* that she has no right to *luff* because, when sighting *abeam* from his normal station and sailing no higher than the leeward yacht, he is *abreast* of or forward of the leeward yacht's *mainmast*. The leeward yacht must respond, but may *protest* if she considers the hail improper.

Mast abeam

Mast band Metal band round a wooden mast, to which *rigging* is attached, or which provides protection against *chafe* in way of *gaff jaws*.

Mast beam Strong *deck beam* fitted forward and aft of a keel-stepped mast; with the *mast partners* forms a framework at the deck around the hole through which the mast passes.

Mast bend See *flexible mast*.

Mast bend controller Fitting for racing dinghies which pushes or pulls the mast forward and aft in the slot or hole at deck level, so that the mast can be bent as required more accurately than by using wedges. A number of types are available, some of which apply considerable power.

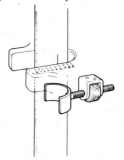

Mast coat (US **mast boot**) Waterproofed gaiter or cover which is fitted round the mast at deck level to prevent water from seeping into the cabin.

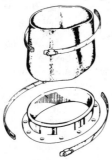

Mast collar or **mast pot** Metal band with flange which acts as mast coat.

Master station When linked radio signals are transmitted from a chain of stations, the main transmitter is the master and the remainder slaves. In some navigation systems the master triggers the slave into action, in others the transmissions are *phase*-locked or timed with extreme accuracy. A *hyperbolic position line* is obtained by comparing the difference in time of reception of the signals, or the difference in phase between the master and any one of the slaves.

Mast fittings All fittings attached to the mast, such as *tangs, spreader roots, halyard sheaves*. Must be light in weight but as strong as possible because they may be inaccessible in the event of damage.

Mast gate 1. Device at the bottom of the mast track which is opened to enable the slides to be fed onto the track. 2. Racing dinghy fitting which closes the slot at deck level through which the mast passes. Adjustable in the fore-and-aft direction so that *mast bend* can be varied. Now largely superseded by mast bend controllers.

Masthead The top part of the mast, often tapered, above which is the masthead fitting or *truck*. The *mainsail halyard sheave* is fitted here, and the sheaves for the *headsail* and *spinnaker* as well if the boat is masthead-rigged.

Masthead fitting A fitting attached to the masthead to which any of the following may be fastened: *backstay, forestay, topmast shroud,*

masthead light, wind direction indicator, anemometer and, possibly, a *loop aerial*. May have *sheaves* for the *topping lift, spinnaker halyard* etc.

Masthead float A hollow, foam-filled or inflatable chamber fitted at the masthead of a *multihull* to prevent her from *turning turtle* if she is *knocked down*. Some inflate automatically if the boat heels beyond a certain angle.

Masthead fly (US) A small *pennant* or device at the masthead; swivels to show the wind direction.

Masthead light or **steaming light** A white light exhibited at or near the masthead over the *fore-and-aft line* by a *power-driven vessel under way*. Shows an unbroken light over an arc of the horizon of 225°, from dead *ahead* to 22.5° *abaft the beam*

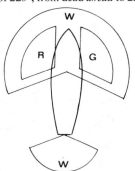

Power driven including vessels with sails and anxiliary engine operating: side lights masthead light stern light

on either side (US Inland: 20 point forward or bow light, and see *range light*). Range of *visibility* varies with the size of vessel, and is prescribed in the *IRPCS* or other *rule of the road*. A *sailing vessel* using *auxiliary* power must exhibit a masthead light, even when her sails are hoisted. See also *IMO*.

Masthead rig A yacht with the *forestay* attached to the masthead, enabling the maximum area of

foretriangle to be used for *headsails*. A popular rig for modern offshore racing boats. With *seven-eighths* and *three-quarter* (fractional) *rig* the forestay does not extend to the masthead.

Mast heel The lower end of the mast, which either slots into a matching *mast step* on *deck* or on the *keel*, or is stepped in a *tabernacle*, or is attached to a *track*. May be square, round or have a tenon, shaped to fit the aperture in the step.

Mast jack A jack fitted beneath the heel, so that the mast can be raised or lowered to alter *rigging* tension and *mast bend*.

Mast partners Strong framework fitted at the deck round the hole through which a keel-stepped mast passes.

Mast section The section of a mast determines its weight, strength and flexibility and, consequently, the amount of *standing rigging* required. A rounded *leading edge* is preferable aerodynamically, because *form drag* is lower than with a square leading edge. Larger diameter section is stronger and the walls can be thinner, resulting in a lighter mast, but form drag is less if the diameter is smaller, although this inevitably means thicker walls.

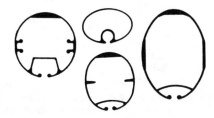

Weight and form drag are lower when small diameter is combined with thin walls, but this has to be paid for by increased *windage* owing to the need for extra standing rigging. Numerous compromises can be made depending on the degree of flexibility required, whether a track or groove is to be used, etc. One advantage of hollow masts is that internal halyards can be fitted, and this reduces windage.

Mast step Fitting into which the matching *mast heel* fits, or to which it is attached, whether the

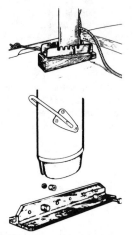

mast is *stepped* on *deck* or on the *keel*. Often designed to enable the mast foot to be moved forward or aft, so that mast *rake* and/or *balance* can be adjusted. Is often just a socket in the *keelson* in which the mast heel fits. Some expensive mast steps made for racing boats enable fine adjustments to *tune* to be made when under way.

Mast strut A variable strut running from the forward side of a dinghy's mast some two feet above the *partners* down to the foredeck. Acts as a *mast bend controller*.

Mast track A metal or plastics track attached to the after side of the mast from the *masthead* to near the *gooseneck*, used in place of a *groove* or *lacing*. Various sections are available. *Slides* sewn to the *luff* of the *mainsail* slide in or on the track,

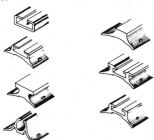

which is closed by a gate at the bottom after all the slides have been fed on. Similar tracks are often fitted to the boom (and gaff) to hold the foot (and head) of a sail to a spar. A second track may be fitted especially for the storm trysail.

Mast wedges 1. In dinghies, wooden wedges of varying thickness can be inserted into the slot where the mast passes through the deck to hold a *flexible mast* in the position desired. 2. In larger boats, wedges are fitted round a keel-stepped mast at deck level to hold it firm. They fill the space between mast and deck, and a *mast coat* is fitted over them to prevent water from entering the cabin.

Mat See *chopped strand mat*.

Match racing Two boats only compete; they sail round a prescribed *course* and comply with the IYRU *racing rules* as in a normal race. The competition may be to find the better boat (e.g. *America's Cup*) or the best *helmsman* as in Congressional Cup racing, in which case each one of a number of helmsmen match races against every other in turn, changing boats for each race; the winner is the helmsman who has won most races.

Maturing or **setting time** The time it takes for a *polyester resin* to harden completely and become stable after *catalyst* and *accelerator* have been added.

Maxi raters A group of offshore racing yachts with an *IOR rating* near the upper limit of 70 ft.

Mayday The internationally recognized *radio telephony distress signal* used when transmitting a distress call and message; may only be sent in a case of imminent danger when immediate aid is required to save life. From the French m'aidez, help me.

Mean Higher High Water, MHHW When there is a marked difference between successive *high water* heights during a day, MHHW is the average level of the higher of the two high waters over a long period.

Mean High Water, MHW The average level of *high water* heights over a long period. US charts frequently use MHW as the datum level above which are given *vertical clearances* and the heights of features that do not *cover*.

Mean High Water Springs, MHWS The average level of all *high water* heights at *spring tides* throughout a year, i.e. of the heights when *range* is greatest. Most UK charts use MHWS as the datum level from which are given *vertical clearances* and the heights of features that do not *cover*.

Mean Lower Low Water, MLLW When there is a marked difference between successive *low water* heights during a day, as occurs with *mixed tides*, MLLW is the average level of the heights of the lower of the two daily low waters over a long period. US charts covering the Pacific coast use MLLW as the datum level for *soundings*, and for features that *cover* and *uncover*.

Mean Low Water, MLW The average level of *low water* heights over a long period. US charts covering the Atlantic coast use MLW as the datum level for *soundings* and for features that *cover* and *uncover*. MLW is also the datum for *tides* in the area.

Mean Low Water Springs, MLWS The average of all *low water* heights at *spring tides* throughout a year, i.e. of sea level at LW when *range* is greatest. UK *fathom charts* use MLWS as the datum level for *soundings* and for *drying features*.

Mean Sea Level, MSL The average level of the sea over a certain period, taking into account all states of the *tide*.

Means of propulsion Under the *IYRU racing rules,* a boat may only be propelled by the natural action of wind and water on *sails, hull* and *spars,* except when recovering someone who has fallen overboard or when assisting another vessel. For example *oars* and *paddles* can be used only for steering in an emergency, *sounding poles* may not be used to propel her by punting, and *pumping* (q.v.) is prohibited except in certain conditions.

Mean solar time Time in relation to the *mean sun*. Often referred to simply as mean time, as in *Greenwich Mean Time, Local Mean Time* etc. The *local hour angle* of the mean sun. The mean solar year over 100 years averages 365 days, 5 hrs, 48 mins, 48 secs, the mean solar day is 24 hours, divided into 60 minutes, each of 60 seconds.

Mean sun A fictitious sun which is assumed to move at a constant speed, whereas the speed of the *true sun* varies. The total time that it takes the mean sun to travel round the *ecliptic* is the same as that taken by the true sun. Mean time is based on the *local hour angle* of the mean sun. The *equation of time* is the excess of mean time over *apparent solar time* (based on the true sun). The rate of travel of the mean sun is 15° *longitude* per mean solar hour.

Measured distance and **measured mile** An accurately measured distance, often one *nautical mile* in length, against which the speed of a vessel can be checked, e.g. on trials. The *log* or *speed-ometer* can also be *calibrated* over a measured distance. The vessel is at one end of the distance when pairs of marks (US ranges) on land are seen to be in line, and buoys are also sometimes laid near the shore to ensure correct headings for the runs. More accurate measurements can be obtained in waters where there is little *tidal stream* or *current,* but even so speed is usually checked by sailing in both directions at the same rpm to find the average time taken on the two runs.

Measurement 1. Racing boats are measured differently according to whether they race in *handicap, development* or *one-design classes*. Development class rules only limit certain measurements, such as overall *length, beam, sail area,* and these are checked by the measurer. One-design class rules are more comprehensive, many measurements have to be taken and often very little *tolerance* is permitted. The measurements of boats for an *International Offshore Rule rating* is complicated, time-consuming and expensive, but the rating certificate is valid for four years; any alterations to the hull, rig, trim etc invalidate the rating certificate and the boat has to be remeasured. See also *tonnage,* length, beam, *draft, depth,* sail area.

Measurement certificate A certificate issued after a boat has been measured, certifying that she complies with *class* rules. It is the owner's responsibility to maintain her in the condition on which her certificate was based.

Measurer A person authorized by a *class* or by a national or international authority to measure sailing dinghies or yachts. A measurement fee usually has to be paid.

Mechanical advantage MA The ratio of load to effort. 1. *Tackles:* the pull on the *hauling part* multiplied by a figure equal to the number of parts of the *fall* at the moving *block* (but an allowance of about 10% has to be made for friction when the rope passes over a block). 2. *Winches:*

$$MA = \frac{\text{radius of handle}}{\text{radius of drum and sheet}} \times$$

$$\frac{\text{number of handle revolutions}}{\text{number of drum revolutions}}$$

Meet To meet her is to apply a certain amount of *helm* to keep the boat on *course* by checking a tendency to *yaw* or swing, perhaps in response to a following sea.

Mega- Greek, meaning large, as in megaphone (loud voice). prefix used with *SI* units, abbr M, as in Megahertz, MHz: multiply by one million, 10^6.

MEKP Methyl ethyl ketone peroxide; *catalyst* for *polyester resin*.

Member Any part of the structure of a *hull,* whether longitudinal or transverse, horizontal or vertical.

Meon anchor See *Danforth anchor*.

Mercator projection To simplify navigation, the 16th Century Flemish cartographer Gerhard Kremer, who preferred to use the Latin form of his name, Gerardus Mercator, invented a map projection wherby the chart is taken to be a cylinder, touching the earth at all points along the *equator*. A rectangular grid is formed of *parallels of latitude,* drawn parallel to the equator, and *meridians* drawn at right angles to them. The representation of the earth on a mercator chart becomes increasingly distorted towards the poles because, as can

be seen in the figure, the outlined area on earth becomes larger at the top of the chart in the E–W direction as a result of drawing the meridians parallel to each other, instead of converging as they do on the earth. The area on the chart is also 'stretched' north and south towards the pole so that the portion of earth represented remains the correct shape. A straight line cuts all meridians at the same angle, and mercator charts are therefore used for *rhumb line* sailing. Almost all charts covering coastal waters are mercator projection.

Meridian A *semi-great circle* which is perpendicular to the *equator* and joins the *geographical north* and *south poles*. At all places on a meridian the sun's meridian passage at noon occurs at the same moment, and *longitude* east or west of the *prime meridian* is the same. See also *magnetic* and *celestial meridians*.

Meridian passage The upper meridian passage occurs when a *heavenly body* is on the *observer's meridian*, i.e. it is due north or south of the observer; the body is then at its maximum *altitude* and the *local hour angle* is 0°. The lower meridian passage cannot often be observed. The sun's

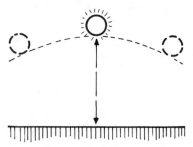

meridian passage occurs at *apparent noon*, and the time of meridian passage can be found by applying the vessel's *longitude* (in units of time) to the time of the sun's meridian passage at Greenwich, which is printed in the *Nautical Almanac*; longitude is added if westerly and subtracted if easterly.

Messenger 1. Lighter line attached to a heavier one, such as a *tow-rope* or *mooring line*, so that the heavier rope can be pulled to the towing vessel or quay. 2. Light line that is rove through an awkward lead, such as down the inside of a hollow mast, often during construction, so that cables, halyards etc may be pulled through later.

Metacentre The point of intersection between the plane of the centreline (i.e. the direction of the forces of gravity and *buoyancy* when the boat is floating upright) and the vertical line which indicates the direction of the upthrust of buoyancy through the *centre of buoyancy*, when the boat is at a small angle of heel. There are two metacentres, one relating to *transverse* and one to *longitudinal stability*.

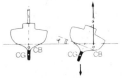

Metacentric height = GM

Metacentric height, $\overline{GM}$ The height of the metacentre above the *centre of gravity* when a boat is at a small angle of *heel*; this indicates a boat's *stability*. If the metacentre is above the CG, metacentric height is positive and the boat is in a condition of *stable equilibrium*; if it is below the

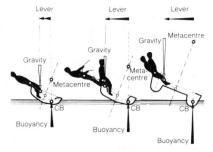

CG, metacentric height is negative and the boat is *unstable*; when the metacentre and the CG coincide equilibrium is *neutral*. The value of metacentric height is determined both by the position of the CG and by hull shape, i.e. by how far the *centre of buoyancy* shifts sideways when the boat starts to heel.

Meteorological navigation Essentially involves the selection of the safe course to sail in view of the expected development of the weather, but in the broadest sense takes into account *global wind circulation, ocean currents* etc. When making long voyages, it is advisable to refer to *Ocean Passages of the World* and to the *Routeing* (US Pilot) charts which show the pattern of weather at monthly intervals, so that full use can be made of favourable winds and currents, and so that the known tracks of *tropical revolving storms* can be avoided as far as possible. Large ships can obtain advice as to the best route during a passage from shore-based meteorologists and master mariners.

Meteorology Science relating to the development of weather in the earth's atmosphere, and weather forecasting.

Metre (US meter) Basis of the metric system: *SI* basic unit of length, abbr m. The standard metre, established in 1795 as one ten-millionth part of a quadrant of the earth through Paris, is a platinum–iridium bar, kept at Sèvres. For conversion factors see *foot*, *speed* and *pressure*.

Metre (US meter) classes Classes rated under the second *International Rule* of 1920, including the 6-, 8-, 10-, 12- and 23-metres. The 5.5-metre formula is:

$$0.9 \left(\frac{L \times \sqrt{S}}{12 \times \sqrt[3]{V}} + \frac{L + \sqrt{S}}{4} \right) =$$

Maximum 5.5 m or 18.04 ft.

L being length, defined in the rule, in metres or feet, S sail area in sq m or sq ft, V displacement in cu m or cu ft.

Metric chart Measurements are given in metres, as opposed to feet, or feet and fathoms.

Metric system Measurement system based on the metre. The c.g.s. (centimetre, gramme, second), m.k.s. (metre, kilogramme, second) and f.p.s. (foot, pound, second) systems have been superseded by *SI* units for scientific work.

MHHW *Mean Higher High Water*, q.v.

MHW *Mean High Water*, q.v.

MHWS *Mean High Water Springs*, q.v.

Micro- 1. Prefix meaning small, as in microscope. 2. Prefix used with *SI* units, abbr μ, 10^{-6}, one-millionth.

Micro Class A *development class* which provides competition for small boats with limited accommodation. The measurements are controlled, with the following maxima: LOA 18 ft (5.5 m), beam 8.04 ft (2.45 m), draft with daggerboard, centreboard or bilgeboards 3.6 ft (1.1 m), draft with fixed or retractable keel 3.28 ft (1 m), displacement series-produced 1103–1323 lb (500–600 kg) displacement one-off 993–1,213 lb (450–550 kg), sail area 199 sq ft (18.5 sq m). Micro-Cuppers have no *lifelines* (guardrails), but carry sufficient *buoyancy* to render them unsinkable, and must be *self-righting* from a 90° angle of heel with a 10 kg weight attached to the masthead. They have *toe-straps* in the cockpit so that the crew can *sit out*, and are designed for *trailing*.

Micrometer sextant or **drum sextant** When taking a *sight* or measuring an angle, the approximate measurement is found by disengaging

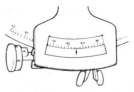

the *index bar* from the toothed rack and moving it quickly along the *arc*. The micrometer drum has a worm wheel which engages in the rack, and the drum is turned to find the precise angle. One full rotation of the drum moves the index bar one degree, i.e. 60 minutes along the arc. The drum is inscribed so that the minutes can be read directly and, although more expensive than a *vernier sextant*, it is so much easier to read and so precise that errors are largely eliminated.

Microspheres or **microballoons** Tiny air-filled cells, with a diameter under 1 mm and therefore measured in microns. When mixed with *resin* are used for many purposes on board, such as filling hollows or dents in a *GRP/FRP laminate*, or *fairing* in the roots of the *spreaders* to reduce *windage*. Very low *density*, and look like powder.

Mid-channel (US fairway) buoy *Aid to navigation* that marks the centre of a channel. The colour, *light* and *topmark* are distinctive to avoid confusion with *port* and *starboard hand marks*. Should normally be left to port. *IALA A: spherical (pillar* or *spar)*, red and white vertical stripes, one red spherical topmark, light white *isophase*, *occulting* or *long flash* every 10 secs. US: *can* or *nun*, black and white vertical stripes, lights white *morse code* A, octagonal black and white *daymark*. See front endpapers.

Middle ground Shoal or bank which divides a fairway into two channels that reunite further along. Middle ground buoys (Uniform system), *bifurcation* or *junction buoys* (US) or *cardinal buoys* (IALA A) are laid at either end where the channels divide and converge.

Midget Ocean Racing Club, MORC US club similar to the British *Junior Offshore Group*. Runs *offshore races* for the two smallest divisions, i.e. for boats under 30 ft overall length.

Midnight sun The sun that does not set, being above the horizon throughout 24 hours, as seen near one of the poles in summer in *latitudes* higher than the *polar circles*, 66°33′ N and S. The polar circles also limit the region where the sun does not rise above the horizon in winter.

Midships See *amidships*.

Midship section The *section* on the *lines plan* mid-way between the perpendiculars forward and aft where *stem* and *stern* intersect the *designed* *waterline*. Maximum *beam* does not necessarily coincide with the midship section.

Midship section coefficient The ratio of the immersed midship section area to that of its circumscribing rectangle with sides equal to breadth and draft:

$$C_M = \frac{A_M}{B \times T}$$

Values for yachts are small by comparison with those for ships because yachts have deep keels; the value for a racing boat with a fin keel is smaller than that for an offshore cruiser with wine-glass sections.

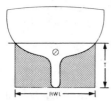

Mildew Fungal growth that flourishes in dark, warm, moist conditions in unventilated areas, making unsightly spots on canvas, sailcloth, clothing etc. It can form in the weave of synthetic fibres but they are not harmed.

Mile Unit of length. On land the statute mile is 1760 yards = 5280 ft, = 1.609 kilometres = 0.868976 n.miles; speed is measured in statute miles per hour. The longer international *nautical mile* is 6076.12 ft, 1852 m, and equals 1.15078 statute miles; speed is measured in *knots*, one knot being one nautical mile per hour. The geographical mile is 6087.2 ft, and is the length of one minute of *longitude* at the *equator*, i.e. the circumference of the earth divided into 21,600 parts. Approximately, 1 statute mph = 1.6 km/hr = 0.45 m/sec = 0.87 knots = 1.47 ft/sec.

Millibar Unit of pressure, used especially for measuring *atmospheric* pressure. One thousandth of a *bar*. *Barometers* are graduated in mb. 1000 mb = 750 mm or 29.5 in of mercury.

Minimum speed Some races have to be sailed at a minimum speed if the race is to count in a *series*. The speed may be given in *knots*, but more often there is a *time limit* before which the leader has to finish. The *race committee* may declare the race abandoned if no competitor can sail at the minimum speed required, but if one finishes within the time limit the others may sail on and finish the race (unless otherwise stipulated).

Mini Ton Class The smallest of the *level rating classes*, the maximum *rating* being 16.5 ft. The class races annually for the Mini Ton Cup, the Coupe Internationale du Cercle de la Voile de Paris, in a series consisting of three Olympic races

over courses about 14 n.miles long and two off-shore races lasting about 10 and 15 hours, run during daylight hours within 10 miles of the coast, and where places of refuge are available. The number of crew is three.

Minute Unit of measurement. One minute equals 60 seconds. 1. Of angles and arcs, one-sixtieth of a *degree* (q.v.). One minute of *longitude* at the *equator* is 6087.2 ft in length. The International *nautical mile* adopted by the International Hydrographic Organization is 6076.12 ft (1852 m). *Distances* on charts are measured against the *latitude* scale bordering the sides, and one minute equals one nautical mile. 2. Of time, one-sixtieth of an hour. One minute of time can be expressed as 15 minutes of longitude, and one minute of longitude as four seconds of time.

Mirage Atmospheric phenomenon that occurs in high temperatures when approaching a coast. The *refraction* of light waves reflected by different layers of heated air makes objects beyond the horizon appear to be higher and closer than they really are; any estimate of distance is then unrealistic.

Mirror 1. Widely distributed two-man racing dinghy with spinnaker, designed by Jack Holt and Barry Bucknell for home construction by the *stitch-and-glue* method. LOA 10 ft 10 in (3.3 m), beam 4 ft 7½ in (1.41 m), weight rigged 135 lbs (61.2 kg), sail area 69 sq ft (6.4 sq m), plus spinnaker 65.5 sq ft (6.1 sq m). 2. See *horizon* and *index glass*.

Miss distance When operating *radar*, the closest that two vessels will approach each other if neither alters course or speed, as found with the aid of a *plotting diagram*.

Miss stays To fail to *go about*.

Mist The transparency of the *atmosphere* is reduced by minute water particles in suspension in the air. *Visibility* is between 0.5 and 1 n.mile (1–2 km), and *relative humidity* is over 95%. The symbol on weather maps is the figure 8 lying on its side (c.f. *haze*).

Mitre (US miter) The central seam of a *diagonal cut sail*; roughly bisects the angle at the *clew* and runs at right angles to the *luff*. See *sail* fig.

Mitre (US **miter**) **cut** See *diagonal cut.*

Mixed tide A tidal undulation which has marked *diurnal* and *semi-diurnal* components. As is common along the US Pacific coast, there is great *diurnal inequality* between the heights of successive *high waters* and successive *low waters;* for example in San Francisco one tide may have a *range* of 7 ft and be followed the same day by one with a range of only 2 ft.

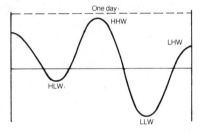

Mizzen or **mizen** (US or **jigger**) The *fore-and-aft sail* set on the mizzenmast.

Mizzenmast (US or **jigger**) 1. The smaller aftermast of a *ketch* or *yawl.* 2. In *sailing ships* with three or more masts, the third mast from forward, aft of the *mainmast.*

Mizzen spinnaker A small *spinnaker* set on the mizzen mast of a *ketch* or *yawl.* Under the *IOR* the sail has to be shaped to conform to the rule governing *mizzen staysails,* and is set without a pole.

Mizzen staysail *Staysail* set by a *ketch* or a *yawl* on a *reach* or *run,* with the *head* at the mizzen masthead and the *tack* attached near the mainmast, to make full use of the free space between masts. *Overlaps* the mizzen, and is generally sheeted to the mizzen boom. Is not taxed heavily by the *IOR.*

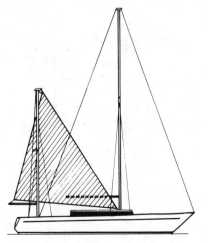

MLLW *Mean Lower Low Water,* q.v.

MLW *Mean Low Water,* q.v.

MLWS *Mean Low Water Springs,* q.v.

Model testing Many factors contributing to the performance of a full size vessel are evaluated in a towing tank or wind tunnel. A scale model is made and measurements are taken of such factors as hull *resistance, aspect ratio* of the *rig,* etc. These are then scaled up to provide figures for the full size vessel in accordance with the principle of dynamic similarity. Many expensive high-performance racing yachts, such as *America's Cup 12-metres* and *Admiral's Cup* boats are tested as models before being built.

Moderate Wind moderates when it blows less strongly; seas become smaller and less dangerous when they moderate.

Moderate breeze *Beaufort force* 4, 11–16 *knots.*

Moderate gale (US) **Near gale** (WMO) *Beaufort force* 7, 28–33 *knots.*

Modulation Information to be transmitted by radio is superimposed on a *carrier wave* by varying its *amplitude* (AM, amplitude modulation), or its *frequency* or *phase* (FM, frequency modulation). FM is usual for short range VHF transmission, while SSB (*single sideband*), which is AM with the carrier and one sideband suppressed, is now required for medium and long range high and medium frequency transmission.

Moisture content The amount of moisture in timber expressed as a percentage of fully dry timber:

$$\frac{\text{wet weight} - \text{dry weight}}{\text{dry weight}} \times 100$$

e.g. $\quad \dfrac{36 - 31}{31} \times 100 = 16\%$

Timber has to be seasoned until the moisture content drops to about 15–18% before it is used for boat-building. Green wood contains too much moisture, would shrink excessively as it dries, and paint etc would not adhere. When the *relative humidity* of air is about 90% (16 °C), moisture content is about 27%, but drops at a relative humidity of 75% to about 17%. Dryer timber swells too much when it becomes wet.

Mole A breakwater, often made of stone or concrete. Vessels can moor alongside the sheltered side.

Mole hill Remote working position at which power is applied to a *winch.*

Moment or **torque** The tendency of a force to

turn the body to which the force is applied; is measured by multiplying the magnitude of the force by the perpendicular distance of the axis from the line of action of the force (as in the figure illustrating *righting lever*, force G × moment arm H).

Monel An alloy of nickel (60–70%) and copper (25–35%) plus small quantities of other metals. Monel fastenings such as bolts combine strength with resistance to *corrosion*. Often used for shafting and tanks.

Monkey's fist A special fancy knot made at the end of a *heaving line* so that it will carry further.

Monofil A *yarn* formed by a single *filament* or *extrusion* of synthetic fibre. Cf. *multifil*.

Monohull As opposed to a *multihull* (i.e. a *catamaran, trimaran* or *proa*) a conventional boat with a single *hull*.

Monsoon Monsoon winds can be compared to *land* and *sea breezes,* but the change is seasonal instead of diurnal, and affects vast tracts of ocean instead of limited coastal waters. The main areas affected are the Indian Ocean, China Sea and the Gulf of Guinea. The winds blow from sea to land during the summer when the land is hot, but from land to sea during the winter.

Month There are a number of different months, apart from the calendar month which varies from 28 to 31 days, including: the sidereal month of 27 d 7 h 43 m 11.5 s, the period between successive transits of the moon across the same star; the *lunar month* or lunation (q.v.) of 29 d 12 h 44 m 2.87s; the anomalistic month of 27 d 13 h 18 m 37 s, the time taken by the moon to go from *perigee* to perigee.

Moon A satellite of earth, whose monthly orbit and phases are extremely important for the prediction of *tides*. See *phase*.

Moonraker, moonsail *Square sail* set above the *skysail* in light weather.

Moor 1. To secure a vessel to a mooring buoy, *piles*, on a *trot* or to the shore or alongside. She may also let go her *anchor* and fall astern to lie stern on (at right angles) to a *pontoon* or *dock,* secured by *stern lines*, often plus *breast ropes* running to piles either side. 2. Mooring ship is to lie to two anchors so as to require less *swinging room.* In tidal waters, when one anchor is dropped upstream and the other downstream, one will hold her when the tidal stream is *flooding* and the other when it is *ebbing.* Two anchors are also laid to increase *holding power*, the load being distributed between them in heavy weather, when seas run

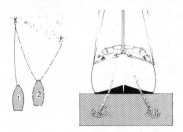

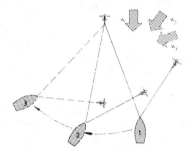

high, or when the wind shifts. Running or flying moor; the first anchor is let go before the vessel loses way, and the second after an interval. Dropping moor; after letting go the first anchor, the vessel drops back for some distance before the second anchor is let go.

Moor alongside To secure a boat alongside another boat, pier, quay, pontoon etc with mooring lines or fasts. *Breast ropes* may be required in addition to *head* and *stern lines* and *springs*.

Mooring The *ground tackle* laid to keep a vessel at a certain position in a harbour when she has secured to, or picked up the mooring buoy; this is connected by a buoy pendant (chain, rope or wire rope) to an *anchor* or *clump* on the bottom. The pendant must be long enough to allow for the rise and fall of the *tide*. Mooring swivels are essential,

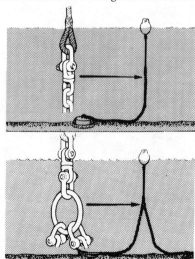

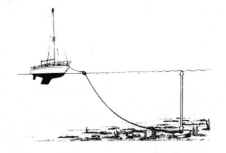

especially if there is more than one anchor or clump, so that *anchor cables* do not get twisted. A larger boat must not use a mooring laid for a smaller boat because either the pendant will part or the mooring will drag.

Mooring bollard, cleat or **bitt** Many different types and shapes of deck fittings are sold under a variety of names, their purpose being to enable mooring lines to be secured to the boat. They should be through-bolted with a *backing plate* to provide a reliable anchorage and spread the load. e.g. *sampson post, crosshead bollard, staghorn.*

Mooring buoy A floating buoy that indicates the position of *ground tackle* laid to keep a boat in a certain position. Sailing boat moorings often have a small pick-up buoy with a rope strop or a handle, or a rod buoy with a raised handle. These are attached to a lighter line with which the stronger buoy pendant is hauled on board so that it can be secured on the foredeck. Other mooring buoys are larger, and the vessel secures to them.

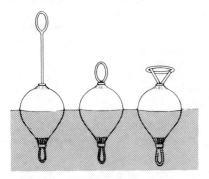

Mooring lines (UK or **ropes,** US or **fasts**) Strong ropes with which a vessel is moored. *Bow lines* and *head ropes* lead forward from the bow, *stern lines* run aft from the stern, *breast ropes* run at right angles to the *fore-and-aft line. Springs* run aft from a point forward, and forward from a point aft.

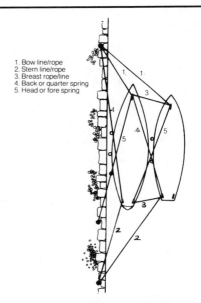

1. Bow line/rope
2. Stern line/rope
3. Breast rope/line
4. Back or quarter spring
5. Head or fore spring

Mooring spring or **shock absorber,** or **rubber snubber** A strong spring or piece of rubber which absorbs the sudden load on a mooring line, caused by the response of a light boat to oscillations of the water, such as the wash of passing vessels. Various gadgets sold under a number of trade names are all designed to prevent *snubbing.*

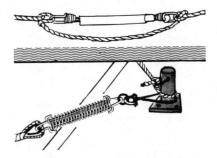

Morse code A communication code devised in 1836 by Samuel Morse, letters, numbers and signs being represented by different combinations of long and short signs (dashes and dots), with pauses between combinations. The length of a dash is three times that of a dot, a pause between parts of the same letter equals the length of one dot, between letters the length of three dots, and between words seven dots. In this dictionary the alphabet code is given under the first entry for each letter. The numerals are:

$1 = \cdot — — — —$ $2 = \cdot\cdot — — —$ $3 = \cdot\cdot\cdot — —$
$4 = \cdot\cdot\cdot\cdot —$ $5 = \cdot\cdot\cdot\cdot\cdot$ $6 = — \cdot\cdot\cdot\cdot$
$7 = — — \cdot\cdot\cdot$ $8 = — — — \cdot\cdot$ $9 = — — — — \cdot$
$10 = — — — — —$
Other special groups are: $ä = \cdot — \cdot —$
$à = \cdot — — \cdot —$ $ch = — — — —$ $è = \cdot\cdot — \cdot\cdot$
$\phi ö = — — — \cdot$ $ü = \cdot\cdot — —$

Signals can be made visually with a *signalling lamp,* or acoustically either with a *foghorn* or tapped out and transmitted by radio telegraphy.

Morse code light and **fog signal** A light exhibited by an *aid to navigation,* aero beacon etc, and a *fog signal* made by siren or horn by an aid to navigation. One or more morse code characters are reproduced by flashes or sounds of varying duration. US: Morse code letter A is exhibited by *mid-channel marks,* short-long. Chart abbr for morse is Mo.

Motion Apart from the normal forward or astern motion of a boat through the water, and *leeway* and *set* which move her sideways, the word motion describes a boat's rotation about several axes,

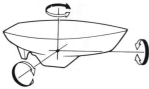

mainly in response to seas. She rotates about her horizontal fore-and-aft axis when she *rolls* from side to side; she *pitches* when she rotates about her horizontal athwartships axis, rocking like a seasaw; she *yaws* when she alters course to port or starboard, pivoting about a vertical axis.

Motor boat Boat propelled by an internal combustion engine; no sails. The US Motor Boat Act divides motor boats into four classes based on their overall length; the equipment that has to be carried varies with the class. Class A, under 16 ft (4.9 m): Class 1, 16 ft and over but under 26 ft (7.9 m), Class 2, 26 ft and over but under 40 ft (12.2 m); Class 3, 40 ft and over.

Motor sailer *Cruising* boat, with two equally efficient methods of propulsion enabling her to make much the same speed under engine as under sail in a full sail breeze; generally of medium to *heavy displacement.* Advantages: cheap wind power is used whenever possible; the engine is available to assist in heavy weather or light breezes; in case of damage there is an alternative means of propulsion; easier to handle in congested or confined waters; a cruise is more likely to be completed according to schedule. However performance in either mode is inferior to that of a true sailing boat or power vessel. May be referred to as a fifty-fifty or, if sail or motor predominates, as a sixty-forty.

Mould (US **mold**) 1. A template or pattern of the transverse shape of the *hull,* set up on the *keel,* connected by *ribbands* to other moulds and firmly braced so as to provide a temporary framework around which a wooden hull is built. 2. A *GRP/ FRP moulding* may be *laid up,* or an iron *ballast keel* cast in a matrix or hollow female mould. 3. A *GRP/FRP moulding* is formed, or the veneers of a *moulded plywood hull* are glued over a male mould or plug. Normally a wooden hull is built keel upwards. 4. Moulds are used for matched die pressure laminating, wet glass being formed into shape between an upper female mould and a lower male mould; for vacuum forming, resin is drawn from a reservoir to impregnate the dry glass mat lying between the two moulds. 5. Used as a verb in connection with 2, 3 and 4. See also *mould loft.* 6. *Mildew.*

Moulded and sided (US **molded and sided**) The dimensions of a member are given as moulded (vertical thickness of *beams* and *keel,* thickness between the athwartships or curved sides of *frames*) and sided (fore-and-aft thickness of beams and frames, athwartship thickness of keel).

Moulded (US **molded**) **dimensions** The dimensions of the *hull* within the *skin, planking* or *plating,* i.e. at the *moulds* around which the hull is constructed and at the outboard edges of the *frames* to which the skin is fastened. The moulded lines and dimensions differ by the width of the planking or plating from the designer's lines drawings and *table of offsets,* which relate to the outside of the hull. Moulded depth is the vertical distance between the underside of the deck at the sides and the upper side of the keel; moulded breadth is the maximum horizontal breadth over a frame. See headroom figure.

Moulded (US **molded**) **plywood construction** A strong but light hull is made of three or more layers of veneers, glued together over a male mould or *plug,* and *cured* either at normal temperature (cold moulding) or by heating in an autoclave. Complicated hull shapes can be made, and the method is as suitable for keelboats or motor boats as for dinghies.

Moulding (US **molding**) 1. A boat, or part of a boat etc, made inside or over a mould. 2. One of the dimensions of a *member* (see *moulded and sided*).

Mould (US **mold**) **loft** A large covered space, often in the roof, on the floor of which the *lines* of the vessel to be built are drawn full scale, so that *moulds* and *templates* of the *members* can be measured and cut to shape.

Mousing Turns of twine taken across the open part of a hook to prevent accidental unhooking.

MSL *Mean Sea Level*, q.v.

Mud A fine soft black sediment of clays or silts, often containing organic matter. Found in many bays and rivers where streams and currents are slow-moving. Channels cut deeply into mud, which is rarely hard enough to walk on.

Mud berth A boat may be *laid up* for the winter in a mud berth, and she settles into a hollow in the mud close by the shore.

Mule or **main backstaysail** Light-weather sail set on a *close reach* on the main *backstay* of a *yawl* or *ketch*, and sheeted to the *mizzen masthead*.

Multifil Several *filaments* twisted together to form one *yarn*. The *denier* or *decitex* of the yarn is the sum of the decitex or denier numbers of the several filaments, e.g. 3×20 d'tex filaments = 60 d'tex yarn, 5×30 denier filaments = 150 denier yarn. Cf. *monofil*.

Multihull As opposed to a *monohull*, a boat with more than one *hull*, i.e. a *proa*, *catamaran* or *trimaran*.

Multimitre (US **multimiter**) See *spider web cut*.

Multiplait Rope formed by plaiting *strands* together, instead of *laying* them. Has proved particularly satisfactory for towing, anchoring and mooring lines.

Muscle box Compact, powerful fitting used in place of a normal *tackle* to increase pulling power. The *sheaves* and *fall* are completely enclosed, reducing *windage* to a minimum; the *mechanical advantage* varies from about 4:1 to 8:1.

Mushroom anchor Is shaped like a mushroom and is usually laid where the bottom is soft to provide a permanent anchorage for a *mooring* because, over a period, it sinks deeply into the ground and has no protruding parts on which the buoy pendant could catch when the boat swings.

Mushroom ventilator A *ventilator* with a domed top that may be transparent to admit light. Is watertight when the dome is screwed down at sea over a rubber sealing ring, and is unscrewed in harbour to admit air.

Mylar DuPont trade name for *polyester* film used in a sandwich construction with conventional woven fabric to form a composite *sailcloth*. Two films are bonded each side of a woven core, or the film forms the core between two layers of woven cloth, or one layer of film is bonded to one layer of cloth. The resulting material is light weight (typically 2–4 oz/sq yd) with a high resistance to stretch, but there is lack of durability (due largely to ultraviolet degradation) and a slight danger of delamination. The name has become synonymous with sandwich constructions involving woven cloth and film made from other plastics such as *polypropylene*, polycarbonate, *nylon* or *polyurethane*.

N

N = **November:** blue and white chequered *code flag.* As a single letter signal means 'No, negative' or 'The significance of the previous group should be read in the negative'. This signal may only be given visually or by sound; for voice or radio transmission the signal is 'No'. *morse code:* — • (dash dot). When racing N means 'All races are *abandoned*', N over X means 'All races are abandoned and will shortly be re-sailed', N over First *Substitute* (US repeater) means 'All races are *cancelled*'. See also N *over C.*

NACA sections or **profiles** The US National Advisory Committee for Aeronautics has devised a series of foil profiles, both *cambered* and symmetrical, of varying dimensions. The values for *lift* and *drag* have been established, and are useful when designing and developing *mast sections, wing sails, centreboards* etc.

Nacelle A small additional *hull,* or a bulge beneath the *bridgedeck* of a *multihull* to provide headroom beneath the boom for the helmsman, or space for an *auxiliary engine.*

Nadir The point on the *celestial sphere* exactly opposite the observer's *zenith,* i.e. where the extension of the line between zenith, observer and the earth's centre meets the celestial sphere.

Nail sick Said of a boat when her hull fastenings are rusty and loose; the woodwork decays.

Narrow channel Under the *IRPCS* a vessel keeps to the side of the channel on her *starboard* hand. *Sailing vessels* and vessels under 20 m in length may not impede vessels which can navigate safely only within a narrow channel.

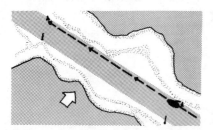

Narrows An area where a channel, river etc becomes even narrower.

National class A *class* of racing boats, generally widely distributed in a country, recognized and usually administered by the national authority, which is also the measuring authority and may issue sail numbers.

National letter Letter displayed on the *mainsail,* and sometimes on the *spinnaker,* denoting the nationality, especially of *international class* boats. The size and position are prescribed in the *racing rules.*

A	Argentina
AL	Algeria
AR	Egypt
B	Belgium
BA	Bahamas
BL	Brazil
BR	Burma
BU	Bulgaria
CB	Columbia
CI	Grand Cayman
CP	Cyprus
CR	Costa Rica
CY	Sri Lanka
CZ	Czechoslovakia
D	Denmark
DR	Dominican Republic
E	Spain
EC	Ecuador
F	France
G	Federal republic of Germany
GO	German Democratic republic
GR	Greece
GU	Guatemala
H	Holland
I	Italy
IL	Iceland
IND	India
IR	Ireland
IS	Israel
J	Japan
K	United Kingdom
KA	Australia
KB	Bermuda
KBA	Barbados
KC	Canada
KH	Hong Kong
KJ	Jamaica
KP	Papua, New Guinea
KR	Rhodesia
KS	Singapore

KT	Trinidad and Tobago
KZ	New Zealand
L	Finland
LX	Luxembourg
M	Hungary
MA	Morocco
MO	Monaco
MS	Mauritius
MT	Malta
MX	Mexico
MY	Malaysia
N	Norway
NK	Democratic republic of Korea
OE	Austria
P	Portugal
PH	Philippines
PR	Puerto Rico
PU	Peru
PZ	Poland
RC	Cuba
RI	Indonesia
RM	Roumania
S	Sweden
SA	South Africa
SL	El Salvador
SR	Union of Soviet Socialist Republics
TA	Republic of China, Taiwan
TH	Thailand
TK	Turkey
U	Uruguay
US	United States of America
V	Venezuela
VI	Virgin Islands
X	Chile
Y	Yugoslavia
Z	Switzerland

Natural scale The ratio of a length measured on a *chart*, say between a *fix* and a symbol denoting a *lighthouse*, to the actual distance over the water between the vessel and the lighthouse itself. A scale of e.g. 1:100,000 may be more easily understood when written as a fraction ¹/₁₀₀,₀₀₀. 1:20,000 would be a larger scale, and 1:200,000 smaller. On a 1:20,000 metric chart, 1 cm = 20,000 cm = 200 m but, given a scale of 1:200,000 1 cm = 200,000 cm = 2,000 m = 1.08 n.miles. Similarly with feet and fathoms charts: large scale of 1:12,500, 1 in = 0.17 n.miles, medium scale 1:75,000, 1 in = 1.03 n.miles. The scale of *mercator charts* varies with *latitude* and increases towards the *poles*.

Nautical almanac Official annual publication, issued jointly by the US Naval Observatory and HM Nautical Almanac Office at Greenwich. Gives the positions of *heavenly bodies*, i.e. *Greenwich Hour Angle* and *declination* hourly of the sun, moon and planets, *Sidereal Hour Angle* and declination every third day for 57 stars, and hourly GHA *Aries*, together with other information that enables the vessel's position to be found by taking *sights* of heavenly bodies.

Nautical mile Unit of length at sea, based on the length of one *minute* of arc measured along the *meridian*, i.e. one minute of *latitude*. Because the earth is not a perfect sphere, the length of one minute of latitude varies slightly; it is shorter at the *equator* than at the poles, but averages 6077 ft. The international nautical mile adopted by the International Hydrographic Organization is 1852 metres, 6076.12 ft; the sea mile is the length of one minute of latitude at a given position. Speed at sea is based on the international nautical mile (see *knot*).

Nautical tables Books for navigational purposes with tabulated data such as altitude and azimuth tables, vertical danger angles, distance tables etc.

Nautical twilight The periods when it gradually becomes less dark before sunrise and darker after sunset; starts in the morning and finishes in the evening when the sun's centre is 12° below the *rational horizon*.

Naval architect Qualified person who designs a vessel, and is responsible for seeing that her strength, stability and seaworthiness are adequate to meet the forces that arise in all specified weather conditions.

Navel pipe See *chain pipe*.

Navigable Said of waters that can be navigated safely by vessels. *Aids to navigation* such as *buoys* marking navigable waters are laid to meet the needs of commercial and naval vessels; they do not necessarily mark the limits of waters navigable by sailing yachts and dinghies which draw less water.

Navigable semicircle Of a *tropical revolving storm* (q.v. for fig.) in the northen hemisphere, the semicircle to the left of its path, i.e. away from the direction of *recurvature*. This is where the vessel can be navigated most safely. See also *dangerous quadrant*.

Navigate To guide a vessel from one place to another knowledgeably. Also to sail from one place to another in a vessel.

Navigation 1. The art and science of guiding a vessel safely from one place to another using all the skills and instruments necessary. In sailing boats the skipper is usually responsible unless he appoints one of the crew navigator. *Coastal* (terrestrial) *navigation* or pilotage, when the vessel is mainly in sight of land, is based on visible terrestrial objects and *aids to navigation* such as *buoys*, together with *dead reckoning*. A *radio direction finder* is required for navigation with the aid of *radio beacons*, and some boats carry *radar*. Navigational systems such as *Decca, Loran, Omega* and *satellite navigation* involve sophisticated electronic equipment and special *charts*. *Celestial* or astro-*navigation* on the open sea is based on observation of *heavenly bodies*. In all cases the broad principle is the same: the navigator lays off on a chart the safe *course* to steer from the vessel's position to the objective, taking into account the *tidal stream or current (vector diagram)*, wind, *dangers* and so on. The vessel's progress is checked regularly by *fixing* her position by at least two *position lines*. An *observed position* is found by taking *sights* of heavenly bodies, and a fix by taking *bearings* with a *hand-bearing compass* or a *direction finder,* by measuring angles with the *sextant,* by taking a *line of soundings* with the *lead* or *echo sounder,* etc. An *estimated position* is worked up from a previous fix or observed position, and is calculated from the *compass course* steered and the distance sailed *through the water* as measured by the *log,* together with the effects of the tidal stream or current and *leeway.* 2. Old-fashioned term for a *canal,* hence the (UK) term navvy: one who laboured on the navigations.

Navigational triangle See *PZX triangle.*

Navigation lights *Lights exhibited by vessels* between sunset and sunrise and, when necessary, by day to enable a vessel's position, course and occupation to be recognized.

Navigator The member of the crew responsible for navigation, and in charge of the instruments and books on board.

Navy The warships of a nation and the military personnel who serve in them or in shore establishments. The term merchant navy relates to the commercial shipping of a country.

Neap tides or **neaps** *Tides* (q.v. for fig.) that occur at or near the time when sun and moon are in *quadrature. Range* is least and *tidal streams* (US *tidal currents*) run least strongly. Neaped: see *beneaped.*

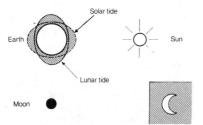

Near gale (WMO) **Moderate gale** (US) *Beaufort force* 7, 28–33 *knots.*

Netting A large-mesh net is often lashed along the *lifeline* (guardrail), especially at the *foredeck* to prevent *headsails* from being blown overboard

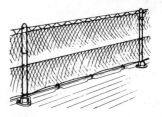

when being hoisted or lowered, or along both sides as a protective measure if small children are carried regularly. Smaller mesh may be used for stowage racks or *bunkboards.* Netting is sometimes spread between the hulls of smaller *catamarans.*

Neutral equilibrium A state of equilibrium when the *metacentre* and the *centre of gravity* coincide; a *heeled* boat in this state has no tendency to *right* herself, nor to *capsize.*

New moon The phase of the moon when she is in *conjunction* with the sun; her dark side faces the earth and she is invisible. *Spring tides* usually, but not invariably, occur one–two days afterwards (as they do just after full moon).

Newton *SI* unit of force, abbr N: one Newton is the force required to give a mass of one kilogramme an acceleration of one metre per second per second. For conversion factors see *pound, pressure.*

Nicopress US trade name for a patented system which replaces *wire splicing,* similar to *Talurit,* q.v.

Night effect or **sky wave effect** *Bearings* of a *radio beacon* obtained with a *direction finder* during the night or at twilight are frequently unreliable because *sky wave* signals reflected from the *ionosphere* are often as strong or stronger than the reliable *ground wave* signal. An unsteady *null* is characteristic of sky wave reception.

Nimbostratus (Ns) Thick, low-lying, grey sheet cloud; rain often falls continuously.

Nip A sharp bend in a rope is a bad nip; see also *freshen the nip.*

Nominal range The *luminous range* of a light on a vessel or an *aid to navigation* when meteorological *visibility* is 10 *nautical miles.* Nominal range depends on the *intensity* of the light:
3 n. miles – 15 *candela*
5 n. miles – 75 cd
8 n. miles – 480 cd
10 n. miles – 1,400 cd
15 n. miles – 14,000 cd
20 n. miles – 110,000 cd
25 n. miles – 770,000 cd
30 n. miles – 4,900,000 cd

Non-directional radio beacon See *omnidirectional radio beacon.*

Non-slip deck paint Contains sand to provide a textured surface that gives a good foothold, even when wet.

Noon The moment of the sun's *meridian passage* at a place. Apparent noon is when the visible *true sun* is on the *meridian*, mean noon when the *mean sun* is on the meridian. The daily *Greenwich Mean Time* times of the meridian passages of sun, moon and planets at Greenwich are given in the *Nautical Almanac.*

Noon sight See *latitude by meridian altitude.*

North The main *cardinal point*, 000° or 360° on the *compass rose* and *compass card. True north* is the direction of the geographical north pole; *magnetic north* is often expressed as the direction to which a *compass needle* points when not subject to *deviation; compass north* is the direction to which the needle points when disturbed by forces in addition to terrestrial *magnetism.*

Northerly To the north, as of courses, currents etc, but from the north in the case of wind.

Northern Adjective that differentiates between two similar areas, features etc by locating them with reference to the *cardinal point*, e.g. northern hemisphere, northern *quadrant* which is bounded by NW and NE.

Northill anchor Type of *anchor* popular in the US; has two *flukes* and a removable *stock* which passes through the *crown.*

Northing The distance a vessel makes good in a northerly direction.

North pole The end of the axis about which the earth rotates that is 90° north of the *equator, latitude* 90° N. True *meridians* connect the north and south poles. Sometimes called geographical north pole. See also *celestial pole.*

North Star The Pole Star: indicates the direction of true north at night. See *Polaris* and *latitude by Polaris.*

Northward Direction; towards the north, as in sailing northward.

Norwegian stern A *stern* where the *hull* curves to a point, both above and below the *waterline.* The *rudder*, hung on the *sternpost*, is immediately accessible in the event of damage and, as in the figure, extends from deck level virtually to the lowest point of the *keel.* Although the pointed stern divides following seas, *reserve buoyancy* is

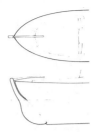

not so great as that provided by an overhanging *counter.* Colin Archer designed many boats of this type, based on Norwegian pilot cutters, and the Trans-Atlantic voyages of Erling Tambs in 'Teddy' and 'Sandefjord' are famous.

Nose dive or **boring** Terms sometimes used to describe the unfortunate tendency of the *bows* to dive beneath a wave instead of lifting to it. Is most likely to occur when boats have a fine *entrance* and little *reserve buoyancy* forward, especially when *running* or *reaching* fast in high seas. May be countered in dinghies and light displacement craft by shifting crew weight aft.

Notation See *graduation.*

Notice of Race Details about a *race, series* or *regatta*, published or sent to clubs and competitors. Includes information as to the racing, class and special rules that will apply, the date, time and place where the race will be held, and particulars concerning entrance fees, closing date for entries, prizes, *scoring system*, time and place for receiving *sailing instructions*, etc.

Notices to Mariners Official notices published weekly and summarized periodically, detailing alterations to *lights*, buoyage etc so that charts, *Pilots*, and the *Lists of Lights* and *Radio Signals* can be kept up to date. Also gives information about *dangers* and other important matters concerning the vessel's safety. UK notices prefixed T are temporary, those prefixed P are preliminary.

Not under command A vessel unable to manoeuvre as required by the *IRPCS* through some exceptional circumstance such as rudder damage. Such a vessel exhibits in a vertical line two black *balls* by day, and two *all-round* red lights by night; when making way through the water she also exhibits *side lights* and a *stern light.* Only vessels below 7 m in length are exempt from this requirement.

N over C *Code flags* flown as a *distress signal*, meaning 'I am in distress and require immediate assistance'.

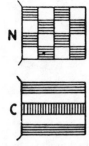

Null The *bearing* of a transmitting *radio beacon* at which the signal becomes extremely faint or disappears when the rotating *loop, ferrite rod* or *goniometer* control of a *direction finder* is turned. Often no signal is heard through an arc of some 5°; the bearing is then found by turning the aerial back and forth, and is half way between the points where the signal just becomes audible. A null meter enables the null to be found visually and more easily. In some sophisticated DFs the bearing is obtained from a maximum signal, as opposed to a null, and is displayed on a cathode ray tube. The word null may be used in other applications and, in general, infers an area or point of minimum response.

Numbering Every US vessel with propelling machinery, except one that is *documented,* has to have an identification number and certificate. These indicate the state where she is used most often and give her individual number, e.g. if in Maine, ME-4632. The numbers are displayed on the forward half of the vessel. A powered dinghy is numbered, unless she is a *tender* to a numbered boat and has an engine of under 10 hp; she then displays the parent boat's number plus the figure 1, i.e. ME-4632-1. In some states sailboats and rowboats also have to be numbered. Foreign craft visiting the US temporarily are exempt.

Nun buoy US *aid to navigation* shaped like a truncated cone, but may come to a point. Red *starboard hand mark* in US navigable waters. See also *junction, mid-channel* and *conical* (UK) buoys and front endpapers.

Nylon *Polyamide* fibres used for making rope and *sailcloth*. Nylon is also made into tough fittings such as *cleats* and *fairleads*. The word derives from the two cities where it was invented, New York and LONdon.

O = Oscar: red and yellow *code flag*. As a single letter signal means '*Man overboard*'. *Morse code:* — — — (dash dash dash).

Oak Mainly used for grown *frames, stem, sternpost, keel* etc, but sometimes for *planking*. Not easy to work because grain is interlocked, but crooks are an advantage when shaping curved members. There are several varieties of varying weights; *specific gravity* 0.68–0.95.

Oakum Tarred fibres with which *seams* are *caulked*, picked from old hemp ropes, often a task allocated as a punishment in the 19th century.

Oar Wooden or light alloy pole with a *blade* at one end. When *rowing* or pulling a dinghy, two oars are shipped in *rowlocks* (crutches, US oarlocks), occasionally between *thole pins*. Leather is often nailed round the oar at the fulcrum to give protection from *chafe*. To *scull* over the stern, one oar is shipped in a semi-circular notch in the *transom* (occasionally in a rowlock). An oar can be used to steer a small boat if the *rudder* breaks.

Oarlock (US) See *rowlock*.

Obscured The sector over which a *direction* or *sector light* cannot be seen; chart abbr (UK) Obscd, (US) OBSC.

Observed position The vessel's position at sea found by observation of *heavenly bodies*, i.e. at the point where two *position lines* or *transferred position lines* intersect.

Observer's meridian The celestial *meridian* which passes through the observer's *zenith*.

Obstruction 1. When racing, is any object that can be passed on one side only, e.g. a shoal, the shore, a pier, or any object including a vessel under way that is large enough to require a yacht, when not less than one overall length from it, to make a substantial alteration of course to pass on one side or the other. 2. A *danger* to navigation; may be marked, often by a *buoy* or *beacon*. Chart abbr (UK) Obstn, (US) Obstr.

Occlusion or **occluded front** When a *depression* starts to die and fill, the faster moving *cold front* overtakes the *warm front* ahead, and all the warm air between them is lifted. In the case of the cold occluded front, colder air replaces less cold air ahead of it; with a warm occluded front, cold air replaces colder air. Increasing cloud and freshening

winds signal the approach of an occlusion, and it is accompanied by gusts and precipitation, the wind *veers* and *visibility* is moderate to poor. After it has passed the wind decreases and probably *backs*, there are some showers as the sky clears, and pressure rises. On a weather map is shown as a line with triangles and semicircles alternately.

Occulting light A *rhythmic light* exhibited as an *aid to navigation; eclipses* at regular intervals, the duration of light in each *period* being longer than the duration of darkness. Chart abbr Oc, formerly Occ.

Occulting

Period

Ocean 1. The body of water that surrounds the continents and covers over 70% of the surface of the earth. 2. One of the seven oceans, i.e. Arctic, Antarctic, North and South Atlantic, Indian, North and South Pacific.

Ocean current The horizontal movement of water in the oceans. *Surface currents* are of interest to sailors, and are caused mainly by the *global circulation of winds*, by *pressure gradients* in the water and by variations in *salinity*. A current flows roughly at 2% of wind speed, but this depends partly on *fetch* and the duration of the wind, and may also be increased or decreased by water temperature and *density*, or when the depth of the current is reduced where the ocean is shallower or shelves. The pattern of surface circulation is similar to the global wind pattern and, apart from seasonal

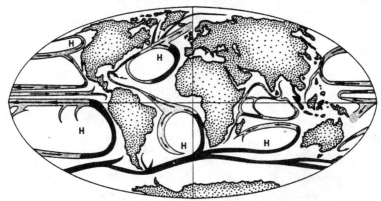

variations, the direction and speed of ocean currents varies little. Full details are given in the monthly *Routeing* (US Pilot) *charts*, and in *Ocean Passages of the World*. When making ocean passages, a boat takes advantage of currents, say by keeping in low latitudes to benefit from the Equatorial Current when sailing westward in the Atlantic, or by making use of the east-setting Southern Ocean Current when sailing eastward round Cape Horn and the Cape of Good Hope. See also *countercurrent*.

Oceanography The study of the oceans, including physical features, marine life, phenomena etc.

Ocean Passages of the World A book, published by the Hydrographer of the Navy, designed to assist the navigator to plan ocean passages; covers waters not dealt with by coastal *Pilots*. Gives information about routes, with recommendations and cautions, and about winds, weather, ice, currents etc. The US Pilot charts and UK *Routeing charts* give additional information for passage-making over the oceans.

Ocean racing See *offshore racing*.

Octant Precision instrument with which either

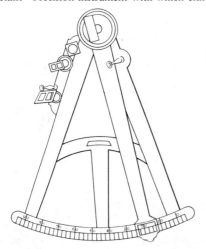

the *altitude* of a *heavenly body*, or the *vertical* and *horizontal angles* subtended by objects such as landmarks may be measured. Operates in exactly the same way as a *sextant* (q.v.), but the *arc* is one eighth of a circle and is graduated from 0–90°. Historically, the octant preceded the sextant, and the figure shows Hadley's 1731 instrument, made not long after Newton discovered the principle of measuring angles in about 1700.

ODAS Ocean Data Acquisition System buoy. Is fitted with sensors to check and record temperature, salinity etc. May be anchored or free floating.

Offing Some distance from the shore, clear of shoals etc. To keep an offing is to keep a safe distance from the shore. Also the part of the sea that is visible from the shore.

Off-lying Of *dangers*, near the coast but not necessarily connected to it.

Offsets See *table of offsets*.

Offshore A direction away from the shore, i.e. seaward. Is sometimes applied to waters relatively close to the coast, as to be blown offshore, offshore wind, but sometimes to activities much further from land, as in offshore racing.

Offshore racing As opposed to *passage racing* or *round-the-buoys* racing etc mainly takes place far from land. Most offshore races are over a distance of between 200 and 700 n.miles, the *courses* normally being round islands or *aids to navigation* such as light buoys, light vessels, lighthouses etc. The race may end at the departure point or elsewhere, e.g. *Bermuda, Fastnet, Sydney-Hobart* and *Southern Ocean Racing Conference* races. Long-distance races of over 1000 n.miles, run at regular or irregular intervals either across part of or an entire ocean, such as *OSTAR, Transpac* are also classed as offshore races. *IOR*-rated yachts and *Ton classes* frequently compete in offshore races, which are run world-wide, including the Agulhas Race, 500 n.miles from Simonstown, round the

Cape of Good Hope and Cape Agulhas to Mossel Bay and back to Cape Town: China Sea Race, 600 n.miles, Hong Kong to Manila: Middle Sea Race, 630 n.miles, Malta, round Lampedusa, Pantellaria and Sicily, and back to Malta: Round Britain Race, 1865 n.miles in all, run in five stages. The longest races of all, of course, are Round-the-World Races which have been run for single-handers as well as fully-crewed boats; generally there are a number of stops en route. See also *Admiral's Cup, Onion Patch, Southern Cross* series.

Offshore Racing Council, ORC International organization which controls offshore racing. The main sub-committees are the Executive, the International Technical Committee (ITC) which deals with the *International Offshore Rule* (IOR) and recommends rule changes, the *Level Rating Classes* Committee which formulates rules for the Ton classes, and the Special Regulations Committee which is concerned with equipment and safety. There are also Measurement, *Time Allowance* and *One-Design* committees. Council members represent countries with offshore racing fleets.

Offshore wind Wind that blows from the land towards the sea or a large body of water.

Off the wind 1. When said of the boat, not sailing close to the wind, i.e. *reaching* with *sheets eased* out. 2. When said of the *helmsman,* allowing the boat to sail to *leeward* of her *close-hauled course,* usually due to lack of concentration.

Off watch Period when a crew member is not on watch but sleeping or relaxing. He is nevertheless needed when it is a case of all hands on deck.

Oil bag A canvas bag, filled with thick heavy oil. This is *streamed* on a line to *windward,* whether over the stern or the bow, to reduce the force of heavy breaking seas when *hove to,* or lying *a-hull.* A thin film of oil spreads quickly over the water, creating an extensive and relatively quiet area round the boat. (Some experts suggest that detergent is equally effective.)

Oilskins or **oilies** or **slickers** Waterproof clothing worn in foul weather. Originally garments for fishermen and seamen made of cloth treated with linseed oil, but are now lighter and more flexible being made of PVC or polyurethane-coated materials. Should be generously cut to fit over pullovers, jacket and trousers, and bright in colour, such as yellow or orange, so that a person in the water can be spotted more easily.

OK *International class* dinghy, *hard-chine,* for single-handed racing, built of *GRP/FRP* or *marine plywood;* designed by Knud Olsen. LOA 13 ft

2 in (4.01 m), beam 4 ft 8 in (1.42 m), weight stripped 159 lbs (72 kg), sail area 90 sq ft (8.4 sq m).

Olympic Class A *class* of racing boats selected by the *IYRU* for Olympic Games racing. The 1984 classes are the *Finn* (one-man boat), *470* and *Flying Dutchman* (two man), *Star* and *Soling* (keelboats), *Tornado* (multihulls), and *Windglider* (sailboard). Former Olympic classes include the *Dragon,* 12 sq m Sharpie and *5.5*-metre.

Olympic course A triangular *course* composed of three *windward legs,* all the same length, two *broad reaches* and one *run. Marks* are laid on the circumference of a circle in such a way that the direct line between the *leeward* and *weather marks* (at one end of the *starting* and *finishing*

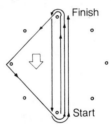

lines respectively) is in line with the direction of the *true wind;* the *reaching mark* is level with the centre of the circle. Two *classes* may use the same course, but sometimes each class has a separate course. Larger boats sail 11.2 n.miles, single-handed classes 8.5 n.miles.

Olympic points See *scoring system.*

Omega A *hyperbolic navigation* system which, with only eight *phase*-locked transmitters, provides world-wide coverage because transmissions are made on very low *frequencies* of 10.2, 11.333 and 13.6 kHz. This gives a range of 5000 miles, while accuracy is about 1 n.mile by day and 2 n.miles by night. The eight stations transmit in sequence every ten seconds, and the receiver on board compares the phase difference of at least two of the most suitable stations. As with *Loran,* the information can be referred to a special Omega *chart* over-printed with hyperbolic *position lines,* but the latest type displays *latitude* and *longitude.* Omega can also be used for submarine navigation in shallow depths, for example when making long passages submerged.

Omnidirectional, non-directional (US **circular**) **radio beacon** As opposed to a *directional radio beacon* (q.v.) transmits a signal all round the horizon; chart abbr (UK) RC, (US) RBn.

Omni(range) or **VOR** (US) Aeronautical navigation system, which can only be used by boats when they are within 10–20 miles of the transmitter because VHF range is restricted to line of sight.

One-design class A *class* of racing boats all built to the same design; they race without *handicap*. The construction rules are precise; *tolerances* allowed for building errors and sail measurements are small. Most *national* and *international classes* are one-design (there are some international *development classes). Manufacturers' classes* are one-design, and are usually even more strictly controlled. Some one-design classes are the *Flying Dutchman, 505* and *420.* One-design racing classes have recently been adopted for *offshore racing.*

One-man boat A sailing dinghy suitable in size and fitted out for single-handed sailing. The *Finn* is the *Olympic* one-man *class.*

One-minute rule A rule that may be enforced when a large fleet is racing, normally after one or more general *recalls.* If any part of a yacht, her crew or equipment is on the course side of the *starting line* during the last minute before the *starting signal* is made she is disqualified.

One Ton Class A *level rating class,* the maximum *rating* being 27.5 ft. A typical boat's measurements are LOA 36.5 ft (11 m), beam 9.8 ft (3 m), sail area 590 sq ft (55 sq m), displacement 13,900 lbs (6.3 tonnes). Races are run annually for the One Ton Cup, the Coupe Internationale, presented by the Cercle de la Voile de Paris. Formerly this was competed for by 6-metres designed to the pre-1906 *International Rule,* but in 1965 the cup was reallocated for level racing. Originally boats were rated under the *RORC* rule, but they are now rated under the *IOR.* Five races are sailed; three Olympic courses, counting single points, about 27 n.miles long; one shorter offshore race, 1.5 points, lasting about 27 hours is about 160 n.miles long, based on an average speed of about 6 knots; a longer offshore race, double points, is 325 n.miles long and lasts about 54 hours. The number of crew is seven.

Onion Patch series A four-race biennial series consisting of a 175-mile *offshore race* from Oyster Bay NY to Newport RI, two *Olympic courses* off Newport and the *Bermuda Race.* Like the *Admiral's Cup* is open to international teams of three boats. Called after the US nick-name for Bermuda.

Onshore Towards the shore, from seaward, as onshore wind.

Onshore wind A wind that blows from the sea or a large body of water to the land.

On the wind *Close-hauled,* q.v.

Open 1. When two *leading* marks (US ranges) are not in line they are said to be open. To open is deliberately to sail a course that separates two marks or features. 2. Unprotected against weather (of boat, harbour etc).

Open boat An undecked boat, such as a *dinghy* or *tender.*

Open harbour Not sheltered from the sea.

Opposition When one *heavenly body* is on the opposite side of earth to another, such as sun and moon at full moon, they are in opposition (c.f. *conjunction*).

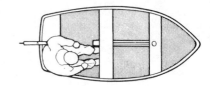

Optimist *International class* dinghy built of *marine plywood* or *GRP/FRP* for children aged between 7 and 15 years; designed by Clark Mills. LOA 7 ft 6½ in (2.3 m), beam 3 ft 8½ in (1.13 m), minimum hull weight 77 lbs 35 kg, sail area 35 sq ft (3.25 sq.m).

Orbital motion In waves, water particles move in a circular orbit, the diameter of which is equal to wave height. They orbit in the same direction as the wave is travelling, moving forwards as the crest passes, then downwards, backwards beneath the troughs and then up towards the surface. The effect can be observed by watching a bird floating on the surface; it is carried forward on the wave crests but moved back in the troughs virtually to its original position. Particles further beneath the surface also follow cirular orbits, but move more slowly round orbits that become smaller as depth increases. Orbital motion ceases at depths equal

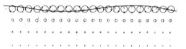

to half wave length. The forward component of orbital velocity, just ahead of the crest, accelerates a boat running downwind, and can be made use of to *surf* down the face, sometimes for a considerable period. This can be dangerous, even for a larger cruising boat when seas are high, because orbital velocity increases with wave height and may cause her to *broach* if a breaking crest thrusts her forward while her bow is decelerated in the trough. When water depth is less than half wave length, the circular orbits become flattened and elliptical; waves at the surface become steeper and unstable and, as in surf, break forcefully.

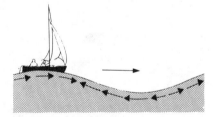

ORC *Offshore Racing Council*, q.v.

Osmosis Water is absorbed through tiny pin-holes, e.g. in the *gelcoat* of a *GRP/FRP* hull. Over a period the *laminate* beneath absorbs water, *blistering* occurs, and the moulding deteriorates.

OSTAR The Observer Single-handed Trans-Atlantic Race which, since 1960, has been run every four years across the Atlantic from England to the USA.

Ounce In the f.p.s. system, the avoirdupois ounce is a unit of weight, one-sixteenth of a pound. 1 ounce = 28.3495 grammes; 1 gramme = 0.0352739 oz. See also *cloth weight*.

Outboard 1. Outside the vessel, e.g. *self-steering gear* is shipped outboard. 2. Towards the side of the vessel. 3. Abbr for outboard engine.

Outboard engine Portable engine for dinghies

or larger boats, usually mounted on the *transom* or *counter*, sometimes over one side or in a *well* aft. Generally can be tilted forward to raise the *propeller* in shallow water.

Outdrive Also called inboard-outboard, stern-drive, Z-drive. Installation that combines the advantages of *inboard* and *outboard engines*. The power unit is mounted inboard near the stern, and is coupled to the gears, shaft and propeller which are in an outboard drive unit. The latter can usually be turned and tilted in the same way as an outboard engine.

Outer jib A third *headsail*, set forward of the *staysail* and *inner jib*.

Outfall buoy Laid where a sewer discharges into the sea.

Outfoot To sail faster than another boat.

Outhaul A line or *tackle*, which may be combined with a mechanical device such as a screw or worm, with which the mainsail *clew* is hauled out towards the end of the *boom*. The term may be applied to other ropes that haul an object *outboard*.

Outpoint To sail closer to the wind than another boat, to *point* better.

Outrigger 1. A *spar* or support which projects outboard. Under the *IYRU racing rules*, a sail may be sheeted to a *boom* regularly used for a *working sail* and permanently attached to the mast to which the *head* of the working sail is set, but not to an outrigger, which is any fitting so placed that it could exert outward pressure on a sheet at a point from which a vertical line would fall outside the hull or deck planking. The *spinnaker pole* and the boom of a *boom headsail* are not classed as out-riggers. 2. A small boat with a float that provides lateral stability (US alternative term for *proa*). 3. The hulls either side of a *trimaran*, or the sub-sidiary hull of a *proa*.

Outsail To sail faster than another boat.

Outside yacht Under the *racing rules*, the outside yacht has to give *room* to an inside yacht(s) when *rounding* a *mark* of the *course*, provided that the inside yacht has established an *overlap* before she is within two of her overall lengths of the mark.

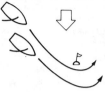

Overboard Over the side, implying movement, as in fall overboard, *man overboard*.

Overcanvassed Describes a boat that is carrying too much sail for the weather conditions, or one with too large a sail area relative to her *displacement*. It rarely pays to carry too much sail, especially when *on the wind* because hull *resistance* increases when the boat *heels*, speed is reduced and *leeway* increased.

Overcast When the sky is completely covered with a layer of cloud.

Overfalls Turbulent water where there is a sudden change in depth, or where two *tidal streams or currents* meet.

Overhand knot Simplest of *stopper knots*. The end crosses the *standing part* and is brought up through the *bight* that is formed.

Overhang The part of the *hull* that extends beyond the *waterline* either forward or aft. The combined length of the forward and aft overhangs is the difference between *length overall* and *waterline length*. Formerly long overhangs were preferred because of the additional *reserve buoyancy* provided and the greater *sailing length* obtained when *heeled*, but they are now avoided for modern offshore sailing boats on the grounds of seaworthiness, and to keep excess weight from the ends of the boat.

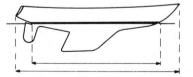

Overhaul 1. To pull the *blocks* of a *tackle* further apart. 2. To sail or motor faster than a vessel ahead and overtake her.

Overlap 1. Under the *racing rules*, two yachts overlap when neither is *clear astern* (q.v.) or when,

although one is clear astern, an intervening yacht overlaps both of them. 2. One sail is said to overlap another, for example the *genoa* overlaps the *mainsail*, when the *clew* of the genoa extends further aft than the *luff* of the mainsail.

Overriding turn (US)   See *riding turn*.

Overstand When *beating* towards an objective, such as the *weather mark* of the *course*, to stay longer than is necessary on one *tack*. After *going about*, the boat has to *bear away* on the new tack to return to the mark.

Overtaking light The *stern light;* the navigation light that is seen by an overtaking vessel when she approaches the vessel she is overtaking from a direction more than two points abaft her beam.

Overtaking vessel Under the *IRPCS*, if a vessel, whether *sailing* or *power-driven*, comes up with another from a direction more than 22.5° abaft the other vessel's beam, she has to keep out of the way of the vessel she is overtaking. Similarly under the *racing rules* a yacht *clear astern* keeps clear of a yacht ahead.

Over the ground *Courses, speeds* and *distances* sailed are either described as made good over the ground (sometimes called tracks), in which case allowance has been made for the effects of *tidal stream* or *current* and *leeway,* or as *through the water,* in which case no allowance has been made. The course sailed by the boat through the water is indicated by the pecked line, but the course made good over the ground will be along the solid line because she is being *set* by the tidal stream. See also *vector diagram* 2.

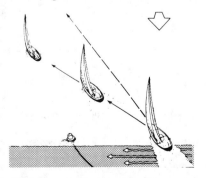

P = Papa: blue *code flag* with a white rectangle, the Blue Peter. As a single letter signal means: in harbour, 'All persons should report on board as the vessel is about to proceed to sea'; at sea, worn by fishing vessels 'My nets have come fast upon an obstruction'. *Morse code:* • — — • (dot dash dash dot). When racing means 'The class designated by the *warning signal* will start in five minutes exactly.'

Paddle 1. A short light *oar* for propelling a dinghy by paddling; no *rowlock* is used. Should be carried by all sailing dinghies without oars. 2. To use a paddle or to *row* very gently.

Paint 1. Marine paints and varnishes are specially formulated to protect boats from the effects of weather and salt water. Only the right paints and *primers* for the construction material must be used. *Topside* paints are abrasion- and water-resistant; *bottom* paints are either of the soft *antifouling* type, or hard paints designed to be scrubbed; deck paints are non-slip. Many paints are applied straight from the tin, but *two-pack* products have to be mixed together first. Careful preparation of the surface is essential if a good *finish* is to be obtained. 2. The spots of light on the *radar* display, produced or painted by the radial sweep when echoes are returned from *targets*.

Painter The line at the bow of a *dinghy* or *tender* by which she is *towed* or *made fast*.

Paint remover Liquid applied to soften paint or varnish so that it can be scraped off more easily with a putty knife. The area must be neutralized as directed before new paint is applied. Must not be used on painted *GRP/FRP* hulls and mouldings.

Paint sick Said of a boat that has acquired excessive layers of paint. They have to be removed.

Palm 1. A sailmaker's palm is worn when stitching sail cloth to provide the sailmaker with a thimble. A leather strap with an opening for the thumb fits round the sewing hand and, at the base of the thumb, has a socketed metal cup with which the needle is forced through the heavy cloth. 2. A *roping* palm, with a deep needle guard, is used

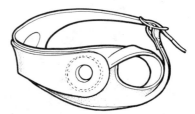

especially for roping. 3. Of the *anchor*, is the flat part of the *fluke*.

Pan-pan The internationally recognized radio telephony *urgency* signal used when transmitting a message concerning the safety of a vessel or person. The message takes priority over all traffic except *distress* messages which are preceded by the word Mayday. From the French, panne, breakdown.

Panel See *cloth*.

Paper former Paper rope with a flexible wire core, round which a *GRP/FRP* rib is *laminated* into a *moulding* to provide reinforcement, say in place of the *frame* of a wooden hull. The paper does not itself increase strength; this is provided by the laminate around the former.

Parachute flare A *distress* rocket which ejects a red flare that floats down slowly on a parachute. Is visible for up to 25 n. miles at night, and is fired from the hand to a height of 1000 ft (300 m), burning for 40 secs at 40,000 *candela*. Some parachute flares incorporate small *radar reflectors* which can be picked up as echoes on a radar screen.

Parallax The difference in direction, or change of apparent position, that results from viewing an object from a different place. Errors occur, e.g. when the helmsman steers while sitting on the side deck instead of being directly forward or aft of the *lubber line*, or when he is not on the boat's centre-line and is keeping the boat on a specific course by lining up the stem or mast with a point on shore. In *celestial navigation*, parallax is the angle between the *true altitude* of the *heavenly body* relative to the centre of the earth and the altitude of the body above the horizontal plane throught the observer's eye, the latter being *sextant altitude* corrected for *index error*, *dip*, *refraction* and *semi-diameter*. The correction to be applied for parallax is included in the *altitude correction tables*

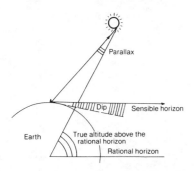

for the sun, but the moon is very much closer to the earth, and a separate table is provided for horizontal parallax, which is tabulated hourly. Parallax is greatest when the heavenly body is on the *horizon,* and decreases to nil at the *zenith.*

Parallel of latitude A *small circle* connecting all places on the earth which are the same *latitude* north or south of the *equator* (see *latitude*).

Parallel rule or **ruler** or **rules** Navigational instrument with which lines can be transferred to and from a *compass rose* on a *chart,* e.g. to lay off a *true* or *magnetic bearing* or to find the *course* to steer. May be two rulers held parallel to each other by two pivoting arms, or a single large ruler with inset rollers. The former is opened and closed

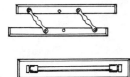

to transfer the line, and the latter is rolled across the chart; in both cases the edge of the ruler stays parallel to the original course or bearing. Most are made of transparent plastic, and many are marked in degrees round the edges.

Parbuckle One end of a line or rope is made fast; the other is taken down beneath an object that is roughly cylindrical, such as a spar, and up to the crew who raises the object by hauling on the line.

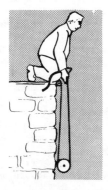

Parcel To protect rope from the weather, tarred canvas strips are bound round rope after it has been *wormed,* working with the lay. A *serving* is then applied against the lay to hold the parcelling in place. The old rhyme runs 'Worm and parcel with the lay, turn and serve the other way'.

Parrel Rope, wire, collar etc which holds a *yard* or *gaff* to a *mast,* allowing the spar to be hoisted, lowered and to move laterally. Wooden parrel beads may be strung on the rope between the *jaws* of a gaff to make it easier to hoist. Parrels may also be used in place of *hoops* or *lacing* to hold the *luff* of a sail to the mast, especially that of a *trysail.*

Part 1. The section of the *fall* (the line or rope) rove through the standing and moving *blocks* of a *tackle;* there are *standing, running* and *hauling parts.* 2. Of rope or cable, to break under strain, whether because the load is too great or as a result of *chafe.*

Partners See *mast partners.*

Passage 1. A narrow navigable channel, often between reefs, islands or shoals. 2. A journey by sea between two places.

Passage racing A race run between two harbours, generally along a coast.

Patch Piece of cloth stitched to a sail, either as reinforcement where the load is greatest (i.e. at *clew, tack* and *head*), or to provide protection against *chafe* at vulnerable places. May also be sewn and/or glued to the sail to repair damage.

Patent log Mechanical *log* that has been in use for many decades and is still preferred by many sailors. A rotator is towed astern of the boat at the end of a log line, which is plaited so that it will not snarl or stretch. The rate at which the rotator turns varies with the speed of the water streaming

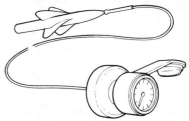

past, and the log line turns with the rotator, actuating the mechanism of the register mounted in a shoe at the stern. Distance is registered in tenths of *nautical miles,* and boat speed in *knots* is also sometimes displayed.

Path 1. The intended route of a vessel. 2. The route that the centre of a *depression* or *tropical revolving storm* is expected to follow.

Pawl Short lug which drops into a toothed wheel or rack to prevent it from running back, e.g. as in a *windlass, ratchet block, roller reefing gear* etc.

Pay To fill a *seam* with *caulking* compound, *marine glue* or *pitch*.

Pay off The vessel's *head* pays off when it falls off from the wind, turning to *leeward*.

Pay out To let out a line or rope gradually.

P-bracket A metal support, for the *propeller shaft* after it has emerged from the hull. Usually a round casting which contains a *cutless bearing*, attached to the hull by a single arm.

Peak 1. The after end of the *gaff* to which the peak of a *gaff sail* is attached. The *sheet* of a *jib-headed topsail* is led to the peak. 2. The upper aftermost corner of a four-sided *fore-and-aft sail* where *head* and *leech* meet. 3. The *forepeak* and *afterpeak* are at the ends of the boat and are used for stowage or as watertight compartments.

Peeling a spinnaker To change *spinnakers*, the second being set before the first is lowered so that the boat is not left *baldheaded*, thus reducing speed. Two spinnaker sheets and halyards are required, but only one guy plus a stripper (a short length of line with a snaphook at one end which holds the second tack).

Pelican hook Hinged hook that can be opened when under load by knocking back the ring. Often fitted in a *lifeline* (guardrail) to provide a *gangway* to make it easier to board the boat when lying alongside, or to recover a person that has fallen overboard.

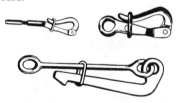

Pelorus or **dumb compass** Instrument with which *relative bearings* are taken. Has a card graduated from 0–360° and sights but, unlike a *magnetic compass*, has no magnetized needle. The pelorus is mounted in the *fore-and-aft line*, generally temporarily in a special shoe, sometimes in *gimbals;* dead *ahead* bears 0°, *abeam* to *starboard* 90°, dead *astern* 180° and abeam to *port* 270°. To obtain a *compass bearing*, the relative bearing has to be added to the vessel's *heading* at the moment the bearing is taken; 360 is subtracted from the total if the figure exceeds that amount. Although a *hand-bearing compass* is easier and quicker to use, a pelorus is useful when checking whether

vessels are on *collision courses,* when finding distance off with a *four point bearing* or *bearing angles on the bow*, and when *swinging ship* to check *compass error*.

Penalty 1. In the case of a gross infringement of the *racing rules*, a person may be disqualified by the national authority from competing in races for a period. 2. Instead of disqualifying a boat when a rule is infringed, the racing instructions may specify that a *720° turn* may be performed by the boat or a percentage penalty applied, such as a place worse than the boat's own place equal to 20% of the starters. 3. When a yacht is measured for an *IOR rating* a number of the measurements taken may be corrected to include penalties, for example if the length of the *spinnker pole* exceeds the J measurement. Hence a penalty pole is a spinnaker pole that is longer than the base of the *foretriangle*.

Pendant 1. A short length of line or wire rope attached at one end to a *spar, cringle* etc; at the other end is often attached to a *block* through which a *tackle* is rove. 2. A tapering *flag*, such as the code flag and *answering pendant;* see end papers. See also *broad pendant*. 3. A span of wire at the *head* or *tack* of a *jib* to increase the *luff* length, or to raise the tack above the deck (also strop).

Pennant 1. Alternative spelling of pendant (2), i.e. a tapering *flag*, usually triangular. 2. On a *wind arrow*, represents 50 *knots* (see *feather*).

Perch (US or **bush stake**) Sapling or withy, rammed into soft mud to mark the edge of a minor channel. Some are painted red (*port hand*) and black (*starboard hand*), others carry *topmarks* to indicate to which side they should be left. In some countries port hand perches are left bushy (flattish tops), but starboard hand perches are trimmed clean (pointed tops).

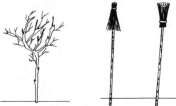

Perigee   The point in the moon's orbit when she is nearest to the earth. Perigee *tides* of greater than average range occur at this time (c.f. *apogee*).

Period   1. Of a light: the time that it takes a *rhythmic* or *alternating light*, exhibited as an *aid to navigation*, to complete one sequence, e.g. *group flashing* (3), from the start of the first of the three flashes to the start of the next group of three. The period has to be known if the light is to be identified, and is printed on *charts* and in the *List of Lights* (UK excluding light buoys under 8 m high). See *character*, fig. 2. Of a wave: the interval between the passage of two successive crests past a stationary point. 3. See *rolling period*.

Perlon   Trade name for German *polyamide* fibres used for making rope.

Personal Flotation Device, PFD   US term for *life-jacket, life vest*. US Coast Guard approved PFD Types I and II are designed to turn an unconscious person from a face down position so that he floats vertically or tilted slightly backwards. Type I, for offshore sailing, provides minimum buoyancy of 22 lbs (10 kg) for adults, 11 lbs (5 kg) for children;

Type II, inshore waters, 15½ lbs (7 kg) and 7 lbs (3 kg) respectively. Type III, as II but does not turn an unconscious person face upwards; allows greater freedom of movement and is suitable for inland waters, sailing close by the shore etc. Type IV, minimum buoyancy 16½ lbs (7.5 kg) is designed to be thrown. Type V covers miscellaneous approved designs.

Phase   1. One element of the sequence of a *rhythmic* or *alternating light,* i.e. the duration of the light or of the *eclipse*. 2. With regard to waves; consider two wheels A and B on a common shaft, each with an identical reference mark on the circumference; when one is moved through 360° the other follows precisely at all points of rotation, and they rotate 'in phase'. If wheel A is released from the shaft so that it no longer rotates exactly in step with wheel B 'phase slip' occurs. If wheel A were locked to the shaft, its reference mark about 60° from that of wheel B, they would rotate in 'phase locked' fashion, but would be 60° 'out of phase', either advanced or retarded depending on the reference used; expressed another way, the wheels would have a phase difference of 60°.

Phase of the moon   The shape of the moon's illuminated surface changes as the moon alters her position in relation to the earth and the sun, and *tides* are greatly affected by her movement as she orbits the earth. At new moon, when between earth and sun, she is invisible; at full moon she has completed half her orbit and is fully illuminated on the opposite side to the sun; these are roughly the periods of *spring tides*. The first quarter is when she has covered 90° of her orbit and is *waxing;* the last quarter is when she has covered 270° and is *waning;* at these times sun and moon are in *quadrature* and tidal *range* is low, i.e. *neap tides*.

Phonetic alphabet   The words used for radio communication are given in this dictionary under the first entry for each letter, e.g. A = Alfa; together with numerals they are listed under *radiotelephony*.

Phosphorescence   See *bioluminescence*.

Pick up a mooring   In order to pick up a *mooring* or other floating object when a boat is under sail, either the sails have to be eased right out or the boat *shoots* into the wind, so as to reach the object when she has ceased to move over the ground.

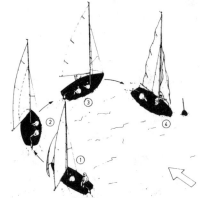

Pier   A wooden, stone, metal or concrete structure which is often built on *piles* so that water may flow under it; juts out from the shore, roughly at right angles. Sometimes vessels can moor at the pierhead, which may be T- or L-shaped. The inshore end is the root.

Pigment   Colouring material added to paints, gelcoat etc.

Pile   Stout timber, concrete or metal post driven vertically into the river or sea-bed. Boats on pile *moorings* are secured fore-and-aft between them. Piles also support structures such as piers, wharves etc.

Pillar   A vertical member that supports *thwarts, deck beams* etc.

Pillar buoy *Aid to navigation* with a tall structure rising from the centre. Exhibits a considerably higher light than a normal channel buoy. Also called *high focal plane buoy.*

Pilot 1. A qualified professional, authorized to navigate vessels in and out of harbour or through channels in a certain locality. He is not a member of the crew, but waits at a pilot station or in a pilot cutter, ready to board a vessel requiring his services. The red and white pilot flag is worn when there is a pilot on board. Sometimes the navigator of a sailing boat is nicknamed the pilot. Is more widely applied as a verb, and an amateur is often said to pilot a boat. 2. Official publication intended for large vessels, but contains much information of interest to small boat sailors, such as details of the *coast, dangers, currents, tidal streams,* harbour regulations, *meteorology* and other information required when sailing along a coast or into a harbour. Each volume covers a particular area, and some countries print a series of pilots covering the entire world. The term is also sometimes applied to unofficial guides or sailing directions written by individual authors expressly for small boat sailors.

Pilotage or **piloting** Navigation largely within sight of the coast or in restricted waters, using visual aids and *soundings* but exclusive of *celestial navigation.* Some people include the use of electronic aids in the definition of pilotage. See *coastal navigation.*

Pilot berth A *berth* for use at sea, with a wooden or canvas *bunkboard.* Often fitted above and outboard of a settee so that both can be used simultaneously.

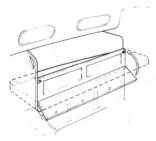

Pilot Chart (US) See *Routeing chart.*

Pilot cutter Alternative term for *pilot vessel,* namely a vessel in which pilots wait, ready to board incoming vessels requiring their services, or to which they transfer after piloting an outward bound vessel.

Pilot vessel or **pilot cutter,** q.v. Under the *IRPCS* a pilot vessel on duty at night exhibits two *all-round lights,* the upper white and the lower red, at or near the *masthead,* in addition to *side* and *stern*

lights when *under way* or the appropriate lights when at *anchor.* By day a British pilot vessel wears a red and white flag, the upper half white and the lower half red, so that she can be identified. A vessel with a pilot on board wears International *Code flag H, hoist* white, *fly* red. When on duty in *restricted visibility* a pilot vessel may sound four short *blasts* as an identity signal. A vessel requiring the services of a pilot wears Code flag G.

Pinch To sail so close to the wind that the sails lose driving power. The boat sails slowly and, although she *points* higher, she makes more *leeway.*

Pine Wood with a high resin content, used for decks, spars and masts. There are many varieties; *specific gravity* 0.45–0.66.

Pinholes Tiny holes in the *gelcoat* which lead to *osmosis* because water can penetrate to the *laminate* beneath.

Pinrail Strong rail fitted horizontally at the side of a *sailing ship;* carries *belaying pins* to which the *running rigging* is *belayed,* and on which the coiled ropes are hung. Similar to a *fiferail* which is fitted round the mast.

Pintle A *rudder fitting* with a long pin, which is slipped into the *gudgeon* to form a hinge about which the rudder pivots. Pintles and gudgeons are fitted in pairs; normally the pintle of one pair is attached to the rudder and the gudgeon to the *stern,* while the other pintle is attached to the stern

and the gudgeon to the rudder. It is easier to *ship* the rudder if one pintle is slightly longer. The spring retaining clip (black in the figure) prevents the rudder from being lifted off accidentally when it hits flotsam or the bottom.

Pipe berth (US) or **pipe cot** (UK) The occupant sleeps on canvas stretched between a pipe frame. Often fitted forward as a spare *berth* or for sail stowage, and usually hinges up to the side when not in use.

Piston end fitting A *spinnaker pole* end fitting

which operates similarly to a piston hank; often has a line attached to a ring on the plunger so that it can be pulled open from a distance. Generally fitted to both ends of the pole, one being attached to the *spinnaker guy* or *tack;* the other is clipped to an eye or pushed into a *bell* on the mast.

Piston hank or **snap** (US) A *hank* sewn to the *luff* of a *staysail;* has a spring-loaded plunger which is opened to hank the sail to the *stay.*

Piston, hand or **deck pump** A simple pump operated by raising and lowering a lever or handle manually. A flexible washer or a hard rubber ball at the bottom of the barrel allows water to enter the chamber when the piston is raised, but closes when the piston descends so that water is forced out through the outlet at the top. *Capacity* varies with swept volume, i.e. with the length and diameter of the chamber. Most piston pumps have to be primed, and some discharge onto the deck.

Pitch 1. The distance that a *propeller* (q.v.) would advance during one complete revolution in a solid medium. This varies with the angle of the blade to the hub. In practice the distance that a propeller advances is shorter (the difference being *slip*), but this is offset to some extent by the *wake factor,* q.v. Pitch is said to be coarse or fine,

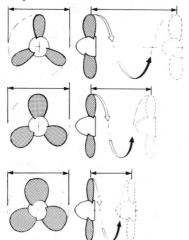

theoretical advance being greater when it is coarse. Fine pitch is required for lightweight, high speed boats and fast revving engines; coarse pitch for heavy boats, slow revving engines and when high power output is desired, e.g. for towing. 2. The *motion* of a boat in a seaway as she see-saws back and forth about her horizontal athwartships axis, *bow* and *stern* rising and falling alternately. Her pitching motion depends partly on her length in relation to the length of the wave. A small boat may pitch to a standstill when heading into short steep seas, whereas a longer, more powerful boat will not be stopped by them. When seas are very high and long, a small boat will sail up the face of a wave and down the other side, whereas a large vessel's bows would drive under the wave. 3. Tarry substance formerly used for *paying seams,* now replaced by *caulking* compound.

Pitchpole The boat is turned *stern* over *bow* in high seas by a breaking *following sea* that lifts the stern high and forces the bows down. May occur when she is *overcanvassed,* or when running under *bare poles.* Few boats survive and then usually with a broken mast.

Plaited rope See *braided rope.*

Plan 1. See *body plan.* 2. Large scale and very detailed *chart* of a small area such as a harbour. The *natural scale* varies from 1:50,000 to 1:5000.

Plane Whereas most vessels are supported purely by the static force of *buoyancy,* the verb to plane is widely used to describe the state of a boat that is supported partially by *dynamic lift.* When sailing fast, a correctly handled lightweight racing dinghy with large sail area is lifted above her own *bow wave;* she partly escapes from the wave system she has generated and, when planing, displaces less than her own weight of water. Very beamy boats with flat *sections* aft plane well, provided *resistance* is low and *wetted area* small. More precisely, the state described above is *semi-planing;* a boat is really planing when she skims over the water supported entirely by dynamic lift.

When a boat jumps onto a plane, rapid acceleration causes the *apparent wind* to shift

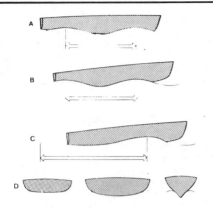

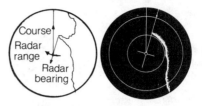

further forward, and the crew have to move their weight further aft, simultaneously *hardening* in the sails to keep her on the plane. In the figure boat A is displacement sailing, B the transition point, C planing. D shows the sections of a typical planing hull, from right to left at the bow, amidships and aft. Speed when planing often considerably exceeds displacement or *hull speed* (see also *speed to length ratio*).

Planet Like the earth is a satellite of the sun. Venus, Mars, Jupiter and Saturn are planets bright enough for *sights* to be taken, and their *Greenwich Hour Angle* and *declination* are given hourly in the *Nautical Almanac*.

Planing hull, boat or **dinghy** A lightweight hull designed so that the boat will plane in winds of about force 4 at a minimum *speed to length ratio* of about 1.6.

Plank A length of timber which covers the *deck beams* (deck planking) or forms part of the outside *skin* of a wooden vessel. As a verb, to cover with planking.

Planking Collective term for the planks or *strakes* that form the *skin* or *deck* of a vessel. A strake is a single line of planking, laid from *bow* to *stern*, and is often made up of several planks. See *construction* fig.

Plank sheer See *covering board*.

Plankton Microscopic plants (phytoplankton) and animals (zooplankton) that float in the sea; from the Greek word for wanderer. They mass near the surface in immense colonies like white clouds, and their movement is largely restricted to drifting in currents. A source of food for a great variety of marine creatures, up to and including the whale in size.

Plan Position Indicator, PPI The type of display normally used in a marine *radar* set (see *radar*). Relative motion display is general in small boat

radars, the vessel's position being stationary at the centre of the screen while echoes of moving and stationary objects move on the screen relative to the vessel. In most small radars the vessel's *head* points to the top of the PPI; bearings taken from the display are *relative bearings* (i.e. dead ahead is 000°, abeam to starboard 090° or green 90, dead astern 180°, abeam to port 270° or red 90). If the PPI is compass stabilized the top becomes north, the heading line marker indicates the vessel's *course*, and bearings are *compass bearings*. True motion display is confined at present to larger ships' radars; the spot of light representing the ship moves across the screen, echoes from stationary objects do not move, and echoes from moving vessels are seen to move across the screen at the appropriate speed and in the true direction.

Plastics Man-made materials of high molecular weight and plastic (i.e. can be formed or shaped) at some stage of manufacture. Generally polymers built up from monomer molecules by addition or condensation *polymerization*. May be thermoplastic (will soften or melt repeatedly) or thermosetting (lose their plasticity). Many marine applications, ranging from boatbuilding (*GRP/FRP*) to paints, ropes, sailcloth and fittings.

Plating Metal plates of varying thickness, welded or riveted to form the *shell* and/or *deck* of a vessel.

Play 1. To play a *sheet* is to adjust it continuously, holding it instead of *cleating* it, and *spilling wind* in the gusts to keep the boat upright. 2. Movement of rudder, steering wheel, gooseneck or other equipment in their fittings or housings. May be allowable or excessive.

Plot 1. To find the boat's *position* by laying off *lines of bearing, position lines* etc on a *chart*, or to draw a boat's *course* to steer or her course made good on the chart. 2. The picture on the radar screen at any time.

Plotting diagram Diagram representing the *radar screen;* the vessel's position is at the centre, and the position of another vessel is plotted at equally spaced time intervals (e.g. after 3 and 6 mins) to find their relative courses and speeds, and to determine whether there is a *risk of collision* by measuring the *miss distance*, or *closest point of approach* (CPA).

Plotting instruments The traditional instrument

for plotting *courses* and *bearings* on *charts* is the *parallel ruler*, but it is not entirely satisfactory for sailing boats because chart tables are small, and the ridges where charts have to be folded to fit into small stowage spaces often cause the ruler to slip. Many alternative instruments have been designed, and are broadly termed rulers, *protractors*, plotters or *set squares*, but there is little consistency as to which term is applied to which type of instrument by the various manufacturers. Almost all are transparent and engraved in degrees, either from 0–180° or 0–360°. One type has a long plotting arm that rotates about the centre of a compass rose, which is marked in degrees and mounted in a square grid base. The grid is aligned with a *parallel of latitude* or a *meridian* on the chart, and *true bearings* are obtained when 0° on the rose is aligned with true north, or *magnetic bearings* when the rose is turned to allow for local *variation*. Square grid-type plotters, ruler-type course plotters with degrees marked in a semi-circle and parallel lines along the length, set squares and rulers graduated round the edge provide true bearings, obtained by referring the bearing to a nearby meridian. See also *station pointer, dividers.*

Plough (US **plow**) **anchor**   Alternative name for the *CQR anchor* (patented), and for many imitations of the CQR. The horn and wings are shaped like a plough share, and hold particularly well in sand or mud into which they dig deeply and quickly. The shank is hinged so that it can move without breaking out the anchor. *Holding power* is good, and at least twenty to sixty times anchor weight.

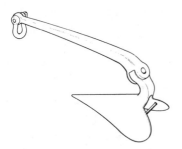

Plug   1. A male *mould*, made as a full-scale model, say of a boat's *hull*. For *GRP/FRP* construction, a *female mould* is *laid-up* over the plug; the hulls are then laid-up inside the resulting female mould, which is braced to prevent distortion. The outside of the plug and the inside of the female mould both correspond to the designer's lines. 2. A bung put in a drain hole in the bottom of a boat 3. Alternative term for *dowel*, q.v. 4. To plug the tide is to sail against a *foul tidal stream.*

Plummer block (US or **pillow block**)   Bearing that supports the *propeller shaft* forward of the *stern tube.*

Pod   1. See *nacelle.* 2. To enable machinery to be changed easily, the engine and propeller may be fitted in a pod, the lower part of which forms part of the *hull*. A watertight fit is obviously essential. The pod can be removed complete with machinery, when engine repairs are necessary, and a second fitted in its place.

Point   1. 11°15′, see *point of the compass.* 2. Where land projects from the shore, or where the line of the coast changes sharply. 3. Verb relating to the ability of a *close-hauled* boat to sail close to the wind; she is said to point well when she can sail very close to the wind, to point high

when sailing as close as possible, to point badly if she sails at too broad an angle to the wind, whether owing to her design, awkward seas, incorrectly trimmed sails or poor helming. 4. Ornamental tapering of a rope's tail.

Point of sailing   The boat's *course* relative to the direction of the wind. As in the figure showing a boat on *port tack,* no boat can sail closer to the true wind than about 40°. She is said to be *close-hauled* when sailing as close to the wind as possible with her sails fully *hardened* in. As the helmsman *bears away* and the crew *ease* the sheets gradually, she first sails on a *close reach* with the apparent wind still *forward of the beam*, then on a *beam reach* with the *wind abeam* and then on a *broad reach* with the wind roughly over the *quarter*. Finally, with sails eased fully and at right angles to the centreline, she is on a *run* with the wind blowing over the stern.

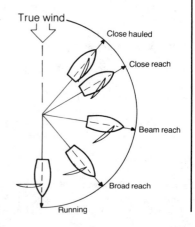

Point of the compass Formerly all *compass cards* were divided into 32 points, the cardinal points (north, east, south and west) being 90° apart, with the intercardinal points (north-east, south-east, south-west and north-west) midway between them. One point is 11°15′, and on many cards every point is subdivided into quarter points, each of 2° 48′ 45″ For instance one of the four *quadrants* (from south to west), including intermediate points and by-points, runs in sequence: S, S × W, SSW, SW × S, SW, SW × W, WSW, W × S, W.

Points reefing The area of a *mainsail* is reduced by gathering the lower part to the *foot*, instead of rolling it round the boom as in *roller reefing*. The *luff* and *leech cringles* are brought down with *reef pendants* and the *bunt* is either *laced* to the boom or, more frequently, gathered with *reef points*. *Jiffy reefing* is similar but quicker. See also *reefing systems*.

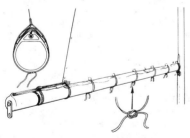

Polar circle Geographical limit of one of the polar regions, i.e. the Arctic circle, 66°33′ N and the Antarctic circle 66°33′ S.

Polar diagram The position of a point lying in a plane is determined by two co-ordinates, the first being the distance of the point from a fixed point called the origin, the second being the angle between a reference line passing through the origin and the line between the point and the origin. The figure shows a polar diagram obtained by plotting the values for *lift* and *drag*, measured at various *angles of attack*. The vertical y scale gives the coefficient of lift or cross wind force, the horizontal

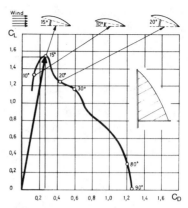

x scale gives the coefficient of drag, and the line from the origin to the circle marked 15° indicates the coefficient of total force at an angle of attack of 15°. The sail force curve is plotted for angles of attack up to 90°, and can be compared with curves obtained when *camber* is varied, or with those of sails of different *aspect ratio*. Polar diagrams can be plotted on a square grid, as in the figure, or on a grid like a spider's web with a series of concentric circles crossed by radial lines (see *economical speed* fig.)

Polar distance The arc between the *elevated pole* and the *heavenly body*, side PX in the *PZX triangle*. 90° minus *declination* when declination and elevated pole are both north or both south, 90° plus declination when they have opposite names. See PZX triangle fig.

Polar front Separates continental-polar air or maritime-polar air from maritime-tropical air, i.e. between the easterlies that come from polar regions and the temperate westerlies. This is where *depressions* breed.

Polaris The North or Pole Star, star alpha in the constellation of Ursa Minor. Polaris moves in a circle with a diameter of about 1.5° around the *celestial north pole*, and indicates the approximate direction of *true north* at night. The relative positions of true north and Polaris change very gradually; in about 2000 years the diameter of the circle will be about 15°. See *latitude by Polaris*.

Pole 1. A long piece of wood with which a boat is propelled manually in shallow water. The pole is thrust onto the bottom of the river or sea at the bow, and the crew pushes the boat forward with his feet as he walks towards the stern. The *boathook* or an *oar* can also be used to pole the boat along. 2. The extremities of the axis about which earth rotates are the north and south poles. 3. Coll the *spinnaker pole*, q.v.

Pole mast Mast made in one piece, a single *spar* as is normal in today's sailing dinghies and keelboats. In sailing ships, mast length depended on the grown timber available, and the height required could only be achieved by adding sections above each other, the *lower mast* being a pole mast which carried other masts above it.

Pollution control Apart from the discharging of oil, which is prohibited and for which offenders are fined, the disposal of refuse is a problem, especially inland. In the US throwing refuse overboard can lead to a heavy fine. Sewage discharge is subject to contol in some waters, such as the River Thames. In the US only approved Marine Sanitation Devices may be installed; the regulations specify no-discharge type MSDs for freshwater lakes and reservoirs, but approved macerator-chlorinator MSDs can be fitted for other waters.

Polyamide Synthetic thermoplastic material produced by the condensation *polymerization* of adipic acid with diamide; numbers denote the composition, such as 6.6 nylon, the first 6 indicating the number of carbon atoms in the diamide and the second 6 the number of carbon atoms in the acid. Melting point is high and mechanical properties are excellent. Nylon and perlon fibres are made up into rope and sailcloth, and in sailing boats are generally used for anchor cables and spinnakers because they have great *elasticity* and *recover* well. Polyamides are attacked by acids and are affected by sun and weather, but they do not rot and can be dyed. Other trade names include Antron, Dederon, Nivion and Nylfranc. High water absorption reduces *tensile strength,* and *chafe* is a problem. *Specific gravity* 1.14, melting point about 200 °C, water absorption about 4%, elongation 15−70%.

Polycondensation A chemical change in a substance in which larger molecules are formed but smaller molecules, such as water, are eliminated. The process can be repeated to produce *polyamides* and *polyesters,* as well as phenolic resin and urea-formaldehyde resin etc.

Polyester A polymer formed fom a polyhydric alcohol and a polybasic acid. See also below.

Polyester resin A fluid solution of unsaturated polyester in styrene, which *polymerizes* without the elimination of volatile molecules, changing from a flammable fluid to a transparent solid that does not melt and is virtually unaffected by water. When making a *GRP/FRP moulding,* polyester resin is combined with reinforcing materials such as *chopped strand mat,* cloth, *rovings* or tape to form a solid *laminate* such as a hull, either by pressure moulding, *spray moulding* or *hand lay-up.* The quality of the product depends on the correct choice of *catalyst* and *accelerator* to match the resin, as well as on manual skill. Various types

of polyester resins and additives are sold; some provide a more resilient laminate, others one that is fire retardant, resistant to chemicals or easier to mould.

Polyester, saturated Molten polymer is extruded through fine nozzles. The filaments are cold drawn and then heat-treated to reduce *elasticity,* so that the rope or woven material made from the fibres does not lose its shape. Discovered in England by Whinfield and Dickson in 1941, and sold under a number of trade names such as *Dacron,* Diolen, *Lavsan,* Polyant, *Tergal, Terital, Terlenka, Terylene, Tetoron, Trevira* and Vestan, depending on the country of manufacture. *Specific gravity:* 1.4−1.7.

Polyethylene (also **polythene**) A thermosplastic material produced by the *polymerization* of ethylene; has very good chemical resistance and excellent insulating properties. Is very light, impervious to water, and is used for fluid containers, tubing etc. Fibres made by extruding molten polyethylene are made up into lightweight rope that floats and is used for mooring lines, nets etc. Sold under trade names such as *Hostalen, Lupolen* and *Trofil. Specific gravity:* 0.92−0.96, melting point about 120 °C, water absorption 0%, elongation 10−20%.

Polymerization A reaction that converts a compound of low molecular weight into one of high molecular weight. When making a *GRP/FRP moulding* the monomer molecules of the unsaturated *resin* combine into chains or larger molecules as the resin changes from a liquid to a solid state. Before applying the resin to the reinforcing materials, a *catalyst* is mixed with the resin to initiate polymerization, and *accelerator* is then added to enable the reaction to occur at room temperatures. See also *plastics.*

Polypropylene A thermoplastic material pro duced by the *polymerization* of propylene, the main use at sea being in the form of rope fibres. The ropes float but, being relatively hard and inflexible, are not as easy to make fast or to splice as ropes of other materials, such as nylon or polyester (which are also stronger). Some trade names are *Herculon, Hostalen P, Meraklon, Nestron, Novolen, Ulstron,* and *Vestalen. Specific gravity:* 0.90, water absorption 0%, elongation 15−25%.

Polystyrene A thermoplastic material produced by the *polymerization* of styrene, normally only used at sea for cheap rope and, in expanded form, for flotation material.

Polyurethane A thermoplastic material produced from polyols and isocyanates, used in the manufacture of adhesives, foams and surface coatings.

Some tough and abrasion-resistant paints and varnishes are sold as *two-pack* products, and the *hardener* has to be well mixed with the base before application. *Pot life* is normally at least two hours, but varies with ambient temperature, which must be over 5 °C, 15 °C being ideal. Polyurethane coatings are suitable for all materials such as *GRP/FRP hulls*, steel, light alloy, *ferro-cement* and fabrics.

Polyurethane foam Substances added to polyurethane liberate carbon dioxide when water is present, and cause foaming. The additives vary with the requirement, e.g. to make buoyant blocks. Can be poured to fill hollow spaces before it hardens and so keep a boat afloat when full of water. Foam varies from flexible to rigid according to its composition, and is flame-resistant.

Polyvinylchloride, PVC A thermoplastic material produced by the *polymerization* of vinyl chloride. Much used on board because it is resistant to weathering, water and many chemicals. Does not catch fire easily in spite of a relatively low melting point, but nevertheless should not be used for fuel lines or filters. Can be glued and welded in its solid state (tubing for engine, galley and bilge pumps, fendering etc). Becomes soft and pliable when plasticizers are added and, having low conductivity, is used to insulate cables as well as for floor coverings, upholstery etc.

Pontoon A watertight tank or float; may be used for raising wrecks, to provide additional *buoyancy,* in *floating docks* etc. Frequently has planks laid on top to provide a catwalk, stage or platform alongside which boats can moor. In tidal waters pontoons are normally secured to piles, so that they rise and fall with the *tide.*

Poop A short raised *deck* aft, extending to the sides over the after accommodation.

Pooped A boat is said to have been pooped when a *following sea* overtakes her and breaks over the *stern,* flooding over the *deck* and into the *cockpit.*

Pop rivet A rivet that can be closed working only from one end. A special tool draws a mandrel in the centre of the rivet towards it, and expands the inner end of the rivet. Pop rivets are used to fasten fittings to hollow light alloy *spars* etc.

Porosity More drive is obtained from sailcloth

with low porosity, because the more porous the cloth the more easily can air pass through it to equalize high pressure to windward and low pressure to leeward.

Port 1. The left hand side when looking towards the *bow,* both inside and outside the boat, as port sheet winch, port hand mark, alter course to port. The opposite side is *starboard.* The *side light* exhibited to port is red, and is screened to shine over an arc from dead ahead to two points abaft the beam to port, i.e. over an arc of 112.5°. 2. An opening in the side of a vessel. 3. A commercial harbour where a vessel can lie in safety. A port of refuge is one which a vessel enters to shelter from a

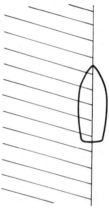

storm or from imminent danger and, under international law, she must be allowed to stay for at least 24 hours to carry out repairs, take on stores etc, even if she does not have the papers, visas etc that are normally required. The port of registry (US home port) is the port where a vessel is based and registered; the name is carved or painted on ships and sailing boats. In the UK smaller sailing boats usually only paint on the initials of the owner's yacht club.

Port hand buoy or **mark** A *lateral system* mark; when a vessel approaches from seaward, or is sailing clockwise round a land mass, a port hand buoy marks the left hand side, e.g. of the fairway; it is left to port on entering a harbour or estuary, but to *starboard* when outward bound. *IALA A:* red *can* buoy and *topmark,* red light. *US* and Canadian *buoyage:* black can buoy, rectangular *daymark,* odd number, white or green light. See endpapers.

Porthole Circular opening in the side of a boat to admit light or air. See *scuttle,* and below.

Portlight or **scuttle** Frame fitted to the side of the hull, with toughened glass to admit light. Round, oval or rectangular, and either fixed or opening, the latter being screwed down tight to prevent water entering. Some have a hinged *deadlight*

which, in the US, is an alternative term for a fixed portlight.

Portsmouth Yardstick A *handicap* system based on past performance, introduced in 1951 in Portsmouth to enable boats belonging to different established *classes* to compete against each other without incurring the expense involved with complicated measuring systems. The numbers in the table are measures of average performance in the class, not of winners, and are defined as times over a common but unspecified distance. A fast boat has a lower number than a slower boat, because she should take less time to cover the same distance. Thus a Finn, Portsmouth number 110, should take 110 minutes to cover the same distance that a Flying Dutchman, Portsmouth number 94, covers in 94 minutes. Primary yardstick numbers, allocated after many years of experience and attested by many clubs, rarely require correction, e.g. OK 118, Cadet 152. Secondary yardsticks are less well attested and sometimes require modification, e.g. Optimist 176. Provisional numbers, which can be modified in the light of further experience, are based on limited information, e.g. Europe 122. The Yardstick system is extended to production cruisers. Several different handicapping systems are based on the Portsmouth numbers, which are reviewed annually.

Port tack A sailing boat is on port tack when she is carrying her *mainsail* to *starboard*.

Port tack yacht When two sailing boats approach each other on opposite *tacks,* the one on the *port tack* keeps out of the way of the other. Port tack gives way both under the *IRPCS* and under the *IYRU racing rules,* but the wording in the two rules differs slightly. C.f. US *Inland rules of the road.*

Position The position of a vessel is given as her *latitude* north or south of the *equator,* and her *longitude* east or west of the *prime meridian.* An *observed position* is found by taking *sights* of *heavenly bodies; a fix* is obtained by observing terrestrial objects or by taking *radio bearings;* a *dead reckoning* position is calculated by plotting the vessel's course and speed on from a previous fix; an *estimated position,* plotted on from a DR position, additionally takes into account the effects of *leeway* and *tidal stream* or *current.*

Position approximate and **position doubtful** The abbreviations PA or PD are printed on *charts* when the exact position of a *danger* has not been confirmed.

Position line (US **line of position,** LOP) A line drawn on the *chart* by the navigator; the vessel should be at some point on the line, which can be obtained in many ways such as by taking a sight of a *heavenly body,* with a *transit* (US range), or with a *line* (US chain) *of soundings.* Most position lines are straight, and are obtained by taking *bearings* with the *hand-bearing compass,* or bearings on a reasonably close *radio beacon* with a *direction finder,* but those found by *sextant* are either plotted as arcs of a circle (*vertical* and *horizontal sextant*

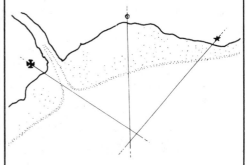

angles) or as straight lines (sights, because the radius of the circle is so immense); those obtained from linked radio station transmissions, such as *Loran, Decca* and *Omega* are *hyperbolic.* Radio bearings from distant radio beacons have to be corrected for *half-convergency* before the position line can be laid off on a *mercator* chart. At least two position lines are required to fix the vessel's position. See also *bearing, transferred position line.*

Postponement A race may have to be delayed for many reasons, such as lack of or too much wind. The International Code *answering pendant* is displayed, and may be flown above a ball, shape or flag to indicate the postponed starting time, which is decided by the *race committee.*

Potable water (US) See *drinking water.*

Pot life After the *catalyst* has been added, the period during which a *resin* or paint remains sufficiently fluid to be applied. Pot life can be varied by adjusting the quantity of *accelerator* added to resin.

Pound 1. The boat pounds in heavy seas when the *bows* come down heavily after being lifted by a wave. She is also said to pound when she bumps on the ground as a result of wave action. 2. Unit of weight and mass:
1 lb = 0.453592 kg: 1 kg = 2.20462 lb.
1 Newton = 0.224809 lbf = 0.101972 kgf: 1 kgf = 9.80665 N = 2.20462 lbf: 1 lbf = 4.44822 N = 0.453592 kgf. See also *density* and *pressure* for conversion factors.

Power 1. In small boats relates to mechanical propulsion, as opposed to sail; e.g. under power when propelled by the *auxiliary engine*. 2. The rate of doing work or expending energy, measured in watts (see *horsepower*).

Power-driven The *IRPCS* define a power-driven vessel as one propelled by machinery. Therefore any vessel which is under both sail and power is classed as power-driven and, so that other vessels may know that she is not a *sailing vessel* for interpretation of right of way, she must exhibit forward where it can best be seen a black *cone*, apex downwards. The lights prescribed by the

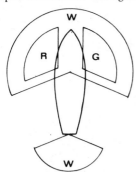

Power driven including vessels with sails and auxilliary engine operating:
side lights
stern light
masthead light

IRPCS and other rules such as US *Inland rules*, vary with the size and condition of the vessel, but when a sailing boat *under way* at night starts her engine and proceeds under sail and power, or power alone, she is required by the IRPCS to exhibit a *masthead light* in addition to her *side* and *stern lights*. See also *rule of the road, restricted visibility* and *IMO*.

Power output The power output of an engine is measured in *kilowatts* or *horse power* in accordance with the requirements of a standard, such as the US SAE, British BS or German DIN standards. Brake power is measured at the engine flywheel, and shaft horse power (SHP) at the propeller shaft, i.e. at the gearbox output coupling.

Power ratio Of a *winch*: the ratio of the distance travelled by the handle to that travelled by the outside of the drum, i.e. the amount of sheet or halyard pulled in; with a single-speed winch a power ratio of 7:1 is obtained with a handle 7 times longer than the radius of the drum. The

power ratio can be increased by decreasing drum diameter, increasing the length of the handle, or by selecting a different gear.

Power to weight ratio The ratio of the output of an engine in *kilowatts* or *horse power* to weight in kg or lbs. Weight often relates to the engine alone, but may be that of the complete installation, or of the boat complete with the power unit installed.

Pram A flattish-bottomed boat with a *transom* forward as well as aft, normally only seen as small *tenders* or *sailing dinghies* such as the *Optimist, Cadet* and *Mirror*. Can carry a greater load than a dinghy of the same length with a normal pointed *bow*, but is stopped more easily by slamming into head seas.

Pratique Certificate indicating that a boat has been released from *quarantine*.

Precipitation The condensation of moisture in the *atmosphere* into particles of liquid or ice, which do not remain in suspension within a cloud but fall towards the ground, e.g. as rain, hail, sleet, snow, drizzle.

Preparatory signal Before starting a *race*, the signal normally made by breaking out *code flag P* (accompanied by an acoustic signal). Indicates that the *class* will start in exactly five minutes time. The *racing rules* come into force at that moment and, although a boat may be *anchored*, she must be *afloat*, off her *moorings* and may not thereafter be propelled manually or by engine.

Pressure The force acting on a surface per unit of area. In *SI* units the Pascal or Newton per square metre, in the f.p.s. system pounds per square inch.
$1 N/sq m = 1.01972 \times 10^{-5}$ kg/sq cm = 1.45038 $\times 10^{-4}$ lb/sq in:
1 lb/sq in = 6894.76 N/sq m = 0.0703068 kg/sq cm
1 kg/sq cm = 98066.5 N/sq m = 14.2234 lb/sq in.
Water pressure increases with depth; wind pressure increases as the square of wind speed. See also *bar, millibar, dynamic pressure* and *atmospheric pressure*.

Pressure gradient The rate at which pressure changes between two points. The steeper the pressure gradient, the more closely spaced are the *isobars* on a *weather map*, and the stronger will the wind blow.

Prevailing wind The wind direction that occurs most frequently at a place at a certain period.

Preventer 1. Temporary additional *rigging*, which duplicates part of the *standing rigging* in heavy weather. 2. A *foreguy*, rigged to the *mainboom* in heavy weather to prevent an *accidental gybe*.

Preventer backstay See *running backstay*.

Pricker A sailmaker's tool with which he makes ·holes in canvas, or holds it to the wooden floor.

Prime meridian or **Greenwich meridian** *Longitude* 0°, from which longitude is measured in degrees, minutes and seconds east and west up to 180°. The *meridian* running through Greenwich, London.

Primer The first coat of *paint* applied to a surface. The composition varies according to the material to which it is applied; this may be porous wood that absorbs water, iron that rusts, an extremely hard *GRP/FRP laminate,* or light alloy. In the latter case, applying the wrong primer could lead to *corrosion*. Special etching primers are available to provide a good key to smooth GRP/FRP. Primers must provide good adhesion for the *undercoat* applied next, as well as protecting the surface beneath.

Primus stove One- or two-burner cooking stove (Swedish patent) that burns alcohol or paraffin (kerosene). Air is pumped into the fuel container to increase the pressure before the stove is lit.

Prismatic coefficient (sometimes **Cylindrical** or **Longitudinal coefficient**) The ratio of the immersed volume of the *displacement* to the volume of a prism, the cross section area of which is equal to the area of the *midship section* and the length of which is equal to *waterline length*.

$$Cp = \frac{\text{displacement}}{A_m \times LWL}$$

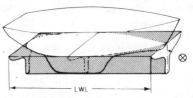

The prismatic coefficient is equal to the *block coefficient* divided by the *midship section coefficient*, and gives an indication of the fullness or fineness of the ends; a yacht with fine ends has a lower prismatic than one designed to plane fast, which has fuller ends. Values for sailing boats vary between about 0.50 and 0.70.

Privileged vessel A term used especially in US *rules of the road* for the vessel that does not have to keep clear when two vessels meet. Her duty as the *stand-on* vessel is to maintain her course and speed.

Proa (US or **outrigger**) A boat with two *hulls*, originally sailed in Indonesia and Polynesia. Instead of *going about*, the boom and sail are swung through 180° so that, when the boat sails away on the opposite tack, the stern becomes the bow and vice versa. The smaller *outrigger* or float is always to *leeward* of the slim, double-bowed

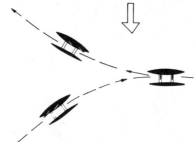

main hull which carries the mast and sail. On the other hand, the outrigger of a flying proa, which is more closely related to the Polynesian original, is always to *windward*. The modern *schooner*-rigged proa 'Cheers' competed in the 1968, 1972 and 1976 OSTARs.

Profile plan or sheer plan The part of the *lines plan* which shows the side view of a hull as a series of vertical fore-and-aft sections called *buttock* lines. Normally the bow is to the right.

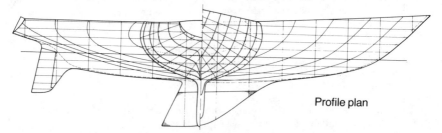

Profile plan

Prohibited anchorage A vessel may not *anchor* in the area, probably because of underwater cables.

Prohibited area An area within *Territorial Waters* which vessels may not enter, and in which they may not *anchor*. Is shown on *charts,* detailed in *Pilots* or *Notices to Mariners,* and the limits may be marked by *buoys.* An area may be permanently prohibited owing, say, to mines, underwater explosives etc, or only at certain times such as when a firing range is in use. Warning signals may be made, and the area may be patrolled to prevent vessels from entering. Chart abbr for prohibited is prohib.

Projected area If a light were shining to *windward* of a boat at the level of the *centre of effort,* the area of the shadow cast by a sail on a vertical surface directly to *leeward* would be roughly the same as the area of the sail. When the boat *heels* the *masthead* tilts towards the surface of the water, and the area of the sail's shadow would then be smaller. Similarly the area of sail projected at right

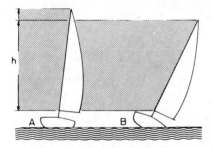

angles to the wind becomes smaller when the boat heels, and the CE is closer to the water than when the boat is upright. When sailing under cliffs in offshore breezes, the wind slants downwards and a boat can be knocked flat by a gust when she is already heeling, because the sail is still at right angles to the wind.

Projection Method whereby part, or all, of the curved surface of the three-dimensional earth is represented on a two-dimensional flat *chart* or map. There is inevitably some distortion. *Mercator* projection is used for most of the charts carried aboard sailing boats, and *gnomonic* for very small scale charts, polar areas and large scale *harbour plans.* Polyconic projection is used for the Great Lakes and US inland waters.

Projector compass Normally found on board larger vessels; the image of part of the card and the *lubber line* are seen at a position remote from the *compass.* The course can therefore be read in more than one place, say in the wheelhouse and below.

Propagation At medium, low and very low radio *frequencies,* propagation is by *ground wave* and, normally, the lower the frequency the stronger the

wave and the greater the range. Long range navigation systems transmit on LF and VLF. Ground wave propagation at LF and MF provides reliable *bearings* for *direction finding* purposes. Long distance marine radio communication is at medium and high frequency. HF waves are reflected by the *ionosphere* and return to the earth as *sky waves* which, although unsuitable for direction finding, travel great distances around the earth in a series of *skips.* At very high frequency and higher frequencies, range is much shorter and propagation is by direct wave (line of sight). VHF is suitable for short range communication, and super high frequency for *radar* because, whereas low frequency waves penetrate buildings, cliffs etc, SHF waves are reflected.

Propeller or **screw** (US coll **wheel**) The screw that is rotated by an engine to propel a vessel. Is usually made of bronze, cast iron, nickel-aluminium-bronze alloy or polyamide, and the *blades* may be fixed, folding, feathering or *variable pitch.* The number of blades varies, but two, three or four is usual for small boats. When viewed from astern, a left-handed propeller rotates in a counterclockwise direction, and a right-handed propeller rotates clockwise to drive a boat forward. Propeller bias affects handling (see *wheel effect*). As the propeller rotates it screws its way through the water and thrusts the boat forward by drawing in water from ahead, accelerating it and discharging it aft. The boat makes *sternway* when the propeller is rotated in the opposite direction. Propeller diameter is that of the circle described by the tip of the blades; the blade-area ratio is the ratio of the area of the propeller blades to the area of that circle. Propeller pitch varies with the angle of the blade to the hub, and is the distance that a propeller would advance during one complete revolution in a solid medium. The pitch to diameter ratio is one of the factors that affects propeller efficiency, which is the ratio of the useful output delivered by

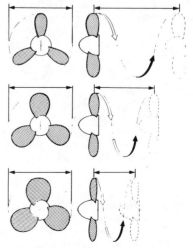

the propeller to the power delivered to the propeller. For example if 10 kW is delivered to the propeller and it delivers 5 kW, propeller efficiency is 50%, the balance being lost to friction, turbulence etc. A large slow-revving 3- or 4-bladed propeller of coarse pitch will usually deliver great power at slow boat speed, while a small high-revving 2-bladed propeller of fine pitch will give high speed but low power. Blade area, number and pitch, and the speed of revolution (through a *reduction* gearbox) are calculated by the naval architect or engine installation expert, based on the type of hull, the power of the engine and the boat's role.

Propeller shaft Metal rod which rotates, transmitting power from the engine to the propeller, which is mounted on the shaft.

Proper course In the *racing rules* is defined as any course which a yacht might sail after the *starting signal,* in the absence of the other yacht or yachts affected, in order to finish as quickly as possible. The course sailed before *luffing* or *bearing away* is not necessarily that yacht's proper course. There is no proper course before the starting signal is made. When on a free *leg,* a yacht may not bear away below her proper course to prevent a *leeward yacht* or one *clear astern* from passing her when they are within three of her overall lengths.

Protest 1. Is made when a yacht is accused of infringing one of the *racing rules,* often by the crew of another competing yacht. For example, if a yacht does not give another *room* at a *mark* of the *course,* or if she touches a mark when *rounding,* the protesting yacht must display a protest flag (*code flag B* is often used) at the first reasonable opportunity and keep it flying until she has finished, unless otherwise prescribed in the *sailing instructions;* she should also inform the yacht concerned. After the finish the protest is lodged in writing, the *race committee* or *jury* call a hearing and the yacht is disqualified if she is deemed to have infringed a rule. An appeal may be made to the national or international authority by the disqualified yacht. In a points *series* it is often more advantageous to retire after breaking a rule, because the penalty for disqualification is greater than that for retiring. 2. A declaration made under oath before a notary public concerning a misfortune that has occurred at sea, and possible or actual loss or damage incurred. Details of the occurrence and of the measures taken are given.

Protractor An instrument used for *plotting* courses and bearings on a *chart.* The term is applied to various instruments such as *set squares,* the *station pointer* and various patent protractors. Generally the patent type consists of a *compass rose* on a transparent plastics circle or square with

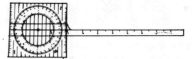

a rotating arm. The instrument is aligned with a *meridian,* and a course can be laid off with the arm without reference to a compass rose on the chart.

Proword Procedural word used in R/T with a specific meaning, e.g. 'out' means 'I have finished my transmission, do not expect a reply, but am switching to receive in order to continue listening out on this frequency.' See *radiotelephony* for list of some common prowords.

Psychrometer Instrument for measuring *humidity.* Small sling psychrometers can be used on board sailing boats, and have two thermometers, one dry and one kept wet with a piece of gauze wrapped round the bulb. Both record the same temperature when *relative humidity* is 100% but if air is dryer, a lower temperature is recorded by the wet bulb when the psychrometer is whirled round the head, because water evaporates from the wet gauze.

Pull To *row:* hence pulling boat, a boat propelled by *oars.* The navy prefers the term pull, and small boat sailors either pull or row, but rowing is heard more frequently.

Pulley *Block* with a *sheave* used in a *tackle* to change the *lead* of a line.

Pulpit (US or **bow rail**) Stainless steel frame which encircles the *forestay,* and to which the *lifelines* (guardrails) are secured at the *bow.* The uprights are firmly bolted close to the sides to give the crew room to change sail safely in all weathers. A *stern pulpit* is similar and fitted round the *stern.* US: a pulpit may also be a projecting plank ahead of the *stem* of fishing boats, on which the crew can stand.

Pump 1. Manually, electrically-, or engine-driven device for raising or moving a fluid, such as the galley and fuel pumps. See also *bilge, diaphragm, submersible electric* and *piston pumps.* 2. As a verb: to pump out, pump dry, pump ship is to remove water from the *bilges* with a bilge pump. 3. See *pumping.*

Pumping To trim the sail, especially the *mainsail,*

in and out repeatedly and quickly to increase boat speed. This is forbidden by the *racing rules,* except when *planing* or *surfing* conditions exist, and then only to make the boat start to plane or surf, but not to keep her on the plane.

Purchase Any mechanical means of increasing an applied force; a system of geared wheels, an arrangement of *levers,* or a *tackle* in the form of blocks and a line.

Pushing Under the *IRPCS,* when a pushing vessel and a vessel being pushed are a composite unit, the lights exhibited by the unit are those of a *power-driven* vessel. When not a composite unit the pushing vessel exhibits the same lights as a *towing vessel,* except for the towing light.

Pushpit Coll for *stern pulpit,* q.v.

Put 1. The *helm* is put up, i.e. *tiller* moved to *windward,* to make the boat *bear away;* it is put down, tiller to *leeward,* to make her *luff up;* it is put over to make her alter course. 2. A vessel is said to put to sea, put in etc.

Put about 1. To *go about.* 'Put her about' is an instruction to the helmsman to make a tack. 2. To cause another boat to go about, e.g. when meeting on opposite tacks the boat on *port tack* is put about by the one on *starboard tack.*

Put in To enter a harbour or anchorage.

Put off To leave in a boat, whether from land or from a vessel.

Putty knife Tool with a long flexible blade, used to remove old paint, or to prepare a surface for painting by filling cracks and hollows with *stopping* or filler.

Pyrotechnic Any type of rocket, *flare* etc used for signalling etc.

PZX Triangle (Also called instantaneous, navigational and celestial triangle.) The spherical triangle which has to be solved by trigonometry if a *position line* is to be obtained as a result of taking a *sight* of a *heavenly body.* The corners of the triangle are Z, the observer's *zenith,* P, the *elevated celestial pole* and X, the position of the body on the *celestial sphere.* The sides are PZ, *co-latitude* ($90°$ minus the observer's *latitude*), PX *polar distance* ($90°$ plus or minus the *declination* of the body) and ZX, *zenith distance* ($90°$ minus the *true altitude* of the body). The two important angles are ZPX, the *hour angle* at the pole, and XZP at the zenith, the *azimuth.*

If two sides of a spherical triangle and the angle between them are known, the values for the remaining side and angles can be calculated but,

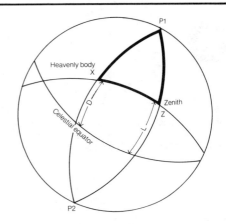

D = Declination
P_1X = Polar distance, $90°$ minus declination
L = Observer's Latitude
P_1Z Co-latitude, $90°$ minus observer's latitude (or $90°$ minus L)
ZX = Zenith distance, $90°$ minus Altitude
XP_1Z = Hour angle
P_1ZX = Azimuth angle

although declination and the *Greenwich Hour Angle* are given in the *Nautical Almanac* (the *local hour angle* is obtained by adding easterly longitude or subtracting westerly longitude from the GHA), the vessel's *latitude* will not be known; nor will her *longitude.* The *intercept method* therefore places the vessel at an *assumed position* (q.v.), which is a certain number of miles from the body's *geographical position.* Calculated zenith distance at the assumed position is compared with true zenith distance, which is found by measuring the *altitude* of the body with the *sextant,* and the difference between CZD and TZD gives the length of the *intercept,* q.v. When *Sight Reduction Tables* are used, the tabulated altitude (Hc) of the heavenly body at a *chosen position* (q.v.) is found in the tables, and is compared with the body's true altitude at the observer's position. The difference between the two figures, say $5'$, indicates how much closer the vessel is to the geographical position of the body (or how much further away from it). The intercept is then measured along the *true bearing* of the body (also found in the tables, Z), 5 miles from the chosen position. It is drawn towards the body if true altitude is greater than Hc, but away from the body if Hc is greater. The position line is drawn at right angles to the terminal point of the intercept. There are other methods of finding the intercept, such as the haversine method, or with the help of a calculator.

Q = **Quebec:** yellow *code flag*. As a single letter signal means 'My vessel is healthy and I request free *pratique*'. *Morse code:* — — • — (dash dash dot dash).

Quadrant 1. One quarter of a full circle; the area contained within two radii of a circle at 90° to each other. *Cardinal system* buoys are laid in north, east, south and west quadrants, e.g. the west cardinal mark is laid to the west of a *danger* in the quadrant bounded by NW and SW. 2. The rudder quadrant is fitted to the head of the *rudder stock*. 3. Obsolete nautical instrument for measuring the *altitude* of a *heavenly body*.

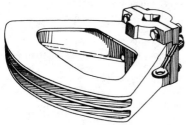

Quadrantal error Term that relates to *deviation* of the *magnetic compass* and *direction finder* error. Deviation changes from easterly to westerly and vice versa every 90°; DF error changes from positive to negative and vice versa in successive quadrants.

Quadrature When two *heavenly bodies* are 90° apart, e.g. when the moon is half way between *conjunction* and *opposition*, and at 90° to the sun, they are said to be in quadrature. These are roughly the times of *neap tides*.

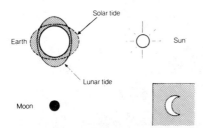

Quadrilateral jib To gain area, some light *genoas* had the *leech* extended in the form of a straight-edged *roach,* controlled by a second upper *clew*. The sail was eventually outlawed by the authorities controlling racing.

Quality of the bottom The composition of the *sea-bed,* details of which are given on *charts;* i.e. colour, texture (small, soft, coarse etc) and content (sand, mud, clay, shingle, pebbles, rocky etc).

Quant A long pole with a fork or disc at the lower end, used to propel a small boat (quanting) by pushing on the bottom; inland waters.

Quarantine A vessel is kept in isolation, and her crew may not go ashore after arriving from a foreign country, until *pratique* has been granted by the health authorities. If she is known to have been in contact with a fatal or dangerous disease such as yellow fever or typhoid, the vessel stays in a quarantine anchorage. The yellow flag Q is flown when a vessel arrives from abroad to inform the authorities that she is healthy and requesting pratique: Q over the first *substitute* (US repeater) indicates that an infectious disease is suspected, and Q over *L* indicates that there is an infectious disease aboard.

Quarantine buoy A *mooring buoy* in the roads of a *port,* to which a vessel moors when in quarantine, or a buoy which marks a quarantine anchorage; generally yellow.

Quarter 1. The side of the hull between *amidships* and *astern*. 2. Directions from the boat are given as (UK) on the quarter, 45° from right astern; fine on the quarter, between right astern and 45°; broad on the quarter, between 45°and *abeam:* (US) broad on, 45° from right astern; abaft the beam, from abeam to broad on; on the quarter, from broad on to astern. 3. Of the moon, the first quarter is when she is *waxing* and half way between new and full moon, the last quarter is when she is *waning*, half way between full and new moon.

Quarter berth A *berth* that extends under the *side deck* between the *cockpit* and the *hull;* the occupant's head is close by the *companionway*. Often allocated to the *navigator* to provide quick access to the cockpit, and may be designed to provide him with a seat when working at the chart table.

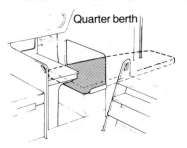
Quarter berth

aground; she sinks deeply into it and may need outside assistance to get free.

Quarter block Fitted at the quarter, often as a *lead* for a *spinnaker sheet.*

Quartering wind and **sea** Wind that blows from a direction half way between *abeam* and *astern,* i.e. from over the quarter; similarly waves that approach the boat from the same direction.

Quarter knee Horizontal knee that joins the *gunwale* to the *transom.*

Quarter spring See *back spring.*

Quarter Ton Class A *level rating class,* the maximum *rating* being 18.5 ft. A typical boat's measurements are LOA 24.5 ft (7.47 m), LWL 19 ft (5.8 m), beam 8 ft (2.4 m), displacement 3100 lbs (1.4 tonnes), sail area 300 sq ft (28 sq m). The Quarter Ton Cup, donated in 1968 by the Société des Régates Rochelaises, was originally competed for by boats with an *RORC* rating and complying with *Junior Offshore Group* regulations; now they are rated under the *IOR.* Five races are sailed: three Olympic courses (single points) about 20 n.miles long, a short offshore race lasting about a day (1.5 points) about 100 n.miles long, and a longer offshore race (double points) about 200 n.miles long lasting about two days. The number of crew is four.

Quay A brick, concrete, stone etc structure with an almost vertical side, built along the shore or river bank. Vessels can lie alongside in deep water to load and unload cargo. Often has tracks for cranes and trains, and a road for transport vehicles.

Quick light (formerly quick flashing light) A white or coloured light, exhibited as an *aid to navigation,* that flashes continuously 50 or 60 times a minute (*IALA A*), or not less than 60 times a minute (US). Chart abbr Q, formerly Qk Fl.

Quick flashing
▮▼▼▼▼▼▼▼▼▼▼▼▼▼▼
↔
Period

Quicksand The *sea-bed* of wet sand supports very little weight at *low water,* the sandy particles being so loose that a man sinks in quickly. Becomes even softer when the *tide* rises, and can endanger a boat or large vessel that has *run*

R

R = Romeo: red *code flag* with a yellow cross. *Morse code:* •—• (dot dash dot). Flag with no meaning allocated in the code book, because the sound signal is made by vessels at *anchor* in *fog* as a warning 'Keep clear, you may run into me' (and the flag would not be seen).

Rabbett or **rebate** A groove cut in the *keel, stem, sternpost* etc of wooden boats. The keel rabbett takes the *garboard strake;* the stem and sternpost rabbetts take the *hood ends* of the *planking.*

Rabies control The importation of animals into the UK is strictly controlled, and violation leads to heavy fines or imprisonment. For example dogs arriving from abroad are kept in quarantine in special kennels for six months, whether they have arrived on board a visiting foreign boat, or have accompanied a British boat abroad, landed and returned to the UK.

Race 1. A competition involving several boats that sail round a prescribed *course* in the shortest possible time. Boats race in *classes,* q.v. In *series racing,* the winner is the boat that has performed best on average over the series, normally the one to accumulate the lowest total of points. Boats are generally measured to check that they comply with class building rules (where applicable), or to obtain a *rating* (some *handicap classes*). Normally boats race under the *IYRU racing rules,* except at night during *offshore races* when the *IRPCS* come into force. See also offshore, *passage, level* and *team racing.* The first recorded yacht race was between King Charles II of England and his brother the Duke of York on 1st October 1661; the King's 'Katherine' lost to the Duke's 'Anne' going from Greenwich to Gravesend, but made up for it on the return journey. 2. A strong stream or *current.* Occurs where two currents meet, where the water *shoals,* in *narrows* and constricted channels, and off headlands. Seas are more vicious, especially when the race is running at maximum speed at *spring tides.*

Race committee Those responsible for the arrangement and conduct of a *regatta, race* or *series* of races, including *starting, shortening course, postponing* or *abandoning* a race, selecting a *course,* timing the finishers and appointing a *jury* to judge *protests.* The authorities and duties of a race committee are prescribed in *IYRU racing rules* 1–14.

Race officers Officials appointed by the race committee to *start* and *finish* a race or races. The *course, preparatory, warning, starting* and, if necessary, *recall, abandonment, postponement* or *cancellation signals* are made by the race officers, who are positioned at one end of the starting and finishing lines, often in a *committee boat.* They may also select and shorten the *course,* arrange for *rescue boats,* record results etc.

Racing dinghy A sailing dinghy that is designed for racing, usually in a *one-design* or *development class;* often competes in *handicap races.* The term embraces many types of dinghy, varying from a small relatively slow and cheap boat such as the *Optimist* which is designed to be raced by one young child, to a highly-tuned, sophisticated and expensive machine, such as the *Flying Dutchman.*

Racing flag Square *flag* to an owner's personal design, made of very light material; often flown at the *masthead* in place of the *burgee* when racing. See also *wind direction indicator.*

Racing rules The rules formulated by the *IYRU* are based on the *International Regulations for Preventing Collisions at Sea,* but are far more comprehensive and specific, because racing inevitably involves sailing at very close quarters. Precise rules lay down which boat has *right of way* in all circumstances, such as when *starting, rounding marks* or approaching *obstructions.* Normally boats race under the internationally agreed IYRU rules, and must comply with them from the *preparatory signal,* made five minutes before the *starting signal,* until they have *finished* or retired, or until the race is *abandoned* or *cancelled.* When long-distance racing offshore, the racing rules are only in force during daylight hours; at night the competitors comply with the *IRPCS.* A yacht that infringes any rule may either be *disqualified* or penalized (see *penalty*). The 78 rules, many of them sub-divided, are reviewed every four years just after the Olympic Games, and no amendments are made in the interim. Any additions or alterations to the IYRU rules are advertized in the *sailing instructions* for a particular race or series.

Racing strategy Broadly, relates to long-term

plans when racing, especially over long distances, taking into account such factors as the development of *weather, tidal streams* or *currents* and *navigation,* e.g. when deciding which tack to choose.

Racing tactics Short-term tactics employed to bring an advantage over other competitors, e.g. by choosing the right place to start, the quickest route to the finishing line, when to *cover* an opponent, how to get a *clear wind, blanket* or *backwind* an opponent; also *false tacks, splitting tacks, safe leeward position* etc. *Racing rules* can be used to gain an advantage, but must not be infringed.

Rack 1. Stowage racks are required for items such as navigation instruments, bottles or crockery, and have cut-outs to match the shape of the items so as to hold them securely in place. 2. To bind two ropes together with a small line that is passed alternately under and over them (see *seizing*).

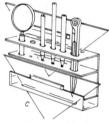

Racon *Radar beacon* with a *transceiver;* reacts to a radar signal received from a vessel by transmitting its own reply signal, often with an identifying code. This appears on the vessel's display

unit, usually as a solid line from the echo to the circumference of the screen. Also termed a transponder or responder beacon.

Radar Electronic instrument which detects and locates distant objects. The main components are the *scanner (directional aerial),* transceiver (which transmits and receives signals) and display unit. The scanner rotates slowly at about 23–30 rpm, transmitting ultra high *frequency* radio pulses (9320–9500 MHz) of high power in a very narrow beam. Typically, between 1000 and 3000 pulses are transmitted per second by small boat radars (pulse repetition rate), and pulse lengths are therefore extremely short, 0.05–0.8 microseconds. The pulses travel at the speed of light (162,000 n.miles per second), and are reflected back to the scanner by objects in their path.

The display unit has a cathode ray tube (CRT) with a phosphor-coated screen *(plan position indicator,* PPI, q.v.), which glows brightly when bombarded by electrons. The vessel's position is at the centre, the ship's *head* pointing to the top of the PPI. At the same instant as a pulse is transmitted, the electron beam within the CRT is swept outwards from the centre to the circumference of the screen; the *bearing* of this trace corresponds with the bearing of the pulse transmitted by the scanner. No electrons flow during flyback, when the beam returns to the centre of the screen. When a pulse is reflected from a *target,* the received signal is amplified and passed to the CRT, and the electron flow is increased instantaneously, thus brightening a spot on the screen. This bright echo continues to glow after the beam has moved on (afterglow), and indicates the target's position,

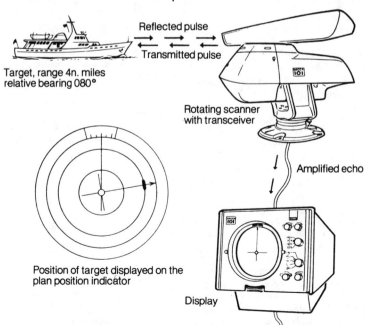

Reflected pulse

Transmitted pulse

Target, range 4n. miles relative bearing 080°

Rotating scanner with transceiver

Amplified echo

Position of target displayed on the plan position indicator

Display

the *relative bearing* of which is read on the bearing scale surrounding the PPI. The range of the target is known because the distance between the spot of light and the centre is proportional to the distance travelled to and from the target by the pulse. The distance to the target is estimated with the aid of electronically generated range rings, which form a series of concentric circles on the PPI. Alternatively some radars are fitted with a variable range marker, which enables a single ring to be super-imposed on the target and the precise range read from a digital display.

When the scanner rotates, transmitting a succession of pulses on different bearings, the trace rotates at the same speed on the PPI, and echoes returned from targets light up, painting a plan-like picture of the area around the vessel. This is similar to what would be seen if an extremely powerful searchlight were rotated at night; it is not a bird's eye view because objects may be hidden behind a target, e.g. a smaller fast-moving boat behind a large anchored ship.

The normal controls are: range selector – typical small boat range scales are ½, 1½, 3, 6 and 12 miles, sometimes also 24 miles; brilliance – controls electron flow; gain – controls the bright-ness of the echoes; tuner – matches the receiver to the transmitted signal's frequency; anti-clutter (see *clutter*). Some radars have a bearing cursor, which is rotated manually to find the exact bearing of an echo, a variable range ring, which is adjusted to give exact target distance, and centering controls with which the vessel is positioned exactly in the centre of the PPI. Many radars transmit pulse rates and lengths to suit the range in use; a short pulse gives a more detailed, clear picture for shorter ranges, while the longer pulse provides lower *resolution* but brightens long range echoes.

The maximum range of radar depends largely on the power of the equipment and the height of the scanner and target (but see *refraction*). Normally the radar beam curves downwards slightly towards the earth, and range is slightly greater than the visible horizon. Range to the radar horizon in nautical miles can be estimated roughly as 1.23 √height in feet (2.24 √height in metres). Thus, in normal atmospheric conditions, and given a scanner 17 ft above sea level (1.23 × √17 = 5 m), and a target 24 ft high (radar horizon 6 m), radar range will be 11 miles. Minimum range is also important and is often about 25 yards.

Interpretation of the radar picture requires practice; flat surfaces such as buildings and cliffs reflect echoes better than rounded surfaces such as conical buoys (*radar reflectors* are often fitted to aids to navigation). Interpretation is easier with a radar chart which shows radar conspicuous objects such as piers, steep coasts, *racons* etc. Radar networks are established in some rivers, harbours etc, and enable navigation in the fairway to be controlled by radio communication, e.g. a vessel can be recommended a course to steer to avoid shipping not visible on her screen owing to local topography.

A vessel's position can be fixed accurately by finding the range and bearing of three identified targets – a method which eliminates *compass error*.

Radar beacon A beacon which transmits signals that are visible on a radar screen. See *racon* and *ramark*.

Radar detector May be a scanning instrument or a hand-held device that detects the presence of radar aboard another vessel, and indicates the direction of that vessel. Enables avoiding action to be taken if the other, possibly much larger, vessel is found to be on a *collision course*.

Radar reflector Generally an octahedral device, consiting of three square or rectangular metal plates assembled at right angles to each other so as to enhance the reflection of radar energy. Wooden and *GRP/FRP* boats are poor reflectors of radar signals, and often carry a radar reflector in the *rigging* or on a mount clear of the *superstructure* to improve their radar visibility. A corner reflector should be hoisted or mounted so that one of the

internal corner cells faces skywards, i.e. with an aperture open to the sky in the 'rain catching' attitude, not hung by a corner; the minimum recommended height is 8 ft (2.5 m) above sea level. Fine woven mesh radar reflectors and spherical types offer less wind resistance. Radar reflectors are fitted to many *aids to navigation*.

Radial or **sunray cut** The *cloths* are not seamed together vertically or horizontally, as in *diagonal* or *horizontal cut* sails, but radiate from the *clew*, increasing in breadth towards the *luff*.

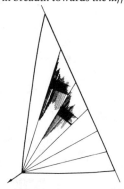

Radiation The transfer of heat from one body to another by electro-magnetic waves, e.g. the heat of the sun.

Radiation or **ground fog** Develops when the ground cools on a clear windless night, and when the air just above the surface is very moist. May drift seaward to affect coastal waters, as well as lakes and rivers inland.

Radio beacon A transmitting station, generally on land but sometimes in a light vessel or *lighthouse* offshore; transmits a signal so that the *bearing* of the beacon can be obtained (see *radio direction finding* and *direction finder*). Range varies from about ten miles, for beacons (US marker beacons) that guide vessels into and out of harbours, to roughly two hundred miles for land-fall beacons. *Omnidirectional* beacons transmit their signals in all directions, but *directional* beacons transmit only in a certain direction. Marine radio beacons are sited by the coast so that the bearing is not affected by *refraction*; they operate on *frequencies* between 285 and 350 kHz. Aero beacons are often sited inland, and bearings may not be reliable; they operate on frequencies between 160 and 415 kHz.

Radio direction finding (RDF) A *direction finder* (q.v.) is a radio receiver with a *directional aerial,* which enables the navigator to find the direction from which a radio signal arrives. Provided that the position of the transmitting radio beacon is known, the *relative* or *magnetic bearing* of the signal provides a *position line.* Many marine radio beacons operate continuously, transmitting a combination of dots and dashes (in European waters these are morse code letters which assist the operator to identify the beacon, e.g. Mizen Head MZ), and a very long dash so that an accurate bearing can be obtained. Frequently groups of up to six radio beacons transmit in sequence on the same *frequency,* each transmission lasting one minute so that the sequence recommences every six minutes. If there are less than six beacons in a group, the sequence could be ABCABC, AABBCC, ABCADC or some other pattern; details of frequencies, call or identification signs and transmission times are published in the US Lights Lists (together with radio beacon charts), in the UK List of Radio Aids and in various nautical almanacs, which also list those aeronautical beacons that are sited sufficiently near the coast to be useful to the mariner (bearings on beacons inland are unreliable owing to *refraction*). Radio waves follow a great circle path, and the bearing obtained is a great circle bearing which, when the beacon is far distant, has to be corrected for *half-convergency* before it can be plotted on a *mercator chart.* DF bearings are subject to instrumental and installation errors, and DF sets have to be calibrated (see *calibration*). Errors are also caused by increased sky wave activity at night (see *night effect*).

A vessel far from land can *home* on a radio beacon or, when a vessel is in *distress* nearby, on the distress signal being transmitted. If the position of a vessel in distress is not given or is incorrectly given, location is still possible if several ships, shore stations or aircraft take bearings when the distressed vessel is transmitting. Chart abbr for radio direction finding station, (UK) RG, (US) RDF.

Radiogoniometer See *goniometer.*

Radio range (US) See *directional radio beacon.*

Radio silence When a *distress* call has been made, radio silence is imposed on all stations in the area, or on any station which interferes with distress traffic; the distressed ship or the station controlling the distress traffic sends instructions as follows:
(a) SEELONCE (French pronunciation of silence) requires full radio silence on specific frequencies.
(b) PRUDONCE (French pronunciation of prudence) indicates that essential radio traffic may be resumed (with caution).
(c) SEELONCE FEENEE (silence fini – ended) indicates that normal working may be resumed.
See also *silence periods*

Radio telephony (R/T) By international agreement specific *frequencies* are allotted for ship-to-ship and ship-to-shore communication:

High Frequency (HF): maritime bands near 4, 8, 12, 16 and 22 MHz for long distance communication; given a sufficiently powerful transmitter, range is over 1000 miles, exceptionally up to 5000 miles.
Medium Frequency (MF): 1605–3800 kHz, includes the international *Distress,* Safety and Calling frequency, 2182 kHz; used for communication up to about 200 miles.
Very High Freqency (VHF): 156–175 MHz; range, which is rather greater than the visual distance to the horizon and limited by aerial height, is normally up to 25 miles but occasionally up to 50 miles.

Licences are required and, in particular (a) the set must comply with government specifications: (b) the use of transmitting and receiving apparatus on board must be authorized, in the UK by the Home Office, in the US by the Federal Communications Commission: (c) the operator's competence must be certified; the FCC issues a Restricted Permit to an applicant of at least 14 years without test or examination, provided that he certifies that he knows the relevant laws and regulations, is able to transmit and receive in English and keep a rough log; the UK Restricted Certificate of Competence (VHF only) is issued after a relatively simple examination has been passed.

Many small boats carry only VHF equipment, which enables them to contact port authorities, *coast stations, pilots, marinas,* nearby vessels etc. Specific channels are assigned for different types of communication:

Channel 16 (156.80 MHz) is the Distress, Safety and Calling channel.
Channel 6 (156.30 MHz) (also mandatory) is the Intership Safety Channel.
Channel 22 (157.10 MHz) is used in the US for non-distress communication with the *Coast Guard.*
Channel 67 (156.375 MHz) is designated in the UK for yacht 'safety' communication purposes.

Apart from cases of distress (see *distress procedure*), procedure is briefly as follows: (a) Listen on the appropriate calling frequency, VHF Channel 16, MF 2182 kHz (UK 2381 kHz is used for public correspondence from 0900–1700 hrs local time daily except Sundays) to ensure that no distress traffic is being sent; only messages concerning distress, urgency and safety may be transmitted during radio silence periods, which are two periods of three minutes every hour, starting at the hour and half hour. (b) Transmit the name of the station being called not more than three times, followed by 'this is' (or DELTA ECHO) and the name or identification of the calling station not more than three times stating which working channel he has available. (c) The coast station replies and informs the calling station to which working frequency he must transfer. (d) Calling station transfers.

The Phonetic Alphabet and Figure Code used internationally is as follows:
(accentuated syllables are underlined):
A Alpha (<u>AL</u> FAH)
B Bravo (<u>BRAH</u> VOH)
C Charlie (<u>CHAR</u> LEE or <u>SHAR</u> LEE)
D Delta (<u>DELL</u> TAH)
E Echo (<u>ECK</u> OH)
F Foxtrot (<u>FOKS</u> TROT)
G Golf (GOLF)
H Hotel (HOH <u>TELL</u>)
I India (<u>IN</u> DEE AH)
J Juliett (<u>JEW</u> LEE <u>ETT</u>)
K Kilo (<u>KEY</u> LOH)
L Lima (<u>LEE</u> MAH)
M Mike (MIKE)
N November (NO <u>VEM</u> BER)
O Oscar (<u>OSS</u> CAH)
P Papa (PAH <u>PAH</u>)
Q Quebec (KEH <u>BECK</u>)
R Romeo (<u>ROW</u> ME OH)
S Sierra (SEE <u>AIR</u> RAH)
T Tango (<u>TAN</u> GO)
U Uniform (<u>YOU</u> NEE FORM or <u>OO</u> NEE FORM)
V Victor (<u>VIK</u> TAH)
W Whiskey (<u>WISS</u> KEY)
X X-ray (<u>ECKS</u> RAY)

Y Yankee (<u>YANG</u> KEY)
Z Zulu (<u>ZOO</u> LOO)
0 Nadazero (NAH-DAH-ZAY-ROH)
1 Unaone (OO-NAH-WUN)
2 Bissotwo (BEES-SOH-TOO)
3 Terrathree (TAY-RAH-TREE)
4 Kartefour (KAR-TAY-FOWER)
5 Pantafive (PAN-TAH-FIVE)
6 Soxisix (SOK-SEE-SIX)
7 Setteseven (SAY-TAY-SEVEN)
8 Oktoeight (OK-TOH-AIT)
9 Novenine (NO-VAY-NINER)
   Decimal point Decimal (DAY-SEE-MAL)
   Full stop Stop (STOP)

Where there are no language difficulties, the first two syllables of numerals may be omitted, as wun, seven, niner, etc. Some words used as signals, to give instructions, or procedurally (prowords) are listed below:

<u>MAYDAY</u> (French, m'aidez – help me): the distress signal.
<u>PAN PAN</u>: the urgency signal.
<u>SECURITE</u> (pronounced say-cure-e-tay): the safety signal.
SEELONCE (French pronunciation of silence): imposes *radio silence.*
PRUDONCE (French pronunciation of prudence): restricted working may be resumed after radio silence.
SEELONCE FEENEE (French, silence fini – end of silence): normal working may be resumed.
OVER: the speaker has finished what he has to say and is switching over to receive because he expects a reply from his correspondent (short for over to you).
OUT: the speaker has finished what he has to say, does not expect a reply, and is switching to receive so that he may continue monitoring the frequency (short for listening out).
OFF: as Out, but the speaker is switching off his radio.
(Note that the phrase 'over and out' should never be used because it is contradictory).
READ BACK or SAY AGAIN: repeat the whole message.
I SPELL: before spelling a word or abbreviation.
CQ or CHARLIE QUEBEC: All ships.
ROGER: message received and understood (from the US Army phonetic alphabet used in World War II, R Roger stood for Right).
Citizens' Band radio operates in the 27 MHz frequency band and can be useful at sea for inter-ship communication when sailing in close company (about 5 miles).

Radome Housing for the radar *scanner;* is transparent to radar pulses, protects the scanner from weather and damage, and reduces the amount of power required to rotate the aerial.

Raft A floating structure carried aboard larger

ships for life-saving purposes. Sailing boats carry inflatable *liferafts*, q.v.

Rafting or **raft up** Two or more boats tie up alongside each other, whether when *anchored* or on a *mooring; ground tackle* must be strong and heavy enough to take their combined weight without *parting* or *dragging*.

Rail UK: the top of the *bulwarks*. US: more widely applied to the top of the sides of a boat, the *gunwale*. See *construction* fig. US: also the *lifeline* (guardrail) that is rigged round the sides through *stanchions* to prevent the crew from falling overboard. See also *toe-rail*.

Rain Precipitation, the water drops being over 0.5 mm in diameter (drizzle, the droplets are much smaller and more closely spaced). Rain showers are of short duration, and are often heavy. Rain clutter (radar), see *clutter*.

Raise To raise a light or land is to approach until it becomes visible above the horizon.

Raised deck The *deck* forward of the *cockpit* is raised at the sides to provide extra headroom and more spacious accommodation. *Camber* is usually more pronounced to shed spray and water taken aboard.

Rake The *fore-and-aft* angle which the *mast* or other part of a boat (such as *stem, stern* or *rudder*) makes with the vertical. Altering mast rake enables the boat's *balance* to be adjusted by shifting the position of the *centre of effort* relative to that of the *centre of lateral resistance*. Normally a mast is raked 2–5° aft, but if a boat has more than one mast the mast(s) further aft usually have more rake than the forward mast(s). Also used as a verb, to rake the mast.

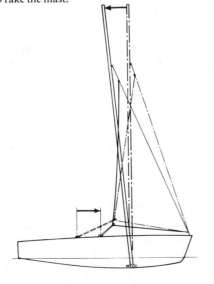

Ramark *Radar beacon* that transmits continuously (c.f. *racon*).

Range 1. To lay out the *anchor cable*, ready for anchoring. 2. Objects that provide a *line of bearing* when they are *in line* (UK *transit*). Range marks include those at either end of a *measured distance*, and those marking a range (UK *leading line*). The latter often also carry range lights. A natural range enables the crew to check whether the *anchor* is

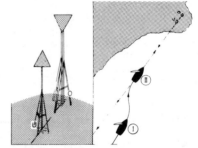

holding; for example, if a bush on shore stays in line with a tree further inland the anchor is holding, but if they open it is *dragging* (see *transit*). The word range is rarely used in these contexts by UK small boat sailors. 3. See also *geographical, luminous* and *nominal range, radar* for radar range, range rings, and entries below.

Rangefinder Optical instrument that enables range or *distance* off to be determined by measuring the angle subtended by an object or landmark of known height. A simple home-made rangefinder is described under *kamal*.

Range light 1. US Inland rules of the road: 32-point white light, exhibited further aft and higher than the forward 20-point light by larger *power-driven* vessels *under way*. 2. US: one of two leading lights marking a range. When the two lights are in line, the boat is on the range and, while she is within the limits marked on the *chart*, is clear of *hazards*.

Range of stability The range of *heeling* angles at which the *righting moment* of a boat is positive, and from which she returns to an upright position when the heeling force is removed. See *stability curve*.

Range of tide The difference between sea level at *high water* and sea level at the preceding or following *low water*. Range at *springs* is greater than that at *neaps*. The range of a particular *tide* varies considerably from place to place. See *tide* fig.

Rap full *Close-hauled* or *close reaching* with the sails drawing and full of wind.

Ratchet block and **winch** A *block* with a serrated

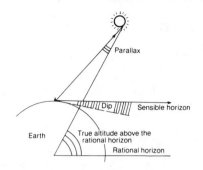

sheave, which grips the sheet, and a *pawl* which permits it to turn in one direction only, thus taking much of the load. Many are designed so that the ratchet can be disengaged when required, especially in light breezes. Most often used aboard racing dinghies. The term ratchet *winch* is used in the US for winches varying from *snubbing winches* to *coffee grinders* in size.

Rate 1. (US drift) The speed at which a *tidal stream or current* runs, given in *knots* and tenths of knots. 2. The daily loss or gain of a *chronometer* or *deck watch;* when the time-piece gains the error has to be deducted, when it loses error is added.

Rating A figure obtained by taking certain measurements of a boat so that her potential performance can be compared with those of other boats of different designs and sizes. The measurement rules are often long and complicated, and may relate to measurements such as *waterline length, beam, displacement* and *sail area,* or to lengths between specified positions such as *girths* (see *International Offshore Rule*). Although a boat's rating is given in feet or metres it does not indicate her actual length. A *time allowance* system is applied to the various ratings of boats competing in a race, and *elapsed time* is converted into *corrected time* to find the winner.

Rating certificate A certificate issued after a boat has been measured, giving her rating under the relevant measurement rule. The *International Offshore Rule* rating certificate lists the measurements taken and the calculations made; it is valid for four years, unless the boat is sold or changes are made, such as structural alterations, different sails or rig, shifting ballast etc.

Ratio A number of different ratios are used to compare different types and designs, based on the measurements of the boats. Included in this dictionary are *ballast, displacement to length, length to beam, length to draft, sail area to displacement, sail area to length* and *sail area to wetted area ratios.* Other ratios used include fin keel to sail area and wetted area to displacement. See also *aspect ratio, gear ratio, power ratio, power to weight ratio,* and *speed to length ratio.*

Rational or **celestial horizon** A *great circle* on the *celestial sphere,* the plane of which passes through the centre of the earth and is perpendicular to the line between the observer's *zenith* and the earth's centre. The *true altitude* of *a heavenly body* is its angular distances above the rational horizon (c.f. *sensible* and *visible horizons*).

Ratlines Short lines attached across pairs of *shrouds* with *clove hitches,* or *seized* to them to serve as steps when going *aloft.* Normally only seen aboard older or larger vessels.

RDF *Radio direction finder,* q.v.

Reach 1. Verb and noun: a boat is on a reach when she is neither *close-hauled* nor *running.* She is close reaching when the wind is *forward of the beam,* on a beam reach when the wind is *abeam,* and broad reaching when the wind is *abaft the beam.* As the helmsman *bears away* to alter course from a close reach to a beam reach and then to a broad reach, the sails are *eased* out further, and the seas become progressively easier, while *leeway* and the angle of *heel* decrease. When reaching, which is the fastest *point of sailing,* the helmsman can bear away or *luff up* as he pleases. 2. A straight stretch of a river.

Reaching genoa or **reacher** Full cut, high-clewed *headsail* set on a reach in light to moderate winds; cloth weight 2½–4 oz US, 3–5 oz UK, 100–170 g/sq m.

Reaching mark When racing, a *mark* of the *course* laid roughly midway between the *weather* and *leeward* marks, and far enough to one side of the direct line between them to provide two *broad reaches* during a race. Also known as a wing mark.

Reaching spinnaker See *star-cut.*

Reaching strut See *jockey pole.*

Ready about The helmsman's warning that he intends to *go about* very shortly. The crew prepares by uncleating the *headsail sheet,* and waits for the boat to turn into the *eye of the wind* after he has said *lee-o* (US hard a-lee), and put the *helm* down, before letting the sail fly.

Recall A yacht that starts a race too soon (i.e. if

any part of her hull, crew or equipment is on the course side of the *starting line* or its extensions when the *starting signal* is made) is recalled and has to return to the other side of the line, keeping clear of other boats that are starting or have started, before she can herself start racing. *Code flag X* is broken out after the starting signal, an acoustic signal is made, and the recall number(s) or letter(s) may be displayed (unless some other procedure has been prescribed in the *sailing instructions*). When many boats are over the line there may be a general recall, the first *substitute* (US repeater) being displayed and a sound signal made. New *warning* and *preparatory signals* are then made, and the *round-the-ends* or *one-minute rule* may come into force.

Reciprocal course and **bearing** The *course* or *bearing* that differs by 180°. If a vessel sailing on a course of 120° *true* or *magnetic* meets a vessel head-on, the other vessel's course will be the reciprocal course of 300°. Similarly if the true or magnetic bearing of a coastguard station from a vessel is 105°, the reciprocal bearing of that vessel from the coastguard station is 285°.

Recover 1. *Sailcloth* stretches to a greater or lesser degree under load, and is said to recover when it reverts to its original shape after the load is removed. 2. To bring a person or some object that has fallen over the side back on board. The figure shows one method of recovering a helpless man from the water. 3. A boat is said to recover, e.g. from a *knockdown*, when she returns to an *even keel*.

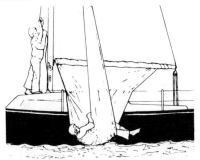

Recovery line Light line attached to the mid-point of a spinnaker to speed up the take-down process.

Rectifier Electrical device that allows a current to flow in one direction only; thus it can make alternating current (AC) into direct current (DC).

Rectilinear tidal stream (UK) or **reversing tidal current** (US) A *tidal stream* (US *tidal current*) that reverses in direction after *slack water* (c.f. *rotary*).

Recurvature The vertex or point of recurvature

of a *tropical revolving storm* (q.v. for fig.) is the most westerly point on its path, where it turns away from the *equator* to follow a north-easterly path in the northern hemisphere or south-easterly in the southern.

Reduction gear Gearing which converts a high input rotational speed into a lower output rotational speed. Reduces the high speed of rotation of an *inboard* or *outboard engine* to a speed better suited to the *propeller*. Given a ratio of $3:1$, when the engine is running at 1500 rpm, the propeller will rotate at 500 rpm.

Reduction of soundings *Soundings* on charts are referred to *chart datum*, and a sounding taken in tidal waters therefore has to be adjusted by subtracting the *height of the tide* above chart datum at the time it was taken before it can be compared with a sounding on the chart.

Reed A rather weak high-pitched *fog signal* emitted by an *aid to navigation*. Chart abbr UK Reed, US Horn.

Reeds Nautical Almanac Invaluable annual publication which covers British and adjacent European waters; a separate volume covers the East Coast of the United States. Contains similar information to the *Nautical Almanac* in condensed form, plus details of *buoyage*, *tides*, signals, radio stations as well as first aid and weather hints, the *International Regulations for Preventing Collisions at Sea*, glossaries etc.

Reef 1. To reduce the area of sail, especially the *mainsail*, when the wind *freshens* and the boat is *overcanvassed* (see *reefing system*). 2. The part of the sail taken in when reefing. When one reef is tucked in, that part of the sail beneath the lowest line of reef points or eyelets that is gathered to the boom. The second reef is the part of the sail between the first and second rows of reef points or eyelets. In *square sails* the part between the head and the row of reef points next below it. 3. An area of rocks or coral. Although a reef may be partially or wholly submerged, its position can be seen because seas break over it, even when there is little wind. Chart abbr Rf.

Reef band Reinforcing strip of canvas at the line of reef points or eyelets; on a *mainsail* is sewn parallel to the *boom*, on a *headsail* parallel to the *foot*.

Reef cringle A round *thimble* which is sewn into the *luff* and *leech* of the *mainsail* at the same level as a row of reef points. Sail area is reduced by pulling down the reef cringles with reef pendants, but for *jiffy reefing* the luff cringle is slipped over a hook on the boom.

Reef earing Short line with which the reef cringle is brought down to the boom when reefing.

Reef eyelet One of a line of small metal eyes sewn or pressed hydraulically into a reef band; *lacing* is passed through them, round the *foot* of the sail and hauled tight to gather the *bunt*.

Reefing claw, boom claw or **claw ring** A fitting which encircles the *boom* like a claw, with rollers at the top opening and an eye underneath, to which the *mainsheet block* is attached. The position along the boom can be altered as desired, generally by means of a line attached to the after end of the boom, and the sail can be rolled around the boom when reefing, neither of which is possible if the mainsheet block is shackled to a fixed *boom*

strap. A double claw, or two claws with a spacer between, can be fitted to distribute the load over a greater part of the spar and, to obviate the need for blocks, the spacer may incorporate *sheaves* set fore-and-aft, the mainsheet being rove over them.

Reefing hook Small hook on the boom over which the luff cringle is slipped when *jiffy reefing*. See also *hook reefing*.

Reefing systems The area of a sail can be reduced in several ways: (a) the sail can be *furled* round a wire or *luff spar* with *furling gear*: (b) when *roller reefing* dinghies, the *mainsail* is normally rolled around the *boom*, which is pulled partly off the *gooseneck* and rotated as often as necessary. The boom of larger boats is rotated mechanically, usually by *worm gear* or a *through-mast* system. c) with *jiffy, points* or *slab reefing*, the sail is not rolled round the boom. The lower portion of the sail (one or more reefs) is brought down to the boom to which the reef cringles are secured. Each reefing system has its protagonists: roller reefing is quick and may require less effort than points reefing, but jiffy reefing is even quicker. The main

disadvantages of roller reefing are: there is often a triangular gap left above the gooseneck; the *luff rope* builds up awkwardly when more than a certain number of rolls have been taken (to avoid this sails are often taped here instead of being roped); the more rolls that are taken the more the end of the boom droops. This last can be prevented by tapering the boom, or by inserting light wooden laths between the layers of sail. Generally sails set better when points or jiffy reefed, and in both these two systems no reefing claw is required if the boat has a *centre mainsheet*; the *kicking strap* (or *boom vang*) can still operate efficiently when the sail is reefed. See also *flattening reef*.

Reef knot or **square knot** A knot that is easy to make and to undo, used to join two ropes or lines of the same size. The *bight* of each line lies over or under both parts of the other. A useless *granny knot* is the result of making it wrongly. A reef knot is used especially when tying in a reef, and may be made with a bighted or slipped end for quick release.

Reef pendant A strong line with which the *luff* or *leech cringle* is pulled down to the boom when reefing. The leech pendant is permanently rove, and runs from one side of the boom, through the reef cringle and down to a *cheek block* or *bee block* on the other side of the boom. In larger boats it is often shackled to a *tackle*. The reef pendants take the main load when the sail is reefed, the points merely confining the sail.

Reef points Short light lines which are sewn to the sail parallel to the boom, and which confine the *bunt* along the *foot* of a reefed sail. They are tied with a reef knot beneath the foot, unless the foot is fed into a groove, in which case the reef points encircle the boom.

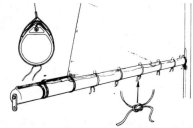

Reel winch See *halyard winch.*

Reeve To pass the end of a rope or line through a hole or aperture such as an *eye, thimble, block* or *sheave.* The past tense is rove, the opposite is unreeve. See *tackle* for reeving a rope purchase to advantage or disadvantage.

Reference station (US) See *standard port.*

Reflector Many US *aids to navigation,* especially those in inland waters, are painted with a border that reflects light, so that they can be found and identified easily at night. See also *radar reflector.*

Reflector compass Generally a larger *magnetic compass,* the *lubber line* and card of which are enlarged and reflected. Often enables the helmsman to steer from two alternative positions.

Refloat to cause a boat to float again, e.g. after *running aground.* She may be refloated by the rising *tide,* or have to be *towed* or *kedged* off by the crew, and they may have to *lighten* her by taking off gear, stores and crew. It often helps to *heel* her over well so as to reduce her *draft,* perhaps by suspending a heavy object outboard from the end of the boom.

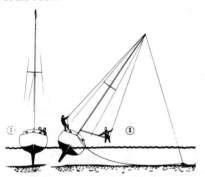

Refraction The bending of light rays and radio waves when they pass from a medium of a certain *density* to another of different density. 1. Because the light ray from a *heavenly body* is bent as it passes through the layers of the earth's *atmosphere,* the body appears to be higher than it really is. Refraction is nil when the body is at the observer's *zenith,* but increases to over 30′ as the body nears the *horizon.* The *altitude correction tables* in the *Nautical Almanac* include the value for average refraction, and there is an additional table for non-standard conditions. 2. *Radar* range is affected when the difference between the temperature of sea and air exceeds about 6 °C. Sub-refraction occurs when the air is cool and the sea warm; the beam bends upwards and range decreases. Super-refraction, when the air is warmer than the sea, causes the beam to bend downwards, and range increases. Ducting is an extreme form of super-refraction; the pulse is contained in a layer of

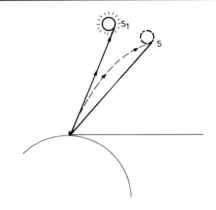

atmosphere, and range may be vastly increased. 3. The path of radio waves is bent when crossing the coast from land to sea, especially when crossing at oblique angles. Marine *radio beacons* are sited at the coast to avoid coastal refraction, which may cause radio *bearings* on inland aero beacons to be unreliable. 4. See also *wind,* paragraph 3.

Regatta A programme of races organized on one or more days. Often there are races for sailing boats only, but other water sports may be included.

Register The mechanism of a *patent log,* driven by the spinning *rotator* at the end of a log line. Often records speed in *knots* as well as distance sailed through the water in tenths of *nautical miles.*

Registration All UK vessels over 15 tons have to be registered by the owner with a Registrar of British Ships at a port of registry, but many owners of smaller pleasure yachts elect to do so, particularly if they intend to go foreign, or so as to obtain either a mortgage or a *warrant* to wear a privileged *ensign.* The documents required are evidence of ownership (i.e. the builder's certificate in the case of a new boat, plus Bills of Sale relating to all transfers of ownership since she was built if she is not new), a Declaration of Ownership and a Certificate of Survey (Tonnage Measurement – a simplified measurement formula is used for vessels under 45 ft 13.6 m overall length – see *tonnage).* The Registrar issues a Carving and Marking Note to the owner, and she is given a number which is glassed in or carved on the main beam with her tonnage if she is over 45 ft in length, or as instructed if she is smaller. The owner pays the registry fee and is then issued with the Certificate of Registry. US, see *documentation.*

Relative bearing The direction of an object relative to the vessel's *fore-and-aft* line, 0° being dead *ahead,* 090° or green 90 *abeam* to *starboard,* 180° dead *astern* and 270° or red 90 abeam to *port.* The relative bearing is added to the ship's *heading* at the moment the *bearing* is taken (360 is subtracted if the total exceeds 360), and is then

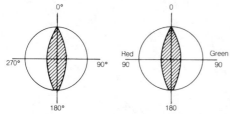

corrected to a *true* or *magnetic bearing* before being laid off on the chart. Approximations are often used, e.g. an object may be said to be two points *abaft* the beam, or *fine on* the starboard bow/quarter.

Relative humidity The amount of moisture in the air at a given moment, expressed as a percentage of the amount of moisture that would be present in saturated air. The lower the relative humidity the dryer the air, i.e. 95–100% is very damp. At *dew point,* when relative humidity is 100%, air is saturated, can hold no more moisture, and water droplets form, say as *fog, drizzle* or *condensation.* Air can hold approximately the same weight of moisture in grammes per cubic metre as the number of degrees of its temperature above 0 °C. Thus, when air temperature is 28 °C and 14 g of moisture is present in one cubic metre of air, relative humidity is 50%, the air is semi-saturated and could hold a further 14 g of moisture. At the same temperature, air with 22 g/cu m vapour concentration has a relative humidity of about 80%. The value of relative humidity is also 50% when air temperature is 10 °C and the amount of vapour held is 5 g/cu m, just as above when air temperature is 28 °C and vapour concentration is 14 g/cu m.

Relative motion The motion of a vessel or object in relation to another object. For example the relative motion of two boats *crossing* on different courses will be such that they will collide if the bearing of one from the other does not change, and a vessel therefore checks, by taking bearings if

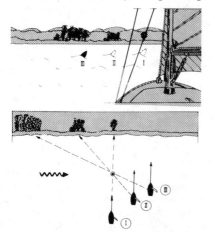

necessary, that the other vessel will either cross her bow or pass astern. Similarly when crossing a *tidal stream* or *current* a boat may see a buoy dead ahead, anchored some distance from the shore. As she sails further the buoy will appear to move upstream along the coast and pass landmarks on shore, whereas in fact it is the vessel that is being set downstream while the buoy is motionless. Relative motion display: see *Plan Position Indicator.*

Relative wind See *apparent wind.*

Release agent A parting agent that is applied to the inside of a *female mould* or to the outside of a *plug* before *laying-up* a *moulding,* to enable the laminate to be removed from the mould.

Relieving tackle A *tackle* attached to the *tiller* or *wheel,* or direct to the *rudder head,* rigged to assist the helmsman, or if *steering gear* is damaged.

Remote control A mechanical, hydraulic or electrical link which enables some part of the boat's equipment, such as the engine or rudder, to be controlled from a distance.

Render Said of a rope or line when it runs smoothly through a block or aperture. Also said of a rope or line when it slips under strain.

Renting (US) Synonymous with *chartering,* but on a commercial basis.

Repeater 1. Instruments often have to be sited where they cannot be seen by the helmsman, and repeater dials for *log, echo-sounder* and/or *wind speed and direction indicator* may be installed in the cockpit. 2. A repeater *compass* can be mounted anywhere on board, and well away from the master compass, the movements of which it follows exactly. The master compass can then be sited where *deviation* is least. 3. US: *code flag,* see *substitute.*

Rescue or **safety boat** (US or **crash boat**) A boat that accompanies dinghies and small keelboats during a *race* to provide assistance when required, say in the event of damage to gear, or if the crew cannot right a dinghy after *capsizing.*

Reserve buoyancy Additional *buoyancy* in the parts of a boat above the *waterline* that are water-tight, such as the *overhangs.* A boat that is leaking and partly filled with water may continue to float on account of her reserve buoyancy, but she will be more deeply immersed.

Resin See *polyester* and *epoxy resin.*

Resistance or **drag** Undesirable component of total aerodynamic or hydrodynamic force; acts in the same direction as that of the *apparent wind,* or in the direction opposite to that of the boat's motion through the water. Total resistance or drag is made up of a number of components, the most important of which are *frictional resistance* (caused by water sliding over the *wetted surface* and air over the sail), *induced drag* (results from pressure being higher on one side of a foil than on the other), *form drag* (caused by the shape of the body) and *wave-making resistance* (resulting from velocity and pressure changes when a boat moves over the surface of water). At slower speeds skin friction is the most important component of hydrodynamic resistance, but at higher speeds wave-making is the predominant factor. When *close-hauled*, induced resistance owing to *leeway* is important at small angles of *heel*, but when the boat heels further resistance owing to heeling becomes the major factor (see *force* figure D(air) and R(hull resistance).

Resolution The ability of a *radar* to show, as separate echoes, two *targets* that are close in terms of *range* and *bearing*. Range resolution is largely governed by pulse width, angular resolution by beam width.

Resorcinol glue Waterproof resin adhesive (phenol and formaldehyde) with a powder *catalyst;* strong and resists moisture and bacteria.

Restricted class See *development class.*

Restricted visibility May be owing to snow, heavy rain, fog etc. In such conditions vessels are required to proceed at a safe speed, suitable for the conditions, and to navigate with extreme caution. Under the *IRPCS* lights must be *exhibited* and *sound signals* made by day and by night. The sound signals are mostly made by *whistle* at intervals of not more than one or two minutes as follows:

(a) *power-driven,* making way through the water; one prolonged *blast;* 2 minute intervals.

(b) power-driven, *under way* but stopped and making no way; two prolonged blasts in succession; 2-minute intervals.

(c) *Sailing vessels,* vessels *towing* and other classes that are unable to manoeuvre freely; three blasts in succession, one prolonged followed by two short; 2-minute intervals.

(d) A vessel being towed, or the last (manned) vessel of a tow; four blasts in succession, one prolonged followed by three short; 2-minute intervals.

(f) At *anchor,* a *bell* rung forward rapidly for 5 seconds at 1 minute intervals; if 100 m in length or more a *gong* is sounded aft for 5 seconds immediately after the bell has been rung. Three blasts may also be sounded as a warning, one short, one prolonged, one short.

(g) *Aground,* as anchored, but three strokes are given on the bell immediately before and after

ringing; an appropriate whistle signal may also be sounded.

(h) A vessel under 12 m in length is not obliged to give the above signals but must make some other efficent sound signal at 2-minute intervals.

(i) A *pilot vessel* on duty may additionally sound an identifying signal of four short blasts.

US Inland, Great Lakes and *Western Rivers* rules differ considerably, e.g. sailing vessel on *starboard tack,* one blast; on *port tack* two blasts; wind *abaft the beam* three blasts, all at one-minute intervals.

Retire A yacht retires when she ceases to race, whether owing to damage or to infringing a *racing rule.* When competing in a *series,* a boat often scores additional penalty points if she is disqualified after a *protest,* and it is therefore to her advantage to retire promptly or to perform an alternative penalty, i.e. a *720° turn.*

Retractable, drop or **lifting keel** As opposed to a fixed *keel,* one that can be drawn into the *hull,* say to make transportation overland easier.

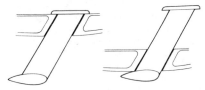

Rev counter Abbreviation for revolution counter and coll for *tachometer,* q.v.

Reverse gear Most boats have either a *variable pitch propeller* or a reverse gear to enable them to make *sternway* under power because, usually, the engine output shaft rotates in only one direction. The gear is fitted between the engine and the *propeller shaft,* the direction of rotation of the shaft being reversed when the gear is engaged. Reverse and *reduction gear* reduces the revolution rate as well.

Reverse sheer *Freeboard* amidships is higher than that at the *bow* and *stern;* the sheer line curves upwards. Sometimes called hogged sheer.

Reversing tidal current (US) See *rectilinear stream.*

Reynolds Number A dimensionless number, named after the British physicist Osborne Reyolds (1842–1912). The formula is

$$Re = \frac{V \times L}{v}$$

where V is velocity of flow in feet or metres per second, L is the characteristic length (e.g. of the *chord* of a sail or of the immersed hull) and v is the kinematic viscosity of the fluid. At 15 °C the kinematic viscosity of fresh water is 1.14×10^{-6} sq m per second, of salt water about 1.19×10^{-6} sq m/sec, of air about 1.46×10^{-5} sq m/sec, depending on the *density*. At 59 °F the kinematic viscosity of fresh water is 1.23×10^{-5} sq ft/sec, of salt water about 1.28×10^{-5} sq ft/sec and of air about 1.57×10^{-4} sq ft/sec. When the Reynolds number rises to a certain critical value, fluid flow changes from *laminar* to *turbulent*, the thickness of the *boundary layer* increases, and this results in a higher coefficient of *frictional resistance*, whether of airflow over a sail or of water over the underwater body, keel, rudder etc. The wetted area therefore has to be kept as smooth as possible to preserve laminar flow.

Rhumb line   A line on the surface of the earth which cuts all *meridians* at the same angle. On the earth's surface is a curve that spirals towards the *pole* without reaching it (A). On *mercator* charts a rhumb line appears as a straight line, but on *gnomonic* projection charts it is curved. The rhumb line distance between two points is longer than the *great circle* distance and, whereas rhumb line sailing is normal for shorter distances, sailing boats making a long voyage are more likely to follow a shorter great circle course, broken up into a series of rhumb lines.

B

Rhythmic light   Whereas a *fixed light* shows a continuous steady light a rhythmic light shines intermittently, and can be identified from its *character* and *period*. The character of *flashing*, *occulting, group flashing* and *occulting, isophase* and *morse code lights* is determined by the relative duration of light and darkness.

Rhythmic rolling   When a boat is on a *run* with the sail at right angles to the wind, the *wake*

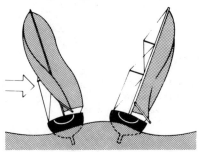

behind the sail moves from side to side and causes the boat to *roll* rhythmically, leaning first to one side until *righting moment* returns her to an upright position, then to the other side, and so on. The angle of roll often increases each time she rolls, sometimes to an uncomfortable or even dangerous degree, especially when seas contribute to the oscillating motion, and if the headsail is *boomed out* to windward.

Rib   A colloquial term for one of the vertical *transverse members* to which *planking* or *plating* is fastened. *Frame* or *timber* is technically preferable.

Ribband   Strips of wood nailed longitudinally to the *moulds* or *frames* to hold them in place during construction. The ribbands may be removed as the boat is planked. Ribband-carvel: see *batten-seam planking*.

Ride   To lie at *anchor* or on a *mooring*, free to swing and react to the waves, e.g. ride easily.

Ride down   To use body weight, especially to haul down a sail.

Ride out a storm   To survive a storm at sea, either lying to a *sea anchor*, running under *bare poles* or *hove to*. Also to remain at *anchor* or *berthed* during a storm, rather than getting *under way*.

Ridge   A narrow area of relatively high pressure between two *low* pressure areas, extending outwards from an *anticyclone*. Weather is usually fine, but of shorter duration than that in a high. See *anticyclone* fig.

Riding light   Alternative term for the *anchor light*, q.v.

Riding turn (US **overriding turn**)   Occurs when a turn is taken on a *winch* if the rope is guided wrongly. An earlier turn rides over a later turn and jams.

Rig   1. A sailing boat is described by her rig. *Square-rigged* boats are the exception nowadays, virtually all boats being *fore-and-aft rigged*. Most are *bermudan-rigged* (US *marconi-rigged*), and some are *gaff-rigged*. The most common rigs are: *cat* – one *mast*, no *headsail: sloop* – one mast, one headsail (may be *masthead-, seven-eighths-* or *three-quarter-rigged*): *cutter* – one mast, two headsails: *ketch* and *yawl* – two masts, the lower *mizzenmast* aft: *schooner* – two or more masts, the *foremast* being lower or the same height as the *mainmast* which is stepped further aft. Other boats set a *lugsail* or *spritsail*, or may be *lateen-* or *gunter-rigged*. 2. As a verb, to prepare gear ready for working, e.g. rig a lifeline, and awning etc, and fit a vessel with rigging.

Rig allowances   A boat with a single *mast*, rigged as a *sloop* or a *cutter*, is aerodynamically more efficient than boats with other rigs such as *yawls*, *ketches* and *schooners*. Under the *RORC* rule a percentage of measured sail area was allowed free to enable them to race on fair terms with single-masted boats: bermudan-rigged yawl 4%, gaff cutter 6%, bermudan schooner 8%, gaff yawl 13%, bermudan-rigged ketch 13%, gaff schooner 18%, gaff ketch 20%. This was not adopted in the *International Rule* which recognizes only sloops (single-masted), yawls (two masts, the shorter mast aft) and schooners (two masts, the shorter mast forward).

Rigger   The person who rigs a vessel, i.e. *steps* the *mast*, fits the *standing* and *running rigging*, makes the necessary *splices* etc.

Rigging   All the ropes, lines, wires and gear used to support the *masts*, and to control the *spars* and *sails*. Divided into *standing rigging* which supports and *running rigging* which controls.

Rigging list or **plan**   A plan or list drawn up by the designer to supplement the *lines drawings*. Gives details of the rigging, such as the length, diameter and material to be used for all the standing and running rigging; also lists *fittings*, *blocks*, *slides* etc, and indicates where they are to be placed.

Rigging screw   Fitting with which the tension of *stays*, *shrouds*, *life-lines* (guardrails) etc is adjusted. Termed *turnbuckle* (q.v.) in the US and sometimes bottlescrew in the UK.

Rigging screw cover   Short tubular cover, usually of hard PVC; tapers at the top where the *shroud* wire passes through. Fitted to reduce *chafe* on sails and sheets.

Right   1. To return a small boat to an upright position after she has *capsized*. This is only possible when the *buoyancy* (flotation) *bags* etc of a dinghy are properly distributed. A *keelboat* rights herself automatically after *heeling* to a gust, owing to her low *centre of gravity*. 2. Right *rudder* is the equivalent of *port helm*.

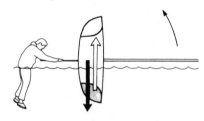

Right bank   When facing downstream, the river bank on the right.

Right-hand lay or **Z-twist** (US also **plain laid**) Rope made with *strands* sloping to the right, in the same direction as the thread of a corkscrew. Most ropes used on board are right-hand laid, and must be *coiled* clockwise. See also *rope-making*. Also used of twist of filaments when making *thread* for *cloth* weaving. Opposite is S-twist or left-hand lay

Right-hand propeller   Viewed from aft the *blades* rotate clockwise to move the boat forward (see also *wheel effect*).

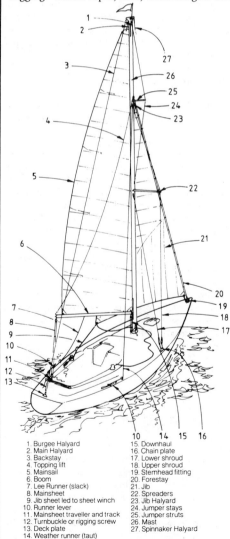

1. Burgee Halyard
2. Main Halyard
3. Backstay
4. Topping lift
5. Mainsail
6. Boom
7. Lee Runner (slack)
8. Mainsheet
9. Jib sheet led to sheet winch
10. Runner lever
11. Mainsheet traveller and track
12. Turnbuckle or rigging screw
13. Deck plate
14. Weather runner (taut)
15. Downhaul
16. Chain plate
17. Lower shroud
18. Upper shroud
19. Sternhead fitting
20. Forestay
21. Jib
22. Spreaders
23. Jib Halyard
24. Jumper stays
25. Jumper struts
26. Mast
27. Spinnaker Halyard

Righting lever or **arm** The horizontal distance between the line of action of the force of gravity acting vertically downwards through the *centre of gravity* and that of buoyancy acting vertically upwards through the *centre of buoyancy* when it has shifted, e.g. to *leeward* when the boat *heels* to

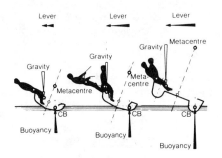

wind pressure. The longer the righting arm the greater the righting moment, whether this is due to hull form or a low CG (*ballast*). *Sitting* (US hiking) *out* or *trapezing* increases the length of the righting arm.

Righting moment The product of *righting lever* and *displacement*. If the *centre of gravity* is to *leeward* of the *centre of buoyancy*, righting moment is negative (*capsizing moment*) and the boat capsizes. Righting moment curve: see *stability curve*.

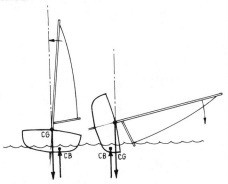

Right of way The rights and obligations of sailing yachts meeting when racing in daylight are laid down in the IYRU *racing rules*, (but at night the IRPCS come into force). Basically a *port tack yacht* keeps clear of a *starboard tack yacht*, a *windward yacht* keeps clear of an *overlapping leeward yacht* and a yacht *clear astern* keeps clear of a yacht clear ahead. Racing at close quarters calls for many additional rules that specify which yacht has right of way, e.g. at the start, when rounding marks, changing tacks, at obstructions etc. The term right of way is not used in the IRPCS which, essentially, specify the duties of vessels to keep out of the way of other vessels (see *rules of the road*). Nevertheless the terms stand-on vessel and privileged vessel are virtually synonymous.

Right rudder (US) An order to direct the vessel's head to starboard.

Ring bolt A bolt with a ring to which lines, lashings or a block may be attached.

Rip current Fast-moving and relatively narrow *current* that flows offshore from surf beaches, often scouring a rather deeper channel as it returns water that has been piled up on the beach by surf and wind.

Ripples Capillary waves that have a *period* of under 1 second and are very small, being an inch or so high. If the wind increases they grow into waves, but if the wind drops the surface becomes smooth almost immediately.

Rise of floor See *deadrise*.

Riser or **rising** *Fore-and-aft member* fastened to the sides of a small boat to support the *thwarts*.

Rising 1. At the visible rise of sun and moon, the upper *limb* appears above the *horizon* but the centre is still below it. An *azimuth* can be taken at sunrise or moonrise, and the times of visible sunrise and moonrise are tabulated in the *Nautical Almanac* for every third day (sun) and daily (moon) for an observer with no *height of eye*, at various *latitudes* on the *Greenwich meridian*; 16' is allowed for *semi-diameter* and 34' for horizontal *refraction*. 2. See *riser*. 3. A rising *barometer* indicates an increase in *atmospheric pressure*.

Rising piece A feature of more costly *sextants*; enables the *telescope* to be moved laterally. Moving it to one side increases the distinctness of the *heavenly body*, moving it the other way makes the *horizon* clearer.

Rising tide When the water level rises during the *flood*, between *low water* and *high water*, as opposed to a falling tide.

Risk of collision The *IRPCS* state that every vessel shall use all available means appropriate to the circumstances to determine if risk of collision exists. They deliberately do not define the condition but state that, if there is any doubt, such risk shall be deemed to exist. This is because circumstances vary so widely and, for example, prescribing a circle of danger based on two vessels moving at high relative speed would be inappropriate for two much slower vessels. Except when both vessels are racing under their own *racing rules,* risk of collision automatically brings the IRPCS Steering and Sailing rules into force. See *rule of the road.*

Rivet A metal fastening with a burred end; fastens plates to each other or to members, and is difficult to remove. Rivets are now largely superseded by welding. *Pop rivets* are used when one side only is accessible. The planks of a *clinker-built* hull are riveted with copper nails.

Roach The part of a *fore-and-aft sail* which extends beyond the straight line between two corners. Most frequently applied to the *leech* roach, which extends beyond the line between *head* and *clew* and which is supported by *battens.* In most *classes* leech roach is limited, often by prescribing maximum batten length, because free sail area is increased and the fullness or *camber* of the sail is affected. The *luff* roach extends similarly beyond the line between head and *tack,* and the *foot* roach beyond that between tack and clew. These areas are often referred to as the luff and foot *round.*

Roach reef See *flattening reef.*

Roads or **roadstead** An *anchorage,* possibly outside a port, where *holding ground* is good and there is some protection from wind and sea, although much less than in the port.

Roaring Forties The belt, roughly 40–50° south, where strong westerly winds blow throughout the year. So called because of the noise of the wind in the rigging. 50–60° S is sometimes similarly called the Furious Fifties. See *global winds* fig.

Rock (a) The height of a rock that does not *cover* is given above *MHWS* on most UK charts, and above *MHW* on US charts; it is printed between brackets on or by the rock. (b) An asterisk denotes the position of a rock which covers and uncovers, but Admiralty charts more often show the extent of the rocky area enclosed by the symbol for rocks. *Drying heights* are given above *chart datum,* either as an underlined figure (sometimes in brackets) or UK as 'Dries × ft or m', US 'Uncov × ft or m'. (c) The symbol for a rock *awash* at chart datum is a vertical cross with dots in each quadrant. (d) On UK charts a simple vertical cross marks the position of a rock less than 6 ft (2 m) below the surface, on US charts it marks the position of a submerged rock, the depth of which is not known. Chart abbr R or Rk.

Rocker The upward curvature of the *keel* towards *bow* and *stern.*

Rode The cable attached to the anchor, whether chain, rope or wire rope (see *anchor cable*). See also *wind-rode* and *tide-rode.*

Rod rigging A single, cold-drawn, stainless steel rod used for *standing rigging* in place of wire rope. May be round or streamlined (lenticular), presents a completely smooth surface to the wind, and does not *stretch,* even when under heavy load; a rod forestay may have a groove for the headsail luff rope. The *terminals* are directly attached to the *chain plates,* and the desired tension is obtained by turning the rod, which has an exterior thread.

Roll 1. The periodic rotating movement of a boat about a horizontal *fore-and-aft* axis as she leans alternately to *port* and *starboard.* The angle to which she inclines either side of the vertical is the angle of roll (see also *rolling period*). A boat rolls on a *run* as a result of the changing direction of the *heeling force* of the wind, and this is often accentuated by seas. She may roll violently in a *swell,* particularly when there is little or no wind to steady her, and when the sails are *furled.* Waves can also cause a boat to roll when reaching, and rolling can become dangerous if the boat's natural rolling period coincides with the period of the waves. It is then best to alter course if possible. Generally the periods only coincide for a short time, and the boat will roll particularly violently at that time. Stabilizers are fitted to larger vessels to reduce rolling and ease motion. 2. One complete turn of the boom in *roller reefing.*

Roller jib A *jib* or other *headsail* which is *furled* by rolling it around itself or round a *luff spar* or a *luff wire.* High stress thrust races at *head* and *tack* enable the sail to be *reefed* by rolling it part way.

Roller reefing A method of *reefing* whereby sail area is reduced by rolling part of the sail around the *boom* (c.f. *points* and *jiffy reefing*). The simplest system is frequently seen in dinghies where the round *goose-neck* pin has squared shoulders; the boom is pulled away from the mast, rotated

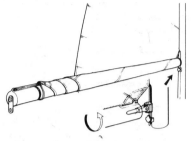

about the round part of the pin as often as necessary, and is then thrust towards the mast, the square hole in the boom end fitting slipping over the shoulders to prevent the boom from unrolling. A more sophisticated type of gooseneck is spring-loaded to hold the boom close to the mast. Mechanical roller reefing systems such as *worm gear* or ratchet and pawl are fitted on the boom, and there are also *through-mast* systems.

Rolling hitch A hitch with which a smaller rope or line is attached to a larger, or a line to a spar, when the direction of pull is along the rope or spar. Basically a *clove hitch*, but an extra turn, taken in the direction of pull, jams the hitch effectively.

Rolling period The time a boat takes to roll from an upright position to the maximum angle of inclination on one side, right over to the other extreme angle of roll on the other side, and back to an upright position. Sometimes the period is taken to be half this, from one extreme angle to the other. The natural period of rolling inherent in a boat's design can be used to give a rough indication of her *metacentric height*. The period is timed when she has been made to roll in still water, say by the crew shifting their weight rapidly from side to side. The natural period of roll, T, is given by the formula

$$T = \frac{1.1 - r}{\sqrt{\overline{GM}}}$$

where $\overline{GM}$ is metacentric height and r is the radius of gyration, the value of which varies from 0.3 beam to 0.5 beam, depending upon the type of boat and her transverse weight distribution. A *stiff* boat has a shorter rolling period than a *tender* boat, and her motion is rapid. Dinghies with form stability have a shorter rolling period (3–4 seconds) than ballasted keelboats which have a period of 5–10 seconds. The lower figure indicates greater metacentric height and better *transverse stability*.

Roll tack A method of *going about* in a sailing dinghy whereby the crew roll the boat from heeling one way to heeling the other as the dinghy passes through the eye of the wind. Helps *gather way* on the new tack quickly, especially when the wind is very light.

Rond anchor L-shaped *anchor* with a single *fluke*, for use on a river or canal bank, often as a permanent mooring anchor.

Room Space in which to manoeuvre. In the *racing rules*, a yacht often has to give room to another competitor, e.g. to *round* a mark or to pass an *obstruction*. She may also hail for room to *tack*. See also *searoom*.

Root 1. Inshore end of a pier or similar structure. 2. Of a *spreader*, the end near the mast.

Root berth The occupant sleeps on canvas stretched between the side of the boat and a removable bar, which is supported on brackets or posts. Can be rolled up against the side when not in use.

Roove See *burr*.

Rope *Cordage* made of natural or synthetic *fibres*; *wire rope* is made of steel. Fibre ropes may be *braided* or *laid* in various ways (see *rope-making*). In the UK the term conventionally relates to cordage over an inch in circumference, but the trend is to call most of the ropes used on board sailing boats *lines*. In the US rope is usually termed a line as soon as it has been put to a specific use. Rope is measured either by its diameter or its circumference (see *cordage*).

Rope-making To make *right-hand lay* or Z-twist rope, the *fibres* are first spun right-handed into *yarns*, secondly the yarns are twisted left-handed into *strands*, third the strands are laid right-handed to form the rope. A *hawser-laid* rope has three strands laid right-handed. *Shroud-laid* rope has four strands laid up round a *heart* made of the same fibres. *Cable-laid* rope is made by laying up left-handed three three-stranded right-hand laid ropes. *Left-hand lay* or S-twist ropes are rarely used on board, and the fibres, yarns and strands are all spun, twisted and laid in the opposite directions to Z-twist. The harder the strands are twisted the more inflexible the rope; it is then described as hard-laid or short-jaw (opp soft-laid, long-jaw). *Braided rope* has 8–16 strands plaited together by machine, sometimes around a central *core* which may be of the same or different material. Rope measurements: see *cordage*.

Rope to wire splice Wire rope *sheets* and *halyards* are often given a fibre rope *tail* to make handling easier. The splice should be *parcelled* and *served* to prevent protruding raw ends (gashers or whiskers) from damaging the crew's hands. Both *laid* and *braided rope* can be spliced to wire.

Ropewalk Now a long shed where rope is laid up. Formerly rope was made in the open air, and the term persists in street names, as Walk Lane, Ropewalk Road.

Roping To sew a *bolt-rope* to the edge(s) of a sail, either to provide strength, such as when roping a big *trysail*, or to enable the sail to be fed into a *groove* in a spar. The sailmaker uses a roping *palm*.

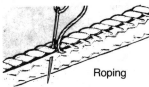

Roping

RORC *Royal Ocean Racing Club*, q.v.

RORC Classes Boats rated under the *IOR* vary from about 20 to 75 ft in length, and their ratings from 16 to 70 ft. The RORC divides them into eight classes by *rating*, because it is impossible to compare the performance of, say, a 25 ft boat with that of a 65-footer. The measurements of boats in these classes is approximately:

Rose See *wind rose, compass rose, current rose.*

Rotary tidal stream (US **tidal current**) During one tidal cycle the directuion towards which the water flows gradually changes through all the *points of the compass* (c.f. *rectilinear*, US reversing).

Rotating mast A mast that can turn about its own axis, like that of a Finn. Banned by the *IOR*.

Rotator A metal spinner with vanes; rotates when the boat moves through the water and actuates the *patent log's* register on board, to which it is connected by the log line.

Rotor ship Experimental ship with a method of propulsion developed by the German engineer Anton Flettner (1885–1961). One or more vertical cylinders rotate in the wind and, owing to Magnus effect (pressure is low on one side of a cylinder that is rotating in a moving fluid) the resultant *lift* propels the vessel. Some vessels were fitted with Flettner rotors in the 1920's, and interest seems to have re-awakened recently in view of the oil shortage.

Round 1. To sail around a point, headland, cape etc. 2. To sail around a *mark* of the *course* when *racing*. The mark must be left to *port* or *starboard* in accordance with the *sailing instructions* and, often, the *committee boat* displays a red flag when marks are to be left to port or a green flag when they are to be left to starboard. 3. Luff and foot round, see *roach*.

Round bilge (US **round bottom**) The most common hull form; the sides curve round and merge into the bottom with no *chine*.

Roundly Quickly.

Round stitch The stitch with which, e.g. a *bolt-rope*, or the after end of a *batten pocket* is sewn to the edge of a sail. See *roping* fig.

Round-the-buoys race Coll for inshore races round marks; usually short.

Round-the-ends Under the *racing rules, code flag I* is displayed one minute before the *starting signal* to indicate that, if any part of a yacht's hull,

Class	Rating	LOA, ft	LWL, ft	Beam, ft	Displacement	Sail area,
I	33.0–70.0	72.8	65	19.5	80,000	2,450
II	29.0–32.9	45	32	11.8	22,650	700
III	25.5–28.9	37	28	10.5	14,500	620
IV	23.0–25.4	35	27	10.2	11,000	480
V	21.0–22.9	32	22	9.0	7,800	370
VI	19.5–20.9	29	21	8.8	6,600	350
VII	17.5–19.4	24.5	19	7.2	3,000	300
VIII	16.0–17.4	21	18.3	6.8	2,200	215

crew or equipment is on the *course* side of the *starting line* or its extensions before her starting signal, she must return to the pre-start side of the line across one of its extensions. Normally applies after a general *recall*, but may also be enforced at the first start.

Round turn A complete turn of rope or line around an object such as a spar, bollard or cleat. The rope completely encircles the object.

Round turn and two half hitches A frequently used knot, more suitable for smaller sizes of cordage.

Round up or **round to** To *head up* into the wind, e.g. when coming *head to wind* and lowering sail prior to *anchoring*.

Routeing chart (US **Pilot chart**) A very small scale *chart* used when planning voyages, UK *natural scale* 1:13,800,000. Shows the ocean routes recommended for each month of the year with *currents*, meteorological conditions, *wind roses* etc.

Rove Past tense of *reeve*, q.v.

Roving Glass filaments bundled together without twisting. May be used in *GRP/FRP mouldings* to provide unidirectional reinforcement, or may be chopped for *spray moulding* or to make mat. Woven roving is a coarse heavy cloth, and is expensive. It is used where loads are greatest, expecially to provide longitudinal reinforcement in the keel and chine areas. Given the same weights, a GRP/FRP mat and roving laminate is two to four times stronger than sheet steel.

Row To propel a boat such as a *dinghy* or *tender* with two or more *oars*, as opposed to *sculling* over the stern with one oar or *paddling* over the side. See also *pull*.

Rowboat (US) or **rowing boat** (UK) Small boat propelled by *oars*.

Rowlock 1. (US **oarlock**): a U-shaped metal or plastics fitting with a pin which engages in a hole in the *gunwale*. Shipped for rowing and unshipped

when the boat is sailing or made fast (see *crutch*). 2. A U-shaped opening in the *washstrake* of a double-banked *pulling* boat; provides the fulcrum for the *oar*.

Royal The *square sail* set above the *topgallant* or upper topgallant on the royal mast, or on the upper part of the topgallant mast; the sixth sail counting up from the deck when upper and lower *topsails* and topgallants are carried above the main *course*.

Royal National Lifeboat Institution, RNLI Private organization supported entirely by voluntary subscription. About 250 *lifeboats* are maintained at many stations around the coasts of the UK, Eire and the Channel Islands, ready to assist vessels in *distress*. Latterly many inshore lifeboats have joined the fleet; these *inflatables* with powerful *outboard engines* have proved very effective near the coast. All crews are volunteers, with the exception of the motor mechanic at the station.

Royal Ocean Racing Club, RORC British club founded in 1925 as the Ocean Racing Club, because the Royal Cruising Club did not wish to organize *offshore racing*. Initiated many major offshore races. Prior to the adoption of the *International Offshore Rule*, many yachts were rated under the RORC Rule, which was amended and adapted from time to time. The 1957 Rule was:

$$Rating = \frac{0.15\,L\sqrt{SA}}{BD} + 0.2\,(L + \sqrt{SA}) \pm \text{stability}$$

allowance − propeller allowance + draft penalty

The rule was also adapted for smaller offshore boats racing with the *Junior Offshore Group*. At this period the *Cruising Club of America's* Rule was in force on the western side of the Atlantic. Currently the RORC organizes British offshore racing.

Royal Yachting Association, RYA Formerly the Yacht Racing Association, founded in 1875 to control British yacht racing and design. By 1952, when the name was changed, activities had extended to include all matters concerning UK yachting, sailing and motor boating interests. Affiliated to the *IYRU*.

Rubber snubber See *mooring spring.*

Rubbing strake (US **rubrail** or **sheerguard**) An additional projecting *strake* or wale fitted around the sides, usually at deck level, to protect the *topsides* when coming or lying alongside. See *construction* fig.

Rub down or **sand down** Surfaces are rubbed or sanded down before paint or varnish is applied to ensure good adhesion, and to obtain a smooth finish. Bare wood is rubbed down dry; *wet-and-dry* sandpaper is used between coats of paint and varnish.

Rudder Flat or streamlined control surface at or near the *stern*. Acts like a *trim tab* fitted to the *hull*, and is designed primarily to make a boat alter course, but also contributes to the side force that resists *heeling force* and reduces *leeway*. When the rudder blade is deflected, pressure increases on the upstream side and decreases on the downstream side, the resultant hydrodynamic force being composed of a useful side force (*lift*) and *resistance* or drag (Fig A). Lift, acting at right angles to the direction of motion, causes the stern to swing in the opposite direction to that in which the rudder blade is deflected, and the hull takes up an attitude at an angle to the water flowing past, which then acts on the whole hull; the boat pivots about an axis roughly amidships at the *centre of gravity,*

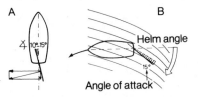

and the bow turns towards the side to which the rudder is deflected. Resistance, acting in the opposite direction to forward motion, is harmful and slows the boat; this is one reason why excessive *weather helm* is undesirable.

Rudder force acts through the rudder's *centre of pressure* and varies with the area, profile shape and *aspect ratio* of the blade, with boat speed, with the depth of water at which the rudder operates and with the *angle of attack*. Maximum lift and minimum resistance are obtained at an angle of attack (not helm angle) of between 15° and 35°, depending on the aspect ratio of the rudder. The helm angle (between the rudder or *tiller* and the *centreline*) is not always the same as

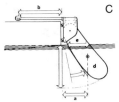

the angle of attack (between the rudder and the direction of water flow across the blade). The two angles are the same when the boat is sailing a straight course, perhaps with slight lee or weather helm, but once the boat starts to turn the stern swings towards the direction of water flow, the angle of attack becomes much smaller than the helm angle, and the rudder can be put further over without *stalling* (Fig B). Rudder *torque*, the product of rudder lift force and the distance (a' in Fig C) between the centre of pressure of the blade and the axis through the *rudder stock* or *pintles* about which the blade pivots, determines the amount of effort applied to the tiller to keep a boat on course, or to put the helm over to alter course. The greater the torque the greater the effort required, and rudder fittings, stock etc must therefore be stronger.

The area and shape of the blade vary with the type of boat and her speed (Fig D). Fast racing dinghies sailed in rough water often have a high aspect ratio blade, as left. That in the centre is less

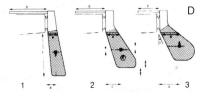

extreme, and *chord* length is greater at the tip than at the waterline, where efficiency is lowest owing to disturbed water flow close astern of the hull. Right is a typical lower aspect ratio rudder for a slower general purpose dinghy. *Yawing moment* is the product of rudder area and the moment arm, i.e. the distance between the boat's centre of gravity about which she pivots and the rudder's centre of pressure. The greater the yawing moment the smaller the *turning circle*.

Unbalanced rudders (sometimes called flap rudders) are hung on the after end of the ballast keel, on a skeg or on the transom, and are the most common type; they are hinged at the *leading edge*. *Spade rudders* have no bottom support and are often *balanced*, part of the area being forward of the rudder stock about which they pivot. Many dinghies have *lifting rudders*.

Rudder angle See *helm angle*.

Rudder blade The part of the rudder on which water flow acts. The section may be flat, or streamlined with a rounded *leading edge* and tapering *trailing edge*. The blade of a *lifting rudder* pivots between *cheeks* that are attached to the stock.

Rudder fittings All those fittings which connect the rudder to the hull, such as *pintles, gudgeons, quadrant* and the rudder brace or strap, which is a strip of metal fitted horizontally across a rudder, the forward end of which often carries a pintle or gudgeon.

Rudder head The upper end of the rudder stock, to which the *tiller* is connected.

Rudder quadrant A metal quadrant which is fitted at right angles to the rudder stock of a boat steered by a *wheel*. The *steering wires* attached to the quadrant apply leverage to the rudder, and run in the two grooves along the circumference, so that the direction of, and tension on the wires is constant at all helm angles. Alternatively a toothed pinion may mesh with a toothed quadrant to provide turning power.

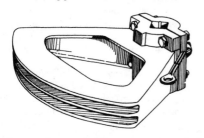

Rudder stock (US or **rudder post**) The vertical or near vertical part of the rudder, to which the blade is attached. May be at the *leading edge* of an unbalanced rudder, or a certain distance abaft the leading edge of a *balanced rudder*. When the rudder is hung beneath the hull on a *skeg* or abaft the *keel*, the stock is housed in the rudder trunk. The *tiller* or rudder quadrant is attached to the head of the stock, which is turned to deflect the blade.

Rudder stops Projections fitted to limit the angle to which the rudder can be deflected.

Rudder trunk Watertight casing through the after part of the hull, in which the rudder stock is housed. Extends from the bottom of the hull either to the *deck* or to the *sole* of a *watertight cockpit*, depending on the position of the *tiller*. See *construction* fig.

Rule of the road A general term for the regulations that govern the conduct of vessels in relation

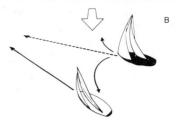

to each other, so as to prevent *collisions*. The *International Regulations for Preventing Collisions at Sea* are in force on the high seas and in many countries, but some other countries such as the USA, have additional regulations which are in force in inland waters, harbours etc. The basic right of way rules are virtually universal and, with certain exceptions for specific situations, may be summarized as follows:

SAILING VESSELS: Whether racing or not (A) when two sailing vessels are approaching each other on opposite tacks, a *port tack yacht* keeps clear of a *starboard tack yacht*; (B) when they are on the same tack, a *windward yacht* keeps clear of a *leeward yacht*; (C) an *overtaking yacht* keeps out of the way of any vessel she is overtaking; further regulations are required when racing (see *racing rules*). The *IRPCS* add that if a vessel on port tack sees another to windward but cannot be sure which tack she is on, say because a spinnaker is hiding her mainboom, the port tack leeward yacht keeps out of the way of the windward yacht.

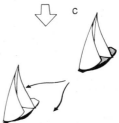

POWER-DRIVEN VESSELS: (D) when meeting *head-on* or nearly so, both alter course to *starboard*; (E) in a *crossing* situation, the vessel that sees the other on her starboard hand has to keep clear; in the two figs the sailing boat ranks as power-driven because she is using her auxiliary engine. (C) overtaking vessel always keeps clear and, when a vessel, whether sailing or power-driven, is in any doubt as to whether she is overtaking another or not, she must assume that she is overtaking and keep clear.

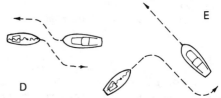

RESPONSIBILITIES BETWEEN VESSELS: under the IRPCS, when sailing vessels meet power-driven vessels the latter keep clear, except when being overtaken, but a sailing vessel has to give way to *vessels* whose *manoeuvrability is restricted*, those *engaged in fishing, constrained by draft* and *not under command*, and also has to give way in *narrow channels* and *traffic separation zones*. Sections of the US rules of the road differ considerably (see *Inland rules of the road*).

Run 1. The distance covered by a vessel between ports or, in the case of a day's run, between noon and noon or in 24 hours. 2. Noun and verb, *point of sailing;* the boat is running or on a run when she sails in the same direction as the wind is blowing, with her *sheets eased* right out. Air flow is fully *turbulent*, the sails are *stalled*, and sail *drag* alone thrusts the boat forward. The *apparent wind* is slower than the *true wind*, the difference being boat speed (see apparent wind). In spite of setting a *spinnaker* and, perhaps, other extra sails, the boat does not sail as fast as on a *broad reach* with a quartering wind, or as on a *beam reach* with the wind abeam. 3. The after part of the *underwater body* where it rises towards the *stern* and becomes finer; usually defined by the *buttock lines*.

Runabout Small, open, high-performance power boat.

Run aground To sail into water that is less deep than the boat's *draft* and to touch the bottom. Often the boat cannot get clear until she is *towed* off, *kedged* off, or *refloats* when the *tide* rises.

Run before a storm To run downwind in heavy weather with the minimum of *canvas* set, or under *bare poles*. Only advisable when wave speed or *orbital* velocity do not exceed boat speed, because of the risk of *broaching*. A *sea anchor* or *warps* can be *streamed* to slow the boat, but it may be safer to *heave to*.

Run down 1. To collide with another, usually smaller, vessel. 2. To sail parallel to a coast. 3. Running the *longitude* is to sail along a *meridian;* to run the easting down is to sail eastward along a *parallel of latitude*.

Runner 1. See *running backstay*. 2 The simplest *tackle* with one *single block;* for example a *mainsheet* with the *standing part* attached to the transom and the block to the end of the boom to provide a *mechanical advantage* of 2:1 less friction. Normally the mainsheet is rove through a second block fixed to the transom to provide a horizontal pull, i.e. as a double whip.

Runner, highfield or **backstay lever** A lever that tensions the *running backstay* quickly. The *leeward* running backstay is slacked off completely to allow the boom to be squared off on a run, and has to be

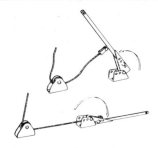

hooked back on and *set up* with the lever prior to *tacking* or *gybing*.

Running Adjective which relates to something that is movable, rather than fixed e.g. running part, rigging and bowsprit. The opposite is *standing*. See also run (2) for point of sailing.

Running backstay or **runner** or **preventer backstay** A *backstay* that supports the mast from aft at an angle, and that can be slacked off. Is often attached to the mast at the level of the upper *spreaders*, and runs down to the *side deck* beside the *cockpit*. Only the *weather* runner is set up when sailing, the *leeward* runner being slacked off to avoid hindering the set of the sail. A lever is used for tensioning (see *runner lever* and *rigging* fig).

Running fix Frequently there is only one identifiable object on which a *bearing* can be taken. The running fix can then be used to determine the vessel's position, a second bearing being taken of the same object after an interval, or a second bearing of a different object that cannot be seen simultaneously. The first bearing is taken and the *position line* is laid off on the chart. The vessels sails on for a period of, say, half an hour and the second bearing is then taken. The navigator lays off line AB representing the *course* and *distance* sailed *through the water* during the half hour,

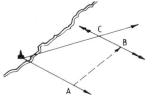

from any point on the position line (and when in tidal waters lays off a further line from B to represent the *set* and *rate* of the *tidal stream or current* during the half hour). Then he transfers

(US advances) the position line, drawing it through point B (or the end of the tidal stream vector) and parallel to the original position line. The second position line is then laid off and point C, where it cuts the transferred position line, is the vessel's position at the time the second bearing is taken.

Running lights *Lights exhibited by vessels* when *under way.*

Running moor Two *anchors* are let go, the second after the boat has moved some distance ahead of the first.

Running part All the middle parts of the *fall* of a *tackle* that move through blocks, i.e. all except the *standing* part.

Running rigging All the moving cordage and wire rope that *hoists, trims, lowers* and controls sails or gear, i.e. *rigging* which runs through *blocks,* over *sheaves* or through *fairleads* etc. Includes *halyards, sheets, topping lift, downhaul, outhaul, barber hauler, reef pendant, cunningham* etc.

Running square sail A *square sail,* formerly often set on a *yard* forward of the mast by larger cruising yachts making long passages in winds of constant direction and strength, and especially in the *trades. Twin running sails* are now preferred.

Run out To use the dinghy to take a rope away from the boat to which it is attached. The rope may be run out to a pier, to another vessel, to a pile etc. After running aground the *kedge* may be run out and let go in deeper water so that the crew can pull the boat free and refloat her.

Rust Red to reddish-brown oxide of iron formed on the surface of iron or steel that is unprotected and exposed to both air and water or moisture. Adheres loosely to the surface, and has to be removed to prevent further *corrosion,* sometimes by *shot-blasting.* The surface is then protected with suitable paint. Steel boats may be zinc sprayed or *sheathed* with plastics for protection.

S = Sierra: white *code flag* with a blue rectangle. As a single letter signal means 'I am operating astern propulsion'. *Morse code:* • • • (dot dot dot). When racing means: at or near the *starting line*, 'sail the *shortened course* prescribed in the *sailing instructions*'; at or near the *finishing line* 'finish the race either at the prescribed finishing line at the end of the round still to be completed by the leading yacht . . .' or 'in any other manner prescribed in the sailing instructions . . .'; at or near a rounding *mark*, 'finish between the nearby mark and the *committee boat*'.

Sacrificial anode or **plate** A small zinc or magnesium plate or casting fastened, for example, to a steel *hull* near a bronze *propeller* so that it will corrode instead of the hull because zinc and magnesium are less noble in the *galvanic series*. Has to be replaced after a period.

Saddle 1. Half round metal fitting on the inboard end of a *gaff*, usually with *parrel* beads round the mast, to enable the gaff to run easily up and down the mast. 2. Wooden block on a spar shaped to support another spar attached to it, e.g. between the *jib-boom* and the *bowsprit*.

Safe leeward position A racing term; the *leeward yacht* of two *close-hauled* on the same *tack* is in the safe leeward position when she is about half a boat's length ahead of the other boat, and about a boat's breadth to leeward. The wind is accelerated between the sails of the boats, to the leeward

boat's benefit, and the wind exhausted from her sails is deflected, *backing* the *headsail* of the *windward yacht*, which is unable to overtake and generally has to tack or try to break through the other boat's *wind shadow* to get a *clear wind*.

Safety boat See *rescue boat*.

Safety equipment A useful list is that specified for offshore races by the *Offshore Racing Council* to ensure the safety of all the crew in the event of a collision of the boat sinking. *Life-jackets* with whistles and *safety harness* for each member of the crew: *life-raft; horseshoe-shaped lifebuoy* with light and *drogue* (plus a *dan buoy* for long-distance races well offshore): *distress signal flares: heaving line*. Other gear that particularly affects safety includes *fire extinguishers, bilge pumps, bilge sniffers* and blowers, *anchor, storm sails, jury steerng gear, pulpits* and *lifelines, drinking water, foghorn, radar reflector, seacocks,* construction details such as *self-draining cockpit* and hatchways, window guards, distress radio transmitters, suitable navigation equipment, *navigation lights,* spare *chandlery, cordage* and *wire-rope,* as well as tools.

Safety harness (sometimes just **harness**) A webbing harness that fits over the shoulders and round the chest; some also have a leg strap. A *lifeline,* which should have two non-magnetic *snap hooks* (one half way along, the other at the end) is

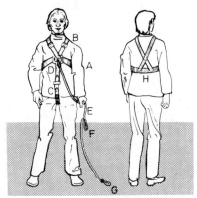

attached to an *eye* on the chest so that the crew can snap himself on to a solid part of the superstructure or to a lifeline rigged specially for the purpose, when working on deck or in the cockpit in a seaway. One harness is provided for each member of the crew. The points to check when selecting a harness are indicated in the figure.

Safety signal (radio communication) When a message (usually transmitted by a coast station) contains an important navigational or meteorological warning, it is preceded by the safety signal which is the spoken word SÉCURITÉ (pronounced say-cure-e-tay) or TTT in morse code (radiotelegraphy). The message is generally addressed to all stations, the signal being sent on a *distress frequency,* often towards the end of a three minute *silence period.* When 2182 kHz is used the message following the call is sent on the working freqency named.

Safe water marks *IALA A* safe water marks are red and white vertically striped *spherical (pillar* or *spar)* buoys with spherical *topmarks* when carried. Lights are white *isophase, occulting* or *long flashing* every 10 seconds. See endpapers.

Safe working load Of rope, usually taken as one-sixth of the *breaking load.*

Sag 1. A *forestay* sags to *leeward* when it is not sufficiently taut, or because either the forestay or the *jib halyard* has stretched. This affects sail *camber* and the *angle of attack* adversely, and the boat cannot *point* so high. 2. A boat that sags to leeward makes excessive *leeway.*

Sagging The *hull* distorts and bends downwards amidships because, when wave lengths approximately match the boat's length, she is supported at either end by wave crests, and tends to be sucked down into the trough between them. The designer allows for this by enabling the hull to be slightly flexible. Sagging is only dangerous if a boat has very long *overhangs.* The opposite is *hogging.*

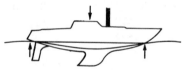

Sail 1. Separate pieces (*cloths* or panels) of *canvas* (sailcloth) are sewn together by the sailmaker to form a sail of the desired shape, which is spread to convert the wind's energy into forward propulsion. Rectangular *square sails* are set athwartship on *yards,* whereas quadrilateral or triangular *fore-and-aft sails* are set along the centreline. *Lateen,* lug-, sprit-, *gaff, gunter* and *bermudan* (US *jib-headed* or *marconi*) sails differ in shape. *Working sails* such as the *mainsail, jib,*

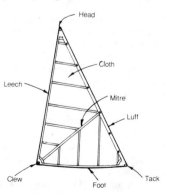

genoa and *mizzen* are made of cloth heavy enough for moderate to fresh winds, while *light-weather sails* are set when *running* and *reaching* (e.g. *spinnaker, big boy*) and in lighter breezes; they are made of lighter cloth. *Heavy-weather sails,* such as the *trysail* and *storm jib,* are smaller and may be made of heavier cloth. The parts of a sail are shown in the figure. A sail is hoisted by a *halyard* and trimmed by a *sheet.* 2. To leave a harbour, whether under sail, *power* or *oars.* 3. To travel in any vessel, including *power-driven* craft. Sail was originally the only form of propulsion available for long-distance voyaging, and the word continued to be used after the introduction of steam and internal combustion engines. 4. A boat is under sail when she is propelled solely by the action of the wind on her sails (*IRPCS* definition of sailing vessel). 5. As a noun, to go for a sail, the implication being a trip of a few hours, not racing.

Sail a boat dry Instead of *bailing* out water, it is sucked out of the bilges of a *sailing dinghy* that is sailing fast when the *self-bailer* is lowered or the *transom flaps* are opened.

Sail area Either the area of a single sail, or of several sails, e.g. that of the *working sails* is *headsail* and *mainsail* combined, or headsail, *mainsail* and *mizzen* of a *yawl* or *ketch.* The nominal area can be calculated from the *sail plan,* which gives the lengths of the sides of each sail. Measured sail area, for *handicap* purposes, is usually based on the actual area of the mainsail, measured when lying on a flat surface, plus about 75%, 85% or 100% of the *foretriangle* area, depending on the particular *rating rule.* The *luff* and *foot roaches* are usually excluded because their purpose is to provide *fullness,* and the *leech* roach is often limited by measuring breadth at half height, or by specifying maximum *batten* lengths; some rules require measurement of all roaches (for example certain *catamarans*). *Black bands* on mast and spars (or bands of another colour on a black spar) indicate the limit to which sails may be hoisted or extended when racing. *Spinnaker* areas are hard to measure, and may be taken for nominal purposes as luff times foot minus 10%; some classes require a more accurate measurement with complicated calculations.

Sail area ratios When comparing different boats, several different ratios include the area of sail carried.

SAIL AREA TO DISPLACEMENT is often taken as sail area in sq ft divided by *displacement* in tons to the $^{2/3}$ power

$$\frac{SA}{D^{2/3}}$$

Alternatively, sail area may be divided by displacement, the figure obtained giving the number of sq ft of sail carried per ton. A Flying

Dutchman with 200 sq ft of sail, weighing 364 lbs with a crew of 340 lbs, has a SA/D$^{2/3}$ ratio of 433, and a SA/D ratio of 636 sq ft per ton. A 12-metre, displacing 31 tons and carrying 1700 sq ft of sail; 172, or 55 sq ft per ton: an offshore racer, 410 sq ft of sail, 2.7 tons; 211, or 152 sq ft per ton.

SAIL AREA TO LENGTH is the square root of sail area divided by waterline length. The same 12-metre, LWL 48.7 ft, would have a SA/L ratio of 0.85, which is the same as that of the offshore racer with a 23.7 ft LWL.

SAIL AREA TO WETTED AREA is the ratio of sail area to the area of the hull beneath the waterline, and gives an indication of the boat's performance, especially in lighter winds because, at slower speeds, *frictional resistance* forms the major part of total resistance. That of the offshore racer with a wetted area of 145 sq ft is 2.83.

Sailbag Bag made of sailcloth in which a sail is stowed. The opening is closed with a *lacing* through *eyelets,* and there is often a strap at the bottom so that it can be held by a hand or foot. May have a hook by which it is attached to the *lifeline* (guardrail) or *pulpit* when changing sails. Alternatively may be a sausage-shaped bag with an opening along one side. Each bag should be labelled with the name of the sail it contains.

Sailboard A simple but unconventional sailing craft; has a normal sail set on a *mast, stepped* on an unsinkable *hull* which is like a long surfboard. The universally-jointed mast can be *raked* in all directions and, as there are no *stays, shrouds* or *sheet,* it is supported by the boardsailor who holds the *wishbone* boom and *trims* the sail with his hands. A *daggerboard* and small *skeg* provide *lateral resistance* and *directional stability* and, there being no *rudder,* the sailboard is steered by altering the relative positions of the *centre of effort*

and the *centre of lateral resistance,* i.e. by raking the mast further forward to *bear away* or further aft to *luff up*. Cannot *heel* like a normal boat; instead the mast is raked to windward in fresher winds, and the boardsailor hangs beneath the boom. Many designs have appeared since the original Windsurfer, which has international status. The *Windglider* achieved Olympic status for 1984.

Sailboat (US) or **sailing boat** (UK) A small vessel propelled by the force of the wind on her sails, now used mostly for cruising and racing. Larger sailing boats may be called yachts, and smaller open boats are more often called sailing or racing dinghies.

Sail changing cartridge A gadget like a magazine with a metal track on which the *piston hanks* of a *staysail* are held close together and open, ready to feed onto the *stay*. It is clamped to the stay when changing *headsails,* and the hanks close over the *forestay* automatically as the sail is hoisted. Considerably reduces the time and effort involved in sail changing.

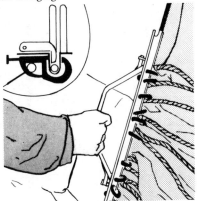

Sailcloth Woven material, originally made of flax, later of cotton and now of synthetic fibres. To avoid *stretch,* the *weft* is woven across the *warp* at high tension, providing firm dense cloth with a high *cover factor* and low *porosity. Fillers* are often added to give the cloth a smooth, almost impermeable surface and to minimize *drag*. Because *bias stretch* and *recovery* vary with the tension of the warp and weft, the appropriate sailcloth has to be selected by the sailmaker for every sail, and the sail is cut so that the tension on the cloth does not pull the sail out of shape (see *cloth construction*). Sailcloth of specific weight is used for varying sizes of sail and differing weather conditions (see *cloth weight*). The material of which awnings, tarpaulins, sail bags etc are made is also called sailcloth, but is often of poorer quality.

Sail cover A sailcloth cover, lashed over a sail that is *furled* on a boom to protect it from the weather, as well as from pollution and the ultra-violet rays that harm synthetic materials.

Sail Drive A transmission system developed by Volvo from the *outdrive*. The engine is mounted inboard, slightly abaft amidships, and drives the propeller through two bevel gears. The transmission unit may be between fin and skeg, or

partly housed in the fin keel (a compact and streamlined method). A smaller hole is required in the hull, and installation is easier because the hole is not slanting like that of a normal transmission system. Any engine can be used and positioned wherever is most desirable.

Sailing chart (US) Small scale *chart* covering a large part of the ocean, the *natural scale* being 1:600,000 or smaller.

Sailing Club Organization whose members are interested in waterborne activities, primarily sailing. See also *Yacht club*.

Sailing dinghy An open or partly decked small sailing boat, usually *una* or *sloop-rigged* with a *bermudan, gaff, gunter, lug-* or *spritsail*. Has a *centreboard* or *daggerboard* and, being easy to *capsize*, is usually fitted with *buoyancy* (US *flotation*) *tanks* or *bags* to keep her afloat when

full of water. *Stability* is due to hull shape, while wind pressure on the relatively large sail area is countered by the weight of the crew who *sit out* (US *hike*) or use a *trapeze*. There are many *racing dinghy classes*, some local, some national, some international. See also *racing dinghy*.

Sailing directions Also called Pilots (UK) or Coast Pilots (US) Official publications, each covering a specific area and providing information useful for navigation in connection with *tides, tidal streams*

or *currents, meteorology, buoyage systems, signals, harbours, coastline* and *dangers*. Unofficial guides are also available, and are written by individual authors specifically for small boat sailors.

Sailing free Not *close-hauled;* sailing with sheets eased out.

Sailing instructions The *racing rules* prescribe that details of how a race will be run must be available for every competing yacht. The instructions include information about *course, marks,* course signals, *classes, starting* time and *line, finishing line, time limit* and any special instructions for that particular race.

Sailing length Term often used in respect of the effective *waterline length* of a sailing boat when she is *heeling*.

Sailing master An expert who takes charge of a sailing yacht, usually for racing, on behalf of the owner. Organizes the racing programme, boat preparation, crew list, and running of the boat during the race; is sometimes also helmsman or foredeck chief. May be paid or amateur, usually the former.

Sailing school A commercial establishment where an individual is taught how to sail. Instruction is often in larger relatively stable dinghies, but may be in keelboats. In many sailing schools the instructors are professionally qualified, and teach a national course.

Sailing ship As opposed to a sailing boat, a large vessel with a wooden or steel hull propelled by wind on the sails. Prior to the invention of the steam engine the only ocean-going vessel, but now used at sea exclusively for *sail training*. Although, strictly, a *ship* is *full-rigged* on all masts, the term embraces all manner of sea-going vessels propelled by wind power; they are differentiated by the number of masts (up to seven), *rig* (e.g. *barque, brig, schooner*), shape of hull (e.g. *clipper*), and purpose (e.g. warships, coasters). Sailing ships reached their peak in world trade at the end of the 19th century, and many are preserved including the 'Cutty Sark' at Greenwich, the USS 'Constitution' in Boston, the 'Falls of Clyde' in Honolulu, HMS 'Victory' at Portsmouth, the 'Charles W Morgan' at Mystic Seaport, the 'Passat' in Travemünde and the 'Pommern' as a museum in Mariehamn.

Sailing triangle Term sometimes use for the *vector diagram* (q.v.) that indicates the velocities of the *true* and *apparent winds* and boat speed (the wind that arises when a boat moves over the ground).

Sailing vessel As defined in the *IRPCS*, any vessel under sail provided that propelling machinery, if fitted, is not being used. This definition is important with regard to responsibilities between vessels, because a boat using her *auxiliary engine* ranks as *power-driven*, whether her sails are hoisted or not, and she must keep out of the way of one being propelled only by the wind; she must exhibit a black *cone* point downwards by day when her sails are hoisted, and the lights of a power-driven (q.v.) vessel by night. Sailing vessels must keep out of the way of *vessels constrained by draft, engaged in fishing, restricted in their ability to manoeuvre,* and *not under command.* When *under way* at night a sailing vessel has to exhibit *side lights* and a *stern light.* Lights must be positioned where they can best be seen and, because she *heels* and a side light near the *gunwale* is often obscured by an *overlapping headsail,* a sailing vessel under 12 m is permitted to use a *tri-colour lantern* (q.v.), one under 20 m may use a *bi-colour lantern* plus stern light or alternatively, two *all-round lights* near the *masthead,* the upper red and the lower green in addition to side and stern lights; the all-round lights may not be exhibited in addition to a tri-colour lantern. A sailing vessel under 7 m in length may draw attention to her presence by means of a torch or white lantern, but if practicable is expected to exhibit side and stern lights. See *rule of the road, restricted visibility,* IMO.

Sail locker Place where sails are stowed, often in the *forepeak* or *forward cabin.*

Sail loft Large area of floor on which the outline of a sail is drawn; the place of business where sails are made.

Sailmaker Makes and repairs sails. A great deal of skill and experience is required to design, cut, sew and finish sails. When making a long voyage a cruising boat should carry at least one crew with sailmaking experience, so that damage can be repaired.

Sailmaker's darn A simple stitch with which a sail can be repaired if the edges do not have to overlap, known domestically as the herring-bone stitch.

Sail needle A needle made specifically for sewing sailcloth; the part just behind the point has a triangular section. Needles are graded to conform with the standard wire gauge, and run from 21 (very small) through 17, 16 and 15 for medium work down to 12 and 11 for the heaviest *roping* needles.

Sail number The number allocated to a boat for identification purposes; is glued or sewn to both sides of the *mainsail,* together with the *class emblem* (if any) and, in an *international class,* the *national letter(s).* Is sometimes displayed on the *spinnaker* as well.

Sailor A person who goes to sea, whether in large ships or small boats. The term is often applied to his propensity for seasickness; he is said to be a good sailor if he is immune, and a bad sailor if he is not.

Sail plan A scale drawing of the *rig,* showing all the sails and their sizes, the positions of *sheet leads* and (sometimes) the *centre of effort.* The total nominal sail area and the area of individual sails can be calculated from the sail plan.

Sail tiers, ties, stops or **gaskets** Light lines, shock cord or strips of canvas used to lash a *lowered* sail to the *boom, pulpit, lifelines* (guardrail) etc to prevent it blowing about. May also be spelt tyers.

Sail track See *mast track.*

Sail training ship A sailing ship used to train young seamen and not for commercial purposes. A number of countries run ships such as 'Sir Winston Churchill' (UK), 'Eagle' (US), 'Christian Radich' (Norway), 'Gorch Fock' (West Germany), many of which compete in the Tall Ships races. Some are *square-rigged,* others are *fore-and-aft rigged.*

St. Elmo's fire or **corposant** Luminous electrical discharge observed at the *masthead,* end of the *boom,* yardarm etc. Occurs during electrical storms and was interpreted in many ways by superstitious seamen, both as a good and bad omen. Many different thoeries are put forward as to St. Elmo's identity.

Salinity The amount of salts (solid materials) dissolved in water, measured in parts per thousand, ‰. The salinity of the sea varies as a result of evaporation, precipitation and the number of rivers that discharge fresh water into an area from about 8‰ in the Baltic to 41‰ in parts of the Red Sea. Salinity in the North Sea is about 34‰, in the Mediterranean about 36‰, in equatorial waters about 35‰, in the Indian Ocean 36‰ and in sub-polar waters about 32‰. The average salinity of rivers is about 0.1‰. Salinity affects the *density* of water, and this has to be taken into account when a boat is measured for a *rating* or *handicap* because the greater the salinity the less she *draws.*

Saloon The main *cabin.*

Saltings Low-lying land that is covered by the sea at some state of the tide.

Salt water As opposed to fresh, the water of seas and oceans. Average *salinity* is 35‰, but varies. See *sea water.*

Salvage A voluntary service which saves a vessel from danger at sea or contributes towards the safety of the vessel, those on board, or her gear and cargo. A salvage award, based on a proportion of the value of the vessel, gear or cargo saved, is made provided the vessel or person(s) on board have been in real danger and provided the service has been performed voluntarily. Awards are made on the basis of no cure – no pay, i.e. the vessel or some property must have been saved. A small boat sailor is advised to use one of his boat's lines when accepting a *tow,* to avoid the possibility of the towing boat basing a claim for a salvage award (or an increase in such an award) on having provided gear which contributed to the safety of the boat and her crew.

Sample of the bottom See *arm the lead.*

Sampson or **samson post** Strong fitting, bolted firmly to the deck, to which a *mooring line, tow-rope* or *anchor cable* is made fast. The figure shows a method of *belaying* that is particularly satisfactory for chain and larger diameter rope because it can be released when under load.

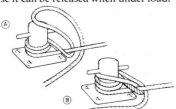

Sand 1. Sediment, the particles of which vary in size from six-hundredths of a millimetre to 2 mm. 2. A *shoal* of sand, which may dry or be permanently submerged. 3. Dry sand was formerly used in a sand glass to measure time, and ran from top to bottom through a narrow neck in a certain time. The half hour sand glass was turned every thirty minutes when all the grains had run through, and the *watch bell* was then struck. A 28-second *log*-glass was used when measuring speed with a *chip log.*

Sandbank A bank of sand, generally marked on the chart, where the water is shallower than the surrounding area.

Sand down See *rub down.*

Sandpaper Paper to which abrasive grains are glued, with which the surface to be painted or varnished is sanded down. See also *wet-and-dry.*

Sandwich construction (UK) or **cored construction** (US) A method of building, used especially for *GRP/FRP hulls.* Two resin and glass *laminates* are separated by a light-weight *core* of pressure-resistant material that holds them apart. Quality depends mainly on how well the laminate is bonded to the core. The strength to weight ratio and insulation are good, and there is little hull distortion,

even without *frames* or longitudinal reinforcement. The core may be of foamed plastics, end-grain balsa, aluminium, GRP/FRP honeycomb, phenolic resin-impregnated paper etc. The term is also applied to similar construction with a core between layers of plywood or moulded wood. See also *mylar.*

Sand yacht or **land yacht** A three-wheeled vehicle which, like a sailing boat, relies on the wind for propulsion. Races are held where sand is hard and firm. There are records of land yachts in China in the 6th century AD, and they have been sailed in the Netherlands since the Middle Ages. Similar to iceboats in appearance.

Sargasso Sea Sub-tropical sea area where there is little wind or current, lying roughly between 30–50°W, 20-30°N. Large quantities of sargassum plants, a floating tropical *kelp,* concentrate here and cover large areas, especially near the centre where they impede the passage of boats.

Satellite navigation The ship's position is fixed with the aid of signals transmitted by orbiting satellites, one of which is normally available every 35–100 minutes. The satellite transmits a signal, which contains updated coded information about variations in orbit and time. The signal is received on board, the change in *frequency* as the satellite approaches or moves away (*Doppler effect*) is measured, and the information is converted by a computer on board into *latitude* and *longitude.* The ship's position is sustained between satellite fixes by dead reckoning or some other continuous system.

Scale Proportional representation of an object. *Charts* are drawn to a natural linear scale (see *natural scale*), say of 1:80,000; one inch or centimetre on the chart then represents 80,000 inches or centimetres on the earth, i.e. 1.1 n.miles or 0.43 n.miles respectively. In the case of areas, a ratio of, say, 1:10 is multiplied or divided by 100, and volume by 1000 when scaling up or down. Thus, if a scale model is made of a boat 10 m LOA with 50 sq m of sail, displacing 500 kg, the model will be 10:10 = 1 m long, sail area will be 50:100 = 0.5 sq m and displacement will be 5000:1000 = 5 kg. See also *Beaufort scale.*

Scandalize 1. To reduce the area of sail set, particularly by *topping* the *boom,* or lowering the *peak* and *tricing up* the *tack* of a *gaff sail.* 2. Formerly, to trim the sails and yards untidily as a sign of mourning.

Scanner The rotating aerial of a *radar* set (q.v.). Transmits and receives radio pulses, enabling the *bearing* and range of an object to be established from echoes on the *display.* Most larger radar aerials are of the slotted waveguide type, but some have parabolic reflectors. The wider the scanner the narrower is the horizontal beamwidth, and the greater is the accuracy (small boat radar beamwidth is about 2.5–3°). Vertical beamwidth is greater to allow for rolling and heeling, 23–30°. Side lobes (energy usually transmitted to either side of the main beam) are reduced as much as possible.

Scantlings Originally the dimensions of *timbers,* but now extended to members made of any material. Acceptable scantlings are specified by the *classification societies* such as *Lloyds* and the *ABS.*

Scarph or **scarf** Joint between two wooden or plywood members, both of which are tapered, fastened and often glued. The length of the scarph should be at least six times the *moulding,* and is often nearer double that. A hook scarph has a step in the centre of the joint; the taper of a lip scarph

has a step at either end instead of becoming progressively finer. Scarphs are used, for example, to join the *stem* and *sternpost* to the *keel, spars* may be scarphed, and so on. In *planking* is preferable to a *butt joint* because the cross-section is not increased and the weight of a butt strap is saved.

Scend 1. Vertical movement of waves or swell against a harbour wall, pier etc. 2. The rising motion of the *bow* when it is lifted by a wave crest while the stern falls into a trough.

Schooner A *sailing ship* or *yacht* with two or more *masts, fore-and-aft rigged.* Derivation of the word is doubtful, but may be of North American

origin; it is widely used to describe a vessel with a *foremast* shorter than, or the same height as the *mainmast* which carries the *mainsail.* There are many types, such as *topsail, fore-and-aft, staysail* and *wishbone* schooners. (See also *three-mast* and *seven-mast schooners*).

Scooter A form of *ice-boat* which also scoots across water. Developed on Great South Bay of Long Island, it has two sets of runners under each bilge, is steered by altering the sheet of its balanced jib (a boom jib, the boom of which is pivoted some distance abaft the tack), and its high speed of 50–60 m.p.h. enables it to shoot across open water leads or cracks in the ice.

Scope 1. Relates to the length of *anchor cable* or rode *veered,* measured from the *bow* to the anchor on the bottom, defined as the ratio of the amount of cable veered to the depth of the water in which the boat is floating. A minimum of 3–4 times the depth of water is generally recommended for chain cable, but half as much again is needed for rope cable, especially if no length of chain is inserted between the rope and the anchor. The rise of *tide* has to be allowed for, and more cable is veered when the wind *freshens.* 2. See *screen* (radar).

Scoring system Under the Olympic scoring system, the winner of each race receives 0, and subsequent finishers points on an ascending scale; the champion is the sailor with the lowest total of points accumulated over the *series,* which normally consists of seven races; the worst result is discarded. 1st finisher 0 points, 2nd 3 points, 3rd 5.7 points, 4th 8 points, 5th 10 points, 6th 11.7 points; thereafter place plus 6 points, i.e. 7th 13 points. The points for other boats, including those that finish but retire or are disqualified are those that would be scored by the last boat if one more entry had been received. Other scoring systems, or modifications to the Olympic system, are used by different authorities and clubs, the principle normally being similar apart from the points scored by retiring and disqualified boats; frequently one that retires scores a lower number of points than one disqualified.

Scow 1. UK: a small, slow, beamy *sailing dinghy,* usually *clinker-built* with a *lugsail.* 2. US: an open, beamy, *bilgeboard* sailboat with a *flat bottom,*

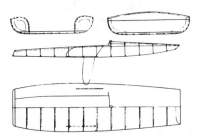

straight sides, low *freeboard,* twin *rudders* and square *bow.* Particularly popular in North American inland waters on account of the high speeds achieved. 3. To *scow an anchor* (also termed becueing) is to attach the *anchor cable* to the *crown* and *stop* it to the ring; a *foul anchor* can then be tripped by snapping the stop.

Scraper A sharp tool, often triangular, sometimes with one curved side, with which paint, varnish etc is scraped off.

Scratch boat In a *handicap* race, the boat that has to give time to all the others. Theoretically the fastest boat but, if she is to win the race, not only must she cross the finishing line first but she must have sufficent time in hand for her *corrected time* to be less than those of the slower boats finishing later which have a greater *time allowance.*

Screen 1. A board fitted to prevent the light exhibited by a lantern from being seen beyond the prescribed *sector.* 2. A screen is often fitted to *ventilators* to keep mosquitoes and other flying insects out of the cabin. 3. Screen (UK) or scope (US): the face of the *radar* or *sonar* cathode ray tube.

Screw 1. The *propeller,* q.v. 2. A *fastening.*

Screw aperture An opening left in the *deadwood* or in the *rudder* to provide space in which the *propeller* rotates.

Scud 1. Thin, low, fast-moving clouds, driven by the wind. 2. To *run* before a strong wind with very little or no sail set.

Scull 1. To propel a small boat with one *oar* over the *stern.* Usually a semi-circular notch is cut out of the *transom* to provide a fulcrum, and the oar is worked back and forth, making a figure of eight pattern in the water. 2. Naval and racing: to propel a boat with a pair of sculls, i.e. what sailing men call *rowing.* Also the small, light racing boat propelled by sculls.

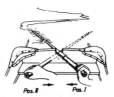

Pos. II   Pos. I

Scupper Drain hole in the *toe-rail, foot rail* or *bulwarks;* allows spray or water on deck to flow overboard. See *construction* fig.

Scuttle 1. UK: a round, glazed window in the side of the *hull* or *coach-roof;* can be opened to admit air but is watertight when closed. May have a *deadlight* cover to prevent water entering if the glass is broken by heavy seas. Frequently called porthole or portlight. 2. US: *hatch* or opening in the *deck* or in a *bulkhead,* and the cover to it. 3. To sink a vessel deliberately, e.g. by opening the *seacocks.*

Sea A word frequently used with different meanings. 1. The salty water that covers 70% of the earth, i.e. the water that makes up the oceans. 2. A large expanse of water, smaller than an ocean, often either partly (e.g. North Sea) or wholly (e.g. Dead Sea) enclosed by land. Seven seas: term now used loosely to mean the entire ocean, but originally the Mediterranean, Red and China Seas, Persian Gulf, Indian Ocean and the waters off east and west Africa; these were the waters bordering the lands settled by Greeks and ruled by Persian Kings. 3. A wave or waves, hence *choppy, green, head, steep, cross* and *following seas.*

Sea anchor or **drogue** A device streamed from *bow* or *stern* to hold a vessel bow or stern on to the wind or sea; slows her and helps to prevent her from *broaching.* Often a conical or tapering canvas bag, held open at either end by a metal frame with a *bridle* attached to a rope that is made fast on board. Opinions are divided as to the advisability of streaming a sea anchor.

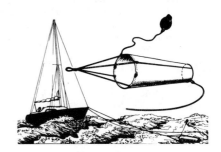

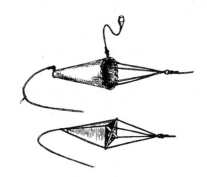

Sea-bed The bottom of the sea; details of its composition are given on *charts,* and samples can be obtained by *arming the lead.*

Seaboat A good seaboat behaves well in rough seas, but a poor seaboat behaves less satisfactorily.

Sea boots Whereas fisherman's boots reach up to the thighs, those used by yachtsmen only reach about half way up the shins, and have non-slip soles.

Sea breeze A daytime wind which blows close by the coast in temperate, sub-tropical and tropical latitudes. Land is heated more quickly than the sea by the sun's rays, the air above it rises and is replaced by cooler air flowing in from the sea. The sea breeze is normally strongest, *force* 3–4, in the early afternoon, and drops away in the evening to be replaced by a *land breeze* at night.

Sea clutter See *clutter.*

Seacock Operates like a stop-cock to prevent water entering the hull; one is fitted at every inlet and outlet below or near the *waterline,* such as the sink outlet, engine cooling water inlet, cockpit drains, and heads tubing. Is usually part of the *skin fitting,* or immediately next to the hull, and may be a screw-down wheel valve or a gate valve operated by turning a handle through 90°.

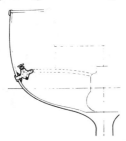

Sea criterion The *Beaufort Scale* includes a description of the state of the sea when the wind is blowing at speeds from *force* 0 to force 12. The description relates to the deep sea, and waves near the coast are often steeper but less high. *Swell* and *tidal streams or currents* also affect the state of the sea.

Sea fog See *advection fog.*

Sea gate Closes the entrance of a harbour, basin or dock to provide shelter from high seas; normally hung in pairs.

Sea horizon See *visible horizon.*

Seakindly Said of a boat that rides and performs well in heavy weather, reacting safely to the seas.

Sea legs The ability to keep one's feet in spite of the boat's *motion.* To get one's sea legs is to become accustomed to her motion and to recover from feeling seasick.

Seam 1. The space between the planks of a *carvel-built* boat, the longitudinal joining of *plating,* or the planks of a *laid deck.* Seams are often *caulked* (sometimes *splined*) to provide a watertight hull or deck. 2. Join between two pieces of *sailcloth.* A zigzag stitch is used when making a sail, but repairs can only be made in this way on board if the boat carries a sewing machine. The alternative is to repair sails with a *sail needle,* sailmaker's *palm* and either a *sailmaker's darn* or a *round* or flat seaming *stitch.* Adhesive repair tape is an excellent alternative, and holds not just for hours but for weeks, even under heavy load.

Seaman General term for a person whose profession is at sea. More precisely relates to a person's behaviour and competence. Seamanlike is a complimentary term.

Seamanship General term covering all the skills and arts which, combined with experience and the ability to improvise, enable a sailor to face every situation at sea, i.e. boat handling, repairs and maintenance, navigation, weather lore, knowledge of the right of way rules etc.

Search and rescue, SAR The whole co-ordinated operation of searching for and rescuing mariners (and aircrew) in *distress.* HM *Coastguard* and the US Coast Guard are responsible for co-ordinating measures, which frequently involve the use of life-boats, aircraft, helicopters and, sometimes, nearby shipping. See also *Automated Mutual-Assistance Vessel Rescue System.*

Searoom Room in which a vessel can manoeuvre without difficulty, with no *obstructions* and no danger of *running aground.*

Seasickness The organs that enable a human to balance are disturbed by the *motion* of the boat; he feels giddy, sweats clammily, is miserable and apathetic, and vomits. Seasickness is accentuated by lack of fresh air, inactivity and anxiety, but the body adapts after a time. People are affected differently, and pills can be obtained which help most people by sedating the balancing organs.

Sea smoke or **Arctic sea smoke** Low-lying *fog* that forms when sea temperature is considerably higher than the very cold air flowing over it (c.f. *advection fog* when the reverse is the case). The cold air absorbs moisture, becomes saturated, and fog forms. The particular danger for small boats is that sea smoke is often only 33–66 ft (10–20 m) high and, whereas a *look-out* on a large ship can see all round the vessel, the *visibility* of the man in a small boat is very restricted. Most common in the Antarctic and Arctic, but also occurs in the Baltic, off Maine and Nova Scotia and in the Gulf of St. Lawrence.

Sea state scale　Much like the *Beaufort scale,* but grades seas according to their height and character. The World Meteorlogical Office scale is given first, followed by the US Hydrographic Scale in brackets.

0 = calm, glassy, 0 ft (calm 0 ft)
1 = calm, rippled, 0–0.5 ft (smooth 1 ft)
2 = smooth, wavelets, 0.5–1.66 ft (slight 1–3 ft)
3 = slight, 1.66–4 ft (moderate 3–5 ft)
4 = moderate, 4–8 ft (rough 5–8 ft)
5 = rough, 8–13 ft (very rough 8–12 ft)
6 = very rough, 13–20 ft (high 12–20 ft)
7 = high,20–30 ft (very high 20–40 ft)
8 = very high 30–45 ft (mountainous 40 ft)
9 = phenomenal, over 45 ft (confused)

The Beaufort scale includes probable and minimum wave heights.

Sea stay　Trade name of a particular *headfoil* (q.v.).

Sea wall　A wall built of stone or concrete to prevent erosion, or to protect low-lying land near the coast or an estuary from being flooded by the sea.

Seaward　Towards the sea.

Sea water　The *salinity* or salt content of sea water varies, but the average is 35 parts per thousand (35‰). Sea water contains approximately 27.2‰ sodium chloride (cooking salt), 3.8‰ magnesium chloride, 2.0‰ magnesium sulphate and small quantities of calcium, potassium, bromide etc. Sea water should not be drunk under any circumstances, mainly on account of the high sodium chloride content. Mass *density* varies with temperature, salinity and pressure, but is about 64 lb/cu ft and 1.025 tonnes/cu m; *specific gravity* is about 1.025.

Seaway　A stretch of water where there are waves, whether wind-raised waves or swell, but often a combination of both.

Seaworthy　A vessel that is fit to go to sea, and to withstand wind and waves in heavy weather. A sailing boat must be large enough, strongly built, *self-righting* and properly *fitted out.* Generally has a *watertight* or *self-draining cockpit,* and is able to *ride out a storm* and *claw off* a *lee shore.* A too lightly built or inadequately equipped or manned boat is unseaworthy, as are dinghies and open centreboard boats.

Second　Unit of measurement of time, and of angles and arcs such as *latitude* and *longitude.* One-sixtieth of a *minute,* q.v. A boat making one *knot* sails 6076 ft (1852 m) in one hour, 101.26 ft (30.87 m) in one minute and 1.69 ft (0.514 m) in one second. The last figures provide a convenient

measure when calculating speed with the *Dutchman's log.* See under *Co-ordinated Universal Time* for definition of *SI* second.

Secondary channel　Less easy to navigate than the main ship channel, but may be marked by *buoys, perches* etc; often unlit.

Secondary depression　A low pressure area that forms within the area of an existing *depression,* often where the *isobars* bulge. Sometimes a family of depressions forms, one following the other, each with its own *fronts.* See *anticyclone* fig.

Secondary port (US **subordinate station**)　A port, harbour or locality for which daily predictions are not published in the *Tide Tables,* but the times and heights of *high* and *low water* can be found by applying the *tidal differences* given in the tables to the high and low water heights and times given for a nearby *standard port* (US reference station).

Section　1. Shows the shape of a solid object when it is cut by a plane. The *mast section* (q.v. for fig) shows the shape of the mast walls when cut horizontally; the *track* in the *mainsheet track* fig has an X-section, etc. 2. In the *lines drawings* the word section relates to the vertical transverse sections shown in the *body plan* (they appear as straight lines in the *half-breadth* and *profile plans*). The vertical fore-and-aft sections are called *buttocks,* the horizontal sections *waterlines.*

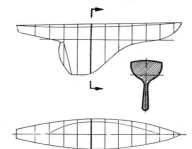

Sector light　A light which is exhibited by a *lighthouse* or *beacon* erected on land or in shallow

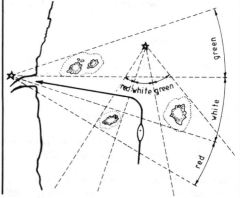

water, and which can be seen only within an arc limited by *bearings*. The limits of the sectors are marked on *charts*, the bearings being given as *true bearings* from seaward on charts and in the *List of Lights*. A sector light may exhibit different colours, have different *characteristics* in two or more sectors, or show an intensified light over a certain sector. Some sector(s) may be *obscured*.

Sécurité The internationally recognized spoken safety signal used before transmitting a message containing an important meteorological or navigational warning. Usually used by a shore station, but may be sent by a ship to warn of a sudden danger to navigation. From the French, it is pronounced say-cure-e-tay.

Seiche Rise and fall of water in a partly enclosed lake, bay, basin harbour etc due to some disturbing force such as a change in *atmospheric pressure* or *ground swell,* but not to *tide*-raising forces. Water level oscillates about a nodal point, and there is no *orbital motion* of water particles.

Seismic sea wave See *tsunami.*

Seize To bind two ropes together, or a rope to a *spar* with light line. An *eye* is made in the end of the line and drawn tight around one rope. For a flat seizing, which is used when the load on both ropes is equal, a series of turns is taken round both ropes; the end is passed back between the ropes and over the series of turns, drawn tight and the seizing is finished with a *clove hitch*. Round seizing

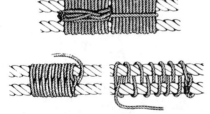

is similar, but a second series of turns is taken above the first. Racking seizing is used when the load on the ropes is unequal or the pull is in opposite directions; figure of eight turns are taken around the ropes (under and over alternately), followed by a series of straight turns taken between them. a rose seizing is used to attach an eye to a spar.

Self-bailer A device fitted in the bottom of a sailing dinghy to empty water from the *bilges*. When pushed down beneath the hull the water flowing past reduces local pressure and sucks water out of the dinghy, provided that she is moving fast enough; at slower speeds it must be shut to prevent water from entering. A *transom flap* serves the same purpose. Self-bailing cockpit: see *self-draining*.

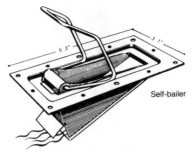

Self-bailer

Self-draining or **self-bailing cockpit** A *watertight cockpit* with drains through which rain, spray or water shipped on board is led to the sea. The drains are usually crossed to discourage water from entering when the boat *heels* and, to comply with *ORC* requirements, must empty the cockpit at all angles of heel. *Seacocks* are fitted at the skin or shell for safety.

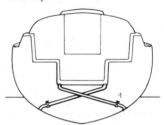

Self-righting Said of a boat that returns to an upright position from any angle of *heel,* and even after *turning turtle. Lifeboats,* in particular, must be self-righting. A *keelboat* rights herself if her *ballast keel* is heavy enough and the *centre of gravity* low enough to turn her upright after *capsizing,* always provided that *hatches, cockpit* etc are absolutely watertight so that she does not sink in the process. A boat may also have sufficient *buoyancy compartments* or flotation material to keep her afloat when full of water.

Self-steering gear Device which enables a boat to keep to the desired *course* without assistance from the *helmsman*. The simplest method, often used when *trade wind* sailing, is to sheet *twin jibs* to the *tiller* so that the change of wind pressure on the sails when the boat *luffs up* or *bears away* returns her automatically to her course. *Vane gear* operates mechanically; the vane, set at an angle to the wind, keeps the boat on a course which is

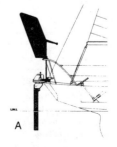

related to wind direction. The vane may be connected directly to the tiller, but more efficient systems have a separate pendulum rudder, or actuate a *trim tab* on the *trailing edge* of the main *rudder*, which is moved to counter any tendency to luff or bear away. Electrically-powered *autopilots* keep a boat on a *compass course*.

Self-tailing winch A *winch* with tapering grooved jaws above the drum. The crew takes three or four turns round the drum, and then leads the sheet or downhaul into the jaws, which grip it tightly for about three-quarters of a turn. When the sheet is hardened a lever eases the *tail* out of the jaws, leaving them free to continue gripping the sheet as it comes off the drum. The sheet does not have to be cleated.

Self-trimming jib A *jib* that shifts from one side of the boat to the other automatically when she is *tacked* or *gybed* (see *boom jib*).

Semi-balanced rudder The upper part of the *rudder* is hung on the *skeg* and is unbalanced, but the lower part beneath the skeg is *balanced*. The rudder area and *stock* can be smaller than those of an unbalanced rudder, and less effort is required from the helmsman.

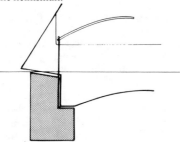

Semi-diameter *Apparent altitude* has to be corrected to allow for the half diameter of sun and moon, because it is the altitude of the upper or lower *limb* that is taken with the *sextant*, whereas the positions of the bodies given in the *Nautical Almanac* relate to their centres. The daily semi-diameter of the moon, and that of the sun every third day, is given in the Nautical Almanac. The correction for semi-diameter is included in the *Altitude Correction Tables*.

Semi-diurnal tide (Semi-diurnal means twice daily). There are two *high waters* and two *low waters* in each *lunar day*, the tidal cycle repeating roughly every 12 hrs 25 mins, whereas a *diurnal tide* has one tidal cycle daily. Semi-diurnal tides are governed largely by the *phase of the moon*.

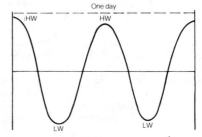

Semi-great circle Half a *great circle*, e.g. the *prime meridian, longitude* 0°, and all other *meridians*.

Semi-planing The interim state between displacement sailing and *planing,* when a boat is supported partly by *byoyancy* and partly by *dynamic lift*. A boat described as a planing dinghy is really semi-planing.

Semi-rigid sail A *wing sail,* the forward third of which is a symmetrical profiled yard with a *groove* at the *trailing edge*. The groove holds the cloth sail, which is often *fully-battened*. Together they form an efficient *aerofoil* pivoting on a mast. The rig was successfully used by 'Lady Helmsman' in the *International Catamaran Challenge Cup* races, but is forbidden in most international classes.

Sennit Three to nine strands of cordage are plaited in various patterns, such as common, square, flat. Used to make mats, chafing gear etc.

Sense When the *loop* or *ferrite rod aerial* of a *direction finder* is rotated to find the *bearing* of a *radio beacon*, two *nulls* are obtained, 180° apart. A separate sense aerial is often fitted because, although there is normally little possibility of confusion, an error of 180° could occur, say when taking the bearing of a radio beacon on an island or light vessel.

Sensible horizon The horizontal plane tangent to the earth at the observer's position; it is parallel to the *rational horizon* which passes through the earth's centre, and perpendicular to the line between the earth's centre and the observer's *zenith*. The *apparent altitude* of a *heavenly body* is its angular distance above the sensible horizon, and has to be corrected for *refraction, semi-diameter* and *parallax* to obtain the *true altitude*.

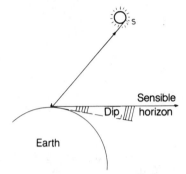

Series (US **stock**) **production** Virtually identical boats, generally *GRP/FRP,* built in quantity. Sometimes there are alternative accommodation lay-outs for the same hull moulding.

Series racing Instead of competing in a single race, boats take part in a number of separate races held over a period, occasionally during a single day, more often over consecutive days or during an entire season. In Championship and Olympic series, the winner on points, generally over seven races, is the boat that has accumulated the lowest total (see *scoring system*), each boat often being allowed to discard the worst result. There may be prizes for the winners of individual races, as well as prizes for the leading boats on points.

Serve To cover and protect a splice, or part of a rope, with turns of *small stuff* would round tightly against the *lay,* often after *worming* and *parcelling.* The serving is generally treated to make it waterproof

Serving mallet Tool used when serving a rope to keep the *small stuff* being applied at a constant and greater tension. The head of the mallet is grooved to fit the rope or line being served.

Servo rudder and **tab** A component of *self-steering gear;* may be a tab, fitted on the *trailing edge* of the main *rudder* and turned by the *vane,* so that water flowing past moves the rudder in the opposite direction, or a pendulum servo rudder that operates indipendently of the main rudder.

Set 1. The direction to which a *tidal stream or current* flows (c.f. wind, which is described by the direction from which it blows). A vessel is said to be set when she is carried by a tidal stream in a certain direction; if she has been set 3 miles to the north-west, drift is 3 miles and set is north-west. 2. A sail is said to set well or badly. 3. See also *set sail.*

Set flying To set a sail that is attached only at *head, tack* and *clew,* the *luff* being neither *hanked* to a *stay* nor held to a *mast.*

Set sail 1. To start out on a voyage, passage or for a short sail, whether *under sail* or *power.* 2. To hoist or spread a sail.

Set square Two transparent set squares are used for *plotting;* at least one is graduated in degrees from 0–180°, often round the edge, the centre

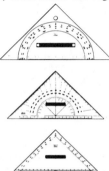

point being at the centre of the hypotenuse. The *course* or *bearing* is referred to a *meridian* by sliding one set square along the edge of the other, as shown in the figure.

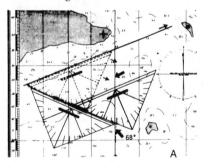

Setting At the visible set of sun and moon, the upper *limb* disappears below the *horizon* but the body's centre is lower. An *azimuth* can be taken at sunset and moonset, the times of visible sunset and moonset being tabulated in the *Nautical Alamanac* for every third day (sun) and daily (moon) for an observer with no *height of eye* at various *latitudes* on the *Greenwich meridian;* 16' is allowed for *semi-diameter* and 34' for horizontal *refraction.*

Set up the standing rigging To tauten the *standing rigging,* e.g. with *turnbuckles* (UK or rigging screws), *backstay adjusters* or *lanyards.* The *leeward runner* is set up before *tacking* or *gybing.*

Seven-eighths rig *Rig* with the *forestay* attached about $7/8$ths of the way up the mast. The *fore-triangle* is smaller than that of a *masthead-rigged* yacht.

Seven-mast fore-and-aft schooner. The largest *sailing ship* built was called the 'Thomas W Lawson', and had seven *fore-and-aft* rigged masts. She was a failure because, unlike *square-rigged* vessels, the many *gaff sails* and *topsails,* set one behind the other, could not all be trimmed to the optimum *angle of attack*. Her masts were named by the crew after the days of the week.

720° turn An alternative penalty to disqualification, performed after infringing one of the right-of-way *racing rules*. The yacht exonerates herself by making two full 360° turns at the first opportunity after the incident, and must keep clear of all other yachts while doing so.

Sextant Precision navigational instrument with which angles are measured, i.e. the *altitude* of a *heavenly body* (*celestial navigation*), the *vertical sextant angle* subtended by an object of known height, or the *horizontal sextant angle* subtended by two identified objects (*coastal navigation*). The fixed parts of the sextant are the frame, graduated arc, telescope (sometimes with *rising piece*) and horizon glass, one half of which is clear glass while the other half is silvered to reflect the image received from the index glass. The index bar rotates about the centre of the arc; it has a worm wheel which engages the toothed rack on the arc, and a quick release clamp so that it can be moved quickly along the arc; it carries a *vernier* or *micrometer drum* at the lower end for fine adjustment and, near the pivot, the index glass. Shades are provided for both glasses to protect the user's eye from glare and the sun's rays. To measure the altitude of the sun, the navigator views the horizon through the horizon glass and moves the index bar along the arc to bring down the image of the sun

until it is visible in the horizon glass; then he turns the vernier tangent screw or micrometer drum until the lower *limb* is touching the *horizon*. The degrees of the angle measured are read on the arc opposite the engraved mark on the index bar, and the minutes are read on the vernier or drum. The word sextant is derived from the arc, which is one-sixth of a circle, 60°, but the mirrors enable angles to be measured up to 120°. An *octant* is similar, but the arc is one-eighth of a circle, 45°. The figure shows an inexpensive modern plastics sextant.

Sextant altitude The *altitude* of a *heavenly body* as measured by the sextant; the angular distance of the body above the *visible horizon*. Has to be corrected for *index error, dip, refraction, semi-diameter* and *parallax* to find the *true altitude*.

Sextant errors The errors that are adjustable are (a) collimation, the telescope is not parallel to the plane of the instrument; (b) *index,* the *index glass* is not parallel to the *horizon glass* when the index is at zero; (c) perpendicularity, the index glass is not perpendicular to the plane of the instrument; (d) side error, the horizon glass is not perpendicular to the plane of the instrument.

Shackle 1. Link, usually made of stainless steel, galvanized iron or bronze; connects ropes or wires to sails, *blocks* etc, chain cable to the *anchor,* and is used for many other purposes. The most common type has a bolt (or pin) with a thread on the end; this passes through one lug, across the open end (jaws), and is screwed into the other lug. Some have a captive pin that cannot be dropped overboard (d). A straight or D-shackle (c) is D-shaped, a bow or harp shackle (a) has curved sides, and a twisted shackle (b) has a 90° twist in it. The bolt of a forelock shackle is retained by a forelock or a *split pin* (US cotter pin) that passes through an eye in the bolt beyond the lug. Stainless strip shackles are often longer than the screw bolt type, and may have a retaining bar to prevent the shackle pin from falling out. Some have a hole for use with a *ball terminal,* and many have a captive pin. Never more than about 40% of the *breaking load* should be applied. See also *snap, swivel, spring snap* and *link shackles*. 2. Verb: to shackle on is to connect,

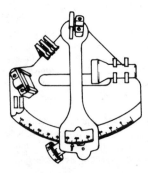

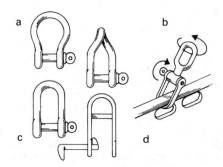

e.g. the *halyard* to the sail, or the *shroud* to the *chain plate* with a shackle. 3. 12½ *fathoms* or ¹/₈th of a *cable*, the standard amount of chain cable between joining shackles; sometimes taken as 15 fathoms.

Shackle spanner, key or **tool,** sometimes **shackler** Simple metal tool with a tapering slot with which shackle bolts, butterfly nuts etc can be turned to tighten them. Many sailor's knives incorporate a shackle spanner.

Shadow pin (sometimes called **sun compass**) A vertical pin in the centre of the *compass card* or on the *azimuth mirror;* the *azimuth* of the sun is found from the shadow cast on the card. It is however easier to check the accuracy of the *compass* with an azimuth at sunset or sunrise. The Vikings set a wooden post on a floating block of wood, the height being such that *latitude* was indicated by the length of the shadow when the sun was in *transit.*

Shaft log, shaft chock or **tube chock** The *member* through which the *propeller shaft* tube passes.

Shake A longitudinal crack in a length of timber, often a wooden spar.

Shake out a reef Either to turn the *boom* to take out a *roll,* or to untie the *reef points* and release the *pendants* so that more area of sail can be set when it has been *hoisted* higher up the mast.

Shallow(s) Adjective: shallow, not deep. Noun: shallows; an area in a river estuary etc where the water is not so deep as it is further upstream or downstream.

Shank The long central part of the *anchor* between the ring and the *crown.*

Shape (US **day shape**) 1. The *IRPCS* specify that certain types of vessels must exhibit signal shapes to indicate their state or occupation, e.g. one black *ball* – vessel at *anchor;* two black balls – *not under command;* three black balls – *aground;* black *cone* point down – *vessel sailing* but using her engine; *basket* or two cones apexes together – *vessel engaged in fishing;* ball over *diamond* over ball – *vessel restricted in her ability to manoeuvre;* diamond – *tow* over 200 m in length. A vessel *constrained by her draft* may exhibit a *cylinder.* 2. To shape a course is to work out the course to steer, and to start along it.

Sharpen up To sail closer to the wind.

Sharpie 1. Type of boat developed in the US with *flat-bottomed* hull, two masts with leg-of-mutton sails, and *centreboards* or *leeboards.* 2. *Hard chine,* flat-bottomed, open sailing dinghy,

such as the 12 sq m Sharpie, which was designed by Kröger with a *gaff rig* in 1928, converted to *bermudan* (US *marconi*) rig and belatedly selected as an *Olympic class* in 1956.

Shear pin Soft metal pin designed to break before a load becomes too great for some other part, say of an *outboard engine* or *self-steering gear,* when hitting *flotsam* or *running aground.*

Sheathing (US or **covering**) Covering which is applied to the *bottom,* and which extends just above the *waterline;* protects the *hull* from attack by marine borers. Traditionally copper or sometimes wood, but now more often a thin *GRP/FRP laminate. Decks* may be sheathed to make them watertight and to provide protection. A PVC or similar waterproof material that wears well, with a rough surface to give a good foothold, may be glued to the deck; alternatively a GRP/FRP laminate may be applied, the final coat of *resin* having non-slip grit added.

Sheave A wheel over which rope or wire runs. May be in a *block* or a sheave box, or fitted in an opening in a spar like the masthead sheave over which the main halyard runs. Single blocks have one sheave, *double, sister* and *fiddle blocks* have two. Often alters the lead of a line, as at the masthead when the downward pull on the halyard is converted to an upward pull on the sail. When a sheave is fitted in an aperture, there must be the minimum of *clearance* between the sheave sides and the sides of the hole so that the line cannot jump out and jam. The sheave must be the right size for the line that runs over it and the sides should not be fully enclosed because the line would *chafe* when pulled sideways. A sheave box may contain one or more sheaves, and can be fastened to the structure wherever required to alter the lead of a rope.

Sheepshank A method of shortening a line on which there is continuous tension. A *half-hitch* is taken over both ends of a double *bight*. The knot will release as soon as tension eases, unless the loops are *stopped* to the *standing parts*.

Sheer 1. The curvature of the *deck* as seen from the side. Normally the deck curves upwards towards *bow* and *stern, freeboard* being least at some point between them. When a boat has reverse or hogged sheer, the curve is convex and freeboard is highest roughly *amidships*. Straight sheer; there is no curvature. Compound sheer; reverse sheer forward combined with straight or normal sheer aft. 2. A boat on a *mooring* or at *anchor* in tidal waters may be given a sheer by lashing the *helm* to one side to discourage her from sheering about, i.e. from swinging wildly from side to side when a gusty wind and the *tidal stream or current* do not

come from the same direction. 3. A vessel is said to take a sheer when she goes off course unexpectedly.

Sheer clamp See *clamp*.

Sheerguard See *rubbing strake*.

Sheer legs Pair of poles that are splayed at the bottom but meet at the top where a *tackle* is attached. Used for *stepping* or unstepping a mast.

Sheer off To turn away from another vessel and, in the case of a human being, to turn away from another person.

Sheer plan See *profile plan*.

Sheer pole A bar or batten fitted across the base of several *shrouds* to prevent them turning.

Sheer strake The uppermost *strake* of the sides, above which the *covering board* is laid. Is often thicker than the rest of the *planking*, and is fastened to the *frames*. A sheerguard or *rubbing strake* may be attached along it outboard.

Sheet 1. Rope, line or wire rope, often rigged as a *tackle*, generally *rove* through *blocks* and attached either to a *boom* or the *clew(s)* of the *sail*, the lateral movement of which it controls. Named after the sail it serves, i.e. *mainsheet, jib, mizzen* and *spinnaker* sheets. A sheet is *eased out* or *hardened* to *trim* the sail to the wind, and is liable to *chafe* through being *made fast* in *jam cleats* and sheet jammers. Heavily stressed and, today, is generally made of *polyester fibres* to limit *stretch*. Must be large enough to handle, flexible, and often has a casing of softer fibres so that it does not slip in the hands or when made fast. 2. To sheet in is to harden in the sail, bringing it closer to the *centreline*. Sheet out is also used occasionally now (esp US and boardsailing). To sheet home is to harden the sheet until it is taut and the sail drawing. 3. See *sternsheets*.

Sheet bend A knot used to *bend* a rope or line to an *eye*, or to join two ropes of different sizes such as a *heaving line* to a *tow-rope*. can also be used for *flags*. A *double sheet bend* (q.v.) is more secure.

Sheeting sails to spars Under the *IYRU racing rules* a sail may be sheeted to a *boom* regularly used for a *working sail* and permanently attached to the mast to which the *head* of the working sail is set, but *outriggers* (q.v.) are not permitted. Under

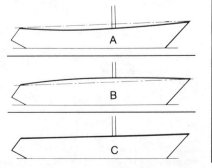

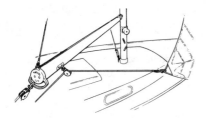

the *IOR* a *headsail sheet* can be led to a fitting on the *mainboom*, and a band of a different colour to the *black band* that limits the E measurement (see IOR) is painted on the boom to limit the position of the *bail* or sheet *block* or *eye*.

Sheet lead See *headsail sheet lead* and *mainsheet*.

Sheet winch A machine for sheeting sails, often used for other purposes as well. After turns have been taken round the drum and the slack of the sheet has been hauled in by hand, the winch is rotated by a handle (US crank) that is inserted above the drum of a top-action winch; the handle can be turned through a full circle, whereas the handle of a bottom-action winch can only be moved through an arc limited by the sheet, and has to be pumped back and forth. Because the

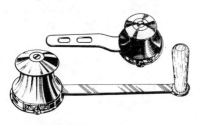

speed ratio is inversely proportional to the *power ratio*, any saving in effort is always made at the expense of speed, and many winches have two or even three gears. Some operate with no reduction of effort at a *gear ratio* of 1:1 when turned clockwise, but at 2:1 when turned counterclockwise, so combining greater initial speed with greater power when required to sheet the sail *home*. *Snubbing winches* may be fitted for the *headsail* sheets of small dinghies, while *coffee grinders* or *cross-linked winches* are required for sheeting the powerful headsails of larger high-performance racing yachts. See also *self-tailing*.

Shelf 1. Longitudinal *member* which supports the *deck beams* and to which they are secured. Sometimes called beam shelf (US clamp or beam clamp). See *construction* fig. 2. An effective method of varying sail *camber* is to sew a zip along the sail above the *foot*, curving up from the *tack* and then down again to the *clew*; the zip is opened to increase *fullness* when *reaching* and *running*, and is closed to flatten the sail for a *beat* (c.f. *flattening reef*).

Shell The outside covering of a steel, light alloy or *GRP/FRP hull*, c.f. *skin*.

Shelving Said of a sea-bed that slopes upwards gradually; the opposite of *steep-to*.

Shielding corrosion A type of *corrosion* suffered by stainless steel if it is deprived of oxygen (which endows it with a form of protective coating).

Shingle Coarse gravel or small pebbles, rounded by the action of the sea.

Ship 1. A sea-going vessel, larger than a boat. 2. Strictly, a three-masted *full-rigged sailing ship* with a full set of *square sails* on each mast; similarly four-mast and five-mast ship (but see *sailing ship*). 3. To ship is to take something on board, especially *seas* in heavy weather. 4. To place fittings or gear in their positions ready for working, e.g. a *rudder* is shipped when hung on the *pintles*. 5. Ship oars: both to place them in *rowlocks*, ready for *rowing*, and to bring them *inboard* when ceasing to row.

Ship canal A *canal* that is connected to the sea, and large enough for sea-going shipping to pass through.

Ship chandler Supplier of marine stores, such as *cordage, blocks, shackles* etc.

Ship husbandry Term that embraces the maintenance of the entire boat, including all work done to maintain and repair *rigging, sails*, machinery and structure.

Shipping Ships collectively, often merchant ships. Also used as an adjective.

Shipping forecast Weather forecast, broadcast several times daily specifically for the benefit of those at sea, giving the weather situation and its anticipated development. Gale and *storm warnings* are given at the beginning and end of the broadcast. Vessels equipped with *weather facsimile* systems can obtain weather map facsimiles from special transmissions. Details of shipping forecast times and *frequencies* can be obtained from national authorities such as the US National Weather Service, or the UK Meteorological Office, and details are printed in publications such as *Reed's Nautical Almanac, Royal Yachting Association* booklet etc.

Shipping lane A busy track across sea or ocean. Over long distances is generally the *great circle* route and, consequently, the shortest distance between two ports or points on coasts, taking weather conditions for the time of year into account. In many congested waters *traffic separation schemes* (q.v.) are in force. Yachts should always hoist *radar reflectors* when near a shipping lane.

Ship's bell Large suspended bell with a rope attached to the clapper. Is struck every half hour to mark the passage of time, the half hours by an uneven number of strokes and the hours by an even number. All four-hour *watches* end with 8 bells, e.g. at noon. Formerly time was measured by a *sand* glass. The ship's bell is also struck in *restricted visibility* when at *anchor* or *aground*.

Shipshape Neat and efficient, as in 'shipshape and Bristol fashion'.

Ship's papers For small pleasure boats, generally consist of the *Certificate of Registry* or some proof of ownership, *customs* paperwork, perhaps receipts from *harbour masters* and, possibly a *warrant* to fly a *defaced ensign*. Also the operator's certificate when R/T is carried.

Shipwreck The loss of a ship at sea, on shore, rocks etc. Under the International Law of the Sea *wreck* (q.v.) includes *jetsam, flotsam, lagan* and *derelict* found in or on the shores of the sea or of any tidal waters.

Shoal An area offshore where water is so shallow that a ship might run aground. Often *buoyed* when near a shipping *channel*. As an adjective shallow; as a verb, of water, to become shallow.

Shoal draft A boat that *draws* less water than would be expected for her size; generally intended for cruising in shallow waters.

Shoal waters Shallow, navigable by small boats that *draw* little water, but not by shipping and therefore often good cruising ground.

Shock cord Elastic rubber strands encased in a sheath of synthetic fibres, useful on board for *lashing* sails to the *boom* or *pulpit*, holding *halyards* clear of the mast etc. Generally has plastic hooks or eyes at either end. Shock-cord reefing: see *hook reefing*.

Shoe 1. Piece of wood on which an object rests, such as the *heel* of a *sheer leg*. 2. A strip fitted beneath the *keel* or *rudder* for protection. 3. Metal fitting, fastened to the structure; takes a *pelorus*, or the register of a *patent log*.

Shoot or **shoot up** When the boat is *luffed up*

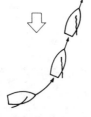

head to wind, she shoots up until she has lost all *way*. For example, when picking up a mooring buoy the helmsman estimates how far she will shoot before coming to a stop. A boat also shoots up when *going about*, and because a heavy keel-boat carries her way further she is put about more slowly than a light centreboard dinghy which loses way almost instantly.

Shoot the sun To take the *altitude* of the sun with a *sextant* or *octant*.

Shore 1. Where the sea meets the land; the limit of the sea. 2. The land. 3. Heavy props that support a vessel under the *turn of the bilge* when she is on land. 4. To prop up a vessel with shores.

Shorten course The *course* prescribed in the *sailing instructions* may be shortened before or during a race by the *race committee*, perhaps owing to lack of wind, too much wind, or because a *mark* in the course has gone *adrift. Code flag S* is flown at or near the *finishing line*, a mark of the course, or the *starting line*.

Shorten in Decrease the amount of *cable veered*, usually preparatory to *weighing anchor*.

Shorten sail To reduce the amount of sail set, whether by *reefing*, partly or completely *furling* a *roller jib*, or by setting a smaller sail in place of a larger.

Short keel Relates to the *fore-and-aft* length of the *keel*. A short keel is typical of the current *fin and skeg* configuration of immersed hull profile.

Short sea Wave length is short in relation to the height of the waves, resulting in steeper seas that are more awkward to take. Generally used to describe relatively small *choppy* seas in coastal waters.

Short splice Joins two ropes or lines of the same size permanently. The ends are unlaid for a shorter distance than when making a *long splice*, and the *strands* of one rope are tucked under those of the other, without reducing their individual diameters.

For natural fibres at least three tucks are required, but a minimum of five is needed for synthetic fibres. Because the diameter is increased, the splice is unsuitable if the rope is to be rove through a block or sheave, but it is stronger than the long splice.

Short tack 1. Or short board: when an objective does not lie directly to *windward,* one tack is shorter than the other (see *long tack*). 2. Short tacking is to change tacks frequently, often in a *narrow channel,* but may be for tactical reasons during a race.

Shot-blasting A steel hull can be blasted with quartz sand under pressure to remove all particles of *rust* etc before primer is applied.

Shower Heavy precipitation of short duration, generally of rain but may be of snow or hail. Showers are associated with cold *air masses,* and occur after a *cold front* has passed. The sky is generally clear, and *visibility* is good between showers, but the wind is *gusty.*

Shroud Part of the *standing rigging;* supports the mast laterally. Sometimes solid *rod rigging* but usually *wire rope* which runs from a point on the mast down to the sides, where it is attached to a *shroud adjuster,* or to a *chain plate* firmly bolted to the sides or *laminated* into the *hull,* or to a *deck plate.* The shroud is tensioned by means of a *turnbuckle* (UK or rigging screw), inserted between the rigging wire and the chain plate; formerly *deadeyes* and *lanyards* were used for tensioning, and lanyards are still used in many small dinghies. Longer *spreaders* and, consequently, a greater angle between the shrouds and the mast at the mast fitting give increased support, and permit smaller wire rope with a lower *breaking strain* to be used. In larger yachts and sailing ships, *ratlines* may be secured between the shrouds either side, to provide steps, for the crew when going *aloft.* Shrouds may also be fitted to provide lateral support for a *bowsprit* or *bumpkin.*

Shroud adjuster A fitting for dinghies which replaces a *turnbuckle* (UK or rigging screw). The *clevis pin,* which is prevented from slipping out by a *split ring,* passes through the two holes and an *eye* in the end of the shroud. Some have a lever system.

Shroud-laid When making rope, four *strands* are laid up *right-handed* round a *heart* of the same material. Less strong than *cable-laid* rope of the same size.

Shroud plate A fitting to which the shrouds are shackled; bolted firmly to the structure.

Shroud roller A tubular plastics roller which is fitted over the shrouds to protect *headsails* and sheets from *chafe.*

Shy Said of a *spinnaker* when set on a *close reach,* the *spinnaker pole* being close to the *forestay* and the *sheet hardened* in fully.

SI (Système internationale d'unités) Internationally agreed system of units, based on the *metre, kilogramme, second* system and used for scientific work. The basic units are metres (m), kilogrammes (kg), seconds (s), *Kelvin* (K, thermodynamic temperature), *candela* (cd, luminous intensity), amperes (A), moles (mol, substance). Multiples and submultiples are given as prefixes:

deca-	(da)	multiply by 10
hecto-	(h)	multiply by 100
kilo-	(k)	multiply by 1000 (10^3)
mega-	(M)	multiply by 10^6
giga-	(G)	multiply by 10^9
tera-	(T)	multiply by 10^{12}
deci-	(d)	multiply by 0.1
centi-	(c)	multiply by 0.01 (10^{-2})
milli-	(m)	multiply by 10^{-3}
micro-	(μ)	multiply by 10^{-6}
nano-	(n)	multiply by 10^{-9}
pico-	(p)	multiply by 10^{-12}

Derived units include: force, *Newton* (N); pressure, Pascal (Pa) or Newton per square metre, also *bar* and *atmosphere;* work, energy, *joule* (J) = newtonmetre; power, *watt* (W), 1 joule per second; frequency, *hertz* (Hz), one cycle per second. Other units include the coulomb (C, electric charge), ohm (Ω, resistance); volt (V, electric potential); farad (F, capacitance); henry (H, inductance), lumen (lm, luminous flux), lux (l), radian (rad, plane angle 57°17′46″). See also the accepted units *litre* and *knot.*

Side Generally refers to direction or to the surface of the *hull* from bow to stern above the bottom or bilge to port or to starboard, as in topsides, side ladder, alongside, port and starboard side, windward and leeward side.

Sided See *moulded and sided.*

Side deck The deck along the side of a dinghy's *cockpit* on which the crew may sit or stand when

Side ladder

hiking out or *trapezing*. In larger boats the deck that runs along the side of the cockpit or between the *coachroof* (US trunk) and the side of the boat.

Side ladder   A *boarding ladder* for larger vessels, with a horizontal platform on which to step when disembarking from the *tender*. Sometimes also applied to a boarding ladder.

Side light   One of the two lights prescribed in the *IRPCS* and other *rules of the road,* to be exhibited by vessels *under way.* Shows an unbroken light over an arc of the horizon of 112.5° from right *ahead* to 22.5° *abaft the beam* (US 10-point light), red to *port* or green to *starboard.* The lantern is screened so that the light is only visible on the appropriate side and through the prescribed arc. See also *bi-colour* and *tri-colour lantern.*

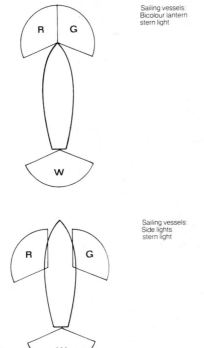

Sailing vessels: Bicolour lantern stern light

Sailing vessels: Side lights stern light

Sidereal   Relating to a star. The word is often used in connection with time, for example the sidereal year is 365 days, 6 hrs, 9 mins, 9.5 secs – the time taken by the earth to complete an orbit in relation to a distant star.

Sidereal Hour Angle, SHA   The angle between the *meridian* that passes through the First Point of *Aries* and the meridian through a *heavenly body,* measured in degrees, minutes and tenths of minutes westward from Aries. This angle changes very slowly and is equal to the *Greenwich Hour Angle* of the heavenly body minus GHA Aries. In the

Nautical Almanac is tabulated every third day for the four navigational planets and the 57 stars suitable for astronomical use. Of the two co-ordinates that fix the position of a heavenly body in the *celestial sphere,* the one that resembles *terrestrial longitude.*

Sight   To take a sight is to measure the *altitude* of a *heavenly body* with a *sextant* or *octant* in order to obtain a *position line.*

Sight Reduction Tables HO 249 and AP 3270 Tables issued jointly by the Admiralty and the US Naval Oceanographic Office in three volumes, one covering 7 stars, the other two covering sun, moon and planets for *latitudes* 0–39° and 40–89° respectively. They give *azimuths* (Z), computed *altitudes* (Hc) and a value (d) for interpolation, together with the interpolation tables required. The navigator selects a *chosen position* and enters the tables with *declination, Local Hour Angle* and the latitude of the chosen position; he finds the *intercept* by comparing the tabulated altitude with the *true altitude* (see *PZX triangle*).

Signal   A message, often a warning, sent visually or acoustically by radio (*morse* or human voice) by light (morse), by *flags* (*International Code*), by siren, *whistle, gong* or *bell* (*sound* and *fog signals*) or by *shapes* (*storm warnings* and in the rigging of vessels). See also *distress signals.*

Signal flag   Apart from *code* signals, flags may be flown for many purposes such as to warn that a firing range is being used, to inform a vessel whether she may or may not enter a port and, when racing, to mark the passage of time (*warning, preparatory* and *starting signals*), to inform competitors whether *marks* are to be left to port or starboard, and whether the *course* is being *shortened,* or the race *abandoned, cancelled* etc. The warships of some countries communicate with a set of flags that differs from the International Code flags.

Signalling lamp   An electric lamp designed for *morse* communication. When the shutters are closed, or the reflecting mirror is tilted, the light is invisible.

Silence periods   On radio telephone *distress, safety* and calling *frequencies* (2182 kHz and 156.80 MHz) two periods of three minutes in each hour are reserved for distress, *urgency* and safety traffic only; radio silence is kept and a listening watch maintained whenever possible for the three minutes past every hour and every half hour. Similarly radio silence and a listening watch are kept on the radio telegraphy distress, safety and calling frequency of 500 kHz during the two three-minutes periods one quarter and three quarters of an hour past every hour.

Simplex operation As opposed to *duplex* (ordinary conversation), simplex *radio telephone* communication is in only one direction at a time. An R/T set is normally on 'receive' until switched manually to 'send' when the operator starts to transmit a message. At the end of the message the speaker says 'over', 'out' or 'off' to indicate that he has finished what he has to say, 'over' when he is switching to receive, ready for an expected reply, 'out' when he is not expecting a reply but is switching to receive to continue monitoring the frequency, and 'off' when he is switching off his set.

Single block *Block* with only one *sheave*. May have a *becket*.

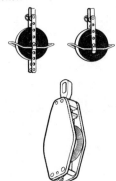

Single-handed To handle a boat alone, with no second person (hand) on board. Often used when referring to a larger boat which would normally be manned by more than one person. Hence Single-handed Trans-Atlantic Race. In the case of single-handed *dividers,* designed to be operated using only one hand.

Single-hander 1. A person who sails alone. One man can only handle a larger boat properly, i.e. change sails, navigate, make repairs etc as well at getting enough rest, if she is properly equipped for single-handed sailing, e.g. with *self-steering gear.* 2. A boat sailed by one person.

Single sideband, SSB When a *carrier wave* is amplitude *modulated,* sidebands are created on both sides; each carries the same information and, in order to save air space on the crowded longer range HF and MF communication frequencies, the carrier wave and one sideband are suppressed. Not only is the air space requirement halved, but less power is needed to transmit the signal. For example, carrier wave frequency 3000 kHz, signal frequencies in sidebands up to 10 kHz, double sideband bandwidth 2990–3010 kHz (20 kHz); SSB bandwidth 3000–3010 kHz (10 kHz). The changeover to SSB in maritime mobile bands between 1605–4000 kHz is now complete.

Single-sticker Coll: a boat with a single mast.

Single up To reduce the number of *mooring lines,* taking in all that are not needed, prior to leaving a dock, pier etc.

Sink 1. Of a boat, to move downwards; she disappears beneath the water when she loses her ability to float, perhaps owing to a leak. Her *displacement* exceeds *buoyancy* because of the additional weight of water inside the hull. 2. To cause something to disappear beneath the water. 3. Of a vessel, sun etc, to go below the horizon when just beyond *geographical range.*

Sinker Weight attached to a rope to hold an object in position, e.g. to anchor a *dan buoy.*

Siren 1. *Fog signal* made by an *aid to navigation;* the sound and power vary considerably. 2. The *whistle* used to give *sound signals.*

Sisal Hairy cordage made of natural fibres obtained from the agave plant which grows in East Africa and Central America. Although strong and relatively cheap it does not wear well and has been replaced by synthetic fibre ropes.

Sister block *Block* with two *sheaves* fitted one above the other on separate pins (B), not side by side on a single pin like a double block (A).

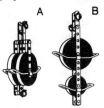

Sister hooks Two hooks on a single eye, facing in opposite directions

Sister ship One of two or more built to the same design.

Sit out (US **hike out,** Australian **swing**) The crew lean(s) out to windward as the wind increases so that the greater *heeling moment* of a fresher wind is countered by greater *righting moment,* and the dinghy stays on an *even keel.* A crew can only sit out effectively if the boat has *toe-straps* or some other device to enable weight to be placed well outboard. See also *hike out.*

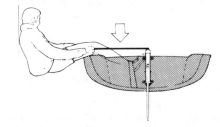

Skeg 1. A solid or hollow part of the hull aft between the *sternpost* and the *keel* (some motor boats). 2. A shallow *false keel* fitted beneath the keel towards the stern of a dinghy, often with handholds cut in it. 3. In *fin and skeg* configuration, a projection near the stern, either completely separate from the fin or connected to it by a *bustle*. Improves *rudder* efficiency and protects the *leading edge* of the rudder which is hung on it.

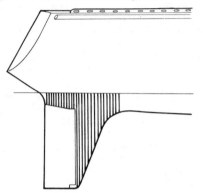

Skin The outside covering of a *planked hull*, c.f. *shell*.

Skin fitting Through-hull fitting where there is a hole in the skin, through which air or water passes, such as at the engine water inlet, piping for the heads etc. A *seacock* is fitted so that the aperture can be closed when not in use, and to prevent the boat from being flooded if there is a leak in the hosing.

Skin friction See *frictional resistance*.

Skipper The master of a fishing vessel and, coll, the master or captain of any vessel. The term is often applied to the man in charge of a keelboat, and even to the helmsman of a dinghy. Also used as a verb.

Skip zone or **skip distance** A *sky wave* travels from the radio transmitter up to the *ionosphere*, from which part is reflected back to earth. The skip zone is the area on the earth between the transmitter and the place where the sky wave returns; no signals are received between the two places.

Skirt Additional pieces of sailcloth, added in the form of *round* to the *foot* of a *spinnaker* or headsail.

Ski yachting Skiing and sailing races combined, held in the spring in Alpine countries. The winner is the person who performs best in both types of race.

Skylight Framework, usually built on a *flush-*

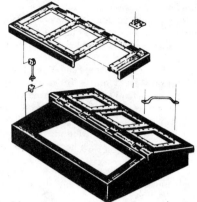

decked boat but may be on the *coachroof* (US trunk), with glazed windows to illuminate the cabin; generally opens to provide ventilation.

Skysail and **skyscraper** Sails set by some sailing ships above the *royal* in light breezes, bent to the seventh yard above the deck when upper and lower *topgallants* and *topsails* are carried. The skysail is square, the skyscraper triangular.

Sky wave Electro-magnetic radio wave which, unlike a *ground wave*, radiates in space; part is reflected back to the earth by the *ionosphere*, and may travel several times round the earth in a series of *skips*. Short wave range is typically 500 to 5000 miles. *Loran* signals are often affected, the sky wave signal being received slightly later than the ground wave, and sky wave corrections have to applied. For sky wave effect see *night effect*.

Slab reefing A term applied in various ways by different sailors, usually synonymous with *jiffy reefing*, but sometimes synonymous with *points reefing* or a *flattening reef*.

Slack 1. Of a rope or line, not *taut*. 2. The part that hangs down when a rope or line is not taut, as in 'to take in the slack', say before a sheet is *winched home*. 3. Of a *bilge*, curves gently.

Slack away or **off** To *ease* or *pay out* a line, sheet, mooring line etc.

Slack or **slow in stays** Said of a boat that *goes about* slowly.

Slack water In tidal waters, the period when a *tidal stream* (US *tidal current*) is non-existent or negligible at the *turn of the tide*.

Slalom race A type of racing with two boats competing against each other; each *beats* to windward, *tacking* frequently to leave a line of markers alternately to *port* and *starboard*, then *reaches* over to the other line of markers and returns to the finish, *gybing* round each marker.

Slam The *forefoot* strikes the water hard when *pitching* into a head sea. This is aggravated if the forefoot is broad and bluff because the water is not parted easily to receive the hull.

Slant A favourable but temporary puff of wind.

Slat Sails slat when they shake vigourously back and forth. The wind does not exert pressure on one side only, and they flutter like flags when the boat *shoots head to wind*, or when the *sheets* are *eased* out until the sails are pointing exactly downwind. *Halyards* are also said to slat when they whip against the mast after the sails have been lowered; to avoid this they are often *frapped* or led to the sides or *pulpit*, so avoiding *chafe* and noise.

Slave station A radio transmitter which is controlled by the signal transmitted by the *master station* to which it is linked (see master station).

Slick Streaks or patches of calmer water, sometimes where there is a concentration of oil or other film on the surface of the water. The area to windward of a boat driven broadside downwind, as when *hove to*, is also calmer than the surrounding area, and seas are less likely to break. The greater the extent and depth of the slick the more beneficial the effect when hove to.

Slickers (US) Foul weather gear, *oilskins*, q.v.

Slide Sewn or seized to the *luff* and/or *foot* of a sail; may be metal or plastics, and internal or external, running in or on the *track* fastened to the *mast* and/or *boom*.

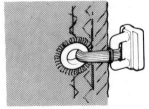

Slider or car Coll for *traveller* or *sliding fairlead*.

Sliding fairlead or **slider** A *track* is fastened to the deck, often with stops to limit the travel of the *fairlead* or *block* for the *headsail sheet*, which can be moved along it to obtain the correct *lead*. May be curved or straight, and fitted fore-and-aft, athwartships, or at an angle to the centreline.

Sliding gunter Alternative term for *gunter* q.v.

Sliding hatch A *hatch*, usually fitted over the *companionway;* is not hinged but slides to provide access, e.g. to the cabin.

Sliding seat (US **hiking board**) A plank which is

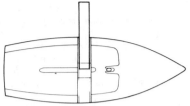

pushed out to one side of a dinghy to enable the crew or helmsman to sit *outboard*. The *trapeze* was a later development. Increased leverage provides greater *righting moment* than when *sitting* (US hiking) *out*. The International 10 sq m canoe and the Toy have sliding seats, and some other classes allow one to be fitted.

Slings Rope or chain for hoisting a heavy object such as a *yard*, or for hoisting a boat out of the water.

Slip 1. To let go quickly, e.g. to let the *anchor cable* run out instead of *weighing anchor*. 2. A *mooring line* is ready to slip when it is passed round a bollard or through a ring on shore, but both ends are held on board; when the boat is ready to sail, one end is released and the line is brought on board by hauling on the other end. 3. A mooring space for one boat in a *marina*. 4. The difference between the theoretical advance of a *propeller* and the actual distance that it advances through the water (i.e. between what it should do and what it achieves). 5. To take a boat out of the water on a slip or slipway. 6. A sloping bed or ramp over which vessels are *hauled out* of the water or *launched*. Extends far enough into the water for boats to be floated into a *cradle*, which is then hauled up the slip on wheels, rollers or tracks.

Slip knot A knot or hitch such as a *clove hitch* made with a bighted end. The knot can be untied quickly, even when under load or wet, by pulling on the end. Slipped *reef knots* are often used for reef points.

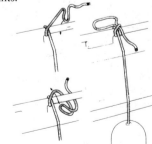

Slippery hitch A hitch that slips under strain or is unreliable.

Slipway An inclined way along which vessels slide when being *launched* or *slipped*, and on which large vessels may be built.

Sloop   A single-masted sailing boat that sets a *mainsail* and one *headsail*. The most common rig for *sailing dinghies* and *keelboats*. Normally *bermudan-rigged* (US *marconi-rigged*), but may also be *gaff-rigged*. *Cutter* rig is similar, but more than one headsail is set in the *foretriangle*. Many present-day offshore racing sloops set more than one headsail in the foretriangle (see *double head rig*) and, to some extent, this invalidates the traditional definition of a sloop.

Slot effect   An interference effect between two or more sails (foils), and one of the most controversial issues, not only in sailing theory but in aero-dynamics. Due to slot effect, the flow separation which might develop on the rear sail can be delayed, or even avoided, if the front sail is properly trimmed. The sail further forward (which may be a genoa, working jib or, under reaching conditions, a *tallboy*) modifies pressure distribution on the sail further aft, making the airflow more resistant to separation, and reducing the possibility of the aerofoil *stalling*.

Small circle   A circle on the surface of the earth, such as any *parallel of latitude* (except the *equator*), the plane of which does not pass through the centre of the earth. C.f. *great circle*.

Small craft chart (US)   Printed especially for small craft. Based on coast charts but are folded small like a map, and often have insets covering specific areas in greater detail.

Small craft advisory (US)   Red triangular flag flown as a warning by day, or red light over white light exhibited at night, when the wind is expected to become too strong (33 knots) or the seas too dangerous for small craft.

Small stuff   All small *cordage* on board, such as *yarn, whipping twine, marline*. Generally defined as cordage under ½ inch in circumference, some-times as under 1 in; for *seizing, whipping* etc.

Smell the ground   Said of a vessel when she is in water so shallow that she is almost touching the *bottom*.

Smoke float   A floating *distress signal* which either marks the position of a man in the water, or that of a boat in distress. May be attached to a

line, and emits orange-coloured smoke, visible from afar.

Snap (US)   The UK equivalent is *hank*, q.v. Holds the *luff* of a *staysail* to the *stay*.

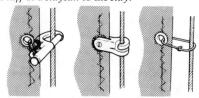

Snap hook   A hook that springs shut when released.

Snap shackle   A *shackle* with a hinged bow that is held closed by a spring-loaded plunger; may have a fixed or swivelling *eye*. Used for attaching sheets, halyards, tensioners etc. The advantages over a screw bolt shackle are that there is no pin to drop overboard, and operation is speedier. See also *spring snap shackle*.

Snarled   Said of a line or rope that is twisted or entangled.

Snatch   1. A boat snatches at her *anchor cable* or rode when it is too short and a *seaway* causes her to bob up and down, jerking short from time to time. 2. To snatch a turn is to take a quick turn round a *cleat, sampson post* etc. 3. Barge term for a *fairlead*.

Snatch block   Part of the shell of the *block* is hinged on one side so that it can be opened quickly to take a line. Most often used for a *mainsheet* so that, when the wind eases, the number of parts can be reduced without having to *unreeve* the whole sheet. May also be used to alter the *lead* of a *headsail sheet*, either by adding a block further forward to shift the lead forward, or by omitting the snatch block forward to shift the lead further aft.

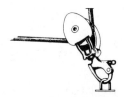

Sneaker See *spinnaker staysail*.

Snotter Ring fitting or rope strop which holds the *heel* of a *sprit* close to the mast.

Snub 1. When lying to an *anchor* or *mooring buoy*, the *anchor cable* or *mooring line* snubs when it jerks taut as the bow lifts to a wave or the *wash* of passing vessels. 2. To stop a line running out by taking a turn round a *bollard, cleat* etc.

Snubbing winch A *winch* with no handle, often used for the *jib sheet* of a sailing dinghy; turns readily in one direction but does not turn the other way, and therefore opposes the pull of the sheet, which is held by the crew.

Snug down Prepare for heavy weather by reducing sail and securing all loose gear etc.

Soft iron spheres Spheres fitted athwartships either side of the *compass card* to reduce *deviation*. Soft iron is easily magnetized when in a magnetic field, but loses its magnetism easily when removed from the field.

Solar cell Converts the energy of the sun into electrical energy.

Solar tide The part of a tidal undulation that is caused by the *tide*-raising forces of the sun. The moon's tide-raising forces are more than double those of the sun because the moon is much much nearer. The period of the solar tide is 12 hrs (c.f. *lunar tide*).

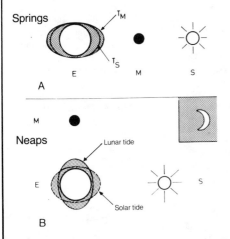

SOLAS Abbreviation for the Convention called by *IMCO* in 1960 in connection with the Safety Of Life At Sea, and attended by representatives from 45 nations. Responsible for the *International Regulations for Preventing Collisions at Sea, traffic separation schemes* the current *International Code Book*, and many other matters concerning the safety of shipping. IMCO is now *IMO*.

Soldier's wind A *fair wind* that enables a boat to sail to her destination and back again without *beating*.

Sole The floor of the *cabin* or *cockpit*.

Soling Three-man keelboat with a spinnaker, designed by Jan H Linge, and an *Olympic class* since 1972. LOA 26 ft 9½ in (8.2 m), beam 6 ft 3 in (1.90 m), displacement 2280 lbs (1035 kg), sail area 233 sq ft (21.7 sq m).

Sonar SOund NAvigation and Ranging. Sonar is very similar to *radar*, but scans the underwater area round the ship and operates at much lower *frequencies* of about 15–250 kHz. A rotating *transducer* is lowered beneath the hull in a soundome, and sends out a sound signal; beam-width varies from about 6–11°. When the sound wave strikes an underwater object it is refllected back to the transducer, the signal is passed to the *display* and the synchronized rotating trace brightens momentarily. The position of the echo on the display gives the *bearing* of the underwater object, the range of which is indicated by the distance between the echo and the centre of the display (c.f. radar), and a picture is gradually built up from echoes all around the vessel. The transducer can be tilted up about 5° above the horizontal and down to 90°. Mainly used to locate fish shoals, submarines etc, but small boat sonars may be installed to give a visual picture of underwater obstructions and channels on a cathode ray tube, or strip chart, or by means of a digital readout or flasher type display.

Sonrib *GRP/FRP mouldings* are reinforced at appropriate places by applying extra layers of glass and *resin* over a former, which may be paper, balsa wood or other light material such as foam. The core merely serves to give the *laminate* the profile required, say semi-circular or top-hat cross-section, and does not itself contribute to strength, which comes from the reinforcement of the virtually hollow GRP/FRP rib.

SOS International *distress signal* made by light, radio or sound. The pattern of three dots, three dashes, three dots ••• — — — ••• is easy to remember and recognize. The words Save Our Souls were attributed to the letters after the signal was internationally recognized in 1912.

Sound 1. A natural waterway or passage connecting two sea areas. 2. To measure the depth of water and obtain a sounding. 3. To measure the depth of a liquid in a tank or well. 4. To make a *sound signal,* e.g. on a *whistle.* 5. The opposite of rotten. 6. Sound waves, such as those made by a *foghorn,* are audible within a limited *frequency* range, but cannot be detected by the human ear at subsonic frequencies below about 20 Hz or at ultrasonic frequencies above about 20 kHz. Sound waves travel through fluids but, unlike electromagnetic light and radio waves, are heavily attenuated (weakened) in space. The velocity of sound in air at 32 °F is 1087 ft (331.4 m) per second, in sea water at standard temperature and pressure 5052 ft (1540 m) per second, and in fresh water 4626 ft (1410 m) per second. Some *radio beacons* sound an acoustic signal synchronized with the radio signal; the approximate range in *nautical miles* can be obtained by multiplying the difference between the time of reception of the two signals in seconds by 0.18 (very roughly, divide the seconds by 5). Range can also be found in the same way if, for example, a puff of smoke is seen when a gun fires, and the number of seconds before the sound is heard is then divided by 5 to give n.miles.

Sounding 1. The distance between the surface of the water and the *seabed.* The depth of water in which a boat is floating, as measured with an *echo sounder, lead and line* or *sounding pole.* 2. On a *chart,* the depth of water in feet, feet and fathoms or metres below *chart datum* (q.v. for fig) at the position where the figures are printed. When a sounding is taken it has to be *reduced* to chart datum, say when taking a *line* (US chain) *of soundings,* or to find maximum and minimum depths at *high* and *low water* at an *anchorage.* 3. In soundings: said formerly of a vessel when floating in water shallower than about 100 fathoms, but now generally when on the *continental shelf.* Off soundings similarly of a vessel floating in water deeper than about 100 fathoms; now beyond the continental shelf.

Sounding pole Wooden or light alloy pole marked at intervals so that depths can be measured when sailing in shallow waters. Can only be used at slower speeds, and must be thrust forward into the water at an angle so that it is upright and touching the bottom when abreast of the man sounding.

Sounding rod Graduated rod for measuring the contents of a fuel or water tank. The graduations are irregularly spaced, unless the tank is of constant horizontal section. Must be longer than the depth of the tank so that it cannot fall in (unless it is housed in a sounding pipe).

Sound signal Audible signal made with a *whistle*

such as is required by the *IRPCS* when vessels manoeuvre in sight of one another (see *manoeuvring and warning signals*), or with a whistle, *bell* or *gong* in *restricted visibility.*

South One of the four *cardinal points;* lies 180° from north.

Southerly To the south, as of courses, currents etc, but from the south in the case of wind.

Southern Adjective that differentiates between two similar areas, courses etc by locating them with reference to the *cardinal point,* such as the southern hemisphere, and southern *quadrant* which is bounded by SW and SE.

Southern Cross Series Races held biennially in Australia, consisting of a 180-mile *offshore race,* two short inshore races and the 630-mile *Sydney_ Hobart* race. Open to international teams which score points in similar fashion as for the *Admiral's Cup.*

Southern Ocean Racing Conference (SORC) A combination of yacht clubs which organizes a series of *offshore races* of varying length (the Southern Ocean Racing Circuit) in the early spring off the coast of Florida.

Southing The distance a vessel makes good towards the south.

Southward Direction towards the south, e.g. to sail southward.

Sou'wester A south-westerly wind; hence a waterproof oilskin hat with a broad brim over the nape of the neck. Has largely been replaced by a hood attached to the collar of a foul weather jacket, but some people still prefer a sou'wester.

Spade rudder *Rudder* with no bottom support; protrudes beneath the hull, and is often *balanced.*

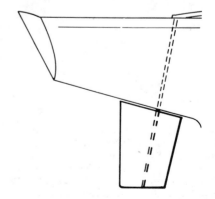

Span In smaller boats, a length of wire usually secured at both ends to an object, such as a *spar.*

For example the *halyard* of a *gaff mainsail* may be attached centrally to the *gaff* span, which is attached at either end of the gaff, and the load is therefore spread to each end of the spar instead of being concentrated at a single point. May be secured at one end only, as in the case of the tack span or strop of a jib which enables the sail to set higher above the deck.

Spanish windlass A simple method of increasing the power applied, e.g. when drawing *seizing* taut or racking two ropes; leverage is provided by a mallet or *marline spike*. The same principle can be used when *slipping* a boat, as illustrated in the figure.

Spanker The *fore-and-aft sail* set on the aftermost mast of a *full-rigged ship* or *barque*, also called *driver*. The aftermost mast of six.

Spanking Of wind, fairly strong but enjoyable; of speed, lively; of appearance, smart.

Spar General term for all the poles, supports etc used on board, whatever the material of which they are made, i.e. *boom, mast, yard, sprit, gaff* etc.

Spar buoy UK: anchored *aid to navigation;* the portion above water looks like a pole or spar. Often considerably taller than a *can* or *conical buoy,* and often carries a *topmark* and/or light and *radar reflector.* US: painted log, moored at one end, being phased out as an aid to navigation.

Specific gravity or **relative density** The ratio of the *density* of a substance relative to the maximum density of pure water at 4 °C (1000 kg/cu m, 62.428 lbs/cu ft), the specific gravity of which is 1.0. In *SI* units specific gravity is numerically equal to density in grammes per cubic centimetre, but is always given as a simple number.

Plastic foams	0.01–0.03
Balsa wood	0.01–0.2
Pine	0.45–0.66
Mahogany	0.56–0.85
Oak	0.68–0.95
Teak	0.88–0.95
Polypropylene fibres	0.90
Polyethylene	0.92–0.96
Pure water	1.0
Salt water	1.02
Polyurethane	1.11–1.28
Cotton	1.54
Polyester fibres	1.4–1.72
Glass fibres	2.5
Aluminium	2.7
Titanium	4.5
Iron	6.9–7.5
Zinc	7.0
Steel	7.6–7.8
Brass	8.4–8.7
Copper	8.5–8.8
Silver	10.5
Lead	11.3
Gold	19.3

Speed The ratio of distance covered to the time taken to cover the distance, regardless of direction, whereas velocity is the same ratio when the body is travelling in a certain direction. In general speech the terms are interchanged and the precise difference is rarely made. Boat speeds at sea are measured in *knots,* i.e. *nautical miles* per hour. Speeds of *tidal streams or currents* are given in knots, except in some inland waters where they are given in mph when the chart is based on statute miles rather than nautical miles. Wind speeds may be given in knots, metres per second, sometimes feet per second or miles per hour. Boat speed through the water is measured with a *log* or speedometer, or can be calculated from the time it takes to cover a *measured distance* or some other known distance; for practical purposes, speed in knots equals distance in feet divided by time in seconds multiplied by 0.6. A sailing boat achieves her maximum speed when *reaching* in winds that are sufficiently strong, with her sails trimmed to the optimum *angle of attack.* Whereas a light racing dinghy can *plane* faster than her maximum *displacement speed,* the *waterline length* of a displacement boat limits her speed (see *hull speed*).

1 m/sec = 3.6 km/hr = 2.23694 mph = 3.28084 ft/sec = 1.943846 knots

1 knot = 0.51444 m/sec = 1.852 km/hr = 1.15078 mph = 1.687811 ft/sec

1 ft/sec = 0.3048 m/sec = 1.09728 km/hr = 0.68182 mph = 0.5924833 knots

See also *over the ground, through the water, light, sound.*

Speed made good to windward Commonly referred to as Vmg. Does not relate to the speed at which a boat sails through the water when *close-hauled* but to the time that it takes her to sail from a position to leeward to an objective to windward, i.e. the rate at which she approaches her objective from dead to leeward. The two factors that affect Vmg are *course* (how close to the wind she *points*) and speed through the water. She sails slower when pointing high, and makes more *leeway,*

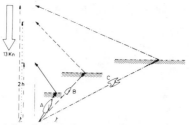

especially if the helmsman *pinches,* but when sailing faster through the water she cannot point so high. In the figure the dinghy (B) sails slower but points closer to the wind, and her Vmg is only slightly slower than that of the catamaran (C) which sails much faster but points less high. See also *windward performance.*

Speedometer Instrument that measures speed through the water, see *log.*

Speed to length ratio The *Froude number,* v/√Lg is modified (g being a constant, acceleration due to gravity, 32.174 ft/sec/sec or 9.807 m/sec/sec) to V/√L. Given boat speed, V, in *knots* and *waterline length,* L, in feet, when V/√L = 1.34 the length of the waves made by the boat matches her waterline length, and this is roughly the limit of displacement speed. *Semi-planing* starts at about V/√L = 1.6 and full *planing* at about V/√L = 3.4 (see also *hull speed).*

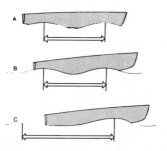

Speed wand A simple hand-held *log* with which speed *through the water* is measured. It is held over the side with the aperture facing forward, and the water level inside the tube rises as boat speed increases.

Speed week Held annually on the south coast of England. Boats sailing in classes are accurately timed over a measured distance. The five classes are based on sail area: 10 sq m Class (107 sq ft); Class A, 13.94 sq m (150 sq ft); Class B, 21.84 sq m (235 sq ft); Class C, 27.88 m (300 sq ft); Open Class, no limit. The Open Class record, held by the *proa* 'Crossbow', stood at 36 knots in 1981, and the Class A record, held by the *hydrofoil* 'Mayfly', was 23 knots. Speed trials have also been held elsewhere. At Long Island, the hydrofoil 'nf²' (the owner's abbreviation for 'neither fish nor fowl') achieved 24.4 knots in class C; in

Hawaii a sailboard (Windsurfer) raised the 10 sq m record to 24.6 knots.

Spell 1. A period spent on duty, e.g. a spell at the *helm* steering the boat for a certain time, or a spell on *look-out* duty. 2. To spell somebody is to take over their duties, to relieve them for a period.

Spencer A *fore-and-aft sail* set abaft the *foremast* or *mainmast* of a *full-rigged ship,* the *head* being extended by a *gaff.*

Spherical buoy Anchored *aid to navigation,* spherical in shape and easily distinguished from *conical* or *can* buoys. *IALA A,* laid to mark *safe water* (red and white vertical stripes) or for special purposes (yellow). See end papers.

Spherical spinnaker Cut of spinnaker with horizontal cloths and no central seam, wider at half height than at the foot.

Spider band Iron *mast band,* usually with *belaying pins,* which takes the *gooseneck* of a *fore-and-aft rigged* vessel's boom.

Spider web cut or **multi-mitre** (US **multi-miter**) A cut suitable for a large *headsail* that is subject to very heavy loads; has two or more *mitres* and particularly small panels to keep stretch to the minimum.

Spill wind If the crew can make use of only part of the *sail area* in gusty weather, or when *over-canvassed,* wind is deliberately spilt from a sail by *easing* the *sheet,* so that only part of the sail fills. This disposes of surplus wind energy, and is most often necessary when racing, especially when beating in single-handed dinghies, because the maximum area of sail is required on the downwind *legs* that follow. Wind can also be spilt by *pointing* slightly too high.

Spindrift Fine spray blown off wave crests by strong winds.

Spinnaker A large symmetrical balloon-shaped sail set when *reaching* and *running;* approximately twice as big as the *foretriangle* area. Sets forward

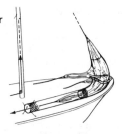

Spinnaker
chute

Spinnaker cuts In the course of time the shape of spinnakers has improved without changing the basic principle that they are set flying. The sail started as a large jib, and gradually increased in size, becoming symmetrical towards the end of the 1920s. In an effort to make larger sails with broader shoulders stand over a wider range of apparent winds, sailmakers changed the cut from vertical, through inverted chevron to horizontal;

of the *forestay*, even when the *halyard sheave* lies beneath the point where the forestay is attached to the mast. Before the sail is set the two sides are called *leeches* or *luffs* and the two bottom corners *clews*, but once it has been hoisted the parts have the same names as a *headsail*, the top corner being the *head* (10), the *weather* side and corner the luff (1) and *tack* (5), the *lee* side and corner the leech (2) and clew (6) and the bottom edge the *foot* (3). The sail is attached only at the three corners, the spinnaker halyard (9) being shackled to the head, the *spinnaker guy* (7) to the tack and the *spinnaker sheet* (8) to the clew. The tack is extended by the *spinnaker pole* or boom (4) which is about half the length of the foot; this is trimmed by the guy. The leech and clew are free to fly out, controlled only by the sheet. The sail is not lowered when *gybing*, but stays full of wind while the spinnaker pole is moved over to extend the opposite side of the sail. At this moment the former tack becomes the clew, the guy becomes the sheet, the luff the leech and vice versa. So large a sail, *set flying*, calls for considerable handling skill, and many devices are employed to ensure that it can be hoisted and lowered quickly, and kept under control. See *spinnaker chute, net* and *sleeve*, also *turtle, in stops*.

Spinnaker chute (US **launching tube**) Tubular container, sometimes of *GRP/FRP* but usually *canvas* or *netting*, connected to a broad opening in the *foredeck*. When the spinnaker is lowered it is drawn into the chute by the downhaul or recovery line, which is attached to the centre of the sail, and the spinnaker is kept stowed in the chute ready to be hoisted again later. The crew does not need to go onto the foredeck. Most often featured on dinghies; on offshore boats a hole in the foredeck is unseaworthy.

some cuts were introduced for no better reason than publicity. Eventually the successful *star-cut* spinnaker was introduced on the ground that, because stresses radiate from the *clews* and *head*, so should the *cloths*. This has been followed by the radial head and tri-radial cuts.

Spinnaker furling See *spinnaker sleeve*.

Spinnaker guy The line which is attached to the spinnaker *tack* and is thrust outboard by the *spinnaker pole*. Is *eased* or *hardened* to trim the spinnaker pole further forward or aft.

Spinnaker net A very wide mesh net of light line, hoisted in the *foretriangle* to prevent the spinnaker from wrapping itself round the *forestay*.

Spinnaker pole or **boom** A *spar* which extends the spinnaker to windward. Generally has the same *end fitting* at either end so that it can be reversed. Its fore-and-aft position is controlled by fore and aft *guys* (*Aus* braces), and its vertical position by the spinnaker pole *topping lift*, which holds it up, and the *downhaul* which prevents it from lifting. Both downhaul and lift are adjustable so that the height of the pole can be altered; the former leads down to the base of the *forestay* or back to the mast, the latter up to the mast at an angle of about 45°. The end fitting usually has a spring piston closure, which is opened to attach the pole to the *tack cringle* or, more often, to enclose the spinnaker guy. If the pole is long, a line attached to the plunger enables the crew to open it from a distance. The inboard end of the pole is attached to an *eye* on the mast, or is shaped to fit into a *bell* or cup. The eye or bell is frequently mounted on a *track* so that the height of the pole at the mast can be adjusted. The pole is set square, held back virtually to the lower shroud, when the boat is on a dead run, but when the spinnaker is set shy for a close reach the pole almost touches the forestay.

Spinnaker recovery line A line attached to the centre of the spinnaker to pull the sail down centre first, either into a spinnaker chute or onto the deck.

Spinnaker sheet 1. Either of the two sheets that will be attached to the *clews* of the spinnaker. 2. When the sail is ready to hoist or is set, the sheet to *leeward* attached to the clew; the other is the *guy;* and is attached to the *tack*. Both are generally led to *quarter blocks* well aft and back into the *cockpit*, often to a *winch*.

Spinnaker sleeve A tubular sleeve of light cloth in which the spinnaker is hoisted; the sleeve is then hauled up above the spinnaker *head* to allow the sail to fill, by hauling up either a bell mouth trumpet or else a stout ring. May also be formed by a coil or a series of linked rings. The sail is furled by reversing the process.

Spinnaker staysail, save-all, demi-bra, or **sneaker** Sail set beneath the spinnaker when *reaching* and *running* to make full use of the area of the *foretriangle*.

Spit A projecting shoal or strip of land connected to the shore.

Spitfire Alternative term for *storm jib*, q.v.

Splice Verb and noun: a permanent and strong join made between two ropes, two wire ropes, or between rope and wire rope. *Long, short* and

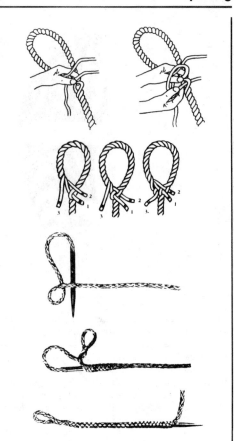

rope-to-wire splices are made by tucking the *strands* of one rope into the other; an *eye splice* provides a permanent eye in the end of a rope. A *marline spike, fid* or *Swedish splicing tool* is used to separate the strands. Manual wire rope splicing has largely been superseded by *swaging, Talurit* (US Nicopress) *splicing* and patented *swageless terminals*. Synthetic fibres are more likely to slip than natural fibres, and therefore more tucks have to be taken when splicing. *Braided* or plaited rope can also be spliced, using a special fid with an eye, and a simple method is shown in the figure; the greater the pull on the line the more firmly does the sheath grip the rope inside. See also *back* and *cut splice*.

Spline 1. Flexible strips of wood used to lay down a curved line when *lofting*. 2. Thin, wedge-shaped strips of wood glued into *seams* to provide a watertight hull, instead of *stopping* or *caulking*.

Split pin See *cotter pin*.

Split ring A ring, rather like a light key ring, with one end protruding so that it can be fed into an eye, often in a *clevis pin*, to prevent accidental withdrawal.

Split tacks When *racing,* to sail on the opposite *tack* to that on which an opponent is sailing, e.g. to get clear of his *dirty wind,* or to avoid being *covered* or involved in a tacking duel.

Spoil ground An area allocated for dumping waste material, marked on *charts* and sometimes *buoyed.*

Spoke One of the hand grips that project beyond the rim of a traditional *steering wheel.*

Sponson Platform projecting outboard from the hull at deck level; often a prolongation of the deck athwartships, but may also be of the hull as in a racing hydroplane.

Spoon bow Whereas a *clipper bow* is concave and curves aft between *stemhead* and *cutwater,* a spoon bow is convex and fuller, roughly resembling a spoon in shape.

Spray Water droplets flung or blown into the air, e.g. when the boat *pitches* into a sea, or when a wave breaks.

Spray hood Folding canvas cover, rather like a child's pram hood, fitted over the *companionway* and forward end of the cockpit. Usually hinges down, or is removable and may be laced to hooks screwed to the *coaming* or *coachroof* (US trunk), or fed into a groove, or secured with press buttons.

Spray moulding To make a *GRP/FRP moulding,* chopped glass *rovings* and *resin* are sprayed simultaneously onto a *mould.* The rovings are chopped into small pieces by a cutter, and blown by compressed air through the resin which is sprayed by two jets, one of which sprays resin and *catalyst* mixed together, and the other a resin and

accelerator mix. Initial costs are higher than for *hand lay-up* and, given the same thickness, the *laminate* is slightly less strong. Control over the thickness of the laminate depends on the skill of the operator, and is not so certain as with hand lay-up.

Spreader or **crosstrees** Metal or wooden struts attached either side of the *mast* at varying heights above *deck* to spread the *shrouds* out sideways, increasing the angle the shroud makes with the mast. This reduces the load and permits the use of smaller diameter *rigging* and a thinner *mast section.* Because spreader length is limited by the boat's *beam,* tall masts often have more than one

pair of spreaders. The fitting connecting the spreader root to the mast is usually rigid, but swinging spreaders can be adjusted both vertically and horizontally; a *flexible mast* often has spreaders that can move through a horizontal arc. The angles made by the outer end of the spreader with the shroud should normally be the same above and below the spreader. The outer end is notched to take the shroud.

Spreader boot or **guard** A plastics cover or wheel that is fitted over the end of the spreader and the shroud to protect the sails from *chafe.*

Spreader lift A short line, leading up to the mast from near the centre of a spreader, fitted to keep a relatively long spreader at the correct angle to the mast, and prevent it from sagging.

Spring 1. When lying *alongside* a pier, quay or another boat, springs are required in addition to *bow* and *stern lines* to prevent the boat from moving forward or aft, and to keep her parallel, regardless of the effects of wind and *tidal stream or current* (see *mooring line* for fig). The head spring runs aft diagonally from a point near the *bow,* and the back spring runs forward diagonally from a point near the *stern.* When leaving a pier with boats moored close ahead and astern, all lines are cast off except one spring; motoring slow

ahead against the head spring causes the stern to swing out, the spring can then be *slipped*, and opposite gear engaged to get clear of the pier. 2. Frequently used in the plural, springs, meaning *spring tides*. 3. A partial fracture or crack in a wooden *mast* or *spar*.

Spring a leak   A leak caused by a plank springing or lifting.

Spring clip   Fitting shaped rather like a rowlock, often screwed to the deck so that a *boathook*, *spinnaker pole* etc can be clipped into it quickly.

Spring snap shackle or **Swedish hank**   *Shackle* that is opened one-handed by pressing a button; this depresses the spring that keeps the shackle closed. May have a fixed or swivelling *eye*.

Spring tide or **springs**   *Tides* that occur at or near the time when the moon is new, the sun and moon being in *conjunction* (Fig 1), and when the moon is full, at which time they are in *opposition* (Fig 2). The *range of the tide* is greatest at spring tides, with higher *high water* heights and lower *low water* heights (see *Tides* for fig). *Tidal streams* (US *tidal currents*) are also strongest at springs. The word has nothing to do with the season of the year, but comes from an old Norse word meaning a swelling.

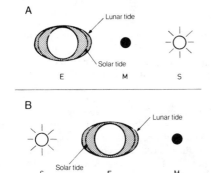

Sprit   A *spar* that runs diagonally across a spritsail and extends the *peak*. Is connected to the *mast* at or near the *tack* of the sail by a *snotter* or *jaw*. See also *bowsprit*.

Spritsail   Quadrilateral *fore-and-aft sail*, generally *laced* to the *mast* and extended by a *spar* (the sprit) which runs diagonally to the *peak*. The corners are the *throat*, peak, *clew* and *tack;* the sides are the *head, luff, leech* and *foot*. May be *loose-footed* or *laced* to a *boom*. Today usually a single sail set in small dinghies such as the Optimist, but formerly was set with a *headsail, topsail* etc like comparable *gaff-rigged* vessels. Spritsail barges sail and race regularly on the East Coast of England today.

Spruce   Strong, flexible wood of the fir family, light in colour and free from knots, from which masts, spars, oars etc may be made; there are several varieties, such as Sitka, Norway spruce etc. *Specific gravity* about 0.50.

Spume   Froth or foam produced when waves break.

Spunyarn   Thin yarn with two or more *strands* twisted together rather than *laid*, often tarred; for *serving, seizing* etc.

Squall   A sudden increase in wind speed that lasts longer than a *gust*. Often blows from a new direction, and may be accompanied by rain, hail, snow etc. The passage of a *cold front* or *occluded front* often brings squalls. A black squall is accompanied by dark rain clouds, whereas a white squall appears from a virtually cloudless sky. Short-lived but violent line squalls are sometimes heralded by a long, low roll-cloud ahead of an advancing cold front.

Square   At right angles to the *keel*, hence square sail. A *spinnaker* may be set square, i.e. with the pole at right angles to the *fore-and-aft line*. Also used as a verb: to square the pole is to set it more squarely to the fore-and-aft line. To square off is to sail more directly down wind.

Square knot   Alternative term for *reef knot*, q.v.

Square rig   A rig used from the early days of sail, the principal sails being rectangular and bent to *yards* which lie across the masts. Seamanship and sail handling skills required are very different from those for *fore-and-aft rigged* sailing yachts.

Square sail   A rectangular sail bent to a *yard* the upper edge being the *head*, the lower the *foot*, the sides the *leeches*. Rarely seen today because *fore-and-aft sails* are more efficient.

Squat A vessel is said to squat when she is trimmed down *by the stern* when making *way*.

Stability The tendency of a boat to remain on an *even keel*, or to return to an upright floating position when her equilibrium has been disturbed, e.g. by water or wind. Two different kinds of stability should be distinguished, static and dynamic. Static metacentric stability is the property of a boat by which the actions of *buoyancy* and weight forces cause her to return to her original upright position. A boat is statically stable if the *metacentre* lies above the *centre of gravity*. Transverse stability is largely governed by hull shape (form stability) and weight (*ballast* stability). As to hull shape, the distance that the *centre of buoyancy* shifts sideways when the boat heels depends largely on overall *beam* and waterline beam and, therefore, on the shape of the transverse *sections*. The position of the centre of gravity is determined by the distribution of ballast and by *draft*. All keelboats are self-righting owing to ballast stability; at small angles of heel their stability is relatively low, but increases to a maximum at 80–90° of heel. Dinghies are not ballasted and rely largely on form stability; they are relatively reluctant to heel initially but capsize when wind pressure increases, unless the crew sit out to windward or use a trapeze to increase *righting lever* and *moment*.

Dynamic stability is the property of a boat to maintain her steadiness or stability only on account of her motion through the water. The motion of the boat is considered following a disturbance such as *rolling* or *broaching*. A statically stable boat may oscillate about the equilibrium position without ever remaining in it (i.e. rolling), and in such a case the boat, although statically stable, may be dynamically unstable. See also *longitudinal stability*.

Stability curve or **curve of stability** or **righting moment curve** Graph showing the stability characteristics of a vessel. *Righting moment* on the vertical axis is plotted against the angle of *heel* on the horizontal axis to show the boat's range of stability. Different types of boats can be compared, such as the characteristics of a *self-righting keelboat*, whose stability is mainly due to ballast, with those of a *capsizable* dinghy, whose stability is mainly due to hull form, or the stability of a

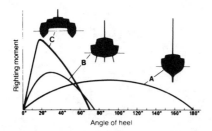

monohull with that of a *catamaran*. An extremely beamy boat such as a catamaran has the greatest transverse stability (at about 20° angle of heel) but, on heeling further, righting moment drops and she may capsize at 70° of heel, the *angle of vanishing stability*. The range of stability of the *bilge-keeler* is smaller than that of the keelboat, and she capsizes at 70° of heel, whereas the keelboat's stability is always positive; righting moment is greatest at 80–90° of heel, although *initial stability* is relatively low.

Stable equilibium A sailing boat is in a state of stable *equilibium* when she is able to counter a force, such as wind pressure or resulting from shifting weight on board, by reaching a new state of equilibium. *Righting moment* equals *heeling moment* and, after removal of the force, she returns to her former state of equilibrium.

Staff Pole or spar from which the *ensign* is flown.

Stage A plank suspended over the side on lines, so that the crew can work on the *topsides*.

Staghorn Type of *bollard*, with cross arms as stong as the upright; *mooring lines* etc may be *belayed* to it.

Stagnation point The point where a moving fluid is brought to rest; in the case of flow round a foil, the positions of the stagnation points near the *leading* and *trailing edges* vary with the *angle of attack*.

Stainless steel Steel that contains at least 12.5% chromium; resists *corrosion* because chrome has a greater affinity for oxygen than iron, and combines with it to form a thin oxide layer which protects the steel from further oxidization. Greater resistance to corrosion is obtained by adding nickel (Ni), molybdenum (Mo) and copper (Cu), as well as some other elements. The usual composition is 18% chrome, 8% nickel plus a small amount of molybdenum, manganese etc.

Stall A *hydrofoil* (*rudder*) or *aerofoil* (sail) stalls when flow is separated from the surface. *Lift* decreases and *drag* increases sharply on account of the *turbulence* over the whole of the leeward or downstream side.

Stanchion Metal post, generally rounded on top but sometimes tapering, with one or more holes

through which the *lifelines* (guardrails) run. Should be spaced no more than 6 ft (2 m) apart (*ORC* maximum is 7 ft, 2.15 m, angled at not more than 10° from the vertical) to provide a safe lifeline around the sides. A stanchion is firmly anchored to the deck by long bolts which pass through the base plate welded to the bottom; alternatively it may fit into a stanchion socket, a pin through socket and stanchion preventing accidental withdrawal. Socket bases often have lugs either side to which can be clipped a line, such as that attached to a *safety harness,* or a lead block. Base plate or socket may be L-shaped, so that it can be bolted to the *toe-rail* or *gunwale* as well as to the deck, distributing the load more widely. Also supports *bulwarks, awnings* etc.

Stand The period during a tidal cycle when the level of water remains constant, either between rise and fall at *high water,* or between fall and rise at *low water.*

Standard port (US **reference station**) A port or harbour for which daily *tidal predictions* have been made. The times and heights of *high* and *low water* are printed in the *Tide Tables,* and those at *secondary ports* (US subordinate stations) can be found by applying the *tidal differences* printed in the same volume.

Stand by 1. A warning to be prepared, e.g. stand by to *gybe* (US jibe), which warning is followed by *gybe-o* when the *helmsman* puts up the *helm;* stand by to lower away warns the crew to prepare to lower sail as a *mooring buoy* is approached. 2. A vessel stands by another when she waits nearby, ready to assist, say when she is leaking or in *distress.*

Stand in To head towards land, a harbour or an anchorage.

Standing As applied to *rigging, tackles* etc, a part that is not moved, such as a standing *backstay* which is set up permanently, as opposed to a *running backstay* which is slacked off when it is to leeward.

Standing block and **part** 1. The standing part of a line is the part that is not used when making a knot, or the part around which a knot is tied. 2. As opposed to *running block and part,* the standing block and part of the *fall* of a *tackle* do not move when power is applied to the *hauling part.*

Standing lug See *lugsail.*

Standing rigging *Wire rope,* or sometimes solid *rod rigging,* which supports *masts* and fixed *spars* but does not control the *sails.* Unlike *running rigging,* remains in position when the boat changes course, *tacks* or *gybes* (with the exception of *running backstays* which are part of the standing rigging but are slacked off and set up under way). The wire construction preferred for keelboats is 1×19, because of its low *stretch;* its inflexibility compared with 7×7 is no drawback for standing rigging. See *shroud* and *stay* which, respectively, support a mast *athwartships* and *fore-and-aft.*

Stand off To head away from the shore, or keep away from some object. To stand off and on is to sail back and forth, away from and towards the land.

Stand-on vessel Under the *IRPCS* the vessel that does not have to keep clear HAS to maintain her course and speed. She MAY take action to avoid a collision when it is apparent that the other vessel is not taking appropriate action, and she MUST take such action as will best avoid a collision when they are so close that no action taken by the *give-way* vessel alone will avoid a collision. The US use the term privileged vessel.

Stand out To head offshore.

Staple A *yarn* may be formed by spinning many short lengths of fibre together, whether synthetic or natural (though filaments are more usual in synthetic cloth construction for sails); the chopped up fibre is called staple fibre.

Star 1. Two-man racing keelboat designed as long ago as 1911 by Francis Sweisgut. Has long been recognized as an international class, and an *Olympic class* from 1932 to 1972, and again in 1980 and 1984. *Gaff-rigged* from 1911–1921, then *bermudan-rigged* (US *marconi-rigged*). Now almost all are made of *GRP/FRP.* LOA 22 ft 8 in (6.91 m), beam 5 ft 8 in (1.73 m), displacement 1460 lbs (662 kg), sail area 285 sq ft (26.5 m). 2. Distant heavenly body that transmits light.

Stars are classified by their magnitude; the brighter the star the lower the magnitude. The *sidereal hour angle* and *declination* of 57 stars is tabulated in the *Nautical Almanac* for every third day.

Starboard The right hand side when looking forward towards the *bow*, both inside and outside the boat, as starboard berth, starboard hand mark. The word stems from the days when a boat was steered by a board on that side. The opposite side is *port*, formerly *larboard*. In days gone by the starboard side of a vessel was the 'best' and senior side, constructed by the senior shipwright. Many customs and laws of the sea can be traced to this, and starboard seniority can be used as an aide-memoire in many cases. An owner boarded his ship on that side, and flew his flag from the

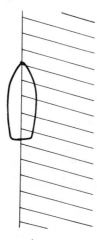

starboard flag halyard. A Naval salute is made up of an odd-number of guns, because the compliment was always fired by guns from alternate batteries aboard ship, starting and finishing with the starboard battery. Starboard tack has right of way over port tack; a power-driven vessel on another's starboard side has right of way; the *IRPCS* sound signal for turning to starboard is one short blast. The *side light* exhibited to starboard is green, and screened to shine over an arc from dead ahead to two points abaft the beam to starboard, i.e. over an arc of 112.5° or 10 points.

Starboard hand buoys or **marks** A *lateral system* mark, on the right hand side when a vessel approaches from seaward or is sailing clockwise round a land mass. It is left to starboard on entering a harbour but to port when outward bound. *IALA A:* green (sometimes black) *conical* buoy and *topmark*, green light. USA, Canada: red *nun* buoy, even number, red or white light, triangular red *daymark*. See end papers.

Starboard tack A sailing boat is on starboard tack when she has the wind on her starboard side and is carrying her *mainsail* to *port*.

Starboard tack yacht When two sailing boats approach each other on opposite *tacks*, the one with the wind on her port side keeps out of the way of the other under the *IRPCS;* under the *IYRU racing rules* the yacht on port tack gives way to the starboard tack yacht. Starboard tack therefore has right of way under both rules, although the wording differs slightly. See also *Inland Waters* (US).

Star cracks Cracks radiating from a central point in the *gelcoat* of a *GRP/FRP laminate,* generally as a result of excessive load or heavy blows which damage both the gelcoat and the laminate beneath; must be repaired.

Star-cut or **reaching spinnaker** A flatter cut *spinnaker,* the panels of which gradually become broader as they approach the centre from the *clews* and *head,* so making a star pattern. Is so flat that it can be set on a *close reach,* sheeted like a *genoa,* but with a *spinnaker pole.* Is more effective than a genoa because the area is greater, and may be made of heavier or lighter *cloth.*

Star identifier A star chart over which the navigator places transparent grids, which are inscribed with varying *latitudes* and *azimuths.* The approximate *altitude* and azimuth of a particular star can be found on the chart before taking a *sight.* Alternatively it can be used to find the name of an observed star, the altitude and bearing of which are known. Other aids to finding and identifying stars include the Planisphere, and the star charts printed in the *Nautical Almanac* and *Reeds.*

Start 1. In the *racing rules,* a yacht is deemed to start a race when any part of her hull, crew or equipment crosses the starting line in the direction of the *course* to the first *mark,* any time after the starting signal has been made. This signal is preceded by the *warning* and *preparatory signals,* generally made 10 and 5 minutes earlier respectively. The aim is to cross the starting line with full way, immediately after the signal is made, with right of way, a *clear wind,* and at the favourable end of the line (which is usually crowded). When *handicap* racing, the *elapsed time* is taken from the time of the starting signal, not from the time that each boat crosses the starting line. 2. To *ease* slightly, especially a *sheet, tackle* etc. 3. A plank is started when its *fastenings* give slightly, usually causing a small leak.

Starting area An area near the starting line, often bounded by marks, where only those boats that are preparing to start in the next race may sail. If boats of another *class* enter, they may be *protested* against and disqualified.

Starting line A starting line may be a line between two *marks*, between a mark and a *mast* or *staff* on the *committee boat*, or the extension of a line through two stationary posts, e.g. on shore; it should be as nearly at right angles to the wind direction as possible. Frequently a starting line is biased, i.e. is not exactly at right angles to the wind, and one end is then slightly nearer the *weather mark*. The helmsman checks which end is

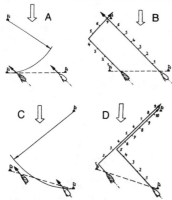

more favourable before the start by *shooting up head to wind* when crossing the line, and takes a *bearing* either of the first mark or of the limit marks at either end. In figs A and B the line is unbiased, and both boats have to cover the same distance to the mark. In C and D the line is not laid at right angles to the wind, and the grey boat at the port end of the line has a shorter distance to sail to the first mark.

Starting signal Visual and acoustic signal made by the *race officers* exactly five minutes after the *preparatory signal*. Both *warning* and preparatory signals are lowered, and an acoustic signal is made to start the race. Any boat on the *course* side of the starting line when the starting signal is made is *recalled*. Time is taken from the visual signal; the acoustic signal merely serves to draw attention to it.

Stationary A term used in *weather forecasts* to indicate that a low, high, front, trough etc is not moving but staying virtually in the same position.

Station buoy (US) A *buoy* laid to mark the position of a nearby *aid to navigation*, such as a *light tower* or buoy (UK watch buoy).

Station circle A circle on a *weather map* indicating the position where observations were made. The *cloud amount* is shown by the amount of the circle that is black, i.e. clear sky by an empty circle. Red and black symbols and figures round

the station circle at specific positions indicate weather details such as air temperature, *dew-point, visibility,* type of low, medium and high cloud, past and present weather, period and height of *seas* and *swell*. Wind direction is indicated by a *wind arrow* flying with the wind, and wind speed by *feathers* and *pennants* on the arrow.

Station pointer (US **three-arm protractor**) Instrument for plotting *horizontal sextant angles;* has three arms, one fixed and two that rotate about the centre point of the metal or plastics disc, which is graduated in degrees. The two arms are locked at the two angles subtended by three identified objects, as measured with a *sextant* or *octant*. The boat's position is at the centre of the disc when the three arms have been aligned with the objects on the chart.

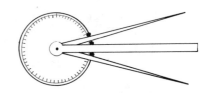

Stations In the *profile* or sheer *plan*, the length of the *hull* between points forward and aft where the *stem* and *stern* meet the *waterline* is usually divided into 10 or 20 equal spaces, so providing 11 or 21 stations. Additional stations may be drawn forward and aft at the *overhangs*. The *sections* in the *body plan* show the shape of the hull at these stations.

Stay 1. Part of the *standing rigging;* provides *fore-and-aft* support for the *mast*, i.e. the *forestay* from forward, the *backstay* from aft (see *Rigging* fig). Frequently named after the mast it supports, while sails are named after the stay to which they are *hanked*. See also *bobstay, jumper stay, running backstay*. 2. Verb: to support a mast with stays and *shrouds*, i.e. attaching them to the mast and deck fittings or *chain plates*, and adjusting the tension with *turnbuckles* (UK or rigging screws), *lanyards* etc. 3. Sailmaker's term for the sides or *leeches* of a *spinnaker*. 4. To go about, see also *in stays*.

Stay adjuster Similar to a *shroud adjuster*, q.v.

Staysail A sail set on a stay, as opposed to a *square sail* set on a *yard* or those *fore-and-aft sails* with *luffs* attached to *masts*. May be *hanked* to the stay or *set flying*. A *cutter* sets a staysail forward of

the mast and abaft the *jib*, *yawls* and *ketches* often set a *mizzen staysail*, and boats with two or more masts, such as *schooners*, may carry a number of staysails, each named after the stay on which it is set.

Staysail schooner A *schooner*-rigged vessel in which the *bermudan* (US *marconi*) or *gaff foresail* is replaced by several smaller staysails set between the two masts, say main staysail and fore-trysail, or *wishbone* staysail. This increases aerodynamic efficiency, and better use is made of the space between the masts, especially if the *foremast* is very short. See also *three-mast staysail schooner*.

Steady 1. Order to the helmsman to keep the boat on her present course, steady as she goes. 2. Of wind, barometer etc, unchanging.

Steadying sail Small sail set by a *motor sailer*, fishing boat etc to reduce *rolling* and *yawing*, especially in a *beam sea*. A cruising *yawl* or *ketch* may also set a *mizzen* to steady her and help her lie at a safe angle to the seas, or more comfortably to a *sea anchor*.

Stealer When *planking* a *hull*, a short tapering plank laid so that succeeding planks are straight. The term is also used for shell *plating*.

Steamer Originally a vessel propelled by steam, as opposed to a *sailing vessel;* later applied to one propelled by any type of machinery.

Steam fog Like *sea smoke*, forms when cold air, passes over considerably warmer water. The cold air becomes saturated, is warmed, and rises like steam.

Steaming light Alternative term for *masthead light*, q.v.

Steel Iron containing about 1.5% carbon and other elements. For boat-building the advantages of greater strength and impact-resistance are offset by cost and the fact that because it is prone to *corrosion*, it has to be protected against *rust*. *Condensation* is a problem, and steel also disturbs a *magnetic compass*. Secific gravity 7.8.

Steep sea The ratio wave height:wave length indicates the steepness of seas. They become steeper and more unstable when depths decrease, and when wind and *tidal stream or current* are opposed.

Steep-to Said of the sea-bed when it slopes down sharply, as opposed to *shelving*.

Steer To control the vessel so that she follows the desired *course*. The helmsman normally turns the *rudder* with a *steering wheel* or *tiller*. In the event of damage to the rudder or steering gear, small boats can be steered with a *paddle* or *oar*, and larger boats with a *jury* rudder. See rudder.

Steerage way Whether she is making *headway* or *sternway*, a boat has steerage way when she is moving fast enough through the water for the rudder to turn her when it is deflected by the helm; she is said to *answer the helm*.

Steering and sailing rules Section B of the *IRPCS* lays down which vessel has to keep clear when they meet, and there is a *risk of collision*. See *rule of the road*.

Steering compass The *compass* which, generally, is mounted close in front of the *helmsman;* he keeps the boat on *course* by keeping the appropriate *graduation* on the card aligned with the *lubber line*. *Deviation* has to be established for various *headings*, and a *deviation table* is drawn up, after which care must be taken not to leave a portable radio or ferrous objects such as tools nearby, because they would deflect the *compass needle*.

Steering gear Everything that connects the steering wheel to the *rudder* and moves it.

Steering oar A long *oar*, rigged over the *stern*, with which the boat is steered; either used as a *jury* rudder or to help when seas are particularly awkward.

Steering pedestal Upright pillar on which the steering wheel is mounted. Is placed centrally in the *cockpit,* and the steering compass is often housed in the top.

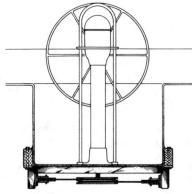

Steering wheel Manually operated wheel with which the helmsman steers the boat.

Steering wires or **cables** Wire ropes that generally run from a drum on the steering wheel spindle, through the pedestal, over the *rudder quadrant* and to the *rudder head.* They move the *rudder blade* when the wheel is turned.

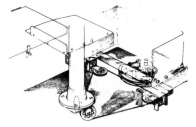

Steeve The upward angle between the *bowsprit* or other outboard *spar* and the horizontal. To steeve up the bowsprit is to raise the outer end to reduce *LOA* when berthing.

Stem 1. The forward *member* that is attached to the *keel* (see *construction* fig). Is *rabbeted* to take the *planking* and often has a stemband for protection. The term is used for the equivalent area of a *GRP/FRP moulding* where the *laminates* overlap. Steel or light alloy stems are of plate or bar metal. 2. To stem the *tide:* when sailing or motoring against a *tidal stream or current,* to make *way over the ground* against it, or at least not to be carried downstream.

Stem band Protective metal strip fastened along the front of the stem.

Stemhead The top of the stem, hence stemhead fitting.

Stemhead fitting Fitting at the stemhead which often has a roller over which the *anchor cable* runs (stemhead or bow roller); is sometimes fitted to one side of the stem. Often also serves as the anchorage for the *forestay* and *headsail tack,* and should enable more than one headsail to be tacked down when changing sails.

Stem knee A *knee* that connects the stem to the *keel.*

Step 1. See *mast step.* 2. To step a mast is to place it in position, whether the mast is stepped on the *keel,* on the *deck,* or in a *tabernacle.* 3. A step-shaped alteration in the line of the bottom of high-speed *planing* power boats. 4. See also *folding step, climbing rung.*

Step off Measure distance on *charts* with *dividers.* When the distance is too long to be measured in a single step, the dividers are set, say to 2 n.miles against the *latitude* scale at about the same latitude as the distance, and the distance is then measured in a series of steps, each of 2 n.miles.

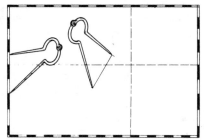

Stern The afterpart of a vessel. The *hull* may end in a *transom stern,* curve to a pointed or *canoe stern,* or have a long, short or raked *counter.* The type of stern depends on the design, the waters where the boat will sail, and the owner's taste.

Stern anchor A boat may be *anchored* by the stern when she is made fast bows on to a pier; in a narrow channel where there is no room to *swing,* she may lie to two anchors, one ahead and one astern.

Sternboard Movement astern, whether the sails are full or not.

Stern-drive Alternative term for *outdrive,* q.v.

Stern gland Packing round the *propeller shaft*

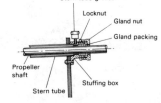

where it passes through the *hull;* is compressed inside a sleeve to prevent water from entering the boat, and is usually greased, either directly by turning a grease cap, or with a remote greaser.

Stern light A white light exhibited from a lantern fitted at the stern on the *fore-and-aft line;* shows an unbroken light over an arc of 135° (US 12 points), i.e. 67.5° from right astern to either side. Also termed overtaking light. See also *tricolour light* and *IMO.*

Stern line or **fast** or **rope** A *mooring line* that runs from the stern to a pier, *pile, mooring buoy* etc. See mooring line fig.

Stern mainsheet The *mainsheet* runs from the end of the *boom* to the stern when lack of space in the *cockpit* of a small dinghy or cruising boat makes the more efficient *centre mainsheet* system impossible. A stronger boom is required, because all the pull is exerted at the outer end.

Sternpost The near-vertical *member* at the after end of the *hull* on which the *rudder* is often hung (see *construction* fig.). Corresponds to the *stem* forward. May extend to the *deck,* as far as the *horn timber,* or to the top of a *transom.*

Stern pulpit or **pushpit** Similar to the *bow pulpit* but fitted round the after end of a boat. The *lifelines* (guardrail) are attached to it either side. Some are split to give access for a *boarding ladder* or stern gangplank.

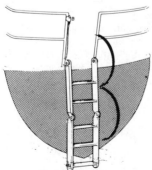

Sternsheets The aftermost part of an *open boat.*

Stern to and **stern on** The stern points towards something, such as *following seas;* stern on when moored with the stern pointing to, say, a *pontoon.*

Stern tube Metal tube which passes through the hull, and in which the *propeller shaft* runs. Has a *stern gland* or *stuffing box* at the inboard end to prevent water entering the boat; sometimes a bearing is incorporated.

Stern wave Part of the wave system generated by a boat moving through water; a transverse wave is formed at the stern between divergent waves which spread out diagonally either side. At maximum *hull speed* the boat is supported at either end by bow and stern waves, and the wavelength equals her *waterline length.* See *bow wave* for fig.

Sternway Movement stern first, as opposed to *headway* when the boat moves forward through the water.

Stevedore's knot A *stopper knot* made like a *figure of eight knot* but with more turns. Easy to make and undo, but does not look neat.

Stick Coll for *mast.*

Stick-boom A boom with a *snotter;* extends a leg-of-mutton sail, as in the US *sharpie* figure.

Stiff A boat that does not *heel* easily is said to be stiff, as opposed to *tender.*

Stitch-and-glue Light small dinghies, such as the Mirror, can be built by this method, which is designed for amateur construction. Plywood panels are sewn together with copper wire and the seams are taped with *resin*-impregnated *glassfibre* strips. When the *GRP/FRP* joint has *cured,* the ends of the copper wire are cut off and the other side of the seam is treated similarly with tape and resin.

Stock 1. The cross-bar of a *fisherman anchor,* set at right angles to the *arms* at the end of the *shank* opposite to the *crown;* lies flat on the sea-bed and turns the anchor to encourage the *fluke* to bite. The stock of some types of *Northill anchor* is at the same end as the arms. Both types of anchor may have fixed or folding stocks, the latter being easier to stow. 2. See *rudder stock.*

Stock anchor A traditional *anchor* with a stock set at right angles to the *arms* and *shank.* If the

anchor has a folding stock, this first has to be set across the shank and secured with a *cotter pin. Holding power* is much less than that of a modern anchor design, and the anchor cable may become *foul* on the upper fluke.

Stockless anchor An *anchor* for larger vessels; has no stock, the *flukes* being rotated and encouraged to bite by tripping palms.

Stock production (UK **series production,** often just **production boat**) A process whereby a number of similar vessels, all virtually identical and built to the same plans, are constructed generally by the same builder.

Stop 1. Stops are fitted to limit the movement of a *traveller, sliding fairlead, rudder* etc. 2. (mainly US): *sail tier*, q.v. 3. Verb: the end of a line may be stopped to the *standing part* after a knot has been made by *seizing* it with *whipping twine.* 4. A leak may be stopped by *caulking,* or by filling a small hole with stopping. 5. A vessel does not stop, she is said to *lose way,* and is stopped by *taking way* off. 6. To put a sail in *stops.*

Stopper Device which holds a rope, often temporarily. A modern stopper, often called jammer, has a cam action and is grooved to hold a *sheet* or *halyard* firmly so that a *winch* is released for other purposes. Cable or chain stoppers take the strain on a cable temporarily and, in small boats, the fitting illustrated takes the weight of *ground tackle* off a *bollard* or *cleat.* See also *devil's claw.*

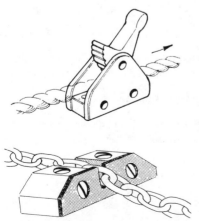

Stopper knot A knot made in the end of a rope or line to prevent it from *unreeving* through a *block, fairlead* etc. For example, a *figure of eight knot.*

Stopping Soft, putty-like compound applied with a putty knife, spatula etc to fill holes, cracks or indentations in a surface prior to painting or varnishing. Various compositions are obtainable, and can be *rubbed down* when dry and hard to provide a smooth surface. May also be used to fill *seams.*

Stopwatch Special waterproof stopwatch designed for *racing,* the face being split into segments, usually coloured, so that the passage of time between the *preparatory signal* and the start can be seen at a glance. Also useful for timing the *period* of a light.

Stopwater A wooden dowel driven into a hole, bored transversely through a joint such as the *keel scarph.* Swells when wet and makes the joint watertight.

Storm Violent disturbance of the atmosphere with winds over *gale* force: WMO *Beaufort force* 10, 48–55 *knots* (US whole gale); WMO violent storm, (US storm) force 11, 56–63 knots. *Tropical revolving storms* such as *hurricanes* often generate much stronger winds, force 12 and over, 64 knots plus.

Stormbound Confined to a port or anchorage by a storm.

Storm jib or **spitfire** Small heavy *jib* set in strong winds on all *points of sailing;* for a large boat may be *roped* on all three sides. *Cloth weight* 5–8 oz US, 6–10 oz UK, 210–340 g/sq m.

Storm sails Sails set in high winds, smaller in area than the *working sails;* made of heavy *cloth* and heavily reinforced.

Storm spinnaker Set by boats *racing offshore* and *reaching* or *running* in *force* 5–7 winds. Narrower, flatter and smaller than a normal spinnaker, especially towards the *head*. *Cloth weight* 1½–2½ oz US, 2–3 oz UK, 65–100 g/sq m.

Storm surge Long wave which is generated by a storm, and which causes sea level to rise above the level predicted. If the storm is severe and of long duration, a storm surge may cause serious coastal flooding, especially if the time of arrival of the surge at places along a coast coincides with the time of *high water springs.*

Storm warnings Visual and radio warnings are given of approaching gales and storms, i.e. *gale* warnings, *force* 8–9; *storm* warnings, force 10–11; *hurricane* warnings, force 12. Visual signals vary from country to country. For example, UK: gale warnings, storm *cones* are hoisted at coastal stations by day and three lights forming a triangle at night; a north cone or lights point upward warn of a gale from a northerly direction within 50–100 miles; a south cone or lights point down, gale from a southerly direction. US: small craft advisory, winds up to 33 *knots*, 38 mph, or sea conditions too dangerous for small craft, one red *pennant* by day and a red light over a white light by night; gale, two red pennants or white light over red, 34–47 knots, 39–54 mph; storm or whole gale, one square *flag* (red with a black centre) or two red lights, winds 48–63 knots, 55–73 mph; hurricane, two flags as above, lights red over white over red, winds over 64 knots, over 74 mph. Chart abbr for a storm signal station is Storm sig. (UK) and S Sig Sta (US).

Stove in Past tense of stave: said of a *hull* that has been broken inwards, perhaps as a result of a collision or of striking some floating object.

Stow To place gear, stores or food in the place allocated, where it is accessible but secure. A place for everything and everything in its place is the rule in a boat; charts in the chart table drawer, sails in the sail locker, bottles, cups and glasses in racks, and so on. Stowed for sea has particular connotations of making especially secure with lashings etc.

Stowage space A compartment, locker or place where stores, equipment, clothing, food etc can be stowed securely but accessibly.

Strainer A coarse filter, e.g. at the engine cooling water inlet or in the bilges at the suction end of the *bilge pump* hose.

Strait A narrow natural waterway or passage that connects two large areas of water, such as Dover Strait between the North Sea and the English Channel.

Strake A line of *planking* or *plating* running continuously along the side of the hull from *stem* to *stern.*

Strand 1. To run a vessel *aground,* whether owing to damage, heavy weather, inaccurate *navigation* or misjudgment of seas, *tidal streams or currents* or wind strength. The term running aground is generally used for less serious occasions when the vessel can be refloated without outside assistance. 2. When making *laid rope,* yarns are twisted together right- or left-handed to form

strands, and three (sometimes four) strands are then laid in the opposite direction to form rope. Strands may also be loosely twisted into twine for *whipping, seizing* etc, or plaited by machine to make *braided* rope. A *wire rope* strand is made up of a number of individual wires twisted together. 3. A sandy beach.

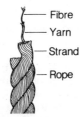

Fibre
Yarn
Strand
Rope

Stratocumulus (Sc) Grey or white sheet or layer cloud, broken or covering the whole sky. Indicates a stable weather situation and light winds.

Stratosphere The part of the *atmosphere* above the *troposphere* where there is little change of temperature with height. The *ionosphere* is above the stratosphere.

Stratus (St) Low-lying continuous layer of cloud, the base of which is rarely above 1650 ft, 500 m.

Stream 1. See *tidal stream.* 2. *Pay out overboard,* e.g. a *patent log* or *oil bag.* A long *warp* or heavy line may be made fast aft and streamed to keep the boat stern on to high following seas; it discourages the crests from breaking, slows the boat and reduces the risk of *broaching.* A *sea anchor* may also be streamed and made fast aft or forward to keep the boat at as safe and comfortable an angle to the seas as possible.

Streamers See *telltales.*

Stretch Although stretch and *elasticity* are often used interchangeably, a material that is elastic *recovers* after a load has been removed, and reverts to its original shape and size, whereas a material that has stretched does not recover. For example, a sheet which has stretched does not revert to its original length and circumference after the sail has been let fly. Natural fibres do not recover well, and lose some of their *tensile strength* when stretched, but the characterisitcs of *synthetic fibres* vary; nylon is both strong and elastic, and nylon rope is therefore suitable for *anchor cables* because its elasticity reduces *snubbing. Halyards,* on the other hand, should stretch as little as possible, and pre-stretched *polyester* is often selected. The construction of wire rope determines how much it stretches.

Stretch is incorrectly but popularly used to denote the amount by which a sail distorts with use. *Sailcloth* does not get any bigger under tension, so that stretch along one edge, e.g. the *luff,* is compensated by contraction in another direction, e.g. across the *chord* of the sail. The characteristics of synthetic sailcloth vary with *cloth construction* and how it is woven, and with the material of which the fibres are made. Some sailcloths are elastic and the fibres lengthen and recover well every time a load is applied and removed; other cloths may stretch once and thereafter behave like elastic fibres.

Stretcher Wooden batten, fitted transversely in the bottom of a *rowing boat,* against which an oarsman braces his feet.

Stretch-luff or **control-luff** As opposed to a *headsail* with a *luff wire* which limits the degree to which the luff can be extended, a stretch-luff genoa is designed to allow greater variation in luff tension and, consequently, greater alteration of sail *camber.*

Strike To lower an object vertically, such as a *topmast* or *yard* in heavy weather. In a battle, when referring to the *ensign,* to strike the colours is to surrender.

Stringer A *longitudinal member* fitted to strengthen the *frames,* such as the bilge stringer, which is fastened to the inner face of the frames at the level of the *bilge* (see *construction* fig). In *GRP/FRP* construction, longitudinal reinforcement is usually *laminated* into the *moulding* where extra strength is required.

Stripper 1. See *paint remover.* 2. A short length of line with a *snap hook* at one end, used when *peeling a spinnaker.*

Strip planking or **edge fastening** A method of construction for wooden hulls. Narrow, almost square planks are each glued and nailed, both to the *frames* and edgewise to the adjacent strip. The hull is extremely watertight, but expensive and difficult to repair.

Stroke 1. A complete *oar* movement, i.e. from the time that an oar dips into the water to the next time it dips in. 2. The rate at which a man rows. 3. The oarsman nearest the stern when two or more are rowing; he controls the rate of striking.

Strong breeze *Beaufort force* 6, 22–27 *knots.*

Strong gale *Beaufort force* 9, 41–47 *knots* in both WMO and US terminology.

Strop A loop of rope or wire rope, fitted round a *spar* or *block,* or to make a *sling;* may also be used to add length to the *luff* of a *headsail.*

Strum box A strainer fitted round the suction end of the *bilge pump* hose to prevent the pump from being choked by debris.

Strut Small projecting rod or bar, such as the *jumper* strut. A strut is often fitted to support the outboard end of the *propeller shaft* (UK often bracket). See also *mast strut.*

Studding sails (pronounced stunsls) Light-weather sails set outside *square sails* on *booms* that extend either side of the *yards.*

Stuffing box Gland fitted round the *propeller shaft,* where it passes through the *hull,* to make it watertight. A metal sleeve is filled with packing, which is compressed to fit tightly round the shaft by screwing up a cap. The *rudder stock* is similarly made watertight where it passes through the hull.

Stump topgallant mast A mast with no *royal* above the *topgallant.*

S-twist See *left-hand lay.*

Submarine cable A cable laid along the *sea-bed.*

Submersible electric pump An electrically-operated *bilge pump* which is fitted in the bilges, the motor being housed in a watertight chamber. An impeller with flexible blades rotates inside an eccentric housing and, when the blades are extended, the partial vacuum in the chamber draws in liquid. As the impeller turns the liquid is transferred from the suction side to the output side, and is forced out when the blades come into

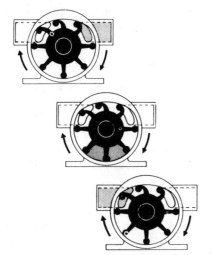

contact with the narrower eccentric section of the chamber. Many of these pumps start automatically when the water in the bilges rises to a certain level.

Subordinate station (US) See *secondary port*.

Sub-permanent magnetism Whereas permanent magnetism is acquired by a steel vessel when she is being built, sub-permanent magnetism is acquired by a vessel from the earth's lines of force when she *heads* in one direction for a long period, either when following one *course* for a long time or when *laid up,* whether on shore or in a mud berth. The effect diminishes gradually, and the *deviation table* should not be drawn up until the residual magnetism has disappeared.

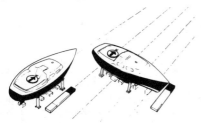

Substitute (US **repeater**) One of three triangular two-coloured *code flags* flown to repeat a letter or number higher in the same *hoist* (see end papers). When racing, the first substitute is the general *recall* signal and means 'The class is recalled for a new start as provided in the sailing instructions'.

Suit A complete set of sails.

Sumlog Proprietary name for a modern mechanical *log* with a large impeller, which is installed beneath the hull and turned by the water streaming past. Rotations are transmitted through a flexible cable to the register, which records speed and distance *through the water.* Electronic impeller Sumlogs are also available.

Sun-ray cut See *radial cut.*

Superstructure All those parts of the structure of a boat that lie above the deck, such as *coachroof* (US trunk), *doghouse, flying bridge* etc, but exclusive of *masts, rigging, spars* and *sails.*

Surf Broken water near the shore, between the shoreline and the outermost breaking seas. The circular *orbital motion* of water particles becomes elliptical when the *sea-bed shelves,* and the waves become steeper and break. As a verb, see *surfing.*

Surface current The horizontal movement of water in the upper layer of the oceans and seas; largely caused by winds that blow persistently from one direction.

Surface wind The wind blowing near the surface in the *boundary layer* of the earth is affected both in strength and direction by friction, and the effect is greater over land, which has a rougher surface than the sea. At sea the surface wind blows at about two-thirds of the speed of the *geostrophic wind,* and is deflected about 20° towards low pressure. Wind speed increases with height (see *wind gradient),* and is considerably stronger at the *masthead* than in the *cockpit.*

Surfacing tissue or **surface mat** A thin tissue of *glass fibres* that is either applied as the final layer of a *GRP/FRP laminate* to provide a smoother surface inside, or is applied to the *gelcoat* to disguise the coarser reinforcing material applied later.

Surfboard A flat, buoyant board often with a small *fin,* used for surfing.

Surfing 1. Riding waves in breaking surf, normally on a surfboard but sometimes without. The sport is particularly popular in Hawaii, and on US and Australian Pacific coasts where the water is warm, and the long *fetch* provides good surf. The surfer speeds inshore on a wave, using the combined effects of the *orbital motion* of water particles, the wave's speed of advance, and the steepness of its face. 2. The same principle is adopted at sea by cruising and racing boats; they can be kept on the face of a breaking wave, often for long periods, and may be accelerated by the breaking crest. A displacement boat may sail faster than *hull speed,* and can increase her speed over the ground by surfing repeatedly, but she slows markedly in the troughs. Boats can only surf when seas are high, and there is then a constant danger of *broaching.*

Surge 1. In abnormal weather conditions, such as a long-lasting storm, the level of the sea may be appreciably higher than that predicted, see *storm surge.* When a negative surge occurs, sea level is lower than that predicted. 2. As a verb is used for two contradictory actions when handling rope or cable: to *ease out* under control, e.g. by letting the turns round a *winch, bollard* or *windlass* slip a little at a time; to let it slip round a winch or *capstan* suddenly when the strain becomes too great.

Surveyor   A qualified professional who examines the *hull, rigging* and all parts of a boat, and reports on her condition. It is advisable to have a second-hand boat surveyed before completing the purchase.

Swage   Instead of making a time-consuming wire *eye splice,* compression *ferrules* or sleeves are squeezed tight round the *wire rope,* the pressure applied being sufficient to force the metal to cold flow between the individual *strands* and hold the wires firmly. Copper ferrules are used with stainless steel, aluminium ferrules with galvanized wire rope. The hand swage in the figure is suitable for wire rope of four different sizes, varying from $5/64$ to $5/32$ in (2 to 4 mm) in diameter. Trade names are (US) Nicopress and (UK) Talurit.

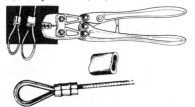

Swaged terminal   Stainless steel *terminal* or end fitting for *standing rigging;* has an eye or fork so that the wire rope can be attached to a mast *tang* or *turnbuckle* (UK or rigging screw), or may have a *ball* or tee *terminal* that engages in a hole in the mast or tang. Roll, power press or rotary hammer swaged terminals can be fitted to wire rope up to $13/32$ in (10 mm) in diameter, but are not removable (c.f. *swageless terminal*).

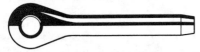

Swageless terminal or **core-and-plug terminal**   Patented *wire rope terminal* with a cone-shaped core over which the individual wires are spread. The tapered housing is screwed over the cone and holds the wires firmly, while a lock nut prevents them from unscrewing. *Breaking load* is generally about 50% higher than that of the wire rope. The same terminal can often be re-used with a replacement cone, or a new terminal fitted to the same piece of wire rope. Trade names are (US) Electroline and (UK) Sta-Lok.

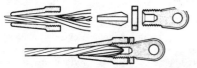

Swallow   The opening in a *block* where rope enters to pass over the *sheave.*

Swallow-tail   As in *broad pendants* and *code flags* A and B, the *fly* has a vee-shaped indentation.

Swamp   A boat is swamped when she is full of water. A centreboard dinghy should still float on account of her *buoyancy* (flotation) *tanks* etc.

Swan neck   Curve in hosing, taking it well above the level of its outlet below or near the *waterline.* Prevents sea-water from entering when the *seacock* is open, and is generally incorporated in engine exhausts and heads discharge piping.

Swashway or **swatchway** or **swash** or **swatch**   A narrow channel through shoals or across a sand-bank; often marked with *perches.*

Sweat up   To tauten a rope, especially a *halyard,* as much as possible.

Swedish hank   See *spring snap shackle.*

Swedish mainsail   *Storm mainsail;* usually the length of both luff and foot are about 75% of those of the regular mainsail; cut flat with pronounced leech hollow, no battens, and a ring for the halyard rather than a headboard. Is more close-winded than a *trysail* but cannot be set without a serviceable mast and boom; the latter can be dangerous in a gale.

Swedish splicing tool   Grooved *marline spike* for easier splicing of hard rope.

Sweep   1. The attractive curve of a boat's hull. 2. A long *oar.*

Swell   Long regular wind-generated *waves* that do not break; may be the precursor of a new wind blowing some distance away, or remain after a wind has dropped. Local winds may generate breaking seas on an existing swell. See also *Douglas scale.*

Swig or **swig up**   To haul a line, especially a *halyard,* taut manually. The lower hand holds a

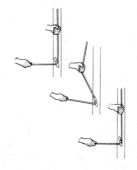

half turn firmly round a *cleat;* the other pulls the halyard horizontally away from the mast, so raising the sail higher; the lower hand then pulls in the slack as the top hand is moved back to the mast. This is repeated until the sail is fully hoisted and the halyard taut. The same method can be used with a *sheet*.

Swing 1. To rotate sideways around a fixed point, such as an *anchor* or a *mooring*, often in response to the changing *set* of a *tidal stream* or shifting winds. 2. Australian: to *sit out* (q.v), hence swinging straps (see *toe-straps*).

Swinging room The area of the circle along the circumference of which a boat at *anchor* or on a *mooring* swings without hitting an *obstruction* such as another vessel, and without *grounding*. In crowded anchorages chain cable is preferable to rope, because less *scope* is required and, consequently, less swinging room.

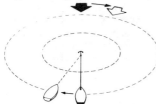

Swinging ship *Deviation* caused by fixtures on board, such as the engine, electronic equipment and electric circuits, can be determined by comparing *compass bearings* on various *headings* with a known *magnetic bearing*, the difference between them being deviation. The vessel is anchored or moored at a position within sight either of one identified object or of two objects in line, the magnetic bearing of which is known; she is then swung round on the spot, and a compass bearing is taken of the object, usually every 20° or 22½°. The difference between the two bearings is entered in the *deviation table*, q.v. A *direction finder* is *calibrated* by swinging ship when within sight of a transmitting *radio beacon* and DF error is found at intervals of about 10° by comparing the DF bearing with the magnetic bearing.

Swivel Many fittings incorporate a swivel that allows one part to turn, whether under strain or slack. There are swivelling *snap hooks, blocks,* and *eyes,* swivel links with a *clevis pin* in both parts, and the swivelling *tang* on the boom cap to which the mainsheet block and topping lift may be shackled. Chain swivel links are fitted in a *mooring pendant*, and a swivel clip is often required when a *flag* is bent to the flag *halyard*, to avoid twisting.

Swivel shackle Many types of *shackle* can be obtained with a swivel *eye* to enable rope to turn without kinking or causing an object to turn with it. For example a swivel snap shackle or swivel

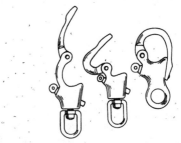

spring snap shackle is often used to shackle the *halyard* to the *spinnaker*.

Sydney–Hobart Race A 630-mile *offshore race,* sailed annually since 1945 when it was first suggested by Capt John Illingworth, who won in 'Myth of Malham'. The course is from Sydney, along the coast of New South Wales, across the Bass Strait to Hobart in Tasmania. About 100 competitors start on Boxing Day, and downwind sailing in fresh winds is normal. Is the culminating race of the *Southern Cross Series*.

Symbols and abbreviations To save space on *charts*, symbols are used for many features such as windmills, lighthouses, rocks, eddies, radio beacons and buoys. Together with abbreviations, they are listed and explained in US chart No. 1, UK No. 5011, and similarly by other national authorities responsible for the publication of charts. Most symbols used are those agreed by the International Hydrographic Organization, and the resulting standardization enables a navigator to interpret charts printed by other countries. US and UK charts are very similar. See also *weather code*.

Synopsis A brief statement giving the outline of the weather situation at a particular time.

Synoptic chart A chart of a considerable area of the surface of the earth, on which is plotted in condensed form information giving a general view of the weather at a particular moment, as if viewed from a satellite.

Synthetic fibres Fibres made from synthetic materials, such as *polyamide, polyester, polypropylene* or *glass*. The first three are spun into *yarns* and *laid* or *braided* into *rope*, or woven into *cloth;* the last is made up into reinforcing material such as *chopped strand mat* or *rovings* for *GRP/ FRP mouldings*.

T

T = Tango Red, white and blue code flag, vertical stripes with red in the hoist (the French ensign has blue in the hoist). As a single letter signal means 'Keep clear of me, I am engaged in pair trawling'. *Morse code:—*(dash).

Tabernacle Three-sided structure, attached firmly to the *deck,* in which the foot of a *lowering mast* is *stepped.* Two steel or wooden *cheeks* provide the bearings for the bolt which supports the mast, and about which it pivots when being raised or lowered. Some tabernacles are knee-high, and some can be moved along a fore-and-aft *track* so that *weather* or *lee helm* can be corrected.

Table At sea a normal fixed table is rarely horizontal because of the boat's *motion.* One solution is to suspend it in the *fore-and-aft line,* and to hang heavy counterweights beneath the points of suspension either end so that it is kept horizontal by gravity when the boat *heels.* See also *tabling.*

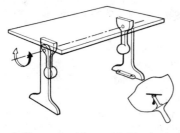

Table of offsets A table provided by the designer with the *lines plan;* gives the co-ordinates of various points at each *station* by tabling the half-breadth measurements for each *waterline,* and the heights of the *buttock lines* above a datum line.

Tabling Hem at the edge of a sail; the verb is to table. A flat seaming stitch or tabling stitch is used when hand-sewing.

Tachometer Instrument that indicates engine rpm or the rotational speed of a *propeller shaft.*

Tack 1. Noun: A sailing boat is on a tack when she is not in the process of *gybing* or tacking; she is on *port tack* when she has the wind on her *port* side and her *mainboom* to *starboard;* she is on *starboard tack* when she has the wind on her starboard side and her mainboom to port. When two boats are on the same tack the *windward boat* has to keep clear; when on opposite tacks port tack gives way to starboard tack (see *rules of the road*). A boat gybes or tacks (2) in order to change tack. 2. Verb: to go about, to change from one tack to another with the *bow* passing through the *eye of the wind.* In the *racing rules* a yacht is deemed to be tacking from the moment she is beyond *head to wind* until she has borne away to a *close-hauled* course (when *beating*), or to the

course on which her *mainsail* is filled (if not beating) and, while tacking she must keep clear of boats that are on a tack. The crew only have to *man* the *headsail sheets* when a boat is tacked, because the mainsail swings over automatically to the opposite side. 3. The lower forward corner of a *fore-and-aft sail* where the *luff* and *foot* meet; to attach the tack to a particular point on deck is to tack down. 4. The windward lower corner of the *spinnaker,* to which the *guy* is attached. 5. In a *square-rigged ship,* the lower *weather* corner of a *course* when close-hauled; also the rope or purchase running forward from the *clew* of the course. When close-hauled the tack to starboard is hauled taut when the ship sails on starboard tack.

Tacking downwind The boat alters course to sail alternately on *port* and *starboard tack, broad reaching* first on one tack and then on the other.

She changes tack by *gybing* instead of tacking, as she would when *beating*. A boat may tack downwind when her objective is dead to *leeward* to avoid a possible *accidental gybe,* or because she can reach her destination faster than on a dead *run* in spite of covering a greater distance over the ground. She sails faster, especially if a *mizzen staysail* is set, because the *apparent wind* is stronger on a broad reach than on a run, and the sails develop greater driving force.

Tacking line A line that leads roughly along the *mitre* of a *genoa* from the *clew* to a *block* on the *forestay* and back into the *cockpit*. When *going about* the line pulls the clew and much of the genoa forward, keeping it clear of the mast, *inner forestay* or *tallboy*. It is released as soon as the bows have passed through the wind, and the genoa is then sheeted home in the usual way.

Tackle 1. A term applied to a collection of gear, such as *ground tackle*. 2. A purchase to increase pulling or hoisting power by means of a rope or line, the *fall*, rove through one or more *blocks*. The *mechanical advantage* (MA) or the reduction in power is equal to the number of parts of the fall at the moving block, less about 10% lost through friction whenever the rope passes through a block. The parts of the fall are the standing part, which does not move when power is applied to the hauling part, and the running parts between the blocks; the blocks are identified as standing and moving. A tackle is rove to disadvantage when the hauling part comes from the standing block, but is

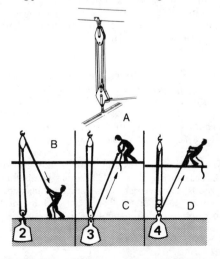

rove to advantage when the hauling part comes from the moving block.

Single *whip:* one single standing block, no MA.
Double whip (B): two single blocks, MA $\times$ 2.
Gun tackle (C): two single blocks, MA $\times$ 3 when rove to advantage.
Luff tackle (D): one double, one single block, MA $\times$ 4 when rove to advantage, MA $\times$ 3 when rove to disadvantage.
Two-fold purchase (A): two double blocks MA $\times$ 5 when rove to advantage, but MA $\times$ 4 when rove to disadvantage.

Tack tackle A tackle sometimes fitted between the *tack* of the sail and the *deck*, but more often attached to a line that leads from the *headsail* tack through a block at the deck. Enables luff tension to be altered as desired after the halyard has been cleated. Also used with *lugsails* to tauten the tack.

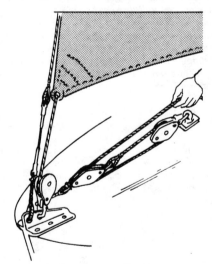

Tactical compass A *compass* designed to enable the helmsman or crew to make quick decisions when *racing*, such as which *tack* or which end of the *starting line* is more favourable, or whether a rival will cross ahead or astern when *beating* to windward. The card or bezel ring may be brightly coloured so as to be easily read from a distance.

Taffrail The *rail* at the *stern;* strictly, covers the head of the counter timbers.

Taffrail log See *patent log*.

Tail 1. A rope tail may be attached to a *block* so that it can be secured where desired. 2. A rope line *spliced* to the end of a wire *halyard* or *sheet* to make it easier to handle. 3. Verb: to tail on a line is to pull on it after turns have been taken round the drum of a *winch* (see also *self-tailing*), or to back up a member of the crew by hauling on the *fall* of a *tackle*, the *anchor cable* etc.

Tail shaft The aftermost part of the shaft, beyond the *stern tube*, to which the *propeller* is attached.

Take in *Lower* or *furl* sails.

Take off The wind is said to take off when it decreases in strength. When the *range of tides* decreases progressively between *springs* and *neaps*, they are said to be taking off or cutting, as opposed to making.

Take the ground To *beach* a vessel deliberately.

Take up *Seams* stop leaking when wooden planking swells (takes up) after immersion.

Take way off To reduce the speed of a boat through the water. In an emergency, say to avoid a *collision*, a boat put about with the *jib* left sheeted on the original side will come to a halt *hove to;* a dinghy can be *luffed head to wind*, or the sheets may be *let fly*, and she will lose way almost instantly; a boat under engine can go full speed astern. Other methods of taking way off include dropping the *anchor*, *shooting up* head to wind or into the *tidal stream*, and checking way with a *mooring line*.

Tallboy (sometimes **slot sail**) A tall, very narrow *headsail* with a short *foot*, mainly carried by offshore racing boats; now largely out of fashion. When set between the *genoa* and the *mainsail* on a *close-hauled* course in winds up to *force 5*, discourages the mainsail from *stalling*. May also be set athwartships on a *run*. *Cloth weight* about 1½–3 oz US, 2–3½ oz UK, 70–120 g/sq m.

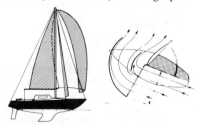

Talurit (US **Nicopress**) Patented systems which replace *wire splicing*. An *eye* is formed in *wire rope*, often round a *thimble*, by leading the wire rope twice through a soft metal *ferrule;* this is squeezed in a hydraulic press, and the metal flows

between the strands and individual wires, gripping them fast.

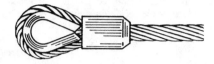

Tandem A *sailboard* designed to be sailed by two people, each controlling one complete rig, which is the same as the rig of a one-man sailboard, i.e. *mast, sail* and *wishbone boom*. The board is longer than the one-man board, has two *mast steps*, one *daggerboard* and a *fin*, and is steered by altering the position of the *centre of effort*. The man aft lets his sail out to make the board *bear away*, while the man forward eases out his sail when the board is to *luff up*. Boards have been sailed with up to seven masts and sails.

Tang Strong fitting, such as stainless steel strip, riveted or bolted to a *mast, spar, pulpit* etc so that part of the *standing rigging, lifeline* (guardrail) etc can be attached to it.

Tank Container for fluids such as fresh water and fuel, often built in. May be metal, *GRP/FRP,* synthetic rubber or plastics. Ballast and trimming tanks are occasionally fitted so that the boat's *trim* can be altered by filling and emptying the tanks.

Taper The end of a rope is unlaid, and the number of *yarns* in each *strand* is gradually reduced so as to decrease the diameter, perhaps to prevent the rope diameter from increasing when making a *long* or *back splice*, or to make it easier to *reeve* a *whipped* line through a *block* or *sheave*.

Target Object, at some distance from the vessel, from which a *radar* pulse is reflected, producing an echo on the *display*.

Tarpaulin Waterproof cover made of canvas or synthetic material; protects a *hatch* or the entire boat when *laid up* for the winter. Adequate *ventilation* is essential to allow air to circulate below.

Tar primer A flexible and abrasion-resistant epoxy *primer* containing tar, applied beneath *antifouling* to metal and *ferro-cement* hulls.

Taut As opposed to slack, a line, rope, wire or the *luff* or *foot* of a sail etc that is under tension.

Teak Wood grown in Burma and the West Indies; shrinks less than all other boatbuilding woods, and is extremely resistant to rot and marine borers. Weathers well, and is ideal for decks because it contains natural oils and therefore needs no varnish, providing a non-slip deck surface. *Specific gravity* 0.88–0.95.

Team racing In normal *races,* a boat is not allowed to hinder another boat or boats in order that a third boat may benefit, i.e. a yacht must compete by individual effort. However team racing is a particular form of the sport, in which two teams at a time race against each other. Each team usually consists of three boats, and teamwork rather than individual skill is decisive. Special tactics and a good knowledge of the *racing rules* are essential. The race is won by the team that accumulates the smallest number of points at the

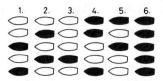

finish, the first boat scoring ¾ point, second boat 2 points, third 3 etc. Boats infringing the rules have penalty points added to their score. In the figure white scores 5¾, 8¾, 9, 9¾ and 10 points while black scores 15, 12, 11¾, 11, 10¾.

Telegraph cable buoy Marks the shore end of a *submarine* telegraph *cable.*

Telescope Optical instrument that magnifies distant objects. Except for those on *sextants* and *octants,* telescopes are no longer used on board, having been superseded by *binoculars.*

Tell-tale compass Usually fitted to the underside of the *deck* or *coachroof* (US trunk) so that those below can see the *course* being steered; often fitted over the owner's bunk.

Telltales 1. 2–3 inch long pieces of wool or very light material, sewn to the sail on both sides to give a visual indication of the character of airflow, in the *boundary layer,* which is of course invisible. They enable the helmsman to check whether his *course* is correct when *close-hauled,* and the crew to check whether the sail is *trimmed* to the correct *angle of attack.* When there is no airflow separation, the telltales lie close to the sail, streaming along towards the *leech,* but where airflow is separated they lift and flutter, or indicate reverse

flow by streaming towards the *luff.* The widely adopted practice of sewing them a few inches

from the luff may not be ideal, disregarding sail size, because a separation bubble often forms close to the sail's *leading edge,* airflow separates and, when the sail is trimmed correctly, it re-attaches quickly, further downwind towards the leech. The position at which telltales are most informative is generally the point of re-attachment, which is found by trial and error, and which is probably 5–10% of sail *chord* length abaft the luff. 2. Light cloth or ribbon, tied to a *shroud* to indicate the direction of the *apparent wind* when racing.

Temperature In *SI* units, thermodynamic temperature is measured in Kelvins, the interval 1 K being the same interval as 1° *Celsius* (centigrade). For conversion factors to and from Fahrenheit, see *Celsius.*

Template A thin pattern of a *member,* such as a *frame,* from which the actual member is shaped.

Tenacity Strength of *yarn* used in *cloth construction* is expressed as grammes per *denier* (rarely as lbs/sq in). If a load of 300 grammes is just sufficient to break a 100 denier yarn, the tenacity is 3 grammes per denier.

Tendency The rate at which *atmospheric pressure* changes, usually over a period of three hours. This is an important clue to future weather because, for example, a rapid fall of pressure generally indicates an approaching *depression* (*isobars* closely spaced round the low pressure centre), whereas a *barometer* rising slowly and steadily often indicates an approaching *anticyclone* (widely spaced isobars around an area of high presure).

Tender 1. A boat that *heels* easily and quickly is said to be tender; may be owing to low *initial stability* (i.e. shape of the *sections*), too high a *centre of gravity,* excessive *tophamper* etc. Although her *motion* in a *seaway* is easier than that of a *stiff* boat, a tender boat is not desirable. When measuring a boat for an *IOR rating,* the tenderness ratio is established by conducting an *inclining test.* 2. Small dinghy in which the crew are transported to and from a larger boat. Can also be used to *run out mooring lines,* when *kedging* off etc. Normally is propelled by *oars,* but some can be sailed and *sculled* as well, and most can propelled by an *outboard.* May be *towed* astern or carried aboard the parent boat when cruising. *Inflatables* are often used as tenders.

Tensile strength The tensile or pulling force that must be applied to break material, a part, rope etc is measured per unit area of cross-section of the material or part (before the load is applied), either in pounds per square inch (f.p.s) or in Newtons per square centimetre and kilonewtons per square metre (*SI*).

Tensioning rack A fitting to which a *centreboard hoist* or a *halyard* can be hooked at various points, thus allowing the position of the board or luff tension to be altered; often combined with a lever.

Teredo navalis Destructive marine mollusc that bores into wood and eats its way through it.

Tergal, Terital and **Terlenka** Trade names for French, Italian and Dutch *polyester* fibres respectively, used for making rope and sailcloth.

Terminal Fitting at the end of *wire rope* by which a *shroud* or *stay* can be attached to the *mast,* a *tang* or a *turnbuckle* (UK or rigging screw). May be a *fork, eye* or *ball* terminal. See also *Talurit, swaged* and *swageless terminals.*

Terrestrial Relating to the earth, as in terrestrial navigation, especially as opposed to *celestial.*

Terrestrial navigation Synonymous with *coastal navigation* and pilotage

Territorial Waters The Territorial Sea is the belt of water surrounding the coasts of a country, and extends a specific number of miles seaward from baselines round the coasts. The limit of three miles is accepted by many countries, but others claim 12 miles and more, and a few claim 200 miles.

Terylene Trade name for British *polyester* fibres used for making rope and sailcloth.

Tetoron Trade name for Japanese *polyester* fibres used for making rope and sailcloth.

Tex The unit for gauging the coarseness of synthetic or natural fibres, *yarns* and *filaments,* based on the weight in grammes of 1000 m of yarn or filament; a spool or cop 1000 m long which weighs 9 grammes has a tex number of 9. Usually divided into *decitex* (one tenth – the accepted unit for sailcloth) and millitex (one thousandth). One tex = 9 *denier.*

Thames Tonnage or **Thames Measurement** (T.M.) Yachts were formerly assessed by the formula

$$\text{Tons} = \frac{(L - B) \times B \times \frac{1}{2}B}{94}$$

L being length from the forward side of the *stem* to the after side of the *sternpost* measured at *deck* level, and B *beam* measured to the outside of the *planking.* The term is little used now because a

five-tonner T.M. could be a *light displacement* offshore racer displacing 2 tons or a 4.5 ton *heavy displacement* cruising boat.

Thimble An eye or ring made of stainless or galvanized steel, brass, bronze or nylon, with a concave groove on the outside in which the rope or wire rope lies. Often held in place by an *eye*

splice, but *Talurit* (US Nicopress) splicing is now more usual for wire rope. Reduces *chafe,* and enables the rope or wire to be shackled to an eye, sail etc.

Thinners Fluid added to *paint, varnish, resin* etc to make it less viscous, say in cold weather; also used for washing out paint brushes. The right thinners must be used, e.g. polyester resin can be thinned by adding styrene.

Thixotropic paste Is added to thicken *polyester resin,* for example when a vertical surface is *hand laid-up.* The more a thixotropic substance is worked, the less viscous it becomes.

Thole pins Two vertical wooden pegs inserted through holes in the *gunwale* in place of a *rowlock* (US oarlock) to provide a fulcrum for an oar when *rowing.* Alternatively, one thole pin with a *grommet* may be used.

Thread Spun-out *staples* of cotton, flax etc; also several filaments of synthetic fibre spun together.

Three-arm protractor (US) See *station pointer.*

Three-mast staysail schooner A *schooner* with three masts and a normal *bermudan* (US *marconi*) or *gaff sail* and boom only on the *mizzenmast; staysails* are set on the *mainmast* and *foremast.*

Three-point problem or **fix with two horizontal sextant angles** Given three identified objects, a *fix* obtained by measuring two horizontal angles virtually simultaneously with the *sextant* is more reliable than one obtained by taking three *bearings* with the *hand-bearing compass;* the sextant measures more accurately and *compass error* is eliminated. Although most easily plotted with a *station pointer,* the fix can be found with tracing paper, on which three lines are drawn from a point (V) at angles corresponding to the two sextant angles measured; the paper is moved over the *chart* until the lines pass through the three objects, and the vessel's position is then at V. The fix can also be plotted geometrically by drawing with a compass the position circles on which the vessel and the objects lie. The centres of the circles are found as in the figure; sextant angle subtended by A and B, 32°, is subtracted from 90° and isosceles triangle AXB is drawn seaward of AB

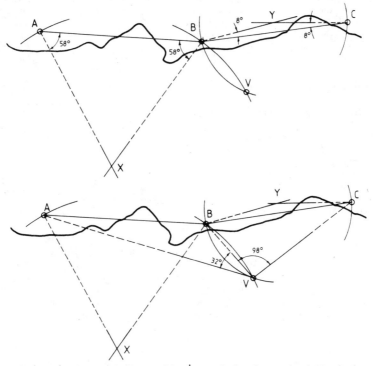

with angles of 58° at A and B; X is the centre of the circle on which A, B and the vessel lie. At 98° the sextant angle subtended by B and C is greater than 90°, and Y the centre of the second circle is found by drawing an isosceles triangle landwards from BC, the angles at B and C being 8° (98° minus 90°). V, the vessel's position, is where the two circles intersect. Should the sextant angle be exactly 90°, the centre of the circle is midway between the objects. The three objects selected should be almost on a straight line at right angles to the observer, or with the centre object nearest, so as to avoid the situation where the observer and all three objects are on the circumference of a single circle, in which case no fix would be obtained because the vessel could be anywhere on the circle.

Three-quarter rig A *sloop* with the *forestay* attached about three-quarters of the way up the *mast*, whereas that of a *masthead-rigged* sloop is

attached at the masthead. *Headsails* and *spinnaker* are smaller than those of a masthead-rigged boat.

Three-Quarter Ton Class A *level rating* class, the maximum *rating* being 24.5 ft. A typical boat's measurements are LOA 34 ft (10.3 m), LWL 25 ft (7.6 m), beam 9.5 ft (2.9 m), displacement 11,000 lbs (5 tonnes), sail area 486 sq ft (45 sq m). The Three-Quarter Ton Cup (the Jean Peytel Trophy) races, which have been sailed since 1974, consist of three Olympic courses about 24 n.miles long which count single points, plus a shorter offshore race planned to last about 27 hours, 150 n.miles, 1.5 points, and a longer offshore race, 54 hours, 300 n.miles, double points. The number of the crew is six.

Throat 1. The upper foremost corner of a quadrilateral *fore-and-aft sail* where *luff* and *head* meet, and to which the throat *halyard* is attached. 2. Sometimes the *jaws* of a *gaff*.

Through-fastening The fastening passes right through the parts being joined, or through a fitting

and a member. For example, a *fairlead* may be through-bolted to the deck, the bolt being secured by a nut beneath the deck and a *backing* plate, which distributes the load more widely over the decking, or a clenched nail plank may be through-fastened to a *frame*.

Through-hull fitting   See *skin fitting*.

Through-mast roller reefing   A method of *roller reefing*: the *mainsail* is reefed by turning the reefing handle, which is forward of the mast. In its simplest form is cheaper than *worm gear*, but more expensive through-mast systems with gears have been developed for larger sailing boats with heavier booms. The handle may then either be at a lower and more convenient position, or on the after side of the mast. The boom rotates so quickly that the system is sometimes used to furl the mainsail in harbour.

Through the water   *Courses, distances* and *speeds* are differentiated as being through the water or *over the ground*. In the latter case allowance has been made for *leeway* and the *set* and *rate* of the *tidal stream or current*, in the former no allowance

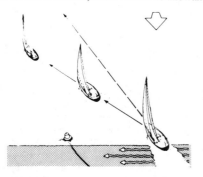

has been made. The boat's course through the water is indicated by the pecked line but, owing to the set of the tidal stream or current, her course over the ground will be along the solid line. See also *vector diagram, 2*.

Thumb cleat   *Cleat* with only one *horn*.

Thumb knot   Alternative term for *overhand knot*.

Thunderstorm   *Cumulonimbus* clouds are seen towering upwards to a height of several miles, their tops spreading out horizontally into a typical anvil shape. Flashes of lightning occur when static electricity is discharged, and the violent expansion of air along the lightning's path is heard as thunder. The time lag between seeing the lightning and hearing the thunder is 3 seconds per kilometre or 5 seconds per *nautical mile*. Thunderstorms are accompanied by heavy rain, perhaps hail, down-draughts and *squalls* from a new direction. The higher the anvil the more violent is the storm.

Thwart   An *athwartships* seat in a small boat, such as that on which an oarsman sits. In *racing dinghies* a thwart is generally fastened to the *centreboard case* and, as a major transverse member, contributes to structural strength.

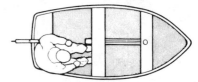

Thwartship   See *athwartship*.

Tidal current (US)   Horizontal movement of water in response to the rising and falling *tides* caused by the tide-raising forces of moon and sun. *Set* and *drift* change continuously and are tabulated in Tidal Current Tables. There are also Tidal Current Charts for some areas, and details are often given on *charts*. This term cannot be used in the UK (where *tidal stream* is used) because the word current relates solely to horizontal movement of water that is not due to tide-raising forces. The direction in which a tidal current is setting can be observed from *eddies* downstream of anchored objects, and the way a boat lies to her *anchor* or *mooring*.

Tidal current charts (US)   The National Ocean Survey publishes sets of twelve small scale charts for various tidal waters, each of which shows the *set* and *drift* of tidal currents in the area, at a certain number of hours after the time of *high* or *low water* at a major *reference station* nearby.

Tidal Current Tables (US)   Tables published annually by the National Ocean Survey, showing for each day of the year the predicted times of *slack water*, the times of maximum *flood* and *ebb current* velocity, and the direction of the flood and ebb currents at specific points. The times are local standard times.

Tidal curve   The change in sea level during a tidal cycle presented graphically in the *Tide Tables;* one curve shows the change in level at *springs* and another the change at *neaps*. The *height of tide* at any time can be read from the curve.

Tidal datum   The datum for *heights of tides* is the same datum as that used for *charts* of the area, i.e. US West Coast, *Mean Lower Low Water*, US Atlantic Coast, *Mean Low Water*, UK *Lowest Astronomical Tide*.

Tidal differences   Figures printed in the *Tide Tables* indicating (a) the difference between the times of *high* and *low water* at *secondary ports* (US subordinate stations), and the times predicted daily for HW and LW at a nearby *standard port*

(US reference station), and (b) the difference in the *heights of tides* at the two places. By applying the tidal differences the navigator can establish the height and time of tides at any secondary port.

Tidal harbour (US **harbor**)   A harbour in which water level rises and falls with the *tide;* not closed off by a lock or gates. Boats often lie on *moorings* or alongside *pontoons.*

Tidal prediction   The *Tide Tables,* which are published annually, tabulate the predicted times and *heights of tides* at many important ports, based on a series of observations over at least a year and on average meteorological conditions.

Tidal river   A river in which water level and flow are affected by *tides.*

Tidal stream (UK)   Horizontal movement of water in response to the rising and falling *tides,* caused by the tide-raising forces of moon and sun.

Set and *rate* alter continuously, and are shown in *tidal stream atlases* and on *charts.* The US term is *tidal current,* which is not used in the UK where current applies only to horizontal movement that is not due to tide-raising forces. The direction in which the tidal stream is setting can be observed from *eddies* downstream of anchored objects, and the way a boat lies to her *anchor* or *mooring.*

Tidal Stream Atlas   A set of chartlets printed by the Admiralty, showing the direction (*set*) and strength (*rate*) of tidal streams in a particular area at hourly intervals before and after *high water* at a *standard port,* usually also before and after high water Dover. The hydrographic authorities of other nations publish similar chartlets covering specific areas where tidal streams are important.

Tidal stream or current   In this dictionary the phrase is used all-embracingly to cover the UK terms *tidal stream* and *current* as well as the US terms *tidal current* and non-tidal current, i.e. to cover the horizontal movement of water whether resulting from *tide*-raising forces or other natural causes.

Tidal waters   Those parts of the ocean, coast and estuaries that are affected by *tides.*

Tidal wave   Popularly but incorrectly applied to a *tsunami* or seismic sea wave, which is caused by underwater earthquakes and which has no connection with *tides.* Tide wave and tidal wave are terms used in respect of the oscillation of water level resulting from tide-raising forces (sun and moon). The time of arrival of the crest of the tidal wave at a place is the time of *high water,* the time of arrival of the trough is the time of *low water.*

Diurnal tide

Semi-diurnal tide
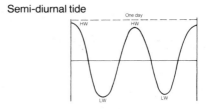

Mixed tide
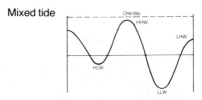

Tide   The vertical rise and fall of the mass of water in the oceans in response to the gravitational forces of sun and moon, i.e. the tidal undulation that results from the difference between the forces exerted on the earth and those exerted on the waters of the earth. *Semi-diurnal* tides have two tidal cycles per *lunar day,* the duration of each cycle being about 12 hrs 25 mins: *diurnal tides* have only one tidal cycle daily: *mixed tides* have two tidal cycles each day, but the *range* of one is very much greater than the range of the other.

Although all tides have diurnal and semi-diurnal components, the range of semi-diurnal tides is governed largely by the *phase of the moon;* range is greatest at *spring tides,* which occur at about the time of full and new moon when sun and moon are in *opposition* and *conjunction* respectively, and when the forces exerted act in the opposite or same direction; range is least (*neaps*) near the quarters when sun and moon are in *quadrature,* and the force of the moon is exerted at right angles to that of the sun. Diurnal tide-raising forces are greatest when the *declination* of sun and moon are

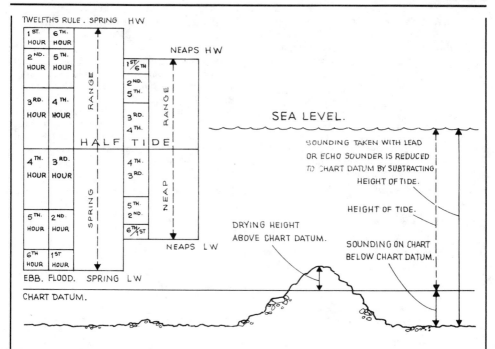

at their maximum, the tides with the greatest range occurring twice a year near the *equinoxes* when both sun and moon are on the equator. Mixed tides occur where both diurnal and semi-diurnal forces have a marked effect, but diurnal factors predominate.

The distance of the moon from the earth as she follows her elliptical orbit also affects the tides, and the range of *perigee* tides, when the moon is closest to the earth, is greater than average whereas the range of *apogee* tides, when she is furthest from the earth, is smaller than average.

Many other factors affect the tides, such as the size, shape and underwater features of the oceans, the shape of the coasts, the depth of the water and the weather, for example a change of *atmospheric pressure* can alter sea level by as much as 1 ft (0.3 m).

Tide gauge   Usually a graduated post or board which shows the *height of a tide*, namely the level of the sea above *chart datum*, so that the depth of water indicated can be related instantly to the *soundings* given on the chart.

Tide-rips   Disturbed water where two streams meet, or where the depth of water changes abruptly. Most noticeable when the tidal stream is running strongly.

Tide-rode   Said of a vessel lying to an *anchor* or at a *mooring* when she heads into the *tidal stream or current* rather than into the wind (see *wind-rode*).

Tide Tables   Official annual publication which, for each day of the year, gives the predicted times and heights of *high water*, and often of *low water* as well, for various *standard ports* (US reference stations). *Tidal differences* and constants are also given, and enable the navigator to find the time and *height of the tide* at many *secondary ports* (US subordinate stations). Often includes tables or curves from which the height of tide can be found at times between HW and LW.

Tide rode

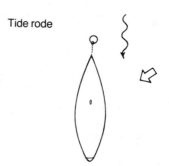

Tideway   The part of a channel, estuary etc where the *tidal stream* (US *tidal current*) runs most strongly.

Tide wind   *Tidal streams and currents* affect the direction and strength of the *apparent wind*, which is the resultant of the *true wind* and the wind that arises when a boat moves over earth's surface (boat speed). When there is no tidal stream or current, the wind that arises from boat speed blows in the opposite direction to that in which she is

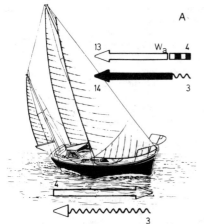

moving through the water, and at the same speed as she is making; when she is being *set* by a tidal stream it blows in the opposite direction to her *track over the ground*. This is most noticeable when drifting with a tidal stream in a *dead calm* because the light tide wind fills the sails and the boat makes *headway*. When the wind is fresh, tactics and seamanship are affected because speed over the ground is increased or reduced by the tide wind. Fig B shows the effect that a 3 *knot fair* tidal

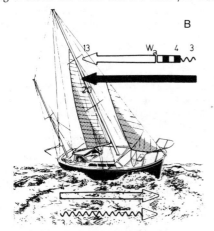

stream has on the seas and the amount of sail that can be set as compared to fig A when the boat is beating against a 3 knot *foul* tidal stream. Although in both cases the true wind is blowing at 13 knots and the boat is sailing at 4 knots, apparent wind speed is 14 knots in fig A but 20 knots in fig B.

Tie in a reef Reduce the area of sail set by bringing down the *luff* and *leech cringles* to the *boom* and gathering the lower, unwanted part of the sail with *reef points*.

Tier See *sail tier*.

Tie-rod A rod fitted to hold two parts of a boat together (see *construction* fig); for example may

be fitted transversely to bind two fore-and-aft members such as *carline* and *shelf* (US clamp), or beneath a *shroud* to transmit the load from the *chain plates* to the *keel*.

Tight Said of a vessel, hatch etc which does not leak.

Tiller A lever, attached at one end to the *rudder head*, and moved at the opposite end by the *helmsman* to deflect the *rudder* to one side. The length depends on the area of the rudder blade, rudder torque and the type of *stern*. Dinghies often have a *tiller extension* (US hiking stick). The tiller is put to *starboard* to turn to *port*, and vice versa.

Tiller extension (US **hiking stick**) A pole or stick attached to the tiller with a universal joint; bridges the gap between the helmsman's hand and the tiller when he is *sitting* or *hiking out*. Its length is at least half the boat's *beam*, and it should have a knob, wedge or other device at the outboard end to prevent it slipping from his grasp.

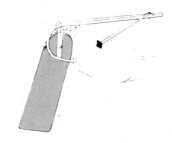

Tiller lines Lines attached to the tiller, either to hold it in a certain position when the boat is steering herself, or to reduce the helmsman's work if the boat is poorly *balanced* (see also *relieving tackle*).

Tiller steering system Simple *automatic pilot* that moves the tiller either with a pushrod or with lines, to keep the boat on a preselected course. This is either a *compass course* or, when controlled by a wind *vane*, a course relative to the wind direction.

Timber 1. Wood ready to be used for boat building. 2. Transverse member (see *construction* fig); whereas *frames* (q.v.) are sawn or laminated, timbers are steamed and bent to the desired shape.

Timber head The part of a timber that projects above *deck* level to support a *bulwark*; may sometimes be shaped for use as a *bollard* in traditional craft.

Timber hitch A simple hitch used to attach a line to a *spar*.

Timber hitch

Time The *SI* unit of time is the second. At sea, time is based on *mean solar time* and is measured in hours, minutes and seconds, just as on land; it is written with four figures using the 24-hour clock system, e.g. 0956 for 56 minutes past 9 a.m. With regard to time when making long voyages, see *zone time, local time* and *Greenwich Mean Time:* with regard to racing, see *elapsed time* and *corrected time:* with regard to celestial navigation, see *apparent solar* and mean solar *time, equation of time.* See *co-ordinated universal time.*

Time allowance A *handicap* class boat is measured in order to determine her *rating,* e.g. under the *IOR,* but it is the time allowance system that enables the *elapsed times* of competitors to be compared by converting them into *corrected time.* Normally time-on-distance, based on the length of the course is preferred in the US, and time-on-time, based on the time the boat takes to complete the course in the UK. Both systems have disadvantages: with time-on-time, calculations cannot be made until the boats have finished racing, and smaller boats may benefit in lighter winds and slow races; with time-on-distance, longer boats benefit when there is a great deal of windward work, the distance actually sailed through the water being longer than the distance on which the allowance is calculated. Attempts are continually being made to produce a system combining the better aspects of each. See also *Portsmouth Yardstick.*

Time limit Unless otherwise prescribed in the *sailing instructions,* provided one boat finishes a race before any advertised time limit the others may finish after than time.

Time Multiplication Factor, TMF or **Time Correction Factor,** TCF When time allowance is based on time-on-time, the TMF which multiplies *elapsed time* to give the boat's *corrected time* may be found from the *RORC* formula

$$TMF = \frac{a\sqrt{R}}{1 + b\sqrt{R}} \text{ where R = rating and}$$

a and b are constants; e.g. RORC 1979, Classes I–IV:

$$TMF = \frac{0.2424\sqrt{R}}{1 + 0.0567\sqrt{R}}$$

Classes V–VIII: $\quad TMF = \dfrac{0.4039\sqrt{R}}{1 + 0.2337\sqrt{R}}$

Other factors are based on less complicated computations.

The TCFs allotted by the RORC from 1936–1972 to racing yachts were obtained from a different formula, but were also based on their ratings and were applied in the same way to give their corrected times. Other TCFs may be found without complicated calculations, for example x seconds per mile against the scratch boat when the allowance is based on time-on-distance.

Time signal The exact time is broadcast regularly by normal radio services and by coastal radio stations so that the accuracy of the *chronometer* or *deck watch* can be checked. May also be made visually or by radio telegraphy.

Time zone An area bounded by *meridians* 15° apart, throughout which the same time is kept. Zone 0, based on the *Greenwich meridian,* is between 7°30'E and 7°30'W.

Tingle A thin patch, usually copper, with which a wooden hull is repaired temporarily to stop a leak.

Titanium (Ti) An expensive metal that is stronger and lighter than aluminium, and of only slightly greater *density* (4.50): is extremely resistant to *corrosion,* and is used for highly stressed fittings, *rod rigging* and even for the *spars* of some racing yachts.

Title The information printed on a *chart* giving details of the chart itself, i.e. its name, the geographical position of a named spot, *chart datum, natural scale,* units used for *soundings* and *heights,* date of publication etc.

Toe-rail 1. A low strip of wood, light alloy section or part of a *GRP/FRP moulding* which runs around the edge of the *deck* between *bow* and *stern* like a low *bulwark.* As in the figure, a light alloy toe-rail may have holes or slots to which the *genoa sheet* lead *blocks,* or a block for a *boom vang* can be shackled. The holes also serve as *scuppers* and allow water to drain overboard. 2. Any low strips secured along a deck to provide a foothold for the crew.

Toe straps (US **hiking straps,** Aus **swinging straps**) A webbing strap under which the crew hook their feet when *sitting out* (hiking out or swinging), fitted on both sides of the *cockpit* of a sailing dinghy. Must be adjustable to suit crews of different heights, so that they can maintain the most effective position for a long period without becoming exhausted.

Toggle 1. U-shaped metal link with a *clevis pin*, often inserted as a universal joint between the *chain plate* and *turnbuckle* (UK or rigging screw) in place of a *shackle*, to align the fitting with the *shroud* or *stay*, and to prevent fatigue or unscrewing caused by vibration. 2. A small piece of wood passed through an *eye* or other aperture to make a quick connection, e.g. when *bending* a *flag* to its *halyard*.

Tolerance Class building rules permit minor inaccuracies to allow for small errors when constructing the hull and when making sails. In some classes tolerances are extremely small; when they are larger they are often exploited to extract even a minimal advantage.

Ton See *tonnage*.
1 long ton = 2240 lbs = 1.12 short tons = 1.016047 tonnes
1 tonne = 0.984207 long tons = 1.10231 short tons
1 short ton = 2000 lbs = 0.893 long tons = 0.907185 tonnes.

Ton classes Coll: *Level Rating classes* such as One Ton, Quarter Ton etc.

Tonnage Of vessels is either a measure of capacity (1), or of weight (2), or is based on external measurements (3). 1. Broadly, gross tonnage is the volume of all that is below the tonnage deck, plus that of spaces between the upper deck and the tonnage deck, and of enclosed spaces on the upper deck. Net tonnage is gross tonnage less the volume of spaces that are non-earning, such as engine room, stores, accommodation and navigation areas. The amount paid for *harbour dues* and *light* dues is based on net tonnage. One ton = 100 cu ft = 2.83 cu m. 2. *Displacement* tonnage is the weight of the vessel, and is equal to the weight of the water displaced by the vessel. For conversion factors see *ton*. 3. In the case of boats built for pleasure, gross and net tonnage are irrelevant apart from payment of dues, and both US and UK authorities use a simplified formula to calculate tonnage, based on length overall, L, overall breadth, B, and depth (internal height) D, all in feet.

US sailboats $\frac{1}{2} \times \frac{LBD}{100}$ Other craft $\frac{2}{3} \times \frac{LBD}{100}$:
UK .0045 LBD
See also *Thames tonnage*.

Tonne *SI* and metric unit of mass: one tonne = 1000 kilogrammes. For conversion factors, see *ton*.

Toothed rack A rack onto which a rope such as the *mainsail halyard* can be hooked, instead of being *cleated*. Tension can be adjusted as required. Often combined with a lever or tackle.

Top A broad platform which rests on the thwartship *crosstrees* and fore-and-aft *trestle-trees* at the *head* of the *lower mast* and the *heel* of the *topmast* of a *sailing ship*. The primary purpose is to extend the topmast *shrouds*, but in sailing men-of-war, fighting tops were manned by men armed with muskets.

Topgallant The *square sail*, set above the *topsail(s)*, bent to the topgallant *yard* on the topgallant *mast*. A vessel carrying upper and lower topsails may also set upper and lower topgallants, in which case they are the fifth and fourth sails counting up from the deck.

Topgallant mast The upper section of a three-part mast, carried on the *topmast*. The section of mast on which the topgallant is set; the *royal* may be set on the upper portion as well.

Tophamper Everything that lies above the *deck*, including *masts, rigging, aerials, coachroof* (US trunk) etc, all of which increase *windage*. Tophamper is a disadvantage, especially when racing, because weight up high increases a boat's angle of *heel*, and this in turn increases *resistance*. Weight is therefore kept to a minimum, particularly *aloft*, for example by using lightweight *titanium masthead fittings*.

Topmark A geometric shape fitted on top of a *buoy* or *beacon* for identification purposes. Different shapes are used to indicate the purpose of the buoy, for example the *IALA A isolated danger* topmark is two large black spheres. Topmarks are not used in US buoyage systems, but two black *cone* topmarks are the major feature of IALA A *cardinal buoyage*. See end papers.

Topmast The mast, next above the *lower mast*, on which the *topsail* is set. May also be the upper part of a *pole mast*.

Topping lift A line which runs over a *sheave* on a *mast* and down to a *spar* that is attached to the mast at one end, such as that attached to the end of the *boom,* which it supports when the *mainsail* is lowered or being *reefed* (see *rigging* fig). The *spinnaker pole* topping lift is rigged to allow the vertical angle of the pole to be adjusted.

Topsail 1. A *fore-and-aft sail,* usually triangular, set above the *mainsail* of a *gaff-* or *sprit-rigged* boat (see *gaff topsail* and *jackyards.*). 2. In *square-rigged ships* the *square sail* above the *course,* bent to the topsail *yard;* frequently divided into upper and lower topsails. The topsail also serves as the *storm sail,* being the last to be left standing. When set on more than one mast of a *sailing ship,* topsails are named after the mast, e.g. main-topsail.

Topsail schooner A *sailing ship* with two or more masts, all *fore-and-aft rigged,* with square sails on the fore topmast in place of the *gaff topsail* of a fore-and-aft rigged *schooner.*

Topsides That part of the sides of a vessel that lies above the *waterline* when she is not *heeled* (as opposed to the *bottom* which is immersed). Coll esp US, on deck as opposed to below decks.

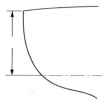

Top up 1. To raise, e.g. the *boom* by tightening the *topping lift.* The boom is then no longer supported by the sail, which can be lowered or reefed. 2. To fill up a tank completely.

Tornado 1. *B-class catamaran* designed by Rodney March. A high-performance racing cata-

maran made of *marine plywood* or *GRP/FRP,* and an *Olympic class* since 1976. LOA 20 ft (6.09 m), beam 9 ft 11 in (3.02 m), hull weight 280 lbs (127 kg), sail area 235 sq ft (21.83 sq m). 2. A funnel of violently whirling air, with a diameter of 150–650 ft (45–200 m) stretches down to the earth from a dark cloud. Winds can be extremely strong, up to 200 *knots,* and there is a strong updraught. A tornado leaves a trail of severe damage, but is of short duration. Usually occurs inland, most frequently in the Midwest and southern US States.

Torque A force that tends to rotate the body to which it is applied; see *moment.* Torque effect, see *wheel effect.*

Tow To pull a vessel or floating object through the water with a tow-rope. A sailing boat may be towed by a power vessel in a *calm* if unable to manoeuvre, perhaps after being *swamped* or damaged; she may be towed off the ground if she has *run aground.* As a noun, the vessel or object being towed. If a boat requires a tow, and the owner and crew of the towing boat are known, a tow can be accepted without risking a claim for *salvage* (q.v.), but it is advisable to use one of the towed boat's own warps as a tow-rope. Better is to agree a charge before accepting a tow because, legally, when a contract of towage has been made the tug cannot normally claim salvage. A *harbour master* is not permitted to claim salvage.

Towing tank An experimental tank in which a *scale* model of a vessel is towed in order to establish factors related to the interaction of hull and water, such as *frictional resistance, stability, wave-making resistance.* In some tanks the model remains stationary while the water is circulated to simulate the boat's motion.

Towing vessel Under the *IRPCS,* a *power-driven* vessel, when towing at night, exhibits two *masthead lights* forward in a vertical line, or three such lights if the tow exceeds 200 metres (or a *diamond shape* by day), in addition to *side* and *stern lights.* She also exhibits a yellow towing light in a vertical line above the stern light, the sector over which it shines matching that of the stern light. The towed vessel exhibits side and stern lights at night and, if the tow exceeds 200 m, a diamond shape by day. There are many differences between the IRPCS and the various US *rules of the road* relating to towed and towing vessels.

Towpath A path beside a canal or river from which a boat can be towed. The tow-rope is made fast to the *mast* or a fitting near the *centre of gravity* about which the boat pivots, because if it were attached to the *bow* the boat would be pulled towards the bank.

Tow-rope (US **towline**) The rope by which a vessel is towed, or with which she tows a floating object.

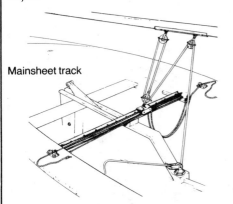

Mainsheet track

Track 1. A metal, light alloy, steel or plastics fitting used for many purposes in connection with sail setting and trimming; on deck, enables the *headsail sheet lead* to be altered; fastened to the forward side of a *mast* allows the inboard end of the *spinnaker pole* to be raised and lowered; C or T section sail *slides* run on or in internal or external tracks on the aft side of the mast and on *spars*. *Mainsheet tracks*, often of T, X or square section, are fitted *athwartships* on the *transom*, in the *cockpit* of a dinghy, on the *deck* or *bridgedeck* of a keelboat etc; the *traveller* (slider or car) runs back and forth as the *boom* passes from one side to the other, and the amount of travel is limited by spring-loaded stops or with a line. 2. The path between one position and another. Ground track is that over the ground; water track is that through the water. 3. The path that has been followed by a storm.

Track angle Direction of a *track*.

Track chart A small scale *chart* which shows the routes normally followed by shipping.

Track made good The mean *track* actually achieved *over the ground* by a vessel during a given period of time.

Trade winds *Global winds* (q.v.) which blow at the surface in the trade wind belt, between the low-pressure *Intertropical Convergence Zone* and the high-pressure belts about 30° north and south of the *equator*. Hot air rises at the ITCZ and, instead of flowing due north and south at high altitude, is diverted to flow towards the north-east and south-east by the earth's rotation. The air then sinks and flows back as a surface wind in the opposite direction, blowing towards the equator as the NE trades in the northern hemisphere and as the SE trades in the southern. The trade wind

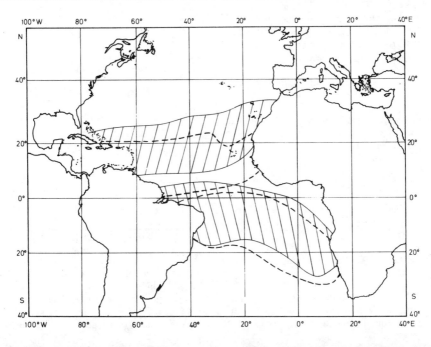

belts move further north during the northern summer and further south during the northern winter, roughly as indicated by the broken lines. Because trade winds blow steadily and virtually constantly, they are useful to sailors who can run or reach across oceans. Formerly a *running square sail* was often set by smaller vessels, but *twin jibs* are now preferred.

Traffic separation scheme In areas where traffic is congested, or where tracks converge, vessels proceeding in opposite directions use internationally agreed one-way lanes. On *charts* the direction in which vessels must proceed in the traffic lanes is indicated by arrows; between the lanes is a separation zone, coloured purple. Regulations regarding behaviour in traffic lanes are strict, and fines for contravention can be very heavy. Among other regulations, a *sailing vessel* and a vessel under 20 m in length may not impede the safe passage of vessels in a traffic lane; when crossing, vessels should do so at an attitude as nearly at right angles to traffic flow as possible, ignoring leeway or tidal set, so as to present the correct profile or navigation lights to ships in the traffic lane and so as to cross in the shortest possible time.

Trailer Framework on which a boat is towed behind an automobile, truck or heavy vehicle. Many types are available; some transport keelboats but most are designed for centreboard dinghies. Vehicles towing trailers are usually subject to a speed limit, often of 50 mph or 80 km/hr.

Trailing edge The downwind or downstream edge of an *aerofoil* or *hydrofoil*, such as the *leech* of a sail or the after edge of the *keel* and *rudder*. Unlike the rounded *leading edge* of a streamlined foil, it tapers.

Trampoline Netting that fills part of the space between the *hulls* of a *catamaran*.

Trans-Atlantic racing The first race took place from the USA to the UK in 1866 between three large American yachts, over 100 ft (30 m) in length, with paid hands crewing; over 20 races have been run across the Atlantic since then. The first single-handed race from the USA to England took place in 1891 and, since 1960, single-handed races (*OSTAR*) have been run every four years in the reverse direction. For trans-Atlantic records, see Blue Ribband.

Transceiver TRANSmits and reCEIVEs radio signals. See also *EPIRB*.

Transducer A component of *sonar, echo sounders, doppler logs* etc which converts electric signals into sound waves and vice versa. May be through-hull or in-hull installed (see *echo sounder*), and many are retractable so that the face can be inspected and cleaned.

Transferred position line (US **advanced** or **retired line of position**) When a *bearing* can be taken of only one landmark, or only one *heavenly body* can be observed, the *position line* obtained can be transferred (US advanced) along the vessel's *track*, and is then drawn parallel to the original position line at a distance based on the vessel's *speed* and *course* made good *over the ground* during the period that elapses before a second position line is obtained. Alternatively a position line obtained later may be transferred back (US retired) along the track to cut an earlier position line. See *running fix.*

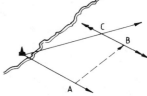

Transit 1. Two fixed objects are in transit when they are seen to be in line (US *range*). A reliable *position line* is obtained without a *hand-bearing compass* when two identified objects on shore such as two *beacons*, or a church tower and a flagstaff, are in transit. The *compass* can be

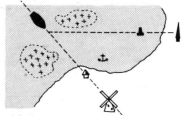

checked for error against a transit. 2. The passage of a *heavenly body* across an *observer's meridian*, at which time it attains its maximum *altitude*. The body's *true bearing* is due north or south of the observer.

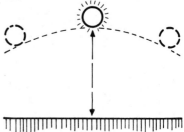

Transom The flat or sometimes slightly curved transverse structure that extends across the *stern* of a hull which has no *overhang* aft. Almost all sailing dinghies have a nearly vertical transom, on which the *rudder* is hung. That of a keelboat may be *raked* forward or aft, generally with the rudder

hung on it, and the *sternpost* extends from the *deck* to the bottom of the *keel*. A transom stern was long preferred for keelboats because the rudder, hung outboard, can be inspected and repaired easily. Some smaller dinghies, such as the Optimist and Cadet, have a bow transom as well.

Transom flap An opening in the transom, normally closed by a flap; this is opened so that water in the *cockpit* can be sucked out automatically when the boat is sailing fast. A *planing dinghy* can often be sailed dry after *capsizing* if she has transom flaps.

Transom knee *Knee* that joins the transom to the *keel*, *hog* or *horn timber*.

Transpacific Race (Transpac) An *offshore race* run for the first time in 1906 from Los Angeles to Honolulu. Originally run biennially, later irregularly but, since 1939, alternately with the *Bermuda Race*. The 2225 n.mile course is sailed in fresh *trade winds* in July or August, and takes about 12 days; 'Windward Passage' sailed the course in 9 days 5 hours in 1971.

Transponder See *racon*.

Transverse bulkhead A *bulkhead* fitted *athwartships*; provides transverse strength and rigidity, which is especially desirable near the mast, and separates two compartments below decks. Generally wooden and may sometimes be watertight.

Transverse members *Members* fitted *athwart- ships* to provide transverse strength and to counter lateral forces such as wind pressure, *buoyancy*, wave action etc. *Frames, timbers, deck beams* and *floors* are all transverse members, and are connected to longitudinal members to form a strong framework.

Transverse stability The ability of a boat to *right* herself, opposing the side forces of wind, waves etc which cause her to *heel* (see *stability*).

Trapeze Gear fitted to fast *racing dinghies* and some *keelboats* to enable the crew to put all his weight outboard to *windward*. The crew wears a trapeze harness or belt with a hook, which he slips into a ring on the lower end of the trapeze wire; this is attached about three-quarters of the way up the mast. He stands out at full stretch, feet on the gunwale, hanging virtually horizontal so that his weight is used with optimum effect to counter *heeling force* and to keep the dinghy on an *even keel* while he trims the headsail. A piece of shock cord keeps the trapeze wire close to the shroud or mast when not in use. Trapeze techniques vary from boat to boat and with the *point of sailing*.

Traveller or car 1. A ring, hoop etc that slides along a *spar* such as a *bowsprit*. 2. A fitting which slides in or on a *track*, such as the *mainsheet* traveller or car which slides along a track or *horse* fitted athwartships as the *boom* passes from one side of the boat to the other. The traveller in the figure has rollers so that it can slide more easily on the X-section track; they also prevent it from tilting. The amount of travel may be limited by adjustable spring loaded plunger stops or by a line which can be cleated. Sometimes the mainsheet of a dinghy is cleated, and the sail played simply with the traveller line. US: the term is also applied to the horse itself.

Travel-lift (US travelling lift) Type of *crane* with which sailing boats or power vessels are lifted out of the water, suspended between framework either side. Runs on wheels.

Traverse Tables Tables based on the solving of a right-angled triangle. The navigator can either find *departure* and *difference of latitude* from *course* and *distance made good*, or can find the course and distance made good from departure and d.lat.

Trawler Under the *IRPCS* a *vessel engaged in fishing* with trawl nets is given separate status from other fishing vessels, and must show different lights.

Treble block A *block* with three *sheaves* on a single pin, used for a *tackle* when all the parts run parallel to one another.

Treenail or **trenail** A *fastening;* a hardwood pin, formerly used to secure wooden members of a hull. Driven through as a fit, and usually wedged at the outer end. Pronounced trunnel.

Trestle-trees Fore-and-aft supports for the *top* of a *sailing ship;* rest on *hounds* or are riveted either side of the *mast.* See also *crosstrees.*

Trevira Trade name for German *polyester* fibres used for making rope and sailcloth.

Triangle of forces/velocities See *vector diagram.*

Triangle of position (US) See *cocked hat.*

Triangular course Often used for races because it provides a good proportion of *reaching, running* and *windward* work. The *Olympic course* is the only course to provide three suitable *marks* regardless of wind direction.

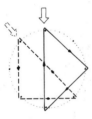

Triatic stay A *stay* in a *fore-and-aft rigged* vessel with more than one *mast;* runs roughly horizontally from one *masthead* to another.

Tri-axial weave A cloth construction which involves two sets of *warp* yarns interlaced at 60° on either side of the *weft* (US fill) in a basket weave pattern. The object is to offer more uniform stretch qualities and a higher resistance to tearing.

Trice up Traditionally to haul up an object, especially with a *tricing line.* Now sometimes to *lash* or restrict an object, trussing it up with a length of line.

Tricing line A line or rope used to haul up an object, particularly the *tack* of a *gaff sail* towards the *jaws.*

Trick Spell on duty, especially at the *helm.*

Tri-colour lantern Under the *IRPCS* the lights prescribed for a *sailing vessel* under 12 m in length may be exhibited from a single lantern at or near the top of the mast. The lantern has different coloured lenses so that *side lights* and *stern lights* are exhibited as required by the regulations. See also *IMO.*

Trim 1. To adjust the sail to the *point of sailing* by hardening or *easing* the *sheet* so that it produces maximum driving force. 2. Esp US: to trim or trim in is synonymous with *hardening,* i.e. to bring the sail closer to the *centreline.* 3. The difference between the boat's *draft forward* and her draft *aft.* The angle that the *designed waterline* makes with the surface of the water in the *fore-and-aft line.* The boat is on an *even keel* when her designed waterline is parallel to the surface of the water, but is trimmed *by the stern* (or by the bow) when she is more deeply immersed aft than forward (or forward than aft). Trim does not relate to lateral inclination (*heeling* and *listing*). To alter the trim of a sailing dinghy, the crew moves further forward when *close-hauled* and further aft when *reaching.* A *keelboat* may be trimmed, say, by moving the *anchor cable* further forward to counter crew weight in the cockpit, or by shifting movable *ballast.*

Trimaran A *multihull* with a central *hull* that is longer and beamier than the *outriggers* or floats

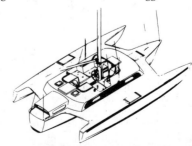

fitted on either side; the cabin is in the central hull. These very beamy craft combine low *frictional resistance* with great *transverse stability*. Cruising trimarans have proved seaworthy and, thanks to their great speed, have performed successfully in Trans-Atlantic and other races. Their weakness lies in the joining of the outriggers to the main hull.

Trim tab 1. A hinged tab at the *trailing edge* of the *keel* of a *fin and skeg* hull; acts like a second smaller *rudder* and is fitted to increase *lift* and reduce *leeway*, especially on *close-hauled* courses.

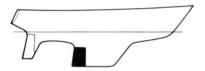

2. Similarly a hinged tab may be fitted to the trailing edge of a rudder to reduce the amount of effort required to alter the rudder angle, especially when the boat has *self-steering gear* or an *automatic pilot*. 3. A hinged horizontal plate, fitted at the bottom of a motor boat's *transom* and raised or lowered to alter her *trim*, usually to assist *planing*.

Trinity House (UK) The body responsible for the installation and maintenance of *lighthouses*, *light vessels* and UK *buoyage* generally. Also licenses *pilots*.

Trip To *break out* the *anchor* by hoisting the *crown* with the tripping line or *buoy rope*.

Tripping line (US usually **trip-line**) 1. A line attached to the *crown* of an *anchor* so that it can be pulled out backwards if the *fluke* has got caught

under a *submarine cable* or rock, or if the *anchor cable* is *foul*. An *anchor buoy* is often attached to mark the anchor's position on the bottom. 2. The line bent to the narrow outboard end of a *sea anchor* or *drogue* so that it can be collapsed and brought back on board.

Trolley Frame with wheels or rollers on which a dinghy is pushed or pulled manually over a ramp or beach.

Tropical revolving storm (US **tropical cyclone**) A storm that originates in the tropics or sub-tropics, often at about *latitude 10°*N or S. Smaller in area than a typical *depression* (US extra-tropical cyclone) and does not have *fronts*, but is often extremely violent. Tropical storms are given different names in different parts of the world, i.e. *hurricane*, *cyclone*, *typhoon*, and occur most frequently at particular times of the year. In the

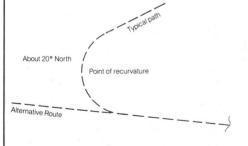

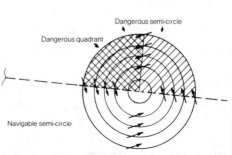

northern hemisphere they initially follow a typical path between W × N and NW and, at about lat 20°, the path often changes direction at the point of recurvature, where the storm swings round to travel in a north-easterly direction. In the southern hemisphere their path is initially between WSW and SSW, and changes to SE beyond the vertex, the point of recurvature. Some storms continue on their original course until they reach a large land mass, where they often cause great damage before they die out; others turn full circle back towards the *equator*.

Winds blow spirally inwards towards the centre where pressure is low, and there is a calm eye, often about 15 n.miles in diameter; winds there are much lighter and the sky is clear or nearly clear. The strongest winds blow near the eye and, to avoid the centre, a vessel tries when possible to keep in the *navigable semicircle* and avoid the *dangerous semicircle*, q.v.

Tropics The area bounded by the tropics of Cancer and Capricorn. The climate is hot and damp, with great differences in temperature between day and night, but temperature differs less between summer and winter.

Tropics of Cancer and Capricorn The highest *latitudes* reached by the vertical sun at noon in the course of the year, latitudes 23°27'N and S. The sun reaches the Tropic of Cancer at the northern summer solstice on June 21, the longest day in the northern hemisphere, and reaches the Tropic of Capricorn on December 21, the longest night in the northern hemisphere, at the northern winter solstice; in the southern hemisphere June 21 is the longest night, December 21 the longest day.

Troposphere The lower part of the earth's *atmosphere* within which weather is formed by the vertical and horizontal movement of *air masses*. In this area temperature decreases markedly with height. The troposphere extends about 7 miles (11 km) upwards in the tropics, about 6 miles (10 km) at the westerlies and about 5 miles (8 km) at the poles. The tropopause is the boundary between the troposphere and the *stratosphere*.

Trot *Mooring buoys* laid in a line; boats moor to them with *bow* and *stern lines*.

Trough 1. The lowest point of a wave. 2. A frontal trough is an area of low pressure, where the *isobars* extend outward from a *low* (see *anticyclone* fig). Weather deteriorates for a period, and the wind may be strong and *veer*. Non-frontal troughs often occur in the rear of a *depression*, and the steeper the *pressure gradient* the worse the weather associated with the trough will be.

Truck Circular block of wood at the top of a *mast*; generally has a *sheave* for the *burgee halyard*.

The very top of the mast is often referred to as the truck.

True Frequently used to differentiate between a value that has been corrected for known errors and one that has not, as in the definitions below.

True altitude The angular distance of a *heavenly body* above the *rational* or celestial *horizon* measured along the celestial *great circle* that passes through the body and the observer's *zenith*; *sextant altitude* corrected for *index error, dip, refraction, semi-diameter* and *parallax*.

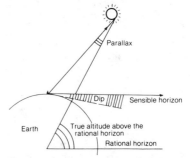

True bearing The angle between the direction of an object and the true north-south *meridian*, from the position of an observer.

True course The *course* relative to true north, i.e. the angle between the vessel's *fore-and-aft line* and the direction of true north. A true course or *bearing* is corrected (US uncorrected) to a *magnetic course* or *bearing* by adding westerly or subtracting easterly *variation*.

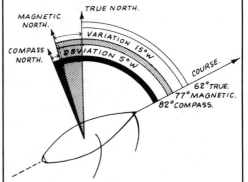

True north The direction of the *geographical north pole*. *Charts* are based on true north.

True sun The sun seen in the heavens. During the course of a year the sun appears to move around a celestial *great circle* called the *ecliptic*, which is inclined at an angle of 23°27' to the earth's *equator* because the earth's axis is tilted. The true sun's path is elliptical and it does not therefore move at constant speed (c.f. *mean sun*).

True wind The movement of air when wind

blows as a result of differences in *atmospheric pressure,* whether owing to global or local effects. Its direction and speed are felt when stationary, as on a pier or a boat at anchor. The *apparent wind* (q.v.) is that felt on a moving vessel, and is the resultant of the true wind and boat speed.

Trunk 1. The *rudder* trunk is a hollow waterproof tube that runs between the *deck* or the *cockpit sole* and the *bottom.* The rudder stock inside is connected to the *tiller* or *quadrant* at the head, and to the *rudder blade* below. 2. The hollow case which houses the *centreboard* (UK usually *centreboard case*). 3. US: the top and sides of a trunk cabin that stand above deck level (UK *coachroof*). A trunk cabin provides headroom below decks. 4. A vertical space, open at top and bottom, in which an outboard engine is suspended, a well.

Trysail 1. or storm trysail: small flat-cut triangular *fore-and-aft sail* made of heavy cloth and strongly reinforced; set *loose-footed* on a mast in place of the *reefed* working *mainsail* in stormy weather. *Cloth weight* normally up to 7–9 oz US, 9–11 oz UK, 300–370 g/sq m. In an emergency the *storm jib* can be set in its place. 2. Fore-and-aft sail with a *boom,* set on the *foremast* or *mainmast* of a *square-rigged ship.* 3. Fore-and-aft sail set between the fore- and mainmasts or main- and *mizzenmasts* of a *staysail schooner.*

Trysail mast Small mast in a *sailing ship,* stepped immediately abaft the *main-* or *mizzenmast;* carries a trysail.

Tsunami or **seismic sea wave** A series of seismic sea *waves* caused by submarine earthquakes, popularly but wrongly called *tidal waves.* They occur most frequently in the Pacific and cannot be detected on the open sea because wavelength may be over 100 miles. They travel very long distances at extremely high speeds (up to 450 *knots*) and, although their height in the open sea is often only about 1.5 ft (0.5 m), they can cause great damage on arrival at distant shores where they build up in shallow waters, sometimes to a height of 65 ft (20 m). The US and New Zealand governments maintain tsunami warning stations in the Pacific.

Tube chock See *shaft log.*

Tubular jam cleat *Cleat,* usually made of nylon but sometimes of metal, tubular in shape with a wedge-shaped slot in the top or side; fitted

especially to sailing dinghies for smaller diameter lines such as spinnaker sheets which can be jammed quickly in the slot.

Tuck 1. The area underwater where the almost vertical part of the *bottom* curves out to meet the side or *bilge.* 2. To weave the individual strands of a rope over and under each other when *splicing.*

Tuck in a reef To reduce the area of sail, by *points* or *jiffy reefing* rather than by *roller reefing.*

Tug A small but powerful motor vessel designed and fitted out for towing larger vessels. The lights and shapes required by the *IRPCS* are detailed under *towing vessel.*

Tumblehome The sides curve inwards towards the centreline at the top near the *gunwale, beam* at deck level being less than maximum beam (see fig), but never less than waterline beam. Many offshore racers have tumblehome amidships, both to improve their *rating* and to reduce *frictional resistance* when the boat is well *heeled.* C.f. *flare.*

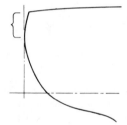

Tune To bring a boat to perfection, so far as performance is concerned. Includes weight trim and hull smoothness, but relates especially to the correct tensioning of the *standing rigging,* which affects the *bend* of the *mast;* this in turn alters sail *camber.* Many devices are fitted for tuning purposes, such as *wheel tensioners, shroud adjusters, backstay adjusters, mast jacks* and *mast bend controllers.*

Tunnel hull A continuously moulded hull of catamaran form with two flotation points and an interconnecting archway between the two. See also *cathedral hull.*

Turbulence Fluid does not follow a smooth regular path parallel to the foil (*laminar* flow), but moves irregularly and perpendicular to the general direction of flow within the *boundary* layer, which

grows considerably thicker. Turbulence starts at a certain critical value of *Reynolds number,* and usually occurs before the point of separation, beyond which eddies form. When a sail is trimmed to too great an *angle of attack*, airflow may become turbulent on the lee side of the sail, but when the sail is trimmed too close, flow becomes turbulent to windward, starting at the luff. This can be seen when *telltales* flutter and stand out from the sail instead of lying smoothly along it. Turbulence also arises where trees, buildings etc interrupt the flow of the wind, and major turbulence on the lee side of obstacles can cause problems, especially for sailing dinghies. Also occurs in water flow, over the hull, keel and rudder.

Turk's head An ornamental knot made on the end of a rope or around an object such as a spar or the tiller.

Turn A loop made round a *cleat, bollard* etc with rope, line or wire. When taken on a *winch*, later turns are taken above those put on earlier to avoid a *riding* (US overriding) *turn* that jams under load.

Turnbuckle (UK usually **rigging screw,** sometimes **bottlescrew** or **turnbuckle**) A fitting inserted between a *chain plate* or *deck plate* and a *stay* or a *shroud* to adjust the tension of the *standing rigging*. The bolt on one end has a right-hand thread, the other a left-hand thread, so that both move in and out simultaneously when the body is rotated, so lengthening or shortening the wire.

The correct tension is maintained by preventing the turnbuckle from unwinding with a lock nut, split pin or wire lashing. Some have forks either end, closed by a *clevis pin*, others are fork and swage, or fork and eye; some have closed bodies, others have open bodies. Turnbuckles are also often used to tension the *lifeline* (guardrail). Formerly a *lanyard* and *deadeye* was used for tensioning rigging, and a lanyard is still sometimes used in an emergency and in small simply rigged dinghies. Racing dinghies usually have light *shroud* and *stay adjusters* instead.

Turning block See *foot block*.

Turning circle The course followed by a boat when the *rudder* is kept at a certain angle; the term is often used in respect of the smallest circle that

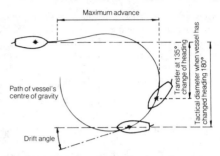

she can make when the rudder is at the optimum *angle of attack*. The roughly circular course is actually followed by the *centre of gravity* (the point about which she pivots) because she turns at an angle. Her bows describe a circle of smaller radius and her stern one of larger radius than the path followed by the centre of gravity. The angle between the tangent at the centre of gravity and her fore-and-aft line is the drift angle. Advance is the distance she covers in the direction of her original course after the helm has been put over (measured parallel to her original course); transfer is the distance covered at right angles to the original course to a particular point, such as the point where she has turned through 135°; tactical diameter is the transfer when her heading has changed 180°.

Turn of the bilge Where the bottom of a *round bilge* boat curves up to meet the *topsides*. The curve of the bilge of a hard bilge boat (A) is smaller than that of a slack bilge boat and, because this provides greater *initial stability,* is seen in sailing dinghies which rely largely on hull form for *stability*. Ballasted keelboats require less initial stability, and may have a slacker bilge (B).

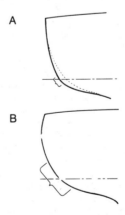

Turn of the tide The time when a *rectilinear stream* (US reversing current) changes direction, say from east-going to west-going or vice versa; *slack water*. Rarely coincides with the times of *high* or *low water*.

Turn to windward See *beat* to windward.

Turn turtle When a *capsized* boat turns right over until the *deck* is horizontal to the surface of the water and the *mast* points down vertically to the bottom, she is said to turn turtle. Some racing dinghies and most multihulls have this tendency, in the absence of buoyancy bags, floats etc.

Turtle A bag which is attached to the *foredeck*, either in the *pulpit* or on the *lee* side, so that the *spinnaker* can be hoisted more easily. The spinnaker is carefully packed into it prior to hoisting, *foot* and *bunt* first; the *head* and *clews* are left to the last so that the halyard and sheets can be shackled to them.

Twelfths rule, or 1, 2, 3, –3, 2, 1, rule An approximate method of estimating *height of tide* during the six hours between *high water* and *low water*, or between low and high water (see *Tide* fig). The *range* of the tide is divided into twelve parts; during the first and sixth hours, water level rises or falls one-twelfth of the range; during the second and fifth, two-twelfths; during the third and fourth, three-twelfths.

12-metre class One of the classes rated under the *International Rule* and, currently, the class to which the boats that compete for the *America's Cup* belong. As this is a *development class,* the measurements differ from boat to boat, but length is approximately 65 ft (20 m), and sail area about 1800 sq ft (167 sq m).

Twilight Period before sunrise and after sunset when it is not yet dark due to light reflected by the atmosphere. The duration of twilight varies according to the observer's *latitude,* being shortest at lower latitudes near the equator and longest near the poles. Both morning and evening twilight are sub-divided into *civil, nautical* and *astronomical twilight* according to how many degrees the sun's centre is below the *rational horizon.*

Twin bilge keels *Bilge keels* fitted either side of the hull near the bilges, instead of a central keel. See bilge keel.

Twine Small stuff, often two twisted yarns, used for sewing *canvas, roping, whipping* etc.

Twing, twang or **twinning line** Similar to a *barber hauler*, but alters the lead of the *spinnaker sheet.*

Twin-grooved forestay A *headfoil* with twin grooves that allow a replacement *headsail* to be hoisted before the first is lowered.

Twin jibs or **twin running sails** Two *headsails* of the same size, *boomed out* by twin poles either side of the mast; set when *running* in *trade winds,* mainly by cruising boats making long passages. *Guys* hold the poles at an angle of about 20° *forward of the beam*, and the mainsail is lowered and stowed.

Twin-screw A power-driven boat with two engines and two propellers.

Twist The *angle of attack* of a sail is not the same along the whole length of the luff, but varies with height. If the hoist length is about 33 ft (10 m), the top part of a sail that is correctly trimmed should set at an angle of attack about 3–5° greater than that at the foot. Up to about 5–10° twist is beneficial, and delays *stalling* at the top of the sail, where the wind frees slightly because wind speed is greater than at the foot (see *wind gradient*) and, in a fractional rig, the mainsail has no headsail in front of it to deflect the wind. Excessive twist is harmful, and is prevented by fitting a *kicking strap* or *boom vang* to hold the boom down, especially on downwind courses when the pull from the mainsheet is largely horizontal.

Twisted shackle *Shackle* with sides deliberately twisted through 90°.

Two-pack or **two-pot paint** and **varnish** As opposed to one-pack products, the two components, base and hardener or *catalyst*, are supplied separately and have to be well mixed together just before application. The mix must usually be applied within 4–8 hours. Toughness, elasticity and resistance both to abrasion and chemicals are superior to those of one-pack products.

Two Ton Class A *Level rating* class, the maximum *rating* being 32 ft. A typical boat's measurements are LOA 44 ft (13.4 m), LWL 31 ft (9.5 m), beam 12 ft (3.6 m), displacement 23,000 lbs (10.5 tonnes), sail area 700 sq ft (65 sq m). The class races annually for the Two Ton Cup, the Europe Cup presented by the Yacht Club Italiano, the conditions being similar to those of the One Ton Cup, but the three Olympic courses are about 30 n.miles long and the two offshore races about 175 and 350 n.miles long. The number of crew is eight.

Typhoon Name given to a *tropical revolving storm* (q.v.) in the China Seas and Western North Pacific areas. Occurs most frequently between May and December.

U = **Uniform:** red and white chequered *code flag.* As a single letter signal means 'You are running into danger'. *Morse code:* •• — (dot dot dash).

Ulstron Trade name for *polypropylene* produced by ICI in England.

Ultimate stability The *IOR* requires rated yachts to be sufficiently stable to recover from a *knock-down,* and a stability test is carried out by pulling the yacht over until the mast is horizontal. A heeling weight (calculated from a formula based on the yacht's rated length, beam and draft, mainsail hoist, foretriangle height and rating) is attached at the top of the foretriangle. The test is passed if the yacht can support this weight, but is failed if the weight makes her heel beyond 90°.

Ultra quick light A light, exhibited as an *aid to navigation,* which *flashes* at a rate of 160 or more times a minute, usually 240–300 flashes per minute; chart abbr UQ.

Ultra quick flashing

Una rig A *rig* with only one sail, set on a *mast stepped* well forward. Although una and *cat-rig* are often used interchangeably, the mast may not be quite so near the *bows* as a typical US cat-rigged boat.

Unbend To unshackle the *sheets* and *halyards* and remove a sail from a *spar* or *stay* so that it is ready to *stow.* Also to undo a *bend,* cast loose.

Uncorrecting (not UK) Whereas a *course* or *bearing* is corrected from *compass* to *magnetic* or magnetic to *true,* uncorrecting is converting from true to magnetic to compass.

Uncovers Said of a feature such as a *rock* or *shoal* which is covered by the sea at *high water* but is exposed at *low water.* Heights of such features are given above *chart datum,* and are underlined on *charts.* Chart abbr uncov. See *drying features.*

Under canvas Propelled only by the wind on the sails.

Undercanvassed Describes a boat with less sail area than would be ideal for her size or potential performance, or for the prevailing weather conditions. Offshore cruising boats designed for long voyages are often sailed single-handed or short-handed, and are therefore undercanvassed, whereas racing yachts carry a lot of sail. Comparisons can be made by calculating the *sail area to displacement ratio* of various boats.

Undercoat One of several layers of paint applied between the *primer* and the topcoat.

Undercurrent A *current* beneath the surface of the water.

Undermanned Said of a vessel without sufficient crew on board. Short-handed is the more usual term for sailing boats.

Under oars Propelled by oars.

Under power Propelled by an engine.

Underpowered Said of a boat with an engine that is not powerful enough, for example if she is unable to *stem* the *tidal streams or currents* in the locality, make *headway* against a fresh wind, or operate safely in congested waters with no sail set.

Underrun To haul a boat along a *mooring line, kedge* rope etc, whether the rope is floating on the water or submerged, by putting the rope over the boat and hauling her along it.

Under sail Propelled only by the wind on the sails.

Under-stand As opposed to *overstand,* to *tack* too early, say for a *mark* or to round a headland; consequently the boat has to *go about* and put in an extra tack.

Under the lee of On the *leeward,* sheltered side of, say, a ship's hull or a headland.

Undertow 1. A strong sub-surface *current* flowing seaward; occurs in breaking *surf* where water runs back into the sea from a beach. Can be dangerous when landing on a beach, but may help when launching a dinghy when there is an onshore breeze. 2. Two words (under tow): being towed.

Underwater body All that part of the *hull* that is immersed, i.e. all beneath the *waterline,* including the *keel, skeg* etc.

Under way In general speech is taken to mean a vessel that is making *way* through the water but, as defined in the *IRPCS,* a vessel under way is one that is not at *anchor,* made fast to the shore, or *aground.* Therefore she need not necessarily be making way through the water and could be *drifting.* She has to exhibit *running lights,* as opposed to those specified for a vessel that is at anchor or aground.

Undock To leave a dock.

Uniform system of buoyage *Buoyage system* used in the Commonwealth, and in European and other waters; is being phased out and replaced by *IALA* Maritime System A, which is now laid in most European waters.

Union Device symbolizing the national union of states or countries; appears in the upper *canton* near the *hoist* of the US and UK *ensigns.*

United States buoyage systems Although there are variations in certain waters, i.e. *Great Lakes, Intracoastal Waterway, Inland Waters* and *Western Rivers,* US buoyage is essentially a *lateral system* with *starboard hand marks* left to starboard when sailing clockwise round North America, when entering estuaries and harbors, and when sailing upstream in rivers or from the north and east towards the south and west in the Intracoastal Waterway. Starboard hand marks are red *nun* buoys, have even numbers, red or white lights and red triangular *daymarks. Port hand marks* are black *can* buoys, have odd numbers, green or white lights and green rectangular daymarks. *Junction marks* are painted with red and black bands, the uppermost band being red if the preferred channel is on the port hand (daymarks triangular, red over black with red borders), but black if it is to starboard (daymarks rectangular, black over red with green borders); lights are white, *interrupted quick flashing. Mid-channel buoys* are can or nun buoys with black and white vertical stripes, and exhibit white *morse code* letter A lights; daymarks are black and white, octagonal (see end papers). The Uniform State Waterway Marking System again is black to port, red to starboard; a white buoy with a black top indicates that a vessel should pass to the north or east of the position, and one with a red top indicates that she

should pass to the south or west. A red and white vertically striped mark indicates that the vessel should not pass between the mark and the shore.

United States Yacht Racing Union, USYRU Organization that promotes racing in the USA. Has individual and club members, and is affiliated to the *IYRU.*

Universal joint A joint invented by Cardano and called a cardan joint in many countries. It allows the parts it connects to move in all directions, such as two rotating shafts that run at an angle to each other. The *gooseneck* is a universal joint.

Universal Rule A *rating* rule for racing yachts and offshore racers introduced at the turn of the century. The rating, given in feet, was:

$$R = \frac{0.2\,L \times \sqrt{S}}{\sqrt[3]{\text{displacement}}}$$

L being length and S sail area. The *J-class,* built to this rule, rated at 76 feet and competed for the *America's Cup* from 1930–37.

Universal time See *Greenwich Mean Time.* C.f. co-ordinated universal time.

Unreeve To pull a line out of a *fairlead,* and *blocks* of a *tackle* etc, i.e. the opposite of to *reeve.*

Unrig To remove the *standing* and *running rigging* before unstepping the *mast,* whether preparatory to putting a dinghy on a trailer or before *laying up* a keelboat for the winter.

Unseaworthy As opposed to seaworthy, a vessel that is unfit to put to sea. All dinghies and most small estuary type cruisers are unseaworthy. Poor seamanship or a seasick crew may also cause a vessel to become unseaworthy.

Unship To remove an object from the position in which it works, such as when lifting the out-board off its bracket.

Unstable equilibrium The condition of a boat such as a dinghy when *stability* becomes vanishingly small; she does not return to an upright position when the force causing her to *heel* is removed. When *righting moment* is unable to counter *heeling moment* the boat *capsizes.*

Up Used either in the sense of raising, as up *anchor,* up *spinnaker,* or to *windward* as up *helm,* i.e. order to put the *tiller* to windward so that the boat will *bear away* from the wind. Up spirits: drinks all round.

Up and down 1. Said of the *anchor cable* when it is vertical. 2. No wind: it blows up and down the mast.

Uphaul A rope or line that raises an object vertically. The traditional words are *hoist* or *lift*, but uphaul may be used, e.g. for the line that raises the *centreboard*.

Upper light Of the two lights that form a *leading line* (US *range*), the higher light which is sited further inland. The vessel is not on the leading line when the two lights are open.

Upstream The direction from which a stream flows; in a river, towards the source.

Upwind The direction from which the wind is blowing, e.g. a landmark may lie dead upwind of the observer. To *windward* of an object, i.e. the windward boat of two is upwind of the leeward boat.

Urgency signal The spoken words Pan-pan or XXX in morse code (radio telegraphy) which precede a message concerning the safety of a vessel or person. The message takes priority over all except *distress* messages.

V

V = **Victor:** white *code flag* with a red cross. As a single letter signal means 'I require assistance'. *Morse code:* ••• — (dot dot dot dash).

Vane 1. Light metal sheet that pivots on a stick at the *masthead* to indicate wind direction, as does a *burgee* or *racing flag*. 2. The wind vane of *self-steering gear* (see *vane gear*) or an *autopilot*.

Vane gear A *self-steering* system with a vane that senses the direction of the *apparent wind* and corrects any deviation from *course* in relation to the wind, either by acting directly on the *tiller*, or on a separate pendulum *rudder* which actuates the tiller (A), or on a *trim tab* fitted to the *trailing edge* of the rudder (B). Because the distance between

A

the vane gear and the *centre of gravity* about which the boat pivots when altering course is relatively great, the vane need not be overlarge and is effective even in light breezes; the vane of the gear illustrated pivots about a vertical axis, and is larger than the vanes which pivot about a nearly horizontal or inclined axis.

B

Vang Rope or line leading to the deck on either side from the *peak* of a *gaff* or *sprit*. Serves to steady the spar and to prevent it from sagging. Stubbornly pronounced wang by Thames bargees and lightermen. Often used (with a V) as an abbreviated form of *boom vang*, q.v.

Variable or **controllable pitch propeller** The *pitch* of the *propeller blades* can be altered, and they are feathered when the boat is under sail. There is no gearbox, and the *propeller shaft* turns in one direction only, the pitch being altered through the feathering position to drive the boat forward or astern. Pitch can also be varied to suit the conditions without altering engine speed, for example when motoring against wind and tidal stream, or when towing.

Variables The high pressure areas, where winds are light and variable, between the NE *trade winds* and the *westerlies* to north of them in the northern hemisphere, and between the SE trades and the westerlies to south of them in the southern hemisphere. Also called the *horse latitudes* or sub-tropical high pressure belt. See also *global winds*.

Variable wind Changeable in direction, and usually associated with light breezes.

Variation The angle between the *true* and *magnetic meridians*. The figure for variation indicates the amount that the needle of a *magnetic compass* is deflected from the true meridian by the earth's magnetic lines of force. Variation not only differs from place to place but from year to year, because the *magnetic north pole* moves. The figure indicating local variation at the date a *chart* is published is usually printed inside or beside the *compass rose*, together with details of *annual*

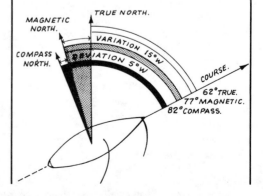

change in variation. Values are given in degrees and minutes easterly (or westerly) when the north end of the compass needle points to the east (or west) of true north. When converting a *magnetic course* or *bearing* to *true*, easterly variation is added, westerly is subtracted. True to magnetic, add westerly, subtract easterly. Unlike *deviation*, which differs with each compass and the ship's *heading*, variation at a particular place is the same for every course.

Varnish Translucent resinous protective coating applied to woodwork to protect it from weathering. Available as a one-pack or two-pack product.

Vector diagram A vector is a quantity that has both direction and magnitude (e.g. velocity, force, acceleration). In a vector diagram an arrow indicates direction, and the length of the arrow indicates magnitude.

1. When a parallelogram of forces is drawn to find the velocity (strength and direction) of the *apparent wind,* arrows are drawn to represent *true wind* velocity and the velocity of the wind that arises because the boat moves over the ground (boat speed). The diagonal drawn from the *centre of effort* where the two winds meet indicates the velocity of the apparent wind (the resultant of true wind and boat speed). The velocity of the true wind can be found similarly, as in the figure. Arrow CA, flying with the wind, indicates apparent wind direction, and arrow AB the boat's course relative to the wind. The lengths of the arrows show true wind speed and boat speed to a common scale. Line BC joining the ends of the arrows shows true wind velocity. It may be important to calculate this before altering course from a *broad reach* or *run* to a *close-hauled* course, because it is easy to underestimate the true wind's strength when sailing downwind. The true wind may be 20% slower than the apparent wind when a slow boat is sailing close-hauled, and up to 30% slower if the boat is fast whereas, when running, the true wind can be 30–40% faster than the apparent wind. Thus the speed of the apparent wind which drives the boat forward may treble when the boat

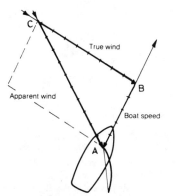

alters course from a run to close-hauled; as *wind pressure* varies as the square of speed, it may be necessary to reduce sail before coming on the wind. (See also *tide wind.*)

2. A vector diagram is also used in *navigation,* for example to find the *course* to steer or the course made good *over the ground* in tidal waters. The sides of the vector triangle represent the course and distance sailed *through the water,* course and distance over the ground, and the *set* and *rate* (US *drift*) of the *tidal stream* (US *tidal current*). In fig (a), the course and speed through the water from a fix at A are known AB, and a second fix places the vessel at point C; the navigator can find the boat's

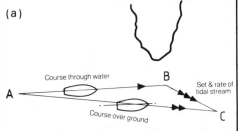

course and speed made good over the ground (AC), and the set and rate of the tidal stream (BC). Alternatively, if both the boat's speed and course through the water (AB) and that of the set and rate of the tidal stream (BC) are known, the boat's track over the ground (AC) from the fix at A to her *estimated position,* C, can be found.

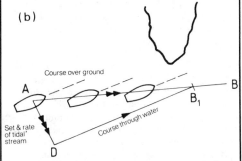

In figure (b), the navigator wishes to sail along the course AB, and draws the line AD to represent the set and rate, say 1 *knot,* of the tidal stream for the next hour. He expects the boat to sail at a certain speed through the water, say 3 knots, and draws a line to the same scale from point D to cut AB at a point 3 miles from D. The line DB$_1$ indicates the course that the boat must steer to make good course AB over the ground. The terms sailing triangle and velocity triangle are sometimes used to mean the navigational and wind vector diagrams respectively.

Vee bottom The *section* (transverse) is vee-shaped, the bottom of the vee being the *keel;* more often termed *hard chine* in the UK. A deep vee hull has a greater *deadrise* angle.

Vee bunks (US)   As fitted in the *fo'c's'le; bunks* that converge at the foot where the boat narrows towards the stem.

Vee drive   Transmission system fitted when the engine is installed further aft than usual. The engine is the opposite way round from normal and the output shaft runs forward to the gear box, from which the *propeller shaft* runs aft at an angle.

Veer   1. To pay out *anchor cable*, rope or line gradually and under control. 2. The wind veers when it shifts to blow from a direction further clockwise, e.g. in the northern hemisphere when a *front* has passed.

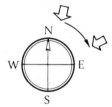

Velocity   The rate at which a moving body travels in a specific direction (c.f. *speed*).

Velocity triangle   A term sometimes used for the *vector triangle* (q.v.) which indicates the velocities of the *true* and *apparent winds* and of boat speed.

Vent   Abbreviated and frequently used alternative for *ventilator*. Sometimes applied to a flexible *cowl*, to the vent-pipe which passes through the structure, and to the breather of a fuel or water tank.

Ventilation   Ventilators provide fresh air for the accommodation on the principle that cold air sinks and hot air rises; forced air is also often provided for the engine compartment. Air will circulate inside the boat when she is lying at her mooring if the inlet ventilators have long tubular ducts reaching down into the *bilges*, and the outlet ventilators have short ducts that terminate at the *deckhead*. When a boat is under way, air must circulate from the *stern* towards the *bow*, and from *leeward* to *windward*, if ventilation is to be effective. No rain or spray should be allowed to enter the cabin or compartment, only air. A boat with a petrol (US gasolene) engine, or one which carries a liquid petroleum gas bottle for lighting or cooking, must be effectively ventilated to prevent the accumulation of dangerous fumes in the bilges; this is a legal requirement in the US in the case of a gasolene-engined boat. See also *flame arrestor, ventilator, wind sail*.

Ventilator   Device which draws fresh air into a boat or compartment, or extracts stale air; usually fitted in pairs. The simplest has a rotating *cowl* which forces air into the cabin when it faces the wind. Air is sucked out on the venturi principle when the cowl is turned to face away from the wind. The *Dorade ventilator* has a separate cowl, and is housed in a box which has drains below to allow spray to run out on deck. These ventilators operate simply on natural principles; other more expensive ventilators are electrically powered, and

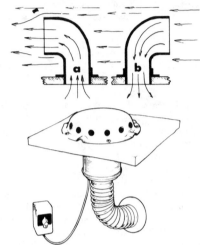

are often fitted to ensure that the engine compartment is adequately ventilated, not just to improve engine performance but to remove dangerous fumes; they should be electrically shielded to avoid sparks. The deck fitting is flat to avoid tripping the crew, strong enough to be trodden on, and has drains to lead spray out on deck. See also *ventilation, louvre, butterfly* and *mushroom ventilators*, and bilge blower under *bilges*.

Ventimeter (US **Elvometer**)   Trade names for wind meters that indicate wind speeds varying from 0–50 knots (0–25 m/sec) by measuring pressure differential. The instrument is held upright with the aperture facing the wind, and the pressure raises a flat disc up a vertical shaft inside the transparent cylinder. Wind speed is read off on

a scale on the side of the cylinder, and is then corrected with a table, often printed on the handle, to allow for the observer's height above sea level which is considerably lower than the 33 ft (10 m) at which wind speeds are normally measured.

Venturi effect See *canal effect*.

Vernier Method of reading fractions of units of a scale, named after the French mathematician Pierre Vernier, but in some countries called nonius,

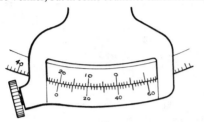

after the Portuguese mathematician Nunez. Is based on the principle that the eye can distinguish an unbroken line from broken lines. For example, the distance between 10 units on the main scale may be divided into 9 units on the vernier; the whole units are read on the upper scale opposite 0 on the vernier, 20° in the figure, and the minutes are given by the unbroken line, 23′ read on the lower scale. These are added to give the measurement, 20°23′.

Vernier sextant The degrees are read directly from the *arc,* and the minutes with the vernier, which is moved along the arc by a tangent screw with an endless worm; this engages in the toothed rack on the arc. Exact readings can be obtained if arc and vernier are clearly engraved, but errors are more likely than when using the more modern *micrometer* or drum *sextant.*

Vertical clearance The height above a datum such as *MHWS* or *MSL* (UK), or *MHW* (US) of an overhead cable, bridge etc. The vertical clearance of the former is taken as the lowest point of the cable, of the latter the highest point of the span.

Vertical sextant angle The angle subtended at the observer's eye by an object of known height above the horizon or water's edge, as measured by

a *sextant.* The distance of the vessel from an object such as a lighthouse can be calculated, and this provides a *position line* which is an arc of the circle, the centre of which is the object, and the radius of which is the distance between the object and the observer. A *fix* is obtained by taking the *bearing* of the object at the same time, or perhaps a second vertical sextant angle of another object. Distance off in *nautical miles* can be found from tables or with the formulae:

$$\text{N. miles} = \frac{\text{height of object (ft)} \times 4}{\text{angle measured in minutes} \times 7}$$

$$\text{or} = \frac{\text{height (ft)}}{\text{angle (mins)}} \times 0.566$$

$$\text{N. miles} = \frac{\text{height of object (m)} \times 13}{\text{angle measured in minutes} \times 7}$$

$$\text{or} = \frac{\text{height (m)}}{\text{angle (mins)}} \times 1.86$$

Very quick light (formerly very quick flashing light) A light, exhibited as an *aid to navigation; flashes* at a rate of 100 or 120 times a minute; chart abbr VQ, formerly V Ql Fl.

Very quick flashing

▲▲▲▲▲▲▲▲▲▲▲▲▲▲▲▲▲▲▲▲▲▲▲▲▲
↔

Vessel In the *IRPCS* is defined as every description of water craft, including non-displacement craft and seaplanes, used or capable of being used as a means of transportation on water. In the regulations vessels are classed as *anchored, aground, not under command, power-driven, pushing, sailing, towing* and as below.

Vessel constrained by her draft In the *IRPCS,* a vessel severely restricted in her ability to deviate from her course, because of her *draft* in relation to the available depth of water. All vessels have to avoid impeding her safe passage, where possible. She may exhibit a *cylinder* by day or three *all-round* red lights by night.

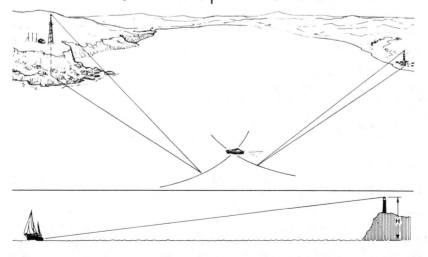

Vessel engaged in fishing The *IRPCS* definition is a vessel fishing with nets, lines, trawls or other fishing apparatus which restricts manoeuvrability; vessels with trolling lines or other apparatus which does not restrict manoeuvrability; and pleasure craft fishing with short lines and other small gear are not accorded the privileges given to commercial fishing vessels by the IRPCS. *Power-driven* and *sailing vessels* keep out of the way of one engaged in fishing, and she keeps out of the way of *vessels restricted in their ability to maneouvre* or *not under command*. She indicates her size and type of fishing by exhibiting various shapes by day, such as two *cones* points together or a *basket,* or at night the lights specified in the IRPCS, such as green over white or red over white *all-round* lights.

Vessel restricted in her ability to manoeuvre (US **maneuver**) In the *IRPCS,* a vessel unable to keep out of the way of other vessels because of the nature of her work, say cable-laying, dredging, minesweeping. *Power-driven* and *sailing vessels* give way to her. Apart from minesweepers, such vessels exhibit, in a vertical line, three shapes by day, *ball* over *diamond* over ball, or three *all-round* lights by night, red-white-red, as well as *navigation lights* when *under way*. Only vessels under 7 m in length are exempted from this requirement.

VHF Very High Frequency, see *frequency, propogation*.

Viscosity The higher the viscosity of a fluid the greater its resistance to flow. The viscosity of *paint* and *resin* often alters with temperature, and *thinners* may have to be added to paint in cold weather to improve flow, or *thixotropic paste* to increase the viscosity of resin. In warm weather the viscosity of paint may be so low that care has to be taken to prevent *curtains* forming on vertical surfaces. Kinematic viscosity: see *Reynolds number*.

Visibility The greatest distance at which an object can be seen against its background. The transparency of the *atmosphere* is measured by selecting objects, such as landmarks or aids to navigation, which are at a known distance from the observer, and checking whether they can be seen or not. Visibility is affected by particles in suspension in the air, dry particles such as smoke, dust and impurities in the case of *haze,* or water droplets in the case of *mist* and *fog*. In fog, visibility is under 0.5 n.miles (1 km), in haze and mist it is between 0.5 and 1 n.mile (1–2 km). Broadly, visibility is described as good, moderate or poor, and the *IRPCS* also use the term restricted. More specifically it is given in yards and nautical miles, or metres and kilometres. The code below is often used when reporting visibility at sea.

	UP TO	
90 dense fog	55 yds	50 m
91 thick fog	220 yds	200 m
92 fog	550 yds	500 m
93 moderate fog	1100 yds	1 km
94 mist or haze	2200 yds	2 km
95 poor visibility	2.2 n. miles	4 km
96 moderate visibility	5.4 n. miles	10 km
97 good visibility	11 n. miles	20 km
98 very good visibility	27 n. miles	50 km
99 excellent visibility	+27 n. miles	+50 km

Visible or **sea horizon** The observed horizon where sea and sky appear to meet (c.f. *rational* and *sensible horizons*).

Vmg abbreviation used frequently in speech and print for *speed made good to windward*, q.v.

Vmg meter an electronic instrument that gives a visual indication of Vmg on a dial. The small analogue computer is fed with signals from the electronic *log* and the *wind speed and direction indicator*.

Voyage A sea journey of some length; often includes a number of *passages*.

W = Whiskey: blue, white and red *code flag*. As a single letter signal means 'I require medical assistance'. *Morse code:* •——(dot dash dash).

Wake 1. Disturbed water left astern by a moving boat. The larger the boat and the smoother the surface of the water, the greater the distance that the wake can be seen. It shows the vessel's path through the water, and can therefore be used to establish the *leeway* angle, which is measured between the wake and the *reciprocal* of the *course* being steered. 2. The disturbed air downwind of an *aerofoil*.

Wake factor Because a moving boat drags water along with her, the speed of her wake is slower than the speed of the boat in relation to undisturbed water nearby. Wake speed is either given (Taylor) as a percentage of the vessel's speed, V, or (Froude) of Va, the speed of advance of the propeller relative to the wake. The Froude formula is:

$$w_f = \frac{V - Va}{Va},$$

and the Taylor formula is:

$$w_t = \frac{V - Va}{V}.$$

The wake factor is important when selecting a *propeller*.

Wall knot A knot made in a line to form a knob that will not pass through an eye or aperture. Is often used in combination with a *crown knot*, and may be made before or after the crown.

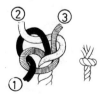

Wane Said of the moon when the illuminated area is decreasing between full and new moon, as viewed from the earth.

Wardrobe All the sails that are provided for a boat.

Warm front The boundary ahead of a moving *depression* where warm air meets cold air and rises over it. Pressure falls ahead of the warm front. The first visible warning is often tufted *cirrus* (mare's tails) at great heights, followed by *cirrostratus;* layer clouds form and it begins to drizzle or rain. *Visibility* is poor and *fog* may form as the front passes, and persist for some time. Winds generally *back* and *freshen* ahead of a front, but *veer* and *moderate* in its rear.

Warning signal Before starting a *race*, a signal made to indicate that the *class* will start in exactly ten minutes time. When a number of classes are started at ten minute intervals, the warning signal is the *starting signal* of the preceding class. The *preparatory signal* is made five minutes after the warning signal.

Warp 1. A term used in *cloth construction* to indicate the lengthwise thread of woven material, at right angles to which the *weft* (US or fill) thread is woven. It is important to know which way the warp runs when cutting or patching sails. 2. Often applies to the heavier lines used for mooring,

kedging or towing, thus the rope or hawser used to move a vessel by warping. 3. To move a vessel by hauling on a warp which may be secured to a *bollard* or to a warping buoy.

Warping buoy Laid to help ships to warp themselves into deeper water, or to turn round in a narrow channel.

Warping drum (US **gipsy**) Drum on the *windlass* that takes rope anchor cable.

Warrant (UK) Authority from the Ministry of Defence to wear a white *ensign,* a *defaced* or undefaced blue ensign, or a defaced red ensign. This privilege is accorded to the vessel, but the owner must be a member of a *yacht club* entitled to fly such an ensign, which is worn with the *burgee* of that yacht club only when the owner is on board or nearby and in effective control of the yacht. The warrant must be kept on board.

Wash The turbulent water left astern by a moving boat.

Washboard (US **hatchboard**) Removable wooden plank fitted in grooves or channels in the *companion hatch* entrance or other aperture to prevent water entering.

Washstrake 1. Vertical *plank* or *strake* fitted at the side of a boat above the *gunwale* to prevent water from coming on board by increasing *free-board.* 2. US: alternative term for *coaming,* q.v.

Watch 1. One of the periods into which 24 hours is divided on board. In smaller boats, watches often differ in timing and duration, and are planned to enable routine work to be carried out, as well as to provide adequate time for the crew to sleep and rest when off watch. In larger boats, the crew is often divided into port and starboard watches, but the skipper, navigator and cook do not keep watch because they must be available at any time.

Naval Watch		*Swedish Watch*	
2000 2400	First	2400 0130	A B
2400 0400	Middle	0130 0300	B C
0400 0800	Morning	0300 0430	C D
0800 1200	Forenoon	0430 0600	D E
1200 1600	Afternnon	0600 0730	A E
1600 1800	1st Dog	0730 0900	A B
1800 2000	Last Dog	0900 1030	B C
		Etc.	

Long Watch			*Storm*	
2000 2400	A	2000 0200	2000 2200	A
2400 0400	B	0200 0800	2200 2400	B
0400 0800	A	0800 1200	2400 0200	C
0800 1400	B	1200 1600	0200 0400	A
1400 2000	A	1600 2000	0400 0600	B

Above are	0600	C
alternatives	0800	
giving long	0800	A
watch by day or	1000	
by night	Etc.	

2. Radio watch is kept by vessels equipped with *radio telephony* or radio telegraphy. Some ships are required to maintain a continuous listening watch but, in the interest of safety of life at sea, all suitably equipped vessels are expected as far as possible to listen on 2182 kHz twice each hour for three minutes starting at the hour and half hour, on VHF Channel 16 at the same period, or on 500 kHz (radio telegraphy) for three minutes after 15 and 45 minutes past each hour.

Watch buoy Laid near a *light vessel* when she is out of sight of land to enable the crew to check her position.

Watching Said of an *aid to navigation* when the buoy is floating and showing above the water.

Waterborne Floating.

Water-jet propulsion The engine propels the boat by expelling water astern, instead of by turning a *propeller.* The direction of the jet of water can be altered to steer the boat or to reverse. Boats with pure jet propulsion are rare.

Waterlight See *lifebuoy light.*

Waterline 1. The line along the *hull* of a boat at the surface of the water in which she floats. Because her actual waterline differs with the load carried, it is rarely the same as her designed waterline, which is shown on the *lines plan,* and which is the waterline at which the designer calculates that she will float. 2. In the lines drawings, one of the curved lines on the *half-breadth plan* that shows the shape of the waterplane; appears as a straight line on the *body* and *profile plans.*

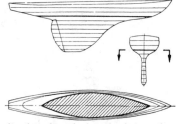

Waterline length The length of a boat from *stem* to *stern* at the waterline; varies with her *displacement,* i.e. according to the number of crew, amount of gear, stores etc on board, and with the *salinity* of the water in which she is floating. Actual waterline length may be greater or smaller than that of her *designed waterline.* Waterline length governs the maximum speed of a *displacement hull,* and affects a boat's *handicap rating.*

Waterlogged Saturated with water and only just afloat. Whereas a boat that has been *swamped* is full of water and can be pumped dry, a waterlogged boat remains *awash*.

Waterplane Horizontal section through the *hull,* the plane being perpendicular to the vertical plane through the boat's *centreline.* Shows the shape and area of the hull at that plane.

Waterplane coefficient, or coefficient of fineness of the waterplane The ratio of the waterplane area at the *designed waterline* to that of its circumscribing rectangle with sides equal to *waterline length* and *beam:*

$$C_{WP} = \frac{A_W}{LWL \times B}$$

The value varies from about 0.60 for boats with fine ends to about 0.70 for full-ended sailing boats, the average being about 0.65.

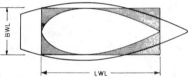

Waterspout The base of a cloud projects downwards like a funnel towards the surface of the sea and merges with a cloud of spray, forming a tube-like column 20–500 ft (6–150 m) in diameter and 1000–2000 ft (300–600 m) high. Generally lasts from 10–30 minutes before breaking. Is a danger to small boats, but can generally be avoided.

Watertight Said of a tank or of an object through which water cannot pass, whether in or out. For example, to provide a watertight hull the *seams* are *caulked,* and a *stuffing box* or *stern gland* is fitted where the *propeller shaft* passes through the hull. The deck may be made watertight by caulking or *sheathing,* and a *mast coat* fitted at the hole where the mast passes through the deck.

Watertight bulkhead A *bulkhead* that prevents water from entering a compartment, or keeps water in the compartment out of the rest of the boat.

Watertight cockpit Well in which the crew sit or

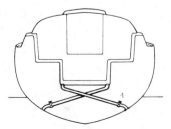

stand, constructed so that water on board does not drain into the *bilges.* The water is led back to the sea through drains or scuppers (see also *self-draining cockpit*).

Waterway 1. A channel navigable by shipping. The term is often applied to canals, channels in lakes, harbours, rivers etc, e.g. inland waterways, Intracoastal Waterway. 2. Gutters along decks, around cockpit lockers, wooden skylights etc; they lead water overboard or prevent it from entering the lockers or the cabin.

Watt *SI* unit of power, 1 Joule per second. See also *kilowatt.*

Wave 1. Oscillation of the surface of water, usually generated by wind, but see below. The highest point of a wave is the crest, the lowest the trough. The horizontal distance between successive crests or troughs is the wavelength, and the vertical distance between crest and trough is wave height. Heights are often overestimated as a result of measuring them from deck level when the

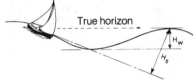

boat is on a crest, instead of from the boat's waterline in a trough. Amplitude is the vertical distance between crest (or trough) and the equilibrium water level, i.e. half height. The interval of time between the passage of two successive crests or troughs past a given point is the wave period, measured in seconds; this can only be measured on land or from an anchored vessel. Wave frequency is the number of complete oscillations per second. The ratio height:length indicates steepness, and the ratio length:period indicates wave speed. Speed, measured in *knots* or metres per second, differs from the speed of a *tidal stream or current* in that the water particles themselves do not travel over the ground but move in a circular orbit (see *orbital motion*).

The period, height and length of waves increase with the strength and duration of wind, and with *fetch.* Immature waves are shorter and steeper, but the period becomes longer and they become higher as they develop. Decaying waves gradually flatten out. Tidal streams and currents affect waves, which become steeper and more vicious when the wind blows in the opposite direction to that in which the stream is setting. Seas are also higher and more confused over *shoals,* where two tidal streams meet, and in *tide-rips* and *races.* Apart from the progressive waves described, there are standing waves and *seiches,* which are reflected from a barrier such as cliffs or a quay wall. Waves that have been generated at some distance and

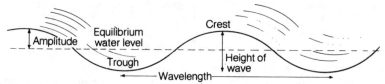

have travelled a long way, and those that persist after a local wind has ceased to blow, are termed *swell*. See also *surf, breakers, storm surge, Tsunami, tidal wave, bow* and *stern waves*. Some exceptionally high waves, recorded in storms, had the following heights (H), lengths (L), periods (T) and speeds (V):

Western Baltic H 9.8 ft 3 m, L 180–280 ft 55–70 m, T 6–7 secs, V 5 knots

Northern North Sea H 26–29 ft 8–9 m, L 590–656 ft 180–200 m, T 11–12 secs, V 8 knots

North Atlantic H 52–59 ft 16–18 m, L 656–820 ft 200–250 m, T 12–14 secs, V 10 knots

Pacific H 111 ft 34 m, L 2600 ft 792 m, T 14.8 sec V 55 knots, the largest recorded.

2. Radio and light waves are electro-magnetic, the electric and magnetic fields lying at right angles to each other and to the direction in which the wave is travelling. Electro-magnetic waves travel at 162,000 n.miles (300,000 km) per second. See also *frequency, ground wave, sky wave, propagation*.

Wave-making resistance or **wave drag** That part of total hull *resistance* that can be attributed to the formation of waves as the hull forces its way through water, the effects of which are visible in the form of divergent and transverse *waves* at *bow* and *stern, wash* and *wake*. Wave-making resistance increases greatly as speed increases, and the length of the waves formed increases to the point where length between crests matches *waterline length;* bow and stern are then supported by crests with a trough between. This limits the speed of a *displacement hull*, and occurs at a *speed to length ratio* of about 1.34.

Waxing Said of the moon when the illuminated area is increasing between new and full moon, as viewed from the earth.

Way A boat makes way when she moves through the water; she makes headway when moving *stem*

first, sternway when moving *stern* first, and leeway when she moves sideways, to *leeward* of her *course*. She carries her way when she continues to move after the propulsive effect of the wind on her sails, of her auxiliary engine or of oars has ceased (i.e. after letting the sails fly, shooting up ito the wind, engaging neutral or stopping rowing). She loses way when she slows and stops moving, and the crew take way off to stop her motion through the water. See also *under way*.

Way enough or **easy oars** Order to oarsmen to stop *rowing*.

Wear To change *tacks* by *bearing away* and *gybing* instead of by *going about*. In spite of losing ground to windward, this may be preferable. *Square-rigged* ships, for example, cannot point anywhere near so close to the wind as *fore-and-aft rigged vessels,* and therefore have to swing round

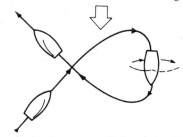

through a much greater arc before their sails fill on the new tack. *Catamarans* have a similar problem owing to their great speed, and often find gybing preferable to *tacking*. The term is now sometimes used as synonymous with tacking so is perhaps best avoided. 2. Vessels are said to wear *flags*. 3. Chafe.

Weather Three alternative meanings: *windward,* survival and atmospheric conditions. 1. Towards or nearer the wind, as in weather helm, weather shore; often interchangeable with windward, as windward or weather mark; opp *lee* and *leeward*. 2. To succeed in passing to windward of an obstruction or feature, such as a headland, rock or mark, especially without having to put in a *tack*. 3. To come safely through a period of strong winds and heavy seas, perhaps by *heaving to, running before a storm* under reduced canvas or *bare poles,* or *streaming* a warp or *sea anchor*. A *squall* or *gust* of short duration may be weathered by, say, *reefing, handing* the sails or *spilling wind*. 4. The weather or atmospheric conditions which most affect the mariner are visibility and wind with associated sea-states.

Weatherbound Unable to leave a port, haven etc on account of bad weather, strong winds, high seas etc.

Weather bow 1. The *bow* to windward. 2. If a boat with the wind free is crossing a *tidal stream or current,* and the water flow strikes the weather bow, she is set to *leeward* of her course and has to *point* higher to reach her destination. If it is a dead *beat* to her objective, it generally pays to *lee bow* the tide first, that is, to sail first on the *tack* that puts the tidal stream on her lee bow, q.v.

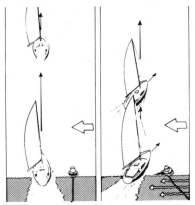

Weather cloth See *dodger.*

Weather code and **symbols** Internationally adopted World Meteorological Organization (WMO) code, used when sending and receiving weather reports, forecasts etc. Groups of letters and numbers are converted into symbols that are plotted on weather maps, such as *wind arrows* indicating wind velocity at a weather station (see *station circle*), symbols indicating the type of *front,* air and sea temperatures, *atmospheric pressure, precipitation,* cloud description and so on. The symbols serve as a meteorological short-hand, and enable more information to be printed and interpreted to give a fuller picture of the weather.

∞	Haze	✳	Snow
=	Mist	▽	Shower
==	Shallow fog	△	Soft or small hail
≡	Fog	▲	Hail
᭰	Drizzle	℞	Thunderstorm
•	Rain	(•)	Precipitation within sight
᭰]	Rain during past hour	ৎ	Tropical storm

Weather deck 1. The uppermost *deck* that is exposed to the elements; may be on different levels. In smaller boats, all the decking that covers the interior. 2. The deck on the windward side of the boat.

Weather facsimile or **weather fax** A special radio receiver traces facsimiles of meteorological charts, giving the navigator full information about the weather and its development. A number of charts such as *isobaric* and *isothermal* charts, charts showing wind direction, the movement of *fronts* etc., are broadcast daily at scheduled times by facsimile transmitters in various countries.

Weather forecast A forecast gives information about the weather and its anticipated development, based on an analysis of reports from weather stations and ships, satellite photographs etc. Forecasts for the ensuing 12 hours are generally given several times daily on the radio and, in various countries, longer term forecasts spanning five days, a week or a month can also be obtained. Shipping forecasts for those at sea are broadcast by national radio, local radio networks, coastal stations etc, and can also be obtained from a meteorological office by telephone. Details of radio frequencies and forecast times are published by the World Meteorological Organization and by national authorities such as the US National Weather Service and the UK Meteorological Office, as well as in publications such as *Reed's Nautical Almanac* and the *Royal Yachting Association* booklet.

Weather helm The tendency of a boat to turn her *bow* to *windward;* the *tiller* has to be be held to weather to keep her on *course.* A boat should have slight weather helm when *close-hauled* in *force* 4 winds, and will then often have slight *lee helm* in lighter breezes. Weather helm on other *points of sailing* and at other times may be caused

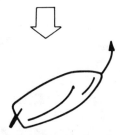

by excessive *heeling,* a wrongly positioned *centreboard,* or by *lifting* sails. When the relative positions of the *centre of effort* and the *centre of lateral resistance* cause excessive weather helm, it can be reduced either by shifting the CLR further aft or the CE further forward (see *balance*).

Weatherly Describes a boat that sails relatively close to the wind and makes little *leeway.*

Weather map or **chart** A map of a geographical area which either shows the weather situation at a certain time, based on reports from weather ships and stations, or shows average weather conditions in an area, based on past records. Abridged maps of anticipated weather are printed daily by some newspapers, but more detailed maps can be obtained from meteorological services, such as the US National Weather Service. A great deal of information is printed on such maps, using the weather code and symbols.

Weather or **windward mark** When racing, the *mark* of the *course* furthest to *windward*, and one end of the finishing line of an *Olympic* or *triangular course*.

Weather report A report of the actual weather observed at a certain time at a station on land or at sea. Forecasts are based largely on weather reports.

Weather runner See *running backstay*.

Weather ship The World Meteorological Organization has established a chain of weather ships to observe and report on weather, and they also assist with *search and rescue* in cases of *distress*.

Weather shore A coast that lies to *windward* of a boat. Unlike a *lee shore*, provides a safe *anchorage* nearby because the wind blows offshore, and does not drive a boat with e.g. a *dragging anchor* towards the land.

Weather tide A *tidal stream* (US *tidal current*) which runs in the opposite direction to that towards which the wind is blowing; seas are shorter, steeper and more dangerous than when the wind is blowing and the tidal stream is setting towards the same direction.

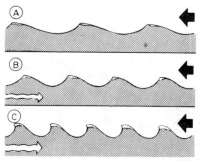

Web frame Transverse member fitted in place of separate *deck beam*, *floor* and *frames* where stresses are great to provide extra strength, e.g. to support longitudinal framing at the *mast* or *bridgedeck*. May be metal, *marine plywood*, or a reinforced *GRP/FRP laminate*.

Weep To leak slowly, for example when water trickles through a *seam*.

Weft (US or fill) A term used in *cloth construction* to indicate the threads woven at right angles to the longitudinal *warp* threads (except in

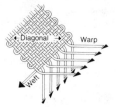

tri-axial cloth, q.v.); generally the weft stretches less than the warp, and sails are often cut to take advantage of this.

Weigh anchor To raise the *anchor*. When it has been brought on deck it is *stowed* and *lashed* on its *bed* or *chocks*. A vessel under weigh is in the act of weighing anchor; when she is *under way* she is not *moored*, *anchored* or *aground* (*IRPCS*), but in general speech is taken to be moving through the water.

Weight The weight of a *sailing dinghy* is generally quoted in pounds or kilogrammes exclusive of sails, spars, loose gear and crew. The *displacement* of *keelboats* may be given in pounds, tons, kilogrammes or tonnes. The actual weight and *trim* of light motor boats with large fuel tanks varies greatly with the amount of fuel that has been consumed. See also *anchor weight*.

Well 1. A sump in the *bilges* into which bilge water drains; is emptied by *bilge pumps*. 2. A small *cockpit*. 3. A hollow trunk in which an *outboard* is shipped. 4. The *anchor* well is a small locker in the *foredeck*, with a cover under which the anchor is stowed; often has drain holes either side.

Well-found Said of a vessel that is well equipped, fitted out and maintained.

West One of the four *cardinal points;* on the *compass rose* and *compass card* lies 270° clockwise from north. The sun sets to the west.

Westerlies The predominantly westerly winds that blow in the temperate zones in *latitudes* higher than about 35°, i.e. towards the poles from the sub-tropical high pressure belt as SW winds in the northern hemisphere and NW in the southern. Many *depressions* form in these regions and, in the northern hemisphere, winds vary greatly in direction and strength. In the southern hemisphere the westerlies often reach gale force in the *Roaring Forties*, and the belt is followed between the Cape of Good Hope, Australia and New Zealand, and Cape Horn when making voyages under sail in an easerly direction. See also *global winds*.

Westerly To the west of currents, deviation etc, but from the west in the case of wind.

Western Adjective that differentiates between two similar areas, places etc, e.g. Western Approaches, and western *quadrant* which is bounded by NW and SW.

Western Rivers The Mississippi river from the source to the Huey P Long bridge in New Orleans, together with its tributaries (not the rivers along the west coast of the USA). In these waters the Western Rivers *rules of the road* are in force, and there are some differences from the *IRPCS*, especially as to *lights exhibited by vessels* and *sound signals* made by them. Western Rivers' *buoyage* is much the same as the basic US system, but there are no mid-channel marks. Black *can* buoys are left to port, and red *nun* buoys to starboard when sailing upstream.

Westing The distance a vessel makes good towards the west.

Westward Direction towards the west, e.g. to sail westward.

Wet Describes a boat that tends to *ship* water.

Wet-and-dry 1. Type of sandpaper, often cloth-backed, to which abrasive particles are glued with waterproof adhesive; can be used dry, but is generally used wet to rub down surfaces and provide a smooth *finish* without making too much dust. 2. Wet-and-dry bulb thermometer: see *psychrometer*.

Wet clothing The weight of clothing worn is limited when racing, because wet clothing, such as several soaking pullovers, increases the crew's weight and, therefore, the *stability* of a racing dinghy when the crew *sits* (US hikes) *out*. For example, pockets etc designed to hold water as *ballast* must be full when the clothing is weighed. The weight limit is normally 44 lbs (20 kg), but in some classes is lower.

Wet dock A basin closed off from the sea by

gates so that the water level does not drop when the *tide* falls. Vessels can only enter and leave at certain times near *high water*, unless there is an entrance lock. A boat moored alongside does not have to adjust her *mooring lines* because the water level is constant.

Wet suit Close-fitting protective clothing made of neoprene and worn mainly by dinghy sailors and boardsailors to provide some thermal insulation from cold winds and water. Long Johns are the most popular, and reach from shoulders to ankles but have no sleeves. A bolero jacket and boots can be worn in addition when required.

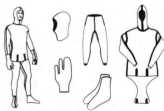

Wetted surface The immersed part of the *hull*, including *rudder*, *keel* or *centreboard*. Varies slightly with the boat's attitude, and affects *resistance*, especially at low speeds in light breezes when *frictional resistance* is the predominant factor of total resistance. The crew *trim* the boat, either to improve the underwater shape by sitting further aft when *planing* and further forward when *close-hauled* to obtain a long narrow wetted area, or to reduce wetted area by sitting to *leeward* when the wind is very light, making the boat *heel* slightly.

Whaleback *Camber* is very marked, and the *deck* almost merges into the *topsides*. Formerly restricted to whalers, but now seen more often because, with *GRP/FRP*, the shape can be moulded without difficulty.

Wharf Structure parallel to the shore and similar to a quay, but built on piles. Vessels can moor alongside.

Wheel 1. The steering wheel which moves the *rudder*. 2. US coll term for the *propeller*.

Wheel effect or **propeller bias** A rotating

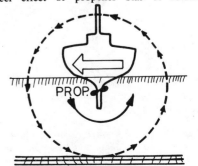

propeller tends to push the *stern* to one side, and this important factor has to be considered when handling a boat under power in confined waters, especially when coming *alongside*. The effect is as if the tip of the blade touched the ground, or moved along the ground like a wheel. When the boat is moving ahead, a *right-hand propeller* turns the stern to *starboard*, and a *left-hand propeller* swings it to *port*. The reverse occurs in astern gear, when a right-hand propeller swings the stern to port. The effect is less marked with an *outboard engine*. Sometimes incorrectly called torque effect.

Wheel steering Instead of a *tiller* directly connected to the *rudder stock,* the rudder is deflected by *steering wires* or rods, which run from a wheel to the *rudder quadrant*. Normally only fitted to larger yachts where muscular power would be inadequate, even if a very long tiller were used, or to those boats where a direct connection between tiller and rudder cannot be made. Less sensitive than tiller steering because of the intervening wires. Hydraulic steering is an alternative to using rods or cables.

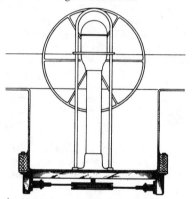

Wheel tensioner or **turnbuckle** or **rigging screw** Fitted aboard larger sailing boats so that the tension of the *backstay* or *inner forestay* can be adjusted when under way. The length of the *stay* can be altered up to 8 ins (200 mm) to *tune* the rig to suit the wind conditions and *point of sailing*. Also used with a *kicking strap*.

Wheel valve A *seacock* or stopcock which closes a pipe; a threaded stopper is screwed down to a bed in the pipe.

Wheft An *ensign* knotted or stopped half way. Formerly was a recognized *distress signal,* and in some countries is still flown to request help.

Whelps Vertical strips or raised ribbing on the barrel of a *capstan* or *winch* drum; helps the rope to grip.

Whip 1. Single whip: a *block* or *sheave* alters the direction of pull, no *mechanical advantage;* e.g. a *halyard* passing over a sheave at the *masthead,* or horizontally for pulling small boats

in and out to a post just off the shore or quay. 2. Double whip; two blocks, the standing part generally being attached to the standing block. See *tackle*. 3. To apply a whipping.

Whipping Twine is bound round the end of a rope to prevent the *strands* unlaying. A whipping should be as long as the diameter of the rope. Common whipping: the turns are taken against the *lay,* half over one end of the twine, the other half over the bight which is then hauled tight and cut off. American whipping is similar, but the two ends are tied with a *reef knot* where they emerge from beneath the turns. West country: half a reef knot is made each side of every turn, and the whipping is finished with a reef knot. A sailmaker's whipping, as in the figure, can also be made without a needle. The rope is unlaid to where the whipping starts, and the twine is led between two

strands, with a bight left hanging down around the adjacent strand, so that twine emerges from between each pair of strands, which are then relaid. After sufficient turns have been taken round the rope with the loose end of the twine, the bight is passed over the end of the same strand that it encircles, and is pulled tight. The whipping is finished with a reef knot between the strands. A heat-shrink plastics sleeve, or rapid-setting plastic fluid may be applied to synthetic fibre rope, and

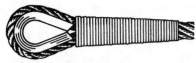

the ends of smaller synthetic fibre ropes can be melted with a naked flame and welded together.

Whipping twine For applying a whipping; generally three- or four-stranded and rather thicker than sewing twine.

Whipstaff A vertical *tiller* which was used for steering before the advent of the *wheel;* it was connected to the end of the tiller, leading up through the deck(s) to the helmsman who pushed it to one or other side about a fulcrum, so moving the tiller in the opposite direction. Now most often found on small harbour *launches,* projecting almost vertically from the *cockpit sole.*

Whirlpool Eddy where a *current* flows virtually in a circle.

Whirlwind A storm that revolves around an almost vertical axis. Is of limited extent, but winds are high.

Whisker pole or **jib stick** Light *spar* that holds the *clew* of a *headsail* out to windward when running *wing and wing.* Usually has a hook at one end that drops into an *eye* on the mast. The other end has a point that is inserted in the clew *cringle.*

Whiskers 1. In *sailing ships,* the horizontal *spars* that project from forward of the catheads to spread the *jib-boom shrouds.* 2. (US) Strands of wire which have parted and stick out sideways to cut the hand; show that the wire is weak. UK gashers.

Whistle 1. Appliance with which *sound signals* are made in *fog, restricted visibility* and when manoeuvring under certain circumstances. The *IRPCS* lay down the frequency, range and minimum audibility required. The two top whistles in the figure (frequently listed in chandlery

catalogues and spoken of as foghorns) are aerosol horns which sound about 500 times on one (exchangeable) container. The left hand bottom whistle is operated by a plunger, and that on the right by blowing through a copper membrane at the mouthpiece; if the mouthpiece is removable it can also be used as a *loudhailer.* Horns powered by 12 or 24 volt batteries are also available. 2. A small whistle, similar to that used to call a dog, may be attached to a *lifebuoy* or *safety harness* so that a person in the water can draw attention to his position.

Whistle buoy An *aid to navigation,* fitted with an automatic whistle; may be operated by compressed air or by the action of waves. Chart abbr Whis.

White horses and **white caps** Breaking waves with white foamy crests. The term does not relate to *surf* breaking on a beach.

Whole gale (US) **Storm** (WMO) *Beaufort* force 10, *48–55 knots.*

Wide berth To give another vessel or obstacle a wide berth is to keep well clear.

Wildcat (US) See *gipsy.*

Willy-willy Obsolescent term for a *tropical revolving storm* that occurs off Northern Australia.

Winch 1. A machine made of manganese bronze, stainless steel, titanium or other lightweight metal (latterly also of plastics) that combines great strength with resistance to *corrosion;* designed to assist the crew to *haul* on a rope or line. Turns are taken round the drum, the slack hauled in and, when the load becomes too great for manual operation, extra power is applied with a winch handle (US or crank). Because speed is inversely proportional to power (see *power ratio*), speed is halved when the power ratio is doubled, and many winches have more than one gear to provide speedy operation initially, followed by additional power

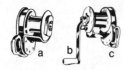

to *sheet* or *hoist home.* Gear ratios vary from 1:1 to about 17:1, and power ratios from about 3:1 to over 65:1. A number of methods are employed to select the gear required. *Halyard* or reel *winches* are designed for wire rope halyards and other lines, which are stored on the drum, for example when the sail is hoisted. *Sheet winches* may be top- or bottom-action, according to whether the handle is inserted above or below the drum; they may be *self-tailing,* and have one or more gears. Winches may be *cross-linked* to provide extra power, or operated from a distance (*coffee-grinder*), and some are electrically-powered. The word winch is generally applied to smaller devices used for smaller sizes of ropes and wire ropes, but the term anchor winch is also sometimes applied to a *windlass* which, essentially, is a mechanism that rotates about a horizontal shaft, whereas winches may be fitted vertically (as sheet winches) or horizontally (when fitted on the mast and used for hoisting sails). 2. As a verb, to use a winch to haul on a rope or wire.

Wind 1. The mainly horizontal movement of air over the surface of the earth, caused by the difference of *atmospheric presure* between two places. Winds may be part of the *global circulation system,* such as *trade winds,* or of local origin and extent, such as *land* and *sea breezes.* Air flows from a high pressure area to a low pressure area, but globally is deflected by *Coriolis force* because the earth rotates. In the northern hemisphere wind blows clockwise and spirally out of a high pressure area, but inwards counterclockwise towards the centre of a low; the reverse is the case in the southern hemisphere, i.e. it spirals inwards clockwise towards a low. The closer the *isobars* are spaced on a weather map the greater the difference in atmospheric pressure (the *pressure gradient* is steeper) and the greater the wind speed.

In the earth's *boundary layer* the speed of wind is greatly reduced by friction (see *wind gradient*); over the sea it blows at about two-thirds of *geostrophic wind* speed, and speed increases with height above sea level. Direction is also affected by friction, and surface winds are deflected about 20° towards low pressure by comparison with geostrophic or *gradient winds.* Topography affects direction and speed in a locality, for example when wind is *funnelled* in a narrow valley.

Wind is also deflected when it passes from land to water and vice versa. On account of the lower frictional drag of water, wind accelerates and blows at a more acute angle to the coastline when over water, but speed is reduced and it crosses at an angle nearer a right angle when blowing from

sea to land. This can be used to good advantage when cruising or racing.

2. As a verb, used by bargemen, meaning to go about (pronounced as 1). See also entries below and *Beaufort scale, apparent* and *true wind.*

Wind abeam The wind blows roughly at right angles to the *fore-and-aft line,* and the boat sails on a *beam reach.*

Windage All those parts of a boat that contribute to total air *drag* increase windage, including *rigging, superstructure, spars* and crew. Windage is helpful when *running,* but a boat normally covers greater distances and spends a greater proportion of time on windward courses when windage reduces her speed, especially when *close hauled.*

Wind arrow Wind direction is shown on weather maps by plotting an arrow flying with the wind towards the *station circle.* Wind speed is indicated by *feathers,* and normally one feather equals 10 *knots,* half a feather 5 knots, and a *pennant* 50 knots. No feather is drawn for a wind speed under 3 knots, one half feather indicating winds of 3–7 knots. Occasionally the feathers relate to the *Beaufort Scale force,* as explained under feather, 2.

Wind direction The direction from which wind blows, as opposed to *tidal streams or currents* which are described by the direction towards which they *set.* In general forecasts wind direction is given in *points of the compass,* as NE winds for example, but shipping forecasts may be more precise and give direction in degrees measured clockwise from north, i.e. 045°. On weather maps, wind direction is indicated by a *wind arrow.* On board a moving boat in the open sea, the direction of a *true wind* blowing above force 3 can be ascertained by taking a *bearing* at right angles to the face of approaching wind-raised seas. In lighter breezes a bearing is taken along the line of the troughs, and 90° is subtracted or added. When wind direction shifts clockwise (from north towards east, south, west), it is said to *veer;* it *backs* when it shifts counterclockwise. When it shifts in relation to the boat's *heading* it is said to *head* when it blows from a direction nearer the *bow* than before, or to *free* when it blows from a direction nearer the *stern.* See also *beam, fair, following, foul, free, head* and *quartering wind.*

Wind direction indicator Any device that

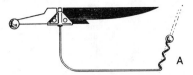

indicates either the direction of the *apparent wind* aboard a moving boat, or that of the *true wind* when the boat is stationary. Generally fitted at the *masthead* where it operates in wind that is not disturbed by the sails and rigging, and may be a *burgee, wind sock, racing flag,* metal or plastics wind *vane,* or a sophisticated electronic *wind speed and direction indicator.* The device in figure A is fitted to the *shroud.* The flag, B, has a metal frame and, like C, has side arms or reference tabs; the flag or arrow should be aligned with them to keep the boat on the optimum *close-hauled* course.

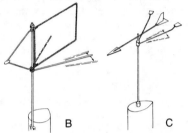

Wind force The strength of wind is normally divided into 12 forces in the *Beaufort scale,* varying from force 0 (calm) to force 12 (hurricane, with a mean wind speed of over 64 *knots*). The scale is sometimes expanded to force 17 (see *Beaufort wind scale*). Speeds may also be given in km/hr, m/sec, and sometimes in mph.

Windglider The class of *sailboard* adopted by the IYRU for the 1984 Olympic games. Constructed of GRP over a foam filling; LOA 3.9 m, beam 0.65 m, weight 23 kg, mast height 4.5 m, sail area 6.5 sq m.

Wind gradient Not to be confused with the meteorological term *gradient wind.* Wind gradient is the term used by some writers when referring to the increase of speed of the *true wind* with height above the surface of the earth, within the *boundary layer.* Friction increases where the surface is rough, e.g. when waves run high in heavy weather. Wind speeds are officially measured at a height of 33 ft (10 m).

Windjammer 1. A colloquial general term loosely used for large sailing vessels and square-rigged ships. 2. US: coll for a sailor who uses sails.

Windlass Sometimes also termed anchor winch. A mechanical device, operated electrically, hydraulically or manually with a lever, fitted on the *foredeck* and usually used to raise the *anchor.* Whereas a *capstan* rotates about a vertical spindle,

a windlass has a horizontal shaft. Most have a *warping drum* (US gipsy) on one side for rope cable, and a *gipsy* (US wildcat) on the other which is recessed to take the links of chain cable. Can also be used for *warping* etc.

Wind over tide The wind blows in the opposite direction to that towards which the *tidal stream or current sets.* The stronger the wind or the tidal stream, the steeper and more vicious do the seas become.

Window 1. In order to enable the crew to see to *leeward,* transparent plastics windows are often sewn into the *mainsail* or *headsail;* the area allowed for a window in a racing sail is limited, and they are prohibited in some *classes.* 2. The term is occasionally used for a glazed port which admits light to the interior and which, usually, can be opened and closed.

Wind pressure The *dynamic pressure* (q.v.) of wind is found from the mass density of air and wind velocity, the formula being $q = \frac{1}{2}mv^2$. Wind pressure therefore increases as the square of wind speed and, consequently, when a *force* 4 wind freshens from 11 to 16 *knots* (an increase of 5 knots or 45%) wind pressure increases from 0.41 to 0.87 lbs/sq ft (112%). It is the pressure of the *apparent wind,* not that of the *true wind,* that is important when sailing, and the apparent wind may be up to nine times stronger when

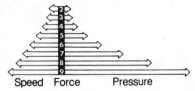

Speed Force Pressure

close-hauled than when *running;* consequently more canvas can be set when sailing downwind than when on the wind, and reaching and running sails may be made of lighter sailcloth. Because wind speed increases with height above water (*wind gradient*), pressure is greater at the head of the sail than at the foot, and this is a point to remember when deciding how many rolls or reefs to take in when the wind freshens.

Wind-rode When a boat is lying at a *mooring,* or is *anchored* in waters where there is a *tidal stream or current* that is not setting in the same direction

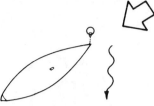

as that to which the wind is blowing, she is said to be wind-rode when she lies head to wind, and tide-rode when she lies to the tidal stream. How the boat lies is largely governed by the relative strengths of the wind and stream, and by the surface of the boat above and below the water. A motor boat with high *superstructure* and little *lateral area* beneath the water is generally wind-rode, as is a dinghy when her *centreboard* is raised, whereas a sailing boat with a *ballast keel* is more often tide-rode. If the wind is *gusty* she will often *sheer* about.

Wind rose 1. On monthly meteorological charts, the frequency of winds at a certain place or in an area, observed and analysed over a long period, is shown by *wind arrows* flying in towards that place, usually at the eight *cardinal* and inter-cardinal *points*. The length of each arrow is proportional to the percentage frequency of wind from that particular direction. The UK wind rose arrow (fig c) is divided into segments which can be measured against the scale of frequency; the inner line indicates winds of *force* 1–3, the next sections respectively force 4, forces 5–6 and force 7, while the last black section indicates force 8 and over.

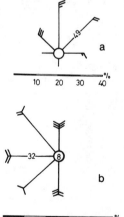

Figs (a) and (b) are German and US wind roses; in both cases the number of *feathers* shows the average force, *Beaufort scale*. Where the percentage frequency is too high to be shown graphically, the line is broken and the percentage given as a figure. The number of *calm* days, and those with light *variable* wind, is indicated by a figure in the centre. 2. Formerly, a *compass card* divided into 8, 16 or 32 parts, often also showing

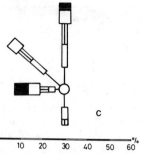

the cardinal and intercardinal points in the form of the eight major winds known to Mediterranean sailors.

Wind sail *Canvas ventilator,* rigged like an enormous *cowl* over a *hatch,* and held open by lines to the *forestay* and/or *mast.* Is rigged in tropical and sub-tropical waters, either when under way or in harbour, to catch the breeze and direct it below. Can be turned round and used as a venturi or suction ventilator to remove air from the cabin.

Wind shadow The area to *leeward* of a sail, trees or other obstructions where wind speed is reduced, direction is affected and air flow is *turbulent.* When sailing extends up to seven times the mast height and its effect is much used in racing to slow a competitor.

Wind shift A sudden change in the direction of the wind, such as occurs when a *front* passes.

Wind sock Flown at the *masthead* to indicate the strength and direction of the *apparent wind.* The light material fills to a greater or lesser extent depending on how hard the wind blows, and is therefore more informative than a simple *burgee* or *racing flag.* Wears well because it does not flutter.

Wind speed 1. The speed of wind is measured at sea and on land by an *anemometer*, a wind gauge, or by a hand-held wind meter such as the *Ventimeter*. On weather maps wind speed, measured at a station at a height of 33 ft (10 m) above sea level, is shown by feathers on arrows flying with the wind to the *station circle*. Several different units are used for wind speed and these can be converted as follows:

1 metre per second = 3.6 km/hr = 1.944 *knots* = 2.237 mph

1 kilometre per hour = 0.54 knots = 0.621 mph = 0.277 m/sec

1 knot = 1.514 m/sec = 1.151 mph = 1.852 km/hr

1 mile per hour = 0.447 m/sec = 1.609 km/hr = 0.869 knots

When listening to weather forecasts it is easy to convert knots to metres per second, divide by two; when accustomed to knots and picking up a forecast in m/sec, multiply by two to obtain knots. 2. Wind speed is reduced by friction as it passes over seas and rough land, but the effect of friction at the surface decreases rapidly with height. 3. Wind speed, as measured on land or on a stationary boat, is not the same as *apparent wind* speed felt on board a moving boat; this varies on every *point of sailing* and is very much greater on a *close-hauled* course than on a *run*. 4. Wind velocity relates to both speed and direction, not speed alone, but the term is usually used less specifically. See also *Beaufort scale*.

Wind speed and direction indicator Electronic instrument that measures the speed and direction of the *apparent wind* when a boat is making way, or those of the *true wind* when she is motionless. Speed is usually measured by an *anemometer*, which is mounted at the *masthead*, together with a *vane* to indicate direction. The information is displayed on dials, often with *repeaters* installed in the cockpit or above the *companion*, so that

they can be read by the helmsman. The wind direction dial may be graduated from 0-360° and/ or have an *expanded scale* for close-hauled work between 0° and about 50–60°; often the close-hauled and running arc is shown on a separate dial. Some electronic wind speed indicators record speed by measuring pressure differential.

Wind speed indicator Instrument which displays

the speed of the wind. May be electronic (see *wind speed and direction indicator, anemometer*) or hand-held (see *Ventimeter*).

Windsurfer The first of the *sailboards*, designed by Jim Drake and Hoyle Schweitzer, originally to enable a surfer to make use of the wind when making his way out against the breaking surf. LOA 12 ft (3.65 m), beam 2 ft 1½ in (0.65 m), weight 60 lbs (27.2 kg), sail area 56 sq ft (5.2 sq m).

Wind tide (US) A rise in the level of water along the shore to *leeward*, caused by wind.

Wind tunnel Apparatus for investigating airflow and its effect on other bodies. A power driven fan provides a wind stream that can be varied in speed, sometimes up to about 90 *knots*. Airflow can be made visible by using smoke or threads. As an example, *lift* and *drag*, the components of total force can be measured so that the efficiency of sails of varying *camber* and *aspect ratio* can be compared. *Anemometers* are tested and *calibrated* in wind tunnels.

Windward The direction from which the wind blows; towards the wind; opp *leeward*. A boat may pass to windward of an object; of two overlapping boats the one nearer the wind is the windward boat. Often interchangeable with *weather*.

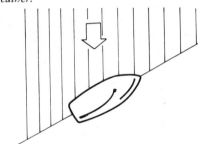

Windward mark See *weather mark*.

Windward performance When the boat's objective or destination lies to windward she has to *beat* up to it on alternate *tacks* because she cannot sail closer than about 35–40° to the true wind. It is the speed at which she works to windward, i.e. the time it takes her to cover the distance to her objective, that is the measure of her windward performance, and this is called Vmg or *speed* (velocity) *made good to windward*, q.v. The rate at which she works to windward depends on how close to the wind she *points* and the speed at which she sails through the water. When she sails fast she cannot point so high, but if she points high she sails slower and makes more *leeway*, especially if the helmsman *pinches*. He has to find the right compromise by keeping the boat moving

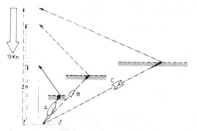

reasonably fast while pointing reasonably high at the same time, and must be sensitive to every shift in wind direction, variation in wind speed and the effect of the waves. No two boats are the same, and *tuning* the rig differently has a marked effect. Some boats perform best to windward when pointing close and sailing more slowly, whereas others make ground to windward faster especially in steep, stopping seas, when the helmsman bears away slightly and sails faster. Slower boats generally perform best at an angle of about 45° to the true wind, faster racing boats at about 40°; *catamarans* sail at even greater angles because their extreme speed draws their apparent wind more ahead.

Windward yacht In the *IRPCS*, when two *sailing vessels* on the same *tack* approach each other and there is a *risk of collision*, the vessel to windward keeps clear of the vessel to *leeward*. In the *IYRU racing rules*, the windward yacht is the one of two on the same tack, neither being *clear astern*, that is on the windward side of the other; the yacht to windward has to keep clear of the other, which is the leeward yacht.

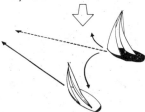

Wind waves Waves raised by wind. The growth of waves is governed largely by the strength and duration of the wind, and by *fetch*. Initially *ripples* form but, as the wind freshens, gravity waves are generated and their height, length and period increase with wind speed. A shows immature waves generated when a fresh wind starts to blow: B, wave period and wind speed coincide: C is the long regular *swell* that remains after the wind has dropped. The descriptions of waves at various wind speeds is given in the *Beaufort Scale* under Sea Criterion, and the *Sea State Scale* grades them by height and character.

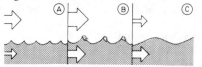

Wing and wing To run with the *mainsail* on one side of the boat and the *headsail* held out or *boomed out* on the other.

Wing mark See *reaching mark*.

Wing sail Unlike a normal cloth sail, is a rigid or semi-rigid *aerofoil* designed to avoid the harmful effect that a normal unstreamlined mast has on airflow. A semi-rigid sail has a profiled yard with a groove at the *trailing edge*, which holds the cloth sail. The yard is uniformly convex on either side, like a profiled centreboard, and pivots on a mast.

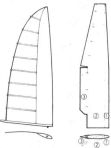

A rigid wing sail, like that used by 'Miss Nylex' when winning the International Catamaran Challenge Cup, often has a movable flap at the trailing edge, and this can be trimmed at an angle to the wind on either tack.

Wire rope Used on board for *standing* and *running rigging, lifelines* (guardrails) etc. Is made of *strands* laid up around a *heart* or another strand, each strand being made up of individual steel wires twisted together. Ordinary lay: the wires are laid up *left-handed* and the strands *right-handed*. Two numbers indicate the construction, the first relating to the number of strands and the second to the number of wires in each strand. Thus 7×19 has 7 strands, each consisting of 19 wires (A).

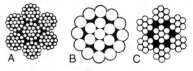

7×7 (C) is often used for standing rigging, and is more flexible than 1×19 (B) but *stretches* more. 1×19 is used exclusively for standing rigging and, although more corrosion-resistant, is relatively inflexible and difficult to splice manually. 7×19 is often preferred for running rigging; it is more flexible than 7×7 or 1×19, stretches less than 7×7 and resists corrosion better. Galvanized wire is sometimes used in fresh water and, although it has to be renewed more frequently than stainless steel, deterioration is easier to detect. Approximate equivalent sizes of wire are as follows (diameters): 2 mm $^5/_{64}$ in; 3 mm $^1/_8$ in; 4 mm $^5/_{32}$ in; 5 mm $^3/_{16}$ in; 6 mm $^1/_4$ in; 7 mm $^9/_{32}$ in; 8 mm $^5/_{16}$ in; 10 mm $^{13}/_{32}$ in;

12 mm $^{15}/_{32}$ in; 14 mm $^9/_{16}$ in; 16 mm $^5/_8$ in; 20 mm $^{13}/_{16}$ in; 24 mm $^{15}/_{16}$ in.

Wire rope grip or **clamp**   See *bulldog grip.*

Wire splice   A *splice* made in wire rope, usually to form an eye. Now largely superseded by *swaged* or *swageless terminals,* or *Talurit* (US Nicopress) splicing which are equally effective but cheaper.

Wishbone   A *boom* made in two halves, which curve outward in an aerofoil shape either side and meet at the after end, where they extend the *clew* of the sail which sets between them. Can be used with a *mainsail* or *staysail,* and allows the sail to take up the shape cut into it, because the *foot* is loose and not held straight by a rigid boom. A *topping lift* may adjust the angle of the wishbone to the mast or stay to alter sail *camber.* The wishbone of a headsail bisects the angle at the clew, following the line of the *mitre* to the *forestay* around which it swings. *Sailboards* have wishbone booms.

Wishbone rig   Nathaniel Herreshoff's wishbone boom has been used with several rigs, often in two-masted boats because the wishbone's sheet can be led over the top of the aftermast and down to the deck. In the case of a wishbone *schooner,* the wishbone staysail set on her *foremast* is smaller and handier than a *foresail,* and is sheeted to the stronger *mainmast;* the *rigging* can therefore be lighter. Wishbone staysails are generally cut with a *mitre* and are *loose-footed.*

Work   Parts of a vessel work when they move in relation to each other, generally because *fastenings* have become loose. The boat may well start to leak.

Working sails   The sails set by a *close-hauled* boat in a *full sail breeze* of *force* 4, namely *mainsail, jib* or *genoa* and, in *yawls* and *ketches,* the *mizzen.* May be *bermudan* (US *marconi*) or *gaff, spritsails, lugsails* etc. *Light-weather sails* are set in lighter breezes and when reaching or running, while *storm sails* are set in heavy weather.

Worm   To fill the spiral grooves in rope with *small stuff,* working with the *lay.* A preliminary step to *parcelling* and *serving.*

Worm roller reefing   A *reefing system* with a simple worm gear; the boom is rotated, and the sail rolled round it, by turning a handle fitted to one side of the boom.

Wreck   In general usage a vessel that is unseaworthy, *abandoned, stranded,* sunk or helpless. When sunk or cast up on the shore and a *danger* to navigation, the position is printed on *charts* and marked by *buoys, light vessels* etc. *Uniform buoyage:* all wreck markings are green. *US buoyage:* buoys are marked WR. *IALA A:* no special wreck marks, they are treated the same as any other danger and are marked with *isolated danger, lateral* or *cardinal* buoys as appropriate. As a verb, to make a vessel useless, say by driving her ashore. 3. Legally the term wreck includes not only the vessel herself, whether sunk, cast up or afloat, but also her gear and cargo, *flotsam, jetsam* and *lagan.* A vessel or her gear and cargo abandoned by her crew is termed *derelict.* The finder of wreck is legally required to hand it over to the Receiver of Wreck; a *salvage* claim can be made when wreck is saved. Chart abbr Wk.

Wrinkled skin   Roughness over a large area of the *gelcoat* of a *GRP/FRP moulding;* breaks through easily, shrinks and cracks open. Usually occurs because the temperature was too low or the atmosphere too humid when the gelcoat was applied, or because too little *catalyst* was added to the *resin.* Another cause could be that the first layer was applied too soon, before the gelcoat had gelled properly. Repairs are essential.

Wung out   Slang, from to wing out (see *wing and wing, goosewinged*).

X = X-ray: white *code flag* with a blue cross.   As a single letter signal means 'Stop carrying out your intentions and watch for my signals'. *Morse code:* — • • — (dash dot dot dash). When racing means 'One or more yachts have started prematurely or have infringed the *round-the-ends* starting rule'.

Y = Yankee: yellow and red diagonally striped *code flag.* As a single letter signal means 'I am *dragging* my anchor'. *Morse code:* — • — — (dash dot dash dash). When racing means that *life jackets* or personal *buoyancy* shall be worn.

Yacht 1. A vessel used for state occasions and representation. 2. A pleasure craft, whether a sailing yacht or motor yacht, used for cruising, voyaging and racing but not for commercial, fishing or naval purposes. The implication is that the boat is of a certain minimum size (*sailing dinghies, tenders, rowing boats* etc are not considered to be yachts). Most sailing yacht

owners prefer the terms sailing boat (UK) or sailboat (US), and call themselves sailors rather than yachtsmen. 3. In the late middle ages, rapid sailing craft used to carry important passengers, dispatches and so on; the word derives from the Dutch, jachten, to hunt or hurry.

Yacht club Organization whose members are interested in waterborne activities primarily sailing, but often including motor boating etc. The following are listed in Lloyd's Register of Yachts as having been founded at the dates given:

1720 Royal Cork Yacht Club, Eire
1770 Lough Ree Yacht Club, Eire
1773 Starcross Yacht Club, England
1775 Royal Thames Yacht Club, England
1815 Royal Yacht Squadron, England
1824 Royal Northern Yacht Club, Scotland
1829 Royal Gibraltar Yacht Club
1838 Royal Hobart Yacht Club, Tasmania
1839 Detroit Yacht Club, USA
1844 New York Yacht Club, USA
1844 Royal Bermuda Yacht Club
1847 Royal Welsh Yacht Club
1849 Southern Yacht Club, New Orleans, USA
1849 Pass Christian Yacht Club, Miss, USA
1852 Royal Canadian Yacht Club
1858 Royal Natal Yacht Club, South Africa
1859 Royal Geelong Yacht Club, Australia
1862 Royal Channel Islands Yacht Club
1866 Royal Ulster Yacht Club, Northern Ireland
1871 Royal New Zealand Yacht Squadron
1873 Royal Malta Yacht Club
1880 Royal Cruising Club, England
1889 Royal Hong Kong Yacht Club
1922 Cruising Club of America
1925 Royal Ocean Racing Club

Yachtmaster The person in charge of a boat. UK: more specifically, the term used by the *RYA* to describe a person who has successfully passed one of the RYA/DoT graded yachtmaster examinations, and should therefore be competent to take charge of a boat and its crew in any conditions likely to be encountered within the qualifying restrictions. The various qualifications are: yachtmaster ocean (anywhere in the world), – offshore (out of sight of land but excluding celestial navigation), – and – coastal (generally within sight of land). Each of these grades can be taken for sail or motor, with appropriate adjustments to the syllabus.

Yachtsman A man who sails a yacht for pleasure; may be a dinghy sailor and is usually a member of a yacht club.

Yankee (not US) A large *jib* with a high *clew,* generally set forward of a *staysail* in lighter winds.

Yard 1. Long powerful *spar* on which a *square sail* is set. Is held centrally to the forward side of the mast with a *parrel,* so that it can be raised and lowered, turned horizontally, or set a-cockbill. 2. The spar to which the *head* of a *lateen* or *lugsail* is bent, and sometimes also used for the *gaff* of a *gunter-rigged* vessel. 3. Measure of length; 1 yard = 3 ft = 0.9144m and 1m = 1.093613 yds. 4. Short for *boatyard.*

Yarn When making rope, natural *fibres* or synthetic *filaments* are spun into yarns which are then twisted into *strands,* and the strands are then *laid* or *braided* into rope. For *sailcloth,* yarns

Fibre
Yarn
Strand
Rope

consisting usually of between 15–100 filaments are twisted together to form one thread. A large number of fine filaments is more flexible than a smaller number of thicker filaments when made up into a yarn of the same *denier* or *decitex*, i.e. of the same total diameter.

Yaw The boat swings first to one side and then to the other side of her *course* when she yaws, pivoting about a vertical axis. Generally most marked when sailing downwind with a *following sea*.

Yawing moment When a *rudder* is put over, the moment which causes the boat to take up an angle of yaw; the hydrodynamic forces acting on the hull then cause her to alter course. The greater the distance between the rudder's *centre of pressure* and the boat's *centre of gravity*, the greater is the yawing moment. When the rudder is hung on the keel, the lever arm is short, and the rudder area has to be larger to obtain the same yawing moment as those of a sailing dinghy or of an offshore racer with *fin and skeg* configuration.

Yawl A boat with two *masts*, the *mizzenmast* aft being considerably shorter than the *mainmast*. Several definitions attempt to differentiate between a yawl and a *ketch* (q.v.) but, essentially, when compared with the area of the *mainsail*, the area of a ketch's *mizzen* is greater than that of a yawl's mizzen. The *International Offshore Rule* does not differentiate between yawls and ketches, and classes all two-masted boats as yawls (if the mainmast is forward) or *schooners* (if the mainmast is aft). The main advantages of yawl rig are that the extra sail aft improves *directional stability*, and it can be lowered quickly and easily when the wind freshens, so reducing sail area and shifting the *centre of effort* further forward; a *mizzen staysail* can be set between the masts when the wind is free; in heavy weather, and when

sailing into port in restricted waters, the mainsail can be *handed* because the boat can be controlled easily under mizzen and headsail alone.

Z = Zulu: black, yellow, blue and red *code flag*. As a single letter signal means 'I require a *tug*'. When made by fishing vessels 'I am shooting my nets'. *Morse code:* ——• • (dash dash dot dot).

Z-drive Trade name for *outdrive*, q.v.

Zenith The point in the *celestial sphere* directly above the observer's head; a line from the zenith to the earth's centre passes through the observer. Point Z in the *PZX triangle*. The *declination* of the zenith is equal to the observer's *latitude*.

Zenith distance The angular distance between the observer's *zenith* and a *heavenly body*, i.e. the complement of *altitude*, obtained by subtracting the *true altitude* of the body from 90°. The side ZX of the *PZX triangle*, q.v. for fig.

Zinc A metal that corrodes more readily than almost all others, being at the less noble end of the *galvanic series*. *Sacrificial plates* made of zinc are fitted to prevent other metals from being corroded. *Specific gravity* 7.0. *Galvanized* iron is coated with zinc for protection against *corrosion*.

Zipper When employed on a sail, may either be used with a *flattening reef* to take out fullness, usually along the foot of the mainsail (see *shelf 2*), or may enclose a sleeve luff round a spar or stay.

Zone time Local mean time at sea is kept in a time zone bounded by *meridians* 15° apart (i.e. one hour difference), and the same time is kept throughout the zone. When sailing eastward into the neighbouring zone, the difference in time has to be added, and clocks are advanced one hour; when sailing westward the difference is subtracted. 1 minute (time) = 15' *longitude*; 1 second (time) = 15'' longitude; 1 degree longitude = 4 minutes (time).

Z-twist See *right-hand lay*.